A Prelude to Neural Networks: Adaptive and Learning Systems

EDITED BY

Jerry M. Mendel
University of Southern California
Los Angeles, California

PTR Prentice Hall
Englewood Cliffs, New Jersey 07632

Library of Congress Cataloging-in-Publication Data

Editorial/Production Supervision: Lisa Iarkowski
Acquisitions Editor: Karen Gettman
Buyer: Alexis Heydt
Cover Design: Karen Marsilio

Formerly published by Academic Press as
Adaptive, Learning, and Pattern Recognition Systems

Prentice-Hall, Inc.
A Paramount Communications Company
Englewood Cliffs, NJ 07632

Printed in the United States of America
10 9 8 7 6 5 4 3 2 1

ISBN 0-13-147448-0

Prentice-Hall International (UK) Limited, *London*
Prentice-Hall of Australia Pty. Limited, *Sydney*
Prentice-Hall of Canada, Inc., *Toronto*
Prentice-Hall Hispanoamericana S.A., *Mexico*
Prentice-Hall of India Private Limited, *New Delhi*
Prentice-Hall of Japan, Inc., *Tokyo*
Simon & Schuster Asia Pte. Ltd., *Singapore*
Editora Prentice-Hall do Brasil, Ltd., *Rio de Janeiro*

To

King-Sun Fu

Pioneer, developer, educator, leader, and inspiration in the fields of adaptive, learning, and pattern recognition systems.

List of Contributors

Numbers in parentheses indicate the pages on which the author's contributions begin.

Colin C. Blaydon (329, 357), School of Business Administration, Tuck School, Dartmouth College, Hanover, New Hampshire 03755

Richard O. Duda (3), Department of Electrical Engineering, San Jose State University, San Jose, California 95192

King-Sun Fu (35, 329, 357, 393)

Rangasami L. Kashyap (81, 329, 357), School of Electrical Engineering, Purdue University, Lafayette, Indiana 47907-1285

Robert W. McLaren (287), Department of Electrical Engineering, University of Missouri, Columbia, Missouri 65211

George J. McMurty (243), College of Engineering, Pennsylvania State University, University Park, Pennsylvania 16802

Jerry M. Mendel (163, 209, 287), Department of Electrical Engineering-Sytems, University of Southern California, Los Angeles, California 90089-2564

Sam S. Viglione (115), McDonnell Douglas Astronautics West, Santa Ana, California 92705

Contents

List of Contributors v
Foreward xi
Preface xiii

PART I PATTERN RECOGNITION

1. Elements of Pattern Recognition

R. O. DUDA

I. Introduction **3**
II. A Recognition Problem **5**
III. The Classical Model **22**
IV. Additions to the Classical Model **31**
References **32**

2. Statistical Pattern Recognition

K. S. FU

I. Statistical Pattern Recognition Systems and Bayes Classifiers . **35**
II. Sequential Decision Model for Pattern Classification **39**
III. Forward Sequential Classification Procedure with Time-Varying Stopping Boundaries **42**
IV. Backward Sequential Classification Procedure Using Dynamic Programming **45**
V. Backward Sequential Procedure for Both Feature Selection and Pattern Classification **48**
VI. Feature Selection and Ordering: Information Theoretic Approach **50**
VII. Feature Selection and Ordering: Karhunen-Loève Expansion **56**
VIII. Bayesian Estimation in Statistical Classification Systems . . . **61**
IX. Nonsupervised Learning Using Bayesian Estimation Technique **66**
X. Mode Estimation in Pattern Recognition **68**
XI. Conclusions and Further Remarks **75**
References **76**

3. Algorithms for Pattern Classification

R. L. Kashyap

I. Introduction 81
II. Nonoverlapping Classes with Reliable Samples 85
III. Nonoverlapping Classes with Erroneously Classified Samples 96
IV. Overlapping Classes 103
V. Multiclass Algorithms 107
VI. Comparison and Discussion of the Various Algorithms . . . 111
References 112

4. Applications of Pattern Recognition Technology

S. S. Viglione

I. Introduction 115
II. Pattern Recognition Mechanisms 117
III. Applications 133
Appendix 158
References 161

5. Synthesis of Quasi-Optimal Switching Surfaces by Means of Training Techniques

J. M. Mendel

I. Introduction 163
II. Quasi-Optimal Control 164
III. The Method of Trainable Controllers 168
IV. Feature Processing 177
V. Applications: A Brief Review 190
VI. Conclusions 191
References 192

Part I Problems 195

PART II ADAPTIVE AND LEARNING SYSTEMS

6. Gradient Identification for Linear Systems

J. M. Mendel

I. Introduction 209
II. System Description 211
III. Gradient Identification Algorithms: Stationary Parameters . . 214
IV. Gradient Identification Algorithms: Time-Varying Parameters 227
V. Noisy Measurement Situation 237
VI. Conclusions 240
References 241

7. Adaptive Optimization Procedures

G. J. McMurtry

I. Introduction 243
II. Unimodal Techniques 247
III. Multimodal Techniques 272
IV. Conclusions 283
References 284

8. Reinforcement-Learning Control and Pattern Recognition Systems

J. M. Mendel and R. W. McLaren

I. Introduction 287
II. Formulation of a Stochastic, Reinforcement-Learning Model 290
III. Reinforcement-Learning Control Systems. 292
IV. Reinforcement-Learning Pattern Recognition Systems . . . 306
References 317

Part II Problems 319

PART III SPECIAL TOPICS

9. Stochastic Approximation

R. L. Kashyap, C. C. Blaydon, and K. S. Fu

I. Introduction 329
II. Algorithms for Finding Zeroes of Functions 332
III. Kiefer-Wolfowitz Schemes 334
IV. Recovery of Functions from Noisy Measurements 336
V. Convergence Rates 345
VI. Methods of Accelerating Convergence 347
VII. Conclusion 350
Appendix 1 350
Appendix 2. 352
References 354

10. Applications of the Stochastic Approximation Methods

C. C. Blaydon, R. L. Kashyap, and K. S. Fu

I. Introduction 357
II. Pattern Classification Examples 358
III. Estimation of Probability Distribution and Density Functions 364
IV. State and Parameter Estimation Methods 371
V. Bang-Bang Feedback Control 383
VI. Conclusions 391
References 391

11. Stochastic Automata As Models of Learning Systems

K. S. Fu

I. Introduction to Stochastic Automata 393
II. Synthesis of Stochastic Automata 399
III. Deterministic Automata Operating in Random Environments 406
IV. Variable Structure Stochastic Automata As Models of Learning Systems 410
V. Generalizations of the Basic Reinforcement Learning Model . 414
VI. Automata Games 417
VII. Conclusions and Further Remarks 428
VIII. Nomenclature. 428
References 429

Part III Problems 433

Index 439

Foreword

One of the legacies of the studies of learning conducted in the 1960s and '70s from the perspective of engineering is the distinction between supervised and unsupervised learning, a distinction suggesting that learning comes in only two fundamental forms: learning from labeled or from unlabeled concepts, examples. In the late 1970s, while searching our library's shelves for theories that reflected learning's greater diversity—and that could encompass learning theories from experimental psychology—my colleagues and I discovered the first edition of "Adaptive, Learning and Pattern Recognition Systems." It is not an exaggeration to say that this discovery had an immediate and lasting influence on our thinking and research. We had seen many books focusing on pattern classification, optimization, or control, but here was a book addressing all of these topics and others, revealing dimensions of learning research and engineering practice that were new to us. Its chapters on reinforcement learning, for example, were among the first we had seen suggesting applications of learning principles not cleanly subsumed by the supervised/unsupervised dichotomy. Moreover, this expanded treatment was not achieved at the expense of substance. Each chapter addressed fundamental issues with clarity and mathematical precision. Rather than being a mere collection of articles, it was a multi-authored textbook, with unified notation and even exercises. *It was a lucky find.*

But what is the relevance of this book now, more than two decades of progress after its first publication? During this period, the study of learning has been shaped by steadily increasing numbers of engineers, psychologists, neuroscientists, and researchers in artificial intelligence. We have seen adaptive filters and controllers become successful in many applications, and the revival of artificial neural networks has kindled unprecedented interest in learning systems. One might expect a twenty-four-year-old technical book to be of some interest historically, but can such a book still be worth reading? In this case the answer is unequivocal:

It is as relevant today as when it was first published. That recent progress has done little to diminish this book's usefulness is a result of its unique breadth and the high quality of its chapters as introductions to basic theoretical frameworks and to unchanging truths about applications. In fact, the book's relevance has probably increased since its first publication because such a large number of researchers are currently focusing on such a small fraction of the approaches it introduces. Future progress will depend as much on expanding our repertoire of basic approaches as on continued refinement of the most familiar ones. *This book is an unmatched resource for modern research on adaptive, learning, and pattern recognition systems.*

Andrew G. Barto
Department of Computer Science
University of Massachusetts
Amherst, Massachusetts

Preface

This book, which was originally published twenty-four years ago, is being republished because its content provides a rich source of background materials for the field of neural networks. In essence, this book was ahead of its time. During the 1960s, there was a lot of activity in the areas of adaptive, learning, and pattern recognition systems. Many of the fundamental concepts which the present field of neural networks exploits were developed during that earlier period. This book provides a bridge between today's "second wave" of neural networks and the "first wave" that occurred in the 1960s. It collects in one place a vast amount of material that should be of great interest to "second wavers."

Pattern recognition (Chapters 1-5) laid the foundation for both supervised and unsupervised feedforward neural networks. Much was learned about training algorithms both for classification and function approximation problems. In the 1960s, we did not refer to the pattern recognition architectures as neural networks. Today's neural networks are vastly more complicated than the 1960s architectures; they are multi-layered and highly interconnected. It is well known today that one usually should not apply a neural network to "raw" data. For example, time-series should first be preprocessed to remove trends and cyclical effects. This is related to the feature extraction problem in pattern recognition, where even in the 1960s it was known that to successfully apply pattern recognition to real-world data a good set of features was needed. Sometimes these features had a physical meaning; other times they were mathematical concoctions. In fact, best results were often obtained when the two types of features were used together (Chapter 4).

Because the 1960s architectures were confined to single "neurons" a backpropagation algorithm was not invented; there was no need for it. However, optimization was a very important part of adaptive, learning, and pattern recognition systems. This book treats optimization from different perspectives, ranging from optimization of deterministic objective functions, to optimization of stochastic objective functions, to adaptive optimization procedures (Chapters 6 and 7). Regarding the latter, in this book you will find some of the very early works on random search algorithms, which can be viewed as the predecessors of simulated annealing algorithms. Gradient optimization algorithms are also very widely studied in this book within the context of general stochastic approximation theory (Chapters 9 and 10) and equation error system identification (Chapter 6). Stochastic approximation theory was widely recognized in the 1960s as an indispensable tool for studying the convergence of recursive algorithms. Today, it is being used to study convergence properties of neural networks.

Reinforcement learning theory had a profound impact on the designs of so-called "learning control systems" in the 1960s. Much of this work was conducted at Purdue University under the direction of Professor King-Sun Fu. Many interesting conceptual ideas were originated; however, because of the lack of adequate computer horsepower in the 1960s, none of these systems came into fruition. In retrospect, I believe that this was also due to the fact that a solid theory of adaptive control did not exist. Adaptive control is one rung lower on the ladder of advanced control system design procedures than is learning control, and usually is tried before the latter is. In the intervening twenty-four years, a solid theory of adaptive control has emerged, so that one can now climb the next rung by introducing learning into a system. In one type of a reinforcement learning control system, the notions of short-term and long-term memory, as well as goals and sub-goals, are very important (Chapter 8). In another type of reinforcement learning control system, stochastic automata are used as models of learning systems (Chapter 11). Today, both reinforcement learning and stochastic automata have been considered in the context of neural networks.

When this book was first issued in 1970, Professor King-Sun Fu was co-editor of it with me. With a change in the book's title and the feeling that his memory should be commemorated in the strongest possible way, we chose to remove his name as editor and to dedicate the book to him instead. He was truly a great pioneer in every aspect of adaptive, learning, and pattern recognition systems. His many books and other publications are testament to his impact on these interrelated fields. Those new to these fields should study his works well; for there is much to be learned from them. I feel fortunate to have known him and to have been profoundly influenced by his works.

Jerry M. Mendel
August 1993

PART I

PATTERN RECOGNITION

1

R. O. Duda

ELEMENTS OF PATTERN RECOGNITION

I. Introduction

The problem of designing or programming machines to recognize patterns is one of the most fascinating topics in the computer and information sciences. It appears in many different forms in a variety of disciplines, and the problems encountered range from the practical to the profound, from engineering economics to the philosophy of science. The great variety of pattern-recognition problems makes it difficult to say precisely what pattern recognition is. However, a good idea of the scope of the field can be gained by considering some typical pattern-recognition tasks.

One of the classic examples of pattern recognition is the recognition of printed characters—alphanumerics, punctuation marks, mathematical symbols, etc. Much engineering effort has been devoted to the reading of machine-printed material, and optical character readers are available that can recognize a variety of styles of machine printing with remarkable accuracy and a speed far exceeding human abilities.

The hallmark of this class of problems is that only a limited number of character types must be distinguished, and each character is derivable from an ideal pattern or template. This means that there is a conceptually easy way of classifying an unknown character—one merely compares it with an ideal version of each of the possible characters and sees which one it most nearly resembles. Though simple, this decision procedure is basic, and with various modifications it finds application in many pattern-recognition tasks.

As the patterns to be recognized become subject to greater distortion and variability, the template-matching approach becomes less and less appropriate. For example, it would be difficult to classify hand-printed characters this way without using a very large number of templates, and for the recognition of cursive script this approach is virtually hopeless. In such cases it is natural to look for features, characteristics which distinguish one type of pattern from all others. For example, one could try to tell an 0 from a Q by looking for the presence of a tail, or to tell a B from an 8 by measuring the straightness of the left side.

Ideally, the use of features reduces the complexity of the problem by extracting from a mass of raw data just that information needed for classification. Moreover, if the results of feature measurement tend to be the same for patterns in the same class, but are noticeably different for patterns in different classes, then there is hope that template matching can be used at the feature level with success.

This general approach to pattern recognition, the extraction of significant, characterizing features followed by classification on the basis of the values of the features, has been applied to many pattern-recognition tasks. Speech recognition, speaker recognition, fingerprint identification, electrocardiogram analysis, radar and sonar signal detection, cloud pattern recognition, blood cell classification, and even weather forecasting and medical diagnosis have all been attacked in this way.

For each application two problems must be solved: the design of a feature extractor and the design of a pattern classifier. The first of these tasks is usually highly problem dependent. Here the designer brings to bear all of his special knowledge about the problem, selecting those features that seem to be most valuable in telling one pattern from another. Since what constitutes a valuable feature depends so strongly on the problem being considered, it is not surprising that little theory is available to guide the design of the feature extractor. Once the feature extractor has been designed, however, a variety of procedures are available for designing the classifier. These procedures differ in the assumptions that are made about the behavior of the features, but these assumptions are usually quite broad, such as assuming that the features are statistically independent. Thus, the methods for designing the classifier are often much more independent of the special characteristics of the particular problem, and the theory of pattern classification is well developed.

But to say that pattern recognition merely consists of feature extraction followed by pattern classification is to grossly oversimplify the situation. For one thing, we have said nothing about how the object or event we wish to recognize is to be located and isolated. Even when the solution is clear in principle, as is the case with optical character recognition, this can be a significant practical problem. If we want to recognize continuous speech or to identify common objects in a photograph, the location and isolation of individual items to be recognized may be one of the hardest parts of the task.

Another important point is that not all pattern-recognition problems are classification problems. At the very least, it may be desirable to be able to reject a pattern if it is quite unlike any of the patterns the system was designed to recognize. Also, in problems where context is important, it is important for the classifier to supply a confidence measure with each decision, and perhaps some alternative choices and their confidences. Finally, in problems such as analyzing involved block diagrams or tracks in bubble-chamber photographs, where the desired output is a description of potentially great complexity, the picture of pattern recognition as feature extraction followed by classification becomes quite inadequate. Thus, while we shall temporarily concentrate on feature extraction and classification, they should not be thought of as constituting the whole of pattern recognition.

II. A Recognition Problem

A. *The Initial Approach*

Many of the ideas we have been discussing can be made clearer by considering a specific example. For this reason and this reason only we shall look at the problem of telling hand-printed B's from hand-printed 8's. We shall assume that a mechanism is available for isolating and digitizing the input data to any degree of precision desired, and we shall consider ways of using this quantized data to recognize the character.

The first thing to note is that the difficulty of the problem depends at least in part upon the degradation resulting from quantization. Fig. 1 shows how a typical hand-printed B appears when reproduced with different degrees of resolution. Clearly, one could not go much below 24-line resolution and still retain enough fidelity to tell that this character is a B and not an 8. In any pattern-recognition problem, the device that senses the physical object or event introduces some distortion and limits the ultimate performance that can be achieved. For an analytical design, it would be nice if one could specify the characteristics required of the transducer on the basis of the performance desired, but this is rarely possible. For our example, we shall assume that a 24×24 black-white representation is adequate, and proceed.

What method shall we use to tell whether or not a given quantized character is a B or an 8? One characteristic that should differentiate

FIGURE 1. A hand-printed B reproduced with 6-line, 12-line, 24-line, 48-line, and unlimited resolution

B's from 8's is the fact that B's have a straight stroke down their left side. Thus, a plausible procedure would be to measure, for example, the straightness of the middle third of that side. If it is sufficiently straight, the figure is called a B; if not, it is called an 8.

Two technical problems remain. One is to decide how to measure straightness, and the other is to decide how straight is "sufficiently" straight. There are a number of ways to measure straightness, for example, by measuring the average radius of curvature or the average second derivative. For no particularly good reason, we shall measure the straightness of a line by the ratio of the distance between its endpoints to its arc length. This will yield a number x between zero and one—the larger the number the straighter the line.

To decide how straight is "sufficiently" straight, we need to know typical values of x for B's and 8's. If we measure the B's and 8's shown in Figs. 2a and 2b, we obtain an average value of 0.92 for the B's and 0.85 for the 8's. Thus, it is reasonable to select some intermediate value x_0, say $x_0 = 0.89$, and use the following rule: *If* $x > x_0$, call the character a B; otherwise call it an 8.

Unfortunately, the results obtained by applying this rule are rather disappointing. About 23 percent of the characters are misclassified, with the majority of the errors being 8's that are called B's. What are the possible reasons for this result? Perhaps the 24-line resolution is inadequate and a better representation of the data is called for. Another possibility is that a better feature extractor is needed: the selection of the particular measure of straightness was certainly arbitrary, and a more careful choice might yield improved results. A third possibility is that a different choice for the threshold value x_0 is called for. Since this is the easiest thing to investigate, we shall consider it first.

B. *Improving the Classifier*

If the straightness ratio x is measured for the 20 B's and the 20 8's in Figs. 2a and 2b, the results range from 0.57 to 1.00. A good way to describe the way these values are distributed is to plot the so-called empirical cumulative distribution function $F_e(x)$, which gives the fraction of cases having a straightness ratio less than x. This has been done in Fig. 3, where $F_e(x \mid \text{B})$ is the empirical cumulative distribution function for the B's, and $F_e(x \mid 8)$ is the empirical cumulative distribution function for the 8's.

The first thing to notice is that $F_e(x \mid \text{B})$ is to the right of $F_e(x \mid 8)$, indicating that the straightness ratio for B's does indeed tend to be greater than the straightness ratio for the 8's. It would be ideal if there were an x_0 having the property that $F_e(x_0 \mid \text{B}) = 0$ and $F_e(x_0 \mid 8) = 1$.

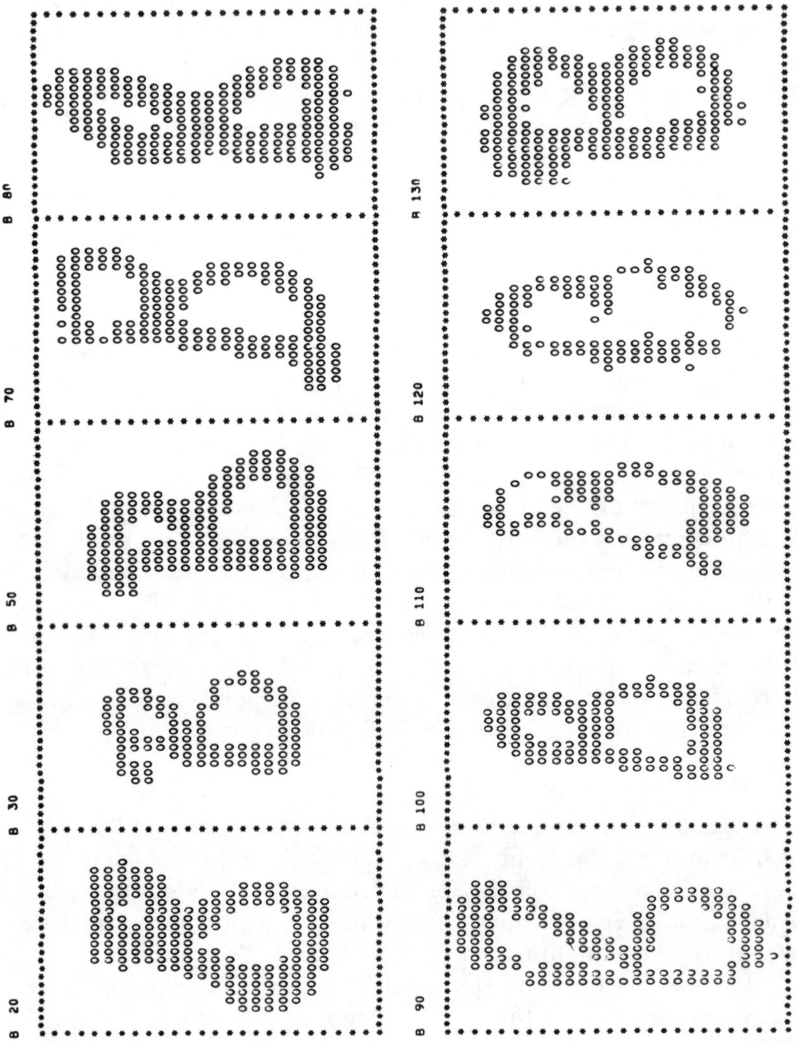

FIGURE 2a. Samples of quantized hand-printed B's

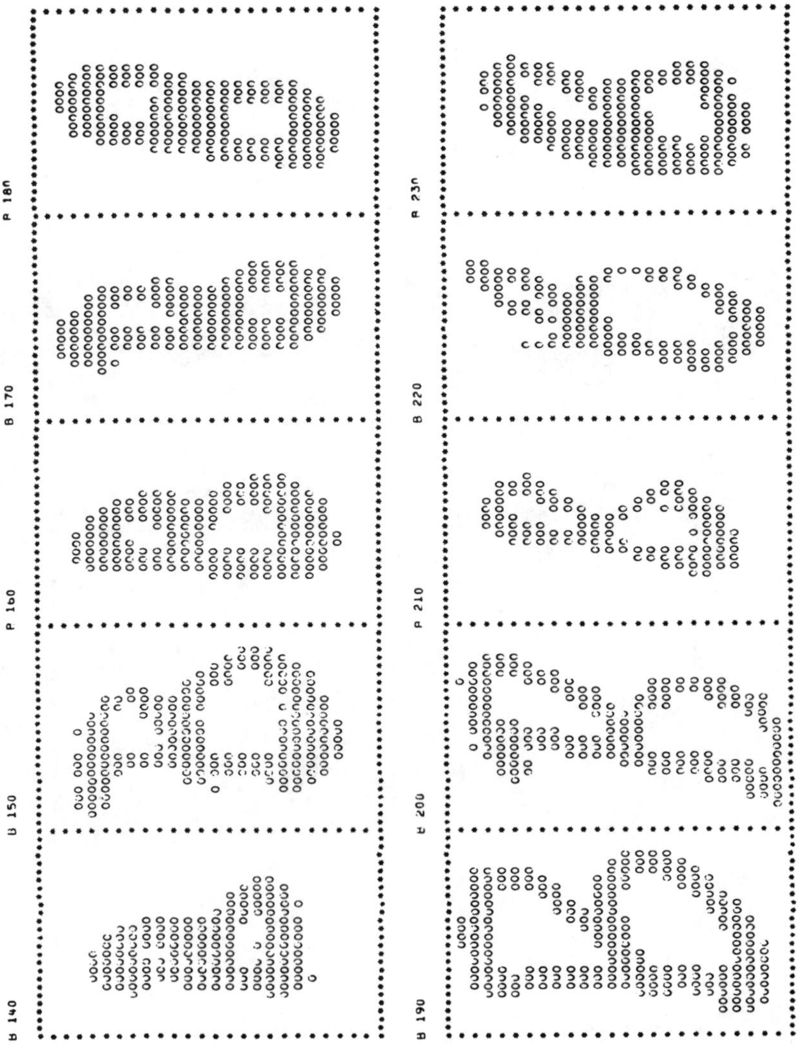

FIGURE 2a (*continued*)

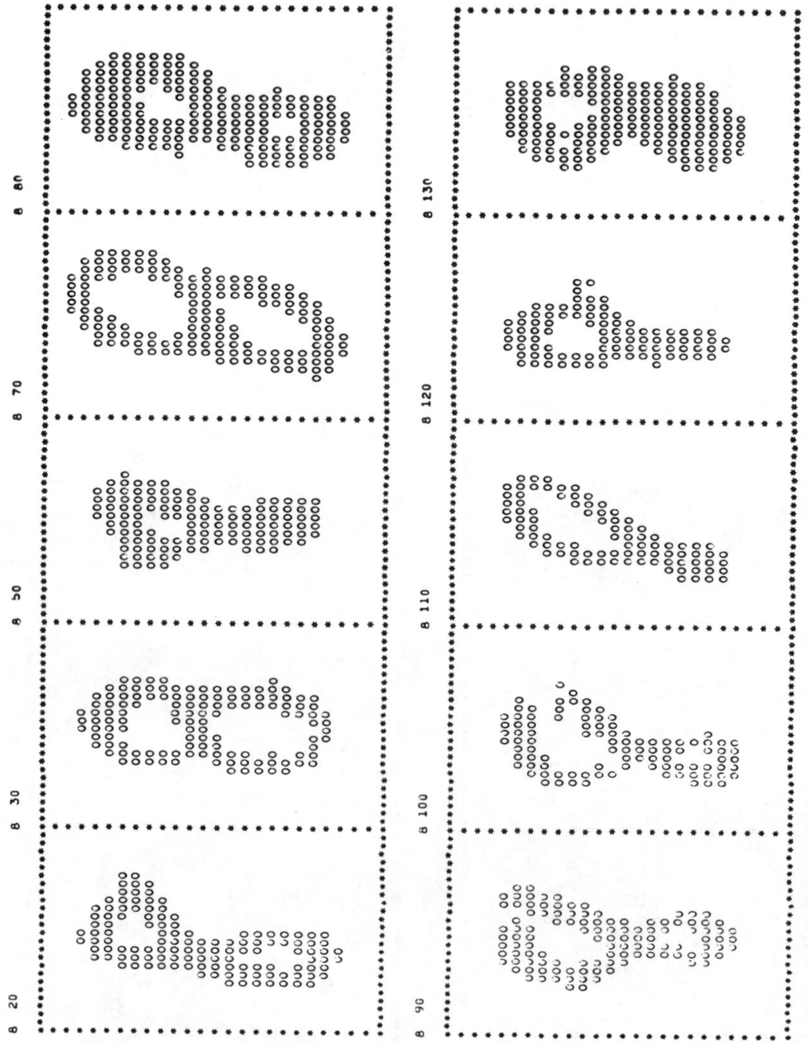

FIGURE 2b. Samples of quantized hand-printed 8's

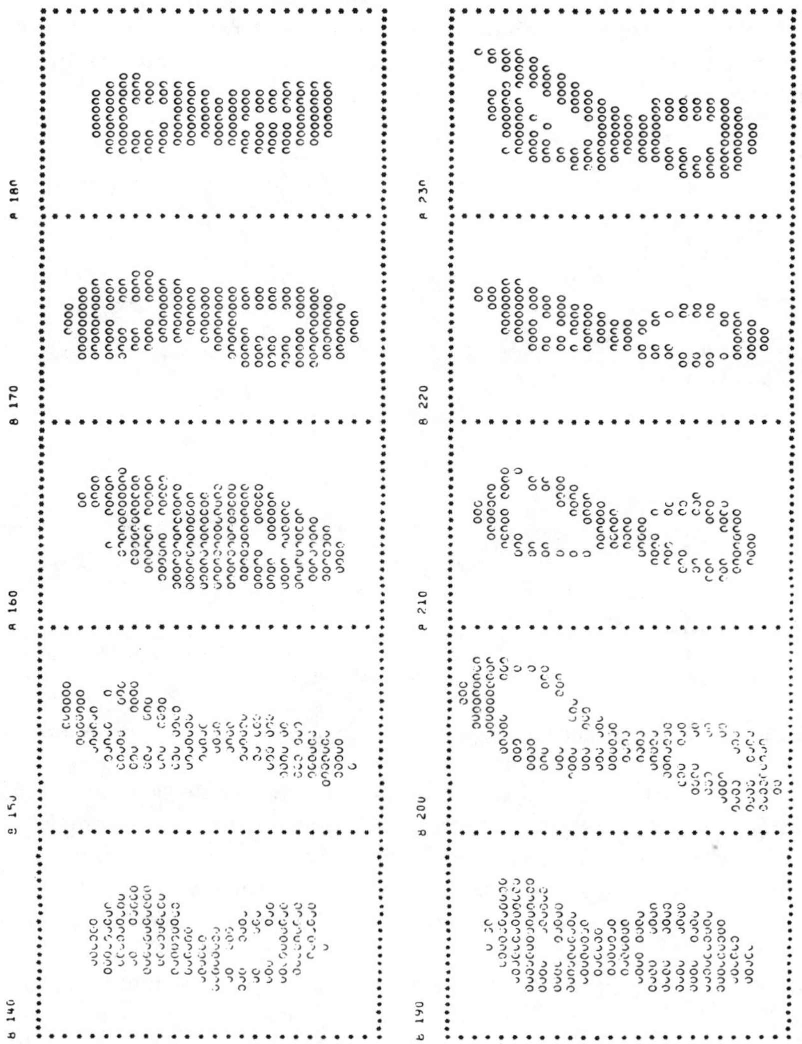

FIGURE 2b *(continued)*

In that case, we could call a character a B if $x > x_0$ and an 8 if $x \leqslant x_0$ without ever making an error. It is clear from Fig. 3 that no such solution exists. No matter what our choice of x_0, there are either some B's having $x \leqslant x_0$ or some 8's having $x > x_0$. Furthermore, it is clear that our previous choice $x_0 = 0.89$ was not at all bad. By taking $x_0 = 0.885$ we can classify one more character correctly and reduce the error rate to 20 percent. However, this improvement is both slight and of dubious significance.

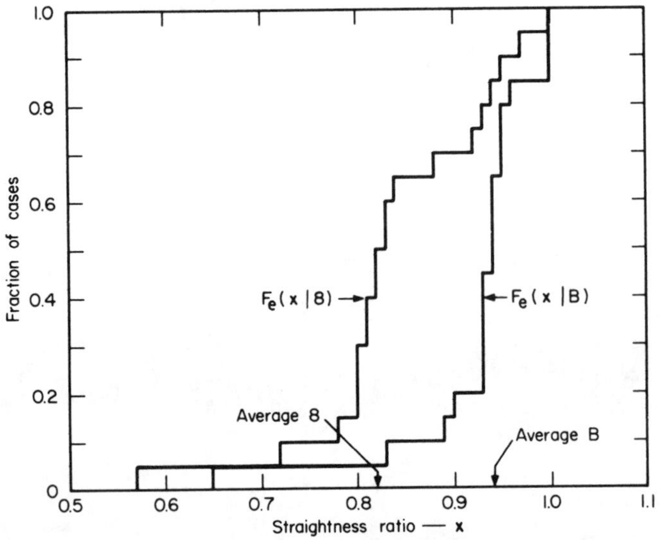

FIGURE 3. Empirical cumulative distribution functions for the straightness ratio

At this point it is natural to ask if there are better decision rules than deciding B if x exceeds some threshold x_0, and if there are, which rule is best? That there are other rules is clear. For example, one could store the values of the straightness ratio for the 40 samples and classify a new pattern by computing $d_i = | x - x(i)|$, $i = 1$ to 40, selecting the class corresponding to the sample for which d_i is smallest.* When applied to the 40 *samples*, this rule is much more effective, reducing the error from 20 to 12.5 percent. However, the only reason it makes any errors at all on the samples is due to ties, and whether or not similar performance could be obtained on new characters is open to serious question.

* This is known as the nearest-neighbor decision rule. In case of ties, one usually selects the most frequently represented class.

Here we have encountered a frequently occurring pattern-recognition problem. Both of the decision rules we have considered have made use of sample patterns, the first in the selection of x_0 and the second in the computation of $d_i = |x - x(i)|$. Both were evaluated by seeing how well they classified these same samples. But it is clear that we really want to know how well the system will perform on new patterns, patterns not included in the set of samples. This is often called the problem of generalization, and its treatment, as well as the treatment of classification generally, is illuminated by viewing it as a statistical problem.

C. *Statistical Approach to Classification*

Let us imagine that we have two very large urns, one containing an infinite number of hand-printed B's and the other containing an infinite number of hand-printed 8's. Suppose we flip a biased coin to decide which urn to choose, so that we select the B-urn with ***a priori probability*** $P(\mathrm{B})$ and the 8-urn with a priori probability $P(8)$, where, of course,

$$P(\mathrm{B}) + P(8) = 1 \tag{1.1}$$

Having selected an urn, we draw a sample and measure the straightness ratio x. In general, we view x as a random variable. Its distribution is presumably different for the B's than for the 8's, since we are trying to use its value to separate the two. Thus, we assume that there exist two *conditional densities* $p(x \mid \mathrm{B})$ and $p(x \mid 8)$. These are related to the cumulative distribution functions $F(x \mid \mathrm{B})$ and $F(x \mid 8)$ by

$$p(x \mid \mathrm{B}) = \frac{dF(x \mid \mathrm{B})}{dx} \tag{1.2}$$

and

$$p(x \mid 8) = \frac{dF(x \mid 8)}{dx} \tag{1.3}$$

A rough idea of the form of $p(x \mid \mathrm{B})$ and $p(x \mid 8)$ can be obtained by differentiating a smooth curve fitted to the empirical cumulative distribution functions of Fig. 3. Of course the results will depend on how the curve is fitted, but they will generally look like the curves shown in Fig. 4.

Suppose that both the a priori probabilities and the conditional densities are known. Then we can use Bayes' rule to compute the so-called ***a posteriori probabilities***

$$P(\mathrm{B} \mid x) = \frac{p(x \mid \mathrm{B})\, P(\mathrm{B})}{p(x)} \tag{1.4}$$

and

$$P(8 \mid x) = \frac{p(x \mid 8)\, P(8)}{p(x)} \tag{1.5}$$

where

$$p(x) = p(x \mid \mathrm{B})\, P(\mathrm{B}) + p(x \mid 8)\, P(8) \tag{1.6}$$

thus assuring that $P(\mathrm{B} \mid x)$ and $P(8 \mid x)$ sum to one. Equations (1.4) and (1.5) show how the observation of the value of the straightness ratio x changes our attitude about whether the B-urn or the 8-urn was selected,

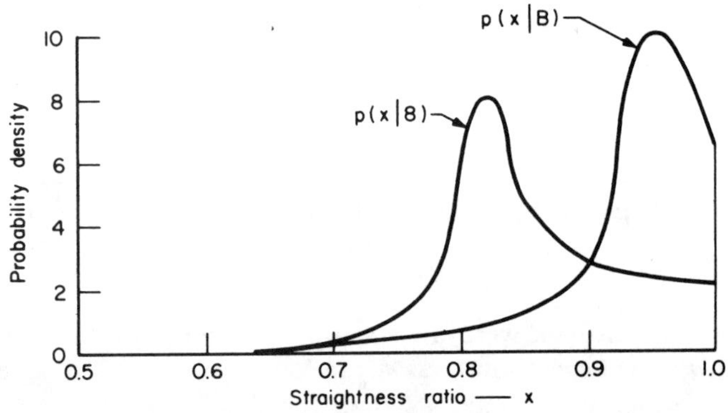

FIGURE 4. Conditional probability densities for the straightness ratio

i.e., whether the character should be called a B or an 8. If we must make a decision, it is reasonable to use the following ***Bayes' decision rule***:

Decide B if $P(\mathrm{B} \mid x) > P(8 \mid x)$; otherwise decide 8.

It will be shown in Chapter 2 that this rule is not only reasonable, it is optimal in the sense that it will minimize the probability of error. To use it, however, we must know or be able to estimate both the a priori probabilities and the conditional densities. In some problems, such as radar signal detection, it is hard to arrive at meaningful values for the a priori probabilities, and in most problems it is difficult to estimate the conditional densities.

In our particular example, we could estimate the a priori probabilities by counting the frequency of occurrence of B's and 8's in a portion of the text being read. For simplicity, however, we shall merely assume that B's and 8's are equally likely a priori. We have already made a rough estimate of the conditional densities from the empirical cumulative distribution functions, and obtained the curves shown in Fig. 4. From Eqs. (1.4) and (1.5), the condition

$$P(\mathrm{B} \mid x) > P(8 \mid x) \tag{1.7}$$

is equivalent to the condition

$$p(x \mid \mathrm{B})\, P(\mathrm{B}) > p(x \mid 8)\, P(8) \tag{1.8}$$

and since we are assuming that $P(\mathrm{B}) = P(8)$, this means that in our case an equivalent decision rule is

Decide B if $p(x \mid \mathrm{B}) > p(x \mid 8)$; otherwise decide 8.

Inspection of Fig. 4 shows that $p(x \mid \mathrm{B}) > p(x \mid 8)$ if x is greater than some threshold value x_0 near 0.9. Thus it happens that we have come full circle and have returned to our original, intuitively suggested decision rule. Now, however, we have a theoretical justification for this rule, and we have a much more general approach for deriving decision rules, the method of statistical decision theory.

D. *Improving the Feature Extractor*

Unfortunately, the major practical result of our attempt to improve the classifier was a demonstration that it was doing about as well as can be expected. If the true conditional densities at all resemble the approximations in Fig. 4, it is clear that the straightness ratio does not have the discriminating power needed to do a good job of separating B's from 8's. It is fair to ask whether this is the fault of this feature or the fault of a low-resolution representation. Inspection of the quantized characters in Fig. 2 makes it clear that most of the problem can be blamed on the feature. While low resolution does make it hard to identify all of these characters with confidence, there is clearly enough information for humans to recognize them with an error rate well below 20 percent. Thus, if any real improvement is to be obtained, it must be the result of finding better features.

One such feature is the ratio of the maximum width of the top half of the figure to the maximum width of the bottom half. This measurement exploits the fact that many hand-printed B's tend to be larger at the bottom, while 8's tend to be larger at the top. Suppose that we measure this top-to-bottom ratio for each of the 40 samples. Then each sample can be thought of as being characterized by two measurements, the straightness ratio x_1 and the top-to-bottom ratio x_2. That means that every sample can be represented as a *feature vector* $\mathbf{x}$ in a two-dimensional *feature space*, where

$$\mathbf{x} = \begin{bmatrix} x_1 \\ x_2 \end{bmatrix} \tag{1.9}$$

If we measure the 40 feature vectors and plot them as points in the $x_1 - x_2$ plane, we obtain the scattering of points shown in Fig. 5. Although there is a certain amount of intermingling of the data, most of the points obtained from B's are separated from those obtained from 8's. Now the problem is to design a classifier that will take advantage of this fact.

E. *Redesigning the Classifier*

The statistical approach to classification can be extended from the scalar case to the vector case with few formal difficulties. We again

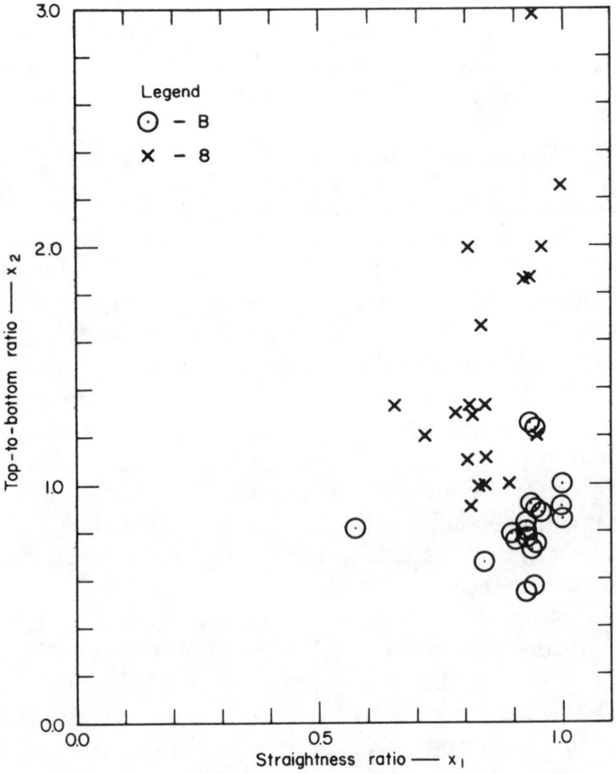

FIGURE 5. Patterns as points in feature space

assume the existence of a priori probabilities and conditional densities, but now the conditional densities are joint distributions $p(\mathbf{x} \mid \mathrm{B})$ and $p(\mathbf{x} \mid 8)$. The decision rule is again to decide B if $P(\mathrm{B} \mid \mathbf{x})$ exceeds $P(8 \mid \mathbf{x})$, and Bayes' rule can be invoked to compute these a posteriori probabilities:

$$P(\mathrm{B} \mid \mathbf{x}) = \frac{p(\mathbf{x} \mid \mathrm{B})\, P(\mathrm{B})}{p(\mathbf{x})} \tag{1.10}$$

and

$$P(8 \mid \mathbf{x}) = \frac{p(\mathbf{x} \mid 8)\, P(8)}{p(\mathbf{x})} \tag{1.11}$$

Once again, the problem is to estimate the a priori probabilities and the conditional densities. The problem of estimating the probabilities $P(\mathrm{B})$ and $P(8)$ is exactly the same as before, and we shall again assume that they are equal. However, the problem of estimating $p(\mathbf{x} \mid \mathrm{B})$ and $p(\mathbf{x} \mid 8)$ is more difficult now, because we have functions of two variables, x_1 and x_2, that must be approximated. The graphical technique we used with one variable would be quite cumbersome to use with two, and would be hopeless for more than two.

The difficulty of estimating the conditional densities depends in part upon the kinds of assumptions one can make. For example, one can greatly simplify the problem by assuming that the features are statistically independent, i.e., by assuming that

$$p(\mathbf{x} \mid \mathrm{B}) = p(x_1, x_2 \mid \mathrm{B}) = p(x_1 \mid \mathrm{B})\, p(x_2 \mid \mathrm{B}) \tag{1.12}$$

and

$$p(\mathbf{x} \mid 8) = p(x_1, x_2 \mid 8) = p(x_1 \mid 8)\, p(x_2 \mid 8) \tag{1.13}$$

since this reduces the problem from a two-dimensional problem to two one-dimensional problems. Suppose that we not only make this somewhat questionable assumption, but that we assume further that the marginal densities $p(x_i \mid \mathrm{B})$ and $p(x_i \mid 8)$ are normal, differing *only* in their mean values. That is, we assume that

$$p(x_i \mid \mathrm{B}) = \frac{1}{\sqrt{2\pi\sigma^2}} \exp\left[-\frac{(x_i - \mu_i^{\mathrm{B}})^2}{2\sigma^2}\right] \qquad i = 1, 2 \tag{1.14}$$

and

$$p(x_i \mid 8) = \frac{1}{\sqrt{2\pi\sigma^2}} \exp\left[-\frac{(x_i - \mu_i^{8})^2}{2\sigma^2}\right] \qquad i = 1, 2 \tag{1.15}$$

Then, from Eqs. (1.12) and (1.13),

$$p(\mathbf{x} \mid \mathrm{B}) = \frac{1}{2\pi\sigma^2} \exp\left[-\frac{1}{2\sigma^2} \| \mathbf{x} - \boldsymbol{\mu}_\mathrm{B} \|^2\right] \tag{1.16}$$

and

$$p(\mathbf{x} \mid 8) = \frac{1}{2\pi\sigma^2} \exp\left[-\frac{1}{2\sigma^2} \| \mathbf{x} - \boldsymbol{\mu}_8 \|^2\right] \tag{1.17}$$

where $\| \mathbf{x} \|$ is the Euclidean norm of $\mathbf{x}$, and $\boldsymbol{\mu}_\mathrm{B}$ and $\boldsymbol{\mu}_8$ are the mean vectors

$$\boldsymbol{\mu}_\mathrm{B} = \begin{bmatrix} \mu_1{}^\mathrm{B} \\ \mu_2{}^\mathrm{B} \end{bmatrix} \tag{1.18}$$

and

$$\boldsymbol{\mu}_8 = \begin{bmatrix} \mu_1{}^8 \\ \mu_2{}^8 \end{bmatrix} \tag{1.19}$$

which represent the averages of the vectors $\mathbf{x}$ corresponding to B's and 8's, respectively.

If the a priori probabilities are equal, $P(\mathrm{B} \mid \mathbf{x}) > P(8 \mid \mathbf{x})$ implies that $p(\mathbf{x} \mid \mathrm{B}) > p(\mathbf{x} \mid 8)$, and vice versa. But from Eqs. (1.16) and (1.17), this is equivalent to $\| \mathbf{x} - \boldsymbol{\mu}_\mathrm{B} \|^2 < \| \mathbf{x} - \boldsymbol{\mu}_8 \|^2$, and leads to the decision rule

Decide B if $\| \mathbf{x} - \boldsymbol{\mu}_\mathrm{B} \| < \| \mathbf{x} - \boldsymbol{\mu}_8 \|$; otherwise decide 8.

This is a simple and appealing decision rule. It says that a pattern $\mathbf{x}$ is classified by comparing it with the average of the patterns in each of the two classes. If $\mathbf{x}$ is closer to the average of the B's than to the average of the 8's, call it a B. This is exactly a template matching procedure, except that the templates $\boldsymbol{\mu}_\mathrm{B}$ and $\boldsymbol{\mu}_8$ are ideal feature vectors rather than ideal hand-printed letters. Whether or not this rule is good depends upon how nearly our various assumptions are satisfied. If they are all satisfied exactly, this procedure is optimal.

The effect of using this decision rule is to divide the feature space into two regions, one in which $\| \mathbf{x} - \boldsymbol{\mu}_\mathrm{B} \| < \| \mathbf{x} - \boldsymbol{\mu}_8 \|$, and one in which $\| \mathbf{x} - \boldsymbol{\mu}_\mathrm{B} \| > \| \mathbf{x} - \boldsymbol{\mu}_8 \|$. These regions are separated by a *decision boundary*, the locus of points satisfying $\| \mathbf{x} - \boldsymbol{\mu}_\mathrm{B} \| = \| \mathbf{x} - \boldsymbol{\mu}_8 \|$. Thus the decision boundary is the locus of points equidistant from $\boldsymbol{\mu}_\mathrm{B}$ and $\boldsymbol{\mu}_8$, i.e., the perpendicular bisector of the line segment from $\boldsymbol{\mu}_\mathrm{B}$ to $\boldsymbol{\mu}_8$. Of course, to find this decision boundary, we must know the mean vectors $\boldsymbol{\mu}_\mathrm{B}$ and $\boldsymbol{\mu}_8$. While we may never know them exactly, we can estimate them from the samples by computing the so-called *sample means* $\mathbf{m}_\mathrm{B}$ and $\mathbf{m}_8$, the arithmetic averages of the feature vectors for the samples. This computation yields $\mathbf{m}_\mathrm{B} = (0.92, 0.84)'$ and $\mathbf{m}_8 = (0.85, 1.51)'$, and leads to the decision boundary shown in Fig. 6.

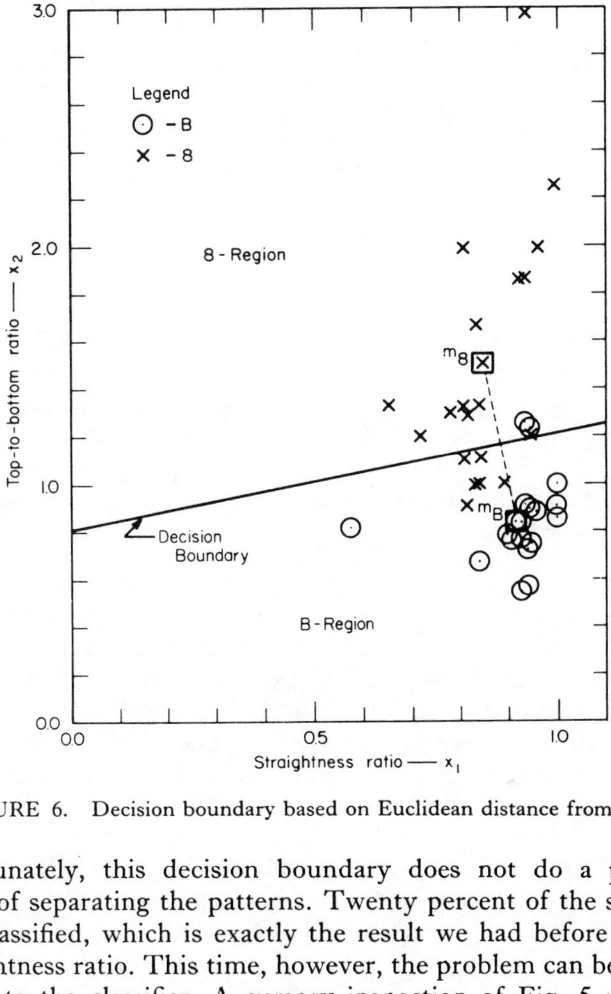

FIGURE 6. Decision boundary based on Euclidean distance from means

Unfortunately, this decision boundary does not do a particularly good job of separating the patterns. Twenty percent of the samples are still misclassified, which is exactly the result we had before using only the straightness ratio. This time, however, the problem can be attributed primarily to the classifier. A cursory inspection of Fig. 5 reveals that both our assumptions of statistical independence and normality can be questioned, and our assumption that the marginal densities $p(x_i \mid \mathrm{B})$ and $p(x_i \mid 8)$ differed only in their mean values is particularly bad. A somewhat better assumption, one that at least takes account of the different scale factors for x_1 and x_2, is to assume that

$$p(\mathbf{x} \mid \mathrm{B}) = \frac{1}{2\pi\sigma_1\sigma_2} \exp\left(-\frac{1}{2}\left[\frac{(x_1 - \mu_1^{\mathrm{B}})^2}{\sigma_1^2} + \frac{(x_2 - \mu_2^{\mathrm{B}})^2}{\sigma_2^2}\right]\right) \tag{1.20}$$

and

$$p(\mathbf{x} \mid 8) = \frac{1}{2\pi\sigma_1\sigma_2} \exp\left(-\frac{1}{2}\left[\frac{(x_1 - \mu_1^{8})^2}{\sigma_1^2} + \frac{(x_2 - \mu_2^{8})^2}{\sigma_2^2}\right]\right) \tag{1.21}$$

where σ_1^2 is the variance of x_1 and σ_2^2 is the variance of x_2. If we define the *covariance matrix* Σ by

$$\Sigma = \begin{bmatrix} \sigma_1^2 & 0 \\ 0 & \sigma_2^2 \end{bmatrix} \tag{1.22}$$

then this can be written in matrix form as

$$p(\mathbf{x} \mid \mathrm{B}) = \frac{1}{2\pi |\Sigma|^{1/2}} \exp[-\tfrac{1}{2}(\mathbf{x} - \boldsymbol{\mu}_\mathrm{B})' \Sigma^{-1} (\mathbf{x} - \boldsymbol{\mu}_\mathrm{B})] \tag{1.23}$$

and

$$p(\mathbf{x} \mid 8) = \frac{1}{2\pi |\Sigma|^{1/2}} \exp[-\tfrac{1}{2}(\mathbf{x} - \boldsymbol{\mu}_8)' \Sigma^{-1} (\mathbf{x} - \boldsymbol{\mu}_8)] \tag{1.24}$$

If we once again assume that the a priori probabilities are equal, the condition $p(\mathbf{x} \mid \mathrm{B}) > p(\mathbf{x} \mid 8)$ leads to the decision rule

> Decide B if $(\mathbf{x} - \boldsymbol{\mu}_\mathrm{B})' \Sigma^{-1} (\mathbf{x} - \boldsymbol{\mu}_\mathrm{B}) < (\mathbf{x} - \boldsymbol{\mu}_8)' \Sigma^{-1} (\mathbf{x} - \boldsymbol{\mu}_8)$;
> otherwise decide 8.

There are two ways to interpret this result. One is to say that we again classify $\mathbf{x}$ as a B if it is closer to the average of the B's than to the average of the 8's, except that we are using a normalized distance [the so-called Mahalanobis distance $(\mathbf{x} - \boldsymbol{\mu})' \Sigma^{-1} (\mathbf{x} - \boldsymbol{\mu})$] to measure closeness. Another is to say that we still use Euclidean distance to measure closeness, but only after scaling the features so that they have unit variance. With either interpretation, we again arrive at a linear decision boundary, since the condition

$$(\mathbf{x} - \boldsymbol{\mu}_\mathrm{B})' \Sigma^{-1} (\mathbf{x} - \boldsymbol{\mu}_\mathrm{B}) = (\mathbf{x} - \boldsymbol{\mu}_8)' \Sigma^{-1} (\mathbf{x} - \boldsymbol{\mu}_8) \tag{1.25}$$

is equivalent to

$$\mathbf{x}' \Sigma^{-1} (\boldsymbol{\mu}_\mathrm{B} - \boldsymbol{\mu}_8) = \tfrac{1}{2}(\boldsymbol{\mu}_\mathrm{B} + \boldsymbol{\mu}_8)' \Sigma^{-1} (\boldsymbol{\mu}_\mathrm{B} - \boldsymbol{\mu}_8) \tag{1.26}$$

which is the equation of a line through $\frac{1}{2}(\boldsymbol{\mu}_\mathrm{B} + \boldsymbol{\mu}_8)$ and normal to $\Sigma^{-1}(\boldsymbol{\mu}_\mathrm{B} - \boldsymbol{\mu}_8)$. If we estimate σ_1^2 by averaging the sample variances for the straightness ratio for both the B's and the 8's, we obtain $\sigma_1^2 = 0.0075$. A similar estimate for the average top-to-bottom ratio yields $\sigma_2^2 = 0.350$. Thus, the estimated decision boundary again passes through $\frac{1}{2}(\mathbf{m}_\mathrm{B} + \mathbf{m}_8) = (0.89, 1.18)'$ but is normal to $\Sigma^{-1}(\mathbf{m}_\mathrm{B} - \mathbf{m}_8) = (9.33, -1.91)'$.

This boundary, shown in Fig. 7, does a significantly better job of classifying the samples, getting all but three correct, for an error rate of 7.5 percent. While one might seek even better performance by

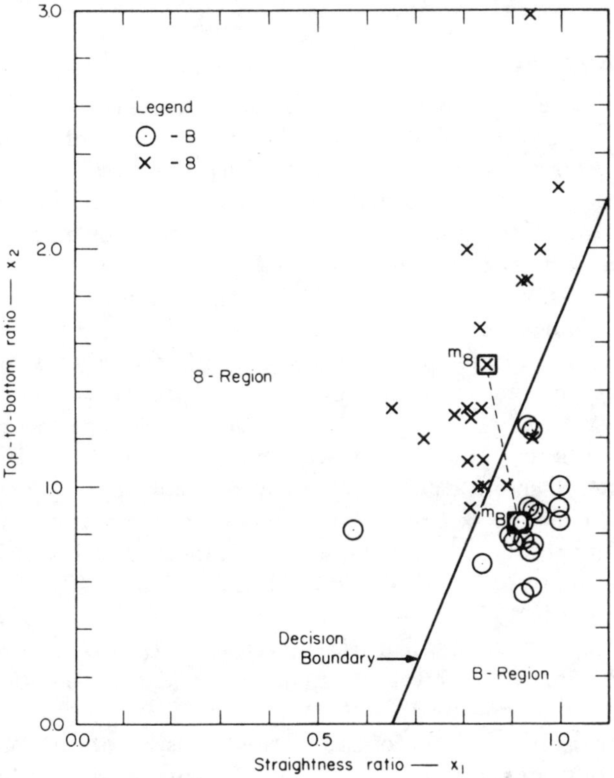

FIGURE 7. Decision boundary based on Mahalanobis distance from means

improving further on the assumptions about the conditional densities, this performance is close to human performance on the quantized data, and is unlikely to be significantly bettered. In fact, even if a more complicated decision boundary could be found that would thread itself through the points and classify all of the samples correctly, there is no guarantee that it would perform better in classifying new B's and 8's—characters other than those used to design the classifier. The important question is not how well the classifier performs on the design data, but how well it works on independent test data. Once again we are faced with the problem of generalization, the question of how well a classifier will perform on independent test data. Rather than trying to solve it, we shall merely remark that, as a rule, the more complicated the decision boundary, the greater the number of design samples needed to fix that boundary and to ensure that good performance on design data will lead to good performance on test data.

III. The Classical Model

A. *Basic Elements*

The example just considered contains elements common to many pattern recognition problems. An object (or event) to be classified is sensed by a transducer and represented in some way, e.g., as a 24×24 binary array. This representation, although basically faithful to the original, is quite complicated to work with, and thus a smaller number of characterizing features are extracted. The values of the features are sent to a classifier, which assigns the input object to one of a fixed number of categories.

This entire process can be viewed mathematically as a mapping. Each input can be viewed as a point $\mathbf{z}$ in object space. The transducer maps each $\mathbf{z}$ into a point $\mathbf{y}$ in representation space. The feature extractor maps each $\mathbf{y}$ into a point $\mathbf{x}$ in feature space. Finally, the classifier maps each $\mathbf{x}$ into a discrete-valued scalar d in decision space, where $d = d_i$ if the classifier assigns $\mathbf{x}$ to the ith category. These mappings are almost always many-to-one, with some information usually being lost at each step. With the transducer, the loss of information may be unintentional, while with the feature extractor and the classifier, the loss of information is quite intentional. The feature extractor is expected to preserve only the information needed for classification, and the classifier preserves only the classification itself.

From an abstract point of view, this division of the problem into representation, feature extraction, and classification is arbitrary. The entire process can be viewed as a single mapping from object space to decision space. The optimum mapping is the one for which the probability of error is minimum. In principle, this problem can be formulated precisely like the classification problem, and can be treated by statistical decision theory.* In practice, this approach is usually hopeless, primarily because the conditional densities for points in object space are usually so complicated that they can never be estimated, let alone used.

The distinctions between representation, feature extraction, and classification are forced upon us for practical, rather than theoretical reasons, and in some problems the boundaries between these operations are far from clear. We shall have little to say about representation, since this topic is extremely problem dependent. Instead, we shall

* If some types of errors are more costly than others, one can assign a cost to each type of error. Then the optimum mapping is the one that minimizes the average cost, or risk. The optimum classifier is still called a *Bayes' classifier*, and the value of the minimum risk is called the *Bayes' risk*.

concentrate on feature extraction and classification, outlining some of the more important general methods of approach to these problems.

B. *Feature Extraction*

The performance of a pattern recognition system often depends crucially on the performance of the feature extractor. This was certainly the case in our B-8 example, where improved performance was only achieved after obtaining better features. The methods by which features are obtained, however, are often intuitive and empirical, drawing upon the designer's knowledge about and experience with the problem. The main guides to feature design are that the features should be invariant to (or at least insensitive to) irrelevant variations, such as limited amounts of translation, rotation, scale change, etc., while emphasizing differences that are important for distinguishing between patterns of different types. In a comprehensive survey of the state-of-the-art in pattern recognition, Nagy (1968) gives many examples of the types of empirically derived features used in practical pattern recognition systems.

Analytical approaches to feature extractor design have been restricted to *feature selection* and *dimensionality reduction*. Both of these approaches assume that a relatively large number of features have somehow been obtained. Taken together, these features are supposed to contain the information needed for classification, but there are so many features that it is not practical to use them all. Feature selection methods seek a smaller number of features by obtaining a subset from the original set, either by discarding poor features or selecting good ones. Dimensionality reduction methods obtain a smaller number of features by forming (usually linear) combinations of the original ones.

Both of these approaches are discussed in some detail in Chapter 2. However, both suffer from the lack of a measure or figure of merit for evaluating features that is both meaningful and computationally feasible. Ideally, one would like that set of features which, when optimally classified, yields the minimum risk. This is the most meaningful figure of merit, and, together with some normality and independence assumptions, it has actually been used for linear dimensionality reduction (Casey, 1965). However, if used without such assumptions, this measure is far from easy to compute.

Many different suggestions have been made for a figure of merit that is both appropriate and at least reasonably easy to compute. These include the ratio of between-class to within-class variance (Miller, 1962), an information or entropy measure (Lewis, 1962; Liu, 1964), divergence (Marill and Green, 1963), mean square error (Tou and Heydorn, 1966), and the Bhattacharyya distance (Kailath, 1967) or Hellinger integral (Kadota and Shepp, 1967). Unless rather suspect assumptions are made, however, none of these measures guarantees that the features finally obtained are optimal, and the ultimate justification for their use lies in the classification performance obtained.

C. *Classification*

1. *The formal solution.* Once a set of features has been selected, the only problem remaining is to design the classifier. This task can be approached in a variety of ways, depending upon the assumptions that can be made about the nature of the problem. Most of these approaches can be viewed in a statistical setting in which the n-component feature vector $\mathbf{x}$ is assumed to be a random vector. In an m-class problem, the ith class is assumed to occur with a priori probability $P(\omega_i)$, $i = 1, \ldots, m$. For patterns in the ith class, the feature vector is assumed to be governed by a conditional density $p(\mathbf{x} \mid \omega_i)$, $i = 1, \ldots, m$. If all errors are equally costly, minimizing the risk is equivalent to minimizing the probability of error. In this case, the formal solution is to compute

$$P(\omega_i \mid \mathbf{x}) = \frac{p(\mathbf{x} \mid \omega_i)\, P(\omega_i)}{\sum_{j=1}^{m} p(\mathbf{x} \mid \omega_j)\, P(\omega_j)} \tag{1.27}$$

for every i and select the category for which $P(\omega_i \mid \mathbf{x})$ is maximum. Equivalent alternatives are to compute the *discriminant functions*

$$g_i(\mathbf{x}) = p(\mathbf{x} \mid \omega_i)\, P(\omega_i) \tag{1.28}$$

or

$$g_i(\mathbf{x}) = \log p(\mathbf{x} \mid \omega_i) + \log P(\omega_i) \tag{1.29}$$

and select the category corresponding to the largest discriminant function. Which form is chosen depends upon the simplicity of the resulting discriminant functions, the last form being particularly convenient when the conditional densities belong to the exponential family.

To implement the formal solution requires knowledge of both the a priori probabilities and the conditional densities, and in most pattern recognition problems neither of these is known exactly. Usually, however, sample patterns from each class are available, and the problem is to estimate the discriminant functions from the samples. The various procedures available for this task differ in the assumptions they make, and we shall examine a few of the most important procedures.

2. *Parametric learning.* If the conditional densities $p(\mathbf{x} \mid \omega_i)$ can be assumed to be known except for the values of some parameters, then

the samples can be used to estimate these parameters, and the resulting estimated densities can be used in the formal solution as if they were the true parameters. The classic example is the multivariate normal case, in which

$$p(\mathbf{x} \mid \omega_i) = \frac{1}{(2\pi)^{n/2} |\Sigma_i|^{1/2}} \exp[-\tfrac{1}{2}(\mathbf{x} - \boldsymbol{\mu}_i)' \Sigma_i^{-1}(\mathbf{x} - \boldsymbol{\mu}_i)] \tag{1.30}$$

where the parameters are the mean vector $\boldsymbol{\mu}_i$ and the covariance matrix Σ_i. Abramson and Braverman (1962) considered the case in which Σ_i was known but $\boldsymbol{\mu}_i$ was unknown, and viewed the estimation of $\boldsymbol{\mu}_i$ from samples as the problem of "learning" the mean vector. Consider the univariate case in which x is normally distributed with unknown mean μ and known variance σ^2. We express the fact that μ is unknown by writing

$$p(x \mid \mu) = \frac{1}{\sqrt{2\pi\sigma^2}} \exp\left[-\frac{1}{2}\frac{(x-\mu)^2}{\sigma^2}\right] \tag{1.31}$$

Suppose that we express any prior knowledge we have of μ by giving μ a normal distribution with mean μ_0 and variance $\sigma_0{}^2$:

$$p(\mu) = \frac{1}{\sqrt{2\pi\sigma_0{}^2}} \exp\left[-\frac{1}{2}\frac{(\mu-\mu_0)^2}{\sigma_0{}^2}\right] \tag{1.32}$$

Then, after observing one sample x_1, we can use this information to change our opinion about the possible true value of μ.* Invoking Bayes' rule, the a posteriori distribution for μ becomes

$$p(\mu \mid x_1) = \frac{p(x_1 \mid \mu)\, p(\mu)}{p(x_1)} \tag{1.33}$$

$$= \frac{1}{p(x_1)\, 2\pi\sigma\sigma_0} \exp\left(-\frac{1}{2}\left[\frac{(x_1-\mu)^2}{\sigma^2} + \frac{(\mu-\mu_0)^2}{\sigma_0{}^2}\right]\right) \tag{1.34}$$

$$= f(x_1) \exp\left(-\frac{1}{2}\left[\mu^2\left(\frac{1}{\sigma^2} + \frac{1}{\sigma_0{}^2}\right) - 2\mu\left(\frac{x_1}{\sigma^2} + \frac{\mu_0}{\sigma_0{}^2}\right)\right]\right) \tag{1.35}$$

$$= f'(x_1) \exp\left[-\frac{1}{2}\frac{(\mu-\mu_1)^2}{\sigma_1{}^2}\right] \tag{1.36}$$

where $f(x_1)$ and $f'(x_1)$ are functions of x_1, but are independent of μ.

---

* Note that we are now using a subscript to denote the sample number rather than the component number.

Thus, the a posteriori distribution for μ is again normal, with mean μ_1 and variance σ_1^2, where

$$\frac{1}{\sigma_1^2} = \frac{1}{\sigma^2} + \frac{1}{\sigma_0^2} \tag{1.37}$$

and

$$\frac{\mu_1}{\sigma_1^2} = \frac{x_1}{\sigma^2} + \frac{\mu_0}{\sigma_0^2} \tag{1.38}$$

The observation of a second *independent* sample x_2 will again give rise to a normal distribution for $p(\mu \mid x_1, x_2)$, and, in general, $p(\mu \mid x_1, \ldots, x_k)$ will be normal with mean μ_k and variance σ_k^2. Furthermore, it follows in exactly the same way that μ_k and σ_k^2 satisfy the recursion relations

$$\frac{1}{\sigma_k^2} = \frac{1}{\sigma^2} + \frac{1}{\sigma_{k-1}^2} \tag{1.39}$$

and

$$\frac{\mu_k}{\sigma_k^2} = \frac{x_k}{\sigma^2} + \frac{\mu_{k-1}}{\sigma_{k-1}^2} \tag{1.40}$$

These relations show that our uncertainty in the value of μ, as measured by σ_k^2, decreases with each observation. Our estimate for the value of μ, μ_k, is a weighted combination of the new sample x_k and our previous estimate μ_{k-1}. It is not hard to solve these difference equations to obtain the following closed-form expressions:

$$\sigma_k^2 = \frac{\sigma_0^2\sigma^2}{k\sigma_0^2 + \sigma^2} \tag{1.41}$$

and

$$\mu_k = \frac{k\sigma_0^2}{k\sigma_0^2 + \sigma^2}\left(\frac{1}{k}\sum_{i=1}^{k} x_i\right) + \frac{\sigma^2}{k\sigma_0^2 + \sigma^2}\mu_0 \tag{1.42}$$

This solution shows that σ_k^2 decreases like σ^2/k for large k. The estimate of the mean, μ_k, is a weighted combination of the mean of the samples and the initial estimate μ_0, approaching the sample mean for large k. Thus, we obtain a nice justification for the intuitively appealing procedure of using the sample mean to estimate the true mean, and we see the relation between parameter estimation and machine learning.

Abramson and Braverman (1962) derived similar relations for the multivariate normal case, showing further that $p(\mathbf{x} \mid \mathbf{x}_1, \ldots, \mathbf{x}_k)$ is multivariate normal with mean $\boldsymbol{\mu}_k$ and covariance matrix $\Sigma + \Sigma_k$. This approach can be further generalized to recursive Bayes estimation of an arbitrary parameter vector $\boldsymbol{\theta}$, leading to formulas like

$$p(\boldsymbol{\theta} \mid \mathbf{x}_1, \ldots, \mathbf{x}_k) = \frac{p(\mathbf{x}_k \mid \boldsymbol{\theta})\, p(\boldsymbol{\theta} \mid \mathbf{x}_1, \ldots, \mathbf{x}_{k-1})}{\int p(\mathbf{x}_k \mid \boldsymbol{\theta})\, p(\boldsymbol{\theta} \mid \mathbf{x}_1, \ldots, \mathbf{x}_{k-1})\, d\boldsymbol{\theta}} \tag{1.43}$$

The usefulness of such relations depends upon whether or not $p(\boldsymbol{\theta} \mid \mathbf{x}_1, \ldots, \mathbf{x}_k)$ maintains a simple form. Spragins (1965) has pointed out that this is closely related to the notion of a *sufficient statistic*, and that simple results can be expected if, and practically only if $p(\mathbf{x} \mid \boldsymbol{\theta})$ is a member of the exponential family—normal, multinomial, poisson, etc. While this family includes most of the commonly encountered distributions, it does not include the simple mixture distribution

$$p(x \mid \theta) = \frac{1}{2\sqrt{2\pi}} \left[\exp\left(-\frac{x^2}{2}\right) + \exp\left(-\frac{(x-\theta)^2}{2}\right) \right] \tag{1.44}$$

This means that attempts to approximate complicated conditional densities with superpositions of normal densities are basically not amenable to the recursive Bayes approach, and that elegant, closed form expressions for estimating the parameters should not be expected. Nevertheless, computationally feasible approximations may be possible, and the recursive Bayes approach supplies the foundations for parametric learning.

3. *Nonparametric learning.* Parametric procedures depend upon the functional forms assumed for the probability densities. Nonparametric procedures are basically independent of these forms, save perhaps for assuming things like continuity, and are said to be *distribution-free.* For example, the estimation of $p(x)$ by differentiating a least-squares fit to an empirical cumulative distribution function is a distribution-free procedure. Another example is the nearest-neighbor rule of Cover and Hart (1967). Such general statistical procedures are treated in detail in Chapters 2 and 3, and we shall not investigate them further at this time. Suffice it to say that very general procedures exchange the need for precise assumptions about functional forms of the densities for the need for a large number of sample patterns to estimate the densities well.

There is another class of distribution-free procedures that reduces the need for a huge number of samples by making more precise assumptions about the functional forms for the discriminant functions. These are the so-called *adaptive procedures.* The most commonly made assumption about the discriminant functions is that they are linear, i.e., that

$$g_i(\mathbf{x}) = (\mathbf{w}_i\,, \mathbf{x}) + c_i \tag{1.45}$$

where $\mathbf{w}_i$ is the ith *weight vector*, $(\mathbf{w}_i\,, \mathbf{x})$ is the inner product of $\mathbf{w}_i$ and $\mathbf{x}$, and c_i is a constant for the ith class (Nilsson, 1965). A vector $\mathbf{x}$ is classified by forming these m linear functions, and by assigning $\mathbf{x}$ to the category corresponding to the largest discriminant function. For the two-category case, it is equivalent to form a single discriminant function

$$g(\mathbf{x}) = g_1(\mathbf{x}) - g_2(\mathbf{x}) \tag{1.46}$$

$$= (\mathbf{w}_1 - \mathbf{w}_2\,, \mathbf{x}) + c_1 - c_2 \tag{1.47}$$

$$= (\mathbf{w}, \mathbf{x}) + c \tag{1.48}$$

assigning $\mathbf{x}$ to ω_1 if $g(\mathbf{x}) > 0$ and to ω_2 if $g(\mathbf{x}) \leqslant 0$. By defining the augmented vectors $\boldsymbol{\alpha}$ and $\mathbf{y}$ by

$$\boldsymbol{\alpha} = \begin{bmatrix} \mathbf{w} \\ c \end{bmatrix} \tag{1.49}$$

$$\mathbf{y} = \begin{bmatrix} \mathbf{x} \\ 1 \end{bmatrix} \tag{1.50}$$

we can write $g(\mathbf{x})$ in the homogeneous form

$$g(\mathbf{x}) = (\boldsymbol{\alpha}, \mathbf{y}) \tag{1.51}$$

The problem of designing such a classifier is the problem of finding an (augmented) weight vector $\boldsymbol{\alpha}$ from a set of sample patterns. The following procedure due to Rosenblatt (1957) is typical of one class of adaptive procedures for solving this problem. Let the samples be considered in a sequence $\mathbf{y}_1\,, \mathbf{y}_2\,,\ldots,$ having the property that each sample appears infinitely often in the sequence. Let $\mathbf{x}_0$ be arbitrary, and let

$$\boldsymbol{\alpha}_{k+1} = \begin{cases} \boldsymbol{\alpha}_k + \mathbf{y}_k & \text{if } (\boldsymbol{\alpha}_k\,, \mathbf{y}_k) \leqslant 0 \text{ and } \mathbf{y}_k \sim \omega_1 \\ \boldsymbol{\alpha}_k - \mathbf{y}_k & \text{if } (\boldsymbol{\alpha}_k\,, \mathbf{y}_k) \geqslant 0 \text{ and } \mathbf{y}_k \sim \omega_2 \\ \boldsymbol{\alpha}_k & \text{otherwise.} \end{cases} \tag{1.52}$$

In words, after $\mathbf{y}_k$ is observed, $\boldsymbol{\alpha}_k$ is either increased by $\mathbf{y}_k$, decreased by $\mathbf{y}_k$, or left unchanged. It is left unchanged if $\boldsymbol{\alpha}_k$ correctly classifies $\mathbf{y}_k$. If $\mathbf{y}_k$ is in Class 1 but $(\boldsymbol{\alpha}_k\,, \mathbf{y}_k)$ is not positive, $\mathbf{y}_k$ is added to $\boldsymbol{\alpha}_k$, thereby increasing the inner product by $\| \mathbf{y}_k \|^2$. Similarly, if $\mathbf{y}_k$ is in Class 2 but

$(\boldsymbol{\alpha}_k, \mathbf{y}_k)$ is not negative, $\mathbf{y}_k$ is subtracted from $\boldsymbol{\alpha}_k$, thereby decreasing the inner product by $\| \mathbf{y}_k \|^2$. This procedure is known as the *fixed-increment error-correction rule.* Corrections to $\boldsymbol{\alpha}_k$ are made if and only if the classification of $\mathbf{y}_k$ is in error, and a fixed multiple of $\mathbf{y}_k$ is added to $\boldsymbol{\alpha}_k$ to make the correction. It is one of a number of rules having the property that after a finite number of corrections it will yield a vector $\hat{\boldsymbol{\alpha}}$ that will classify all of the samples correctly, provided only that such a vector exists.

The properties of this rule and related adaptive procedures will be considered in detail in Chapter 3. These procedures have the virtue that they can be applied to patterns from a wide variety of distributions, and that they control the complexity of the classifier by prior specification. They have the drawback that they optimize performance on the samples, which may not lead to optimum performance on independent data.* Nevertheless, they are frequently used in practice when it is difficult to verify the assumptions needed to derive the optimum classifier.

4. *Unsupervised learning.* Consider again our example problem of designing a system to tell B's from 8's. Suppose that after the system has been designed, it is used by someone whose printing habits change with time. If the classifier can adjust itself to accomodate these changes, higher levels of performance can be obtained. Or consider the problem of obtaining extremely large amounts of hand-printed data to design a classifier. If each character must be identified correctly, very careful and time-consuming human monitoring and checking will be necessary. If the classifier can continually improve its performance on unidentified data coming from typical documents, much painstaking work can be avoided.

The problem of learning from unidentified samples (sometimes called unsupervised learning, or learning without a teacher) presents both theoretical and practical problems. In fact, at one time the problem was thought to be insoluble in principle. With no prior assumptions, successful unsupervised learning is indeed unlikely. However, with appropriate assumptions, solutions can be found.

Consider, for example, the problem of separating B's from 8's on the basis of the straightness ratio, x. Suppose that $p(x \mid \mathrm{B})$ is normally distributed with unknown mean μ_{B} and unit variance, and that $p(x \mid 8)$ is normally distributed with unknown mean μ_8 and unit variance.

---

* One exception to this statement is the least-mean-square rule of Widrow and Hoff (1960), which can be shown to be optimum for the two-class multivariate normal case (Koford and Groner, 1966).

Assuming that B's and 8's are equally likely, we can write

$$p(x \mid \mu_B, \mu_8) = p(x, B \mid \mu_B, \mu_8) + p(x, 8 \mid \mu_B, \mu_8) \tag{1.53}$$

$$= p(x \mid B, \mu_B, \mu_8) P(B) + p(x \mid 8, \mu_B, \mu_8) P(8) \tag{1.54}$$

$$= \frac{1}{2\sqrt{2\pi}} \left[\exp\left(-\frac{(x-\mu_B)^2}{2}\right) + \exp\left(-\frac{(x-\mu_8)^2}{2}\right)\right] \tag{1.55}$$

Thus, if hand-printed B's and 8's are selected randomly, the probability density for the straightness ratio is a mixture of two normal densities. This distribution is completely specified by a parameter vector $\boldsymbol{\theta} = (\mu_B, \mu_8)'$. If we use labeled samples to estimate μ_B and μ_8 roughly to begin with, then we may have a fairly good initial idea of $\boldsymbol{\theta}$, which we can represent by a density $p(\boldsymbol{\theta})$. If we now start receiving unlabeled samples, we can use the recursive Bayes approach to get a better and better idea of $\boldsymbol{\theta}$. From this viewpoint, the distinction between supervised and unsupervised learning disappears, and we see that under appropriate assumptions learning without a teacher is certainly possible.

The basic problem with this solution is that the a posteriori densities $p(\boldsymbol{\theta} \mid \mathbf{x}_1, \ldots, \mathbf{x}_k)$ keep getting more and more complicated as more samples are received. This problem is discussed further in Chapter 2, and a good survey of methods of handling this problem has been given by Spragins (1966). Although most of these approximate methods are difficult to treat analytically, they may perform very well. A good example is provided by the experiments in self-corrective character recognition reported by Nagy and Shelton (1966).

Unsupervised learning is also possible in the nonparametric case. In particular, Ide and Tunis (1967) have shown how the error-correction rules can be modified so that slow changes can be tracked. Finally, a large number of other techniques have been proposed for discovering consistent subsets in a set of patterns, for example, for automatically separating lower-case B's from upper-case B's. These cluster-seeking or mode-seeking techniques usually use some kind of distance measure to decide whether or not two patterns belong in the same subset.

One such method, due to Sebestyen (1962), employs Euclidean distance and an arbitrary distance threshold, r. A set of sample patterns is partitioned into subsets by considering the patterns in sequence. The first pattern $\mathbf{x}_1$ is automatically assigned to the first subset, and the mean of the patterns in that subset, $\mathbf{m}_1$, is set equal to $\mathbf{x}_1$. Then the next pattern $\mathbf{x}_2$ is considered, and the distance $\| \mathbf{x}_2 - \mathbf{m}_1 \|$ is computed. If this distance is less than r, $\mathbf{x}_2$ is also assigned to the first subset, and $\mathbf{m}_1$ is updated so that it is the average of $\mathbf{x}_1$ and $\mathbf{x}_2$. However, if this distance equals or exceeds r, a new subset is created together with its mean $\mathbf{m}_2$. In general, if n subsets have been created and a new pattern $\mathbf{x}$ is introduced, all n distances $\| \mathbf{x} - \mathbf{m}_i \|$ are computed. If the smallest is less than r, $\mathbf{x}$ is assigned to that subset and the corresponding mean vector is updated. Otherwise a new subset is created with mean $\mathbf{m}_{n+1} = \mathbf{x}$.

There are many variations on this theme, the most prominent ones being described in a good survey article by Ball (1965). While some theoretical properties of these procedures have been established, such results are rare and hard to obtain. The theoretical questions that arise in this work penetrate the foundations of the scientific method, and the best justification for such methods is their performance on practical problems.

IV. Additions to the Classical Model

The classical model of pattern recognition involves three major operations: representation, feature extraction, and classification. Though arbitrary and oversimplified, this model allows the formulation and discussion of many important problems, and provides a pleasant way of formalizing the classification problem.

However, in particular applications this model may omit some of the most significant aspects of the problem. For example, in some situations it may be very expensive or time consuming to measure features. In such cases the cost of feature extraction must be added to the cost of making errors in order to obtain a truly minimum-cost classification rule. Sequential decision theory provides a formal approach to this problem, and this topic is considered in some detail in the next chapter.

Another extension to the classical model can be made whenever decisions can be influenced by context. For example, classification of the center character in Fig. 8 as a B or an 8 may be influenced by the nature of the surrounding characters, since a string of letters or a string of numbers may be more likely than a mixture of the two. Compound decision theory (Abend, 1966) provides the theoretical solution to the problem of using context, and its exploitation can result in significantly improved performance (Raviv, 1967; Duda and Hart, 1968).

These extensions invest the classical model with considerable generality. Yet, practical necessity may dictate the use of approximate methods that may at best be only vaguely motivated by theoretical considerations. Procedures for locating, isolating, normalizing, and preprocessing patterns are often purely empirical, and most practical methods of feature extraction remain largely unmarred by theory. Furthermore, for some very interesting pattern-recognition systems, the division of the process into clearly defined stages of representation, feature extraction, and classification may be difficult or unnatural (Greanias *et al.*, 1963; Marill *et al.*, 1963; Roberts, 1965). Nevertheless, the classical model provides a basic framework for many problems, and its analysis provides the theoretical foundations for pattern recognition.

FIGURE 8. The effect of context on pattern recognition

References

Abend, K., Compound decision procedures for pattern recognition. *Proc. NEC 22*, pp. 777–780 (1966).

Abramson, N. and Braverman, D., Learning to recognize patterns in a random environment. *IEEE Trans. Info. Theory 8*, No. 5, pp. S58–S63 (1962).

Ball, G. H., Data analysis in the social sciences. *Proc. FJCC*, Las Vegas, Nevada, 1965. Spartan, Washington, D. C., 1965.

Casey, R. G., Linear reduction of dimensionality in pattern recognition. Ph.D. Thesis, Columbia Univ., New York, 1965; and Research Report RC–1431, IBM, Yorktown Heights, New York, March 1965.

Cover, T. M. and Hart, P. E., Nearest neighbor pattern classification. *IEEE Trans. Info. Theory 13*, No. 1, pp. 21–27 (1967).

Duda, R. O. and Hart, P. E., Experiments in the recognition of hand-printed text: part II—context analysis. *Proc. FJCC*, San Francisco, Calif., 1968. Thompson, Washington, D. C., 1968.

Greanias, E. C. *et al.*, The recognition of handwritten numerals by contour analysis. *IBM J. 7*, No. 1, pp. 14–22 (1963).

Ide, E. R. and Tunis, C. J., An experimental investigation of a nonsupervised adaptive algorithm. *IEEE Trans. Electron. Comp. 16*, No. 6, pp. 860–864 (1967).

Kadota, T. T. and L. A. Shepp, On the best finite set of linear observables for discriminating two Gaussian signals. *IEEE Trans. Info. Theory 13*, No. 2, pp. 278–284 (1967).

Kailath, T., The divergence and Bhattacharyya distance measures in signal selection. *IEEE Trans. Comm. Tech. 15*, No. 1, pp. 52–60 (1967).

Koford, J. S. and Groner, G. F., The use of an adaptive threshold element to design a linear optimal pattern classifier. *IEEE Trans. Info. Theory 12*, No. 1, pp. 42–50 (1966).

Lewis, P. M., The characteristic selection problem in recognition systems. *IRE Trans. Info. Theory 8*, No. 2, pp. 171–179 (1962).

Liu, C. N., A programmed algorithm for designing multifont character recognition logics. *IEEE Trans. Electron. Comp. 13*, No. 5, pp. 586–593 (1964).

Marill, T. and Green, D. M., On the effectiveness of receptors in recognition systems. *IEEE Trans. Info. Theory 9*, No. 1, pp. 11–17 (1963).

Marill, T. *et al.*, CYCLOPS-1: a second-generation recognition system. *Proc. FJCC*, Las Vegas, Nevada, 1963. Spartan, Washington, D. C., 1963.

Miller, R. M., Statistical prediction by discriminant analysis. *Meteorological Monographs 4*, No. 25 (1962).

Nagy, G. and Shelton, G. L., Self-corrective character recognition system. *IEEE Trans. Info. Theory 12*, No. 2, pp. 215–222 (1966).

Nagy, G., State of the art in pattern recognition. *Proc. IEEE 56*, No. 5, pp. 836–862 (1968).

Nilsson, N. J., "Learning machines: foundations of trainable pattern classifying systems." McGraw–Hill, New York, 1965.

Raviv, J., Decision making in markov chains applied to the problem of pattern recognition. *IEEE Trans. Info. Theory 13*, No. 4, pp. 536–551 (1967).

Roberts, L. G., Machine perception of three-dimensional solids. *In* "Optical and Electro-Optical Information Processing" (J. T. Tippett *et al.*, eds.) pp. 159–197. MIT Press, Cambridge, Mass., 1965.

Rosenblatt, F., The perceptron: a perceiving and recognizing automaton. Report No. 85–460–1. Cornell Aeronautical Laboratory, Buffalo, New York, 1957.

Sebestyen, G. S., Pattern recognition by an adaptive process of sample set construction. *IRE Trans. Info. Theory 8*, No. 5, pp. S82–S91 (1962).

Spragins, J., A note on the iterative application of Bayes' rule. *IEEE Trans. Info. Theory 11*, No. 4, pp. 544–549 (1965).

Spragins, J., Learning without a teacher. *IEEE Trans. Info. Theory 12*, No. 2, pp. 223–230 (1966).

Tou, J. T. and Heydorn, R. P., Some approaches to optimum feature extraction. *In* "Computer and Information Sciences" (J. T. Tou, ed.) pp. 57–89. Academic Press, New York, 1967.

Widrow, B. and Hoff, M. E., Adaptive switching circuits. Report No. 1553–1. Stanford Electron. Lab., Stanford Univ., Stanford, Calif., June 1960.

2

K. S. Fu

STATISTICAL PATTERN RECOGNITION

I. Statistical Pattern Recognition Systems and Bayes Classifiers

A pattern recognition system, in general, consists of two parts, namely, feature extractor and classifier.* The function of feature extractor is to extract or to measure the important characteristics from the input patterns. The extracted characteristics are called features, and they are supposed to best characterize all the possible input patterns. Usually, if the cost of extracting features is not considered, the number of features characterizing input patterns can be arbitrarily large. One problem raised in practice is to select a subset from a given set of features. In this case, since the size of the subset is specified by the designer, the size of the feature extractor is also correspondingly determined. The function performed by a classifier is the one of making a proper decision to assign each input pattern to one of the possible pattern classes. The decision is made on the basis of the feature measurements supplied by the feature extractor in a recognition system. The classification criterion is usually the minimization of misrecognitions. A simple block diagram of a pattern recognition system is shown in Fig. 1.

* The division into two parts is primarily for convenience rather than necessity.

Assume that there are m possible pattern classes, $\omega_1, \omega_2, \ldots, \omega_m$, and there are N features, $f_1, f_2, \ldots, f_N$, to be extracted for classification. Let the (noisy) measurements of the N feature be denoted by $x_1, x_2, \ldots, x_N$, where $x_j = f_j + \text{noise}$. Each set of N feature measurements can be represented as an N-dimensional vector $\mathbf{x}$ or as a point in the N-dimensional feature space $\Omega_{\mathbf{x}}$. Let the a priori probability of each pattern class be $P(\omega_i)$, $i = 1, \ldots, m$, and the conditional probability density function of $\mathbf{x}$ for each class ω_i be $p(\mathbf{x} \mid \omega_i)$, $i = 1, \ldots, m$. On the basis of the a priori information $p(\mathbf{x} \mid \omega_j)$ and $P(\omega_j)$, $j = 1, \ldots, m$, the function of a statistical classifier is to perform the classification task for minimizing probability of misrecognition. The problem of pattern classification can now be formulated as a statistical decision problem (testing of statistical hypotheses) by defining a decision function $d(\mathbf{x})$,

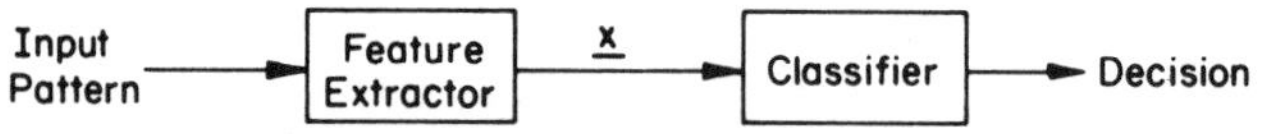

FIGURE 1. A simple block diagram of a pattern recognition system

where $d(\mathbf{x}) = d_i$ means that the hypothesis $\mathbf{x} \sim \omega_i$ ($\mathbf{x}$ is from the class ω_i) is accepted (Chow, 1957; Anderson, 1958; Blackwell and Girshick, 1954; Sebestyen, 1962). Let $L(\omega_i, d_j)$ be the loss incurred by the classifier if the decision d_j is made when the input pattern is actually from ω_i. The conditional loss (or conditional risk) for $d = d(\mathbf{x})$ is

$$r(\omega_i, d) = \int_{\Omega_{\mathbf{x}}} L(\omega_i, d)\, p(\mathbf{x} \mid \omega_i)\, d\mathbf{x} \tag{2.1}$$

For a given set of a priori probabilities $P = \{P(\omega_1), P(\omega_2), \ldots, P(\omega_m)\}$, the average loss (or average risk) is

$$R(P, d) = \sum_{i=1}^{m} P(\omega_i)\, r(\omega_i, d) \tag{2.2}$$

Substitute Eq. (2.1) into Eq. (2.2) and let

$$r_{\mathbf{x}}(P, d) = \frac{\sum_{i=1}^{m} L(\omega_i, d)\, P(\omega_i)\, p(\mathbf{x} \mid \omega_i)}{p(\mathbf{x})} \tag{2.3}$$

Then Eq. (2.2) becomes

$$R(P, d) = \int_{\Omega_{\mathbf{x}}} p(\mathbf{x})\, r_{\mathbf{x}}(P, d)\, d\mathbf{x} \tag{2.4}$$

$r_{\mathbf{x}}(P, d)$ is defined as the a posteriori conditional average loss of the decision d for given feature measurements $\mathbf{x}$.

The problem is to choose a proper decision d_j, $j = 1,..., m$ to minimize the average loss $R(P, d)$, or to minimize the maximum of the conditional loss $r(\omega_i, d)$ [minimax criterion]. The optimal decision rule which minimizes the average loss is called the Bayes' rule. From Eq. (2.4) it is sufficient to consider each $\mathbf{x}$ separately and to minimize $r_{\mathbf{x}}(P, d)$. If d^* is an optimal decision in the sense of minimizing the average loss, then

$$r_{\mathbf{x}}(P, d^*) \leqslant r_{\mathbf{x}}(P, d) \tag{2.5}$$

That is,

$$\sum_{i=1}^{m} L(\omega_i, d^*) P(\omega_i) p(\mathbf{x} \mid \omega_i) \leqslant \sum_{i=1}^{m} L(\omega_i, d) P(\omega_i) p(\mathbf{x} \mid \omega_i) \tag{2.6}$$

For the (0, 1) loss function; that is,

$$L(\omega_i, d_j) = 1 - \delta_{ij} = \begin{cases} 0, & i = j \\ 1, & i \neq j \end{cases} \tag{2.7}$$

the average loss is essentially also the probability of misrecognition. In this case, the Bayes' decision rule is that $d^* = d_i$; that is, $\mathbf{x} \sim \omega_i$ if

$$P(\omega_i) p(\mathbf{x} \mid \omega_i) \geqslant P(\omega_j) p(\mathbf{x} \mid \omega_j) \qquad \text{for all} \qquad i, j = 1,..., m \tag{2.8}$$

Define the likelihood ratio between class ω_i and class ω_j as

$$\lambda = \frac{p(\mathbf{x} \mid \omega_i)}{p(\mathbf{x} \mid \omega_j)} \tag{2.9}$$

Then Eq. (2.8) becomes

$$d^* = d_i \qquad \text{if} \qquad \lambda \geqslant \frac{P(\omega_j)}{P(\omega_i)} \qquad \text{for all} \qquad i, j = 1,..., m \tag{2.10}$$

The classifier that implements the Bayes' decision rule for classification is called a Bayes' classifier. A simplified block diagram of a Bayes' classifier is shown in Fig. 2.

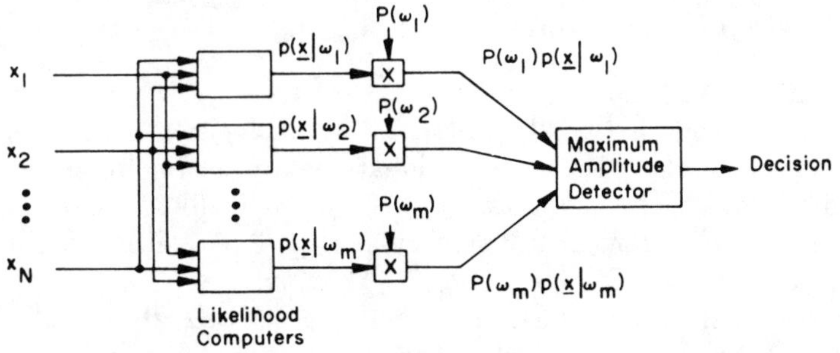

FIGURE 2. A simplified block diagram of a Bayes' classifier

It is noted from Eq. (2.8) that the corresponding discriminant function implemented by a Bayes' classifier is essentially

$$g_i(\mathbf{x}) = P(\omega_i)\, p(\mathbf{x} \mid \omega_i) \qquad i = 1,\ldots, m \tag{2.11}$$

or equivalently,

$$g_i(\mathbf{x}) = \log[P(\omega_i)\, p(\mathbf{x} \mid \omega_i)] \qquad i = 1,\ldots, m \tag{2.12}$$

since for $\mathbf{x} \sim \omega_i$, $g_i(\mathbf{x}) > g_j(\mathbf{x})$ for all $i, j = 1,\ldots, m (i \neq j)$ [Nilsson, 1965]. The decision boundary between ω_i and ω_j is

$$P(\omega_i)\, p(\mathbf{x} \mid \omega_i) - P(\omega_j)\, p(\mathbf{x} \mid \omega_j) = 0 \tag{2.13}$$

or

$$\log \frac{P(\omega_i)\, p(\mathbf{x} \mid \omega_i)}{P(\omega_j)\, p(\mathbf{x} \mid \omega_j)} = 0 \tag{2.14}$$

As an illustrative example, suppose that $p(\mathbf{x} \mid \omega_i)$, $i = 1,\ldots, m$, is a multivariate Gaussian density function with mean vector $\boldsymbol{\mu}_i$ and covariance matrix Σ_i; that is,

$$p(\mathbf{x} \mid \omega_i) = \frac{1}{(2\pi)^{N/2} |\Sigma_i|^{1/2}} \exp[-\tfrac{1}{2}(\mathbf{x} - \boldsymbol{\mu}_i)' \Sigma_i^{-1} (\mathbf{x} - \boldsymbol{\mu}_i)] \quad i = 1,\ldots, m \tag{2.15}$$

Then the decision boundary between ω_i and ω_j is

$$\log \frac{P(\omega_i)}{P(\omega_j)} + \log \frac{p(\mathbf{x} \mid \omega_i)}{p(\mathbf{x} \mid \omega_j)} = \log \frac{P(\omega_i)}{P(\omega_j)} - \frac{1}{2} \log \frac{|\Sigma_i|}{|\Sigma_j|}$$
$$- \tfrac{1}{2}[(\mathbf{x} - \boldsymbol{\mu}_i)' \Sigma_i^{-1} (\mathbf{x} - \boldsymbol{\mu}_i) - (\mathbf{x} - \boldsymbol{\mu}_j)' \Sigma_j^{-1} (\mathbf{x} - \boldsymbol{\mu}_j)] = 0 \tag{2.16}$$

Eq. (2.16) is, in general, a hyperquadric. If $\Sigma_i = \Sigma_j = \Sigma$, Eq. (2.16) reduces to

$$\mathbf{x}' \Sigma^{-1} (\boldsymbol{\mu}_i - \boldsymbol{\mu}_j) - \tfrac{1}{2}(\boldsymbol{\mu}_i + \boldsymbol{\mu}_j)' \Sigma^{-1} (\boldsymbol{\mu}_i - \boldsymbol{\mu}_j) + \log \frac{P(\omega_i)}{P(\omega_j)} = 0 \tag{2.17}$$

which is a hyperplane.

It is noted from Eq. (2.8) that the Bayes' decision rule with (0, 1) loss function is also the unconditional maximum-likelihood decision rule. Furthermore, the (conditional) maximum-likelihood decision may be regarded as the Bayes' decision rule, Eq. (2.8), with equal a priori probabilities; that is, $P(\omega_i) = 1/m$, $i = 1,\ldots, m$.

In the statistical classification systems described above, all the N features are observed by the classifier at one stage. As a matter of fact, the cost of feature measurements has not been taken into consideration.

It is evident that an insufficient number of feature measurements will not be able to give satisfactory results in correct classification. On the other hand, an arbitrarily large number of features to be measured is impractical. If the cost of taking feature measurements is to be considered or if the features extracted from input patterns is sequential in nature, one is led to apply sequential decision procedures to this class of pattern recognition problems (Wald, 1947; Reed, 1960; Fu, 1962). A tradeoff between the error (misrecognition) and the number of features to be measured can be obtained by taking feature measurements sequentially and terminating the sequential process (making a decision) when a sufficient or desirable accuracy of classification has been achieved. Since the feature measurements are to be taken sequentially, the order of the features to be measured is important. It is expected that the features should be ordered such that measurements taken in such an order will cause the terminal decision earlier. The problem of feature ordering is a rather special problem in sequential recognition systems. It is an objective of this chapter to cover some recent developments in the application of stastical techniques to feature selection, feature ordering, mode estimation, and pattern classification.

II. Sequential Decision Model for Pattern Classification

Application of sequential decision procedures to pattern classification was proposed by Fu (1962). If there are two pattern classes to be recognized, Wald's sequential probability ratio test (SPRT) can be applied (Wald, 1947). At the nth stage of the sequential process, that is, after the nth feature measurement is taken, the classifier computes the sequential probability ratio

$$\lambda_n = \frac{p_n(\mathbf{x} \mid \omega_1)}{p_n(\mathbf{x} \mid \omega_2)} \tag{2.18}$$

where $p_n(\mathbf{x} \mid \omega_i)$, $i = 1, 2$, is the conditional probability density function of $\mathbf{x} = (x_1, x_2, \ldots, x_n)'$ for pattern class ω_i. The λ_n computed by Eq. (2.18) is then compared with two stopping boundaries A and B. If

$$\lambda_n \geqslant A, \qquad \text{then} \qquad \mathbf{x} \sim \omega_1 \tag{2.19}$$

and if

$$\lambda_n \leqslant B, \qquad \text{then} \qquad \mathbf{x} \sim \omega_2 \tag{2.20}$$

If $B < \lambda_n < A$, then an additional feature measurement will be taken and the process proceeds to the $(n + 1)$th stage. The two stopping boundaries are related to the error (misrecognition) probabilities by the following expressions:

$$A = \frac{1 - e_{21}}{e_{12}} \quad \text{and} \quad B = \frac{e_{21}}{1 - e_{12}} \tag{2.21}$$

where e_{ij} = probability of deciding $\mathbf{x} \sim \omega_i$ when actually $\mathbf{x} \sim \omega_j$ is true, $i, j = 1, 2$. Following Wald's sequential analysis, it has been shown that a classifier, using the SPRT, has an optimal property for the case of two pattern classes; that is, for given e_{12} and e_{21}, there is no other procedure with at least as low error-probabilities or expected risk and with shorter length of average number of feature measurements than the sequential classification procedure.

For more than two pattern classes, $m > 2$, the generalized sequential probability ratio test (GSPRT) can be used (Reed, 1960). At the nth stage, the generalized sequential probability ratios for each pattern class are computed as

$$u_n(\mathbf{x} \mid \omega_i) = \frac{p_n(\mathbf{x} \mid \omega_i)}{[\prod_{q=1}^{m} p_n(\mathbf{x} \mid \omega_q)]^{1/m}} \qquad i = 1, 2, \ldots, m \tag{2.22}$$

The $u_n(\mathbf{x} \mid \omega_i)$ is then compared with the stopping boundary of the ith pattern class, $A(\omega_i)$, and the decision procedure is to reject the pattern class ω_i from consideration; that is, $\mathbf{x}$ is not from class ω_i if

$$u_n(\mathbf{x} \mid \omega_i) < A(\omega_i) \qquad i = 1, 2, \ldots, m \tag{2.23}$$

The stopping boundary is determined by the following relationship

$$A(\omega_i) = \frac{1 - e_{ii}}{[\prod_{q=1}^{m} (1 - e_{iq})]^{1/m}} \qquad i = 1, 2, \ldots, m \tag{2.24}$$

After the rejection of pattern class ω_i from consideration, the total number of pattern classes is reduced by one and a new set of generalized sequential probability ratios is formed. The pattern classes are rejected sequentially until only one is left which is acceptable as the recognized class. The rejection criterion suggested, though somewhat conservative, will usually lead to a high percentage of correct recognition because only the pattern classes which are the most unlikely to be true are rejected (Fu, 1968).

For two pattern classes, $m = 2$, the classification procedure, Eq. (2.22) and Eq. (2.23), is equivalent to Wald's SPRT and the optimality of SPRT holds. For $m > 2$, whether the optimal property is still valid remains to be justified. However, the classification procedure is close to optimal in that the average number of feature measurements required to reject a pattern class from consideration is nearly minimum when two hypotheses (the hypothesis of a pattern class to be rejected and the hypothesis of a class not rejected) are considered. A general block diagram for a sequential recognition system is shown in Fig. 3.

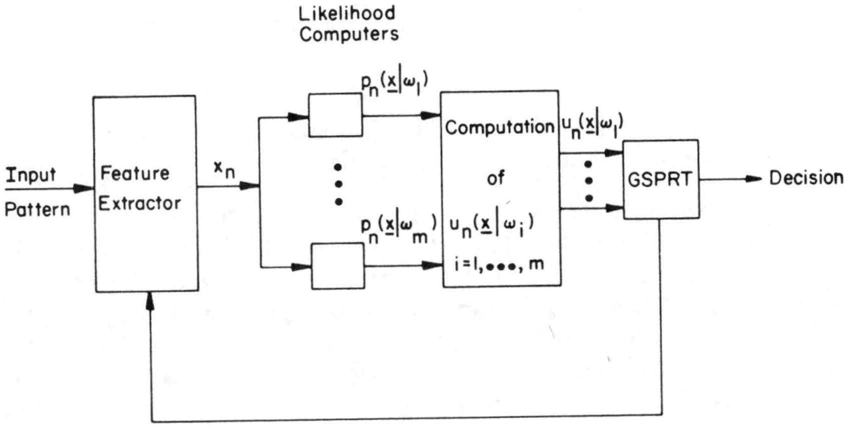

FIGURE 3. A simplified block diagram of a sequential classifier

A pattern classifier using a standard sequential decision procedure, or a SPRT or GSPRT, may be unsatisfactory because: (1) an individual classification may require more feature measurements than can be tolerated, and (2) the average number of feature measurements may become extremely large if e_{ij}'s are chosen to be very small. In practical situations, it may become virtually necessary to interrupt the standard procedure and resolve among various courses of action. The application arises when the feature extractor of a recognition system has only a finite number of suitable feature measurements available to the classifier or when the cost of taking more feature measurements is found to be too high as the number of measurements exceeds a certain limit. In either case, the urgency to terminate the process becomes greater when the available feature measurements are to be exhausted. This can be achieved by truncating the sequential process at $n = N$. For example, the truncated sequential decision procedure for SPRT will be the following: Carry out the regular SPRT until either a terminal decision is made or stage N of the process is reached. If no decision has been reached at stage N, decide $\mathbf{x} \sim \omega_1$ if $\lambda_n > 1$ and $\mathbf{x} \sim \omega_2$ if $\lambda_n \leqslant 1$. In a pattern classifier using truncated GSPRT, at $n = N$ the input pattern is classified as belonging to the class with the largest generalized sequential probability ratio. Under the truncated procedure, the process must terminate in at most N stages. Truncation is a compromise between an entirely sequential procedure and a classical, fixed-sample decision procedure as Eq. (2.8). It is an attempt to reconcile the good properties of both procedures: (1) the sequential property of examining measurements as they accumulate, and (2) the classical property of guaranteeing that the tolerances will be met with a specified number of available measurements.

III. Forward Sequential Classification Procedure with Time-Varying Stopping Boundaries

As described in Section II, the error probabilities e_{ij} can be prespecified in SPRT and GSPRT. However, in SPRT and GSPRT, the number of feature measurements required for a terminal decision is a random variable, which, in general, depends upon the specified e_{ij} and has a positive probability of being greater than any constant. Since it is impractical to allow an arbitrarily large number of feature measurements to terminate the sequential process, one is frequently interested in setting an upper bound for the number of feature measurements within which the pattern classifier must make a terminal decision. An abrupt truncation of the process as described in Section II is an answer. In this section, the problem of terminating the sequential process at a finite number of feature measurements, using a forward computation procedure (i.e., SPRT or GSPRT), is presented. Instead of using abrupt truncation, this problem is studied by considering time-varying stopping boundaries for the sequential classification process (Fu, 1968; Chien and Fu, 1966; Anderson, 1960; Bussgang and Marcus, 1964). The idea of varying the stopping boundaries as a function of time or number of feature measurements enables us to investigate the behavior of a modified SPRT (with time-varying stopping boundaries), as compared with the standard Wald's SPRT with constant stopping boundaries A and B. Since the stopping boundaries are constructed and employed in the direction of the usual time sequence, starting with the first feature measurement, the term "forward procedure" is emphasized here as opposed to the "backward procedure" discussed later in Section IV.

The modified SPRT is formulated as follows: Let $E_i(n)$ be the expected number of feature measurements when $\mathbf{x} \sim \omega_i$, $i = 1, 2$; that is, when a terminal decision is made. Subject to the requirement that the probability of misrecognition will be at most $e_{ij} (i \neq j)$ when $\mathbf{x}$ is classified as from class ω_i, the problem is to give a procedure with time-varying stopping boundaries for deciding between $\mathbf{x} \sim \omega_1$ and

$\mathbf{x} \sim \omega_2$ such that $E_i(n)$ is a minimum. The procedure of modified SPRT can be stated as follows:

Let $g_1(n)$ and $g_2(n)$ be either constants, or monotonically nonincreasing and nondecreasing functions of n, respectively. The classifier continuously take measurements as long as the sequential probability ratio λ_n lies between $e^{g_1(n)}$ and $e^{g_2(n)}$; that is, the sequential process continuous by taking additional feature measurements as long as

$$e^{g_2(n)} < \lambda_n < e^{g_1(n)} \qquad n = 1, 2, \ldots \tag{2.25}$$

If

$$\lambda_n \geqslant e^{g_1(n)} \qquad \text{then} \qquad \mathbf{x} \sim \omega_1$$

and if

$$\lambda_n \leqslant e^{g_2(n)} \qquad \text{then} \qquad \mathbf{x} \sim \omega_2 \tag{2.26}$$

In this formulation, it is seen that the standard Wald's SPRT can be considered as a special case of the modified SPRT where $g_1(n)$ and $g_2(n)$ are constants. The fact that, in general, $g_1(n)$ and $g_2(n)$ can be made functions of n enables us to design a sequential classifier such that the expected number of feature measurements in reaching a terminal decision and the probability of misrecognition may be controlled in advance.

Consider the modified sequential probability ratio test defined in Eqs. (2.25) and (2.26) for which

$$g_1(n) = a'\left(1 - \frac{n}{N}\right)^{r_1} \tag{2.27}$$

$$g_2(n) = -b'\left(1 - \frac{n}{N}\right)^{r_2} \tag{2.28}$$

where $0 < r_1,\ r_2 \leqslant 1$, $a' > 0$, $b' > 0$, and N is the prespecified number of feature measurements where the truncation occurs and the classifier is forced to reach a terminal decision. The graphical representation of $g_1(n)$ and $g_2(n)$ as functions of n is shown in Fig. 4. Let

$$L_n = \log \lambda_n = \log \frac{p_n(\mathbf{x} \mid \omega_1)}{p_n(\mathbf{x} \mid \omega_2)} \tag{2.29}$$

Then the modified sequential probability ratio test is defined in

$$-b'\left(1 - \frac{n}{N}\right)^{r_2} < L_n < a'\left(1 - \frac{n}{N}\right)^{r_1} \tag{2.30}$$

and the violation of either one of the inequalities is associated with the classification of $\mathbf{x} \sim \omega_1$ or $\mathbf{x} \sim \omega_2$. It is noted as $N \to \infty$, Eq. (2.30) defines the standard Wald's SPRT where $a' = \log A$ and $b' = -\log B$. The derivatives of $g_1(n)$ and $g_2(n)$ at $n = 0$ are $-r_1 a'/N$ and $r_2 b'/N$, respectively; they characterize the initial slopes of the convergent boundaries and, therefore, determine the rate of convergence to N when the process is to be truncated.

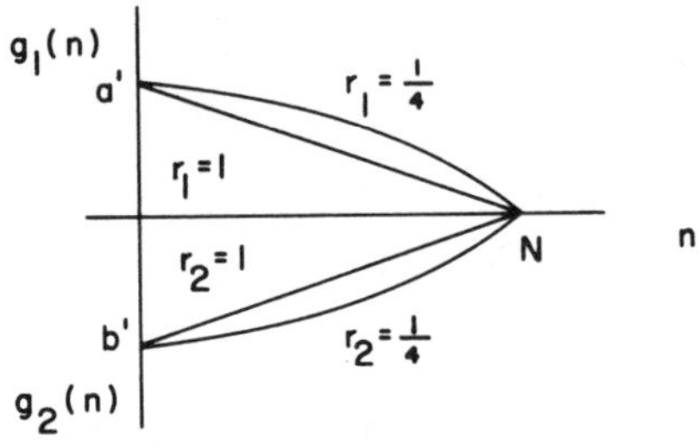

FIGURE 4. A class of convergent time-varying stopping boundaries

Generally speaking, the principle of constructing the time-varying stopping boundaries for Wald's SPRT also applies to the generalized sequential probability ratio test when the number of pattern classes to be recognized is more than two. In a modified GSPRT, the generalized sequential probability ratio for each pattern class is computed at the nth stage

$$u_n(\mathbf{x} \mid \omega_i) = \frac{p_n(\mathbf{x} \mid \omega_i)}{[\prod_{j=1}^{m} p_n(\mathbf{x} \mid \omega_j)]^{1/m}} \qquad i = 1,..., m \tag{2.31}$$

and is compared with the stopping boundary $g_i(n)$, $i = 1,..., m$. As soon as

$$u_n(\mathbf{x} \mid \omega_i) < g_i(n) \tag{2.32}$$

the pattern class ω_i is dropped from consideration, and the number of possible pattern classes is reduced by one for the next computation. The process of forming the generalized sequential probability ratio continues until there is only one pattern class retained, this pattern class would be assigned to the input. Note that the stopping boundaries $g_i(n)$, $i = 1,..., m$, are, in general, functions of time and need not be identical for all classes. Similar to the ones suggested for the modified SPRT, a simple class of convergent boundaries may assume the form as

$$g_i(n) = G_i' \left(1 - \frac{n}{N}\right)^{r_i} \qquad i = 1,..., m \tag{2.33}$$

In fact, the spirit of the modified GSPRT relies on an optimal construction of these functions such that all the pattern classes but one are dropped from consideration by a prespecified number of feature measurements N.

IV. Backward Sequential Classification Procedure Using Dynamic Programming

As mentioned in Section II, many pattern recognition problems may be considered as sequential decision processes in which the number of observations is necessarily finite. The method of modifying the sequential probability ratio test as described in Section III is certainly one approach for solving this class of decision problems. However, the optimality of the original decision procedure is frequently sacrificed, especially in the multiple decision case ($m > 2$). The optimal Bayes' sequential decision procedure which minimizes the expected risk including the cost of observations is essentially a backward procedure (Blackwell and Girshick, 1954). It is intended to show in this section that, as an alternative approach to the modified sequential probability ratio test, the dynamic programming (Bellman, 1957; Bellman *et. al.*, 1961; Lindley, 1961; Dynkin, 1963; Fishburn, 1965; Howard, 1960) provides a feasible computational technique for a class of sequential recognition systems with finite stopping rules. The intuitive argument of using dynamic programming for finite sequential recognition problems can be stated as follows: Consider a sequential decision process. With observations taken one at a time, each stage of the process is a decision problem including both the choice of closing the sequence of observations and making a terminal decision, and the choice of taking an additional observation. It is easy to determine the expected risk involved in the decision when the procedure is terminated, but it is not easy to find the expected risk involved in taking an additional observation. For the case of taking one more observation, the expected risk is that of continuing and then doing the best possible from then on. Consequently, in order to determine the best decision at the present stage (i.e., whether to continue the process or not) it is necessary to know the best decision in the future. In other words, as far as seeking the optimal decision procedure is concerned, the natural time order of working from the present to the future is of little use because the present optimum essentially involves the future optimum. The only alternative to keep the true optimality is to work backwards in time, i.e., from the optimal future behavior to deduce the optimal present behavior, and so on back into the past. The entire available future must be considered in deciding whether to continue the process or not, and the method of dynamic programming provides just such an optimization procedure, working backwards from a prespecified last stage to the very first stage. In the problems of sequential recognition where the decision procedure is to terminate at a finite number of observations, the termination point can be used as a convenient starting point (i.e., the last stage) for backward computation.

The way in which the dynamic programming is carried out in the finite optimal sequential decision procedure is by applying the Principle of Optimality. As stated by Bellman (1957):

"An optimal policy has the property that whatever the initial state and initial decision are, the remaining decisions must constitute an optimal policy with regard to the state resulting from the first decision."

In essence, it is equivalent to saying that if an optimal policy is pursued, then at each stage of the sequential process the remaining decisions must themselves form an optimal policy from the state reached to the terminal point of the process.

Consider the successive observations or feature measurements $x_1, x_2, \ldots, x_n$, $n = 1, 2, \ldots$, with known distribution function $P(x_{n+1} \mid x_1, \ldots, x_n)$ of x_{n+1} given the sequence $x_1, \ldots, x_n$. After the observation of each feature measurement, the decision made by the classifier includes both the choice of closing the sequence of feature measurements and making a terminal decision (to decide the pattern class based on the observed feature measurements), and the choice of making another observation of the next feature measurement before coming to a terminal decision (Fu *et. al.*, 1967; Fu, 1968). Let

$R_n(x_1, x_2, \ldots, x_n) =$ the minimum expected risk of the entire sequential decision process, having observed the sequence of feature measurements $x_1, x_2, \ldots, x_n$;

$C(x_1, x_2, \ldots, x_n) =$ the cost of continuing the sequential process at the nth stage; i.e., taking an additional feature measurement x_{n+1};

and $G(x_1, x_2, \ldots, x_n; d_i) =$ the expected risk of making terminal decision d_i (i.e., the ith pattern class is accepted by the classifier), $i = 1, 2, \ldots, m$ on the basis of the feature measurements $x_1, x_2, \ldots, x_n$.

If the classifier decides to stop the process, the expected risk by employing an optimal decision rule is $\text{Min}_i\, G(x_1, x_2, \ldots, x_n; d_i)$. If the classifier decides to continue the process and to take one more feature measurement x_{n+1}, the expected risk is

$$C(x_1, x_2, \ldots, x_n) + \int R_{n+1}(x_1, x_2, \ldots, x_n, x_{n+1})\, dP(x_{n+1} \mid x_1, \ldots, x_n)$$

where the integration is carried over the admissible region of x_{n+1}. Hence, by the Principle of Optimality, the basic functional equation governing the infinite sequence of the expected risk $R_n(x_1, x_2, \ldots, x_n)$, $n = 1, 2, \ldots$, is

$$R_n(x_1, x_2, \ldots, x_n) = \mathrm{Min} \begin{bmatrix} \text{Continue: } C(x_1, \ldots, x_n) \\ + \int R_{n+1}(x_1, \ldots, x_n, x_{n+1})\, dP(x_{n+1} \mid x_1, \ldots, x_n) \\ \text{Stop: } \underset{i}{\mathrm{Min}}\, G(x_1, \ldots, x_n; d_i) \end{bmatrix} \tag{2.34}$$

In the case of finite sequential decision processes where a terminal decision has to be made at or before a preassigned stage number N (for example, only a maximum of N feature measurements available for observation), the optimal stopping rule can be determined backwards starting from the given risk function (or specified error probabilities) of the last stage. That is, at the Nth stage let

$$R_N(x_1, x_2, \ldots, x_N) = \underset{i}{\mathrm{Min}}\, G(x_1, x_2, \ldots, x_N; d_i) \tag{2.35}$$

and compute the expected risk for stage number less than N through the functional Eq. (2.34). Specifically, starting with the known (or given) value for $R_N(x_1, x_2, \ldots, x_N)$ in Eq. (2.35), we have at $(N-1)$th stage

$$R_{N-1}(x_1, x_2, \ldots, x_{N-1}) = \mathrm{Min} \begin{bmatrix} \text{Continue: } C(x_1, x_2, \ldots, x_{N-1}) \\ + \int R_N(x_1, \ldots, x_N)\, dP(x_N \mid x_1, \ldots, x_{N-1}) \\ \text{Stop: } \mathrm{Min}\, G(x_1, \ldots, x_{N-1}; d_i) \end{bmatrix} \tag{2.36}$$

in which $R_N(x_1, \ldots, x_N)$ is obtained from Eq. (2.35). At $(N-2)$th stage,

$$R_{N-2}(x_1, x_2, \ldots, x_{N-2}) = \mathrm{Min} \begin{bmatrix} \text{Continue: } C(x_1, x_2, \ldots, x_{N-2}) \\ + \int R_{N-1}(x_1, \ldots, x_{N-1})\, dP(x_{N-1} \mid x_1, \ldots, x_{N-2}) \\ \text{Stop: } \underset{i}{\mathrm{Min}}\, G(x_1, \ldots, x_{N-2}; d_i) \end{bmatrix} \tag{2.37}$$

in which $R_{N-1}(x_1, \ldots, x_{N-1})$ is obtained from Eq. (2.36). At second stage,

$$R_2(x_1, x_2) = \mathrm{Min} \begin{bmatrix} \text{Continue: } C(x_1, x_2) + \int R_3(x_1, x_2, x_3)\, dP(x_3 \mid x_1, x_2) \\ \text{Stop: } \underset{i}{\mathrm{Min}}\, G(x_1, x_2; d_i) \end{bmatrix} \tag{2.38}$$

in which $R_3(x_1, x_2, x_3)$ is obtained from the third stage. At first stage,

$$R_1(x_1) = \text{Min} \begin{bmatrix} \text{Continue: } C(x_1) + \int R_2(x_1, x_2)\, dP(x_2 \mid x_1) \\ \text{Stop: } \underset{i}{\text{Min}}\, G(x_1; d_i) \end{bmatrix} \tag{2.39}$$

in which $R_2(x_1, x_2)$ is obtained from Eq. (2.38).

The risk function $R_n(x_1, x_2, \ldots, x_n)$ is then determined for each and every sequence of $x_1, x_2, \ldots, x_n$, $n = 1, 2, \ldots, N$. In addition, the optimal stopping rule is also determined at each stage. That is, if the risk of stopping is less than the expected risk of continuing for a given history of feature measurements, the sequential process is terminated. The actual optimal structure of the resulting procedure is obtained in the course of solving the functional equation (2.34).

V. Backward Sequential Procedure for Both Feature Selection and Pattern Classification

In Section IV, the dynamic programming procedure has been applied to pattern classification problems without considering the ordering of feature measurements. However, in order to terminate the sequential recognition process earlier, the ordering of feature measurements is often rather important. In this section, a more general sequential pattern classifier is considered. The classifier so designed has the additional capability of selecting the best feature for the next measurement. In other words, in the process of sequential decisions, if the decision is to continue taking an additional measurement, it also, in the meantime, selects the best feature for the next measurement.

Let $F_N = (f_1, \ldots, f_N)$ be the set of N features extracted by the feature extractor in their natural order. Let $F_{t_n} = (f_{t_1}, \ldots, f_{t_n})$, $n = 1, \ldots, N$ be a particular sequence of n features measured by the classifier at the nth stage of the sequential recognition process. The remaining features available for further measurements at the nth stage will be $F_n = F_N - F_{t_n}$. Note that the feature f_{t_i} may be any one of the elements in F_N, and the (noisy) feature measurement corresponding to f_{t_i} is represented by a random variable x_i as in the previous formulation. Similar to those in Section IV, the following terms are defined:

$R_n(x_1, \ldots, x_n \mid F_{t_n})$ = the minimum expected risk of the entire sequential recognition process, having observed the sequence of feature measurements $x_1, \ldots, x_n$ when the particular sequence of features F_{t_n} is selected.

$C(x_1, \ldots, x_n \mid F_{t_n})$ = the cost of continuing the sequential recognition process at the nth stage, when F_{t_n} is selected.

$G(x_1, \ldots, x_n; d_i \mid F_{t_n})$ = the expected risk of making terminal decision d_i, $i = 1, \ldots, m$ on the basis of the feature measurements $x_1, \ldots, x_n$ when F_{t_n} is selected.

$P(x_{n+1}; f_{t_{n+1}} \mid x_1, \ldots, x_n; F_{t_n})$ = conditional probability distribution of x_{n+1} when $f_{t_{n+1}}$ is selected given the sequence of measurements $x_1, \ldots, x_n$ on the sequence of features F_{t_n}.

When the classifier decides to stop the process and make a terminal decision at the nth stage, the expected risk is simply

$$\operatorname*{Min}_i G(x_1, \ldots, x_n; d_i \mid F_{t_n})$$

If the classifier decides to take an additional measurement, then the measurement must be optimally selected from the remaining features F_n in order to minimize the risk. That is, the expected risk of measuring the $(n+1)$th feature is

$$\operatorname*{Min}_{f_{t_{n+1}} \in F_n} \Big\{ C(x_1, \ldots, x_n \mid F_{t_n}) + \int R_{n+1}(x_1, \ldots, x_n, x_{n+1} \mid F_{t_n}, f_{t_{n+1}}) \cdot dP(x_{n+1}; f_{t_{n+1}} \mid x_1, \ldots, x_n; F_{t_n}) \Big\}$$

Therefore, by the principle of optimality, the basic functional equation governing the sequential recognition process becomes

$$R_n(x_1, \ldots, x_n \mid F_{t_n}) = \operatorname{Min} \begin{bmatrix} \text{Continue: } \operatorname*{Min}_{f_{t_{n+1}} \in F_n} \{ C(x_1, \ldots, x_n \mid F_{t_n}) \\ + \int R_{n+1}(x_1, \ldots, x_n, x_{n+1} \mid F_{t_n}, f_{t_{n+1}}) \\ \times dP(x_{n+1}; f_{t_{n+1}} \mid x_1, \ldots, x_n; F_{t_n}) \} \\ \text{Stop: } \operatorname*{Min}_i G(x_1, \ldots, x_n; d_i \mid F_{t_n}) \end{bmatrix} \qquad (2.40)$$

Again, Eq. (2.40) can be recursively solved by setting the terminal condition to be

$$R_N(x_1, \ldots, x_N \mid F_{t_N}) = \operatorname*{Min}_i G(x_1, \ldots, x_N; d_i \mid F_{t_N}) \qquad (2.41)$$

and computing backwards for risk functions R_n, $n < N$. The major difference between the solution of Eq. (2.40) and that of Eq. (2.34) lies in the fact that the optimal stopping rules obtained from the present solution are automatically accompanied by a best sequence of features capable of minimizing the expected risk upon termination.

VI. Feature Selection and Ordering: Information Theoretic Approach

As mentioned in Section I, the selection of features is an important problem in pattern recognition, and is closely related to the performance of classification. Also, in sequential pattern recognition systems, the ordering of features for successive measurements is important. The purpose of feature ordering is to provide, at successive stages of the sequential classification process, a feature which is the most "informative" among all possible choices of features for the next measurement so the process can be terminated earlier. The problem of feature ordering may be considered as a problem of feature selection if, at each stage of the sequential classification process, the feature subset to be selected contains only one feature. Approaches from the viewpoint of information theory have been suggested for evaluating the "goodness" of features. Both the divergence and the average information about the pattern classes characterized by the features have been proposed as criteria for feature "goodness." The concept of divergence is closely related to the discriminatory power between two pattern classes with normally distributed feature measurement vector **x**. The use of information measure and divergence as criteria for feature selection or ordering is also implied by the comparison of the expected risks when the Bayes' decision rule is employed for the classification process.

The application of divergence as a criterion for feature selection and ordering has been proposed by Marill and Green (1963). Assume that, for ω_i, **x** is distributed according to a multivariate Gaussian density function with mean vector $\boldsymbol{\mu}_i$ and covariance matrix Σ; that is,

$$p(\mathbf{x} \mid \omega_i) = \frac{1}{(2\pi)^{N/2} |\Sigma|^{1/2}} \exp[-\tfrac{1}{2}(\mathbf{x} - \boldsymbol{\mu}_i)' \Sigma^{-1}(\mathbf{x} - \boldsymbol{\mu}_i)] \tag{2.42}$$

Let the likelihood ratio be

$$\lambda = \frac{p(\mathbf{x} \mid \omega_i)}{p(\mathbf{x} \mid \omega_j)} \tag{2.43}$$

and let

$$L = \log \lambda = \log p(\mathbf{x} \mid \omega_i) - \log p(\mathbf{x} \mid \omega_j) \tag{2.44}$$

Substituting Eq. (2.42) into Eq. (2.44), we obtain

$$L = \mathbf{x}'\Sigma^{-1}(\boldsymbol{\mu}_i - \boldsymbol{\mu}_j) - \tfrac{1}{2}(\boldsymbol{\mu}_i + \boldsymbol{\mu}_j)'\,\Sigma^{-1}(\boldsymbol{\mu}_i - \boldsymbol{\mu}_j) \tag{2.45}$$

and

$$E\{L \mid \omega_i\} = \tfrac{1}{2}(\boldsymbol{\mu}_i - \boldsymbol{\mu}_j)'\,\Sigma^{-1}(\boldsymbol{\mu}_i - \boldsymbol{\mu}_j) \tag{2.46}$$

Define the divergence between ω_i and ω_j as (Kullback, 1959):

$$J(\omega_i\,, \omega_j) = E\{L \mid \omega_i\} - E\{L \mid \omega_j\} \tag{2.47}$$

Then, from Eqs. (2.46) and (2.47)

$$J(\omega_i\,, \omega_j) = (\boldsymbol{\mu}_i - \boldsymbol{\mu}_j)'\,\Sigma^{-1}(\boldsymbol{\mu}_i - \boldsymbol{\mu}_j) \tag{2.48}$$

It is noted that in Eq. (2.48), if $\Sigma = I$, the identify matrix, then $J(\omega_i\,, \omega_j)$ represents the squared distance between $\boldsymbol{\mu}_i$ and $\boldsymbol{\mu}_j$. If a fixed-sample or nonsequential Bayes' decision rule is used for the classifier, then for $P(\omega_i) = P(\omega_j) = \frac{1}{2}$, from Eq. (2.8)

$$\mathbf{x} \sim \omega_i \quad \text{if} \quad \lambda > 1, \quad \text{or} \quad L > 0$$

or

$$\mathbf{x} \sim \omega_j \quad \text{if} \quad \lambda < 1, \quad \text{or} \quad L < 0$$

The probability of misrecognition is

$$e = \tfrac{1}{2}P\{L > 0 \mid \omega_j\} + \tfrac{1}{2}P\{L < 0 \mid \omega_i\} \tag{2.49}$$

From Eqs. (2.45), (2.46), and (2.48), it is concluded that $p(L \mid \omega_i)$ is a Gaussian density function with mean $\frac{1}{2}\,J$ and variance J. Similarly, $p(L \mid \omega_j)$ is also a Gaussian density function with mean $-\frac{1}{2}\,J$ and variance J. Thus,

$$\begin{aligned} e = {} & \frac{1}{2}\int_0^\infty \frac{1}{\sqrt{2\pi J}} \exp[-\tfrac{1}{2}(\xi + \tfrac{1}{2}J)/J]\, d\xi \\ & + \frac{1}{2}\int_{-\infty}^0 \frac{1}{\sqrt{2\pi J}} \exp[-\tfrac{1}{2}(\xi - \tfrac{1}{2}J)/J]\, d\xi \end{aligned} \tag{2.50}$$

Let

$$y = \frac{\xi \pm \frac{1}{2}J}{\sqrt{J}} \tag{2.51}$$

then

$$e = \int_{\frac{1}{2}\sqrt{J}}^\infty \frac{1}{\sqrt{2\pi}} \exp[-\tfrac{1}{2}\,y^2]\, dy \tag{2.52}$$

It is noted that, from Eq. (2.52), e is a monotonically decreasing function of $J(\omega_i, \omega_j)$. Therefore, features selected or ordered according to the magnitude of $J(\omega_i, \omega_j)$ will imply their corresponding discriminatory power between ω_i and ω_j.

For more than two pattern classes, the criterion of maximizing the minimum divergence or the expected divergence between any pair of classes has been proposed for signal detection and pattern recognition problems (Grettenberg, 1962 and 1963). The expected divergence between any pair of classes is given by

$$J(\omega) = \sum_{i=1}^{m} \sum_{j=1}^{m} P(\omega_i)\, P(\omega_j)\, J(\omega_i, \omega_j) \tag{2.53}$$

For the distributions given in Eq. (2.42),

$$J(\omega) = \sum_{i=1}^{m} \sum_{j=1}^{m} P(\omega_i)\, P(\omega_j)(\boldsymbol{\mu}_i - \boldsymbol{\mu}_j)'\, \Sigma^{-1}(\boldsymbol{\mu}_i - \boldsymbol{\mu}_j) \tag{2.54}$$

Let

$$d^2 = \operatorname*{Min}_{i,j} J(\omega_i, \omega_j) \tag{2.55}$$

and

$$J(\omega) \geqslant d^2 \left\{1 - \sum_{j=1}^{m} [P(\omega_j)]^2\right\} \tag{2.56}$$

Hence,

$$d^2 \leqslant \frac{J(\omega)}{1 - \sum_{j=1}^{m} [P(\omega_j)]^2} \tag{2.57}$$

The tightest upper bound of d occurs when

$$1 - \sum_{j=1}^{m} [P(\omega_j)]^2$$

is the maximum. This maximum is $1 - 1/m$ which yields

$$d^2 \leqslant \frac{m J(\omega)}{m - 1} \tag{2.58}$$

The bound, as indicated in Eq. (2.58), can be achieved by taking various combinations of features from a given feature set, or, alternatively, by gradually increasing the number of features, N, such that the feature subset selected will correspond to the case where d^2 is the closest value to $mJ(\omega)/(m - 1)$. In general, there may be more than one feature subset which satisfies the criterion.

In the case that the covariance matrices Σ_i and Σ_j are not equal and the number of classes is more than two, the following approach has been proposed (Fu and Min, 1968). Let $g_i(\mathbf{x})$ be the discriminant function of class ω_i, $i = 1,..., m$. Then the probability of misclassification for class ω_i and class ω_j can be expressed as

$$P_{ij}(\epsilon) = \tfrac{1}{2}P[g_i(\mathbf{x}) > g_j(\mathbf{x}) \mid \omega_j] + \tfrac{1}{2}P[g_i(\mathbf{x}) < g_j(\mathbf{x}) \mid \omega_i] \tag{2.59}$$

with the assumption of equal a priori probabilities. Suppose that a family of linear discriminant functions is chosen for $g_i(\mathbf{x})$ as

$$g_i(\mathbf{x}) = \mathbf{b}_i'\mathbf{x} - c_i \qquad i = 1,..., m \tag{2.60}$$

where $\mathbf{b}_i$ is an N-dimensional vector and c_i is the constant term. Let

$$g_i(\mathbf{x}) - g_j(\mathbf{x}) = (\mathbf{b}_i - \mathbf{b}_j)'\mathbf{x} - (c_i - c_j) = \mathbf{b}_{ij}'\mathbf{x} - c_{ij} \tag{2.61}$$

Then Eq. (2.59) becomes

$$P_{ij}(\epsilon) = \tfrac{1}{2}P[\mathbf{b}_{ij}'\mathbf{x} > c_{ij} \mid \omega_j] + \tfrac{1}{2}P[b_{ij}'\mathbf{x} < c_{ij} \mid \omega_i] \tag{2.62}$$

After defining a standardized variable (Anderson and Bahadue, 1962), Eq. (2.62) can be written as

$$P_{ij}(\epsilon) = \tfrac{1}{2}\{2 - P[\xi < d_j] - P[\xi < d_i]\} \tag{2.63}$$

where

$$d_i = \frac{\mathbf{b}_{ij}'\boldsymbol{\mu}_i - c_{ij}}{(\mathbf{b}_{ij}'\Sigma_i\mathbf{b}_{ij})^{1/2}} \tag{2.64}$$

and

$$d_j = \frac{c_{ij} - \mathbf{b}_{ij}'\boldsymbol{\mu}_j}{(\mathbf{b}_{ij}'\Sigma_j\mathbf{b}_{ij})^{1/2}} \tag{2.65}$$

ξ is the standardized Gaussian random variable. Since, in this case, for linear classifications, the minimax procedure is admissible (Anderson and Bahadue, 1962), it is used here to determine an appropriate criterion for feature selection in multiclass classification problems.

Consider that, in a multiclass classification problem, the performance of classification can be measured in terms of a weighted sum of all pair-wise misclassifications; i.e., the overall performance measure is

$$P(\epsilon) = \frac{1}{m(m-1)} \sum_{i=1}^{m} \sum_{j=1}^{m} P_{ij}(\epsilon) \qquad i \neq j \tag{2.66}$$

From Eqs. (2.66) and (2.63), the condition of minimizing the maximum of $P_{ij}(\epsilon)$ is

$$d_i = d_j = d_{ij} \tag{2.67}$$

Thus, it can be obtained from Eqs. (2.64), (2.65), and (2.67) that

$$d_{ij} = \frac{\mathbf{b}'_{ij}(\boldsymbol{\mu}_i - \boldsymbol{\mu}_j)}{(\mathbf{b}'_{ij}\Sigma_i\mathbf{b}_{ij})^{1/2} + (\mathbf{b}'_{ij}\Sigma_j\mathbf{b}_{ij})^{1/2}} \tag{2.68}$$

When $\boldsymbol{\mu}_i \neq \boldsymbol{\mu}_j$, $\Sigma_i \neq \Sigma_j$, and Σ_i and Σ_j are nonsingular, the value of $\mathbf{b}_{ij}$, which maximizes d_{ij} is of the form

$$\mathbf{b}_{ij} = [\lambda_{ij}\Sigma_i + (1 - \lambda_{ij})\,\Sigma_j]^{-1}(\boldsymbol{\mu}_i - \boldsymbol{\mu}_j) \tag{2.69}$$

where λ_{ij} is a Lagrange multiplier and can be calculated by solving the equation

$$\mathbf{b}'_{ij}[\lambda_{ij}^2\Sigma_i - (1 - \lambda_{ij})^2\,\Sigma_j]\,\mathbf{b}_{ij} = 0 \tag{2.70}$$

with $0 < \lambda_{ij} < 1$. Finally, Eq. (2.63) becomes

$$P_{ij}^*(\epsilon) = 1 - P[\xi < d_{ij}] \tag{2.71}$$

It is noted from Eq. (2.71) that a monotonic functional relationship exists between $P_{ij}^*(\epsilon)$ and d_{ij}. The quantity d_{ij} is denoted as a separability measure between class ω_i and class ω_j, and the divergence $J(\omega_i, \omega_j)$ can be considered as a special case of d_{ij}.

Based on the separability measure d_{ij}, the feature selection criterion is to maximize the expected separability measure for all pairs of classes; that is,

$$\text{Max}\left\{\sum_{i=1}^{m}\sum_{j=1}^{m} P(\omega_i)\,P(\omega_j)\,d_{ij}\right\} \qquad i \neq j$$

If there are several feature subsets satisfying the above criterion, the subset which minimizes the maximum variance of the expected separability measure is selected. The proposed criterion has been tested in real-data crop classification problems with satisfactory results (Fu and Min, 1968).

In practical applications, the monotonic properties demonstrated by Eqs. (2.52) and (2.71) sometimes cannot be obtained; i.e., it is possible to have subsets of features resulting in better classification performance than that using the complete set of features (Estes, 1965; Allais, 1964; Hughes, 1968; Fu and Min, 1968). This is probably mainly due to the deviation of the actual feature distributions from the Gaussian assumption and the error involved in the estimation of parameters $\boldsymbol{\mu}_i$ and Σ_i.

In sequential recognition systems, since the features are measured sequentially, a slightly different approach with a similar viewpoint from information theory can be used for "on-line" ordering of features (Fu and Chen, 1965). In the application of SPRT or GSPRT for classification, the knowledge of what pattern classes are more likely to be true (at the input of the recognition system) is used to determine the "goodness" of features. Let r be the available number of features at any stage of the sequential process, $r \leqslant N$, and f_j, $j = 1,..., r$, the jth feature. The criterion of choosing a feature for the next measurement, following Lewis' (1962) approach, is a single-number statistic which is an expectation of a function describing the correlation among pattern classes, previous feature measurements and each of the remaining features. Such a statistic associated with f_j can be expressed, after n feature measurements, $x_1, x_2, ..., x_n$ are taken, as

$$I_j(n) = \sum_{i=1}^{m} P(f_j, \omega_i, x_1, x_2, ..., x_n) \log \frac{P(f_j, \omega_i, x_1, x_2, ..., x_n)}{P(f_j)\, P(\omega_i)\, P(x_1, x_2, ..., x_n)} \qquad \begin{array}{l} j = 1,..., r \\ N = r + n \end{array} \tag{2.72}$$

Since

$$P(f_j, \omega_i, x_1, x_2, ..., x_n) = P(f_j \mid \omega_i, x_1, x_2, ..., x_n) \cdot P(\omega_i \mid x_1, x_2, ..., x_n)\, P(x_1, x_2, ..., x_n) \tag{2.73}$$

and $P(x_1, x_2, ..., x_n)$ is independent of f_j and ω_i, Eq. (2.72) can be written as

$$I_j(n) = \sum_{i=1}^{m} P(f_j \mid \omega_i, x_1, x_2, ..., x_n)\, P(\omega_i \mid x_1, x_2, ..., x_n) \cdot \log \frac{P(f_j \mid \omega_i, x_1, x_2, ..., x_n)\, P(\omega_i \mid x_1, x_2, ..., x_n)}{P(f_j)\, P(\omega_i)} \qquad j = 1,..., r \tag{2.74}$$

It is noted that $P(f_j \mid \omega_i, x_1, x_2, ..., x_n)$ is the a posteriori distribution of f_j for class ω_i after $x_1, x_2, ..., x_n$ were taken. $I_j(n)$ is the conditional entropy of f_j after n feature measurements $x_1, ..., x_n$ are taken. The feature ordering criterion is the maximization of $I_j(n)$. The ordering procedure is to compute $I_j(n)$ for all $j = 1,..., r$ and select the feature for the $(n + 1)$th measurement which gives the largest value of $I_j(n)$. As the number of feature measurements increases, the a posteriori distribution corresponding to the input pattern class gradually plays a dominant role in $I_j(n)$, and the feature which best characterizes the input pattern class is the most likely to be chosen earlier than the others.

VII. Feature Selection and Ordering: Karhunen–Loève Expansion

An alternative approach is proposed in this section for feature selection and ordering in which the complete knowledge of the probability structure for the input patterns under consideration is not required. The basic viewpoint is essentially that of preweighting the features according to their relative importance in characterizing the input patterns, regardless of the specific classification scheme in a recognition system. Here, "relative importance" is interpreted in the sense of (1) committing less error when the representation of patterns is subject to approximation because of truncated finite measurements, and (2) carrying more information with regard to the discrimination of classes. With this point of view, an optimal feature selection and ordering procedure has been developed under the framework of the Karhunen–Loève expansion (Karhunen, 1960; Watanabe, 1965). The procedure described in the following is considered as a generalized version. A generalized Karhunen–Loève expansion is presented first in the continuous case and then in its corresponding form in the discrete case.

Consider the observation of a stochastic process $\{x(t),\ 0 \leqslant t \leqslant T\}$ over the time period $(0, T)$. The observed random function $\mathbf{x}(t)$ is generated from one of the m possible stochastic processes

$$\{x_i(t)\ 0 \leqslant t \leqslant T\} \qquad i = 1, 2, \ldots, m,$$

corresponding to the m pattern classes, respectively. Let the random functions have the expansion

$$x_i(t) = \sum_{k=1}^{\infty} V_{ik}\phi_k(t) \qquad \text{for all} \quad t \in (0, T) \qquad i = 1, \ldots, m \tag{2.75}$$

where V_{ik}'s are random coefficients satisfying $E(V_{ik}) = 0.$† $\{\phi_k(t)\}$ is a set of deterministic orthonormal coordinate functions over $(0, T)$. Define a covariance function $K(t, s)$ for the m stochastic processes as follows:

$$K(t, s) = \sum_{i=1}^{m} P(\omega_i)\, E[x_i(t)\, x_i^*(s)] \tag{2.76}$$

† This can be achieved by centralizing all the random functions and is therefore assumed without loss of generality.

where $x_i^*(t)$ is the complex conjugate of $x_i(t)$. After substituting Eq. (2.75) into Eq. (2.76), we have

$$K(t, s) = \sum_{k,j} \phi_k(t)\, \phi_j^*(s) \sum_{i=1}^{m} P(\omega_i)\, E(V_{ik}V_{ij}^*) \tag{2.77}$$

Let the random coefficients V_{ik}'s satisfy the conditions

$$\begin{aligned} \sum_{i=1}^{m} P(\omega_i)\, E(V_{ik}V_{ij}^*) &= \sum_{i=1}^{m} P(\omega_i)\, \mathrm{Var}(V_{ik}) = \sigma_k^2 \qquad \text{if} \quad k = j \\ \sum_{i=1}^{m} P(\omega_i)\, E(V_{ik}V_{ij}^*) &= 0 \qquad \text{if} \quad k \neq j \end{aligned} \tag{2.78}$$

Then Eq. (2.76) becomes

$$K(t, s) = \sum_{k=1}^{\infty} \sigma_k^2 \phi_k(t)\, \phi_k^*(s) \tag{2.79}$$

That is, if the expansion in Eq. (2.75) exists for $x_i(t)$, $i = 1,\ldots, m$, and the random coefficients satisfy the conditions in Eq. (2.78), then the covariance function $K(t, s)$ must have the representation as Eq. (2.79). Furthermore, from Eq. (2.79),

$$\int_0^T K(t, s)\, \phi_k(s)\, ds = \int_0^T \sum_{j=1}^{\infty} \sigma_j^2 \phi_j(t)\, \phi_j^*(s)\, \phi_k(s)\, ds \tag{2.80}$$

If the summation and the integration can be interchanged, Eq. (2.80) becomes

$$\begin{aligned} \int_0^T K(t, s)\, \phi_k(s)\, ds &= \sum_{j=1}^{\infty} \sigma_j^2 \phi_j(t) \int_0^T \phi_j^*(s)\, \phi_k(s)\, ds \\ &= \sigma_k^2 \phi_k(t) \end{aligned} \tag{2.81}$$

The expansion in Eq. (2.75) in which $\{\phi_k(t)\}$ is determined by Eq. (2.80) or Eq. (2.81) through the defined covariance function $K(t, s)$ is called the generalized Karhunen–Loève expansion (Chien and Fu, 1967).

The generalized Karhunen–Loève expansion described above has been shown to have the following optimal properties: (1) it minimizes the mean square error committed by taking only a finite number of terms in the infinite series of the expansion, and (2) it minimizes the entropy function defined over the variances of the random coefficients in the expansion. It is noted that the necessary conditions stated in Eq. (2.78) essentially mean that the random coefficients between each pair of coordinate functions among all classes of stochastic processes should be uncorrelated. However, the random coefficients between each pair of coordinate functions for a single class should not be uncorrelated.†

If, instead of that the random function $x(t)$ is continuously observed over $(0, T)$, only the sampled measurements from the random function are taken, then the desired representation becomes

$$\mathbf{x}_i = \begin{bmatrix} x_{i1} \\ x_{i2} \\ \vdots \\ x_{iN} \end{bmatrix} \quad \text{and} \quad x_{ij} = \sum_{k=1}^{\infty} V_{ik}\mu_{kj} \qquad \begin{matrix} i = 1,\dots, m \\ j = 1,\dots, N \end{matrix} \tag{2.82}$$

The V_{ik}'s are random coefficients and μ_{kj} is the jth component of the coordinate vector k in $\{\phi_k\}$ which is a set of orthonormal coordinate vectors. Define the discrete analog of the covariance function $K(t, s)$ for the m stochastic processes to be

$$K(t, s) = \sum_{i=1}^{m} P(\omega_i)\, E(x_{it}x_{is}^*) = \sum_{i=1}^{m} P(\omega_i)\, E\left(\sum_{k=1}^{\infty} V_{ik}\mu_{kt} \sum_{j=1}^{\infty} V_{ij}^*\mu_{js}^*\right)$$

$$= \sum_{k=1}^{\infty}\sum_{j=1}^{\infty} \mu_{kt}\mu_{js}^* \sum_{i=1}^{m} P(\omega_i)E(V_{ik}V_{ij}^*) = \sum_{k=1}^{\infty} \sigma_k^2\mu_{kt}\mu_{ks}^* \tag{2.83}$$

Furthermore, by the orthonormality of the coordinate vectors,

$$\sum_{s=1}^{N} K(t, s)\, \mu_{k,s} = \sum_{s=1}^{N}\sum_{j=1}^{\infty} \sigma_j^2\mu_{jt}\mu_{js}^*\mu_{ks}$$

$$= \sum_{j=1}^{\infty} \sigma_j^2\mu_{jt} \sum_{s=1}^{N} \mu_{js}^*\mu_{ks} = \sigma_k^2\mu_{kt} \tag{2.84}$$

The generalized Karhunen–Loève expansion in discrete case becomes

$$x_{ij} = \sum_{k=1}^{\infty} V_{ik}\mu_{kj} \qquad \begin{matrix} i = 1,\dots, m \\ j = 1,\dots, N \end{matrix} \tag{2.85}$$

where the μ_{kj}'s satisfy Eq. (2.84) and the random coefficient V_{ik} is determined by Eq. (2.86) for each k

$$V_{ik} = \sum_{j=1}^{N} x_{ij}\mu_{kj}^* \qquad i = 1,\dots, m \tag{2.86}$$

† The same conclusion seems to have been reached from the information theoretic point of view by Barabash (1965).

It is noted that Eq. (2.84) is the discrete equivalent of the integral equation defined in Eq. (2.81). The coordinate vectors of the generalized Karhunen–Loève expansion are essentially the eigenvectors determined from $K(t, s)$.

The optimal properties of minimized mean square error and entropy function of the generalized Karhunen–Loève expansion lend to an optimal procedure for feature selection and ordering. By properly constructing the generalized Karhunen–Loève coordinate system through Eq. (2.81) or Eq. (2.84) and arranging the coordinate functions $\{\phi_k(t)\}$ or coordinate vectors $\{\phi_k\}$ according to their descending order of their associated eigenvalues σ_k^2, feature measurements taken according to this order will contain the maximum amount of information about the input patterns whenever the recognition process stops at a finite number of measurements. The following theorem which summarizes the results obtained in this section will furnish a convenient way of constructing an optimal coordinate system.

Theorem 1. Let $\{x_i(t), 0 \leqslant t \leqslant T\}$ and $P(\omega_i)$, $i = 1,..., m$ be the m stochastic processes and their corresponding probabilities of occurrences, respectively. Let the random functions have the expansion

$$x_i(t) = \sum_{k=1}^{\infty} V_{ik}\phi_k(t) \tag{2.87}$$

where the V_{ik}'s are random coefficients with zero mean and $\{\phi_k(t)\}$ is a set of orthonormal coordinate functions over $(0, T)$. Then the necessary and sufficient condition for the set of coordinate functions $\{\phi_k(t)\}$ to be the generalized Karhunen–Loève system defined in Eq. (2.81) is

$$\sum_{i=1}^{m} P(\omega_i)\, E(V_{ik}V_{ij}^*) = \sigma_k^2\delta_{kj} \tag{2.88}$$

where δ_{kj} is the Kronecker delta function and

$$\sigma_k^2 = \sum_{i=1}^{m} P(\omega_i)\, \mathrm{Var}(V_{ik}) \tag{2.89}$$

Note that Theorem 1 also holds for the discrete case with obvious substitutions of corresponding discrete quantities.

From Theorem 1, it is easily seen that the construction of the desired coordinate system can be viewed as finding the coordinate functions (or vectors) in which the coordinate coefficients are mutually uncorrelated so that the conditions in Eq. (2.78) are satisfied. The procedure is basically that of decorrelating the coordinate coefficients over the ensemble of all pattern samples from different classes. In many recognition problems where the covariance functions are real and symmetric, the decorrelation process simply amounts to the diagonalization of the covariance functions under consideration. The actual procedure for feature selection and ordering is summarized into the following steps in terms of discrete case.*

Step 1: Obtain the covariance function $K(t, s)$ defined in Eq. (2.83) from the feature vectors extracted from the given pattern samples. If the components of the feature vectors assume real values, $K(t, s)$ is a real symmetric matrix.

Step 2: Find the eigenvalues and their associated eigenvectors for $K(t, s)$. Let the eigenvectors be normalized and lexicographically arranged according to the descending order of their associated eigenvalues. The set of orthonormal vectors thus obtained constitutes the generalized Karhunen–Loève coordinate system.

Step 3: Make the transformation defined in Eq. (2.86) where the μ_{kj}'s are the components of the orthonormal eigenvectors obtained from Step 2. The resulting V_{ik}'s are the desired coordinate coefficients in terms of the generalized Karhunen–Loève coordinate system.

It is noted that the complete ordering of feature measurements is achieved in the course of rearranging the eigenvectors according to the descending order of their associated eigenvalues. The eigenvalues are nothing but the variances of the transformed coefficients. Also, since the proposed procedure is independent from the classification scheme used in the recognition system, the problem of selecting the feature subset from a given set of features can be viewed as a subproblem of feature ordering. The procedure of completely ordering the coordinate vectors will allow us to select a subset of $r(r \leqslant N)$ feature measurements with minimized mean square error by simply picking out the first r coordinate vectors in the resulting generalized Karhunen–Loève system. Applications of the generalized Karhunen–Loève expansion to feature selection problems in character and crop classifications can be found in Chien and Fu (1968) and Fu and Min (1968).

* The reason for presenting the discrete case here is that most of the practical experiments in pattern recognition are processed with sampled data on a digital computer.

VIII. Bayesian Estimation in Statistical Classification Systems

In previous sections, all the information concerning the statistical characteristics of patterns in each class, such as $P(\omega_i)$ and $p(\mathbf{x} \mid \omega_i)$, is assumed completely known. However, in practice, the information required for optimal design of feature extractors or classifiers is often only partially known. One approach suggested is to design a pattern recognition system which has the capability to estimate the unknown information during its operation. The decisions (feature selections or classifications) are made on the basis of the estimated information. If the estimated information gradually approaches the true information, then the decisions based on the estimated information will eventually approach the optimal decision as if all the information required is known. Therefore, during the system's operation the performance of the system is gradually improved. The process which acquires necessary information for decision during the system's operation and which improves the system's performance is usually called "learning."

Several approaches based on statistical estimation theory have been proposed for the estimation (learning) of unknown information. If the unknown information is the parameter values of a given function such as $p(\mathbf{x} \mid \omega_i)$ or the equation of a decision boundary, parametric estimation techniques can be applied. If both the form and the parameter values of a function are unknown, in general, nonparametric techniques should be used. However, as can be seen later, both cases can be formulated as the problems of successive estimation of unknown parameters.

During the operation of a pattern recognition system, the system estimates the necessary information about each pattern class by actually observing various patterns. In other words, the unknown information is obtained from these observed patterns. Depending upon whether the correct classifications of the observed input patterns are known or not, the learning process performed by the system can be classified into "learning with a teacher" or "supervised learning" and "learning without a teacher" or "nonsupervised learning." In the case of supervised learning, Bayesian estimation (Abramson and Braverman, 1962) and stochastic approximation (Tsypkin, 1966, Chap. 8) can be used to successively estimate (learn) unknown parameters in a given form of feature distributions of each class, $p(\mathbf{x} \mid \omega_i)$. The successive estimation of continuous conditional probabilities of each pattern class can be performed by applying the Potential Function Method (Aiserman *et al.*, 1964, Chap. 3) or stochastic approximation (Fu, 1968, Chap. 8). In nonsupervised learning, the correct classifications of the observed patterns are not available, and the problem of learning is often reduced to a process of successive estimation of some unknown parameters either in a mixture distribution of all possible pattern classes, or of a known decision boundary. In this section, learning schemes using Bayesian estimation techniques are discussed (Abramson and Braverman, 1962; Keehn, 1965; Fralick, 1967; D. Cooper and P. Cooper, 1964).

When the form of the probability density function $p(\mathbf{x} \mid \omega_i)$ is known but some parameters $\boldsymbol{\theta}$ of the density function are unknown, the unknown parameters can be learned (estimated) by iterative applications of Bayes' theorem. It is assumed there exists an a priori density function for the unknown parameter $\boldsymbol{\theta}$ (in general vector-valued) $p_0(\boldsymbol{\theta})$ which reflects the initial knowledge about $\boldsymbol{\theta}$. Consider what happens to the knowledge about θ when a sequence of independent identically-distributed feature vectors $\mathbf{x}_1, \mathbf{x}_2, \ldots, \mathbf{x}_n$, all from the same pattern class, is observed; $p_0(\boldsymbol{\theta})$ changes to the a posteriori density function $p(\boldsymbol{\theta} \mid \mathbf{x}_1, \ldots, \mathbf{x}_n)$ according to Bayes' theorem. For example, the a posteriori density function of θ given the first observation $\mathbf{x}_1$ is

$$p(\boldsymbol{\theta} \mid \mathbf{x}_1) = \frac{p(\mathbf{x}_1 \mid \boldsymbol{\theta})\, p_0(\boldsymbol{\theta})}{p(\mathbf{x}_1)} \tag{2.90}$$

After $\mathbf{x}_1$ and $\mathbf{x}_2$ are observed, the a posteriori density function of $\boldsymbol{\theta}$ is

$$p(\boldsymbol{\theta} \mid \mathbf{x}_1, \mathbf{x}_2) = \frac{p(\mathbf{x}_2 \mid \mathbf{x}_1, \boldsymbol{\theta})\, p(\boldsymbol{\theta} \mid \mathbf{x}_1)}{p(\mathbf{x}_2 \mid \mathbf{x}_1)} \tag{2.91}$$

The central idea of Bayesian estimation is to extract information from the observations $\mathbf{x}_1, \mathbf{x}_2, \ldots, \mathbf{x}_n$ for the unknown parameter $\boldsymbol{\theta}$ through successive applications of the recursive Bayes' formula. It is known that, on the average, the a posteriori density function becomes more concentrated and converges to the true value of the parameter as long as the true value is not excluded by the a priori density function of the parameter.

In each of the supervised learning schemes to be discussed, the iterative application of Bayes' theorem can be accomplished by a fixed computational algorithm. This is made possible by carefully selecting a reproducing a priori density function for the unknown parameter so that the a posteriori density functions after each iteration are members of the same family of a priori density functions (i.e., the form of the density function is preserved and only the parameters of the density function are changed).* The learning schemes are then reduced to the

* Some important results concerning the necessary and sufficient conditions admitting a reproducing density function can be found in Spragins (1965).

successive estimations of parameter values. The following examples illustrate the estimation procedure.

A. *Learning the Mean Vector* $\boldsymbol{\mu}$ *of a Gaussian Distribution with Known Covariance Matrix* Σ

In this case, the unknown parameter $\boldsymbol{\theta}$ to be learned is $\boldsymbol{\mu}$ whose uncertainty can be reflected by assigning a proper reproducing a priori density function $p_0(\boldsymbol{\theta}) = p_0(\boldsymbol{\mu})$. Let

$$p(\mathbf{x} \mid \boldsymbol{\theta}) = p(\mathbf{x} \mid \boldsymbol{\mu}) = \frac{1}{(2\pi)^{N/2} |\Sigma|^{1/2}} \exp[-\tfrac{1}{2}(\mathbf{x} - \boldsymbol{\mu})' \Sigma^{-1} (\mathbf{x} - \boldsymbol{\mu})] \quad (2.92)$$

and assign

$$p_0(\boldsymbol{\theta}) = p_0(\boldsymbol{\mu}) = \frac{1}{(2\pi)^{N/2} |\Phi_0|^{1/2}} \exp[-\tfrac{1}{2}(\boldsymbol{\mu} - \boldsymbol{\mu}_0)' \Phi_0^{-1} (\boldsymbol{\mu} - \boldsymbol{\mu}_0)] \quad (2.93)$$

where $\boldsymbol{\mu}_0$ represents the initial estimate of the mean vector and Φ_0 is the initial covariance matrix which reflects the uncertainty about $\boldsymbol{\mu}_0$. From the reproducing property of Gaussian density functions it is known that, after successive applications of Bayes' formula, the a posteriori density function $p(\boldsymbol{\mu} \mid \mathbf{x}_1, \ldots, \mathbf{x}_n)$, given the learning observations $\mathbf{x}_1, \ldots, \mathbf{x}_n$, is again a Gaussian density function with $\boldsymbol{\mu}_0$ and Φ_0 replaced by $\boldsymbol{\mu}_n$ and Φ_n where

$$\boldsymbol{\mu}_n = (n^{-1}\Sigma)(\Phi_0 + n^{-1}\Sigma)^{-1} \boldsymbol{\mu}_0 + \Phi_0(\Phi_0 + n^{-1}\Sigma)^{-1} \langle \mathbf{x} \rangle \quad (2.94)$$

$$\Phi_n = (n^{-1}\Sigma)(\Phi_0 + n^{-1}\Sigma)^{-1} \Phi_0 \quad (2.95)$$

and

$$\langle \mathbf{x} \rangle = \frac{1}{n} \sum_{i=1}^{n} \mathbf{x}_i$$

Or, in terms of recursive relationship, Eqs. (2.94) and (2.95) can be written as

$$\boldsymbol{\mu}_n = K(\Phi_{n-1} + \Sigma)^{-1} \boldsymbol{\mu}_{n-1} + \Phi_{n-1}(\Phi_{n-1} + \Sigma)^{-1} \mathbf{x}_n \quad (2.96)$$

and

$$\Phi_n = K(\Phi_{n-1} + \Sigma)^{-1} \Phi_{n-1} \quad (2.97)$$

Equation (2.94) shows that $\boldsymbol{\mu}_n$ can be interpreted as a weighted average of the a priori mean vector $\boldsymbol{\mu}_0$ and the sample information $\langle \mathbf{x} \rangle$, with the weights being $(n^{-1}\Sigma)(\Phi_0 + n^{-1}\Sigma)^{-1}$ and $\Phi_0(\Phi_0 + n^{-1}\Sigma)^{-1}$, respectively. The nature of this interpretation can be seen more easily in the special case where

$$\Phi_0 = \alpha^{-1}\Sigma \qquad \alpha > 0 \quad (2.98)$$

Then Eqs. (2.94) and (2.95) become

$$\boldsymbol{\mu}_n = \frac{\alpha}{n+\alpha}\boldsymbol{\mu}_0 + \frac{n}{n+\alpha}\langle \mathbf{x} \rangle \tag{2.99}$$

and

$$\Phi_n = \frac{1}{n+\alpha}\Sigma \tag{2.100}$$

As $n \to \infty$, $\boldsymbol{\mu}_n \to \langle \mathbf{x} \rangle$ and $\Phi_n \to 0$ which means, on the average, the estimate $\boldsymbol{\mu}_n$ will approach the true mean vector $\boldsymbol{\mu}$ of the Gaussian density function.*

B. *Learning the Covariance Matrix Σ of a Gaussian Distribution with Zero (or Known) Mean Vector*

In this case $\boldsymbol{\theta} = \Sigma$ is the parameter to be learned. Let $\Sigma^{-1} = Q$ and assign the a priori density function for Q to be the Wishart density function with parameters (Σ_0, v_0) [Cramer, 1961]; that is,

$$p_0(\boldsymbol{\theta}) = p_0(Q) = \begin{cases} C_{N,v_0} \left| \frac{v_0}{2}\Sigma_0 \right|^{\frac{1}{2}(v_0-1)} \mid Q \mid^{\frac{1}{2}(v_0-N-2)} \exp[\frac{1}{2} \operatorname{tr} v_0\Sigma_0 Q] \text{ on } \Omega_Q \\ 0 \text{ otherwise} \end{cases} \tag{2.101}$$

Ω_Q denotes the subset of the Euclidean space of dimension $\frac{1}{2}N(N+1)$ where Q is positive definite, and C_{N,v_0} is the normalizing constant

$$C_{N,v_0} = \frac{1}{(\pi)^{\frac{1}{4}N(N-1)} \prod_{\alpha=1}^{N} \Gamma\left(\frac{v_0-\alpha}{2}\right)} \tag{2.102}$$

Σ_0 is a positive definite matrix which reflects the initial knowledge of Σ^{-1}, and v_0 is a scalar which reflects the confidence about the initial estimate Σ_0. It can be shown that, by successive applications of Bayes' formula, the a posteriori density function of Q, $p(Q \mid \mathbf{x}_1, \ldots, \mathbf{x}_n)$, is again a Wishart density function with parameters Σ_0 and v_0 replaced by Σ_n and v_n where

$$\Sigma_n = \frac{v_0\Sigma_0 + n\langle \mathbf{x}\mathbf{x}' \rangle}{v_0 + n} \tag{2.103}$$

$$v_n = v_0 + n$$

and

$$\langle \mathbf{x}\mathbf{x}' \rangle = \frac{1}{n}\sum_{i=1}^{n} \mathbf{x}_i\mathbf{x}_i' \tag{2.104}$$

* Because the sample mean, $\langle \mathbf{x} \rangle$, is an unbiased estimate of the true mean vector $\boldsymbol{\mu}$.

Equation (2.103) can be again interpreted as the weighted average of the a priori knowledge about Σ^{-1}, Σ_0, and the sample information contained in $\langle \mathbf{xx}' \rangle$.

C. *Learning the Mean Vector* $\boldsymbol{\mu}$ *and the Covariance Matrix* Σ *of a Gaussian Distribution*

In this case, $\boldsymbol{\theta}$ consists of $\boldsymbol{\mu}$ and Q and $Q = \Sigma^{-1}$. An appropriate a priori density function for the unknown parameter $\boldsymbol{\theta}$ is found to be Gaussian–Wishart; i.e., $\boldsymbol{\mu}$ is distributed according to a Gaussian density function with mean vector $\boldsymbol{\mu}_0$ and covariance matrix $\Phi_0 = u_0^{-1}\Sigma$, and Q is distributed according to a Wishart density function with parameters v_0 and Σ_0. It can be shown that, by successive applications of Bayes' formula, the a posteriori density function of θ, $p(\boldsymbol{\theta} \mid \mathbf{x}_1, \ldots, \mathbf{x}_n) = p(\boldsymbol{\mu}, Q \mid \mathbf{x}_1, \ldots, \mathbf{x}_n)$, is again a Gaussian Wishart density function with parameters v_0, u_0, $\boldsymbol{\mu}_0$ and Σ_0 replaced by v_n, u_n, $\boldsymbol{\mu}_n$ and Σ_n where

$$v_n = v_0 + n \tag{2.105}$$

$$u_n = u_0 + n \tag{2.106}$$

$$\boldsymbol{\mu}_n = \frac{u_0\boldsymbol{\mu}_0 + n\langle \mathbf{x} \rangle}{u_0 + n} \tag{2.107}$$

$$\Sigma_n = \frac{1}{v_0 + n}\{(v_0\Sigma_0 + u_0\boldsymbol{\mu}_0\boldsymbol{\mu}_0') + [(n-1)\,S + n\langle \mathbf{x} \rangle\langle \mathbf{x} \rangle'] - u_n\boldsymbol{\mu}_n\boldsymbol{\mu}_n'\} \tag{2.108}$$

and

$$S = \frac{1}{n-1}\sum_{i=1}^{n} (\mathbf{x}_i - \langle \mathbf{x} \rangle)(\mathbf{x}_i - \langle \mathbf{x} \rangle)' \tag{2.109}$$

Equation (2.107) is the same as Eq. (2.99) except that α is replaced by u_0. Equation (2.108) can be interpreted as follows: The first two terms on the right-hand side are weighted estimates of the noncentralized moments of $\mathbf{x}$; the term $(v_0\Sigma_0 + u_0\boldsymbol{\mu}_0\boldsymbol{\mu}_0')$ represents the a priori knowledge and $[(n-1)\,S + n\langle \mathbf{x} \rangle\langle \mathbf{x} \rangle']$ represents the sample information. The last term at the right-hand side is generated from the new estimate of the mean of $\mathbf{x}$.*

---

* Equations (2.96), (2.103), (2.107), and (2.108) can be shown to fall into the general framework of Dvoretzky's stochastic approximation procedure. Readers may refer to Chien and Fu (1967) and Fu (1968).

IX. Nonsupervised Learning Using Bayesian Estimation Technique

Since the correct classifications of learning observations are unknown in the case of nonsupervised learning, it is almost impossible to precisely associate each learning observation with the distribution of the correct pattern class for updating information. Instead, one approach is to formulate the problem of nonsupervised learning as a problem of estimating the parameters in an overall distribution (called a mixture distribution) comprising the component distributions. The learning observations are considered from the mixture distribution, and the component distributions may be the distributions of each pattern class or the distributions corresponding to the various partitions in the observation space. The parameters of the mixture distribution can be learned (estimated) using Bayesian estimation technique or stochastic approximation. In this section, nonsupervised learning using Bayesian estimation is discussed.

A. *Estimation of Parameters of a Decision Boundary*

Consider n learning observations, denoted by $x_1, x_2, \ldots$, and x_n, that are drawn from one of the two pattern classes, ω_1 and ω_2, that have univariate Gaussian distributions with some unknown parameters. The optimum decision boundary to minimize the probability of misrecognition in classifying observations into one of the two pattern classes is, in general, a function of the a priori probabilities, the means and the variances. For example, in the nonsequential Bayes' classification process (Section I), if the a priori probabilities are equal and the variances are equal, the optimum decision boundary is known to be the mean of the two means. When the learning scheme is a supervised one, the two means can be easily learned from the classified learning observations. In the case of nonsupervised learning, the problem can be viewed as one of estimating the mean of the mixture distribution $p(x)$ where (Cooper and Cooper, 1964)

$$\begin{aligned} p(x) &= \sum_{i=1}^{2} P(\omega_i)\, p(x \mid \omega_i) \\ &= \frac{1}{2}\, \frac{1}{\sigma\sqrt{2\pi}} \exp\left[-\frac{1}{2\sigma^2}(x-\mu_1)^2\right] + \frac{1}{2}\, \frac{1}{\sigma\sqrt{2\pi}} \exp\left[-\frac{1}{2\sigma^2}(x-\mu_2)^2\right] \end{aligned} \tag{2.110}$$

From Eq. (2.110) it is easily seen that the optimum decision boundary is simply the mean of the mixture distribution $p(x)$. The sample mean

$$m_n = \frac{1}{n} \sum_{i=1}^{n} x_i \tag{2.111}$$

is used as an estimate of the mean of $p(x)$. The approach can be extended to the problems concerning unequal a priori probabilities and mixtures of multivariate Gaussian distributions. The solutions to these generalizations are shown to rely on the estimation of higher moments of the mixture distribution (Cooper, 1967).

B. *Estimation of Parameters in Mixture Distributions*

Assume there are two pattern classes ω_1 and ω_2. The form of the probability density function $p(\mathbf{x} \mid \omega_1)$ is known but a parameter $\boldsymbol{\theta}$ is unknown, and $p(\mathbf{x} \mid \omega_2)$ is completely known. The problem is to learn the parameter $\boldsymbol{\theta}$ from the learning observations $\mathbf{x}_1, \mathbf{x}_2, \ldots, \mathbf{x}_n$ with unknown classifications. Since the correct classifications of the learning observations are unknown, each observation can be considered as either from class ω_1 or from class ω_2. If the sequence $\mathbf{x}_1, \ldots, \mathbf{x}_n$ is partitioned into all possible combinations in which the two classes ω_1 and ω_2 can occur, there will be 2^n such combinations. Let z_i^n be the ith partition of the sequence $\mathbf{x}_1, \ldots, \mathbf{x}_n$, then the a posteriori probability density is obtained by

$$p(\boldsymbol{\theta} \mid \mathbf{x}_1, \ldots, \mathbf{x}_n) = \sum_{i=1}^{2^n} p(\boldsymbol{\theta} \mid \mathbf{x}_1, \ldots, \mathbf{x}_n, z_i^n)\, P(z_i^n \mid \mathbf{x}_i, \ldots, \mathbf{x}_n) \tag{2.112}$$

The problem is now reduced to that of supervised learning for each of the 2^n partitions (Daly, 1962). The results of estimation is obtained by taking the weighted sum of the results obtained from each partition with the weights being the probabilities of occurrence of each partition $P(z_i^n \mid \mathbf{x}_1, \ldots, \mathbf{x}_n)$, $i = 1, \ldots, 2^n$. It can be seen from Eq. (2.112) that the number of computations will grow exponentially with n, and for this reason it does not seem to be practical for large numbers of learning observations.

An alternative solution to this problem has been developed in order to avoid the difficulty of exponential growth in computation (Fralick, 1967). By applying Bayes' theorem,

$$p(\boldsymbol{\theta} \mid \mathbf{x}_1, \ldots, \mathbf{x}_n) = \frac{p(\mathbf{x}_n \mid \boldsymbol{\theta}, \mathbf{x}_1, \ldots, \mathbf{x}_{n-1})\, p(\boldsymbol{\theta} \mid \mathbf{x}_1, \ldots, \mathbf{x}_{n-1})}{p(\mathbf{x}_n \mid \mathbf{x}_1, \ldots, \mathbf{x}_{n-1})} \tag{2.113}$$

Assume that the learning observations are conditionally independent; that is,

$$p(\mathbf{x}_{n+1} \mid \boldsymbol{\theta}, \mathbf{x}_1, \dots, \mathbf{x}_n) = p(\mathbf{x}_{n+1} \mid \boldsymbol{\theta}) \tag{2.114}$$

Thus,

$$p(\mathbf{x}_n \mid \boldsymbol{\theta}, \mathbf{x}_1, \dots, \mathbf{x}_{n-1}) = P(\omega_1)\, p(\mathbf{x}_n \mid \boldsymbol{\theta}, \omega_1) + P(\omega_2)\, p(\mathbf{x}_n \mid \omega_2) \tag{2.115}$$

which is a mixture of $p(\mathbf{x}_n \mid \boldsymbol{\theta}, \omega_1)$ and $p(\mathbf{x}_n \mid \omega_2)$. The assumption of conditional independence is the fundamental reasons that there is no need to store all the learning observations. Substituting Eq. (2.115) into Eq. (2.113), a recursive expression for estimating $\boldsymbol{\theta}$ is obtained, as

$$p(\boldsymbol{\theta} \mid \mathbf{x}_1, \dots, \mathbf{x}_n) = p(\boldsymbol{\theta} \mid \mathbf{x}_1, \dots, \mathbf{x}_{n-1}) \left[\frac{P(\omega_1)\, p(\mathbf{x}_n \mid \boldsymbol{\theta}, \omega_1) + P(\omega_2)\, p(\mathbf{x}_n \mid \omega_2)}{p(\mathbf{x}_n \mid \mathbf{x}_1, \dots, \mathbf{x}_{n-1})} \right] \tag{2.116}$$

If $p(\boldsymbol{\theta} \mid \mathbf{x}_1, \dots, \mathbf{x}_{n-1})$, $p(\mathbf{x}_n \mid \boldsymbol{\theta}, \omega_1)$, $p(\mathbf{x}_n \mid \omega_2)$, $P(\omega_1)$ and $P(\omega_2)$ are known, $p(\boldsymbol{\theta} \mid \mathbf{x}_1, \dots, \mathbf{x}_n)$ can be computed by Eq. (2.116). Assume that $P(\omega_1)$ and $P(\omega_2)$ are known. In order to compute $p(\mathbf{x}_n \mid \boldsymbol{\theta}, \omega_1)$ and $p(\boldsymbol{\theta} \mid \mathbf{x}_1, \dots, \mathbf{x}_n)$ for all values of $\boldsymbol{\theta}$, it must be assumed that $\boldsymbol{\theta}$ can be finitely quantized so that the number of computations can be kept finite.

For multiclass problems, if more than one pattern class has unknown parameters, let $\boldsymbol{\theta}_i$ be the unknown parameter associated with pattern class ω_i, $i = 1, \dots, m$. Assuming conditional independence of learning observations $\mathbf{x}_1, \dots, \mathbf{x}_n$ and independence of $\boldsymbol{\theta}_i$, $i = 1, \dots, m$ similar to Eq. (2.116), the recursive equation for estimating $\boldsymbol{\theta}_i$ can be obtained as

$$p(\boldsymbol{\theta}_i \mid \mathbf{x}_1, \dots, \mathbf{x}_n) = p(\boldsymbol{\theta}_i \mid \mathbf{x}_1, \dots, \mathbf{x}_{n-1}) \left[\frac{P(\omega_i)\, p(\mathbf{x}_n \mid \boldsymbol{\theta}_i, \omega_i) + \sum_{j \neq i}^{m} P(\omega_j)\, p(\mathbf{x}_n \mid \omega_j, \mathbf{x}_1, \dots, \mathbf{x}_{n-1})}{\sum_{j=1}^{m} P(\omega_j)\, p(\mathbf{x}_n \mid \omega_j, \mathbf{x}_1, \dots, \mathbf{x}_{n-1})} \right]$$

$$i = 1, \dots, m \tag{2.117}$$

In general, either $p_0(\boldsymbol{\theta}_i)$ or $P(\omega_i)$, $i = 1, \dots, m$, must be different. Otherwise, the computations for all $\boldsymbol{\theta}_i$'s will learn the same thing (since they compute the same quantity) and the system as a whole will learn nothing.

X. Mode Estimation in Pattern Recognition

As pointed out in Chapter 1, the isolation and location of each event to be recognized is an important problem in pattern recognition. Roughly speaking, how many classes or subclasses should we consider in designing a recognition system? Cluster-seeking or mode estimation procedures have been proposed to solve this class of problems.* Many adaptive techniques (Ball, 1965; Patrick and Hancock, 1965; Sebestyen and Edie, 1966) attempt to define regions in the feature space in which data samples are most heavily concentrated. These regions are called clusters. By letting each cluster be considered as a distinct pattern class or subclass, an adaptive classification procedure can be formed. A mode estimation technique is described in this section. The term mode is taken to mean the location of a local maximum of a probability density function. The basic assumption motivating this approach is that the modes of a continuous probability density function are important in describing and analyzing the underlying data structure for recognition purposes.

Goguen (1962) has proposed a nonparametric pattern classification procedure based on the assumption that the modes can be adequately represented. No procedure has been given to isolate these modes. The criterion of optimality in partitioning the observed samples is to minimize the sum of the variances about the modes. Partitioning based on the criterion of minimizing the sum of the distances of the observed samples about the means has been suggested by a number of authors (Ball and Hall, 1965; MacQueen, 1965; Stark, 1962; Singleton, 1967; Forgy, 1966). Direct estimates of the mode, $\tilde{m}$, of a unimodal continuous probability density function $p(x)$ have received only limited attention in the statistical literature. Grenander (1965) considered a statistic based on a weighted average of a set of n order statistics $\{x_{(i)}\}_{i=1}^{n}$. The idea in his method is to make the weights large at values where the probability density function is large. Venter (1967) analyzes the consistency and speed of convergence of the following estimates:

$$\tilde{m}_n = \tfrac{1}{2}[x_{(k_n+r_n)} + x_{(k_n-r_n)}] \tag{2.118}$$

and

$$\tilde{m}_n = x_{(k_n)} \tag{2.119}$$

where $\tilde{m}_n$ is the nth estimate of the mode $\tilde{m}$. $\{r_n\}$ is a sequence of integers depending on the sample size n and such that

$$\frac{r_n}{n} \to 0 \tag{2.120}$$

and k_n is the index determined from Eq. (2.121)

$$k_n = \operatorname{Arg}[\operatorname*{Min}_i\{x_{(i+r_n)} - x_{(i-r_n)} \mid i = r_n + 1,\ldots, nr_n\}] \tag{2.121}$$

* A good bibliography and general discussion of clustering techniques may be found in Ball (1965).

A potential function type of approach to density approximation has been pursued by a number of people (e.g., Aiserman *et. al.*, 1964; Whittle, 1958; Parzen, 1962; Murthy, 1965; Rosenblatt, 1956; Watson, 1963; Specht, 1967) and is typically of the following form:

$$p_n(x_0) = \int \frac{1}{h_n} K\left(\frac{x_0 - x}{h_n}\right) dP_n(x) = \frac{1}{nh_n} \sum_{j=1}^{n} K\left(\frac{x_0 - x_{(j)}}{h_n}\right) \tag{2.122}$$

where $P_n(x)$ is the empirical distribution function; $K(y)$ is a smoothing function; and $\{h_n\}$ is a sequence of suitably chosen positive constants.

Parzen (1962) places conditions on $K(y)$ and $\{h_n\}$ such that p_n converges to $p(x)$ uniformly in probability; that is,

$$p_n(x) \xrightarrow{\text{u.p.}} p(x) \tag{2.123}$$

and shows for a certain class of functions, $\{K(y)\}$, that

$$\tilde{m}_n = \text{Arg}\left(\underset{-\infty < x < \infty}{\text{Max}} (p_n(x))\right) \tag{2.124}$$

is a consistent* estimate of the mode.

Chernoff (1964) analyzes a "naive" estimate of the mode [with $\tilde{m}_n$ as determined by Eq. (2.124)] for $K(y)$ of the following form:

$$\begin{aligned} K(y) &= \tfrac{1}{2} \quad \text{for} \quad |y| \leqslant i \\ &\ 0 \quad \text{otherwise} \end{aligned} \tag{2.125}$$

Note that for this choise of $K(y)$, the density approximation in Eq. (2.122) becomes

$$p_n(x_0) = \frac{P_n(x_0 + h_n) - P_n(x_0 - h_n)}{2h_n} \tag{2.126}$$

and $\tilde{m}_n$ in Eq. (2.124) has the simple interpretation as being the center of that interval of length $2h_n$ which contains the most observations. Loftsgaarden and Quesenberry (1965) have shown that such an estimator is consistent. Their work has been extended recently to the case of estimating multiple modes (Henrichon and Fu, 1968). The procedure of locating these modes is described in the following:

Let (a) $\{x_i\}_{i=1}^{n}$ be a set of independent one-dimensional observations on a random variable x with absolutely continuous distribution function $P(x)$ and corresponding density $p(x)$,

* A consistent estimate is one which converges in probability to the true value.

(b) $\{r_n\}$ be a nondecreasing sequence of positive integers such that

(i) $\lim r_n = \infty$

(ii) $\lim n^{-1} r_n = 0$

and (c) $h_{x_0}(r_n)$ be the distance from some point x_0 to the r_nth closest observation $\epsilon \{x_i\}_{i=1}^{n}$ as determined by some metric (e.g., Euclidean distance).

Let $p(x)$ be uniformly continuous and positive over an interval I_1 and let there exist a unique mode, $\tilde{m}_1 \in I_1$. Let a new estimate of the mode $\tilde{m}_1$ be formed as follows:

$$\tilde{m}_{1n} = x_{(k)} \tag{2.127}$$

where

$$k = \operatorname{Arg}(\operatorname*{Min}_i \{h_{x_{(i)}}(r_n) \mid x_{(i)} \in I_1\}) \tag{2.128}$$

That is, the estimate of the mode is that order statistic contained in the interval I_1 which yields the minimum value of h. Then it can be shown that $\tilde{m}_{1n}$ is a consistent estimate of the mode $\tilde{m}_1$ (Moore and Henrichon, 1968). Now consider the set of l relative maxima (unique), located at modes $\{\tilde{m}_i\}_{i=1}^{l}$ respectively and such that $\tilde{m}_i \in I_i = (a_{2i-1}, a_{2i}]$, $i = 1, \ldots, l$ where

$$a_1 < a_2 \leqslant a_3 \leqslant a_4 \leqslant a_5 \cdots < a_{2l}$$

Further, let $p(x)$ be uniformly continuous and positive over the intervals $\{I_i\}_{i=1}^{l}$. Let the estimate $\tilde{m}_{jn}$ of $\tilde{m}_j$ be determined by

$$\tilde{m}_{jn} = x_{(k)} \tag{2.129}$$

where

$$k = \operatorname{Arg}(\operatorname*{Min}_i \{h_{x_{(i)}}(r_n) \mid x_{(i)} \in I_j\}) \tag{2.130}$$

Then, the set of estimates $\{\tilde{m}_{in}\}_{i=1}^{l}$ converges in probability to the set $\{\tilde{m}_i\}_{i=1}^{l}$.

The method proposed here consists of constructing a primary approximation to the underlying density in the form of a histogram such that different modes will tend to occupy disjoint regions in the histogram. This approach performs the integrating effect of smoothing the local variations in the pointwise approximation. An adaptive histogram approach such as that of Sebestyen and Edie (1966) or an orthonormal series expansion approach (Kashyap and Blaydon, 1967) may provide excellent ways of performing the desired type of smoothing, but these matters will not be pursued here.

The histogram method presented here consists of forming intervals or bins of length, H, where H is determined as in Eq. (2.131).

$$H = C_1 \cdot \operatorname*{Min}_i \{h_{x_{(i)}}(r_n) \mid i = r_n + 1, \ldots, n - r_n\} \tag{2.131}$$

C_1 in Eq. (2.131) is a constant of proportionality and is a parameter to be chosen by the user. This approach tends to smooth the regions of most concentration while at the same time does not let the bin lengths become so large as to average over a greater interval than is necessary.* The first histogram bin is constructed with the left most bin starting at the point $x_{(r_n)}$. Successive bins are formed until the point $x_{(n-r_n)}$ is covered. Next, successive bins which contain the same number of observations are lumped together. Note that at this stage the outliers have been discarded from further processing.

An extrema seeking technique is then applied to this histogram approximation in order to determine appropriate regions in which to search for pointwise maxima. The algorithm for selecting these appropriate intervals (i.e., the set $\{I_i\}_{i=1}^l$) depends on a parameter d, to be specified by the user. This parameter is a distance measure which essentially determines how much local variation in the histogram approximation will be tolerated before a decision to specify an extremum region is made.

The algorithm first seeks histogram intervals to be used in determining pointwise minima between successive modes. Roughly, the criterion used in order to store such an interval is that

(1) there exists an interval to the left such that the difference in the density approximations for these two intervals is greater than d and

(2) there exists an interval to the right such that a similar condition is met. The relative minima are then estimated as the midpoints of these stored intervals. To this set $x_{(r_n+1)}$ and $x_{(n-r_n)}$ are added and the regions $\{I_i\}_{i=1}^l$ are then formed. Equation (2.129) is then applied to determine an estimate for the mode in each region.

For the multidimensional case, in view of computer storage difficulties, a multivariate mode estimation procedure which has merit for use in many cluster organizing situations is suggested. The basic idea is similar

---

* From simulation studies it was noted that pointwise approximations closest to the mode varied considerably from point to point, while in regions remote from the mode, the approximations were fairly smooth.

to that originally proposed by Mattson and Damon (1965), but differs in that the Mattson and Damon approach assumed the existence of a procedure for determining a one-dimensional density and its associated extrema. The proposed estimation procedure is summarized in the following:

Step 1: Compute the maximum eigenvector (principal component) associated with the sample covariance matrix determined from a set of independent sample points (observations).

Step 2: Project the multivariate observations onto this maximum eigenvector to obtain a one-dimensional data set.

Step 3: Apply the one-dimensional mode estimation discussed above to determine the number and locations of the extrema associated with the one-dimensional probability density.

Step 4: Partition the observation space with hyperplanes which are perpendicular to the eigenvector and such that they intersect the eigenvector at the locations of relative minima determined from Step 3.

Step 5: If only one extremum was found in Step 3, repeat the procedure from Step 2 using the next principal component direction (i.e., the eigenvector associated with the next largest eigenvalue of the covariance matrix). If all eigenvectors have been processed and the region (observation space) has not been partitioned by Step 4, compute the location of the mode by addition of the vectors determined from Step 3.

Step 6: Continue the procedure from Step 1 for each new region formed from Step 4.

This procedure is described by means of a two-dimensional example in Fig. 5. The underlying densities are indicated here (rather than their estimates from a set of observations) only so that the procedure might be better understood.

In order to indicate the feasibility of such an approach, a three-dimensional observation set consisting of 500 samples was generated by Monte Carlo techniques according to the following distribution:

$$p(\mathbf{x}) = \tfrac{1}{2}\, p_1(\mathbf{x}) + \tfrac{1}{2}\, p_2(\mathbf{x}) + \tfrac{1}{4}\, p_3(\mathbf{x})$$

where

$$p_i(\mathbf{x}) = \frac{1}{(2\pi)^{3/2}} \exp[-\tfrac{1}{2}(\mathbf{x} - \boldsymbol{\mu}_i)' \Sigma^{-1}(\mathbf{x} - \boldsymbol{\mu}_i)] \qquad i = 1, 2, 3$$

and

$$\boldsymbol{\mu}_1' = (-2, -2, -2)$$
$$\boldsymbol{\mu}_2' = (0, 0, 0)$$
$$\boldsymbol{\mu}_3' = (2, -2, -2)$$
$$\Sigma = \begin{pmatrix} 1 & 0 & 0 \\ 0 & 1 & 0 \\ 0 & 0 & 1 \end{pmatrix}$$

Application of the above procedure resulted in the determination of three modes at the following locations:

$$\tilde{\mathbf{m}}_1' = (+2.08 \quad -1.64, -2.21)$$
$$\tilde{\mathbf{m}}_2' = (-.15, -.18, -.05)$$
$$\tilde{\mathbf{m}}_3' = (-2.16, -1.80, -2.17)$$

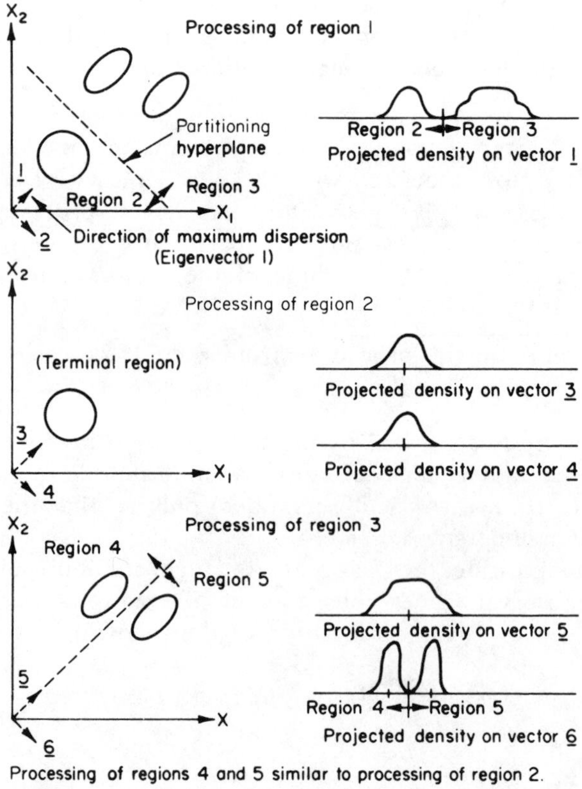

FIGURE 5. A two-dimensional mode-seeking example

In this simulation, although no direct statement on the number of modes to be determined was made, two parameters of the procedure affect the maximum number which can be estimated. The parameter d used in the algorithm was chosen as one-third of the maximum histogram height. Note that a choice of d in this manner indicates that the user prefers to determine only the more prominent modes in the first approximations. In the implementation of the multidimensional procedure, provision was made for the rejection of new regions (Step 4) containing less than a critical number of samples, n_{crit}. Thus the choice of n_{crit} also affects the upper bound on the number of modes which can be found. Note that the procedure did indeed isolate three modes for this simulation. The modes agree approximately with the theoretical modes but possibly other estimation procedures could have yielded closer estimates. For instance mode $\tilde{m}_1$ was estimated from 125 samples by computing the densities along each of the associated eigenvectors. Due to the small number of samples, a good estimate along each direction was not obtainable. The application of the proposed procedure to crop classification problems indicates fairly satisfactory results (Henrichon and Fu, 1968).

XI. Conclusions and Further Remarks

In this chapter, the problem of pattern classification is formulated as a statistical decision problem. Both fixed-sample size and sequential decision procedures are discussed. Forward and backward computational procedures are described for sequential classification systems. Feature selection and ordering problems are studied in terms of the information theoretic approach and the generalized Karhuman–Loève expansion. The dynamic programming procedure has been applied to both feature selection and pattern classification. Bayesian estimation techniques are employed to estimate unknown parameters of a probability density (or distribution) function. A multivariate multiple mode estimation technique is proposed and its computational procedure described. Other nonparametric classification procedures will be discussed in Chapter 3.

Although time-varying stopping boundaries have been used in finite forward sequential classification systems, the forms of $g_1(n)$ and $g_2(n)$ assumed are rather arbitrary. It will be interesting to investigate the relation between $g_1(n)$, $g_2(n)$, and the expected number of measurements $E(n)$. There has not been much quantitative comparison of performance between the forward and the backward sequential classification procedures other than the degree of optimality and computational difficulty. This lack of comparison makes it difficult to determine exactly which procedure is more appropriate for a particular problem at hand. For the Bayesian estimation of unknown parameters, the class of reproducing distribution functions plays an important role in obtaining simple computational algorithms. This may practically limit the applications of the Bayesian estimation techniques. In the mixture formulation of nonsupervised learning, it is not obvious that efficient computational algorithms can be easily obtained for the estimation even if the mixture is identifiable. It would be desirable, from a practical viewpoint, to study the computational problem in mixture estimation, especially in the high-dimensional cases where the number of unknown parameters is large.

Studies of the relationship between the features selected for statistical classification and the number of available pattern samples have received increasing attention recently (Kanal and Chandrasekaran, 1968). Regarding the problem of mode estimation, in view of computational difficulties, a very simple (single) mode estimation technique is proposed and its possible extension to the case of multiple modes is described. Further extension to multidimensional multiple-mode case is discussed only on the basis of the principal-component projection approach which is by no means the best. It would be interesting to study more efficient multiple-mode estimation techniques and their direct extension to multidimensional case.

Because of the limited length of this chapter, many practical applications and other statistical techniques have not been included. Readers interested in practical applications may refer to several other chapters in this book and the references listed at the end of the chapter.

References

Abramson, N. and Braverman, D., Learning to recognize patterns in a random environment. *IRE Trans. Info. Theory 8*, pp. 558–563 (1962).

Aiserman, M. A., Braverman, E. M., and Rozonoer, L. I., The probability problem of pattern recognition learning and the method of potential functions. *Automation and Remote Control 25*, No. 9, pp. 1175–1190 (1964).

Allais, D. C., The selection of measurements for prediction. Tech. Rept. No. 6103–9, Stanford Electronics Lab, Stanford, Calif., 1964.

Anderson, T. W., "An Introduction to Multivariate Statistical Analysis." Wiley, New York, 1958.

Anderson, T. W., A modification of the sequential probability ratio test to reduce the sample size. *Ann. Math. Stat. 31*, (1960).

Anderson, T. W. and Bahadue, R. R., Classification into two multivariate normal distributions with different covariance matrices. *Ann. Math. Stat. 33*, No. 2, pp. 420–431, 1962.

Ball, G. H., Data analysis in the social sciences. *Proc. Fall Joint Comp. Conf.*, Las Vegas, Nevada, 1965. Spartan, Washington, D. C., 1965.

Ball, G. H., A comparison of two techniques for finding the minimum sum-squared error partition. Stanford Research Institute, Menlo Park, Calif., 1967.

Ball, G. H., and Hall, D. J., Isodata, a novel method of data analysis and pattern classification. Stanford Research Institute, Menlo Park, Calif., 1965.

Barabash, Yu. L., On properties of symbol recognition. *Engin. Cybernetics.* No. 5, pp. 71–77 (1965).

Bellman, R., "Dynamic Programming." Princeton Univ. Press, Princeton, New Jersey, 1957.

Bellman, R., Lalaba, R., and Middleton, D., Dynamic programming, sequential estimation and sequential detection processes. *Proc. Natl. Academy of Sciences, 47*, pp. 338–341 (1961).

Blackwell, D. and Girshick, M. A., "Theory of Games and Statistical Decisions." Wiley, New York, 1954.

Bussgang, J. J. and Marcus, M. B., Truncated sequential hypothesis tests. Memo RM–4268–ARPA, Rand Corporation, Santa Monica, Calif., 1964.

Chernoff, H., Estimation of the mode. *Ann. Inst. Stat. Math., Tokyo 16*, pp. 31–41 (1964).

Chien, Y. T. and Fu, K. S., A modified sequential recognition machine using time-varying stopping boundaries. *IEEE Trans. Info. Theory, IT–12*, No. 2, pp. 206–214 (1966).

Chien, Y. T. and Fu, K. S., On the generalized Karhunen–Loève expansion. *IEEE Trans. Info. Theory, IT–13* (1967).

Chien, Y. T. and Fu, K. S., Selection and ordering of feature observations in a pattern recognition system. *Info. and Control 12*, No. 5 (1968).

Chien, Y. T. and Fu, K. S., On Bayesian learning and stochastic approximation. *IEEE Trans. Systems Science and Cybernetics, SSC–3*, pp. 28–38 (1967).

Chow, C. K., An optimum character recognition system using decision functions. *IRE Trans. Electron. Comp. EC–6*, pp. 247–254 (1957).

Cooper, D. B. and Cooper, P. W., Nonsupervised adaptive signal detection and pattern recognition. *Info. and Control 7*, pp. 416–444 (1964).

Cooper, P. W., Some topics on nonsupervised adaptive detection for multivariate normal distributions. *In* "Computer and Information Sciences–II" (J. T. Tou, ed.). Academic Press, New York, 1967.

Cramer, H., "Mathematical Methods of Statistics." Princeton Univ. Press, Princeton, New Jersey (Ninth printing), 1961.

Daly, R. F., The adaptive binary-detection problem on the real line. Rept. 2003–3, Stanford Electron. Lab., Stanford, Calif., 1962.

Dynkin, E. B., The optimum choice of the instant for stopping a Markov process. *Soviet Math. 4*, No. 3, pp. 627–629 (1963).

Estes, S. E., Measurement selection for linear discriminants used in pattern classification. IBM Research Report RJ–331, San Jose, Calif., 1965.

Fishburn, P. C., A general theory of finite sequential decision processes. Tech. paper RAC–TP–143, Research Analysis Corporation, McLean, Va., 1965.

Fix, E. and Hodges, J. L., Discriminatory analysis: nonparametric discrimination: consistency properties. Proj. No. 21–49–004, Rept. No. 4, USAF School of Aviation Medicine, Randolph Field, Texas, 1951.

Forgy, E. W., Improving classification systems for multivariate observations. U.C.L.A. Technical Rept., Los Angeles, Calif., 1966.

Fralick, S. C., Learning to recognize patterns without a teacher. *IEEE Trans. Info. Theory, IT–13*, pp. 57–64 (1967).

Fu, K. S., A sequential decision model for optimum recognition. "Biological Prototypes and Synthetic Systems, I." Plenum Press, 1962.

Fu, K. S. and Chen, C. H., Sequential decisions, pattern recognition, and machine learning. Tech. Rept. TR-EE 65–6, School of Electrical Engineering, Purdue Univ., Lafayette, Ind., 1965.

Fu, K. S., Chien, Y. T., and Cardillo, G. P., A dynamic programming to sequential pattern recognition. *IEEE Trans. Electron. Comp.*, pp. 790–803 (1967).

Fu, K. S. and Min, P. J., On feature selection in multiclass pattern recognition. TR–EE 68–17, School of Electrical Engineering, Purdue Univ., Lafayette, Ind., 1968.

Fu, K. S., "Sequential Methods in Pattern Recognition and Machine Learning." Academic Press, New York, 1968.

Goguen, J. A., Jr., Nonparametric pattern classification by relative maxima. Sylvania ARL Research Rept. No. 310, 1962.

Grenander, U., Some direct estimates of the mode. *Ann. Math. Stat. 36*, pp. 131–138 (1965).

Grettenberg, T. L., A criterion for statistical comparison of communication systems with applications to optimal signal selection. TR No. 2004–4, SEL–62–013, Stanford Electron. Lab., Stanford Univ., Calif., 1962.

Grettenberg, T. L., Signal selection in communication and radar systems. *IEEE Trans. Info. Theory, IT–9*, pp. 265–275 (1963).

Henrichon, E. G. and Fu, K. S., On mode estimation in pattern recognition. *Proc. 7th Symp. Adaptive Processes*, Los Angeles, Calif., 1968.

Howard, R. A., "Dynamic Programming and Markov Processes." Wiley, New York, 1960.

Kanal, L. and Chandrasekaran, B., On dimensionality and sample size in statistical pattern classification. *Proc. Natl. Electron. Conf. 24*, pp. 2–7 (1968).

Karhunen, K., Über lineare methoden in der Wahrscheinlichkeitsrechnung. *Ann. Acad. Sci. Feen., Ser. A I 37*, Helsinki, 1947. (English translation by I. Selin, On Linear Methods in Probability Theory, The RAND Corporation, T–131, Aug. 11, 1960.)

Kashyap, R. L. and Blaydon, C. C., Estimation of probability density and distribution functions. Tech. Rept. TR-EE 67–114, School of Electrical Engineering, Purdue Univ., Lafayette, Ind., 1967.

Keehn, D. G., A note on learning for Gaussian properties. *IEEE Trans. Info. Theory, IT–11*, pp. 126–132 (1965).

Kendall, M. G. and Stuart, A., "The Advanced Theory of Statistics," Vols. 1 and 2. Charles, Griffen and Co., Ltd., London, 1961.

Kullback, S., "Information Theory and Statistics." Wiley, New York, 1959.

Lehman, E. L., "Testing Statistical Hypotheses." Wiley, New York, 1959.

Lewis, P. M., The characteristic selection problem in recognition systems. *IRE Trans. Info. Theory, IT–8*, pp. 171–178 (1962).

Lindley, D. V., Dynamic programming and decision theory. *Appl. Stat. 10*, pp. 39–51 (1961).

Loftsgaarden, D. O. and Quesenberry, C. P., A nonparametric estimate of a multivariate density function. *Ann. Math. Stat. 36*, pp. 1049–1051 (1965).

MacQueen, J., Some methods for classification and analysis of multivariate observations. *Fifth Berkeley Symp. Prob. and Stat.*, 1967.

Marill, T. and Green, D. M., Statistical recognition functions and the design of pattern recognizers. *IRE Trans. Elec. Comp., EC–9*, pp. 472–477 (1960).

Marill, T. and Green, D. M., On the effectiveness of receptors in recognition systems. *IEEE Trans. Info. Theory*, *IT–9*, pp. 11–17 (1963).

Mattson, R. L. and Dammann, J. E., A technique for determining and coding subclasses in pattern recognition problems. *IBM J.*, pp. 294–302 (1965).

Moore, D. S. and Henrichon, E. G., Uniform consistency of some estimates of a density function. Purdue Univ. Statistics Department Mimeograph Series, No. 168, Lafayette, Ind. 1968.

Murthy, V. K., Estimation of probability density. *Ann. Math. Stat. 36*, pp. 1027–1031 (1965).

Nilsson, N. J., "Learning Machine-Foundations of Trainable Pattern Classifying Systems." McGraw–Hill, New York, 1965.

Owen, J., The consistency of a non-parametric decision procedure, Sylvania ARL Eng. Note No. 334, 1962.

Parzen, E., On estimation of a probability density function and mode. *Ann. Math. Stat. 33*, pp. 1065–1076 (1962).

Patrick, E. A. and Hancock, J. C., The nonsupervised learning of probability spaces and recognition of patterns. *IEEE Interntl. Conv. Record*, 1965.

Patrick, E. A. and Hancock, J. C., Nonsupervised sequential classification and recognition of patterns. *IEEE Trans. Info. Theory*, *IT–12* (1966).

Reed, F. C., A sequential multi-decision procedure. *Proc. Symp. Decision Theory and Appl. to Electron. Equipment Dev.*, USAF Dev. Center, Rome, New York, 1960.

Rosenblatt, M., Remarks on some nonparametric estimates of a density function. *Ann. Math. Stat. 27*, pp. 832–837 (1956).

Sebestyen, G., "Decision-making Processes in Pattern Recognition." Macmillan, New York, 1962.

Sebestyen, G. and Edie, J., An algorithm for nonparametric pattern recognition. *IEEE Trans. Electron. Comp.*, pp. 908–915 (1966).

Specht, D. F., Generation of polynomial discriminant functions for pattern recognition. *IEEE Trans. Electron. Comp. 16*, pp. 308–319 (1967).

Spragins, J. D., Jr., A note on the iterative applications of Bayes rule. *IEEE Trans. Info. Theory*, *IT–11* (1965).

Stark, L., Okajima, M., and Whipple, G. H., Computer pattern recognition techniques: electrocardiographic diagnosis. *Comm. ACM 5*, No. 10, pp. 527–532 (1962).

Teicher, H., Identifiability of finite mixtures. *Ann. Math. Stat. 34* (1963).

Venter, J. H., On estimation of the mode. *Ann. Math. Stat. 38*, pp. 1446–1455 (1967).

Wald, A., "Sequential Analysis." Wiley, New York, 1947.

Watanabe, S., Karhunen–Loève expansion and factor analysis—theoretical remarks and applications. *Proc. 4th Prague Conf. Info. Theory*, 1965.

Watson, G. S. and Leadbetter, M. R., On the estimation of a probability density, I. *Ann. Math. Stat. 34*, pp. 480–491 (1963).

Wetherill, G. B., "Sequential Methods in Statistics." Methuen and Company, and Wiley, New York, 1966.

Whittle, P., On the smoothing of probability density functions, *J. Royal Stat. Soc. (Ser. B) 20*, pp. 334–343 (1958).

3

R. L. Kashyap

ALGORITHMS FOR PATTERN CLASSIFICATION

I. Introduction

A general statement of the pattern classification problem involves the consideration of its three fundamental aspects, namely characterization, abstraction, and generalization. *Characterization* involves the selection of the independent variables which characterize the two classes. These independent variables, say $x_1, \ldots, x_m$, are known as features. With every member of all the classes, we can associate an m-dimensional numerical (real) vector $\mathbf{x}$, known as the pattern vector, whose components are the values of the features $x_1, \ldots, x_m$. After choosing the features, we have to choose a decision rule using all the available information for classifying a new sample with pattern vector $\mathbf{x}$ of unknown class. The process of obtaining the decision rule from the given information is called *abstraction.* The ability of the decision rule or classifier mentioned above to correctly categorize the samples of unknown class is called *generalization.* The generalization ability is best stated in probabilistic terms like the probability of correct classification.

The three aspects of the classification problem are not completely independent of each other. Clearly the choice of improper features manifests itself in an unduly complex form for the decision rule to obtain a certain level of performance. Similarly, the ability to generalize may be considered as the criterion for getting the decision function during the abstraction of the problem. The three aspects essentially serve as guidelines in getting the desired solution to the overall problem.

In this chapter, we will assume the knowledge of the features. Our main concern will be the abstraction problem and the generalization ability of the corresponding algorithms. The available information for abstraction *is nothing more* than a set of patterns with known classification, the so called training samples.

To procede further, it is necessary to look at the nature of the classes. For simplicity, we will assume that there are only two classes, namely ω_1 and ω_{-1}. In some problems, we can uniquely associate one class with every pattern $\mathbf{x}$. In such cases, the classes ω_1 and ω_{-1} are said to be nonoverlapping with a separating function $f(\mathbf{x})$ (not necessarily unique) defined below.*

$$\begin{aligned} \operatorname{sgn} f(\mathbf{x}) &= 1 \ \forall \mathbf{x} \sim \omega_1 \\ &= -1 \ \forall \mathbf{x} \sim \omega_{-1} \end{aligned}$$

In such problems, all the information required for classification is contained in $f(\mathbf{x})$.

In some other problems, a pattern $\mathbf{x}$ may sometimes belong to ω_1 and at other times to ω_{-1}. Such classes are said to be overlapping. Here it is necessary to make the notion of a pattern belonging to a class more precise than before. With each class ω_i, we associate a probability density function $p_i(\mathbf{x})$. A pattern $\mathbf{x}$ is said to belong to class ω_i if it is drawn from a population with probability density $p_i(\mathbf{x})$. In addition, we can define two other functions $g_1(\mathbf{x})$ and $g_{-1}(\mathbf{x})$ which specify the aposteriori probabilities of the random pattern $\mathbf{x}$ belonging to the classes ω_1 and ω_{-1}, respectively.

To make the relation between the function $p_i(\mathbf{x})$, $g_i(\mathbf{x})$ clear, let us define the indicator variable y for every pattern $\mathbf{x}$, to denote the observed classification of the latter. For example, let

$$y = i \qquad \text{if} \qquad \mathbf{x} \sim \omega_i \qquad i = \pm 1$$

Let q_i be the apriori probability of the class ω_i. Clearly

$$q_1 + q_{-1} = 1$$

$$* \operatorname{sgn} f = \begin{matrix} 1 \\ 0 \\ -1 \end{matrix} \quad \text{if} \quad f \begin{matrix} > 0 \\ = 0 \\ < 0 \end{matrix}$$

Further, let $\mathbf{x}$ and y have a joint probability density $p(\mathbf{x}, y)$. Then

$$p_i(\mathbf{x}) = p(\mathbf{x} \mid y = i) \qquad i = +1, -1$$

$$g_i(\mathbf{x}) = p(y = i \mid \mathbf{x}) = \frac{p_i(\mathbf{x})\, q_i}{p_1(\mathbf{x})\, q_1 + p_{-1}(\mathbf{x})\, q_{-1}} \qquad i = +1, -1$$

Let us find a decision rule (3.1), optimal in some sense, involving a decision function $d(\mathbf{x})$ to classify patterns with unknown classification.

$$\operatorname{sgn} d(\mathbf{x}) = i \Rightarrow \text{classify } \mathbf{x} \text{ in } \omega_i \qquad i = \pm 1 \tag{3.1}$$

Then, P_d, the probability of misclassification by the use of decision rule (3.1) is given below

$$P_d = \int_{d(\mathbf{x})<0} p(y = 1 \mid \mathbf{x}) \left(\prod_{i=1}^{m} dx_i\right) + \int_{d(\mathbf{x})>0} p(y = -1 \mid \mathbf{x}) \left(\prod_{i=1}^{m} dx_i\right) \tag{3.2}$$

The optimal decision rule, i.e., the decision rule which minimizes the probability of misclassification is found by minimizing P_d with respect to $d(\mathbf{x})$. The optimal decision function, denoted by $g(\mathbf{x})$, is given below

$$g(\mathbf{x}) = p(y = 1 \mid \mathbf{x}) - p(y = -1 \mid \mathbf{x}) \tag{3.3}$$

It is needless to say that, in such problems, all the information required for classification is contained in $g(\mathbf{x})$. Of course, we can treat non-overlapping classes as special cases of overlapping classes in which the optimal decision function $g(\mathbf{x})$ and the separating function $f(\mathbf{x})$ have the following relation

$$g(\mathbf{x}) = \operatorname{sgn} f(\mathbf{x}) \tag{3.4}$$

The basic aim of this chapter is to recover the function $g(\mathbf{x})$ or $f(\mathbf{x})$ from the available information. A number of computing schemes are available for doing this involving various assumptions on $p_i(\mathbf{x})$ or $f(\mathbf{x})$. However, we assume that the only information available to us is a sequence of sample pairs

$$\{(\mathbf{x}(k), y(k)), k = 1, 2, \ldots,\}$$

where $y(k)$ denotes the observed classification of pattern $\mathbf{x}(k)$. Using *only* this information, we would like to recover $g(\mathbf{x})$ or $f(\mathbf{x})$. We will see later that the algorithms which recover $f(\mathbf{x})$ or $g(\mathbf{x})$ using only the samples [without any additional assumptions on $g(\mathbf{x})$ or $f(\mathbf{x})$] will involve computations in the function space and hence, may pose computational difficulties.

We can reduce the computational complexity by either of the two methods. In the first method, one makes specific assumptions on the classes, like the classes being separable by a hyperplane or the probability densities $p_i(\mathbf{x})$ being normal, etc. This method has been pursued by many workers in the field. We will mention them briefly. The main objection to the method is the lack of justification for the assumption.

In the second method, which will be used throughout the chapter, we will seek a "best" approximation of the form in Eq. (3.5) to the unknown function $g(\mathbf{x})$ or $f(\mathbf{x})$

$$\sum_{i=1}^{n} \alpha_i \varphi_i(\mathbf{x}) \tag{3.5}$$

where $\alpha_1, \ldots, \alpha_n$ are the unspecified parameters to be determined by minimizing a suitable criterion function and $\varphi_1(\mathbf{x}), \ldots, \varphi_n(\mathbf{x})$ are known linearly independent functions of the variables $x_1, \ldots, x_m$. This method does not need any assumptions on $g(\mathbf{x})$ or $f(\mathbf{x})$.

The principle reason for the choice of the approximation of the type in Eq. (3.5) is that it allows the analysis and computation to be carried out in the finite dimensional space of the vector $\boldsymbol{\alpha}$ instead of the infinite dimensional space of the decision functions. The second reason is that the functions $\varphi_1(\mathbf{x}), \varphi_2(\mathbf{x}), \ldots,$ can be chosen to reflect the special characteristics of the classes under consideration more clearly than the features $x_1, \ldots, x_m$ themselves whose choice depends heavily on the data processing considerations. By choosing the number n sufficiently large, we can get as close to the true optimal decision function as desired. The functions $\varphi_1(\mathbf{x}), \varphi_2(\mathbf{x}), \ldots,$ are usually chosen among the numbers of the various families of orthogonal polynomials like Legendre, Hermite, etc.

In the following sequel, we will treat the problems involving non-overlapping classes and those involving overlapping classes separately since the former involve the estimation of $f(\mathbf{x})$, the separating function, where as the latter involve the estimation of the optimal decision function $g(\mathbf{x})$. We can get a measure of the generalization of the decision rules by estimating their corresponding probability of misclassification P_d. Later we will compare all the algorithms.

A brief word on notation is in order. Vectors will be indicated by boldface lower case letters. The transpose of the vector is denoted by prime.

$$\mathbf{x}' = (x_1, \ldots, x_m), \qquad \boldsymbol{\alpha}' = (\alpha_1, \ldots, \alpha_n)$$

$$\boldsymbol{\varphi}'(\mathbf{x}) = (\varphi_1(\mathbf{x}), \ldots, \varphi_n(\mathbf{x}))$$

$\boldsymbol{\varphi}$ by itself means $\boldsymbol{\varphi}(\mathbf{x})$. $\mathbf{x}(k)$ stands for the kth pattern. $\boldsymbol{\varphi}(k)$ means $\boldsymbol{\varphi}(\mathbf{x}(k))$. Matrix $A > 0$ or $A < 0$ means A is positive definite or negative definite respectively. Vector $\boldsymbol{\beta} > 0$ means the components $\beta_i > 0$ for all i. $\boldsymbol{\beta} \geqslant 0$ means the components $\beta_i \geqslant 0$ for all i and $\boldsymbol{\beta}$ is not identically zero. A vector $\boldsymbol{\beta}$ is said to be positive or nonnegative if $\boldsymbol{\beta} > 0$ or $\boldsymbol{\beta} \geqslant 0$, respectively. $\| A'A \|$ means the spectral norm of A. The symbol $\nabla_{\boldsymbol{\alpha}}$ stands for the gradient with respect to $\boldsymbol{\alpha}$.

II. Nonoverlapping Classes with Reliable Samples

A. *Linearly Separable Classes*

This is the simplest case of classification. By assumption, there exists a separating hyperplane in the $\boldsymbol{\varphi}$-space separating the two classes, i.e., the separating function $f(\mathbf{x})$ has the following representation

$$f(\mathbf{x}) = \sum_{i=1}^{n} \alpha_i^* \varphi_i(\mathbf{x}) = \boldsymbol{\alpha}^{*\prime} \boldsymbol{\varphi}(\mathbf{x}) \tag{3.6}$$

The simplest choice for the functions $\varphi_i(\mathbf{x})$ is

$$\varphi_i(\mathbf{x}) = x_i \qquad i = 1,\ldots, m$$

$$\varphi_{m+1}(\mathbf{x}) = 1 \qquad n = m + 1$$

Let us recover the vector $\boldsymbol{\alpha}^*$ from a finite set of samples $\{(\mathbf{x}(k), y(k)), k = 1,\ldots, N\}$ where $y(k)$ denotes the class of $\mathbf{x}(k)$. By the definition of separating functions, $\boldsymbol{\alpha}^*$ obeys the following inequalities

$$\left.\begin{aligned} \boldsymbol{\alpha}^{*\prime}\boldsymbol{\varphi}(\mathbf{x}(k)) &> 0 \quad \forall \mathbf{x}(k) \sim \omega_1 \\ &< 0 \quad \forall \mathbf{x}(k) \sim \omega_{-1} \end{aligned}\right\} \tag{3.7}$$

Recalling the definition of $y(k)$, inequalities (3.7) can be rewritten as in Eq. (3.8) where β_k, $k = 1,\ldots, N$ are unspecified positive quantities.

$$\boldsymbol{\alpha}^{*\prime}\boldsymbol{\varphi}(\mathbf{x}(k))\, y(k) = \beta_k > 0$$

or

$$A\boldsymbol{\alpha}^* = \boldsymbol{\beta} > 0 \tag{3.8}$$

where

$$A = \begin{bmatrix} \boldsymbol{\varphi}'(1)\, y(1) \\ \vdots \\ \boldsymbol{\varphi}'(N) y(N) \end{bmatrix} \qquad \boldsymbol{\beta} = \begin{bmatrix} \beta_1 \\ \vdots \\ \beta_N \end{bmatrix}$$

The equalities (3.8) can be solved by the method of linear programming. However, it may be useful to investigate the following method for finding $\boldsymbol{\alpha}^*$ which involves the minimization of the function $J_1(\boldsymbol{\alpha}, \boldsymbol{\beta})$ with respect to $\boldsymbol{\alpha}$ and $\boldsymbol{\beta}$

$$J_1(\boldsymbol{\alpha}, \boldsymbol{\beta}) = \| A\boldsymbol{\alpha} - \boldsymbol{\beta} \|^2 \qquad \boldsymbol{\beta} > 0$$

A gradient method for minimizing $J_1(\boldsymbol{\alpha}, \boldsymbol{\beta})$ can be developed by changing $\boldsymbol{\alpha}$ and $\boldsymbol{\beta}$ alternately in the direction of negative gradient. The algorithm is given below.

$$\begin{aligned} \boldsymbol{\alpha}(k+1) &= \boldsymbol{\alpha}(k) + \rho S A' \mid \boldsymbol{\epsilon}(k)\mid, \quad \boldsymbol{\alpha}(0) \text{ arbitrary} \\ \boldsymbol{\epsilon}(k) &= A\boldsymbol{\alpha}(k) - \boldsymbol{\beta}(k) \qquad\qquad \text{(S-1)} \\ \boldsymbol{\beta}(k+1) &= \boldsymbol{\beta}(k) + \mid \boldsymbol{\epsilon}(k)\mid + \boldsymbol{\epsilon}(k), \quad \boldsymbol{\beta}(0) \geqslant 0, \quad \text{otherwise arbitrary.} \end{aligned}$$

where scalar $\rho > 0$, $S = S'$, ($n \times n$ matrix) and

$$R \triangleq (2\rho S - \rho^2 S A' A S) > 0 \qquad (3.9)$$

The convergence properties of the scheme (S-1) are given in Theorem 1 (Ho and Kashyap, 1965, 1966).

Theorem 1. The algorithm (S-1) converges to a solution of the inequalities $A\boldsymbol{\alpha} > 0$ within $\bar{N}$ steps, if one exists where

$$\bar{N} = \frac{\log \| \boldsymbol{\epsilon}(0)\|^2}{-\log(1 - \lambda)} \qquad (3.10)$$

$$\begin{aligned} \boldsymbol{\epsilon}(0) &= A\boldsymbol{\alpha}(0) - \boldsymbol{\beta}(0), \quad \boldsymbol{\alpha}(0) \text{ is arbitrary}, \quad \beta_i(0) = 1\ \forall i \\ \lambda &= \operatorname*{Min}_{\boldsymbol{\gamma}}(\boldsymbol{\gamma}' A R A' \boldsymbol{\gamma}) \qquad (3.11) \\ \| \boldsymbol{\gamma} \|^2 &= 1 \qquad \gamma_i \geqslant 0 \qquad i = 1,\ldots, N \end{aligned}$$

Proof of Theorem 1: We will prove the theorem by showing that the error $\boldsymbol{\epsilon}(i)$ becomes zero in a finite number of steps. The algorithm (S-1) can be rewritten in terms of $\boldsymbol{\epsilon}(i)$

$$\begin{aligned} \boldsymbol{\epsilon}(i+1) &= (\rho A S A' - I) | \boldsymbol{\epsilon}(i)| \\ \| \boldsymbol{\epsilon}(i)\|^2 - \| \boldsymbol{\epsilon}(i-1)\|^2 &= | \boldsymbol{\epsilon}(i)|' A R A' | \boldsymbol{\epsilon}(i)| \\ &\geqslant \lambda \| \boldsymbol{\epsilon}(i)\|^2 \qquad (3.12) \end{aligned}$$

where the last step follows from the definition of λ. We will show $\lambda > 0$.

By Eq. (3.11), $\lambda \geqslant 0$. λ can be zero only if there exists a nonnegative vector $\boldsymbol{\gamma}$ such that $\| \boldsymbol{\gamma} \|^2 = 1$ and $A'\boldsymbol{\gamma} = 0$. But a theorem of Fan (1956) states that if the inequalities $A\alpha > 0$ have a solution, then the only nonnegative solution γ of equations $A'\gamma = 0$ is the null solution which, of course, does not satisfy the condition $\| \gamma \|^2 = 1$. Hence, $\lambda > 0$. This fact, in conjunction with Eq. (3.12), implies that $\epsilon(i)$ tends to zero as i tends to infinity, leading to a solution of Eq. (3.8). Moreover, since $\beta_i \geqslant 1 \; \forall \; i = 1,..., N$ by choice, any $\alpha(i)$ satisfying the condition $\| \epsilon(i)\|^2 < 1$ is a solution to the inequalities $A\alpha > 0$. Hence, convergence should occur within $\bar{N}$ steps where $\bar{N}$ obeys the following relation

$$\| \epsilon(\bar{N})\|^2 \leqslant (1 - \lambda)^{\bar{N}} \| \epsilon(0)\|^2 < 1$$

Taking logarithms of this equation leads us to the desired expression for $\bar{N}$.

Remarks. (i) We can regard the upper bound $\bar{N}$ as proportional to the log N where N is the number of inequalities since $\| \epsilon(0)\|^2$ is a sum of N terms.

(ii) Note that the statement $\lambda > 0$ is a necessary and sufficient condition for the inequalities $A\alpha > 0$ to possess a solution. Thus, we have a constructive way of verifying the existence of a solution for the linear inequalities.

If our aim is only to check for the existence of a solution for $A\alpha > 0$, we need only compute λ_1 and check whether it is positive.

$$\lambda_1 = \operatorname*{Min}_{\gamma}(\gamma' A A' \gamma) \qquad \| \gamma \|^2 = 1 \qquad \text{and} \qquad \gamma_i \geqslant 0 \qquad i = 1,..., N$$

Some possible choices for S and ρ obeying Eq. (3.9) are listed below in the order of decreasing complexity and decreasing rate of convergence.

Case (i): $S = (A'A)^{-1} \qquad 0 < \rho < 2$

Case (ii): $S = (2 \| A'A \| I - A'A)/\| A'A \|^2 \qquad 0 < \rho < 2$

Case (iii): $S = I \qquad 0 < \rho < \| A'A \|^{-1}$

In particular, in Case (i), if we set

$$\alpha(0) = (A'A)^{-1}A'\beta(0) \qquad \text{with} \qquad \beta'(0) = (1, 1,... 1, 1), \text{ then } \alpha(k)$$

represents the best linear least squares fit for a given $\beta(k)$, i.e., it minimizes $J_1(\alpha, \beta(k))$.

Of course, there are other methods of solving the inequalities $A\alpha > 0$ besides (S-1), like linear programming (Dantzig, 1963), the perceptron algorithm (Novikov, 1963), and relaxation algorithm (Agmon, 1956).

We will rewrite them in matrix notation, as shown below, so as to bring out their similarity to (S-1).

Perceptron: $\boldsymbol{\alpha}(k+1) = \boldsymbol{\alpha}(k) + \rho A'[\operatorname{sgn} | \boldsymbol{\epsilon}(k)| - \operatorname{sgn} \boldsymbol{\epsilon}(k)]$ (S-2)

Relaxation: $\boldsymbol{\alpha}(k+1) = \boldsymbol{\alpha}(k) + \rho A'[| \boldsymbol{\epsilon}(k)| - \boldsymbol{\epsilon}(k)]$ (S-3)

where $\boldsymbol{\epsilon}(k) = A\boldsymbol{\alpha}(k) - \boldsymbol{\beta}(0)$

$$\boldsymbol{\beta}'(0) = [1, 1,..., 1]$$

Let us discuss the various algorithms. When the inequalities $A\boldsymbol{\alpha} > 0$ have a solution, then all the algorithms achieve a solution of the inequalities in a finite number of steps. However, Case (i) of the algorithm (S-1) seems to possess the highest convergence rate among the schemes (S-1) to (S-3). The apparent reason is the introduction of the quantities $\boldsymbol{\beta}(k)$ as variables in the algorithm (S-1). Heuristically, the variable vector $\boldsymbol{\beta}$ allows those row constraints (in the inequalities) which are not satisfied to have different weights at every iteration. In comparing the algorithm (S-1) with the method of linear programming, note that in (S-1), the number of steps needed for a solution is bounded by log N whereas in linear programming, the number of steps is about $2N$ (Saaty, 1959). Thus, when N is large, (S-1) may be preferable to linear programming.

However, in many problems, the assumption about the existence of the separating function of the form in Eq. (3.6) is invalid; i.e., the inequalities $A\boldsymbol{\alpha} > 0$ may not have a solution. In such cases, only the algorithm (S-1) leads to a meaningful result which can be interpreted as a least square fit. The other two algorithms (S-2) and (S-3) will only oscillate without leading to any useful result whereas linear programming gives only an indication of the inconsistency of the inequalities. We will consider this class of problems in the next section.

Example 1. Consider the following classification problem involving the vertices A, B, C, and D of a two-cube whose coordinate vectors (x_1, x_2) are given below

$$A = (1, 1), \quad B = (1, -1), \quad C = (-1, -1), \quad D = (-1, 1)$$

Let

$$A, B \sim \omega_1$$

$$C, D \sim \omega_{-1}$$

Let the φ functions be chosen as follows

$$\varphi_1(\mathbf{x}) = x_1, \quad \varphi_2(\mathbf{x}) = x_2, \quad \varphi_3(\mathbf{x}) = 1$$

The corresponding A matrix is displayed below

$$A = \begin{bmatrix} 1 & 1 & 1 \\ 1 & -1 & 1 \\ 1 & 1 & -1 \\ 1 & -1 & -1 \end{bmatrix}$$

Clearly this problems has a separating hyperplane. This can also be ascertained by evaluating the parameter λ (defined earlier) which is found to be 0.5 and thus, the inequalities $A\boldsymbol{\alpha} > 0$ have a solution.

To find $\boldsymbol{\alpha}^*$, let us use (S-1), Case (i) with

$$\boldsymbol{\alpha}(0) = (A'A)^{-1}A'\boldsymbol{\beta}(0), \qquad \boldsymbol{\beta}'(0) = [1, 1,..., 1]$$

In this case

$$\boldsymbol{\alpha}^* = \boldsymbol{\alpha}'(0) = (1, 0, 0)$$

Separating hyperplane is

$$f(\mathbf{x}) \triangleq x_1 = 0$$

Example 2. Let us again consider the problem of the Example 1 two-cube, with

$$A, C \sim \omega_1 \qquad \text{and} \qquad B, D \sim \omega_{-1}$$

Choosing the φ functions the same as before, the corresponding value of A is given below

$$A = \begin{bmatrix} 1 & 1 & 1 \\ 1 & 1 & -1 \\ 1 & -1 & 1 \\ 1 & -1 & -1 \end{bmatrix}$$

One can ascertain by inspection that the problem does not have a separating hyperplane. Alternately, we can evaluate λ, which is zero, showing $A\boldsymbol{\alpha} > 0$ does not have a solution.

On the other hand, if we chose another set of φ functions as shown below, then the problem has a separating hyperplane in the new φ space

$$\varphi_1(\mathbf{x}) = x_1 \qquad \varphi_2(\mathbf{x}) = x_2 \qquad \varphi_3(\mathbf{x}) = x_1x_2 \qquad \varphi_4(\mathbf{x}) = 1$$

The corresponding separating hyperplane is

$$f(\mathbf{x}) = x_1x_2 = 0$$

B. *Optimal Approximations to the Separating Function*

Since the recovery of the separating function in all its generality may be very difficult computationally, we will be content to find a "best" approximation to the unknown separating function $f(\mathbf{x})$. The approximation $d(\mathbf{x})$ will have the following linear form

$$d(\mathbf{x}) = \sum_{i=1}^{n} \alpha_i \varphi_i(\mathbf{x}) + t = \boldsymbol{\alpha}'\boldsymbol{\varphi}(\mathbf{x}) + t$$

where $\varphi_i(\mathbf{x})$, $i = 1,\ldots, n$ are known functions of $\mathbf{x}$ so that 1, $\varphi_1(\mathbf{x})$, $\varphi_2(\mathbf{x}),\ldots, \varphi_n(\mathbf{x})$ are linearly independent and $\alpha_1, \ldots, \alpha_n$ are the undetermined parameters and t is a known threshold. Since the decision rule (3.13) to be used for classification involves only the sign of $d(\mathbf{x})$, we can assume t to be an arbitrary nonzero constant.

$$\operatorname{sgn} d(\mathbf{x}) = i \rightarrow \text{classify } \mathbf{x} \text{ in class } \omega_i\,, \qquad i = \pm 1 \tag{3.13}$$

We have to chose $\boldsymbol{\alpha}$ by minimizing a suitable criterion $J(\boldsymbol{\alpha})$ which reflects the average misclassification performed by the function $d(\mathbf{x})$ and rule (3.13). Let

$$J(\boldsymbol{\alpha}) = E[V(\boldsymbol{\alpha}, \mathbf{x}) \mid \boldsymbol{\alpha}]$$

where $V(\boldsymbol{\alpha}, \mathbf{x})$ is a suitable loss function associated with every pattern $\mathbf{x}$ and parameter $\boldsymbol{\alpha}$

$$\begin{aligned} V(\boldsymbol{\alpha}, \mathbf{x}) &= 0 \text{ if } \mathbf{x} \text{ is correctly classified by rule (3.13)} \\ &> 0 \text{ if } \mathbf{x} \text{ is misclassified by rule (3.13)} \end{aligned}$$

The first loss function that will be considered is $V_2(\boldsymbol{\alpha}, \mathbf{x})$.

$$\begin{aligned} V_2(\boldsymbol{\alpha}, \mathbf{x}) &= (\operatorname{sgn}(\boldsymbol{\alpha}'\boldsymbol{\varphi}(\mathbf{x}) + t) - \operatorname{sgn} f(\mathbf{x}))(\boldsymbol{\alpha}'\boldsymbol{\varphi}(\mathbf{x}) + t) \\ J_2(\boldsymbol{\alpha}) &= E[V_2(\boldsymbol{\alpha}, \mathbf{x}) \mid \boldsymbol{\alpha}] \end{aligned}$$

To understand the function $J_2(\boldsymbol{\alpha})$, recall $\boldsymbol{\alpha}'\boldsymbol{\varphi}(\mathbf{x})$ is proportional to the projection of the vector $\boldsymbol{\varphi}(\mathbf{x})$ on the hyperplane $\boldsymbol{\alpha}'\boldsymbol{\varphi} + t = 0$. Thus, the minimization of $J_2(\boldsymbol{\alpha})$ with respect to $\boldsymbol{\alpha}$ is equivalent to the choice of the hyperplane with normal $\boldsymbol{\alpha}$ which minimizes the sum of the magnitudes of the projections of the misclassified samples on that hyperplane.

The second loss function $V_3(\boldsymbol{\alpha}, \mathbf{x})$ is

$$\begin{aligned} V_3(\boldsymbol{\alpha}, \mathbf{x}) &= \tfrac{1}{2} \mid \operatorname{sgn} f(\mathbf{x}) - \operatorname{sgn}(\boldsymbol{\alpha}'\boldsymbol{\varphi}(\mathbf{x}) + t)| \\ J_3(\boldsymbol{\alpha}) &= E[V_3(\boldsymbol{\alpha}, \mathbf{x}) \mid \boldsymbol{\alpha}] \end{aligned}$$

Minimizing $J_3(\boldsymbol{\alpha})$ is equivalent to minimizing the average number of misclassifications. $J_3(\boldsymbol{\alpha})$ is a more realistic criterion function than $J_2(\boldsymbol{\alpha})$, but it is harder to find the minimum of $J_3(\boldsymbol{\alpha})$ than that of $J_2(\boldsymbol{\alpha})$.

1. *Modified perceptron scheme.* Let $\boldsymbol{\alpha}^*$ be the minimum of $J_2(\boldsymbol{\alpha})$ with respect to $\boldsymbol{\alpha}$

$$J_2(\boldsymbol{\alpha}) = E[V_2(\boldsymbol{\alpha}, \mathbf{x})] = E[(\operatorname{sgn}(\boldsymbol{\alpha}'\boldsymbol{\varphi} + t) - \operatorname{sgn} f(\mathbf{x}))(\boldsymbol{\alpha}'\boldsymbol{\varphi} + t)]$$

The corresponding optimal approximation function is

$$\hat{f}(\mathbf{x}) = \boldsymbol{\alpha}^{*\prime}\boldsymbol{\varphi}(\mathbf{x})$$

We will obtain an expression for $\boldsymbol{\alpha}^*$, in terms of the unknown functions $f(\mathbf{x})$ and $p(\mathbf{x})$. We note that

$$\begin{aligned} -\nabla_{\boldsymbol{\alpha}} V_2(\boldsymbol{\alpha}, \mathbf{x}) &= \text{negative gradient of } V_2(\boldsymbol{\alpha}, \mathbf{x}) \text{ with respect to } \boldsymbol{\alpha} \\ &= (\operatorname{sgn} f(\mathbf{x}) - \operatorname{sgn}(\boldsymbol{\alpha}'\boldsymbol{\varphi} + t))\, \boldsymbol{\varphi} \end{aligned}$$

To get the gradient of $J_2(\boldsymbol{\alpha})$ from $\nabla_{\boldsymbol{\alpha}} V_2(\boldsymbol{\alpha}, \mathbf{x})$, we use the fact that $J_2(\boldsymbol{\alpha})$ is a smooth function of $\boldsymbol{\alpha}$ and interchange gradient and expectation operation. Thus, $\boldsymbol{\alpha}^*$ is the solution of the following:

$$\begin{aligned} -\nabla_{\boldsymbol{\alpha}} J_2(\boldsymbol{\alpha}) &= -\nabla_{\boldsymbol{\alpha}} E[V_2(\boldsymbol{\alpha}, \mathbf{x})] = -E[\nabla_{\boldsymbol{\alpha}} V_2(\boldsymbol{\alpha}, \mathbf{x})] \\ &= E[(\operatorname{sgn} f(\mathbf{x}) - \operatorname{sgn}(\boldsymbol{\alpha}'\boldsymbol{\varphi} + t))\, \boldsymbol{\varphi}] = 0 \end{aligned} \tag{3.14}$$

However, we cannot use this equation for finding the optimal value $\boldsymbol{\alpha}^*$ since the equation involves the unknown $f(\mathbf{x})$, which we want to estimate.

To solve for $\boldsymbol{\alpha}^*$ based only on the sample pairs $\{(\mathbf{x}(k), y(k)), k=1, 2, \ldots,\}$, we have to use a gradient scheme to minimize $J_2(\boldsymbol{\alpha})$. The gradient of $J_2(\boldsymbol{\alpha})$ is never available to us. However, we can evaluate the stochastic gradient $\nabla_{\boldsymbol{\alpha}} V_2(\boldsymbol{\alpha}, \mathbf{x})$ whose expected value is $\nabla_{\boldsymbol{\alpha}} J_2(\boldsymbol{\alpha})$. Thus, the stochastic gradient scheme can be written down as shown below

$$\boldsymbol{\alpha}(k+1) = \boldsymbol{\alpha}(k) + \rho(k)(y(k) - \operatorname{sgn}(\boldsymbol{\alpha}'(k)\, \boldsymbol{\varphi}(k) + t))\, \boldsymbol{\varphi}(k) \tag{S-4}$$

where $\Sigma_k \rho(k) = \infty$, $\Sigma_k \rho^2(k) < \infty$.

If the samples are independent and if $\boldsymbol{\alpha}^*$ is the unique solution of Eq. (3.14), then $\boldsymbol{\alpha}(k)$ tends to $\boldsymbol{\alpha}^*$ in the following sense

$$\lim_{k\to\infty} E \mid \operatorname{sgn}(\boldsymbol{\alpha}'(k)\, \boldsymbol{\varphi}(\mathbf{x}) + t) - \operatorname{sgn}(\boldsymbol{\alpha}^{*\prime}\boldsymbol{\varphi}(\mathbf{x}) + t)\mid = 0$$

The proof of convergence is a special case of the one to be given in Section III. The conclusions of the theorem are not effected even if the classes ω_i have only a finite number of points like the vertices of a hypercube.

The algorithm (S-4) with $\rho(k)$ as a constant is the perceptron algorithm in its original form (Novikov, 1963). As remarked earlier, it may oscillate when the separating function is not of the form in Eq. (3.6).

We have obtained $\boldsymbol{\alpha}^*$ under the assumption of the availability of the samples in large numbers. When N, the number of samples is small, then the result $\boldsymbol{\alpha}(N)$ obtained from the algorithm using these samples is usually unsatisfactory. The natural way to improve the result is to continue the algorithm by cycling the available samples, that is,

$$\left.\begin{aligned}\boldsymbol{\varphi}(k) &= \boldsymbol{\varphi}(j)\\ y(k) &= y(j)\end{aligned}\right\} \quad \text{if} \quad k = j (\text{mod } N)$$

Let us consider the asymptotic properties of the estimate $\boldsymbol{\alpha}(k)$ obtained by this modification. When the separating functions $f(\mathbf{x})$ has the following form

$$f(\mathbf{x}) = \sum_{i=1}^{n} \alpha_i^* \varphi_i(\mathbf{x}) + t \tag{3.15}$$

then the modified algorithm leads to a hyperplane $\boldsymbol{\alpha}$ separating the samples in the φ space. The proof follows directly from that in Novikov (1963). When the structure of $f(\mathbf{x})$ is unknown, it is experimentally observed that the modification leads to a value of $\boldsymbol{\alpha}$ which approximately minimizes

$$\left(\sum_{k=1}^{N} V_2(\boldsymbol{\alpha}, \mathbf{x}(k))\right)$$

2. *Minimum classification error scheme.* We will minimize $J_3(\boldsymbol{\alpha})$ with respect to $\boldsymbol{\alpha}$. Let the optimal value of $\boldsymbol{\alpha}$ be $\boldsymbol{\alpha}^{**}$

$$J_3(\boldsymbol{\alpha}) = E[V_3(\boldsymbol{\alpha}, \mathbf{x}) \mid \boldsymbol{\alpha}] = E[\tfrac{1}{2} \mid \operatorname{sgn} f(\mathbf{x}) - \operatorname{sgn}(\boldsymbol{\alpha}'\boldsymbol{\varphi} + t) \mid \mid \boldsymbol{\alpha}]$$

Firstly, we note that $V_3(\boldsymbol{\alpha}, \mathbf{x})$ is a function assuming one of two values, 0 or 1, and hence, there is no question of its possessing a smooth gradient function. However, $J_3(\boldsymbol{\alpha})$, usually, is a smooth function of $\boldsymbol{\alpha}$. We can construct an approximation $\hat{\nabla}_{\boldsymbol{\alpha}} J_3(\boldsymbol{\alpha})$ for the gradient of $J_3(\boldsymbol{\alpha})$ using $2n$ sample pairs $\mathbf{x}(2nk + 1), \ldots, \mathbf{x}(2nk + 2n)$ in the following form

$$\begin{aligned}\hat{\nabla}_{\boldsymbol{\alpha}} J_3(\boldsymbol{\alpha}(k)) = \sum_{j=1}^{n} \mathbf{e}_j \frac{1}{2c(k)} \{&V_3(\boldsymbol{\alpha}(k) + c(k)\, \mathbf{e}_j, \mathbf{x}(2nk + 2j - 1))\\ &- V_3(\boldsymbol{\alpha}(k) - c(k)\, \mathbf{e}_j, \mathbf{x}(2nk + 2j))\}\end{aligned}$$

where the n-vectors $\mathbf{e}_1, \ldots, \mathbf{e}_n$ are the unit vectors

$$(\mathbf{e}_j)_i = i\text{th component of } \mathbf{e}_j = \delta_{ij}$$

In this case, the descent scheme for finding the minimum of $J_3(\boldsymbol{\alpha})$ is given in (S-5)

$$\boldsymbol{\alpha}(k+1) = \boldsymbol{\alpha}(k) - \rho(k)\, \hat{\nabla}_{\boldsymbol{\alpha}} J_3(\boldsymbol{\alpha}(k)) \tag{S-5}$$

where the scalar gains $\rho(k)$, $c(k)$ are chosen to satisfy the following conditions

$$\sum_k \rho(k) = \infty \qquad \sum_k \rho(k)\, c(k) < \infty \qquad \sum_k \left(\frac{\rho(k)}{c(k)}\right)^2 < \infty$$

$$c(k) \to 0 \qquad \rho(k) < d_1 c^2(k) \qquad 0 < d_1 < \infty$$

The gradient scheme given above is nothing but the Kiefer–Wolfowitz scheme discussed in detail in the chapter on stochastic approximation.

From the theorem of Venter (1967), it follows that $\boldsymbol{\alpha}(k)$ will tend to $\boldsymbol{\alpha}^{**}$, the optimal value with probability one if the function $J_3(\boldsymbol{\alpha})$ satisfies the following conditions:

(A1) $J_3(\boldsymbol{\alpha})$ must be a continuous function of $\boldsymbol{\alpha}$ with bounded second derivatives.

(A2) $J_3(\boldsymbol{\alpha})$ has a local minimum at $\boldsymbol{\alpha} = \boldsymbol{\alpha}^{**}$.

(A3) $dJ_3(\boldsymbol{\alpha})/d\boldsymbol{\alpha} \neq \mathbf{0}$ if $\boldsymbol{\alpha} \neq \boldsymbol{\alpha}^{**}$.

Assumption (A1) is valid if the probability density $p(\mathbf{x})$ is a continuous function of $\mathbf{x}$. Note that this rules out the possibility of the classes ω_i having only a finite number of points. Assumptions (A2) and (A3) imply that $J_3(\boldsymbol{\alpha})$ can have only one local minimum at $\boldsymbol{\alpha} = \boldsymbol{\alpha}^{**}$ and cannot have any point of local maxima. All values of $\boldsymbol{\alpha}$, such that the hyperplane $\boldsymbol{\alpha}'\boldsymbol{\varphi} + t = 0$ does not intersect the two classes ω_1 and ω_{-1}, are candidates for local *maximum* of the function $J_3(\boldsymbol{\alpha})$. Hence, if we choose the origin to be a member of one of the classes and let $\| \boldsymbol{\alpha} \| > d_2 > 0$ where d_2 is a suitable positive constant, then the hyperplane $\boldsymbol{\alpha}'\boldsymbol{\varphi} + t = 0$ will be close to the origin and presumably pass through one of the classes thus avoiding the possibility of $\boldsymbol{\alpha}$ being a local maximum.

When the number of samples are finite, we cannot say anything about the result of the algorithm on account of the discontinuous nature of $V_3(\boldsymbol{\alpha}, \mathbf{x})$.

C. *Recovery of the Separating Function*

1. *Classes with a finite number of members.* When the two classes have only a finite number of members, it is relatively easy to obtain a separating function which is, of course, not unique. As an example, let us consider the case of patterns being the vertices of an m-cube of side two centered about the origin. Thus, all the components of the patterns will be ± 1. The total number of distinct patterns is less than or equal to 2^m. In this case, it is relatively straight forward to show the existence of a separating function of the following form, the so-called Radmacher–Walsh (Walsh, 1923) expansion,

$$f(\mathbf{x}) = \sum_{i=1}^{n} \theta_i \varphi_i(\mathbf{x}) \qquad n = 2^m \tag{3.16}$$

where the functions $\varphi_i(\mathbf{x})$ are the various products among the variables $1, x_1, \ldots, x_m$ so that no variable is of degree greater than one in any product. In otherwords

$$\begin{aligned}
\varphi_1(\mathbf{x}) &= 1 \\
\varphi_{i+1}(\mathbf{x}) &= x_i \qquad i = 1, \ldots, m \\
\varphi_{m+2}(\mathbf{x}) &= x_1 x_2 \\
\varphi_{m+3}(\mathbf{x}) &= x_1 x_3 \\
\varphi_{m+2+m(m+1)/2}(\mathbf{x}) &= x_1 x_2 x_3 \\
\varphi_{2^m}(\mathbf{x}) &= x_1 x_2 \cdots x_m
\end{aligned}$$

The functions $\varphi_i(\mathbf{x})$ are orthogonal

$$\sum_{\mathbf{x}} \varphi_i(\mathbf{x})\, \varphi_j(\mathbf{x}) = 2^m \delta_{ij}$$

where the summation is over all the vertices of the m-cube. The unknowns, $\theta_1, \theta_2, \ldots, \theta_{2^m}$, can be found by solving the following system of 2^m equations for 2^m unknowns, θ_i, $i = 1, \ldots, 2^m$.

$$\boldsymbol{\theta}' \boldsymbol{\varphi}(\mathbf{x}(i))\, y(i) = 1 \qquad i = 1, \ldots, 2^m$$

For details of solving for $\boldsymbol{\theta}$ without explicitly inverting the associated $2^m \times 2^m$ matrix, see Kashyap (1965).

But, the solution for $f(\mathbf{x})$ obtained above is not very useful for practice for it involves the realization of 2^m terms, which can be a very large number even for moderate values of m. Moreover, in many problems, only a fraction of 2^m vertices are assigned to one of the classes, and the rest are of no consequence. Some effort has been spent on getting a separating function of Eq. (3.16) involving the least number of nonzero coefficients among $\theta_1, \ldots, \theta_{2^m}$. The techniques are largely heuristic. Further details can be obtained from the survey paper by Winder (1966).

2. *Classes are subsets of Euclidean space.* In this section, we shall recursively recover the separating function itself from an infinite set of samples when the pattern vector is continuous. We hasten to remark that the scheme involves computation in the function space in contrast with the computations in the finite dimensional spaces encountered in the earlier section.

The basic idea is to express $f_k(\mathbf{x})$, the estimate of the function $f(\mathbf{x})$, at the kth stage (based on the sample pairs $\{(\mathbf{x}(j), y(j)), j = 1, 2, \ldots, (k-1)\}$ as the weighted sum of k terms

$$f_k(\mathbf{x}) = \sum_{j=1}^{k-1} \gamma_j(k)\, K(\mathbf{x}, \mathbf{x}(j)) \tag{3.17}$$

where $K(\mathbf{a}, \mathbf{b})$ is the so called potential function and $\gamma_j(k)$ are the associated gains. The potential function $K(\mathbf{a}, \mathbf{b})$ where $\mathbf{a}, \mathbf{b}$ are m-vectors has the following properties

$$\begin{aligned} &K(\mathbf{a}, \mathbf{b}) \geqslant 0 \qquad \forall \mathbf{a}, \mathbf{b} \in R^m \\ &K(\mathbf{a}, \mathbf{b}) = \sum_{i=1}^{\infty} \varphi_i(\mathbf{a})\, \varphi_i(\mathbf{b}) \end{aligned} \tag{3.18}$$

where the functions $\varphi_1(\mathbf{x}), \varphi_2(\mathbf{x}), \ldots,$ are orthogonal with a measure μ

$$\begin{aligned} \int \varphi_i(\mathbf{x})\, \varphi_j(\mathbf{x})\, d\mu(\mathbf{x}) &= 0 \qquad \text{if} \quad i \neq j \\ &> 0 \qquad \text{if} \quad i = j \end{aligned}$$

Some candidates for $K(\mathbf{a}, \mathbf{b})$ are

(i) $K(\mathbf{a}, \mathbf{b}) = \exp[-d \,\|\, \boldsymbol{\alpha} - \mathbf{b} \,\|^2] \qquad d > 0$

(ii) $K(\mathbf{a}, \mathbf{b}) = 1/(1 + \|\, \mathbf{a} - \mathbf{b} \,\|^2) \qquad \text{if} \ \|\, \mathbf{a} - \mathbf{b} \,\| < 1$

A natural error correction scheme for computing $f_k(\mathbf{x})$ recursively is given below

$$f_{k+1}(\mathbf{x}) = f_k(\mathbf{x}) + \rho(k)(\operatorname{sgn} f(\mathbf{x}(k)) - \operatorname{sgn} f_k(\mathbf{x}(k)))\, K(\mathbf{x}, \mathbf{x}(k)) \tag{S-6}$$

with

$$\sum_k \rho(k) = \infty \qquad \text{and} \qquad \sum \rho^2(k) < \infty$$

We can look upon the scheme (S-6) as a generalization of (S-4). We can formally represent $f_k(\mathbf{x})$ as

$$f_k(\mathbf{x}) = \sum_{j=1}^{\infty} \alpha_j(k)\, \varphi_j(\mathbf{x}) = \boldsymbol{\alpha}'(k)\, \boldsymbol{\varphi}(\mathbf{x})$$

where $\boldsymbol{\alpha}(k)$ obeys the scheme (S-4). Scalar multiplication of (S-4) by $\boldsymbol{\varphi}'(\mathbf{x})$ throughout and the use of the expansions for $f_k(\mathbf{x})$ and $K(\mathbf{x}, \mathbf{x}(k))$ gives us the scheme (S-6).

It is possible to show that

$$\lim_{k\to\infty} E\,[|\operatorname{sgn} f_k(\mathbf{x}) - \operatorname{sgn} f(\mathbf{x})|] = 0$$

provided that the samples $\{(\mathbf{x}(i), y(i))\ i = 1, 2, \ldots,\}$ are independent and $f(\mathbf{x})$ satisfies some mild conditions.

It is clear from (S-6) that $f_k(\mathbf{x})$ will have the form in Eq. (3.17), i.e., $f_k(\mathbf{x})$ is a sum of about k functions. The storage of such functions for large k on the computer may pose some formidable problems. For further details of the potential function method, see the chapter on stochastic approximation.

III. Nonoverlapping Classes with Erroneously Classified Samples

A. *Introduction*

In the previous section, we have considered the determination of separating function and its approximation when the classification of the training samples is known to us exactly. If the classification of the given (training) samples is erroneous (or unreliable), there is very little that can be done in such a situation if we have no information on the nature of errors. However, if the average number of misclassifications is known, then it is possible to recover the separating function or an approximation to it by modification of the scheme (S-4). This is the topic of this section.

Let $f(\mathbf{x})$ be the separating function. Let z represent the observed (noisy) class indicator of the pattern $\mathbf{x}$.

$$z(\mathbf{x}) = i \qquad \text{if } \mathbf{x} \text{ is observed to belong to } \omega_i, \qquad i = \pm 1$$

Recalling the definition of y, the true class indicator, we can write

$$z(\mathbf{x}) = y(\mathbf{x})\eta \triangleq (\operatorname{sgn} f^o(\mathbf{x}))\eta$$

where η is the measurement noise, assuming one of two values ± 1.

As an example, consider the problem of testing the effectiveness of a particular drug in curing a certain disease. The pattern vector $\mathbf{x}$ represents the various symptoms of the disease in quantified form. Let $y(\mathbf{x})$ be $+1$ or -1 depending on whether the patient with symptom $\mathbf{x}$ has been cured or not, respectively. In a certain trial run, with patients with symptoms represented by $\mathbf{x}(1), \mathbf{x}(2),\ldots$, we record only the responses $z(\mathbf{x}(1)), z(\mathbf{x}(2)),\ldots$, of the patients to the disease where $z(\mathbf{x}) = 1$ if the patient with symptom $\mathbf{x}$ "feels" better after taking the drug and $z(\mathbf{x}) = -1$ otherwise. Clearly $z(\mathbf{x})$ is different from $y(\mathbf{x})$ since there are many cases in which the patient may feel better (i.e., $z(\mathbf{x}) = 1$) even though the drug did not do him any good, by itself (i.e., $y(\mathbf{x}) = -1$). It is needless to say that $y(\mathbf{x})$ cannot be measured exactly in this case.

We pose the following problem: Given a sequence of pattern vectors $\mathbf{x}(1), \mathbf{x}(2),\ldots$ and their associated noisy measurements $z(\mathbf{x}(1)), z(\mathbf{x}(2)),\ldots$ of the true class indicator variables $y(\mathbf{x}(1)), y(\mathbf{x}(2)),\ldots$, find an optimal approximation to the unknown separating function $f^o(\mathbf{x})$.

It is needless to say the problem posed above is identical to the problem with correctly classified training samples, when $\hat{\eta} = 1$.

We note that no definitive statements are available concerning the behavior of the algorithms mentioned in the literature when misclassified training samples are used.

B. *Statement of the Problem*

We will recall the definitions of the separating function $f^o(\mathbf{x})$, the true class indicator $y(\mathbf{x})$, and the observed class indicator $z(\mathbf{x})$. We will make the following assumptions:

(B1): The pattern vector $\mathbf{x}$ can assume any value in a subset $\Omega \in R^m$ and it possesses a probability density $p(\mathbf{x})$ which is nonzero in Ω. Moreover, $p(\mathbf{x})$ is unknown. In addition, there exists a set of linearly independent functions $\varphi_1(\mathbf{x}),\ldots, \varphi_n(\mathbf{x})$ such that

$$E\{\varphi_i^2(\mathbf{x})\} < \infty \qquad \forall\, i = 1,\ldots, n$$

(B2): The successive samples $\mathbf{x}(1), \mathbf{x}(2),\ldots$ are independent.

(B3): The measurement noise $\eta(i)$ is independent of the patterns $\mathbf{x}(j)$ for all i and j. Furthermore,

$$\hat{\eta} \triangleq E\{\eta(i)\} \neq 0 \qquad \hat{\eta} \text{ is known}$$

The problem is to obtain an "optimal" approximation $f^*(\mathbf{x})$ to the unknown separating function $f^o(\mathbf{x})$, using only the sample pairs $\{\mathbf{x}(i), z(\mathbf{x}(i))\}$, $i = 1, 2,\ldots$.

We choose the optimal approximating function $f^*(\mathbf{x})$ in the class of functions given in Eq. (3.19)

$$f(\mathbf{x}) = \sum_{i=1}^{n} \alpha_i \varphi_i(\mathbf{x}) + t = \boldsymbol{\alpha}'\boldsymbol{\varphi}(\mathbf{x}) + t \tag{3.19}$$

where $\varphi_1(\mathbf{x}),..., \varphi_n(\mathbf{x})$ are the known linearly independent functions mentioned earlier, t is a known threshold, and $\alpha_1 ,..., \alpha_n$ are undetermined parameters, whose values are determined by minimizing a suitable criterion function $J(\boldsymbol{\alpha})$. The choice of the functions $\varphi_1(\mathbf{x})$, $\varphi_2(\mathbf{x}),...,$ and the integer n depends on the error $|f^o(\mathbf{x}) - f^*(\mathbf{x})|$ that can be tolerated and the computational complexity of the functions $f^*(\mathbf{x})$.

The criterion function $J(\boldsymbol{\alpha})$ must reflect the magnitude of the average error in classification if we used $f(\mathbf{x})$ as the decision function, in conjunction with the rule in Eq. (3.20). If

$$\begin{aligned} f(\mathbf{x}) &> 0 \quad \text{classify } \mathbf{x} \text{ in } \omega_1 \\ &< 0 \quad \text{classify } \mathbf{x} \text{ in } \omega_{-1} \end{aligned} \tag{3.20}$$

Thus, we can define $J(\boldsymbol{\alpha})$ as

$$J(\boldsymbol{\alpha}) = E\{V(\boldsymbol{\alpha}, \mathbf{x})|\ \boldsymbol{\alpha}\}$$

where $V(\boldsymbol{\alpha}, \mathbf{x})$ is the penalty for misclassifying a sample $\mathbf{x}$.

$$\begin{aligned} V(\boldsymbol{\alpha}, \mathbf{x}) &= 0 \quad \text{if } \mathbf{x} \text{ is correctly classified by the rule in Eq. (3.20)} \\ &> 0 \quad \text{if } \mathbf{x} \text{ is misclassified by the rule in Eq. (3.20)} \end{aligned}$$

Our choice for $V(\boldsymbol{\alpha}, \mathbf{x})$, satisfying the above requirement, is

$$V(\boldsymbol{\alpha}, \mathbf{x}) = |\ \boldsymbol{\alpha}'\boldsymbol{\varphi}(\mathbf{x}) + t\ |\ |\ \operatorname{sgn}(\boldsymbol{\alpha}'\boldsymbol{\varphi}(\mathbf{x}) + t) - \operatorname{sgn} f^o(\mathbf{x})| \tag{3.21}$$

To get a geometrical interpretation of the function $V(\boldsymbol{\alpha}, \mathbf{x})$, let us regard all samples $\boldsymbol{\varphi}(\mathbf{x}(k))$, $k = 1, 2,...,$ as points in the n-dimensional φ-space

$$\{|\ \boldsymbol{\alpha}'\boldsymbol{\varphi}(\mathbf{x}(k)) + t\ |/\|\ \boldsymbol{\alpha}\ \|\} = \textit{shortest} \text{ distance between the point } \boldsymbol{\varphi}(\mathbf{x}(k)) \text{ and the hyperplane } \boldsymbol{\alpha}'\boldsymbol{\varphi}(\mathbf{x}) + t = 0 \text{ (see Fig. 1).}$$

Thus, the minimization of $J(\boldsymbol{\alpha})$ with respect to $\boldsymbol{\alpha}$, yields an $\boldsymbol{\alpha}$ which minimizes the average distance between the misclassified samples and the hyperplane $\boldsymbol{\alpha}'\boldsymbol{\varphi}(\mathbf{x}) + t = 0$.

Let $\boldsymbol{\alpha}^*$ be the value of $\boldsymbol{\alpha}$ which minimizes $J(\boldsymbol{\alpha})$

$$J(\boldsymbol{\alpha}) \geqslant J(\boldsymbol{\alpha}^*)$$

The corresponding *optimal* approximation $f^*(\mathbf{x})$ to $f^o(\mathbf{x})$ is

$$f^*(\mathbf{x}) = \boldsymbol{\alpha}^{*\prime}\boldsymbol{\varphi}(\mathbf{x}) + t$$

It is needless to say that if $f^o(\mathbf{x})$ had the following form

$$f^o(\mathbf{x}) = \sum_{i=1}^{n} \theta_i \varphi_i(\mathbf{x}) + t$$

then

$$f^*(\mathbf{x}) = f^o(\mathbf{x}).$$

Our problem is to recover $f^*(\mathbf{x})$ or $\boldsymbol{\alpha}^*$, using only the sample pairs $\{\mathbf{x}(i), z(\mathbf{x}(i))\}$, $i = 1, 2,\ldots$, obeying assumptions (B1)–(B3) by recursive schemes. It is important to note that we do not have the knowledge of the probability density $p(\mathbf{x})$ of the samples $\mathbf{x}(i)$, $i = 1, 2,\ldots$

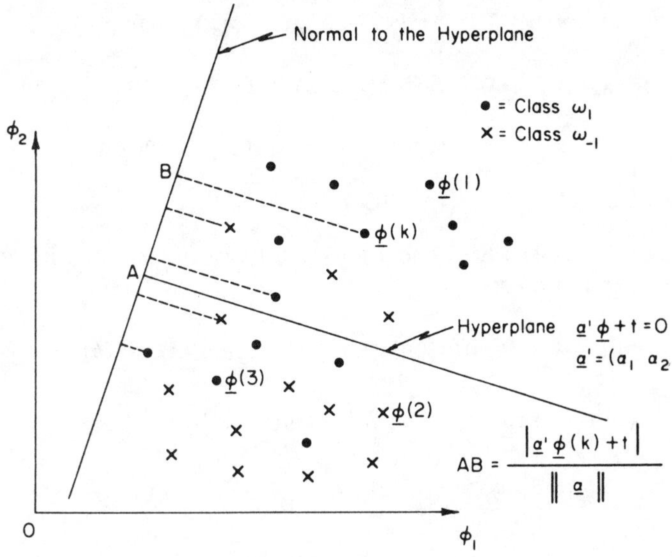

FIGURE 1

C. *The Algorithm and Discussion*

Let $\boldsymbol{\alpha}(k)$ = Estimate of $\boldsymbol{\alpha}^*$ at the kth stage based on the sample pairs

$$(\mathbf{x}(i), z(\mathbf{x}(i))), \qquad i = 1,\ldots, k-1$$

Then we can update $\boldsymbol{\alpha}(k)$ by the gradient method

$$\boldsymbol{\alpha}(k+1) = \boldsymbol{\alpha}(k) + \rho(k) \left.\frac{\partial J(\boldsymbol{\alpha})}{\partial \boldsymbol{\alpha}}\right|_{\boldsymbol{\alpha}=\boldsymbol{\alpha}(k)} \tag{3.22}$$

Since we do not know the probability density $p(\mathbf{x})$, we can never evaluate $J(\boldsymbol{\alpha})$ or $\partial J(\boldsymbol{\alpha})/\partial \boldsymbol{\alpha}$.

We have to be content with the stochastic gradient scheme as in Eq. (3.23)

$$\boldsymbol{\alpha}(k+1) = \boldsymbol{\alpha}(k) + \rho(k)\, \bar{\mathbf{h}}(\boldsymbol{\alpha}, \mathbf{x})|_{x=x(k),\alpha=\alpha(k)} \tag{3.23}$$

where

$$\bar{\mathbf{h}}(\boldsymbol{\alpha}, \mathbf{x}) = (\operatorname{sgn}(\boldsymbol{\alpha}'\boldsymbol{\varphi}(\mathbf{x}) + t) - \operatorname{sgn} f^o(\mathbf{x}))\, \boldsymbol{\varphi}(\mathbf{x}) \approx \frac{\partial V(\boldsymbol{\alpha}, \mathbf{x})}{\partial \mathbf{x}}$$

But, for any given pattern $\mathbf{x}$, we cannot determine $\bar{\mathbf{h}}(\boldsymbol{\alpha}, \mathbf{x})$ since we do not know $\operatorname{sgn} f^o(\mathbf{x})$. So, we will replace the approximate gradient $\bar{\mathbf{h}}(\boldsymbol{\alpha}, \mathbf{x})$ in Eq. (3.23) by a quantity $h(\boldsymbol{\alpha}, \mathbf{x}, z(\mathbf{x}))$ so that $\mathbf{h}$ is observable for any $\mathbf{x}$ and has the same expected value as $\bar{\mathbf{h}}$

$$\mathbf{h}(\boldsymbol{\alpha}, \mathbf{x}, z(\mathbf{x})) = \frac{1}{\hat{\eta}}(z(\mathbf{x}) - \hat{\eta}\operatorname{sgn}(\boldsymbol{\alpha}'\boldsymbol{\varphi}(\mathbf{x}) + t))\, \boldsymbol{\varphi}(\mathbf{x})$$

$$\begin{aligned} E\{\mathbf{h}(\boldsymbol{\alpha}, \mathbf{x}, \mathbf{z}(\mathbf{x})) \mid \boldsymbol{\alpha}\} &= E\{(\operatorname{sgn}(\boldsymbol{\alpha}'\boldsymbol{\varphi}(\mathbf{x}) + t) - \operatorname{sgn}(f^o(\mathbf{x})))\, \boldsymbol{\varphi}(\mathbf{x}) \mid \boldsymbol{\alpha}\} \\ &\quad + E\left\{\left(\frac{\eta}{\hat{\eta}} - 1\right)(\operatorname{sgn} f^o(\mathbf{x}))\, \boldsymbol{\varphi}(\mathbf{x}) \mid \boldsymbol{\alpha}\right\} \\ &= E(\bar{\mathbf{h}}(\boldsymbol{\alpha}, \mathbf{x}) \mid \boldsymbol{\alpha}) \end{aligned}$$

by assumption (B3). Thus, the algorithm in Eq. (3.23) can be written in the following manner:

$$\boldsymbol{\alpha}(k+1) = \boldsymbol{\alpha}(k) + \frac{1}{\hat{\eta}}\rho(k)\, \boldsymbol{\varphi}(\mathbf{x}(k))[z(\mathbf{x}(k)) - \hat{\eta}\operatorname{sgn}(\boldsymbol{\alpha}'(k)\, \boldsymbol{\varphi}(\mathbf{x}(k)) + t)] \tag{S-7}$$

where the gain $\rho(k)$ satisfies the following conditions

$$\rho(k) \geqslant 0, \qquad \sum_{k=1}^{\infty} \rho(k) = \infty \qquad \sum_{k=1}^{\infty} \rho^2(k) < \infty \tag{3.24}$$

The convergence properties of the algorithm are given in Theorem 2.

Theorem 2: Consider the algorithm in Eq. (S-7) with gain $\rho(k)$ obeying Eq. (3.24). Let $E\|\boldsymbol{\alpha}(1)\|^2 < \infty$ and the assumptions (B1)–(B3) be satisfied. Let

$$f_k(\mathbf{x}) = \boldsymbol{\alpha}'(k)\, \boldsymbol{\varphi}(\mathbf{x}) + t \qquad f(\mathbf{x}) = \boldsymbol{\alpha}'\boldsymbol{\varphi}(\mathbf{x}) + t$$

$$f^*(\mathbf{x}) = \boldsymbol{\alpha}^{*\prime}\boldsymbol{\varphi}(\mathbf{x}) + t$$

$$J(\boldsymbol{\alpha}) = E\{f(\mathbf{x})(\operatorname{sgn} f(\mathbf{x}) - \operatorname{sgn} f^o(\mathbf{x})) \mid \boldsymbol{\alpha}\}$$

$$\boldsymbol{\alpha}^* = \operatorname{Arg.}[\operatorname*{Min.}_{\boldsymbol{\alpha}} J(\boldsymbol{\alpha})]$$

Then $f_k(\mathbf{x})$ tends to the optimal approximation $f^*(\mathbf{x})$ in the following manner

$$\lim_{k\to\infty} E\{|\operatorname{sgn} f_k(\mathbf{x}) - \operatorname{sgn} f^*(\mathbf{x})| \mid \mathbf{x}\} = 0, \qquad \forall \mathbf{x} \in \Omega$$

The proof of the above theorem is given in the next section. It is worthwhile to note that even though the algorithm in Eq. (S-7) may *appear* to belong to the family of stochastic approximation schemes, its validity cannot be established from the various stochastic approximation theorems (see Chapter 9).

Comments: (i) The above theorem is valid even when the pattern vector $\mathbf{x}$ can assume only a finite number of distinct (real) values, say $\mathbf{x}^{(1)},\ldots, \mathbf{x}^{(N)}$ provided the assumption (B1) is replaced by the assumption (B1)′.

(B1)′: The probabilities $P(\mathbf{x} = \mathbf{x}^{(i)})$ are not zero and $\sum_{i=1}^{n} P(\mathbf{x} = \mathbf{x}^{(i)}) = 1$.

(ii) The condition $\hat{\eta} \neq 0$ may need some explanation. When $\hat{\eta} = 0$, the probability of the given classification of sample being correct is 0.5; that is, we are not given any information at all about the classification of the training samples. Hence, it is futile to expect the algorithm to converge in the case $\hat{\eta} = 0$.

(iii) Even when $\hat{\eta} = 1$, that is, the classification of the training samples is exactly known, the gain sequence $\rho(k)$ *must satisfy* the condition in Eq. (3.24) if we want the algorithm to converge to the value $\boldsymbol{\alpha}^*$ defined earlier.

D. *Proof of Theorem* 2

Let

$$\tilde{\boldsymbol{\alpha}}(k) = \boldsymbol{\alpha}(k) - \boldsymbol{\alpha}^* \qquad \tilde{\eta}(k) = (\eta(k) - \hat{\eta})/\hat{\eta}, \qquad \boldsymbol{\varphi}(\mathbf{x}(k)) \triangleq \boldsymbol{\varphi}(k) \tag{3.25}$$

Substituting for $z(\mathbf{x}(k))$ from Eq. (3.18) and subtracting $\boldsymbol{\alpha}^*$ from both sides of Eq. (S–7), we get

$$\begin{aligned}\tilde{\boldsymbol{\alpha}}(k+1) = \tilde{\boldsymbol{\alpha}}(k) &+ \rho(k)\, \boldsymbol{\varphi}(k)(\operatorname{sgn} f^o(\mathbf{x}(k)) - \operatorname{sgn} f_k(\mathbf{x}(k)))\\ &+ \rho(k)\, \tilde{\eta}(k)\, \boldsymbol{\varphi}(k) \operatorname{sgn} f^o(\mathbf{x}(k))\end{aligned} \tag{3.26}$$

Scalar multiply Eq. (3.26) with itself and take expectation given $\tilde{\boldsymbol{\alpha}}(k)$

$$\begin{aligned}E\{\|\tilde{\boldsymbol{\alpha}}(k+1)\|^2 \mid \tilde{\boldsymbol{\alpha}}(k)\} = [\|\tilde{\boldsymbol{\alpha}}(k)\|^2] &+ E\{2\rho(k)\, \tilde{\boldsymbol{\alpha}}'(k)\, \boldsymbol{\varphi}(k)\\ &\times (\operatorname{sgn} f^o(\mathbf{x}(k)) - \operatorname{sgn} f_k(\mathbf{x}(k))) \mid \tilde{\boldsymbol{\alpha}}(k)\}\\ &+ E\{2\rho(k)\, \tilde{\eta}(k)\, \tilde{\boldsymbol{\alpha}}'(k)\, \boldsymbol{\varphi}(k) \operatorname{sgn} f^o(\mathbf{x}(k)) \mid \tilde{\boldsymbol{\alpha}}(k)\}\\ &+ E\{\rho^2(k)\|\boldsymbol{\varphi}(k)\|^2((\operatorname{sgn} f^o(\mathbf{x}(k)) - \operatorname{sgn} f_k(\mathbf{x}(k)))^2\\ &+ (\tilde{\eta}(k))^2) \mid \tilde{\boldsymbol{\alpha}}(k)\}\end{aligned} \tag{3.27}$$

The expectation terms in Eq. (3.27) will be evaluated individually.

$$\begin{aligned}\text{II term in Eq. (3.27)} &= 2\rho(k)\, E\{(f_k(\mathbf{x}(k)) - f^*(\mathbf{x}(k))\\ &\qquad \times (\operatorname{sgn} f^o(\mathbf{x}(k)) - \operatorname{sgn} f_k(\mathbf{x}(k))) \mid \boldsymbol{\alpha}(k)\}\\ &= 2\rho(k)[-J(\boldsymbol{\alpha}(k)) - E\{f^*(\mathbf{x}(k))\\ &\qquad \times (\operatorname{sgn} f^o(\mathbf{x}(k)) - \operatorname{sgn} f_k(\mathbf{x}(k))) \mid \boldsymbol{\alpha}(k)\}]\\ &\leqslant 2\rho(k)[-J(\boldsymbol{\alpha}^*) - E\{f^*(\mathbf{x}(k))\\ &\qquad \times (\operatorname{sgn} f^o(\mathbf{x}(k)) - \operatorname{sgn} f_k(\mathbf{x}(k))) \mid \boldsymbol{\alpha}(k)\}]\\ &= -2\rho(k)\, E\{g\{\boldsymbol{\alpha}^*, \boldsymbol{\alpha}(k), \mathbf{x}(k)) \mid \boldsymbol{\alpha}(k)\} \qquad (3.28)\end{aligned}$$

where

$$g(\boldsymbol{\alpha}^*, \boldsymbol{\alpha}(k), \mathbf{x}) \triangleq f^*(\mathbf{x})(\operatorname{sgn} f^*(\mathbf{x}) - \operatorname{sgn} f_k(\mathbf{x})) \qquad (3.29)$$

By assumption (B3),

$$\text{III term in Eq. (3.27)} = 0 \qquad (3.30)$$

By assumptions (B1) and (B3)

$$\text{IV term in Eq. (3.27)} \leqslant \rho^2(k)\, c_1\,, \qquad 0 < c_1 < \infty \qquad (3.31)$$

Substituting Eqs. (3.28), (3.30), and (3.31) in Eq. (3.27) and taking expectation over $\boldsymbol{\alpha}(k)$ we get

$$E\{\| \tilde{\boldsymbol{\alpha}}(k+1)\|^2\} \leqslant E\{\| \tilde{\boldsymbol{\alpha}}(k)\|^2\} - 2\rho(k)\, E\{g(\boldsymbol{\alpha}^*, \boldsymbol{\alpha}(k), \mathbf{x}(k))\} + \rho^2(k)\, c_1 \qquad (3.32)$$

Repeated use of Eq. (3.32) gives us the following expression

$$0 \leqslant E\{\| \tilde{\boldsymbol{\alpha}}(k+1)\|^2\} \leqslant E\{\| \tilde{\boldsymbol{\alpha}}(1)\|^2\} + c_1 \sum_{j=1}^{k} \rho^2(j) - \sum_{j=1}^{k} \rho(j)\, E\{g(\boldsymbol{\alpha}^*, \boldsymbol{\alpha}(j), \mathbf{x}(j))\}$$

or

$$\sum_{j=1}^{k} \rho(j)\, E\{g(\boldsymbol{\alpha}^*, \boldsymbol{\alpha}(j), \mathbf{x}(j))\} \leqslant E\{\| \tilde{\boldsymbol{\alpha}}(1)\|^2\} + c_1 \sum_{j=1}^{k} \rho^2(j) \qquad (3.33)$$

Using Eq. (3.24), Eq. (3.33) becomes

$$\lim_{k\to\infty} \sum_{j=1}^{k} \rho(j)\, E\{g(\boldsymbol{\alpha}^*, \boldsymbol{\alpha}(j), \mathbf{x}(j))\} < \infty \qquad (3.34)$$

Since $g(\boldsymbol{\alpha}^*, \boldsymbol{\alpha}(j), \mathbf{x}(j))$ is nonnegative and $\sum_{j=1}^{\infty} \rho(j)$ is infinite, Eq. (3.34) implies

$$\lim_{j\to\infty} E\{g(\boldsymbol{\alpha}^*, \boldsymbol{\alpha}(j), \mathbf{x}(j))\} = 0 \qquad (3.35)$$

But $g(\boldsymbol{\alpha}^*, \boldsymbol{\alpha}(j), \mathbf{x}(j)) = |f^*(\mathbf{x}(j))|\, |\operatorname{sgn} f^*(\mathbf{x}(j)) - \operatorname{sgn} f_j(\mathbf{x}(j))|$. By assumption (B2), $\mathbf{x}(j)$ is independent of $\boldsymbol{\alpha}(j)$, since the latter is only a function of the samples $\mathbf{x}(k)$, $k < j$. Hence

$$E\{g(\boldsymbol{\alpha}^*, \boldsymbol{\alpha}(j), \mathbf{x}(j))\} = \int_{\mathbf{x}\in\Omega} | f^*(\mathbf{x})|_{\boldsymbol{\alpha}(j)} E\{| \operatorname{sgn} f^*(\mathbf{x}) - \operatorname{sgn}(\boldsymbol{\alpha}'(j)\, \boldsymbol{\varphi}(\mathbf{x}) + t) \mid \mathbf{x}\} \times p(\mathbf{x})\, dx_1 ,..., dx_m \tag{3.36}$$

where the expectation on the right hand side is taken over $\boldsymbol{\alpha}(j)$ given $\mathbf{x}$. Equations (3.35) and (3.36) imply

$$\lim_{k\to\infty} E\{| \operatorname{sgn} f^*(\mathbf{x}) - \operatorname{sgn}(\boldsymbol{\alpha}'(k)\, \boldsymbol{\varphi}(\mathbf{x}) + t)| \mid \mathbf{x}\} = 0$$
$$\forall \mathbf{x} \in \Omega \quad \text{for which } f^*(\mathbf{x}) \neq 0$$

This completes the proof of the Theorem 2.

IV. Overlapping Classes

In this section, we will consider the two class problem where there may not be a unique class associated with every pattern $\mathbf{x}$. As mentioned in Section I, a pattern $\mathbf{x}$ is said to belong to class ω_i, if it is drawn from a population with probability density $p_i(\mathbf{x})$. The decision rule which gives rise to minimum probability of misclassification is given below

$$\operatorname{sgn}(g(\mathbf{x})) = i \Rightarrow \mathbf{x} \text{ is placed in } \omega_i \qquad i = +1 \text{ or } -1$$

$$g(\mathbf{x}) = p(y = 1 \mid \mathbf{x}) - p(y = -1 \mid \mathbf{x})$$

At the cost of repetition, we point to the lack of any information concerning the probability functions $p(y = i \mid \mathbf{x})$, $p_i(\mathbf{x})$, $i = \pm 1$. Our present intention is to recover the function $g(\mathbf{x})$ or a best approximation to it solely from a sequence of sample pairs $\{(\mathbf{x}(k), y(k)), k = 1, 2,...,\}$. We will consider the two cases separately.

A. *Approximations to the Optimal Decision Function*

We seek an approximation to $g(\mathbf{x})$ of the following form

$$\sum_{i=1}^{n} \alpha_i \varphi_i(\mathbf{x}) = \boldsymbol{\alpha}' \boldsymbol{\varphi}(\mathbf{x})$$

The functions $\varphi_1(\mathbf{x})$, $\varphi_2(\mathbf{x})$,..., $\varphi_n(\mathbf{x})$ are linearly independent. The unknown parameters α_1, α_2,. α_n are determined by minimizing a suitable criterion function. The most popular among these is the minimum mean square error criterion function

$$J_4(\boldsymbol{\alpha}) = E(g(\mathbf{x}) - \boldsymbol{\alpha}' \boldsymbol{\varphi}(\mathbf{x}))^2$$

Let $\boldsymbol{\alpha}^*$ be the value of $\boldsymbol{\alpha}$ which minimizes $J_4(\boldsymbol{\alpha})$

$$\boldsymbol{\alpha}^* \triangleq [E(\boldsymbol{\varphi}(\mathbf{x})\,\boldsymbol{\varphi}'(\mathbf{x}))]^{-1}\,E[\boldsymbol{\varphi}(\mathbf{x})\,g(\mathbf{x})]$$

Let $\hat{g}(\mathbf{x})$ = optimal linear approximation to $g(\mathbf{x}) = \boldsymbol{\alpha}^{*\prime}\boldsymbol{\varphi}(\mathbf{x})$.

It is needless to say that if

$$g(\mathbf{x}) = \sum_{i=1}^{n} \theta_i \varphi_i(\mathbf{x})$$

then $\boldsymbol{\alpha}^* = \boldsymbol{\theta}$ and $\hat{g}(\mathbf{x}) = g(\mathbf{x})$.

To evaluate $\boldsymbol{\alpha}^*$ from the samples we will rewrite $J_4(\boldsymbol{\alpha})$ utilizing the fact that $E(y \mid \mathbf{x}) = g(\mathbf{x})$

$$J_4(\boldsymbol{\alpha}) = E(y - \boldsymbol{\alpha}'\boldsymbol{\varphi}(\mathbf{x}))^2 + E(y - E(y \mid \mathbf{x}))^2$$

Since the second term in $J_4(\boldsymbol{\alpha})$ is independent of $\boldsymbol{\alpha}$, $\boldsymbol{\alpha}^*$ also minimizes the first term or $\bar{J}_4(\boldsymbol{\alpha})$

$$\bar{J}_4(\boldsymbol{\alpha}) = E(y - \boldsymbol{\alpha}'\boldsymbol{\varphi}(\mathbf{x}))^2$$

A stochastic gradient method for finding the minimum of $\bar{J}_4(\boldsymbol{\alpha})$ can be written as follows

$$\begin{aligned} &\boldsymbol{\alpha}(k+1) = \boldsymbol{\alpha}(k) + \rho(k)(y(k) - \boldsymbol{\alpha}'(k)\,\boldsymbol{\varphi}(k))\,\boldsymbol{\varphi}(k) \\ &\rho(k) \geqslant 0 \qquad \sum_k \rho(k) = \infty \qquad \sum_k \rho^2(k) < \infty \end{aligned} \tag{S-8}$$

It has been shown (Blaydon and Ho, 1966; Kashyap and Blaydon, 1966) that $\boldsymbol{\alpha}(k)$ in (S-8) tends to $\boldsymbol{\alpha}^*$ in the mean square sense and with probability one if the following conditions are satisfied.

(C1) The samples $\mathbf{x}(k)$, $k = 1, 2,\ldots$, are statistically independent

(C2) $E[\boldsymbol{\varphi}\boldsymbol{\varphi}'] > 0$, $\quad E[\boldsymbol{\varphi}\boldsymbol{\varphi}'\boldsymbol{\varphi}\boldsymbol{\varphi}'] > 0$

(C3) $E\,\|\,\boldsymbol{\varphi}g\,\| < \infty$, $\quad E\,|\,g\,| < \infty$, $\quad E\,\|\,\boldsymbol{\varphi}\boldsymbol{\varphi}'\boldsymbol{\varphi}g\,\| < \infty$, $E\,\|\,\boldsymbol{\alpha}(0)\|^2 < \infty$, $\boldsymbol{\alpha}(0)$ otherwise arbitrary.

We can also compute $\boldsymbol{\alpha}^*$ by minimizing $\bar{J}_4(\boldsymbol{\alpha})$ with the aid of the stochastic version of Newton's method in the hope of getting faster convergence. Note that

$$\frac{\partial^2 \bar{J}_4(\boldsymbol{\alpha})}{\partial \boldsymbol{\alpha}^2} = 2E(\boldsymbol{\varphi}\boldsymbol{\varphi}')$$

If we knew $E(\boldsymbol{\varphi}\boldsymbol{\varphi}')$, then Newton's method will have the following appearance

$$\boldsymbol{\alpha}(k+1) = \boldsymbol{\alpha}(k) + \rho[E(\boldsymbol{\varphi}\boldsymbol{\varphi}')]^{-1}\,\boldsymbol{\varphi}(k)[y(k) - \boldsymbol{\alpha}'(k)\,\boldsymbol{\varphi}(k)]$$

Since we do not know $E(\boldsymbol{\varphi}\boldsymbol{\varphi}')$, we have to recursively estimate it. Thus, the algorithm can be written in the following form

$$\begin{aligned} \boldsymbol{\alpha}(k+1) &= \boldsymbol{\alpha}(k) + B(k+1)\,\boldsymbol{\varphi}(k)[y(k) - \boldsymbol{\alpha}'(k)\,\boldsymbol{\varphi}(k)] \\ B(k+1) &= B(k) - \frac{B(k)\,\boldsymbol{\varphi}(k)\,\boldsymbol{\varphi}'(k)\,B(k)}{1 + \boldsymbol{\varphi}'(k)\,B(k)\,\boldsymbol{\varphi}(k)}, \qquad B(0) > 0 \end{aligned} \tag{S-9}$$

The matrix $B(k)$ in (S-9) has the following interpretation

$$B(k) \triangleq \left(B^{-1}(0) + \sum_{j=1}^{k} \boldsymbol{\varphi}(j)\,\boldsymbol{\varphi}'(j)\right)$$

(S-9) converges to the quantity $\boldsymbol{\alpha}^*$ with probability one under the conditions (C1)–(C3) mentioned earlier. Additional details on schemes (S-8) and (S-9) such as their relative rates of convergence, possibility of relaxation of assumption (C1), etc., can be found in the chapter Stochastic Approximation.

B. *Recovery of Optimal Decision Function*

Given an infinite set of sample pairs $\{(\mathbf{x}(k), y(k)),\ k = 1, 2, \ldots,\}$, it is possible to recover $g(\mathbf{x})$, the optimal decision function involving computations in the function space.

In the first algorithm, the estimate for $f(\mathbf{x})$ is a linear combination of the potential function evaluated at various points. We can regard the scheme as a generalization of (S-8). We will mention it briefly since it has been treated in greater detail in the chapter on stochastic approximation.

Let $g_k(\mathbf{x})$ = approximation to $g(\mathbf{x})$ at the kth stage involving the sample pairs

$$\{(\mathbf{x}(j), y(j)) \qquad j = 1, 2, \ldots, k-1\}$$

The algorithm can be written as follows

$$\begin{gathered} g_{k+1}(\mathbf{x}) = g_k(\mathbf{x}) + \rho(k)(y(k) - g_k(\mathbf{x}(k)))\,K(\mathbf{x}, \mathbf{x}(k)) \\ \rho(k) \geqslant 0 \qquad \sum_k \rho(k) = \infty \qquad \sum_k \rho^2(k) < \infty \end{gathered} \tag{S-10}$$

where $K(\mathbf{a}, \mathbf{b})$ is the potential function mentioned earlier in Section IIC. It is possible to show (Braverman, 1965) that $g_k(\mathbf{x})$ tends to $g(\mathbf{x})$ in probability, if the assumptions (C1)–(C3) are satisfied and in addition $g(\mathbf{x})$ has the following infinite expansion in terms of a set of orthogonal functions $\varphi_i(\mathbf{x})$

$$g(\mathbf{x}) = \sum_{i=1}^{\infty} \theta_i \varphi_i(\mathbf{x}) \qquad \sum_{i=1}^{\infty} \theta_i^2 < \infty$$

In the second algorithm, the unknown function is recovered as a linear combination of another type of function, the so-called window function $H(\mathbf{x})$ evaluated at various points. Let us introduce the function $H(\mathbf{x})$ having the following properties:

$$H(\mathbf{x}) \geqslant 0 \ \forall \text{ all } \mathbf{x} \in R^m$$

$$\text{Sup}|\, H(\mathbf{x})| < \infty$$

$$\int H(\mathbf{x})\, d\mathbf{x} = 1$$

$$H^* = \int \|\, \mathbf{x} \,\|\, H(\mathbf{x})\, d\mathbf{x} < \infty$$

Some examples of the function $H(\mathbf{x})$ [Parzen, 1960; Van Ryzen, 1966] are

$$\text{(i)} \quad H(\mathbf{x}) = \begin{cases} (2C)^{-m} & \text{if } \ |\, x_i \,| \leqslant C, \quad i = 1,..., m; \quad C > 0 \\ 0 \text{ otherwise} \end{cases}$$

$$\text{(ii)} \quad H(\mathbf{x}) = 2^{-m} \exp \left\{ - \sum_{i=1}^{m} |\, x_i \,| \right\} \quad \text{for all } x$$

$$\text{(iii)} \quad H(\mathbf{x}) = \left(\prod_{i=1}^{m} |\, x_i \,| \right) C^{-2m} \quad \text{if } \ |\, x_i \,| \leqslant C, \quad i = 1,..., m; \quad C > 0$$

Define

$$H_k(\mathbf{c}, \mathbf{d}) = (a(k))^{-m}\, H \left(\frac{\mathbf{c} - \mathbf{d}}{a(k)} \right)$$

where **c**, **d** are two m-vectors and the scalar gain $a(k)$ is defined below

$$a(k) = k^{-q} \qquad 0 < q < \frac{1}{2m}$$

Construct the following sequence

$$D_k(\mathbf{x}) = \frac{1}{k} \sum_{j=1}^{k} y(j)\, H_j(\mathbf{x}, \mathbf{x}(j))$$

$$D_{k+1}(\mathbf{x}) = D_k(\mathbf{x}) + \frac{1}{k+1} (\, y(k+1)\, H_{k+1}(\mathbf{x}, \mathbf{x}(k+1)) - D_k(\mathbf{x})) \qquad k \geqslant 0$$

$$D_0(\mathbf{x}) = 0 \qquad \text{(S-11)}$$

Then, it has been shown by Wolverton and Wagner (1967) that

$$\lim_{i \to \infty} \int (D_i(\mathbf{x}) - p(\mathbf{x})\, g(\mathbf{x}))^2\, d\mathbf{x} = 0 \quad \text{with probability one.}$$

It should be noted that, by this method, we get the function $(p(\mathbf{x})\, g(\mathbf{x}))$ and not $g(\mathbf{x})$. But, for the decision rule, it does not matter whether we use $(p(\mathbf{x})\, g(\mathbf{x}))$ or $g(\mathbf{x})$ since both have the same sign everywhere.

V. Multiclass Algorithms

In this section, we will briefly deal with the classification of patterns which may arise from more than two classes. Using only samples of known classification, we would like to arrive at decision rules which categorize any new sample with unknown classification into the proper class. Most of the techniques to be presented here have very close analogy to those mentioned earlier in the two class problem. We will label the classes $\omega_1 ,..., \omega_r$.

As before, we can divide the problems into two categories which are

(i) Nonoverlapping classes.

(ii) At least two classes are overlapping.

In the former case, the information about classification is contained in the separating functions $f_1(\mathbf{x}),..., f_r(\mathbf{x})$ which satisfy the conditions in Eqs. (3.37) and (3.38)

$$f_i(\mathbf{x}) > 0 \Leftrightarrow \mathbf{x} \quad \text{is } \omega_i \qquad i = 1, 2,..., r \tag{3.37}$$

$$f_i(\mathbf{x}) > 0 \Rightarrow f_j(\mathbf{x}) \not> 0 \; \forall j \neq i \qquad i = 1, 2,..., r \tag{3.38}$$

In the case of overlapping classes, recall that we have to make the notion of a pattern belonging to a class precisely as in Section I.

With each class ω_i , we can associate an optimal decision function $g_i(\mathbf{x})$ with the associated decision rule (3.39)

$$\begin{aligned} g_i(\mathbf{x}) &> 0 \Rightarrow \text{classify } \mathbf{x} \text{ in } \omega_i \\ &< 0 \Rightarrow \text{no decision} \end{aligned} \tag{3.39}$$

Thus, the classification problems are entirely characterized either by the functions $f_i(\mathbf{x})$, $i = 1,..., r$ or $g_i(\mathbf{x})$, $i = 1,..., r$. We would like to determine the approximation to these unknown functions using only sample pairs.

As far as the determination of approximations to $f_i(\mathbf{x})$ or $g_i(\mathbf{x})$ is concerned, we need consider only an equivalent two-class problem, the classes being (ω_i) and (not ω_i). This can be done by any of the methods mentioned earlier. Also note that, while determining the approximation to $g_i(\mathbf{x})$, we do not care about other functions like $g_j(\mathbf{x})$, $j \neq i$.

The principal appeal of the above procedure is simplicity. However, it suffers from a serious disadvantage. Suppose the decision rule that is being used is of the form in Eq. (3.39) with the functions $g_i(\mathbf{x})$ replaced by the known approximations $\hat{g}_i(\mathbf{x})$. Since the approximations *do* not satisfy the condition in Eq. (3.40), the regions given by various decision functions may be overlapping

$$\hat{g}_i(\mathbf{x}) > 0 \nRightarrow \hat{g}_j(\mathbf{x}) \leqslant 0 \; \forall j \neq i \qquad j, i = 1,..., r \tag{3.40}$$

To remove this difficulty, we should choose our decision functions and rules so that the entire decision space should be divided into r *nonoverlapping* parts. This implies that we use fewer than r decision functions in the decision rule. The rest of the section will be devoted to the determination of decision rules which give rise to unambiguous decisions.

To begin with, let us assume that the $r = 2^{r_1}$, where r_1 is an integer. We will define the class indicator $\mathbf{y}$ for every pattern $\mathbf{x}$. $\mathbf{y}$ is an r_1-dimensional vector whose components are ± 1. Such a vector can assume only 2^{r_1} different values, $\mathbf{y}^{(1)}, \mathbf{y}^{(2)},..., \mathbf{y}^{(r)}$. We will associate the value $\mathbf{y}^{(i)}$ with class ω_i, for all $i = 1, 2,..., r$. For example, if $r = 4$, $r_1 = 2$. There are four values of $\mathbf{y}$. If

$$\mathbf{x} \sim \omega_1 \qquad \mathbf{y}^{(1)'} = (1, 1)$$

$$\mathbf{x} \sim \omega_2 \qquad \mathbf{y}^{(2)'} = (1, -1)$$

$$\mathbf{x} \sim \omega_3 \qquad \mathbf{y}^{(3)'} = (-1, 1)$$

$$\mathbf{x} \sim \omega_4 \qquad \mathbf{y}^{(4)'} = (-1, -1)$$

We will treat the case of overlapping and nonoverlapping classes separately.

A. *Nonoverlapping Classes*

By definition, there exists the separating functions $f_1(\mathbf{x}),..., f_r(\mathbf{x})$ satisfying Eqs. (3.37) and (3.38).

Equation (3.38) suggests that the possibility of characterization of the classes by functions whose number is smaller than r. As a matter of fact, it is possible to show, after some manipulation, the existence of r_1 functions $h_1(\mathbf{x}),..., h_{r_1}(\mathbf{x})$, so that

$$\operatorname{sgn} \mathbf{h}(\mathbf{x}) = \mathbf{y}^{(i)} \Leftrightarrow \mathbf{x} \sim \omega_i \qquad i = 1,..., r$$

where

$$\mathbf{h}'(\mathbf{x}) = (h_1(\mathbf{x}),..., h_{r_1}(\mathbf{x})) \qquad (r_1\text{–vector})$$

Our aim is to obtain a best approximation to the unknown vector function $h(\mathbf{x})$ solely in terms of the sample pairs $\{(\mathbf{x}(k), \mathbf{y}(k)), k = 1, 2, \ldots,\}$. The approximating function will have the form $A\boldsymbol{\varphi}(\mathbf{x}) + \mathbf{t}$ where A is an $r_1 \times n$ matrix of undetermined coefficients, $\boldsymbol{\varphi}(\mathbf{x})$ is the n-vector of known independent functions mentioned earlier, and $\mathbf{t}$ is an r_1-vector threshold. A is determined by minimizing the criterion functions $\bar{J}_2(A)$ and $\bar{J}_3(A)$ which are analogs of $J_2(\boldsymbol{\alpha})$ and $J_3(\boldsymbol{\alpha})$ mentioned earlier in Section II.

$$\bar{J}_2(A) = E[(\text{sgn}(A\boldsymbol{\varphi}(\mathbf{x}) + \mathbf{t}) - \text{sgn}\,\mathbf{h}(\mathbf{x}))'(A\boldsymbol{\varphi} + \mathbf{t}) \mid A]$$

$$\bar{J}_3(A) = E[\| \text{sgn}(A\boldsymbol{\varphi}(\mathbf{x}) + \mathbf{t}) - \text{sgn}\,\mathbf{h}(\mathbf{x})\|^2 \mid A]$$

As before, we can give algorithms of finding numerically the minimum value of $\bar{J}_2(A)$ and $\bar{J}_3(A)$. As an example, we will give a gradient algorithm for minimizing $\bar{J}_2(A)$. Let

$$A(k+1) = A(k) + \rho(k)(\mathbf{y} - \text{sgn}(A(k)\,\boldsymbol{\varphi}(k) + \mathbf{t}))\,\boldsymbol{\varphi}'(k) \tag{S-12}$$

where

$$\sum_k \rho(k) = \infty \qquad \sum_k \rho^2(k) < \infty$$

Let

$$A^* = \text{Arg}[\underset{A}{\text{Min}}\ \bar{J}_2(A)]$$

$A(k)$ tends to the optimum value A^* with probability one, and in the mean square sense. The final approximating function has the form

$$\hat{\mathbf{h}}(\mathbf{x}) = A^*\boldsymbol{\varphi}(\mathbf{x}) + \mathbf{t}$$

and the corresponding decision rule is

$$\{\text{sgn}(\hat{\mathbf{h}}(\mathbf{x})) = \mathbf{y}^i\} \Rightarrow \{\text{classify } \mathbf{x} \text{ in } \omega_i\}$$

B. *Overlapping Classes*

The optimal decision rule for classification is given below

$$\{p(\mathbf{y} = \mathbf{y}^i \mid \mathbf{x}) \geqslant p(\mathbf{y} = \mathbf{y}^j \mid \mathbf{x})\ \forall j\} \Rightarrow \text{classify } \mathbf{x} \text{ in } \omega_i \tag{3.41}$$

We could like to approximate the probability function $p(\mathbf{y} \mid \mathbf{x})$ using only the samples. As a first step, we will consider only approximation of the form $\mathbf{y}'A\boldsymbol{\varphi}(\mathbf{x})$ where A is an $r_1 \times n$ matrix of undetermined parameters and $\boldsymbol{\varphi}(\mathbf{x})$ is an n-vector of linearly independent functions. The criterion function $\bar{J}_4(A)$ for choosing A is similar to the function $J_4(\alpha)$ introduced earlier.

$$\bar{J}_4(A) = E \sum_{\mathbf{y}} (p(\mathbf{y} \mid \mathbf{x}) - \mathbf{y}' A \boldsymbol{\varphi}(\mathbf{x}))^2$$

where the summation is over all the r values of $\mathbf{y}$. Minimizing $\bar{J}_4(A)$ with respect to A, we get the following equation whose solution gives us the optimum value A^{**}

$$E \left[\sum_{\mathbf{y}} (p(\mathbf{y} \mid \mathbf{x}) - \mathbf{y}' A \boldsymbol{\varphi}(\mathbf{x}))\, \mathbf{y} \boldsymbol{\varphi}'(\mathbf{x}) \right] = 0 \tag{3.42}$$

Note that

$$\sum_{\mathbf{y}} \mathbf{y}' A \boldsymbol{\varphi}(x)\, \mathbf{y} = r A \boldsymbol{\varphi}(x) \tag{3.43}$$

Using Eq. (3.43), Eq. (3.42) gives us

$$E[(\mathbf{y} - r A \boldsymbol{\varphi}(\mathbf{x}))\, \boldsymbol{\varphi}'(\mathbf{x})] = 0 \tag{3.44}$$

or

$$A^{**} = \frac{1}{r} [E(\boldsymbol{\varphi}\boldsymbol{\varphi}')]^{-1} E(\mathbf{y}\boldsymbol{\varphi}')$$

To evaluate A^{**} numerically, we have to solve the regression Eq. (3.44) using sample pairs $\{(\mathbf{x}(k), \mathbf{y}(k), k = 1, 2, \ldots,\}$. This can be done as in (S-8). The resulting scheme (S-13) is given below

$$\begin{gathered} A(k+1) = A(k) + \rho(k)(\mathbf{y}(k) - A(k)\, \boldsymbol{\varphi}(k))\, \boldsymbol{\varphi}'(k) \\ \sum_k \rho(k) = \infty \qquad \text{and} \qquad \sum_k \rho^2(k) < \infty \end{gathered} \tag{S-13}$$

As before, $A(k)$ tends to A^{**} with probability one and in mean square sense.

Having obtained the approximation $\hat{p}(\mathbf{y} \mid \mathbf{x}) = \mathbf{y}' A^{**} \boldsymbol{\varphi}(\mathbf{x})$ for $p(\mathbf{y} \mid \mathbf{x})$, we can use the decision rule (3.41) using $\hat{p}(\mathbf{y} \mid \mathbf{x})$. Because of the fact that $\mathbf{y}$ occurs linearly in $\hat{p}(\mathbf{y} \mid \mathbf{x})$, we can simplify the decision rule as follows

$$\operatorname{sgn}(A^{**} \boldsymbol{\varphi}(\mathbf{x})) = \mathbf{y}^{(i)} \Rightarrow \text{classify } \mathbf{x} \text{ in } \omega_i$$

We could have chosen more sophisticated forms of approximation for $p(\mathbf{y} \mid \mathbf{x})$ by including terms like $y_i y_j$, $y_i y_j y_k$, etc., in it. This will be considered in another chapter.

As a matter of fact, we can recover the entire function $p(\mathbf{y} \mid \mathbf{x})$ by iteration in the function space. Before concluding, we note that our analysis was relevant only for the case when the number of classes r

equals 2^{r_1}, where r_1 is an integer. If r_1 is not an integer, we would have to divide some of the classes into two parts, and thus, increase r so that $\log_2 r$ is an integer.

VI. Comparison and Discussion of the Various Algorithms

We have developed a number of algorithms for finding the optimal approximations to the unknown optimal decision function or separating function based only on the samples. Most of these impose very mild conditions on the unknown function for convergence. All of them are error-correcting type algorithms. For every decision function $d(\mathbf{x})$ obtained from the algorithms in the two-class problems, we can get a measure of its generalization ability by approximately evaluating the probability of misclassification P_d associated with $d(\mathbf{x})$.

$$P_d = 1 + \int_{d(\mathbf{x})<0} g(\mathbf{x}) \left(\prod_{i=1}^{m} dx_i\right)$$

where

$$g(\mathbf{x}) = p(y = 1 \mid \mathbf{x}) - p(y = -1 \mid \mathbf{x})$$

Similarly in the multiclass problem, if we use the decision rule, Eq. (3.41), with $p(\mathbf{y} \mid \mathbf{x})$ replaced by a function $h(\mathbf{x}, \mathbf{y})$, then the corresponding probability of misclassification p_h is given below

$$P_h = \sum_{i=1}^{r} \int_{\Omega_x} p(\mathbf{y} = \mathbf{y}^{(i)} \mid \mathbf{x}) \left(\prod_{j=1}^{m} dx_j\right)$$

where $\Omega_x = \{\mathbf{x} : h(\mathbf{x}, \mathbf{y}) > h(\mathbf{x}, \mathbf{y}^{(i)})$ for some $\mathbf{y}$ among $\mathbf{y}^{(1)},\ldots, \mathbf{y}^{(r)}\}$. We can get reliable estimates of $g(\mathbf{x})$ or $p(\mathbf{y} \mid \mathbf{x})$ only when we have a large number of samples of known classifications.

The choice of the algorithm for any occasion depends on a number of factors like the complexity of the resulting decision function, convergence rate of the algorithm, etc. We will first consider the two-class problems only, though similar comments can be made with respect to multiple-class problems also. The schemes (S-1), (S-4), (S-5), (S-7), (S-8), (S-9) result in a decision function of comparatively simple form whereas schemes (S-6), (S-10), and (S-11) result in decision functions having infinite number of terms in them. Similarly, when the number of available samples is small, it may be preferable to use algorithms having a least square fit interpretation like case (i) of (S-1) and (S-9).

Throughout this chapter, we have made a distinction between problems having overlapping classes and these having nonoverlapping classes. However, it is important to note that we cannot ascertain whether the classes are overlapping or not based only on a finite set of observed distinct sample pairs. As long as no pattern is observed to belong to more than one class and the number of patterns is finite, it is always possible to construct a separating surface to separate the patterns of one class from those of the other. It is clear that the algorithms developed in connection with the overlapping classes can be used with nonoverlapping classes as well. The other part of the question is what happens when we apply algorithms like (S-10) and (S-5) supposedly meant for nonoverlapping classes to a problem with overlapping classes. Recall that the criterion function associated with these algorithms can be rewritten as

$$J_2(\boldsymbol{\alpha}) = \tfrac{1}{2}E[(\operatorname{sgn}(\boldsymbol{\alpha}'\boldsymbol{\varphi}(\mathbf{x}) + t) - y)(\boldsymbol{\alpha}'\boldsymbol{\varphi}(\mathbf{x}) + t) \mid \boldsymbol{\alpha}]$$

$$J_3(\boldsymbol{\alpha}) = E| \operatorname{sgn}(\boldsymbol{\alpha}'\boldsymbol{\varphi}(\mathbf{x}) + t) - y |$$

These criterion functions can be considered to be reasonable whether the classes are overlapping or not. Hence, the value of $\boldsymbol{\alpha}$ we get by minimizing these functions by using algorithms (S-4) and (S-5) respectively still leads to a reasonable decision function. If, in addition, the classes were nonoverlapping, then these decision functions are also optimal approximations to the separating function.

Summing up, a reasonable course of action is to pick an algorithm which has the maximum generalization ability. But, we can get a measure of the generalization ability only when we have a large number of sample pairs.

References

Agmon, S., The relaxation method for linear inequalities. *Canadian J. Math. 6*, pp. 393–404 (1954).

Blaydon, C. C. and Ho, Y. C., On the abstraction problem in pattern recognition. *Proc. National Electron. Conf.* (1966).

Braverman, E. M., On the method of potential functions. *Automation and Remote Control 26*, No. 12 (1965).

Cover, T. M., Classification and generalization capabilities of linear threshold devices. Stanford Electron. Lab., Stanford, Calif., Rept. 6107–1 (1965).

Dantzig, G., "Linear Programming and Extensions." Princeton Univ. Press, Princeton, New Jersey, 1963.

Devyaterikov, I. P., Propoi, A. I., and Tsypkin, Ya. Z., Iterative learning algorithms for pattern recognition. *Automation and Remote Control*, pp. 108–207, January 1966.

Fan, K., On systems of linear inequalities in linear inequalities and related systems. (H. W. Kuhn and A. W. Tucker, eds.), *Ann. Math. Studies, No. 38*, 1956.

Ho, Y. C. and Kashyap, R. L., An algorithm for linear inequalities and its applications. *IEEE Trans. Electron. Comp., EC–14* pp. 683–688 (1965).

Ho, Y. C. and Kashyap, R. L., A class of iterative procedures for linear inequalities. *J. SIAM on Control 4*, pp. 112–115 (1966).

Kashyap, R. L., Pattern classification and switching theory. Tech. Rept. 483, Cruft Lab., Harvard Univ., Cambridge, Mass., 1965.

Kashyap, R. L. and Blaydon, C. C., Recovery of functions from noisy measurements taken at randomly selected points. *Proc. IEEE 54*, pp. 1127–1128 (1966).

Nilson, N. J., "Learning Machines." McGraw–Hill, New York, 1965.

Novikoff, A., On convergence proofs for perceptrons. *Proc. Symp. Math. Theory of Automata, 21*, Polytech. Inst. of Brooklyn, New York, pp. 615–622 (1963).

Parzen, E., On estimation of a probability density and mode. *Ann. Math. Stat. 33*, pp. 1065–1076 (1962).

Saaty, T. L., "Mathematical Methods of Operations Research." McGraw–Hill, New York, 1959.

Sebestyen, G., "Decision Making Processes in Pattern Recognition." Macmillan, New York, 1962.

Van Ryzin, J., A stochastic aposteriori updating algorithm for pattern recognition. Tech. Rept. 121, Dept. of Statistics, Stanford Univ., Stanford, Calif., 1966.

Venter, J. H., On the convergence of Kiefer–Wolfowitz approximation procedure. *Ann. Math. Stat. 38*, No. 4, pp. 1031–1036 (1967).

Walsh, J. L., A closed set of normal orthogonal functions. *Amer. J. Math. 45*, pp. 5–24 (1923).

Widrow, B. and Hoff, M. E., Adaptive Switching Circuits. Tech. Rept. No. 1553–1, Stanford Electron. Lab., Stanford, Calif., June 1960.

Winder, R. O., The status of threshold logic. *Proc. 1st Princeton Conf. Info. Science and Systems*, pp. 59–67 (1967).

4

S. S. Viglione

APPLICATIONS OF PATTERN RECOGNITION TECHNOLOGY

I. Introduction

Pattern recognition is concerned with the investigation of adaptive and analytic techniques for processing large amounts of data, the extraction of useful information to reduce the data, and the classification of the data as required. This research in many ways is closely related to the classification as done by humans—in fact the basis for much of the early work in the field was found in "brain" modeling (Rosenblatt, 1962).

In Chapters 1 and 2, as well as in Nilsson (1965), pattern recognition is discussed in terms of a statistical analysis where each pattern is considered as a vector in n-dimensional space. The goal of the recognition system is to define partitions in this space such that each region can be identified with a class of patterns.

Pattern recognition, as discussed and utilized in this chapter, will encompass both these approaches and will be considered as accomplished by comparing information derived from an input signal with similar data derived from known sample patterns (called paradigms or prototypes). The specification of these paradigms is accomplished adaptively utilizing a learning algorithm. Based on these comparisons, a decision is made as to the nature of the input pattern.

In many real problems, before deriving these paradigms, it becomes necessary to condition or format the input data to a form suitable for subsequent analysis. In performing this conditioning operation it may be possible to enhance the pattern to ease the recognition task. Since the intention of this chapter is to discuss pattern recognition applications, a third functional unit (that of preprocessing the input data) is introduced in the simplified block diagram of Fig. 1, Chapter 2. Various techniques for preprocessing or conditioning the input data are presented. This is followed by a discussion of several techniques for extracting features from the conditioned data and for the design of the classifier. A specific algorithm is detailed which provides for the specification and evaluation of features as the classifier is being designed. Several applications are then presented to demonstrate how these mechanisms of pattern recognition technology can be utilized to classify data resulting from a variety of sensory mechanisms.

The key to pattern recognition is invariance. For example, in photographic imagery analysis, it is desirable that the classification assigned to an object or pattern of interest be independent of the position of that pattern in the field, the aspect at which it is viewed, the background against which it is seen, partial obscuration of the pattern, minor changes within a pattern class, and changes in illumination or background noise. It is not too difficult to provide any one of these invariances. To provide all of the desired invariances with a practical amount of hardware, however, requires that the decision mechanism extract the essence of the patterns to be identified.

In the design of the pattern recognition system, three phases will be considered. These phases are illustrated in the block diagram of Fig. 1. The input pattern is normally a vector quantity made up of many components (i.e., the number of resolvable elements in a photograph, or the output from a bank of narrow band filters), hence the dimensionality of the input space may be large (see Chapter 1).

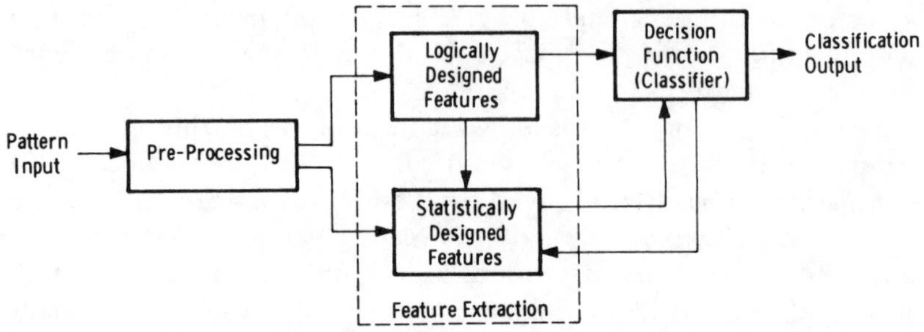

FIGURE 1. Pattern recognition mechanism

The purpose of signal conditioning, or "preprocessing," is to provide a convenient input format, to provide invariance, to provide in many cases a reduction in the dimensionality of the input data, and to emphasize aspects of the input signal which are deemed important. Preprocessing includes techniques such as scanning, edge enhancement, Fourier transformation, and autocorrelation.

An almost universal approach to pattern recognition is to extract properties or features from the original signal, and to perform the recognition on the feature profile of the input signal. This serves several functions. First, by reducing the input pattern to its essential features, the memory required for storing the paradigms is reduced to realistic levels. Secondly, by reducing the input pattern to independent features, a considerable amount of invariance to exact form is obtained. Finally, by extracting more than the minimum number of features required, a degree of invariance to noise and background may be achieved as the decision process then need not require a very high degree of matching between the input pattern and the paradigms.

Feature extraction can be accomplished in two phases. First, the designer constructs detectors for those features that he knows or suspects are important. These may prove to be inadequate, or may provide a format not suitable for the decision mechanism. Statistical feature extraction, in which a sample of preclassified patterns is analyzed, is used to augment the known feature list and to reformat the feature profile.

Most decision mechanisms are based on correlation. The distances of the feature profile from stored paradigms is computed, and are used to provide an appropriate classification for the pattern. There are a variety of methods for obtaining the paradigms, and for combining the distances into a decision.

The following sections describe the three phases of the pattern recognition mechanism in greater detail.

II. Pattern Recognition Mechanisms

A. *Signal Conditioning* (*Preprocessing*)

Perhaps the most arduous task in the field of pattern recognition is that of feature extraction. Difficult pattern recognition problems may involve the recognition of "target shapes," waveform shapes, or may involve a phenomenon which is not easily relatable to the notion of shape and hence may not be describable in geometric or functional terms. For this class of problems statistical design techniques can be used to provide useful features. In applying these statistical algorithms it is necessary to condition the inputs to the recognition device (and also the data base used to design the recognition device). A properly conditioned data base will simplify the design, instrumentation, and operation of the system. The data conditioning is performed by a preprocessor whose role as a component of the recognition system is to perform some or all of the following functions:

1. Enhancement
   (a) Strengthening features (i.e., edges, specific frequencies, etc.) which may be characteristic of the phenomena to be recognized.
   (b) "Centering" the input data within a sensory aperture.
2. Provide invariance to translations, rotations, and scale changes of the input data.
3. "Noise Suppression"
   (a) Suppression of detail present in the input data which may obscure the phenomena to be recognized, making the task of feature extraction more difficult.
   (b) Normalization of input data.
4. Formatting the processed data for acceptance by the recognition device.

Enhancement operations to highlight the boundaries between contrasting regions in photographic or spatial inputs are useful when the background does not contain much fine detail. There are processes that produce edge enhancement in such cases. One such technique is to filter the pattern function, $f(x, y)$, by applying the Laplacian (Kovásznay and Joseph, 1955) operator, $\nabla^2 = \partial^2/\partial y^2 + \partial^2/\partial x^2$. $f(x, y)$ can be obtained by scanning the image for photographic or spatially oriented patterns. Since, in regions where picture intensity is constant, $\nabla^2 f$ is zero, the resulting image consists of the fine detail present in the original. That is, the boundaries of highly contrasting regions are displayed against a dark background. This effect may be enhanced further by a thresholding operation.

Laplacian filtering may be approximated by giving a small region of the field of view a large positive weight while weighting its nearest neighboring regions negatively to balance the positive weight. The filtered brightness at the small element under consideration is a weighted average of brightness at the element under consideration and its neighbors.

"Centering" the input is important to minimize the effect of translation variations. Invariance to translations, rotations, and input scale changes is highly desirable but rarely realizable at the preprocessor level; in many pattern recognition problems these invariances can best be provided by including samples of translated, rotated, or scaled inputs in the design data base. Perhaps the most universal technique used to insure translation invariance is to scan the image (or signal in the case of time series data) with a sample aperture. The sample aperture comprises a window function: only that part of the input data that appears in this window is considered as an input to the recognition system. With this approach, only a small portion of the input to the recognition system is treated at one time. Thus decisions are made only on the portion of the input signal in the aperture. The entire signal is scanned with the aperture, producing a sequence of decisions. Individual decisions in this sequence are normally not influenced by other decisions in the sequence, therefore the sampling aperture is taken to be large enough to cover the entirety of the pattern of interest in the data. It is also desirable to have the pattern of interest as large as possible, with respect to the aperture, so that the figure-ground or signal-to-noise ratio problem is simplified. Scanning with an aperture can provide a considerable amount of invariance to translations. Varying the image to aperture size ratio can also satisfy part of size invariance and background suppression functions of the signal conditioning operation.

The final function to be performed by the preprocessor is the formatting of the processed data for acceptance by the recognition device. It is frequently advantageous to transform the output of the sensor to facilitate further processing of the data, to reduce the dimensionality of the data, and to ease the task of feature extraction. The decision as to the particular transformation to be used is made only after a detailed examination of the input data and depends on the particular recognition task to be performed. Examples of operations and transformations which are being used in pattern recognition applications are:

1. Sampling of input data.
2. Fourier transformation
   (a) Fourier series or the use of a bank of narrow band filters.
   (b) Simultaneous consideration of time and frequency.
   (c) Two-dimensional Fourier analysis using optical techniques
3. Filtering of input data by masking
   (a) Masking operations in the frequency domain.
   (b) Optical matched filter for attention centering.

The Fourier transformations are useful in problems where the amplitude or energy spectrum exhibit significant interclass differences which are easily detected and measured. Fourier series, time-frequency histories, and, in general, orthogonal expansions of one-dimensional functions fall into this category. There is no existing theory which enables the designer to determine which transform will be most beneficial. Direct examination of the transformed data is necessary to determine whether the interclass differences exhibited by the transformed data may be related to the phenomenon to be recognized and not to differences in superfluous detail (or noise) present in the data. In some cases the applicability of the transform is best evaluated by measuring the performance of a recognition system designed using the transformed data base.

For spatial inputs the use of coherent optical techniques to obtain the Fourier spectrum has made it possible to consider rather simple operations in the frequency domain. For example, "masking" in the frequency plane may be used to effect the normalization and enhancement of inputs. The coherent matched optical filter (VanderLugt *et al.*, 1965) can provide a technique for localizing subregions which possess a high probability of containing a given target. If an image containing a given target shape is present in the input plane and a filter (transparency) "matched" to the target is present in the frequency plane, then (ideally) the output plane will display a "bright spot" in the same relative position as the target on the input image. Hence, the coherent matched optical filter detects the presence of the target and its location. A scanning device can be used to detect the location of the birght spot in the output plane of the matched optical filter and this information can then be used to center the aperture at the corresponding point on the image. Such a procedure is known as "Attention Centering." Realistically, noise due to spurious correlations and imperfect matches gives rise to false bright spots or areas. The technique can be used to reduce the time required to scan an image by directing the attention of the recognition system to examine, for final classification, only those regions of the input that correlate highly with the pattern of interest.

B. *Feature Extraction*

Feature extraction is the second phase of signal processing in a pattern recognition system. Techniques for defining features which carry significant information may be divided into human or logical design techniques (known features) and automatic design techniques (statistical features). Usually, when extracting features only a portion of the input pattern is considered at one time. This implies that a subspace (a selected number of sensory inputs) is utilized, a feature extracted, another subspace selected, and the process repeated.

1. *Known features.* Unfortunately, there are no general techniques for the design of feature extractions which utilize the designer's a priori knowledge of the recognition problem. Each case depends upon the specific problem and the knowledge and ingenuity of the designer. In some instances (Gerdes *et al.*, 1966) special scans are used to derive local texture features (e.g., long-line content, high frequency content) which provide a feature profile. In others (Brain *et al.*, 1964), optical correlation is used to extract a very limited number of special features using replicas of actual patterns of interest. In the cloud-pattern recognition problem discussed in Section IIIB, a trained meteorologist examined the photographs and specified features relating to the average gray scale, the size and number of cloud cells, and several other features which proved effective for that task. In applications involving time series data, particularly physiologic signals, detection of specific frequencies and the correlation between frequencies are suggested as features to be extracted.

The importance of such design cannot be overestimated. By utilizing the considerable experience in pattern recognition of the designer, enormous savings in the amount of statistical analysis performed in the automatic design phase can be effected. However, because the designer's knowledge and ingenuity is being tapped in some depth, automatic procedures for accomplishing this task are not readily available.

2. *Statistical feature extraction.* The last step, prior to the design of the decision mechanism, is the extraction of additional features to facilitate the decision making process. These features may be extracted from the data directly, from other features, or from a combination of these. Their purpose is to augment the feature profile descriptions with additional features to facilitate pattern class separation. The techniques for extracting these additional features may be classified by two criteria—the means for choosing the subset of data or inputs from which a feature is extracted, and the means by which the function of this data representing the feature is chosen.

Occasionally, features are extracted by correlating a mask or prototype against the entire input pattern. More often, however, the input data are sampled and only a small fraction is correlated against a prototype. There are a variety of methods for selecting the particular subset of data used for a given feature detector, as well as a variety of approaches to the specification of the prototype pattern.

In the original perceptron work (Rosenblatt, 1962), features were generated randomly. Each feature detector was a linear input threshold unit with a fixed number of input connections. The input connections were selected randomly, as were the weights for each connection. The result of this method is completely random feature detectors. As might be expected, only a small fraction of the features so derived prove useful. Systems employing this method depend upon having many more feature detectors than actually needed for the task, and an effective identification technique for properly evaluating and utilizing their information. In one variation of this approach (Joseph *et al.*, 1963), the evaluation of the feature was determined by examining the weight given to each feature in performing the classification task. Only those units with the largest weights were incorporated in the final network.

Randomly selected input connections are still widely used; most often, however, geometric constraints are placed on the selection of these inputs. A point in the input field is selected as a center, and random connections are drawn from points constrained to be in a local area about this center. In this way, the input connections for a feature detector all come from an area in which the patterns are likely to be coherent.

The statistical technique of discriminant analysis can readily be applied to the generation of features. When so used, distributional assumptions on the input patterns are required. Most often, a multivariate normal distribution is assumed for each class, and although this assumption is not often met, the resultant features are still considerably better than those that are randomly derived. If one assumes that the covariance matrices are equal for the pattern classes, the discriminant analysis results in a linear input threshold unit for the feature detectors. When the variance matrices are assumed not to be equal, quadratic input threshold units result. The specific functions implemented by these techniques as used to generate statistical features will be taken up further in Section IID.

Since the functions of the feature detectors is to reformat and extract the essence of the pattern from the input information so that it will be most readily identified, the technique of Section IID labeled "DAID" permits the set of statistical feature detectors and the decision structure utilizing their information to be developed simultaneously. This can be related to feature extraction and ordering as discussed in Chapter 2. Using DAID, the effects of the distributional assumptions and the element of randomness introduced in subspace selection are softened by selectively evaluating each feature according to its effectiveness in classifying the sample patterns. The technique insures that the feature detectors are complementary, and as the design evolves, attention is concentrated on the hard-to-classify patterns.

C. *Decision Mechanism* (*Classifier*)

The structure common to many pattern recognition systems is shown in Fig. 2. The patterns are conditioned and made available for classification through some media represented by the input array. The number of elements (x_1, x_2,...) in the input determines the dimensionality of the patterns. Features are extracted from the (preprocessed) pattern, and a decision is computed from the resulting feature profile. For the two-class problem a single response unit suffices. For multiple classes additional response units will be required. Many methods are available for specifying the form of the decision function. Using such generic titles as "Forced Learning" and "Error Correction" the decision function is "adapted" to the problem by examining a set of preclassified sample patterns.

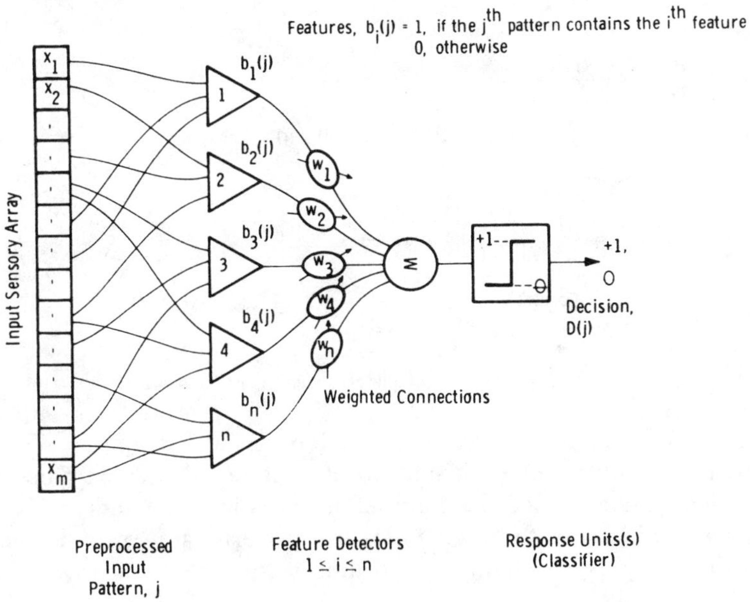

FIGURE 2. Decision network structure

Figure 3 illustrates three design rules for generating linear decision functions. Let $b_i(j)$ be the (binary) output of the ith feature detector for the jth pattern. Let $D(j) = \sum_i w_i b_i(j) - \theta$ where θ is a threshold for the decision element. Then a binary decision is achieved by assigning the jth pattern to class 1 if $D(j) > 0$ and to class 2 if $D(j) < 0$. For computational convenience, the two values of $b_i(j)$ are taken to be "1" and "0." The three techniques differ in the method for assigning values to the parameters w_i and θ, based on the feature profiles of the sample patterns.

In the forced-learning technique (Joseph, 1961), the earliest of the adaptive rules, the weights w_i are defined to be:

$$w_i = p_i - q_i$$

where p_i is the fraction of patterns in class 1 (denoted the "positive" class) possessing the ith feature [i.e., the fraction for which $b_i(j) = 1$] and q_i is the fraction of patterns in class 2 (denoted the negative class)

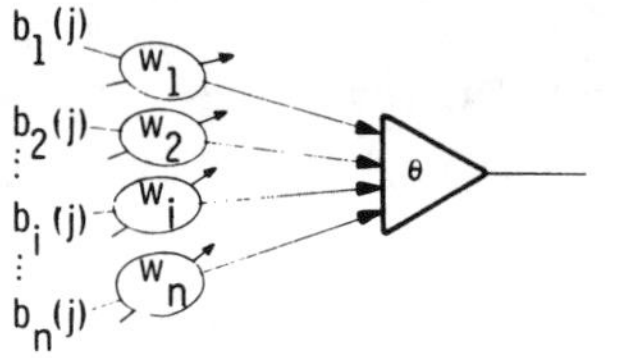

$$D(j) = \begin{cases} 1 \text{ if } \sum_i b_i(j) w_i - \theta > 0 \\ 0 \text{ if } \sum_i b_i(j) w_i - \theta < 0 \end{cases}$$

Forced Learning

$w_i = p_i - q_i$

Sequentially $\Delta w_i(j) = \frac{1}{c} \operatorname{sgn}(j)\, b_i(j)$

Bayes Weights

$$w_i = \ln \frac{p_i}{1 - p_i} - \ln \frac{q_i}{1 - q_i}$$

Error Correction

Adaptively $\Delta w_i(j) = (\text{err}) \operatorname{sgn}(j)\, b_i(j)$

FIGURE 3. Decision function generation

possessing the feature [again the fraction for which $b_i(j) = 1$]. If the number of samples for each pattern class is equal, the weights can be derived adaptively. Let the number of samples per class be "c." Set each weight initially to zero. Then the patterns are examined one by one. The weights are changed according to the following rule.

$$\Delta w_i(j) = \frac{1}{c} \operatorname{sgn}(j)\, b_i(j)$$

where sgn(j) is "1" or "-1" according to whether the jth pattern is "positive" or "negative" and $\Delta w_i(j)$ is the increment to the w_i due to the jth pattern.

The forced-learning technique generally assumes the value of the threshold, θ, to be zero. It can also be taken to be the average value of

$$\sum_i w_i b_i(j)$$

for all sample patterns. Using this average value compensates for feature detectors which are designed to be "on" primarily for patterns of one class and "off" primarily for patterns of the other class. The original forced learning technique was applied to randomly generated feature detectors which did not have this consistent bias.

Note that if b_i has a probability p_i of being "1" for a pattern of class 1, and q_i for a pattern of class 2; and if the b_i are statistically independent, then the optimum values for the weights can be found using the maximum likelihood ratio test and computing the difference of the logarithms of the odds ratio (see Chapter 2). These are called out as "Bayes Weights" in Fig. 3.

The "Bayes Weights" technique was originally derived as an "optimum" solution to the assignment of a decision function under the assumption that the feature detectors were statistically independent. This assumption is not, in general, valid. With this technique, the weights are assigned by the following rule:

$$w_i = \ln \frac{p_i}{1 - p_i} - \ln \frac{q_i}{1 - q_i}$$

where the symbols are as described above. These weights may be computed from the forced learning data if the accumulations of $\Delta w_i(j)$ are kept separately for class 1 and 2 patterns. As with the forced learning, the threshold θ can be taken as the average value of $\sum w_i b_i(j)$.

The adaptive rule for error correction (Joseph, 1961) is similar to that for forced learning in that the feature profile vector of a sample pattern is added or subtracted from the weight vector. This rule is closed-loop, however, and the change is made to the weight vector only if the sample pattern is misclassified by the decision function. It has been shown that if there is any way of assigning the weights to give complete separation of the sample patterns, this rule will arrive at such a set of weights. The technique is nonparametric, and the resultant decision boundary is based on an attempt to get complete separation of a set of sample patterns. The error correction theorem guarantees perfect performance on the sample patterns, provided that a set of weights permitting this exists.

The weights are derived adaptively, in a manner similar to the adaptive derivation of the forced learning weights:

$$\Delta w_i(j) = (\text{err}) \operatorname{sgn}(j)\, b_i(j)$$

The difference is that this weight change is applied only when the jth sample pattern is misclassified ((err) $\operatorname{sgn}(j)\, b_i(j)$). If the sample pattern is correctly classified, the weights are not changed. This modification requires that each sample pattern be processed many times. The error correction theorem specifies that only a finite number of corrections are needed to achieve a solution, but does not specify the number.

The threshold θ is also determined adaptively

$$\Delta\theta(j) = -\text{sgn}(j)$$

Again, this change is made only when an incorrect decision is observed.

Other techniques are available for generating decision functions, both linear and nonlinear. "Iterative design," discussed in Section IID, is a nonparametric technique based on sample pattern separation which minimizes a loss function to achieve the linear discriminant function.

Each of the techniques mentioned above to define feature detectors or to specify a decision function has its own relative merit. The end objective remains to define a partitioning of the input pattern space such that patterns of different classes can be uniquely identified. Iterative design is one of the few techniques which allows the simultaneous generation of subpartitions (feature detectors) and the selection of the features to achieve pattern space partitioning with a minimum number of features. This technique is described in greater detail in the following Section. The use of the technique on several actual pattern recognition problems is taken up in Section III.

D. *A Recognition System Design Technique*

The design technique to be described provides an effective means for designing feature detectors and for developing the linear discriminant function for a response unit. Variations in the technique are presented which differ only in the statistical method for generating features. That portion of the design philosophy which is invariant has been named "iterative design" and involves a loss function reduction. The feature detectors are designed by discriminant analysis giving rise to the design technique acronym DAID (Discriminant Analysis-Iterative Design) [Joseph *et al.*, 1965].

The recognition logic is designed sequentially. As logic units (features) are added to the design, the pattern losses indicate which of the sample patterns require the most attention. In acquiring the data required to generate additional logic units, the loss assigned to a pattern is used to weight the contribution of that pattern to the group statistics. This insures that the logic units thus derived are suitable for the part of the recognition problem as yet unsolved.

Logic units are generated by selecting a subspace of the original signal space, and performing a discriminant analysis in that subspace. For example, in the cloud-pattern recognition task to be discussed, the pattern is presented as a 5625-dimensional vector since the input device providing the input space is considered as a 75×75 sensory array. Only six of these dimensions or elements of the array are utilized for each logic unit or feature, giving rise to a six-dimensional subspace for the discriminant analysis. Subspaces are used since it is usually not practical to perform the discriminant analysis in spaces with high dimensionality, nor is the implementation in analog hardware of the resulting logic unit feasible. No technique has yet been specified for optimally selecting subspaces, so that an element of randomness is used.

Randomly chosen subspaces are not all of equal utility, and often a particular subspace will prove to be of no value at all. For this reason, selection is used. Each time the recognition network is to be expanded by the addition of logic units, more units are generated than are to be added. Only the best of these units are selected. The selection criterion is which unit would result in the greatest decrease in the system loss.

1. *Iterative Design**. Iterative design is an approach to developing the decision structure of Fig. 2 gradually, using information derived from a partially designed structure to highlight difficult problem areas. Each sample pattern is assigned a loss number that depends upon how strongly it is classified by a partially designed machine. The system loss is taken as the sum of the losses of all sample patterns. Each change made in the system reduces the system loss.

Let:

$$b_i(j) = \begin{cases} 1 \text{ if the } j\text{th sample pattern activates the } i\text{th logic unit} \\ 0 \text{ otherwise} \end{cases}$$

let w_i be the weight assigned to the ith logic unit, and let θ be the threshold of the response unit.

β_j is used to denote the linear discriminant, or input to the response unit for the jth pattern.

$$\beta_j = \sum_i^n b_i(j)\, w_i \tag{4.1}$$

* R. D. Joseph and J. A. Daly of the Astropower Laboratory, McDonnell Douglas Corporation are primarily responsible for the following derivation, and that appearing in the Appendix to this chapter.

The network classifies the jth pattern as a class 1 or "positive" pattern if the discriminant exceeds the response unit threshold, that is, if

$$\beta_j - \theta > 0 \tag{4.2}$$

and as a class 2 or "negative" pattern if the discriminant is less than the threshold. The symbol δ is used to indicate the true classification of the jth sample pattern.

$$\delta_j = \begin{cases} 1 & \text{if the } j\text{th pattern is a "positive" pattern} \\ -1 & \text{if the } j\text{th pattern is a "negative" pattern} \end{cases}$$

The loss function used has an exponential form. The loss assigned to the jth pattern is

$$L_j = e^{\delta_j(\theta - \beta_j)} \tag{4.3}$$

This form has many desirable features, but does not permit the analytic optimization of the linear discriminant function. A relaxation technique as presented in the following paragraphs is utilized instead.

Given that $N - 1$ logic units (features) have been incorporated in the design, and a discriminant function established, a population of logic units that are candidates for inclusion in the network is made available by statistical techniques described in Section IID2. The iterative design algorithm calls for the addition to the network of that candidate unit which results in the lowest system loss. Denote by I_+ the set of indices, j, for which $\delta_j = 1$, and by I_- the set of indices for which $\delta_j = -1$. For a given candidate for the Nth logic unit, let I_N be the set of indices j for which $b_i(j) = 1$ and by $\bar{I}_N$ those for which $b_i(j) = 0$: Thus the symbol $\sum_{j \in I_+ \cap I_N}$ would mean "the summation over all values of j for which the jth pattern is 'positive' *and* activates the Nth unit."

The system loss,* if the candidate unit is added, and the weights $w_1, \ldots, w_{N-1}$ are held fixed, is

$$SL = 2\sqrt{\Big(\sum_{j \in I_+ \cap I_N} L_j\Big)\Big(\sum_{j \in I_- \cap I_N} L_j\Big)} + 2\sqrt{\Big(\sum_{j \in I_+ \cap \bar{I}_N} L_j\Big)\Big(\sum_{j \in I_- \cap \bar{I}_N} L_j\Big)} \tag{4.4}$$

The change in the value of the threshold is given by:

$$\Delta\theta = \frac{1}{2} \ln \frac{\sum_{j \in I_- \cap I_N} L_j}{\sum_{j \in I_+ \cap I_N} L_j} \tag{4.5}$$

---

* For a derivation of Eqs. (4.4), (4.5) and (4.6) see the Appendix.

and the weight of the candidate unit by:

$$w_N = \Delta\theta - \frac{1}{2}\ln\frac{\sum_{j\in I_-\cap I_N} L_j}{\sum_{j\in I_+\cap I_N} L_j} \tag{4.6}$$

Once the Nth unit for the machine has been selected, the coefficients of the linear discriminant are readjusted, and the pattern losses recomputed. With the exponential loss function, this is also accomplished iteratively—each weight, w_i being adjusted in turn. Several adjustments for each weight each time a unit is added seem to be adequate. Each time a weight is changed, the threshold is also adjusted. These changes are defined by

$$\Delta w_i = \Delta\theta - \frac{1}{2}\ln\frac{\sum_j L_j b_i(j)(1 - \mathrm{sgn}(j))}{\sum_j L_j b_i(j)(1 + \mathrm{sgn}(j))} \tag{4.7}$$

$$\Delta\theta = \frac{1}{2}\ln\frac{\sum_j L_j(1 - b_i(j))(1 - \mathrm{sgn}(j))}{\sum_j L_j(1 - b_i(j))(1 + \mathrm{sgn}(j))} \tag{4.8}$$

Despite the computational difficulties it engenders, the exponential loss function offers some desirable features. It permits the approximate calculations described above to be accomplished with ease. It has an exponential rate of change, insuring that most attention is given to those patterns which are most poorly classified. It does not become constant, insuring that the decision boundary will be placed as far as possible from correctly classified sample patterns.

2. *Discriminant Analysis.* A number of techniques are available for generating populations of logic units required by the iterative design procedure as candidates for inclusion in the decision network. These techniques use the loss numbers assigned to the sample patterns by the iterative design process to weight the importance of these patterns—the populations of units thus generated tend to emphasize the remaining problem difficulties. Each of the techniques involves strong distributional assumptions concerning the distribution of the pattern classes in the selected subspaces. The effects of these assumptions on the network design are softened by the iterative design algorithm, which selects, on the basis of performance, only a small fraction of the units generated.

Discriminant analyses are used to generate a logic unit, given a subspace. Each logic unit, or feature detector, dichotomizes the patterns in its *subspace*. An "optimum" discriminant function is computed to partition the subspace. The patterns falling on one side of the resulting surface defined by that discriminant function are associated with one pattern class; those falling on the other side are associated with the second pattern class. The two pattern classes are assumed to have multivariate normal distributions in that subspace. The statistical data which must be extracted from the patterns is thus limited to the first two moments, but this does not seem to be a serious shortcoming when considered in light of the overall design philosophy. The selection and iterative design procedures evaluate and weight logic units according to their actual performance on the sample patterns rather than the performance predicted for them by the discriminant analysis. The assumptions which are made concerning the mean vectors and the covariance matrices of the two distributions appear to effect the system performance noticeably. These assumptions control the nature of the differences between distributions which are to be exploited.

The n-variate normal density function, in matrix form, is

$$\frac{1}{(2\pi)^{n/2}|\Sigma|^{1/2}} \exp\{-1/2(\mathbf{x}-\boldsymbol{\mu})'\,\Sigma^{-1}(\mathbf{x}-\boldsymbol{\mu}\} \tag{4.9}$$

where $\mathbf{x}$ is the pattern vector, $\boldsymbol{\mu}$ is the (column) mean vector, Σ is the covariance matrix, and $|\Sigma|$ is the determinant of the covariance matrix. A subscript "+" will denote those parameters which apply to the distribution of the class of positive patterns; a subscript "—" those pertaining to the distribution of the negative patterns; and for those parameters which apply to both distributions, no subscript will be used.

The Neyman–Pearson Lemma (1936) specifies the likelihood ratio test as the optimum decision rule in the subspace. A pattern with measurement vector $\mathbf{x}$ turns the unit on if:

$$\frac{\dfrac{1}{(2\pi)^{n/2}|\Sigma_+|^{1/2}} \exp\{-\frac{1}{2}(\mathbf{x}-\boldsymbol{\mu}_+)'\,\Sigma_+^{-1}(\mathbf{x}-\boldsymbol{\mu}_+)\}}{\dfrac{1}{(2\pi)^{n/2}|\Sigma_-|^{1/2}} \exp\{-\frac{1}{2}(\mathbf{x}-\boldsymbol{\mu}_-)'\,\Sigma_-^{-1}(\mathbf{x}-\boldsymbol{\mu}_-)\}} > \lambda_1 \tag{4.10}$$

By taking logarithms this inequality is seen to be equivalent to:

$$(\mathbf{x}-\boldsymbol{\mu}_+)'\,\Sigma_+^{-1}(\mathbf{x}-\boldsymbol{\mu}_+) - (\mathbf{x}-\boldsymbol{\mu}_-)'\,\Sigma_-^{-1}(\mathbf{x}-\boldsymbol{\mu}_-) < \lambda_2 = -\ln \lambda_1{}^2 + \ln \frac{|\Sigma_-|}{|\Sigma_+|} \tag{4.11}$$

Taking into account the symmetric properties of the covariance matrix an alternative form is given by:

$$\mathbf{x}'(\Sigma_+^{-1} - \Sigma_-^{-1})\,\mathbf{x} - 2\mathbf{x}'(\Sigma_+^{-1}\boldsymbol{\mu}_+ - \Sigma_-^{-1}\boldsymbol{\mu}_-) < \lambda_3 = \lambda_2 - \boldsymbol{\mu}_+{}'\Sigma_+^{-1}\boldsymbol{\mu}_+ + \boldsymbol{\mu}_-{}'\Sigma_-^{-1}\boldsymbol{\mu}_- \tag{4.12}$$

The constant λ_1 (and hence λ_2 and λ_3) is chosen to reflect differences in the a priori probabilities of the pattern classes, and differences in the costs associated with the two types of errors (false alarms and missed identifications). The discriminant function,

$$D(\mathbf{x}) = \mathbf{x}'(\Sigma_+^{-1} - \Sigma_-^{-1})\,\mathbf{x} - 2\mathbf{x}'(\Sigma_+^{-1}\boldsymbol{\mu}_+ - \Sigma_-^{-1}\boldsymbol{\mu}_-) - \lambda_3 \tag{4.13}$$

is specified by estimating $\boldsymbol{\mu}_+$, $\boldsymbol{\mu}_-$, Σ_+, and Σ_- from the sample patterns. It is, of course, a quadratic function of the measurements taken from the pattern to be classified, and thus specifies a quadratic surface as the decision boundary for the logic unit.

The well-known result given above is the general discriminant analysis solution for multivariate normal distributions. In the subsequent sections special cases which occur when certain restrictions are placed on the estimates of the mean vectors and covariance matrices are examined. These restrictions can be chosen to serve one or more of three purposes—to simplify the estimation process, to simplify the implementation of the discriminant function, or to conform to actual constraints on the patterns.

A. ORIENTED HYPERPLANE. The first constraint to be considered is the assumption that the covariance matrices are equal, that is, that $\Sigma_+ = \Sigma_- \equiv \Sigma$. While this assumption simplifies the estimation process since there is only one covariance matrix to estimate and invert, its primary purpose is to simplify the implementation of the discriminant function, which becomes from Eq. (4.13)

$$D(\mathbf{x}) = -2\mathbf{x}'\Sigma^{-1}(\boldsymbol{\mu}_+ - \boldsymbol{\mu}_-) - \lambda_3 \tag{4.14}$$

This function is implementable by the linear input threshold device. A weight vector for such a unit is given by $\Sigma^{-1}(\boldsymbol{\mu}_+ - \boldsymbol{\mu}_-)$ and the threshold by $\ln \lambda_1 + 1/2(\boldsymbol{\mu}_+ + \boldsymbol{\mu}_-)'\,\Sigma^{-1}(\boldsymbol{\mu}_+ - \boldsymbol{\mu}_-) = -\lambda_3/2$. This technique of generating logic units is called the "Oriented Hyperplane" technique (Fig. 4a). The name stems from the fact that the decision boundary of a logic unit is a hyperplane which cuts (bisects for $\lambda_1 = 1$) the line segment joining the means $\boldsymbol{\mu}_+$ and $\boldsymbol{\mu}_-$, but in general has some orientation other than perpendicular with respect to that line segment.

B. PERPENDICULAR BISECTOR. The second special case to be considered is a further restriction of the Oriented Hyperplane case given above. The additional assumption is that the common covariance matrix is a multiple of the identity matrix $\Sigma = cI$. This assumption (that the measurements taken from the patterns to be classified are independent with equal variances) has the effect of greatly simplifying the estimation process. An implementation of the decision boundary with a linear input threshold device uses $(\mu_+ - \mu_-)$ for a weight vector, and has $1/c \ln \lambda_1 + 1/2(\mu_+'\mu_+ - \mu_-'\mu_-)$ for a threshold. If λ_1 is taken to be "1" then it is not necessary to estimate the parameter "c." If an equal number of positive and negative sample patterns are available, the weight vector can be obtained with adaptive hardware by adding the measurement vectors for positive patterns to the existing weight vector and subtracting the measurement vector for negative patterns.

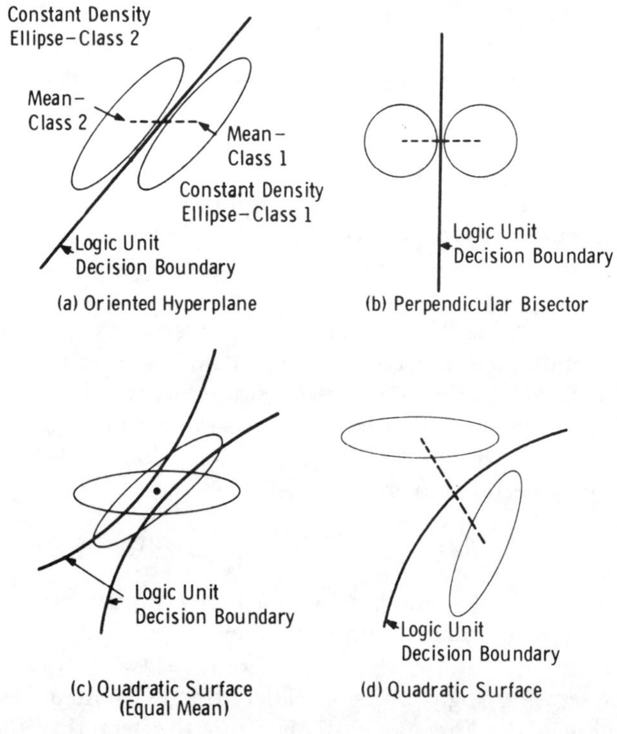

FIGURE 4. Discriminant functions

A difference in the number of sample patterns could be accounted for by a gain adjustment for negative patterns.

This technique for generating logic units is called "Perpendicular Bisector." The name is derived from the fact that the decision boundary of Fig. 4b is a hyperplane perpendicular to the line segment joining the means, and bisecting it when $\lambda_1 = 1$.

C. QUADRATIC SURFACE. In the third special case considered, the covariance matrices are again allowed to vary, but the mean vectors are constrained (equal means).

If both pattern classes are assumed to have the same mean vector as shown in Fig. 4c then Eq. (4.13) becomes

$$D(\mathbf{x}) = \mathbf{x}'(\Sigma_{+}^{-1} - \Sigma_{-}^{-1})\,\mathbf{x} - 2\mathbf{x}'(\Sigma_{+}^{-1} - \Sigma_{-}^{-1})\,\boldsymbol{\mu} - \lambda_3 \tag{4.15}$$

where

$$\lambda_3 = -\ln \lambda_1{}^2 + \ln \frac{|\Sigma_-|}{|\Sigma_+|} - \boldsymbol{\mu}'(\Sigma_{+}^{-1} - \Sigma_{-}^{-1})\boldsymbol{\mu} \tag{4.16}$$

The quadratic weights are taken from the first term of $D(\mathbf{x})$. The linear weights from the second term and the threshold from the constant as before.

This technique for generating logic units is called "Quadratic Surface." In the most general case, illustrated in Fig. 4d, where these constraints are not imposed on the means and the covariance matrices of the pattern classes, a general second-order quadratic surface again results directly from Eq. (4.13). Note that for this general case the quadratic terms are the same as those derived for the equal means case just discussed, however the linear terms and the threshold will differ.

III. Applications

A. *Pattern Recognition Applied to Sleep State Classification*

1. *Design approach.* The electroencephalograph (EEG) recording has long served as a clinical aid for the diagnosis of mental disorders and brain defects, and has been quite useful in the study of epilepsy. More recently EEG has provided a tool for categorizing sleep periods of normal subjects. The EEG signal successively assumes several well-defined patterns throughout the course of a normal night's sleep. Dement and Kleitman (1957) classified these patterns into the following sleep states:

Stage 1. Low voltage signal with irregular frequency.
Stage 2. 13–15 Hz sleep spindles and "K" complexes in a low voltage background.
Stage 3. Sets of large delta waves (1–3 Hz) appear frequently.
Stage 4. EEG composed almost entirely of delta waves.

Most subjects move through this succession of patterns in the first hour of sleep. After stage 4 sleep, the EEG pattern returns to a low voltage irregular waveform; this phenomenon is accompanied by bursts of rapid eye movement (REM). This sleep state has been termed stage REM. Through the rest of the sleep period the EEG alternates between stage REM and stages 2 or 3 in cycles ranging from 90 to 120 minutes. The categorization of sleep has led to more accurate determination of various phenomena occurring during sleep; for example, a high correlation has been established between dreaming and the occurrence of REM.

The present method of visually classifying EEG records in the awake and various sleep categories requires a great deal of time on the part of a skilled encephalographer. With the routine collection of this type of data, a means of automatically screening the data must be developed. The pattern recognition techniques previously described offer an approach to the analysis of EEG waveforms and to the development of a method of scoring the records automatically.

The implementation of the design approach is illustrated in Fig. 5. The first step in the preprocessing of the EEG data involves converting

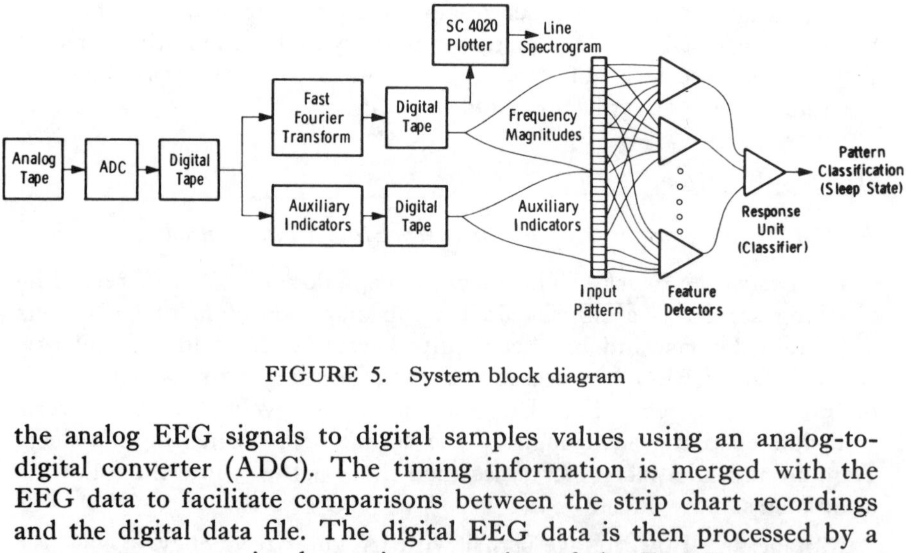

FIGURE 5. System block diagram

the analog EEG signals to digital samples values using an analog-to-digital converter (ADC). The timing information is merged with the EEG data to facilitate comparisons between the strip chart recordings and the digital data file. The digital EEG data is then processed by a computer program implementing a version of the Fast Fourier transform (FFT). Line spectrograms may then be plotted on a computer recorder. An example of this type of plot is shown in Fig. 6. The sleep patterns are then the magnitudes of the frequency components covering the range from 0–26 Hz for each 16.4-second interval, and serve as inputs to the recognition system. In addition, specific properties can be extracted from the EEG data to assist in the scoring process. For example, the presence of "K" complexes in the EEG records assists in distinguishing stage 2 from all other sleep states. The "K" complex consists of one or two large voltage slow waves at 0.8–4 Hz that may be followed by a spindle burst (short period of 13–15 Hz activity) and usually lasting less than 4 seconds (Kiloh *et al.*, 1966). A "K" complex detector output could then be added to the frequency data to provide another input to the recognition system.

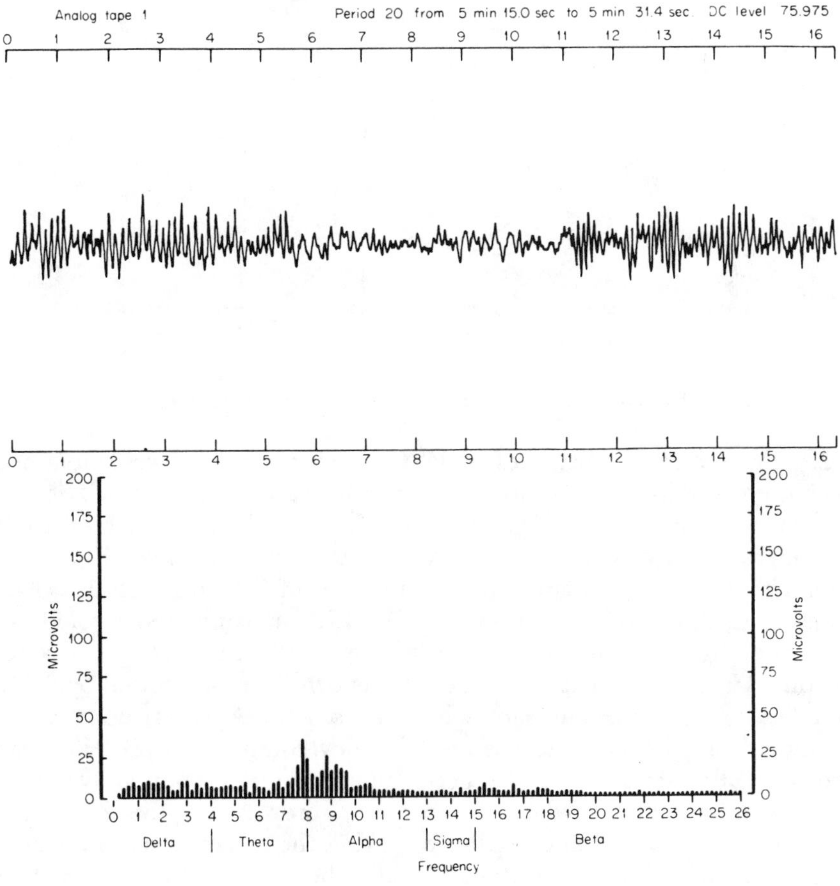

FIGURE 6. An example of EEG data accompanied by the resulting spectral analysis of the 16.4-second interval

Since systems designed by the DAID procedure normally split the input patterns into two categories, a convenient method for classifying sleep states is to design several recognition systems with each system assigned a specific dichotomy as illustrated in Fig. 7. Such a decision tree or discrimination net can be implemented with six pattern recognition devices. The decisions which experience has proven to be least difficult appear close to the top of the net. The more difficult discriminations, such as separating stage 1 from stage REM, are performed in the lower portion of the net.

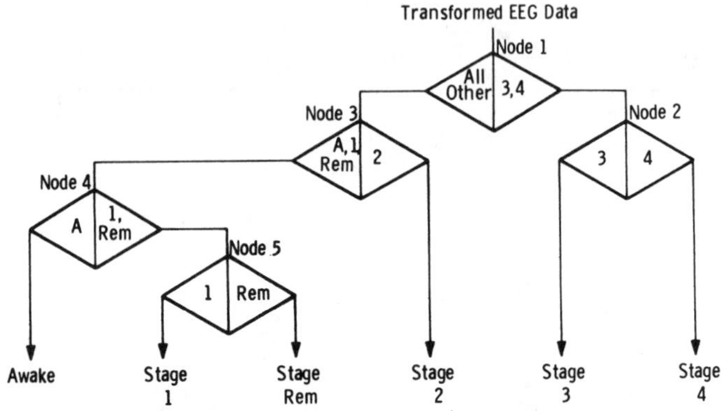

FIGURE 7. Decision tree for scoring sleep records

2. *Preprocessing*. Samples of EEG sleep recordings were obtained from the Navy Medical Neuropsychiatric Research Unit in San Diego.* The data consisted of a single channel of EEG (right parietal with left ear reference electrode) plus a time code mark spaced at 10-second intervals. The data, obtained from a number of subjects includes sleep stages 1, 2, 3, 4, REM, and awake. The EEG is converted into 11 bit plus sign digital form at a sampling rate of 125 samples per second. At this sample rate each 16.4-second epoch is represented by 2048 sampled data points. The sampled data from the ADC is input to the computer and the sine and cosine frequency components present in an epoch of EEG are extracted by performing a Fourier analysis over each 16.4-second interval of data. From these components, the amplitude spectrum is computed and finally, by taking the square root of the sum of the squares of each component pair, the mean square intensities. The 2048 sampled data points representing one epoch are transformed into 1024 frequency components covering the band from 0–62.5 Hz. To consolidate the information scattered throughout the 1024 frequency components into a consistent pattern of a much smaller dimensionality for input to the recognition system, an averaging of approximately

* The EEG data was made available by L. C. Johnson and his staff at the NMNRU.

three adjacent values is performed, resulting in 312 frequency components over the same frequency range. Those frequency components covering the immediate range of interest (0–26 Hz) are then extracted providing 130 frequency components for each time epoch.

The extraction of the frequency coefficients is accomplished using Fast Fourier analysis, a computer algorithm developed by Tukey and Cooley (1965). They considered the calculation of the Fourier coefficients for a period consisting of N data points as the multiplication of an N-vector by an N by N matrix. Using the folding properties of the sine function they factored this matrix into m sparse matrices where m was proportional to $\log_2 N$. This resulted in a procedure requiring $N \log_2 N$ rather than N^2 operations required by other techniques.

For the 16.4-second periods the 1024 extremely accurate coefficients for frequencies ranging from 0 to 62. 5 Hz can be computed in only seven seconds of SDS 930 computer time. Another second of computer time is required to combine the coefficients and extract the desired 130 values covering the range from 0–26 Hz. This operation is performed every 15 seconds allowing for a slight overlap of the spectrum with the following epoch. Each epoch's set of 130 components, associated with an indication of the particular sleep stage of the subject during that 16.4-second period, comprises one input pattern to be used in the design of various pattern recognition systems.

3. *Pattern recognition.* The Discriminant Analysis-Iterative Design (DAID) technique was used to design the pattern recognition system for classifying this EEG data. The recognition structure is similar to that shown in Fig. 2. Each feature detector connects to a set of six randomly selected inputs. The training set of patterns is input to the system, the data are assumed to have multivariate normal distributions in the six-dimensional subspace, and the first two moments of the pattern classes in that six-dimensional subspace are then computed. The optimum quadratic discriminant function (see Section IID2) is then computed with no constraints imposed on the mean or the covariance matrices of the pattern classes (in that subspace). The output of the statistical feature detector is 0 or 1 if the discriminant expression evaluated for a particular pattern is positive or negative, respectively.

The output of the ith feature detector is multiplied by a numerical weight, w_i, and summed with the other weighted property filter outputs in the response unit (see Fig. 2). The response unit generates the final decision function for the system classification. Each sample pattern, j, is assigned a loss L_j (see Section IID1). The loss will be less than "1" if the pattern is correctly classified and greater than "1" if it is incorrectly classified. The magnitude of the loss reflects the degree of confidence in the decision. System loss, *SL*, is defined as the sum of the individual pattern losses. The response unit input weights and threshold are adjusted to minimize the system loss using the cyclic relaxation process.

At the beginning of the design procedure, the pattern recognition system contains no feature detectors. As the design progresses, features are added sequentially and selectively to the growing decision network. At each cycle in the design procedure, 15 candidate feature detectors are generated, by discriminant analysis, for possible inclusion in the decision network. Overall system performance on the entire training sample of patterns is measured as each candidate feature in turn is evaluated. The five candidates which prove to be the most useful in separating the pattern classes are then included in the system. The weights between the feature detectors and the response unit are then readjusted by the iterative design process and the cycle repeated. Fifteen new candidates are generated. The performance of the first five units previously selected plus each candidate unit in turn is measured. The five additional feature detectors selected thus complement those features already incorporated in the system and the ten response unit input weights are readjusted. Additional features are added in this manner until a desired performance level of classification on a generalization set of patterns is achieved.

When the required performance is reached or the simulated design terminated, the design program prints out the parameters used to specify the discriminant function computed by each feature detector; the weight, w_i, associated with each feature; and the response unit threshold, θ. These parameters, together with the input connection list printed for each unit are sufficient to specify the recognition system design completely. In the test, or operational phase, the function computed by each feature detector, and the response units, are mechanized in terms of these input connections and the associated weights and thresholds. The classification of an unknown pattern is accomplished automatically and rapidly without any further requirement for system design modification.

4. *Results.* A design experiment consisted of the recognition of patterns from EEG data obtained from subjects other than the subject used to design the systems. The systems were designed on patterns obtained from subject B, described as a high alpha (presence of significant 8–10 Hz activity in his awake, eyes closed EEG records) subject, and tested on patterns obtained from subject L, a low alpha subject. To

perform this experiment, a two-hour recording from subject B and a three-hour recording from subject L were utilized. Both subject's recordings include data taken while they were awake and in sleep stages 1, 2, 3, 4, and REM.

Four recognition systems were designed.

System	Distinguished Between	
1	Sleep stage 2, or any other sleep stage and the awake state	(2 V all)
2	Sleep stage 3, or any other sleep stage and the awake state	(3 V all)
3	Sleep stage REM or any other sleep stage and the awake state	(R V all)
4	Sleep stage REM or sleep stage 2	(R V 2)

Systems 1, 3, and 4 were designed by training on 80 percent of subject B's patterns from the particular stages under consideration, and tested on the remaining 20 percent. It was then further tested on all of the patterns from subject L. System 2 was designed by training on all of subject B's patterns from the particular stage under consideration, and tested on all of the patterns from subject L. Table I presents the results of these experiments.

TABLE I

PERFORMANCE OF SYSTEMS TRAINED ON A HIGH ALPHA SUBJECT

	Training Results		Generalization Results	
System	80% Subject B	100% Subject B	20% Subject B	100% Subject L
2 V all	94	—	83	68
3 V all	—	89	—	66
R V all	94	—	92	76
R V 2	99	—	98	67

A second experiment was a preliminary attempt to evaluate the feasibility of the decision tree described. The subject chosen for the first decision tree was classified as a high alpha subject. Recognition systems were designed and tested using the standard DAID computer program and a complete overnight sleep record from this subject. Eighty percent of the subject's patterns were used for the system design; the remaining 20 percent were reserved as a generalization sample. Based upon performance on this test sample, five systems were selected for the appropriate nodes of the decision tree shown in Fig. 7.

The performance of each of these systems is summarized in Table II.

TABLE II

CLASSIFICATION PERFORMANCE AT EACH NODE

Node 1	Stages 3 and 4	vs.	All other patterns
	3, 4		98.2% correct
	All others		96.1% correct
Node 2	Stage 3	vs.	Stage 4
	Stage 3		92.9% correct
	Stage 4		81.0% correct
Node 3	Stage 2	vs.	Awake, Stage 1, REM
	Stage 2		95.4% correct
	A, 1, REM		98.8% correct
Node 4	Awake	vs.	Stage 1, REM
	Awake		100% correct
	Stage 1, REM		93.5% correct
Node 5	Stage 1	vs.	REM
	Stage 1		66.7% correct
	REM		83.3% correct

The five recognition system designs were then stored in the computer by a program developed to implement the decision tree concept. This program was given the task of classifying the patterns representing the entire eight hours of the subject's baseline sleep. The percentage of patterns correctly identified is shown for each class in Table III. These

TABLE III

SUMMARY OF DECISION TREE CLASSIFICATION PERFORMANCE ON 7-1/2 HOURS OF SLEEP

Class	Number Correct	Total Patterns	Percentage Correct
Stage 1	40	53	75.5
Stage 2	819	869	94.2
Stage 3	63	72	87.6
Stage 4	180	210	85.7
Awake	41	41	100.0
REM	299	341	87.7
All Classes	1442	1586	91.0

results serve only as an indication of the feasibility of the decision tree concept since the eight-hour interval of sleep contained many patterns that were also used in the training set. However, with this reservation in mind, it appears that the recognition system performed in a rational manner. The greatest percentage of classification errors was made in confusing stage 1 with REM. Given only the EEG pattern, this is also the most difficult discrimination for the human scorer. The second greatest percentage of errors occurred in separating stages 3 and 4. The EEG patterns associated with these stages are very similar. Human scorers base their discrimination on whether the EEG shows more than or less than fifty percent of the activity to be in the form of low frequency waves (2 Hz or less) with peak-to-peak amplitudes greater than 75 μv (Kales and Rechtschaffen, 1968) an inherently subjective procedure. It was noted that most of the recognition system's errors occurred near the region of the transition from stage 3 to stage 4 sleep. It also appeared that in several cases the recognition system was making a finer discrimination than the human. For example, the system indicated several isolated awake periods in what was nominally termed stage 1 sleep. Examination of these records showed distinct 9 Hz alpha bursts indicating that the subject may actually have been roused for a few seconds.

5. *Summary.* The procedure discussed has proved to be an effective method of processing EEG data. The use of the FFT for rapid frequency transformation and the DAID recognition system for pattern classification illustrate a technique for on-line scoring of sleep records.

B. *Video Pattern Recognition**

On April 1, 1960, TIROS I was launched into orbit to prove the feasibility of meteorological satellites. A succession of TIROS and NIMBUS satellites have supplied meteorologists with a staggering number of photographs. A feeling for the dimension of the collection, transmission, and processing tasks may be gained by considering that the television cameras on a NIMBUS satellite deliver 96 pictures with a total of 5×10^8 bits of data per orbit. All of these data are stored aboard the spacecraft and transmitted to data acquisition stations on earth. As an approach to increasing the transfer rate of significant video

* This work (Joseph *et al.*, 1968) was supported under contract NAS 12–30 from the Electronics Research Center of the National Aeronautics and Space Administration. The "Known Features" specified in Table IX were derived by E. M. Darling, Jr., NASA Technical Officer for this program.

information from unmanned spacecraft the possibility of performing pattern recognition prior to transmission was considered. It is envisioned that the data to be transmitted would then be simply a few numbers characterizing the imagery in a sampling aperture. From these, the boundaries separating large homogeneous areas could be computed and the original scene could be reconstructed on earth from idealized models of the pattern class.

The pattern recognition design techniques investigated were considered in the context of the design philosophy discussed in Section II. The process of recognition is composed of three parts—signal conditioning, feature extraction, and computation of the decision.

1. *Areas of Investigation.* Pattern recognition systems were designed experimentally for recognition tasks which might arise in spacecraft imagery. To accomplish this empirical evaluation, five recognition tasks were defined on seven classes of patterns. Four of the pattern classes represented features of the lunar terrain, the remaining three classes being textural patterns occurring in satellite cloud imagery. For these experiments, the signal conditioning consists of a limited degree of size and position normalization, resolution regulation, and contrast and brightness control.

Five adaptive techniques for designing the decision mechanism were selected. In addition, two methods for statistically designing feature detectors were chosen. Both of these methods provide binary output feature detectors; one technique using linear switching surfaces, and the other, quadratic surfaces.

An important area in pattern recognition, which had not received any attention, is that of statistically designing feature detectors to augment a set of known features. A set of known features for the cloud pattern tasks was designed and a subset of these features was applied to the lunar data. Augmented systems were designed for both cloud pattern tasks, and the three lunar terrain pattern tasks.

The pattern recognition techniques under consideration share a common structure. As shown in Fig. 2 of Section IIC, features are extracted from the conditioned pattern, and the decision function is computed from the feature profile of the pattern.

2. *Generation of the Pattern Files.* A. ORIGIN OF THE PATTERN SETS. Four of the pattern classes were prominences occurring in the lunar terrain: (1) craters with no conspicuous central elevations, (2) craters with one or more conspicuous central elevations, (3) rima, and (4) wrinkle ridges. Three classes were types of cloud cover as seen

from satellites: (1) noncumulus cloud cover, (2) cumulus clouds-solid cells, and (3) cumulus clouds-polygonal cells.

Figure 8 illustrates samples of the lunar terrain patterns obtained from Air Force Lunar Atlases. From these sources 198 examples were selected and categorized as shown in Table IV.

TABLE IV

LUNAR TERRAIN PATTERNS

Feature	No. of Examples
Craters, no conspicuous central elevation	53
Craters, one or more conspicuous central elevation	53
Rima (rilles or trenches)	52
Wrinkle ridges	40

The cloud patterns, taken from actual NIMBUS imagery, are categorized in Table V. Examples of each cloud type are illustrated in Fig. 9. The "pattern" in these cases is not a single cell, but an assemblage of many cells.

TABLE V

CLOUD PATTERNS

Feature	No. of Examples
Noncumulus	108
Cumulus, Polygonal Cells	96
Cumulus, Solid Cells	119

B. PREPROCESSING. Some preprocessing, consistent with the capability of present satellite instrumentation systems, was performed to obviate the need for a larger sample of patterns for the recognition experiments. The crater patterns varied in diameter from 10 km to 100 km. To accommodate these size variations a simple size normalization was performed. The diameter of the largest was specified to be no greater than $1\frac{1}{2}$ times the diameter of the smallest crater in the set. The ridges and rima presented a more difficult problem in size normalization. They did not have a convenient dimension comparable to the diameter of the craters, and they varied considerably both in width and length. As a compromise, it was decided to normalize the size of these patterns so that the distance across the patterns was approximately 10 percent to 15 percent of the width of the aperture

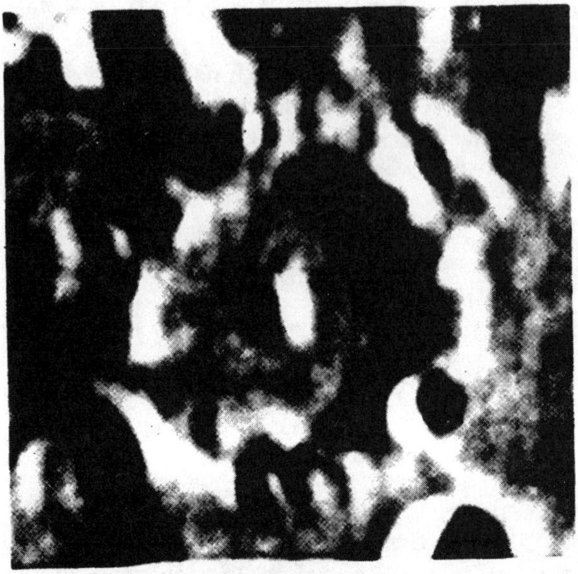

Crater with Central Elevation

(a)

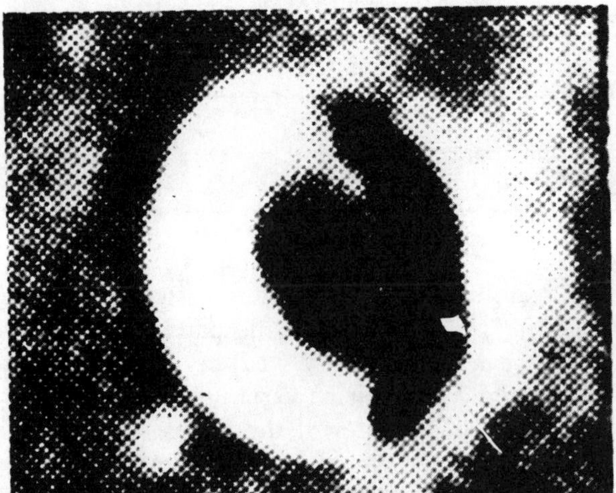

Crater without Central Elevation

(b)

FIGURE 8. Lunar terrain patterns

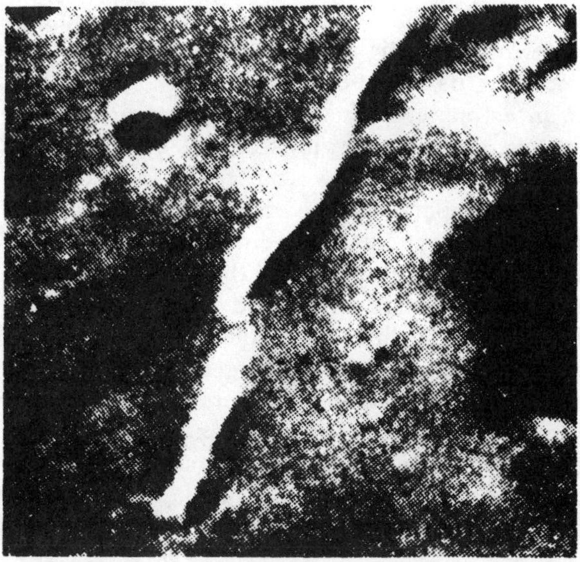

Rima

(c)

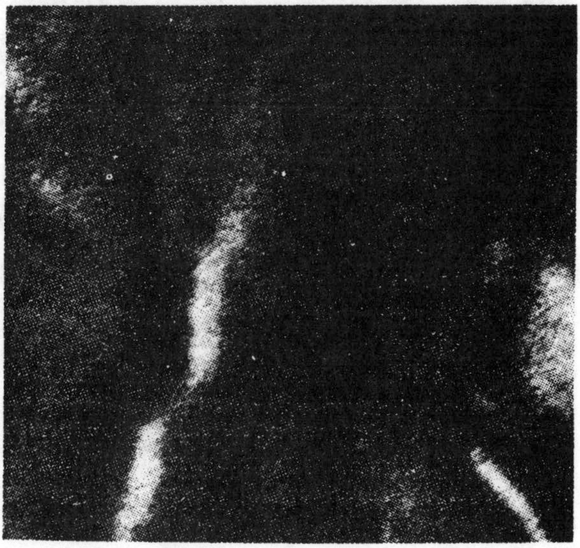

Lunar Ridge

(d)

used for the craters. This achieved sufficient resolution across the pattern to determine the light side and shadow side of the ridge or rima while retaining its linear characteristic.

To obtain an estimate of the resolution required for recognition of the lunar patterns, typical examples were selected from the four pattern groups and placed before a slow scan television camera. The minitor display was photographed as the distance between the TV camera and the photograph was increased in five steps. Examination of pictures taken of the TV monitor indicated that observers could accurately distinguish between craters with and craters without conspicuous elevations with about 25 lines of resolution across the crater. It was decided to make the largest crater no larger than 80 percent of the width of the aperture. Since the smallest craters were to be no smaller than two-thirds the size of the largest craters, a 50 × 50 point picture gave at least 25 lines of resolution across the smallest crater. The results for ridges and rima were not so well defined. It was difficult to measure the width of these patterns on the face of the monitor precisely. However,

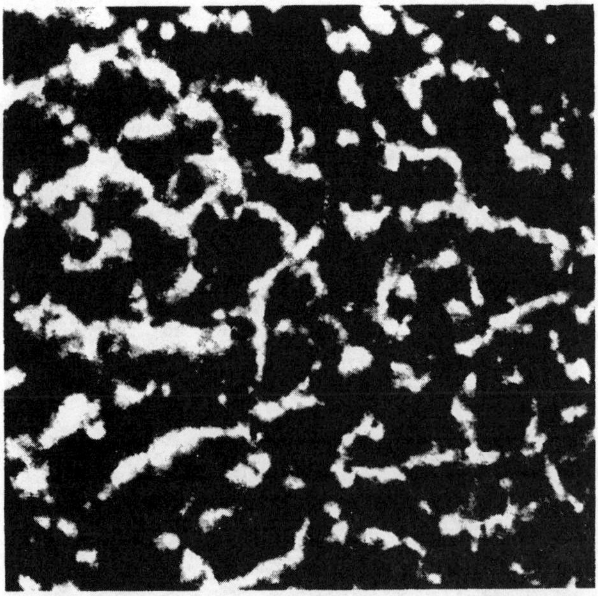

Cumulus, Polygonal Cells

(a)

FIGURE 9. Cloud patterns

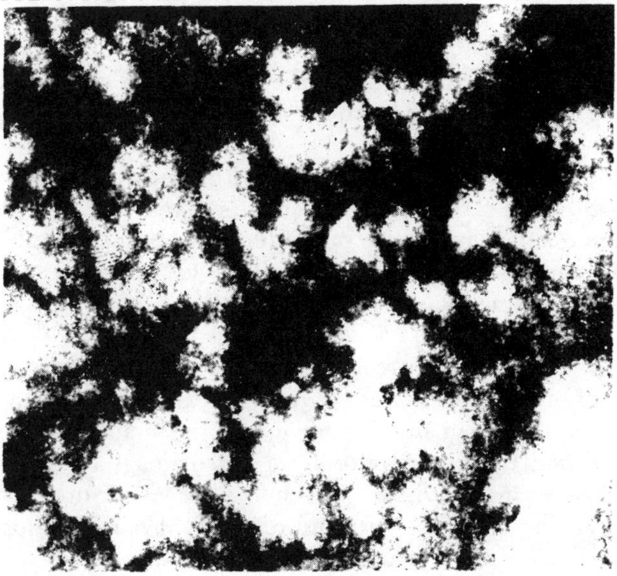

Cumulus, Solid Cell
(b)

Noncumulus
(c)

it was felt that at least 5 to 8 resolvable elements across the ridge or rima were necessary to determine the bright side and the dark side, and that the 50 × 50 raster would be adequate for the recognition system.

A similar experiment was performed with the NIMBUS data. It was determined that the 50 resolvable elements across the aperture did not give sufficient detail to recognize individual cells in the cumulus patterns. The digital pattern processing program was modified to achieve a resolution of 75 elements across the aperture.

C. PHOTOGRAPHIC-TO-DIGITAL CONVERSION. The procedure for converting the photographic pattern sets to pattern files stored on digital magnetic tapes, in a form suitable for use in the simulation experiments, was accomplished by first developing a video image of the photograph with the slow scan television system. The video output was then recorded on analog magnetic tape and replayed through analog-to-digital conversion equipment creating a set of digitized video tapes. The digitized tapes were processed to obtain the correct resolution, enhance the contrast, and eliminate "between picture" noise. Finally the processed pictures were edited to separate training and generalization samples and to provide translated versions of the recorded pictures.

Each of the basic lunar patterns was initially recorded in three rotations, differing by about 15°, providing from 120 to 150 digital pictures for each set. By taking translations and rotations of the basic patterns, the editing process resulted in a set of 1,000 training and 200 generalization patterns for each of the four basic pattern sets. For the NIMBUS photographs an editing program was also employed to provide several translations and a 180° rotation of the stored patterns to expand the pattern files. The editing process again produced a set of 1000 training and 200 generalization patterns for each of the three basic pattern sets.

3. *Experimental programs.* A. DECISION FUNCTIONS. The techniques used for designing decision functions (the response unit of Fig. 2) in this experiment were discussed in Section IIC. They are Forced Learning, Bayes Weights, Error Correction, Iterative Design, and MADALINE (Widrow, 1962). The first four techniques derive linear functions of the binary feature profile vectors for the computation of the decision and differ principally in the method used to derive the weight and threshold required to mechanize the decision function. The fifth technique generates a piecewise linear function in the feature space.

B. STATISTICAL FEATURE DETECTORS. Two techniques for generating binary feature detectors, or logic units, were used in the initial experiments; one yielding units with linear switching surfaces and one yielding quadratic input units. The linear units proved to be considerably less effective than the quadratic units and will not be discussed.

Each unit has a limited number of randomly selected input connections; thus, each views the patterns as projected on a subspace of the signal space. The switching surface for the unit is derived from the analysis of the moments of the sample patterns as projected into this subspace. The DAID (see Section IID) computer program was used to generate the quadratic logic units. The DAID program designs the set of units (statistical features) sequentially, five units being added to the list in each pass. A decision function is defined concurrently, using the iterative design algorithm. The loss function of the iterative design method is used to control the overall system design.

The selection process of the iterative design algorithm is used to obtain the five units added to the system in each pass. Fifteen six-dimensional subspaces (of the signal space) are chosen by selecting their coordinates randomly. Within a randomly selected subspace, the switching surface of a unit is defined by the general quadratic expression of Eq. (4.11) with $D(\mathbf{x}) = 0$. The 15 candidate property filters are then evaluated, and five are selected—those which provide the greatest decrease in the system loss. Their output weights are assigned and the output weights of the previously retained units are updated. Two cycles through the sample patterns are required in each pass. In the first cycle, mean vectors and covariance matrices are collected; in the second, the activities of the units for the sample patterns are computed and stored. Using this technique, 310 logic units or statistical feature detectors were designed for the basic lunar pattern recognition task discussed in Section 3c below. For the cloud-pattern recognition task, 400 units were designed. In both cases the output weights for each unit were discarded and the design techniques of Section 3a above were used to reassign the decision function, or to effect the partitioning of the feature space.

C. RECOGNITION TASKS. The three tasks concerned with differentiating between prominences of the lunar terrain are:

(1) Task CVC: Separate craters with central elevations from craters without central elevations.

(2) Task RVR: Separate wrinkle ridges from rima.

(3) Task CVR: Separate the composite class of craters with and without elevations from the composite class of ridges and rima.

Of the three tasks, separating the craters with central elevations from those without is the most difficult. Although the craters themselves are usually well defined, the central elevations are not. The elevations, which are the significant portion of the image in this task, cover less than one percent of the sensory field. Separating the ridges from the rima represents a task of intermediate difficulty. The patterns in general are not well defined. Inspection of computer printouts of the patterns revealed that a number of samples are not readily classified by the observer, even though the significant portions of the patterns are larger than in the crater problem, covering perhaps 5 to 15 percent of the sensory field. The task of separating the craters from the ridges and rima is the easiest of the three; as the significant pattern characteristic, the crater, is usually well defined and may constitute more than 30 percent of the image.

The remaining two tasks involved cloud textures in NIMBUS photographs. In these cases the cloud patterns covered a major portion of the sampling aperture.

(4) Task PVS: Separate cumulus polygonal cells from cumulus solid cells.

(5) Task NVC: Separate noncumulus cloud cover from the composite class of cumulus polygonal and solid cells.

4. *Results.* A. LUNAR DATA. Table VI presents the results achieved on the three classification tasks. The recursive techniques (MADALINE, Error Correction, and Iterative Design) were able to separate the training sample effectively and in general out-performed the nonrecursive techniques, except for the CVC task where performance was generally poor. It can be seen that the generalization performance is tied to the size of the significant pattern characteristic present in the field. The percentage of correct classification increased markedly from the CVC to the RVR task and was near perfect on the CVR task. Considering that upon examination of the data a number of patterns existed for which the classification by an observer could not be made accurately, and some in which the ridge or rima was difficult to locate, the generalization performance appeared encouraging and led to the further experiments discussed in subsequent sections.

TABLE VI

LUNAR PATTERNS CLASSIFICATION RESULTS
310 Daid units

	Recognition Task					
	Percentage Correct on Design Patterns			Percentage Correct on Generalization Patterns		
Design Technique	CVC	RVR	CVR	CVC	RVR	CVR
Forced Learning	82.60	81.20	78.50	62.75	71.0	74.75
Bayes Weights	84.10	82.60	82.60	63.75	75.25	77.50
Error Correction	92.80	100.00	99.25	59.75	70.25	99.25
Iterative Design	92.10	100.00	99.50	59.00	73.75	99.50
MADALINE	100.00	95.80	94.35	58.00	75.75	89.5

B. NIMBUS DATA. The performances achieved are shown in Tables VII and VIII. For the three recursive techniques, two blocks of data are shown. The first block shows the cycle in the recursive process at which the best performance on the training patterns is achieved, and the classification and generalization performance at that point. The second block indicates the cycle and performance levels for best generalization performance. The total number of cycles examined is also indicated.

Both the iterative design and MADALINE achieved perfect or near perfect separation of the training patterns. The best generalization performances are achieved by iterative design and MADALINE. Iterative design and error correction achieve their best generalization performance very early in the design. This has been observed consistently, and may be characteristic of these two techniques. Figure 10 shows the performance of the iterative design technique on a cycle-by-cycle basis. The solid lines represent classification performance, the broken lines show generalization performance. Of the three high performance techniques, MADALINE, as illustrated in Fig. 11, shows the least sacrifice in generalization performance when classification performance is used as the criterion for terminating the design.

More advanced desings for Tasks PVS and NVC were accomplished using a modified form of the DAID program (labeled QSID). Generalization performance of 87.5 and 86.0 were achieved, using 50 and 100 feature detectors for these tasks, respectively. The performance level was not significantly altered by this design but the number of feature detectors required were reduced drastically, lending itself well to a hardware implementation.

TABLE VII

CUMULUS VS. NONCUMULUS—400 DAID UNITS

Technique	Classification %	Generalization %
Forced Learning	78.00	81.25
Bayes Weights	77.90	82.50

	Total Cycles	For Best Classification			For Best Generalization		
		Classif. %	Gen. %	Cycles	Classif. %	Gen. %	Cycles
Error Correction	365	95.15	81.75	81	92.20	85.75	6
Iterative Design	78	100.00	84.25	78	93.45	86.25	2
MADALINE	63	100.00	85.50	63	99.80	86.00	59

TABLE VIII

SOLID CELLS VS. POLYGONAL CELLS—400 DAID UNITS

Technique	Classification %	Generalization %
Forced Learning	86.10	81.00
Bayes Weights	86.10	82.00

	Total Cycles	For Best Classification			For Best Generalization		
		Classif. %	Gen. %	Cycles	Classif. %	Gen. %	Cycles
Error Correction	192	92.40	80.50	34	89.30	83.00	1
Iterative Design	47	98.50	82.75	47	90.50	85.50	1
MADALINE	112	99.85	85.00	76	97.40	85.50	72

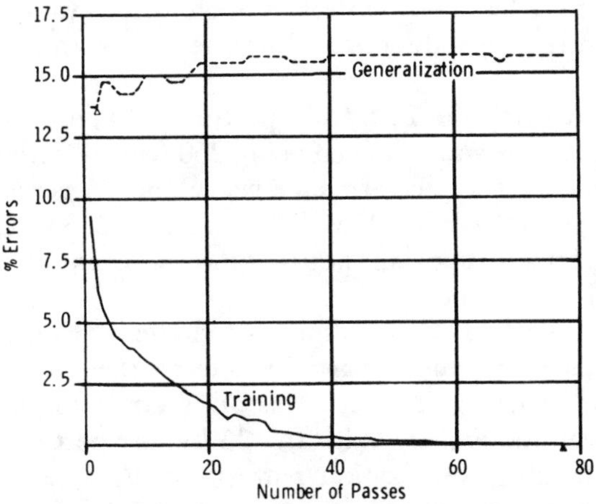

FIGURE 10. Iterative design—cumulus vs. noncumulus

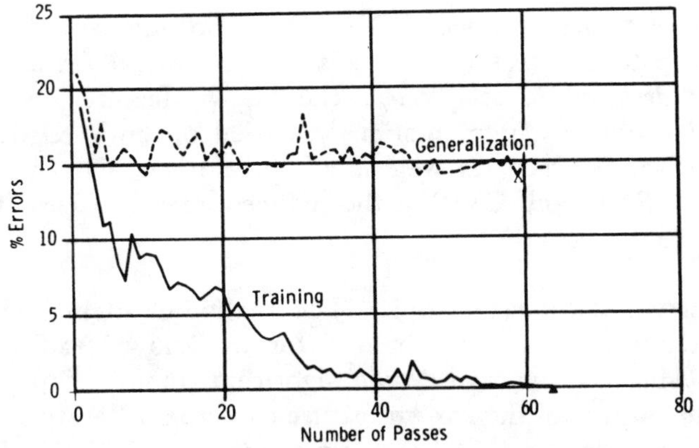

FIGURE 11. MADALINE—cumulus vs. noncumulus

C. REDUCED APERTURE PATTERNS. In an approach toward improving the signal-to-noise ratios in the poorly defined patterns such as those involved in the CVC and RVR task, reduced scanning apertures were used. Subapertures of 15 by 15 and 25 by 25 were applied to each sample lunar pattern, training and generalization. The subapertures were positioned to include as much as possible of the significant characteristics of the patterns. The effect of reducing the aperture is greater on the craters than on the ridges and rima. This is because part of the ridges and rima are sacrificed as the aperture size is decreased, while none of a central elevation is lost. The craters with elevations thus gain quadratically with aperture size reduction, while the ridges and rima gain only linearly.

For Task RVR using the 25 by 25 aperture, 100 percent classification of the training patterns was achieved using 260 feature detectors designed by DAID. Generalization performance was about 75 percent. Using the 15 by 15 aperture on Task RVR, and a network of 235 feature detectors, generalization performances showed a more substantial improvement, reaching a level of 84.5 percent.

The results on Task CVC show more dramatic improvements than on Task RVR. This is no doubt partially due to the quadratic effect on crater patterns of aperture reduction as opposed to the linear effect on ridges and rima noted earlier. With the 25 by 25 aperture, 82.5 percent was achieved on the generalization patterns using a set of 140 feature detectors. When the aperture is reduced to 15 by 15, another large increase in performance is noted. Only 65 feature detectors are needed to produce a 96.25 percent correct generalization performance.

5. *Augmentation of Known Features.* The augmentation of a set of known feature detectors with a set of statistical feature detectors *specifically designed to complement* the known features is a virtually untouched problem. Augmentation was tried on both NIMBUS tasks (Tasks PVS and NVC), as well as all three lunar pattern recognition tasks (CVC, RVR, and CVR) at the reduced aperture sizes of 25 by 25 and 15 by 15.

A. AUGMENTATION TECHNIQUE. The method of augmentation was as follows: A linear decision mechanism for the known features was first designed using the iterative design algorithm (modified to process the continuous outputs of the known feature detectors). Iterative design was used for three reasons: (1) design times are short, (2) the designs are optimized in terms of the pattern losses used in the rest of the process, and (3) compensation for variation of means and variances between feature detectors is automatic. After this design was complete, each sample pattern in the training set was assigned a loss value. This portion of the system design was held fixed for the rest of the process. The losses for the training samples were used as initial values for the sample pattern losses in the QSID program. Thus, the statistical features are selected to complement the known features.

After the set of augmenting statistical features was selected, the decision mechanism generated by the QSID program was discarded. That portion of the decision mechanism was redesigned by applying the iterative design algorithm, again using initial values for losses of the training patterns. Performance on the sample patterns was determined by adding the decision functions for the known and statistical feature sets. Again, the use of the iterative design algorithm made the equal weighting of these two decision functions automatic.

B. KNOWN FEATURES. The set of 29 known features listed in Table IX was specifically designed for recognizing cloud patterns. Fifteen of these 29 known features (numbers 1–14 and 29) relate to general characteristics of a two-dimensional brightness field. The remaining features are specifically tailored to the cloud-recognition problem. These 15 features were also used in the lunar terrain-recognition experiments.

TABLE IX

KNOWN PROPERTIES

1. Mean Brightness		15. Mean Cloud Segment		
2. Brightness Variance		16. Number of Clouds		
3.	0	17. Mean Cloud Size		
4. Relative Frequency	1	18. Variance Cloud Size		
5. (proportionate number	2	19.	1–25	Number of
6. of resolution elements)	3	20.	26–100	resolution
7. of Each	4	21. Number of	101–225	elements
8. Gray Level	5	22. Clouds in	226–400	comprising
9.	6	23. Each Sampling	401–900	a sampling
10.	7	24. Aperture	901–1600	aperture
11. Information in the *X*-Direction (adjacent points)		25.	1601–2500	(ranges from
		26.	2501–3600	5 × 5 to
12. Information in the *Y*-Direction		27.	3601–4900	75 × 75
		28.	4901–5625	element).
13. Mean Gray Level Area (connected regions of constant gray level)		29. 0.80 contour area (auto-correlation function)		
14. Variance, Gray Level Area				

Most of the entries in Table IX are self-explanatory. The following definitions are offered for those which are not.

Information in the X and Y Directions: Let $P(I)$ be the unconditional probability of brightness I, $0 \leqslant I \leqslant 7$, calculated from a particular pattern.

$P(J \mid I)$ is the probability of brightness J, given that the brightness is I at the adjacent point.

$H_q(J \mid I)$ is the conditional information of J given I where q is either X or Y.

$$H_q(J \mid I) = \sum_{I=0}^{7} P(I) \sum_{J=0}^{7} P(J \mid I) \log P(J \mid I)$$

Mean Gray Level Area: The average size of connected areas of constant brightness, I for $0 \leqslant I \leqslant 7$.

Variance, Gray Level Area: The variance of size for connected areas of constant brightness, I for $0 \leqslant I \leqslant 7$.

0.80 *Contour Area*: The area bounded by the y-axis and 0.80 autocorrelation contour.

C. AUGMENTED SYSTEMS. Table X presents the results obtained both with the known features alone, and with known features augmented by statistical features. On Task PVS a significant performance decrease was encountered, and on Task CVC at the 15 × 15 aperture an insignificant performance change occurred. These failures are not disappointing, as performances with the known features alone are 97 percent and 96 percent, respectively. On Task CVR at both apertures, and on Task CVC at 25 × 25, very substantial reductions in the error rates accompanied the augmentation. The likelihood that these improvements occurred by change is quite remote as illustrated by the last column of Table IX. A modest performance improvement is noted on Task NVC. The reduction in the error rate is only one-third to one-half as large as those achieved in the better cases. For Task RVR the reductions in

TABLE X

GENERALIZATION PERFORMANCES

Task	Aperture	Known Features	Known Features plus Augmenting Statistical Features	Percentage Decrease in Error Rate	Probability of Chance Occurrence
NVC	75 × 75	90.00	92.75	27.5	0.083
PVS	75 × 75	97.00	94.25	−91.7	.029
CVR	25 × 25	92.00	97.00	62.5	.0009
	15 × 15	81.50	96.00	78.4	$< 10^{-10}$
RVR	25 × 25	78.50	80.00	7.0	.300
	15 × 15	81.00	82.75	9.2	.260
CVC	25 × 25	71.50	85.75	50.0	.00003
	15 × 15	96.00	96.25	6.2	.426

the error rates were relatively small. Nonetheless, in at least half of the test cases on which augmentation would be important to a designer, substantial performance increases were achieved. Thus, the augmentation process appears to be a valuable one, particularly when it is most appropriate—when the known features alone do not produce high performance levels.

6. *Summary.* Using only statistically derived feature detectors, recognition systems were designed to give more than 84 percent correct generalization decisions on all five tasks. For three of the tasks performances near 85 percent were obtained; on one task 96 percent was obtained; and on the fifth task, 99.5 percent was achieved. To accomplish this, the size of the sampling aperture had to be reduced for two of the tasks. The importance of choosing the proper aperture size was strongly emphasized on one task, for which performance rose from 64 percent with a 50×50 aperture to 96 percent with a 15×15 aperture.

Two of the tasks, for which 86 percent and 87.5 percent were obtained, were cloud-pattern tasks. Using only 15 known features, recognition systems were designed which achieved 90 percent and 97 percent correct decisions on these tasks. Augmenting the logically designed or known, feature detectors with statistically designed feature detectors raised the 90 percent figure to 92.75 percent.

Experiments with known features and techniques to augment the known features with statistically designed feature detectors were performed. As a result it was demonstrated that, where possible, known feature detectors should be designed for each recognition task. Augmentation of these known features with statistically designed features should then be attempted and the resulting performance evaluated. An improvement in performance can be expected particularly where it is needed most—where known feature performance is low.

In view of the quality of the sample patterns, many of which are difficult for a human observer to identify, it is felt that the performances obtained are sufficiently good to demonstrate the feasibility of performing on-board classification using spaceborne pattern recognition systems.

APPENDIX

Iterative Design

The following derivation is provided for Eqs. (4.4), (4.5), and (4.6) of Section IID1. The output form the ith feature detector (see Fig. 2) is defined as b_i.

Let:

$$b_i(j) = \begin{cases} 1 \text{ if the } j\text{th sample pattern activates the } i\text{th feature detector;} \\ 0 \text{ otherwise} \end{cases}$$

w_i = the output weight assigned to the ith feature detector

θ = the threshold of response unit;

β_j = the linear discriminant, or input to the response unit for the jth patterns;

M = number of feature detectors in the system at any time;

$$\beta_j = \sum_{i=1}^{M} b_i(j)\, w_i \tag{4.A.1}$$

$$\delta_j = \begin{cases} 1 \text{ if the } j\text{th pattern is of class 1 (positive pattern)} \\ -1 \text{ if the } j\text{th pattern is of class 2 (negative pattern)} \end{cases}$$

I_+ = set of patterns for which $\delta_j = 1$

I_- = set of patterns for which $\delta_j = -1$

For a given candidate for the Nth feature detector:

I_N = set of patterns for which $b_N(j) = 1$

$\bar{I}_N$ = set of patterns for which $b_N(j) = 0$

An exponential form for the pattern loss is utilized:

$$L_j = \exp \delta_j(\theta - \beta_j) \tag{4.A.2}$$

and the system loss is:

$$SL = \sum_j L_j = \sum_j \exp[\delta_j(\theta - \beta_j)] \tag{4.A.3}$$

The weight, W_N, to be assigned to the candidate feature detector and the change in the response unit threshold, $\Delta\theta$, required to minimize the system loss is as follows:

Find W_N and $\Delta\theta$ such that the system loss, with the Nth candidate added,

$$SL = \sum_j L_j \exp[\delta_j(\Delta\theta - b_N(j)\, W_N)] \tag{4.A.4}$$

is a minimum. Consider first the weight assigned to the Nth candidate:

$$\frac{\partial(SL)}{\partial W_N} = 0 = \sum_j \{-\delta_j b_N(j)\, L_j \exp[\delta_j(\Delta\theta - b_N(j)\, W_N)]\} \tag{4.A.5}$$

Equation (4.A.5) can be partitioned into the contributions made by those patterns contained in I_+ (that is, $\delta_j = 1$) and those in I_- ($\delta_j = -1$).

$$\sum_{j\in I_+} - b_N(j) L_j \exp[\Delta\theta - b_N(j)\, W_N] + \sum_{j\in I_-} b_N(j) L_j \exp - [\Delta\theta - b_N(j)\, W_N] = 0 \tag{4.A.6}$$

Accounting for the activity of the Nth feature detector Eq. (4.A.6) becomes:

$$\sum_{j\in I_+\cap I_N} - L_j \exp[\Delta\theta - W_N] + \sum_{j\in I_-\cap I_N} L_j \exp - [\Delta\theta - W_N] = 0 \tag{4.A.7}$$

$$\exp[-(\Delta\theta - W_N)] \sum_{j\in I_-\cap I_N} L_j = \exp(\Delta\theta - W_N) \sum_{j\in I_+\cap I_N} L_j \tag{4.A.8}$$

$$\frac{\sum_{j\in I_-\cap I_N} L_j}{\sum_{j\in I_+\cap I_N} L_j} = \exp[2(\Delta\theta - W_N)] \tag{4.A.9}$$

Taking the ln of both sides of Eq. (4.A.9) provides the value for the weight of the candidate unit:

$$W_N = \Delta\theta - 1/2 \ln \left\{\frac{\sum_{j\in I_-\cap I_N} L_j}{\sum_{j\in I_+\cap I_N} L_j}\right\} \tag{4.A.10}$$

To determine the change in the response unit threshold, Eq. (4.A.4) is differentiated with respect of $\Delta\theta$ and set to 0:

$$\frac{\partial(SL)}{\partial\Delta\theta} = 0 = \sum_j \delta_j L_j \exp[\delta_j(\Delta\theta - b_N(j)\, W_N)] \tag{4.A.11}$$

$$\sum_{j\in I_+} L_j \exp[\Delta\theta - b_N(j)\, W_N] = \sum_{j\in I_-} L_j \exp - [\Delta\theta - b_N(j)\, W_N] \tag{4.A.12}$$

Since the activity of all units affect the response unit threshold, Eq. (4.A.12) may be partitioned into components arising from contributions made by all patterns, not only those acting on the Nth unit. Taking this into account and factoring out $e^{\Delta\theta}$:

$$e^{\Delta\theta}\left\{\sum_{j\in I_+\cap I_N} L_j\, e^{-W_N} + \sum_{j\in I_+\cap \bar{I}_N} L_j\right\} = e^{-\Delta\theta}\left\{\sum_{j\in I_-\cap I_N} L_j\, e^{W_N} + \sum_{j\in I_-\cap \bar{I}_N} L_j\right\} \tag{4.A.13}$$

From Eq. (4.A.8):

$$e^{\Delta\theta} \sum_{j\in I_+\cap I_N} L_j\, e^{-W_N} = e^{-\Delta\theta} \sum_{j\in I_-\cap I_N} L_j\, e^{W_N}$$

Therefore Eq. (4.A.13) becomes:

$$e^{\Delta\theta} \sum_{j\in I_+\cap \bar{I}_N} L_j = e^{-\Delta\theta} \sum_{j\in I_-\cap \bar{I}_N} L_j \tag{4.A.14}$$

and the change in response unit threshold is:

$$\Delta\theta = 1/2 \ln \left\{\frac{\sum_{j\in I_-\cap \bar{I}_N} L_j}{\sum_{j\in I_+\cap \bar{I}_N} L_j}\right\} \tag{4.A.15}$$

The system loss when the Nth feature detector is added can be derived in the same manner as above. Partitioning Eq. (4.A.4) into its components:

$$SL = \sum_{j\in I_+\cap I_N} L_j \exp[\Delta\theta - W_N] + \sum_{j\in I_-\cap I_N} L_j \exp - [\Delta\theta - W_N]$$

$$+ \sum_{j\in I_+\cap \bar{I}_N} L_j \exp(\Delta\theta) + \sum_{j\in I_-\cap \bar{I}_N} L_j \exp - (\Delta\theta) \tag{4.A.16}$$

From Eq. (4.A.9):

$$e^{\Delta\theta - W_N} = \left\{\frac{\sum_{j\in I_-\cap I_N} L_j}{\sum_{j\in I_+\cap I_N} L_j}\right\}^{1/2} \tag{4.A.17}$$

and:

$$e^{-(\Delta\theta - W_N)} = \left\{\frac{\sum_{j\in I_+\cap I_N} L_j}{\sum_{j\in I_-\cap I_N} L_j}\right\}^{1/2} \tag{4.A.18}$$

From Eq. (4.A.15):

$$e^{\Delta\theta} = \left\{\frac{\sum_{j\in I_-\cap \bar{I}_N} L_j}{\sum_{j\in I_+\cap \bar{I}_N} L_j}\right\}^{1/2} \tag{4.A.19}$$

and:

$$e^{-\Delta\theta} = \left\{\frac{\sum_{j\in I_+\cap \bar{I}_N} L_j}{\sum_{j\in I_-\cap \bar{I}_N} L_j}\right\}^{1/2} \tag{4.A.20}$$

Combining Eqs. (4.A.17) through (4.A.20) with Eq. (4.A.16) gives:

$$SL = \sum_{j\in I_+\cap I_N} L_j \left\{\frac{\sum_{j\in I_-\cap I_N} L_j}{\sum_{j\in I_+\cap I_N} L_j}\right\}^{1/2} + \sum_{j\in I_-\cap I_n} L_j \left\{\frac{\sum_{j\in I_+\cap I_N} L_j}{\sum_{j\in I_-\cap I_N} L_j}\right\}^{1/2}$$

$$+ \sum_{j\in I_+\cap I_N} L_j \left\{\frac{\sum_{j\in I_-\cap I_N} L_j}{\sum_{j\in I_+\cap I_N} L_j}\right\}^{1/2} + \sum_{j\in I_-\cap I_N} L_j \left\{\frac{\sum_{j\in I_+\cap I_N} L_j}{\sum_{j\in I_-\cap I_N} L_j}\right\}^{1/2}$$

$$SL = \left\{\sum_{j\in I_+\cap I_N} L_j\right\}^{1/2} \left\{\sum_{j\in I_-\cap I_N} L_j\right\}^{1/2} + \left\{\sum_{j\in I_-\cap I_N} L_j\right\}^{1/2} \left\{\sum_{j\in I_+\cap I_N} L_j\right\}^{1/2}$$

$$+ \left\{\sum_{j\in I_+\cap I_N} L_j\right\}^{1/2} \left\{\sum_{j\in I_-\cap I_N} L_j\right\}^{1/2} + \left\{\sum_{j\in I_-\cap I_N} L_j\right\}^{1/2} \left\{\sum_{j\in I_+\cap I_N} L_j\right\}^{1/2} \qquad (4.A.21)$$

Combining terms reduces this to:

$$SL = 2\sqrt{\Big(\sum_{j\in I_+\cap I_N} L_j\Big)\Big(\sum_{j\in I_-\cap I_N} L_j\Big)} + 2\sqrt{\Big(\sum_{j\in I_+\cap I_N} L_j\Big)\Big(\sum_{j\in I_-\cap I_N} L_j\Big)} \qquad (4.A.22)$$

References

Brain, A. E., Duda, R. O., Hall, D. J., and Munson, J. H., Graphical data processing research study and experimental investigation. Quarterly Progress Rept. 5, Stanford Research Institute, Menlo Park, Calif., July-Sept. 1964.

Cooley, J. W. and Tukey, J. W., An algorithm for the machine calculation of complex Fourier series. *Math. of Computation 19*, No. 90, pp. 297–301 (1965).

Dement, W. C. and Kleitman, N., Cyclic variations in EEG during sleep and their relation to eye movements, body motility and dreaming. *Electro-encephalography and Clinical Neurophysiology 9*, pp. 673–710 (1957).

Gerdes, J. W., Floyd, W. B., and Richards, G. O., Automatic target recognition device. Tech. Rept. No. RADC–TR–65–438, Jan. 1966.

Joseph, R. D., Contributions to perceptron theory. Ph.D. Thesis, Cornell Univ., Ithaca, New York, 1961.

Joseph, R. D., Kelly, P. M., and Viglione, S. S., An optical decision filter. *Proc. IEEE 51*, No. 8, pp. 1098–1118 (1963).

Joseph, R. D., Runge, R. G., and Viglione, S. S., Research on the utilization of pattern recognition techniques to identify and classify objects in video data. *Nasa Contractor Rept.* NASA CR–99, prepared by Astropower Laboratory, Douglas Aircraft Co., Newport Beach, Calif., March 1968.

Joseph, R. D. and Viglione, S. S., Design of a Cloud Pattern Recognition System, *Final Rept. on Contract Nas 5-3866*, prepared for NASA, Goddard Space Flight Center by Astropower Laboratory, Douglas Aircraft Co., Newport Beach, Calif., Sept. 1965.

Kales, A. and Rechtschaffen, A. (eds.), A manual for standardized terminology, techniques, and scoring system for sleep stages of human subjects. National Institute of Health Publication No. 204, 1968.

Kilo, L. G. and Osselton, J. W., "Clinical Electroencephalography." Butterworths, Washington, D. C. 1966.

Kovàsnay, L. S. G. and Joseph, H. M., Image Processing. *Proc. IRE*, pp. 560–570, May 1965.

Neyman, J. and Pearson, E. S., "Statistical Research Memoirs." Vol. I. University College, London, England, 1936.

Nilsson, N. J., "Learning Machines: Foundations of Trainable Pattern-Classifying Systems." McGraw–Hill, New York, 1965.

Rosenblatt, F., "Principles of Neurodynamics: Perceptrons and the Theory of Brain Mechanisms." Spartan Books, Washington, D. C., 1962.

VanderLugt, A., Rotz, F. B., and Klooster, A., Jr., Character reading by optical spatial filtering. *In* "Optical and Electro-Optical Information Processing" (J. T. Tippett *et al.*, eds.), Chap. 7, pp. 125–141. MIT Press, Cambridge, Mass., 1965.

Widrow, B., Generalization and information storage in networks of ADALINE "neurons." *In* "Self-Organizing Systems" (M. C. Yovits, G. T. Jacobi, and G. D. Goldstein, eds.), pp. 435–461. Spartan Books, Washington, D. C., 1962.

5

J. M. Mendel

SYNTHESIS OF QUASI-OPTIMAL SWITCHING SURFACES BY MEANS OF TRAINING TECHNIQUES

I. Introduction

Control system design problems can, as pointed out in Chapter 8, be conveniently viewed as collections of mappings from an input space into an output space. It has been said, for example, that "... the very problem of automatic control as a whole can be considered to be the problem of assigning the input situation to one or another class, and to generate the optimal response as a function of that class" (Aizerman *et al.*, 1964a). This mapping interpretation for control problems permits the control engineer to apply pattern recognition techniques to their solutions. In this chapter, we will investigate how training algorithms can be applied to the problem of designing multilevel, quasi-optimal controllers for dynamic processes. By multilevel, we mean that the controller is capable of only a finite collection of control actions; by quasi-optimal, we mean that the controller is slightly suboptimal. (These concepts are further clarified in Section II.)

Many of the results which are presented here in the context of a control system application are also suitable for other types of applications in which training algorithms may be, or have been, used. Examples of such applications are (1) reconstruction of the characteristics of a function generator from perfect measurements or from noisy measurements (Aizerman *et al.*, 1964c; Duda *et al.*, 1963); (2) determination of a confidence level (Aizerman *et al.*, 1964b); (3) real-time trainable speech-recognition systems (Talbert *et al.*, 1963); and (4) weather prediction (Duda *et al.*, 1963). In all of these applications, it is possible to introduce a vector space, Ω_X, and some function, $f(\mathbf{x})$, defined on Ω_X in such a way that the process of learning occurs. During the learning process, points $\mathbf{x}^1, \mathbf{x}^2, \ldots, \mathbf{x}^k, \ldots$ from Ω_X, together with some information about $f(\mathbf{x})$ at these points, are presented. The result of learning is the synthesis of a function which in a certain sense approximates $f(\mathbf{x})$.

Why not use more conventional approximation techniques for these problems? There are a number of reasons. First, as pointed out by Aizerman *et al.*, (1966), the usual approximation techniques are often practically inapplicable to the solution of such problems, mainly because points $\mathbf{x}^1, \mathbf{x}^2, \ldots, \mathbf{x}^k, \ldots$ cannot be chosen at will but are presented independently in an irregular manner. They may, for example, be presented in accordance with a certain probability distribution which is not known a priori. Second, the space, Ω_X, is often multidimensional, and this hampers the application of ordinary approximation techniques. The sequential nature of the learning approach makes it quite amenable to multidimensional situations. Finally, information about the values of the function, $f(\mathbf{x})$, at the points, $\mathbf{x}^k$, may be incomplete. In the quasi-optimal controller application, for example, only the sign of $f(\mathbf{x}^k)$ is given.

Multilevel control and reasons for quasi-optimal control are discussed in Section II. The structure of a trainable controller, training in the context of the multilevel control application, and a collection of sub-problems that must be solved when pattern recognition techniques are used to synthesize multilevel controllers, are the topics of Section III. The details of two-feature processing techniques are discussed in Section IV, and a brief review of applications that have been reported on in the literature is given in Section V.

II. Quasi-Optimal Control

Multilevel controllers often result from applications of optimization theory to dynamic systems in which the control is subject to realistic constraints such as saturation.

Consider a linear time-invariant system described by the vector differential equation

$$\dot{\mathbf{x}}(t) = A\mathbf{x}(t) + \mathbf{b}u(t) \tag{5.1}$$

where $\mathbf{x}(t)$ is an $n \times 1$ state vector, A is an $n \times n$ constant matrix, $\mathbf{b}$ is an $n \times 1$ control distribution vector, and $u(t)$ is a normalized scalar control that is bounded in amplitude

$$| u(t) | \leqslant 1 \tag{5.2}$$

The solution for $\mathbf{x}(t)$ from Eq. (5.1) is (Athans and Falb, 1966)

$$\mathbf{x}(t) = e^{At}\mathbf{x}_0 + e^{At} \int_0^t e^{-A\tau}\mathbf{b}u(\tau)\, d\tau \tag{5.3}$$

If the initial state, $\mathbf{x}_0$, and the final state, $\mathbf{x}(t_f) = \mathbf{0}$, are given, then these states are related by the expression

$$\mathbf{x}_0 = -\int_0^{t_f} e^{-A\tau}\mathbf{b}u(\tau)\, d\tau \tag{5.4}$$

A control which satisfies Eq. (5.4) drives the system from its initial state, $\mathbf{x}_0$, to $\mathbf{0}$.

Example 1. We wish to find the time-optimal control, $u_T^*(t)$, which satisfies Eqs. (5.2) and (5.4) and minimizes the response time, t_f.

From Pontryagin's minimum principle, the optimal control, $u_T^*(t)$, minimizes the Hamiltonian $H(\mathbf{x}, \boldsymbol{\psi}, u)$ where

$$H(\mathbf{x}, \boldsymbol{\psi}, u) = \boldsymbol{\psi}'(t)\, \dot{\mathbf{x}}(t) + 1 \tag{5.5}$$

(for a more precise formulation of this problem and other optimal control problems, see Athans and Falb, 1966), and $\boldsymbol{\psi}(t)$ is the n-dimensional adjoint vector, which is the solution of the adjoint system of the system described by Eq. (5.1):

$$\dot{\boldsymbol{\psi}}(t) = -A\, \boldsymbol{\psi}(t), \qquad \boldsymbol{\psi}_0 \text{ unknown} \tag{5.6}$$

Minimization of $H(\mathbf{x}, \boldsymbol{\psi}, u)$ is, of course, subject to the constraints in Eqs. (5.2) and (5.4), and results in the following choice for $u_T^*(t)$:

$$u_T^*(t) = -\text{sgn}[\mathbf{b}'\boldsymbol{\psi}(t)] \tag{5.7}$$

The bistable nature of the optimal control is depicted in Fig. 1.

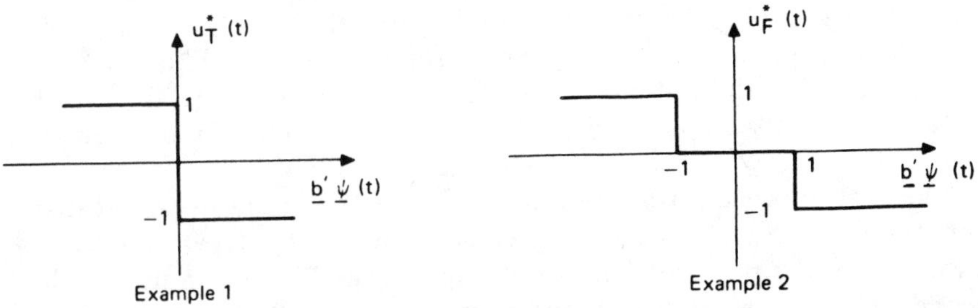

FIGURE 1. Optimal controls for Examples 1 and 2

Example 2. Four formulations of fuel-optimal problems exist. The first minimizes fuel consumption without restricting response time. The second minimizes fuel consumption with response time fixed a priori. In the third, fuel consumption is minimized with the response time bounded by a multiple of the minimum time corresponding to each initial state; with this method, the minimum time must be known as a function of the state. The last method, to which our attention is directed below, minimizes a linear combination of the consumed fuel and elapsed time.

We want to find the control, denoted $u_F{}^*(t)$, which satisfies Eqs. (5.2) and (5.4), and minimizes the cost-functional

$$J_F = \int_0^{t_f} [|\, u(t)| + K]\, dt \tag{5.8}$$

where t_f is free, and K is a specified positive constant. The Hamiltonian for this problem is

$$H(\mathbf{x}, \boldsymbol{\psi}, u) = \boldsymbol{\psi}'(t)\, \dot{\mathbf{x}}(t) + |\, u(t)| + K \tag{5.9}$$

where the adjoint vector is defined in Eq. (5.6).

From Pontryagin's minimum principle, the optimal control, $u_F{}^*(t)$, minimizes this Hamiltonian, subject to Eqs. (5.2) and (5.4). Performing the optimization, one finds

$$\begin{aligned} u_F{}^*(t) &= 0 \quad \text{if } |\, \mathbf{b}'\boldsymbol{\psi}(t)| < 1 \\ u_F{}^*(t) &= -\text{sgn}[\mathbf{b}'\boldsymbol{\psi}(t)] \quad \text{if } |\, \mathbf{b}'\boldsymbol{\psi}(t)| \geqslant 1 \end{aligned} \tag{5.10}$$

Hence, the optimal control for this problem is a three-level control (tristable). It is also depicted in Fig. 1.

Two approaches have been taken for implementing optimal controllers. In the first, optimal control is computed as an explicit function of time and initial state (initial conditions). This control is denoted $u^*(t)$ in the rest of this chapter. In the second, optimal control is computed as an explicit function of the system's state variables. This control is denoted $u^*(\mathbf{x})$ in the rest of this chapter; it differs from $u^*(t)$ in that $u^*(t)$ is an open-loop control whereas $u^*(\mathbf{x})$ is a closed-loop (feedback) control (see Fig. 2).

The first approach has often been suggested as a means for realizing optimal controllers. It is a natural consequence of applying Pontryagin's minimum principle, and has been demonstrated in Examples 1 and 2 above. In those examples, it was shown that $u_T{}^*(t)$ and $u_F{}^*(t)$ depend upon the solution to the adjoint system in Eq. (5.6). The solution of the adjoint system, however, depends—in some unknown manner—upon the system's initial conditions, $\mathbf{x}_0$. Usually, one must solve a two-point boundary value problem in order to determine the dependence of $\psi(t)$ on a specific value of $\mathbf{x}_0$. Thus, the first approach must always have available a computer capable of rapidly computing the optimal control for every initial condition, and usually requires an on-line digital computer.

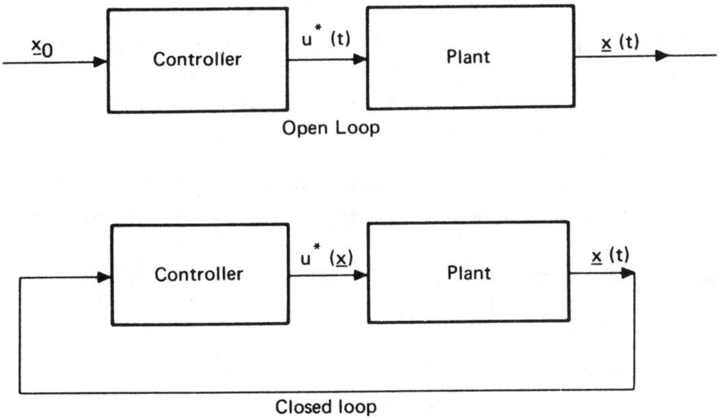

FIGURE 2. Open- and closed-loop controls

In the second approach, a large computer capacity is used during the design phase, when the controller is being obtained as a function of the system's states. The resulting controller is frequently referred to as a *switching function* or *switching surface*, since it is capable of deciding which control action should be applied, at every instant of time, as a function of the system's present states (Fig. 3, for example). Usually, as discussed by Smith (1964), a much smaller computer capacity is needed in the controller to evaluate the switching function, and often, the switching function can be mechanized using only analog equipment.

Although the second approach is more practical than the first, it has rarely been used because the optimal switching surfaces for higher than second- or third-order systems have an extremely complicated dependence upon the system's state variables. In only the simplest cases, such as the system in Fig. 3, can expressions for these surfaces be expressed in closed form (see Athans and Falb, 1966, for additional examples). As an alternative, control engineers have turned to quasi-optimal switching functions. These functions give slightly suboptimal performance, but are more feasible to implement than are the optimal switching functions. Three methods have been suggested for designing quasi-optimal switching functions (Smith, 1964):

1. An easily realizable functional form for the quasi-optimal switching function can be assumed, and the parameters set to minimize the cost-functional for a typical set of initial conditions.
2. The optimal switching surface can be determined in some manner, and then this surface can be approximated by some readily implemented, quasi-optimal surface.
3. Open-loop optimal controls can be determined in some manner for a small but representative collection of initial conditions, and then these controls can be used to obtain a quasi-optimal switching function by means of training techniques.

Because our interest here is in training techniques, our attention in the rest of this chapter is directed to the third method—trainable controllers.

Plant: $$\begin{pmatrix} \dot{x}_1 \\ \dot{x}_2 \end{pmatrix} = \begin{pmatrix} \lambda_1 & 0 \\ 0 & \lambda_2 \end{pmatrix} \begin{pmatrix} x_1 \\ x_2 \end{pmatrix} + \begin{pmatrix} \lambda_1 \\ \lambda_2 \end{pmatrix} u(t)$$

$$u_T^*(\underline{x}) = -\mathrm{sgn} \left\{ x_2 - \frac{x_1}{|x_1|} \left[(1 + |x_1|)^{\lambda_2/\lambda_1} - 1 \right] \right\}$$

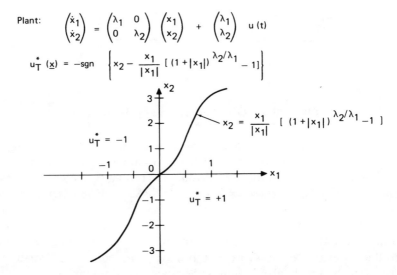

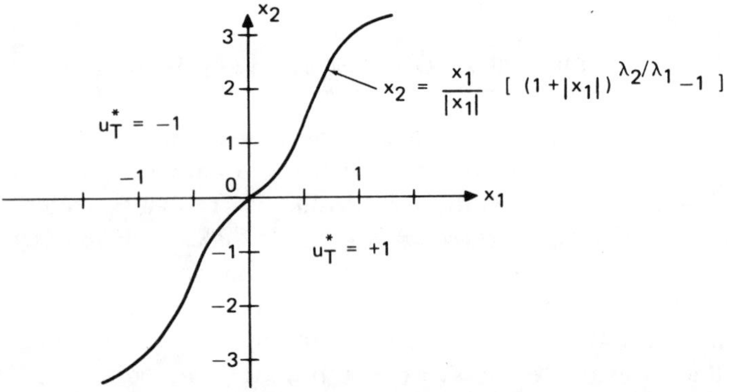

FIGURE 3. Time-optimal switching surface and function for a plant with two real time constants

III. The Method of Trainable Controllers

A. *Trainable Controllers*

A trainable controller (Mendel and Zapalac, 1968) achieves mappings of points from a feature space, Ω_X, into control categories. It includes discriminant functions which define a quasi-optimal switching surface.

These functions are specified during training by use of a training set that is derived from a set of open-loop optimal controls.

The structure of a trainable controller is depicted in Fig. 4. Information (features) from the feature space is processed in the φ-Units. In these units, the features (state variables and, perhaps, plant parameters or linear combinations of state variables) are processed either individually (quantization and encoding) or collectively (multivariable polynomials), as shown in Fig. 4. The output of a φ-Unit is transmitted to $l-1$ N-Units (networks). Each N-Unit is an adaptive linear threshold element (Fig. 5), the weights of which are adjusted during training. Hence,

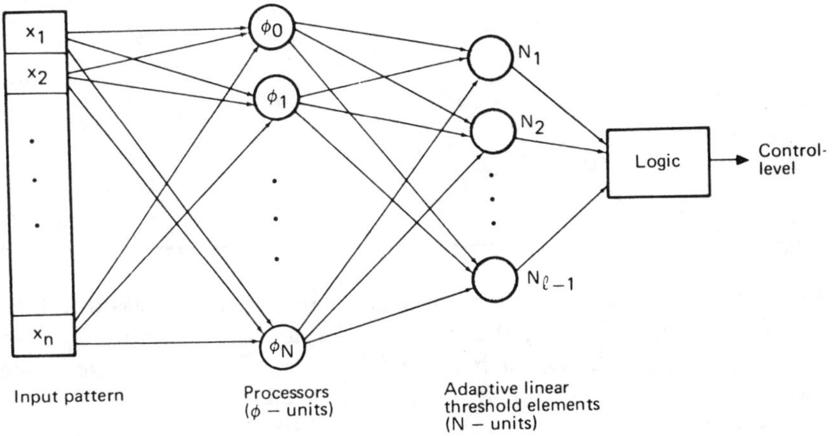

FIGURE 4. Trainable controller

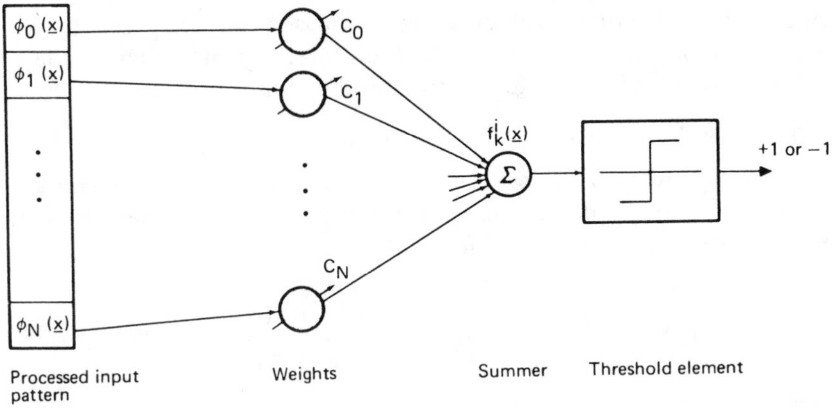

FIGURE 5. N-unit (N_i)

the input to the Logic-Units is an $(l-1)$ vector of $+1$'s and -1's. This vector is decoded in the Logic-Unit into the appropriate control-level. The logic for coding and decoding control-levels appears in the Table.

TABLE

LOGIC FOR CODING CONTROL LEVELS AND DECODING OUTPUT OF TRAINABLE CONTROLLER

Control Level	N-Unit N_1	N-Unit N_2	N-Unit N_3		N-Unit N_{l-2}	N-Unit N_{l-1}
1	+1	−1	−1	···	−1	−1
2	−1	+1	−1	···	−1	−1
3	−1	−1	+1	···	−1	−1
·				·		
·				·		
·				·		
l-1	−1	−1	−1	···	−1	+1
l	−1	−1	−1	···	−1	−1

Example 3. To illustrate an application of the Table, assume three control-levels such as $+1$, 0, and -1 (Section II, Example 2). Two N-Units are required, and each control-level is transformed into a two-bit word: $+1 \leftrightarrow (1, -1)$, $0 \leftrightarrow (-1, 1)$, and $-1 \leftrightarrow (-1, -1)$.

Observe, from the Table, that the ith N-Unit, N_i, learns a switching function that separates the ith control-level from the other levels. Hence, it is possible to view multilevel training as a collection of two-level (category) training problems (other techniques for handling multi-category classification problems are discussed in Chapters 1 and 3 and in Chaplin and Levadi, 1967); therefore, our attention in the rest of this chapter is directed to the two-level training problem.

B. *Two-Level Training*

A brief review of the two-level classification problem, in the context of control, is in order at this point. We can assume that a set of training samples exists for each *control-level* (A and B):

$$L(A) \triangleq \{\mathbf{x}^j(A): j = 1, 2, \ldots, N(A)\}$$
$$L(B) \triangleq \{\mathbf{x}^{j'}(B): j' = 1, 2, \ldots, N(B)\} \tag{5.11}$$

where

$$N(A) + N(B) = N' < \infty \tag{5.12}$$

In the present application, the training samples are obtained from open-loop optimal controls and trajectories.

A training sequence, denoted S_X, is constructed. S_X is an infinite sequence of patterns

$$S_X = \mathbf{x}^1, \mathbf{x}^2, \ldots, \mathbf{x}^k, \ldots \tag{5.13}$$

such that

1. Every $\mathbf{x}^k$ in S_X is a member of $L(A) \cup L(B)$.

2. Every element of $L(A) \cup L(B)$ may occur infinitely often in S_X.

It is further assumed that there exists a switching function, $f(\mathbf{x})$, such that

$$\begin{aligned} f(\mathbf{x}) &\geqslant 0 \quad \text{if } \mathbf{x} \sim A \\ f(\mathbf{x}) &< 0 \quad \text{if } \mathbf{x} \sim B \end{aligned} \tag{5.14}$$

for all $\mathbf{x} \in \Omega_X$. The two-level classification problem can then be considered to be the problem of determining a set of parameters, $C_i(k)(i = 0, 1, \ldots, N)$, such that with $\epsilon > 0$ (see Chapter 3)

$$\begin{aligned} f_k(\mathbf{x}^j) &\geqslant \epsilon \quad \text{if } \mathbf{x}^j \sim A \\ f_k(\mathbf{x}^j) &\leqslant -\epsilon \quad \text{if } \mathbf{x}^j \sim B \end{aligned} \tag{5.15}$$

for all N' training samples. $f_k(\mathbf{x})$ denotes the kth successive estimate of $f(\mathbf{x})$, and is given by the expression

$$f_k(\mathbf{x}) = \sum_{i=0}^{N} C_i(k)\, \varphi_i(\mathbf{x}) \qquad k = 1, 2, \ldots, K, \ldots \tag{5.16}$$

The convergence of the training procedure should occur in a finite number of steps if the two control-levels are separable by $f_k(\mathbf{x})$. [As pointed out in Chapter 3, $f_k(\mathbf{x})$ is nonunique.] The convergence is in a sense that no more error correction is needed for classifying the samples from $L(A)$ and $L(B)$. Letting

$$r_k = \tfrac{1}{2}[\operatorname{sgn} f(\mathbf{x}^k) - \operatorname{sgn} f_{k-1}(\mathbf{x}^k)] \tag{5.17}$$

this means that when

$$r_k = 0 \quad \text{for all } \mathbf{x}^k \in L(A) \cup L(B) \tag{5.18}$$

convergence is said to have occurred.

The parameters, $C_i(k)$, in Eq. (5.16) are updated by means of the following algorithm:

$$\left.\begin{aligned} C_i(k) &= C_i(k-1) + \gamma_k r_k \varphi_i(\mathbf{x}^k) \\ C_i(0) &= 0 \end{aligned}\right\} \tag{5.19}$$

Choosing γ_k suitably leads to either the fixed-increment or relaxation algorithms that were discussed in Chapter 3.

C. *Synthesis Procedure and Related Subproblems*

Figure 6 depicts the various subproblems and their interrelationships that must be studied when multilevel, quasi-optimal controllers are synthesized by means of pattern recognition techniques. Thus far in this section, we have touched briefly on the subproblems of: selection of a trainable controller; training sample and sequence; and training.

Feature extraction refers to the process of extracting a collection of properties which are known to be—or suspected to be—of value, and which are sufficient for convergence of the training process. In some applications, these properties are extracted from either raw data or preprocessed data. In the multilevel, quasi-optimal controller application, the features usually correspond to states, linear combinations of states, and plant parameters. Choosing important, perhaps optimal, features is difficult; however, techniques for obtaining such features have begun to appear in the literature (Heydorn and Tou, 1967). Fortunately, in control system applications, much a priori information is available about "important" features.

Two types of *feature processing* will be of interest to us here: (1) polynomial processing, and (2) quantization-encoding processing. Polynomial processing has the advantage of leading to analytical expressions for $f_k(\mathbf{x})$. Such expressions, which are in terms of the state variables (and possibly plant parameters), may be very useful if one wishes to perform additional analyses of the nonlinear control system. In addition, these expressions may suggest simpler nonlinear feedback control laws for the system. Usually, not as much information about features is required when polynomial processing is employed; however, as is usually the case when less information is used during a design, the resulting controller may be rather complicated because of the requirement for computing multivariable polynomials on-line.

Quantizing and encoding has the advantage of leading to relatively simple and highly reliable processors. A disadvantage of this type of processing is that analytical expressions for $f_k(\mathbf{x})$ are not obtained in the original feature space, but are obtained instead in the encoded space. To date, no technique exists for transforming the expression for the separation function from the encoded space back to the original feature space. Both polynomial processing and quantization-encoding processing are discussed further in Section IV.

A computer flow diagram for the *training and testing-after-training subproblems*, both of which are intimately related, is given in Fig. 7.

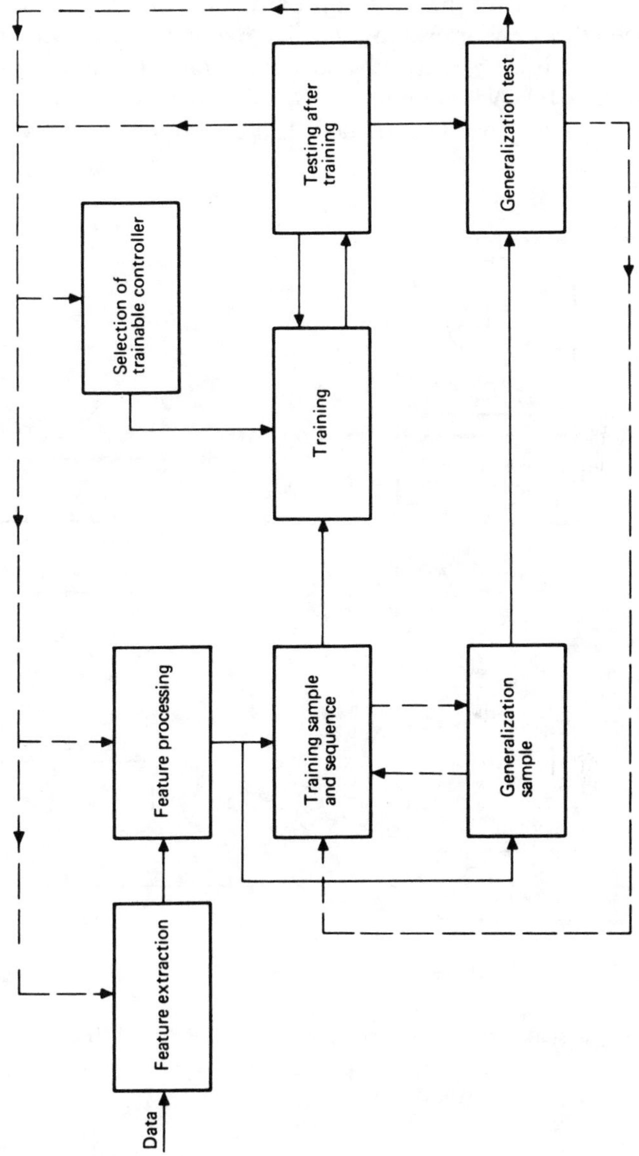

FIGURE 6. Pattern recognition subproblems for multilevel, quasi-optimal controller synthesis

After the entire training sample is in the computer, an element of S_X is generated (randomly, sequentially, etc.), and its classification is determined with the present approximation to $f(\mathbf{x})$. If the classification is incorrect, a new approximation is generated by means of Eqs. (5.19) and (5.16). If it is correct, the approximation is left unchanged. Training is continued for N'' elements of S_X (the number N'' is specified ahead of time, and may be less than N'), after which we pass to the testing phase.

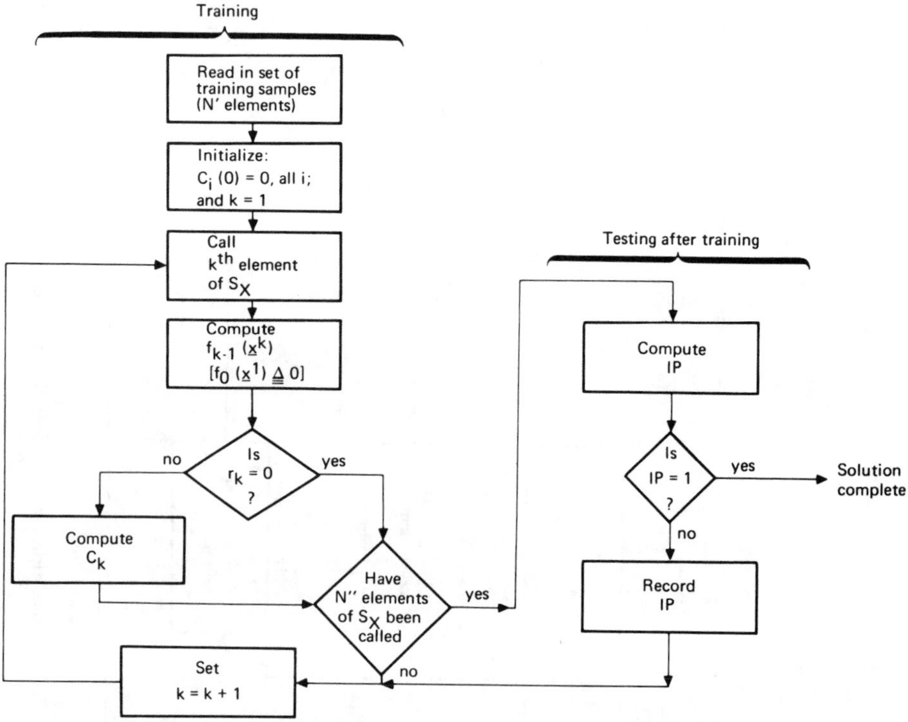

FIGURE 7. Flow diagram for training and testing after training subproblems

During testing, an index of performance (IP) that demonstrates the convergence of the learning process is computed for the N' training samples. The IP is given by

$$IP = \frac{N_{cc}}{N'} \tag{5.20}$$

where N_{cc} is the *n*umber of *c*orrectly *c*lassified elements of the N' training samples. When the IP equals unity, perfect classification has been achieved, a solution has been found, and the program terminates. If the IP is less than unity, the entire process is repeated until convergence occurs.

Generalization refers to the ability of the trained controller to correctly classify patterns from within a region of interest of the feature space after being trained to correctly classify patterns from only a part of the feature space.

Generalization samples are defined analogously to training samples. It is assumed that there exists, for each control level, a set of samples that has not been used during training:

$$\begin{aligned} G(A) &\triangleq \{\mathbf{x}^i(A) : i = 1, 2, \ldots, M(A)\} \\ G(B) &\triangleq \{\mathbf{x}^{i'}(B) : i' = 1, 2, \ldots, M(B)\} \end{aligned} \tag{5.21}$$

where

$$M(A) + M(B) = M' < \infty \tag{5.22}$$

Generalization samples are also obtained from open-loop optimal controls and trajectories, and are usually obtained at the same time as the training samples.

A *generalization test* consists of evaluating an index of performance, IP_G, that is very similar to the index of performance in Eq. (5.20):

$$IP_G = \frac{M_{cc}}{M'} \tag{5.23}$$

M_{cc} is the number of correctly classified elements of the M' generalization samples. It is very rare, in practical applications, for $IP_G = 1$, even if $IP = 1$; hence, one must be prepared to accept a controller design for which $IP_G < 1$. In the final evaluation of the trained, quasi-optimal controller, one usually simulates the nonlinear control system with the trained controller in the loop, and evaluates the performance of the overall system (Mendel and Zapalac, 1968).

It is possible that even though IP is close to unity, IP_G is far from unity. This could occur if the training samples were not *representative* of the system's behavior, as is illustrated in Fig. 8. Two approximations to $f(\mathbf{x})$ are shown: IP_G for $f_k^1(\mathbf{x})$ is 0.625, whereas for $f_k^2(\mathbf{x})$ it is unity. These two approximations could be obtained merely by presenting the training samples in different orders during training.

We remarked earlier in this section that convergence of $f_k(\mathbf{x})$ to $f(\mathbf{x})$ is in a sense that $IP = 1$ for the samples from $L(A)$ and $L(B)$; thus, successful training does not necessarily imply a closeness of fit between $f_k(\mathbf{x})$ and $f(\mathbf{x})$. It should be obvious, however, that if a closeness of fit can be achieved between $f_k(\mathbf{x})$ and $f(\mathbf{x})$, convergence of $f_k(\mathbf{x})$ to $f(\mathbf{x})$ in the sense of unity, *IP*, is highly likely. In addition, if $f_k(\mathbf{x})$ and $f(\mathbf{x})$ are not close in fit, poor generalization is likely, as demonstrated in Fig. 8.

Hence, we see that, in order to achieve good generalization results, we must achieve a closeness of fit between $f_k(\mathbf{x})$ and $f(\mathbf{x})$, as well as unity, *IP*. One way to achieve this is to choose the training samples judiciously, such as, for example, by including only those points close to switch points. This type of training sample can be obtained from open-loop optimal control histories. If IP_G is poor, or if *IP* is poor,

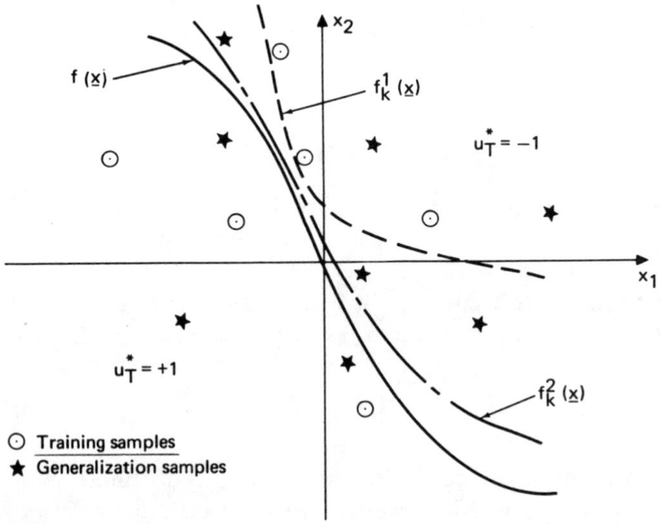

FIGURE 8. Example illustrating *IP* and IP_G for two approximations to $f(x)$

a different structure may be chosen for the trainable controller, features may be processed differently, training samples may be made more representative (along with generalization samples), or features may be added or deleted from the feature-vector. This is implied in Fig. 6 by the dashed lines. The order in which such changes are made is largely arbitrary and depends to a large extent on the experience of the designer.

In this section, we have emphasized the commonalities of the different trainable controllers that have been described in the literature. In the next section, the subproblem of feature processing is elaborated upon, and, as we shall see, it is in the processing of features that we find the main differences between the various trainable controllers.

IV. Feature Processing

Two feature-processing techniques are discussed in this section. In the first technique, features are processed as polynomials. Because we usually have a collection of features—$(x_1, \ldots, x_n)$ in Fig. 4—we will be interested in multivariable polynomial processing. The literature on approximation theory abounds in discussions of single-variable polynomials, especially on the classical orthonormal polynomials (Hermite, Legendre, etc.); however, it is difficult to find comprehensive discussions of multivariable polynomials in the literature. Because such polynomials are the basis for our first type of processor, they will be discussed in detail below.

In the second feature-processing technique, features are first quantized and then encoded. Quantization and encoding, along with some useful theoretical results about the types of surfaces that can be realized by means of a single linear threshold element, are also discussed below.

A. *Polynomial Processing*

Recall the expression for the kth successive estimate of $f(\mathbf{x})$, $f_k(\mathbf{x})$:

$$f_k(\mathbf{x}) = \sum_{i=0}^{N} C_i(k)\varphi_i(\mathbf{x}) \tag{5.24}$$

where $k = 1, 2, \ldots$. In this paragraph, $\varphi_i(\mathbf{x})$ $(i = 0, 1, \ldots, N)$ are assumed to be multivariable polynomials. We will be interested in obtaining answers to the following two questions which occur in connection with Eq. (5.24):

(1) How does one construct multivariable polynomials?

(2) How many terms are there in Eq. (5.24) ($N =$?)?

Before answering these questions, we will make a few additional remarks about Eq. (5.24).

1. *Φ Functions and the Method of Potential Functions.* In Eq. (5.24), $f_k(\mathbf{x})$ depends linearly upon the parameters $C_0(k)$, $C_1(k), \ldots$, and $C_N(k)$. If the $\varphi_i(\mathbf{x})$ are linearly independent, real, single-valued functions of $\mathbf{x}$ that are independent of these parameters, then $f_k(\mathbf{x})$ is a Φ function (Nilsson, 1965), and the trainable controller in Fig. 4 is a Φ machine.

Next, we will derive Eqs. (5.24) and (5.19) from a seemingly different point of view. Our purpose for doing this is to demonstrate that this seemingly different point of view leads to our previous results exactly, and is therefore not different from Nilsson's Φ function approach.

The Soviets (Aizerman *et al.*, 1964a) define the *potential function*, $K(\mathbf{x}, \mathbf{y})$, as

$$K(\mathbf{x}, \mathbf{y}) = \sum_{l=0}^{N} \varphi_l(\mathbf{x})\, \varphi_l(\mathbf{y}) \tag{5.25}$$

where the $\varphi_i(\mathbf{x})$ are bounded from above and are some complete set of functions, so that $K(\mathbf{x}, \mathbf{y})$ is bounded. The kth successive estimate of $f(\mathbf{x})$ is given by $f_k(\mathbf{x})$ ($k = 1, 2,\ldots$), where it is assumed that

$$f_k(\mathbf{x}) = f_{k-1}(\mathbf{x}) + r_k K(\mathbf{x}, \mathbf{x}^k) \tag{5.26}$$

and r_k is as in Eq. (5.17). The solution to Eq. (5.26) is

$$f_k(\mathbf{x}) = f_0(\mathbf{x}) + \sum_{m=1}^{k} r_m K(\mathbf{x}, \mathbf{x}^m) \tag{5.27}$$

which, with the help of Eq. (5.25), can also be written as

$$f_k(\mathbf{x}) = f_0(\mathbf{x}) + \sum_{l=0}^{N} C_l(k)\, \varphi_l(\mathbf{x}) \tag{5.28}$$

where

$$C_l(k) = \sum_{m=1}^{k} r_m \varphi_l(\mathbf{x}^m) \tag{5.29}$$

and $l = 0, 1,\ldots,$ and N. This last equation can also be written as

$$C_l(k) = C_l(k-1) + r_k \varphi_l(\mathbf{x}^k) \tag{5.30}$$

where $k = 1, 2,\ldots,$ and $C_l(0) \triangleq 0$. Upon comparison of Eqs. (5.28) and (5.24), and (5.30) and (5.19), one concludes that the potential function and Φ function approaches are identical when $\gamma_k = 1$ and $f_0(\mathbf{x}) = 0$. γ_k need not in general be set equal to unity, for if the expression for $f_k(\mathbf{x})$ in Eq. (5.26) is broadened by replacing r_k with $\gamma_k r_k$, the convergence of the potential function algorithm is not disturbed.

In their original work (Aizerman *et al.*, 1964a), the Soviets required that the set of functions $\{\varphi_i(\mathbf{x})\}$ be orthonormal, a requirement which was later relaxed to the requirement that the set $\{\varphi_i(\mathbf{x})\}$ be complete in some sense (Aizerman *et al.*, 1966, and Braverman, 1965). Hence, the $\varphi_i(\mathbf{x})$ do not have to be orthonormal although orthonormal polynomials are easily constructed, and are known to have properties that are quite desirable for approximations. In fact, due to the equivalence of potential functions and Φ functions, the $\varphi_i(\mathbf{x})$ can be chosen quite generally so long as they are bounded, real, single-valued, and linearly independent.

Equation (5.26) sometimes provides us with a more convenient way to successively approximate $f(\mathbf{x})$; that is, instead of defining a system of functions, $\{\varphi_i(\mathbf{x})\}$, and constructing $f_k(\mathbf{x})$ from Eqs. (5.24) and (5.19), we directly prescribe $K(\mathbf{x}, \mathbf{y})$ in a form convenient for computation. It is necessary then to guarantee the expandability of $K(\mathbf{x}, \mathbf{y})$ in the form in Eq. (5.25). The following theorem is useful (Braverman, 1965).

Theorem 1. Let Ω_X be: (a) a bounded region of an n-dimensional Euclidean space, E_n, or (b) a discrete finite set of points in E_n. Let $K(|\mathbf{z}|)$, $\mathbf{z} \in E_n$, be a continuous function whose multidimensional Fourier transform is positive at any point $\boldsymbol{\omega} = (\omega_1, \ldots, \omega_n)'$.

Then the potential function, $K(|\mathbf{x} - \mathbf{y}|)$, can be expanded in a series of the form in Eq. (5.25), where $\varphi_i(\mathbf{x})$ is a complete system of functions in L^2-Space.

The proof of this theorem follows from the theory of symmetric kernels in the theory of integral equations, and Mercer's theorem; it is found in Braverman (1965). Also observe that Theorem 1 only indicates the condition guaranteeing the required expandability of the potential function, but says nothing about the concrete system of functions in Ω_X generated by the given potential function. By means of this theorem, one can show, for example, that

$$K(\mathbf{x}, \mathbf{y}) = \exp[-\alpha^2 \| \mathbf{x} - \mathbf{y} \|^2] \tag{5.31}$$

is expandable as in Eq. (5.25). The details of such an expansion can be found in Specht (1966).

For the present application, it has been found more convenient to work directly in terms of Eq. (5.24) rather than Eq. (5.26); hence, our attention is now directed to answering the two questions posed at the beginning of this paragraph.

2. *Multivariable Polynomials.* It is assumed below that each component, x_j ($j = 1, 2, \ldots, n$), of the feature vector, $\mathbf{x}$, is defined over some open, closed, or semiopen interval such as

$$x_j \in (b_j, h_j) \quad \text{or} \quad x_j \in [b_j, h_j] \quad \text{or} \quad x_j \in [b_j, h_j) \tag{5.32}$$

It is also assumed that all of the variables are normalized to the same interval of interest; that is,

$$\forall x_j \in [m, M] \qquad j = 1, 2, \ldots, n \tag{5.33}$$

This is easily accomplished by means of the following transformation:

$$x_j = \frac{M - m}{h_j - b_j} x_j' + \frac{h_j m - b_j M}{h_j - b_j} \tag{5.34}$$

in which x_j' denotes the original variable that is defined over some range of values specified by b_j and h_j, as in Eq. (5.32) for example. This normalization is done for computational reasons.

Associated with each component of $\mathbf{x}$ will be a system of polynomials, $F_{i_j}(x_j)$, which can be expressed in terms of x_j by means of the following expansion:

$$F_{i_j}(x_j) = \sum_{m_j=0}^{i_j} a^j_{m_j}(i_j)\, x_j^{m_j} \tag{5.35}$$

where $i_j = 0, 1,\ldots$. The dependence of $a^j_{m_j}(i_j)$ on j and i_j is so that different values may be assigned to each of these coefficients; however, it is often the case that some or many of the coefficients are zero.

Example 4. The simplest polynomial is obtained by setting all of the coefficients except the i_jth equal to zero, and the i_jth coefficient equal to unity. In this case,

$$F_{i_j}(x_j) = x_j^{i_j} \tag{5.36}$$

Associated with $\mathbf{x}$ is a set of multivariable polynomials whose elements are denoted $Q_{i_1,\ldots,i_n}(\mathbf{x})$ and are defined as

$$Q_{i_1,\ldots,i_n}(\mathbf{x}) = F_{i_1}(x_1)\, F_{i_2}(x_2) \cdots F_{i_n}(x_n) \tag{5.37}$$

where i_1,..., and i_n range from 0 to I. The range of values for which these polynomials are defined is given by the n-dimensional hypercube in Eq. (5.33). Reasons for defining multivariable polynomials as in Eq. (5.37) will be given shortly. First, let us investigate a number of useful properties of these polynomials.

3. *Properties of Multivariable Polynomials. Property* 1. Let $d(Q)$ denote the *degree* of $Q_{i_1,\ldots,i_n}(\mathbf{x})$. From Eqs. (5.37) and (5.35),

$$d(Q) = \sum_{l=1}^{n} i_l \tag{5.38}$$

Let us order the multivariable polynomials according to degree. To this end, we group together all of the polynomials of degree, ξ, into a subset, q_ξ,

$$q_\xi \triangleq \{Q_{i_1,\ldots,i_n}(\mathbf{x}) : d(Q) = \xi \text{ and } i_1 ,\ldots, \text{ and } i_n \text{ range from 0 to at most } \xi\} \tag{5.39}$$

where $\xi = 0, 1,\ldots$. Generating the elements in q_ξ—and determining how many elements there are in this set—are problems which are related to the well-known *signature problem* in combinatorial analysis (Lehmer, 1964). $(i_1, \ldots, i_n)$ is the *signature* of the multivariable polynomial in Eq. (5.37). The signature problem is concerned with obtaining all of the values of $i_1, \ldots,$ and i_n, subject to the constraints in Eq. (5.39). Although it is possible to obtain the signatures by hand, their number increases very rapidly as the number of features, n, and $d(Q)$ increase.

Property 2. Let $e(n; q_\xi)$ denote the number of elements of q_ξ in Eq. (5.39). Then

$$e(n; q) = \frac{(\xi + n - 1)!}{\xi!(n-1)!} = {}_{(n+\xi-1)}C_\xi \tag{5.40}$$

which can be proved by means of combinatorics (MacFarlane, 1963). Quite obviously, it is impractical to compute by hand the $e(n; q_\xi)$ signatures required for each q_ξ. A flow diagram (easily programmed for a digital computer) that presents a sequential solution to the signature problem is shown in Fig. 9. First, a set of monotone signatures $(\delta_1, \delta_2, \ldots, \delta_{n-1})$ is generated, where

$$\delta_1 \geqslant \delta_2 \geqslant \cdots \geqslant \delta_{n-1} \geqslant 0 \quad \text{and} \quad \delta_i \leqslant \xi \tag{5.41}$$

Next, the signatures, $(i_1, i_2, \ldots, i_n)$, are obtained from $\delta_1, \ldots, \delta_{n-1}$ and ξ, as indicated. Observe that for a fixed value of ξ,

$$i_1 + i_2 + \cdots + i_n = \xi \tag{5.42}$$

as required in Eq. (5.39), and that the outer loop in Fig. 9 guarantees that signatures will be generated for all $\xi \leqslant \xi_{\max}$.

Example 5. For $n = 3$ and $\xi = 2$, signatures for the polynomials of degree 2 are generated from the routine in Fig. 9, in the following order: $(i_1, i_2, i_3) = (0, 0, 2), (0, 1, 1), (0, 2, 0), (1, 0, 1), (1, 1, 0)$, and $(2, 0, 0)$.

Let us now collect all of the polynomials in Eq. (5.37) of degrees 0, 1,..., and ξ into the sets, $\mathcal{Q}_\xi$, where

$$\mathcal{Q}_\xi = \{q_0, q_1, \ldots, q_\xi\} \tag{5.43}$$

and $\xi = 0, 1, \ldots$.

Property 3. Let $e(n; \mathcal{Q}_\xi)$ denote the total number of elements in $\mathcal{Q}_\xi$; that is to say,

$$e(n; \mathcal{Q}_\xi) = \sum_{j=0}^{\xi} e(n; q_j) \tag{5.44}$$

Then

$$e(n; \mathcal{Q}_\xi) = \frac{(\xi + n)!}{n!\,\xi!} \tag{5.45}$$

When $\mathbf{x}$ is a six-vector, for example, $e(6; \mathscr{Q}_6) = 924$. This means that the collection of multivariable polynomials in six variables, up to and including polynomials with sixth-degree terms, contains 924 elements.

Our interest is in approximations of $f(\mathbf{x})$ of the form $\sum_{i=0}^{N} C_i\varphi_i(\mathbf{x})$, where the $\varphi_i(\mathbf{x})$ are multivariable polynomials. How are the $\varphi_i(\mathbf{x})$

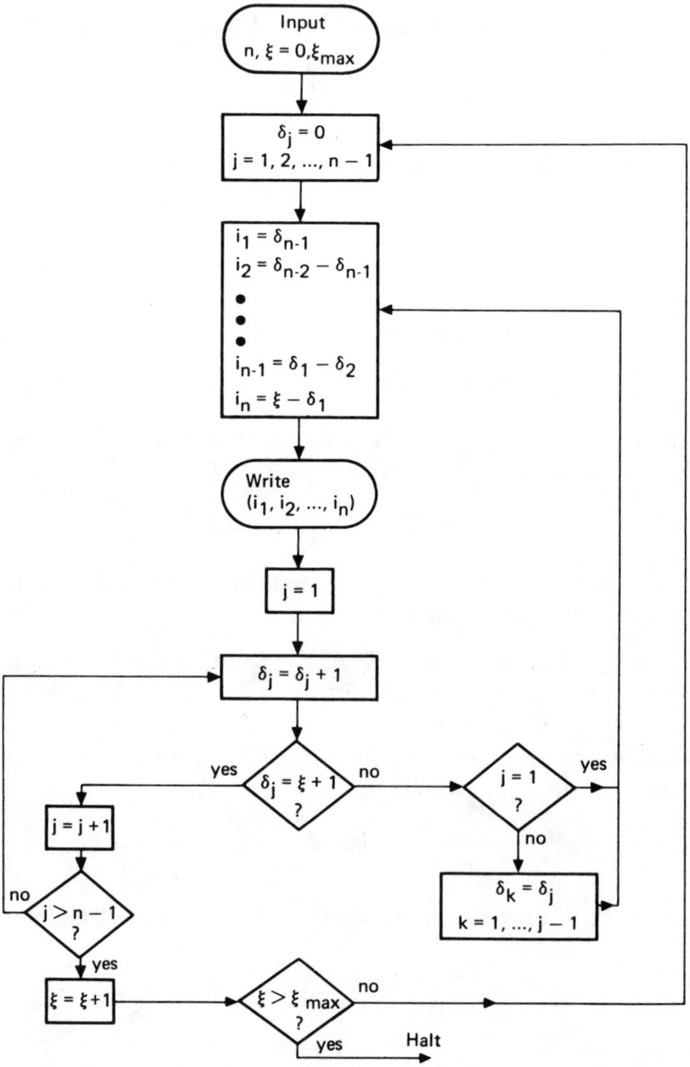

FIGURE 9. Computer flow diagram for generating signatures

obtained from the functions in Eq. (5.37)? The simplest way to obtain them is to associate succeeding values of i with successive solutions of the signature problem. This is easily done on the computer. Such associations provide mappings from signatures $(i_1, \ldots, i_n)$ to the index variable, i. We know from Property 3 that there will be exactly $e(n; \mathscr{Q}_\xi)$ such mappings once n and ξ are fixed.

During the course of our development, we have provided answers to the two questions that were posed at the beginning of this paragraph, for a very general class of multivariable polynomials. First, we have shown that such polynomials can be generated from Eqs. (5.37) and (5.35); and second, that for these polynomials there will be

$$N = e(n; \mathscr{Q}_{\xi_{\max}}) - 1 \tag{5.46}$$

terms in Eq. (5.24). $f_k(\mathbf{x})$ will contain terms in $x_1, \ldots,$ and x_n of degree less than or equal to $\xi_{\max}$.

4. *Examples of Multivariable Polynomials.* Specific systems of polynomials can be found in a number of different ways. Nilsson (1965) suggests using the following polynomials:

$$Q_{i_1,\ldots,i_n}(\mathbf{x}) = x_1^{i_1} \cdots x_n^{i_n} \tag{5.47}$$

where

$$i_1, \ldots, \text{ and } i_n = 0 \quad \text{or} \quad 1 \tag{5.48}$$

In this case [the prime notation is used to emphasize that Eqs. (5.49) and (5.50) are different from Eqs. (5.39) and (5.43), respectively]

$$q_\xi' = \{Q_{i_1,\ldots,i_n}(\mathbf{x}) : d(Q) = \xi \text{ and } i_1, \ldots, \text{ and } i_n = 0 \text{ or } 1\} \tag{5.49}$$

and

$$\mathscr{Q}_\xi' = \{q_0', q_1', \ldots, q_\xi'\} \tag{5.50}$$

The signatures for these polynomials are easily computed by hand. They cannot be obtained from the Signature Program in Fig. 9 because the basis for that program is Eq. (5.39), not Eq. (5.49).

It is a straightforward matter to show, using combinatorics, that

$$e(n; q_\xi') = \frac{n!}{\xi!(n-\xi)!} = {}_nC_\xi \tag{5.51}$$

and, therefore, that

$$e(n; \mathscr{Q}_\xi') = 1 + \sum_{j=1}^{\xi} {}_nC_j \tag{5.52}$$

The obvious advantage of these polynomials over the more general ones in Eqs. (5.37) and (5.35) is that there are not nearly so many of them. Using these polynomials, there will only be

$$N = \sum_{j=1}^{\xi} {}_nC_j \tag{5.53}$$

terms in Eq. (5.24). Another advantage of the polynomials in Eqs. (5.47) and (5.48) is that they are much easier to implement than are the more general polynomials. The disadvantage of these polynomials is that they contain, at most, first-degree terms in the variables, $x_j (j = 1, 2, \ldots, n)$; hence, they may not provide enough variety for successfully approximating $f(\mathbf{x})$.

The simplest class of polynomials for which arbitrary powers of each variable can be included is obtained from Example 4 and has elements given by the following expression:

$$Q_{i_1, \ldots, i_n}(\mathbf{x}) = x_1^{i_1} \cdots x_n^{i_n} \tag{5.54}$$

where $i_1, \ldots,$ and i_n range from 0 to ξ. For these polynomials, all of the results that were obtained for the general polynomials in Eqs. (5.35) and (5.37) apply, and the number of terms in Eq. (5.24) is given by N in Eq. (5.46).

As a last example of how to generate multivariable polynomials, we require that the polynomials in Eq. (5.37) be orthonormal. Courant and Hilbert (1953) prove that products of orthonormal polynomial functions, $F_{i_1}(x_1), \ldots,$ and $F_{i_n}(x_n)$, are again orthonormal when all variables are normalized to the same range of values. Actually, a more general theorem is proved by Courant and Hilbert for when the variables are not all normalized to the same range; however, because of Eq. (5.34), the more general result is not needed in the present development. By means of this multiplication theorem, it is simple to compute multivariable orthonormal polynomials. First, one chooses systems of orthonormal polynomials for the $F_{i_j}(x_j)$ in Eq. (5.37). Classical systems such as Hermite and Legendre polynomials (Abromowitz and Stegun, eds., 1964) are well-documented and are easily generated by means of simple recursive relationships. Then, the single-variable orthonormal polynomials are multiplied together in order to obtain the $Q_{i_1, \ldots, i_n}(\mathbf{x})$.

Just as for the preceding system of polynomials, there will be $e(n; \mathcal{Q}_\xi) - 1$ terms in Eq. (5.24) when the $\varphi_i(\mathbf{x})$ are orthonormal. When orthonormal polynomials are used, however, each $\varphi_i(\mathbf{x})$ is a complicated function of $x_1, \ldots,$ and x_n, so that the exact dependence of $f_k(\mathbf{x})$ on terms of the form in Eq. (5.54) must still be determined by expanding the $\varphi_i(\mathbf{x})$, and combining similar terms in x_1 ,..., and x_n and their many products. This is usually very tedious to do because each $\varphi_i(\mathbf{x})$ contains many products, and there will usually be quite a few of the $\varphi_i(\mathbf{x})$. Fortunately, such an expansion for $f_k(\mathbf{x})$ is not necessary during training because the entire training process can be carried out directly in terms of the $F_{i_j}(x_j)$.

5. *Discussion.* In a synthesis of a multilevel, quasi-optimal controller in which polynomial discriminants are used during training, one should first try to approximate $f(\mathbf{x})$, using the simpler polynomials. If it is not possible to obtain acceptable values for IP and IP_G using the simpler polynomials, more complicated polynomials should be tried. Such an approach is in keeping with our earlier discussions about the dashed lines in Fig. 6 that emanate from the Testing After Training and Generalization Test boxes, and lead to the Feature Processing box.

Various techniques for implementing polynomial-discriminant functions, $f_k{}^i(\mathbf{x})$ (Fig. 5), have been suggested. Among these are:(1) parallel/analog, (2) sequential/hybrid, and (3) sequential/digital (Douglas Aircraft Company Report SM–48464–F, 1967). The term *parallel* refers to the fact that all $l - 1$ discriminants (Fig. 4) are separately implemented. The term *analog* indicates that the trainable controller's x_j inputs are analog voltages. In the sequential approach, the general expression for $f_k(\mathbf{x})$ is implemented once, in hardware, or by means of a computer program. The coefficients and input values are specified, and the expression is evaluated sequentially for each of the $l - 1$ units. The term *hybrid* refers to the fact that the feature-vector inputs are supplied in both analog and digital form to the φ-Units. The term *digital* implies that the feature-vector inputs (as well as weights) to the φ-Units are all binary. Cost, power, size, and weight comparisons of these three techniques for a trainable controller with 256 quadratic multivariable polynomial discriminants have been made; they are reported on extensively in Douglas Aircraft Company Report SM–48464–F. The main results are that the sequential/hybrid and sequential/digital techniques compare much more favorably than the parallel/analog technique.

B. *Quantization–Encoding Processing*

In a second type of feature processing, features are first quantized and then encoded. This type of feature processing has received considerable attention by numerous investigators, and is very well-documented in the literature (for example, Mendel and Zapalac, 1968, and Smith, 1964 and 1966); hence, our discussions are brief. It is convenient, for this type of feature processing, to reinterpret the trainable controller and N-Unit, in Figs. 4 and 5, as shown in Fig. 10.

The φ-Units are quantizer/encoders. Each component, x_i ($i = 1,..., n$), of the feature vector enters only one φ-Unit, wherein it is quantized into one of N_i levels that is then encoded, by means of a suitable code, into a partial pattern vector of dimension $N_i + 1$. One element of each partial pattern vector is fixed a priori. Reasons for doing this will be discussed shortly. Each component of the partial pattern vector is weighted, and appropriate values are obtained for these weights by means of training.

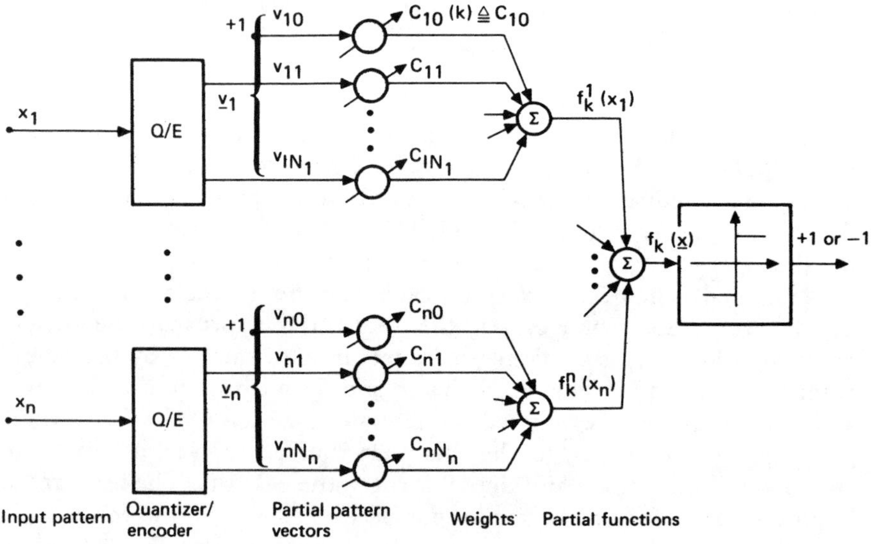

FIGURE 10. Trainable controller with quantization and encoding of features (ADALINE)

Quantization and encoding achieve a transformation from Ω_X to Ω_V, where Ω_V is the *encoded space* and is of much higher dimension than Ω_X. Training occurs in terms of the encoded variables, and $f_k(\mathbf{x})$ is not obtained as an explicit function of x_1 ,..., and x_n. As can be seen from Fig. 10, $f_k(\mathbf{x})$ is obtained as an explicit function of the encoded variables; that is to say,

$$f_k(\mathbf{x}) = \sum_{i=1}^{n} f_k^{\,i}(x_i) = \sum_{i=1}^{n} \sum_{j=0}^{N_i} C_{ij}(k)\, v_{ij} \tag{5.55}$$

from which it follows that, if $N + 1$ denotes the total number of weights in Eq. (5.55),

$$N + 1 = n + \sum_{i=1}^{n} N_i \tag{5.56}$$

Uniform or nonuniform quantization can be used. For the present application, the *output level* from the quantizer is unimportant because of the encoding which precedes quantization; hence, rather than associate an output level with each variable, it is more expedient to associate an identification number, denoted $\hat{x}_{ij}$, with the quantized variable, x_i. This is easily accomplished by numbering the quantum zones from 1 to N_i starting at the negative extreme (Fig. 11). Each

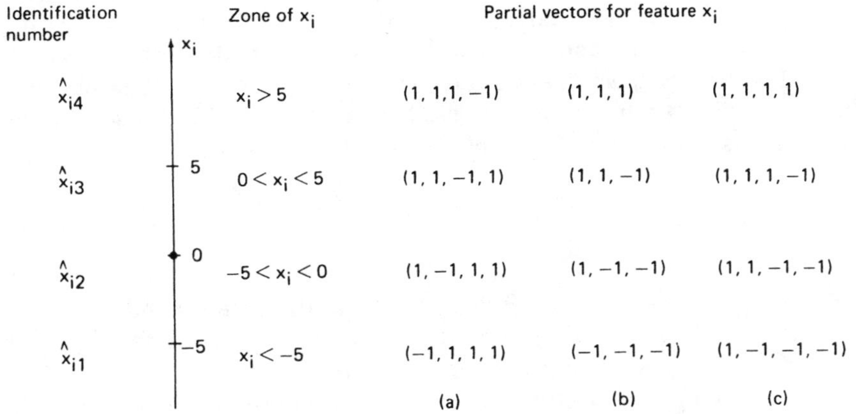

FIGURE 11. Codes: (a) Single-element code, (b) Multielement code, (c) Augmented multielement code

identification number is then encoded. In other applications for training techniques, such as function approximation in the sense of closeness of fit, the output level from the quantizer is important; if the statistical distribution associated with the appearance of a feature is known or can be estimated, optimum output levels can be determined (Max, 1960).

Smith (1964 and 1966) has shown that when the encoder represents the zones of the features with linearly independent codes, the trainable controller can closely approximate many different functions. Although many of his results are in the context of the closeness-of-fit type of function approximation problem, they are useful and provide valuable insight for the present decision surface application, because, as we mentioned in Section IIIC, good generalization ability usually requires a closeness of fit between $f_k(\mathbf{x})$ and $f(\mathbf{x})$, as well as a large value for *IP*.

A linearly independent code is a code for which the set of partial pattern vectors representing the quantum zones of a feature either (1) are linearly independent, or (2) will be linearly independent if the dimension of the partial pattern vector is increased by the addition of the same constant element to each vector. Examples of different codes (Smith, 1966) are given in Fig. 11. The single element (termed single element because -1 appears only once in each partial vector) and augmented multielement codes are linearly independent, whereas the multielement code is not. The augmented multielement code is obtained by augmenting a $+1$ to each partial vector in the multielement code, thereby making it a linearly independent code. Generally speaking, $+1$'s and 0's or -1's and 0's could be used in the codes instead of $+1$'s and -1's; however, using $+1$'s and -1's permits every C_{ij} to be changed during training each time a misclassification occurs. This is seen when Eq. (5.19) is rewritten in terms of the encoded variables,

$$\begin{aligned} C_{ij}(k) &= C_{ij}(k-1) + \gamma_k r_k v_{ij}(x_i{}^k) \\ C_{ij}(0) &= 0 \end{aligned} \tag{5.57}$$

for $i = 1, 2, \ldots, n$, and $j = 0, 1, \ldots, N_i$. On the other hand, if $+1$'s, or -1's and 0's, are used, even if $r_k \neq 0$, it is possible for $C_{ij}(k)$ to equal $C_{ij}(k-1)$, since $v_{ij}(x_i{}^k)$ may equal zero.

The following very useful theorems have been proved by Smith (1964).

Theorem 2. When linearly independent coding is used to represent the independent variables, $x_1, \ldots,$ and x_n, as partial patterns, the *ada*ptive *line*ar threshold element (Adaline) *function generator* can realize any function (except for "round-off" error due to quantization) of the form:

$$f(\mathbf{x}) = \sum_{i=1}^{n} f_i(x_i) \tag{5.58}$$

where $f_i(x_i)$ is any nonlinear function of x_i.

Theorem 3. When features are individually coded, and when the encoded features are algebraically independent, the Adaline function generator can realize *only* the functions that can be expressed in the form of Eq. (5.58).

Smith shows that using a linearly independent code ensures the possibility of a unique solution for the C_{ij} such that $f_k(\mathbf{x})$ matches $f(\mathbf{x})$

at *some point* within each quantum zone. In fact, if $f(\mathbf{x})$ is known at one point in each quantum zone, and if a linearly independent code is used for each feature, the C_{ij} can be solved for algebraically by matrix inversion. Nonrealizable functions for the Adaline function generator can be described as those functions for which

$$\frac{\partial^2 f(\mathbf{x})}{\partial x_i \, \partial x_j} \neq 0 \tag{5.59}$$

where x_i and x_j are features.

Example 6. The function, $x_1^3 + 5x_2 - 16x_2^4$, can be approximated by means of a single adaptive linear threshold element, whereas the function, $x_1^3 + 5x_1x_2 - 16x_2^4$, cannot be.

Therefore, we see that if the switching function, $f(\mathbf{x})$, contains cross-product terms in the feature variables, it cannot be closely matched by a single adaptive linear threshold element with features $x_1, \ldots,$ and x_n. Smith suggests the addition of features that are linear combinations of the original features in order to obtain cross-product terms. Unfortunately, in the present application, one does not know the form of, or the expression for, $f(\mathbf{x})$ ahead of time. Our information is about the sign of $f(\mathbf{x})$ at a training sample rather than the value of $f(\mathbf{x})$. It is still possible to use Smith's theorems for our application. One approach is to train, initially using the trainable controller and features in Fig. 10. If *PI* is too small, add additional features that are linear combinations of the original features, since a small value for *IP* is suggestive of cross-products in $f(\mathbf{x})$.

We have shown that quantization and encoding of features form threshold logic-element inputs which are nonlinear functions of the features. This method of processing is attractive because it is more readily implemented than are polynomial processors. The trainable controller in Fig. 10 can be implemented by means of a special-purpose computer or integrated circuitry, and is *very reliable* (Mendel and Zapalac, 1968). Reliable, as used here, refers to the controller's capacity to maintain satisfactory system performance even when weights change their values. Such changes could occur, for example, because of electronic failures caused by aging or exposure to an unexpected environmental hazard. The reliability of the controller in the face of such changes is due to the very distributed form of the solution, when linearly independent codes are used to encode the features. Such coding provides a good deal of redundancy (linearly independent codes are not minimal codes); thus, a change in one weight affects only a small region of the feature space.

V. Applications: A Brief Review

Many applications of the techniques we have described in the preceding sections, to the synthesis of multilevel, quasi-optimal controllers, have been described in the literature. Space limitations allow us only a brief review of some of these. Interestingly enough, all of the reported applications have one thing in common: they are for two-level controllers.

Some of the systems for which quasi-, time-optimal controllers have been synthesized are: $1/s^2$ (Smith, 1964; and Smith Jr. *et al.*, 1964), $1/s^3$ (Smith, 1964), $b/s(s - a)$ where $-1 \leqslant a \leqslant 1$ and $0.25 \leqslant b \leqslant 1.6$ (Smith Jr. *et al.*, 1964), $1/s(s^2 + 1)$ (Mendel and Zapalac, 1968), a third-order model for the longitudinal motion of F101B aircraft (Smith, Jr. *et al.*, 1965), and a fourth-order model of a rigid aerospace vehicle (Smith, Jr., 1962).

Many of these studies were more interested in demonstrating the feasibility of the synthesis technique than in applying it to real-world problems. Such is usually the case, however, when a new synthesis technique emerges; hence, one should not judge those studies too harshly or as completely impractical, since much was learned about the synthesis technique that will be of value when the technique is applied to more difficult problems. Additionally, if feasibility cannot be demonstrated for the simplest multilevel controller—the two-level controller—then it is not very likely that the synthesis technique will be applicable to more difficult problems. Feasibility has been demonstrated for all of the above systems, and the technique now awaits application to more difficult problems.

There is yet another reason why applications to-date have been limited to two-level controllers. It has to do with the difficulties associated with obtaining training samples for multilevel controllers. Often, two-point boundary value problems must be solved; such problems become increasingly more difficult and computationally time-consuming as the number of control levels increases.

Elaborate system simulations may be required in order to generate the necessary data. It has even been suggested, in an application in which the feasibility of realizing a switching surface model for man-in-the-loop was investigated (Mendel *et al.*, 1967), to let man be in the loop to assist in obtaining the training samples.

The problem of obtaining data for the set of training samples is common to all pattern recognition problems. Often, such data must be obtained as a part of a different and even larger study. For example, in order to train a device to distinguish lunar features (Chapter 4), representative photographs of these features had to be obtained. To obtain these photographs, NASA designed, launched, and orbited the Surveyor spacecraft which photographed the moon and telemetered these photographs back to earth—indeed, a formidable task.

In all but one of the above studies, quantization and encoding feature-processing was used. The main difference in these studies was in the way the training samples were chosen. Smith (1964), for example, trains the trainable controller on a set of training samples that border the optimal switching surface. The time-optimal switching surfaces are known a priori for his plants because they are so simple. For high-order plants which are more typical of real-world systems, it is usually impossible to obtain such a set of training samples. Smith, Jr. (1962) trains on a set of samples uniformly distributed in the quantized feature space. For example, in the control of a fourth-order rigid aerospace vehicle, the four-dimensional feature space was quantized into 524, 288 hypercubes. The trainable controller was trained on a set of 400 training samples chosen at uniform intervals in the four-space. This represents only 0.076 percent of the total hypercubes.

Controllers have been obtained for the system $1/s(s^2 + 1)$ by Mendel and Zapalac (1968) and Byrne and Mendel (1968) which use quantization-encoding or polynomial processing. This system can be associated with simplified pitch-plane dynamics for a fin-controlled aerospace vehicle during one flight condition. For quantization and encoding of features, it was demonstrated that: (1) quantization can be coarse without degradation of closed-loop system performance; (2) the size of the set of initial conditions for which open-loop optimal controls (determined for their application by means of a special-purpose computer program for solving a two-point boundary value problem) must be determined is very small compared to the totality of hypercubes in the quantized state space (for example, 10 out of 8,000); (3) the number of training samples is small compared to the totality of hypercubes (for example, 600 out of 8,000 or only 7.5 percent); (4) the trained controller is relatively insensitive to changes in the weights (Mendel and Zapalac varied *all* weights plus or minus 20 percent, and observed that it took from 15 percent to—at most—30 percent longer for the system to reach from one to two quantum zones of the origin of their three-dimensional state space); and (5) excessive data-processing time is not required.

VI. Conclusions

The reader who expected to find a detailed, step-by-step exposition on how a trainable controller is synthesized for a specific system, is, no doubt, disappointed; however, he can find many expositions of that type in the literature. This chapter was written for those interested in the big picture, and contains enough information so that they can try solving some of their problems using training techniques. By presenting the big picture, we have demonstrated that the application of training techniques to the synthesis of multilevel, quasi-optimal controllers has reached the point where generalizations can be made. In short, the details of individual studies have suggested a general design approach which, although it has only been tested for two-level control, is applicable to multilevel control, and awaits such applications.

Much of the material in Sections III and IV is appropriate for other applications. For example, feature processing is common to all applications. We expect that, in the future, multivariable polynomial feature-processing will receive more attention than it has. In Douglas Aircraft Company Report SM–48464–F (1967), for example, much better generalization was obtained with quadratic discriminants than with linear discriminants. Of course, practical (light, small volume, inexpensive, etc.) implementations of high-degree multivariable polynomial discriminants must be found.

We have spoken about training only in the context of error-correction training algorithms. It is possible to use some of the other training algorithms, discussed in Chapter 3, to obtain a solution. Comparative analyses of these algorithms in the context of the multilevel control application remain to be performed.

In certain control problems, we are not certain about the membership of the feature vector in a specific control category. For such problems, statistical pattern recognition concepts (Chapter 2) are appropriate, and Fig. 6 must be modified accordingly. No doubt, this area will receive considerable attention in the not-to-distant future.

References

Abromowitz, M. and Stegun, I. A. (eds.), "Handbook of Mathematical Functions with Formulas, Graphs and Mathematical Tables." National Bureau of Standards Applied Mathematics Series 55, Washington, D. C., 1964.

Aizerman, M. A., Braverman, E. M., and Rozonoer, L. I., Theoretical foundations of the potential function method in pattern recognition learning. *Automation and Remote Control 25*, No. 6, pp. 821–837 (1964a).

Aizerman, M. A., Braverman, E. M., and Rozonoer, L. I., The probability problem of pattern recognition learning and the method of potential functions. *Automation and Remote Control 25*, No. 9, pp. 1175–1190 (1964b).

Aizerman, M. A., Braverman, E. M., and Rozonoer, L. I., The method of potential functions for the problem of restoring the characteristic of a function converter from randomly observed points. *Automation and Remote Control 25*, No. 12, pp. 1546–1556 (1964c).

Aizerman, M. A., Braverman, E. M., and Rozonoer, L. I., Potential functions technique and extrapolation in learning systems theory. *Proc. Interntl. Federation on Auto. Control Congr., 3rd, London, England, 1966*. Butterworth, London, England, 1966.

Athans, M. and Falb, P. L., "Optimal Control: An Introduction to the Theory and its Applications." McGraw–Hill, New York, 1966.

Braverman, E. M., On the method of potential functions. *Automation and Remote Control 26*, No. 12, pp. 2130–2138 (1965).

Byrne, W. E. and Mendel, J. M., Methodology and general purpose FORTRAN IV programs for the synthesis and utilization of multivariable polynomial discriminant functions. *In* "Self-organizing control systems," Vol. 7. Douglas Aircraft Co., Santa Monica, Calif., 1968.

Chaplin, W. G. and Levadi, V. S., A generalization of the linear threshold decision algorithm to multiple classes. In "Computer and Information Sciences" Vol. 2 (J. T. Tou, ed.), pp. 337–355. Academic Press, New York, 1967.

Courant, R. and Hilbert, D., "Methods of Mathematical Physics," Vol. 1. Interscience Publishers, New York, 1953.

Duda, R. O., Machanik, J. W., and Singleton, R. C., Function modeling experiments. Stanford Research Institute Rept., Contract NONR 3438(00), Stanford Research Institute, Menlo Park, Calif., 1963.

Heydorn, R. P. and Tou, J. T., Some approaches to optimum feature extraction. *In* "Computer and Information Sciences" Vol. 2 (J. T. Tou, ed.), pp. 57–89. Academic Press, New York, 1967.

Lehmer, D. H., The machine tools of combinatorics. *In* "Applied Combinatorial Mathematics" (E. F. Beckenbach, ed.). Wiley, New York, 1964.

MacFarlane, A. G. J., A method of computing performance functionals for linear dynamical systems. *J. Electron. and Control 15*, pp. 383–393 (1963).

Max, J., Quantizing for minimum distortion. *IRE Trans. Info. Theory 6*, No. 1, pp. 7–12 (1960).

Mendel, J. M., Harding, C. F., and Byrne, W. E., Feasibility of realizing a pattern recognition model for man in the loop. *In* "Self-organizing control systems," Vol. 6, Rept. No. DAC–60603, Douglas Aircraft Co., Santa Monica, Calif., 1967.

Mendel, J. M. and Zapalac, J. J., The application of techniques of artificial intelligence to control system design. *In* "Advances in Control Systems: Theory and Applications" Vol. 6 (C. T. Leondes, ed.). Academic Press, New York, 1968.

Nilsson, N. J., "Learning Machines: Foundations of Trainable Pattern-Classifying Systems," McGraw–Hill, New York, 1965.

Smith, F. W., Contactor control by adaptive pattern-recognition techniques, Rept. No. 6762–1. Stanford Electron. Lab., Stanford Univ., Palo Alto, Calif., 1964.

Smith, F. W., A trainable nonlinear function generator. *IEEE Trans. Auto. Control 11*, No. 2, pp. 212–218 (1966).

Smith, Jr., F. B., "A logical net mechanization for time-optimal regulation." *NASA Tech. Note* TN D–1678 (1962).

Smith, Jr., F. B., Lee, J. F. L., Butz, A. R., and Prom, G. J., Trainable flight control system investigation. Rept. No. FDL–TDR–64–89. Wright–Patterson Air Force Base, Dayton, Ohio, Aug. 1964.

Smith, Jr., F. B., Lee, Y. S., Butz, A. R., and Glasser, W. A., Logic-networks for flight control applications, Rept. No. AFFDL–TR–65–216, Wright–Patterson Air Force Base, Dayton, Ohio, 1965.

Specht, D. F., Generation of polynominal discriminant functions for pattern recognition, Rept. No. 6764–5. Stanford Electron. Lab., Stanford Univ., Stanford, Calif., 1966.

Talbert, L. R., Groner, G. F., Koford, J. S., Brown, R. J., Low, P. R., and Mays, C. H., A real-time adaptive speech recognition system. Rept. No. 6700–a. Stanford Electron. Lab., Stanford Univ., Stanford, Calif., 1963.

Research on the utilization of pattern recognition techniques to identify and classify objects in video data, Rept. No. SM–48464–F, Douglas Aircraft Co., Santa Monica, Calif., 1967.

PART I PROBLEMS

Chapter 1 Problems

1. Consider the one-dimensional, two-class problem in which the a priori probabilities $P(\omega_1)$ and $P(\omega_2)$ are equal, and

$$p(x \mid \omega_i) = \frac{1}{\sqrt{2\pi\sigma_i^2}} \exp\left[-\frac{(x-\mu_i)^2}{2\sigma_i^2}\right] \qquad i = 1, 2$$

   (a) Show that $P(\omega_1 \mid x) > P(\omega_2 \mid x)$ if

$$\frac{(x-\mu_1)^2}{\sigma_1^2} + \log \sigma_1 < \frac{(x-\mu_2)^2}{\sigma_2^2} + \log \sigma_2$$

   (b) Sketch $P(\omega_1 \mid x)$ and $P(\omega_2 \mid x)$ for the case $\mu_1 = -1$, $\mu_2 = 1$, $\sigma_1 = \sigma_2 = 1$. Repeat for the case $\mu_1 = \mu_2 = 0$, $\sigma_1 = 1, \sigma_2 = 2$.

   (c) Under what condition can the decision rule be cast in the form of deciding ω_i if $x > x_0$? What is x_0 ?

2. A decision rule divides feature space into regions, all points in the ith region R_i being assigned to the ith category. Consider the one-dimensional, two-class problem in which the x-axis is divided into two (not necessarily connected) regions R_1 and R_2.

(a) Show that the probability of error is given by

$$P_e = P(\omega_2) \int_{R_1} p(x \mid \omega_2)\, dx + P(\omega_1) \int_{R_2} p(x \mid \omega_1)\, dx$$

(b) Sketch two simple conditional densities, weighted by the a priori probabilities, and give a graphical interpretation of this expression.

(c) The minimum-error-rate classifier assigns x to ω_1 if $P(\omega_1 \mid x) > P(\omega_2 \mid x)$, and to ω_2 otherwise. Using the same sketch as in part (b), make a graphical comparison between P_e for this rule and P_e for any other nonoptimal rule.

3. Suppose that the n features used to classify a pattern are binary, with x_i being either 0 or 1 for $i = 1$ to n. Suppose further that the features for patterns in the same category are statistically independent, with

$$P(x_i = 1 \mid \omega_1) = p_i \qquad i = 1 \text{ to } n$$

and

$$P(x_i = 1 \mid \omega_2) = q_i \qquad i = 1 \text{ to } n$$

(a) Show that

$$P(\mathbf{x} \mid \omega_1) = \prod_{i=1}^{n} p_i^{x_i}(1 - p_i)^{1-x_i}$$

and

$$P(\mathbf{x} \mid \omega_2) = \prod_{i=1}^{n} q_i^{x_i}(1 - q_i)^{1-x_i}$$

(b) Show that $P(\omega_1 \mid \mathbf{x}) > P(\omega_2 \mid \mathbf{x})$ if

$$\sum_{i=1}^{n} w_i x_i + w_0 > 0$$

where

$$w_i = \log\left(\frac{p_i}{q_i}\,\frac{1 - q_i}{1 - p_i}\right) \qquad i = 1, 2, \ldots, n$$

and

$$w_0 = \log\left(\frac{P(\omega_1)}{P(\omega_2)}\right) + \sum_{i=1}^{n} \log\left(\frac{1 - p_i}{1 - q_i}\right)$$

(c) What happens to w_i if $p_i = q_i$? If $p_i > q_i$? If $p_i < q_i$? How do the a priori probabilities affect the decision rule?

4. Consider the problem of learning the probability that an event will occur. Let x be a binary random variable, with

$$P(x = 1 \mid \theta) = \theta$$
$$P(x = 0 \mid \theta) = 1 - \theta.$$

That is, the parameter θ to be estimated is the probability that $x = 1$. Suppose that in the absence of any other information about θ we assume a uniform a priori distribution,

$$p(\theta) = \begin{cases} 1 & 0 \leqslant \theta \leqslant 1 \\ 0 & \text{otherwise} \end{cases}$$

(a) Show that after one observation x_1, θ has the a posteriori distribution

$$p(\theta \mid x_1) = \begin{cases} 2\theta p(\theta) & \text{if } x_1 = 1 \\ 2(1-\theta)\, p(\theta) & \text{if } x_1 = 0 \end{cases}$$

and sketch $p(\theta \mid x_1)$ versus θ. What is the expected value of θ given x_1? For what value of θ is $p(\theta \mid x_1)$ maximum?

(b) Show that if n independent observations $x_1, \ldots, x_n$ are made, and if k of these have the value 1, then

$$p(\theta \mid x_1, \ldots, x_n) = \frac{(n+1)!}{k!(n-k)!}\, \theta^k (1-\theta)^{n-k} p(\theta)$$

(c) Using this result, show that for a new independent sample x,

$$P(x = 1 \mid x_1, \ldots, x_n) = \int_{-\infty}^{\infty} \theta p(\theta \mid x_1, \ldots, x_n)\, d\theta = \frac{k+1}{n+2}$$

Hint:

$$P(x \mid x_1, \ldots, x_n) = \int_{-\infty}^{\infty} p(x, \theta \mid x_1, \ldots, x_n)\, d\theta$$

(d) Show that the value of θ for which $p(\theta \mid x_1, \ldots, x_n)$ is maximum is $\theta = k/n$. Sketch $p(\theta \mid x_1, \ldots, x_n)$ versus θ and describe its behavior as $n \to \infty$ for the case $k = fn$.

5. Suppose that the following data are given:

Class 1:

$$\mathbf{x}_1 = (0, 0)'$$
$$\mathbf{x}_2 = (3, 0)'$$

Class 2:

$$\mathbf{x}_3 = (-1, 0)'$$
$$\mathbf{x}_4 = (0, 2)'$$

(a) Add a unit third component to these vectors and apply the fixed-increment error correction rule

$$\boldsymbol{\alpha}_{k+1,} = \begin{cases} \boldsymbol{\alpha}_k + \mathbf{y} & \text{if } (\boldsymbol{\alpha}_i, \mathbf{y}) \leqslant 0 \text{ and } \mathbf{y} \sim \omega_1 \\ \boldsymbol{\alpha}_k - \mathbf{y} & \text{if } (\boldsymbol{\alpha}_k, \mathbf{y}) \geqslant 0 \text{ and } \mathbf{y} \sim \omega_2 \\ \boldsymbol{\alpha}_k & \text{otherwise} \end{cases}$$

with $\boldsymbol{\alpha}_0 = \mathbf{0}$, cycling through the four patterns in sequence until the solution $\hat{\boldsymbol{\alpha}} = (2, -2, 1)'$ is obtained. How many corrections are required?

(b) Sketch the patterns in the $x_1 - x_2$ plane, together with the decision boundary $(\hat{\boldsymbol{\alpha}}, \mathbf{y}) = 0$. In addition, show the boundary corresponding to the nearest-mean decision rule, where one decides ω_1 if $\| \mathbf{x} - \mathbf{m}_1 \| < \| \mathbf{x} - \mathbf{m}_2 \|$.

6. Suppose that the following four patterns are given without category information:

$$\mathbf{x}_1 = (0, 0)'$$
$$\mathbf{x}_2 = (3, 0)'$$
$$\mathbf{x}_3 = (-1, 0)'$$
$$\mathbf{x}_4 = (0, 2)'$$

(a) Show that the application of Sebestyen's clustering method with $r = 2.5$ leads to two subclasses, with

$$\mathbf{m}_1 = (-\tfrac{1}{3}, \tfrac{2}{3})'$$

and

$$\mathbf{m}_2 = (3, 0)'$$

(b) What happens if $r < 1$? If $r > 3$? Is there any value of r for which $\mathbf{x}_1$ and $\mathbf{x}_2$ fall in one subclass, and $\mathbf{x}_3$ and $\mathbf{x}_4$ fall in the other?

Chapter 2 Problems

1. In the sequential classification system using Wald's SPRT, show that for given error probabilities e_{12} and e_{21} an appropriate choice of the upper and lower stopping boundaries respectively is

$$A = \frac{1 - e_{21}}{e_{12}}$$

$$B = \frac{e_{12}}{1 - e_{12}}$$

2. In using the SPRT for a sequential classification system suppose that $x_1, x_2, \ldots$ are independent feature measurements with $p(x_j \mid \omega_i)$, $i = 1, 2$, $j = 1, 2, \ldots$, a univariate Gaussian density function with mean μ_i and variance σ^2. Show that the SPRT becomes that if

$$\sum_{i=1}^{n} x_i \geqslant \frac{\sigma^2}{\mu_1 - \mu_2} \log A + \frac{n}{2}(\mu_1 + \mu_2), \qquad \text{then} \quad \mathbf{x} \sim \omega_1$$

$$\sum_{i=1}^{n} x_i \leqslant \frac{\sigma^2}{\mu_1 - \mu_2} \log B + \frac{n}{2}(\mu_1 + \mu_2), \qquad \text{then} \quad \mathbf{x} \sim \omega_2$$

and if

$$\frac{\sigma^2}{\mu_1 - \mu_2} \log B + \frac{n}{2}(\mu_1 + \mu_2) < \sum_{i=1}^{n} x_i < \frac{\sigma^2}{\mu_1 - \mu_2} \log A + \frac{n}{2}(\mu_1 + \mu_2)$$

then an additional measurement x_{n+1} will be taken.

3. Derive Eq. (2.68), and determine the relationship between d_{ij} and divergence $J(\omega_i, \omega_j)$.

4. Show that the generalized Karhunen–Loéve expansion has the following optimal properties:
    1. It minimizes the mean square error committed by taking only a finite number of terms in the infinite series of the expansion.
    2. It minimizes the entropy function defined over the variances of the random coefficients in the expansion.

5. Derive Eqs. (2.94) and (2.95).

6. Derive Eq. (2.124).

7. (Project) This is a project of pattern classification using nonparametric techniques.

    Step 1: Choose a set of data with known number of pattern classes. The following are the possibilities.

    (1) Weather information
    (2) EKG data
    (3) Multispectral data
    (4) Any other data of your own choice

    Step 2: Choose a set of features based on your own subjective judgement.

Step 3: Program the computer to classify the data you have selected using a linear classification technique. Choose your training samples for weight-vector adjustment. Perform:

(1) a two-class classification experiment (with training)
(2) a multiclass classification experiment (with training) $[m > 2]$

Step 4: Extend Step 3 using a polynomial discriminant function or a piecewise linear discriminant function. (This part is optional.)

After you have finished the project, write a report including the following:

(1) A brief description of the classification techniques used.
(2) Data selected.
(3) Features selected.
(4) Results from training (including the training sequence used and the training procedure applied).
(5) Results of classification (in terms of percentage of correct recognition with unknown patterns).
(6) Conclusions and discussions.
(7) Computer flow diagram and program.

8. (Project) This is a project of pattern classification using statistical approaches.

Step 1
and Step 2:

Same as Steps 1 and 2 for Problem 7.

Step 3: Assume that the distribution of the feature vector selected is multivariate normal for each pattern class. The mean vectors and the covariance matrices for each class can be computed from the training samples (using sample mean and sample covariance).

Step 4: Program the computer to perform a multiclass classification experiment using Bayes' classification technique, with:

(1) equal covariance matrices
(2) unequal covariance matrices

Step 5: Extend Step 4 using a sequential classification procedure (optional).

9. (Project) This is a project of feature selection and ordering.

Step 1: Same as Step 1 for Problem 7.

Step 2: Choose arbitrarily a set of N features (they may be the same set of features used in Problems 7 and 8).

Step 3: Apply divergence criterion for feature selection of a two-class recognition problem. Program the computer to select the best feature subset with 1 feature, with 2 features,..., etc.

Step 4: Extend Step 3 to a multiclass recognition problem.

Step 5: (Optional) Compare the results obtained in Steps 3 and 4 with the results obtained by using any other approach (of your own choice).

Your report should include:

(1) A brief introduction of the technique used.
(2) Data selected for the experiment.
(3) Initial feature set (Step 2).
(4) Feature subsets selected in Step 3 and Step 4.
(5) Curves which indicate the relationship between the probability of correct recognition and the divergence (or d_{ij} in Step 4).
(6) Comparisons of the experimental results with theoretical results, and further discussions of your experiments.

Chapter 3 Problems

1. Consider the classification problems in which the patterns $\mathbf{x}_1, \mathbf{x}_2, \ldots,$ are the coordinate vectors of the vertices of a four-cube. We mention only members of ω_1, the remaining belong to ω_{-1}. The vertices are identified by the decimal number representation of their binary coordinate vectors.

Determine a hyperplane of type

$$\sum_{i=1}^{4} \alpha_i x_i + \alpha_0 = 0$$

separating the classes ω_1 and ω_{-1} if one exists. If not, find non-negative weights $\beta_1, \beta_2, \ldots,$ so that

$$\sum_{\substack{i \\ \mathbf{x}_i \sim \omega_1}} \beta_i \mathbf{x}_i = \sum_{\substack{j \\ \mathbf{x}_j \sim \omega_{-1}}} \beta_j \mathbf{x}_j$$

(a) $\omega_1 = \{0, 1, 2, 3, 4, 5, 6, 8\}$
(b) $\omega_1 = \{0, 1, 2, 3, 4, 5, 8\}$
(c) $\omega_1 = \{0, 1, 2, 3, 4, 9\}$
(d) $\omega_1 = \{0, 1, 2, 3, 4, 13, 15\}$

2. Among the cases (a), (b), (c), and (d) in Problem 1 in which a separating hyperplane does not exist, choose suitable functions $\phi_1(\mathbf{x})$, $\phi_2(\mathbf{x})$,..., so that the classes have a separating hyperplane in the ϕ space.

3. Establish the convergence of the perceptron scheme by nonprobabilistic methods given that the classes have finite membership and they possess a separating hyperplane.

4. Construct the membership of two classes so that they are linearly separable in a suitable chosen ϕ space, but $\boldsymbol{\alpha}^{*\prime}\boldsymbol{\phi}(\mathbf{x}) = 0$ is not a separating hyperplane, where $\boldsymbol{\alpha}^*$ is defined below

$$\boldsymbol{\alpha}^* = \operatorname*{Arg\,Min}_{\boldsymbol{\alpha}} \left[\sum_{i=1}^{N} (\boldsymbol{\alpha}'\boldsymbol{\phi}(i)\, y(i) - 1)^2 \right]$$

and N is the total membership of the classes.

5. In classification problems involving photographs, it is convenient to regard the pattern as a matrix instead of a vector. If X denotes the pattern matrix and the decision function is of the form

$$\operatorname{tr}(\alpha X) + t = 0$$

where α is a matrix of same dimension as X, reunite the perceptron and relaxation algorithms to arrive at a suitable gain matrix, α, which uses matrix training patterns.

6. Suppose we are given a set of samples $\mathbf{x}(i)$, $i = 1, 2,...$, belonging to classes ω_1 and ω_{-1}. A reasonable decision rule for classifying a new sample $\mathbf{x}$ is as follows

$$\left(\sum_{\substack{i \\ \mathbf{x}(i)\in\omega_1}} \|\mathbf{x} - \mathbf{x}(i)\|^2 - \sum_{\substack{j \\ \mathbf{x}(j)\in\omega_{-1}}} \|\mathbf{x} - \mathbf{x}(j)\|^2 \right) \begin{matrix} < 0 & \text{classify } \mathbf{x} \text{ in } \omega_1 \\ > 0 & \text{classify } \mathbf{x} \text{ in } \omega_{-1} \end{matrix}$$

Is there is a relation between this decision rule and that obtained by using Algorithm (S-1), case (i)?

7. Obtain the "best" linear decision functions of the form

$$\sum_{i=1}^{2} \alpha_i x_i + \alpha_0 = 0$$

to classify the situations pictured below, where the distribution of each class is uniform and the a priori probabilities of the classes are inversely proportional to the area covered by the class. Use the criterion functions $J_2(\boldsymbol{\alpha})$ and $J_3(\boldsymbol{\alpha})$ mentioned in Section IIB. Verify your results by sampling the two classes and using the algorithms mentioned in the text.

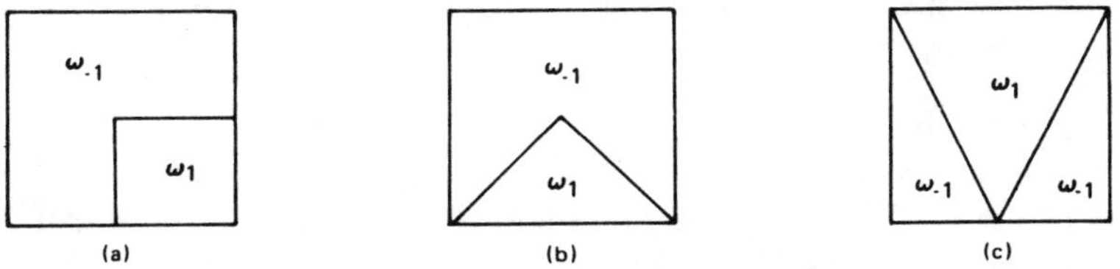

8. Suppose you are given a finite number of samples. Classify them into two classes so as to maximize $\| \mathbf{m}_1 - \mathbf{m}_{-1} \|^2_{(K_1+K_{-1})^{-1}}$ where $\mathbf{m}_1$ and $\mathbf{m}_{-1}$ are the sample means of the two classes and K_1 and K_{-1} are the sample covariance matrices of the two classes.

Chapter 4 Problems

1. Given the set of sample patterns in two-dimensional space (x_1, x_2) as listed below, use the maximum likelihood criteria of Section IID2 to derive the optimum decision surface, assuming that the density functions of the pattern classes are multivariate normal. Derive the decision surface for the four cases:
   - (a) Perpendicular bisector
   - (b) Oriented hyperplane
   - (c) Constrained quadratic surface (equal means)
   - (d) General quadratic surface

POSITIVE PATTERNS	NEGATIVE PATTERNS
$S_1^+ = (2, 10)$	$S_1^- = (6, 12)$
$S_2^+ = (1, 13)$	$S_2^- = (7, 8)$
$S_3^+ = (5, 13)$	$S_3^- = (8, 5)$
$S_4^+ = (4, 15)$	$S_4^- = (8, 11)$
$S_5^+ = (8, 16)$	$S_5^- = (9, 3)$
$S_6^+ = (7, 19)$	$S_6^- = (10, 8)$
$S_7^+ = (10, 20)$	$S_7^- = (11, 6)$
$S_8^+ = (9, 22)$	$S_8^- = (12, 2)$

2. Design an analog (or digital) circuit to mechanize the discriminant function resulting from the perpendicular bisector case of Problem 1a.

3. Design a circuit to mechanize the function resulting from the quadratic surface case of Problem 1d. Note the differences in hardware complexity and attendant hardware constraints in the mechanization of the logical functions in this problem and in Problem 2.

4. From the discussion of the characteristics of the "K" complex presented in Section IIIA1, derive a feature detector which will assist in detecting the presence of "K" complexes (and associated spindles) in the EEG data.

5. Develop at least three features which can be used to distinguish between the craters and the ridges and rima discussed in Section IIIB.

Chapter 5 Problems

1. Find other functions that satisfy Theorem 1. Describe how they, as well as $K(\mathbf{x}, \mathbf{y})$ in Eq. (5.31), might be implemented.

2. Derive Eqs. (5.40) (5.51), and tabulate $e(n; q_\xi)$ and $e(n; q_\xi')$ for $n = 1, 2, \ldots, 6$ and $\xi = 0, 1, \ldots,$ and 6.

3. Prove Theorems 2 and 3.

4. Prove that a function realizable by one linearly independent code is realizable by any linearly independent code (Smith, 1964, 1966).

5. Show that when each feature, $x_j (j = 1, \ldots, n)$, is quantized into m zones, and when the n threshold weights in Fig. 10 (Chapter 5) are replaced by a single threshold weight (why can this be done?), the total number of weights in Fig. 10 is

$$N_{q/e} = n(m - 1) + 1$$

6. Compare the number of weights required for polynomial processing with $N_{q/e}$ (Problem 5). Make a table showing values of ξ and m for which $N \simeq N_{q/e}$, and do this for $n = 1, 2, 3,$ and 4. Why can't a strict equality be used? For $n = 3$ and $m = 20$, what maximum-degree polynomials must be used such that $N \simeq N_{q/e}$?

7. (Project) Assume the existence of the switching surfaces shown below. Obtain trainable controllers for quantization-encoding and

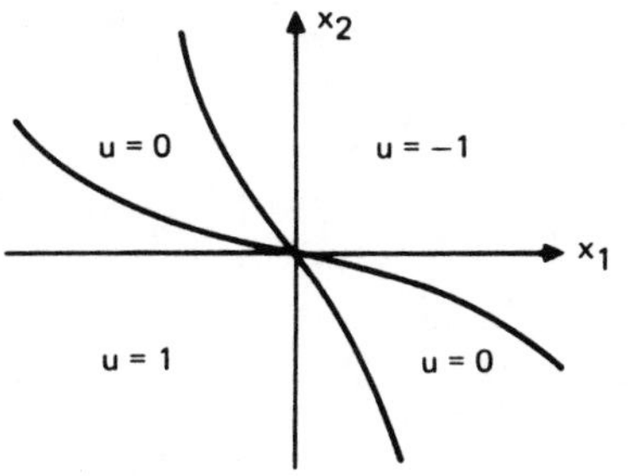

polynomial processing, such that $N \simeq N_{q/e}$ (Problem 6). Use the same training and generalization sets for all designs. Tabulate IP and IP_G for the polynomials in Eqs. (5.47), (5.48), and (5.54), and for Legendre and Hermite polynomials, as well as for quantization-encoding processing. Sketch some of the quasi-optimal switching surfaces.

PART II

ADAPTIVE AND LEARNING SYSTEMS

6

J. M. Mendel

GRADIENT IDENTIFICATION FOR LINEAR SYSTEMS

I. Introduction

Identification refers to the characterization of a system. It includes the measurement or estimation of a system's important features and is, loosely speaking, synonymous with feature extraction. Identification may be required in two basically different situations. In the first or *static situation*, identification is solely for the purpose of recognition. Identifying lunar craters in satellite photographs, to estimate the number of craters per square mile on a portion of the moon's surface, is an example of identification in a static situation. Feature extraction techniques, discussed in Viglione's chapter, are quite useful in the static situation. In the second or *dynamic situation*, identification is required as a prelude to action. Action results from decisions and modifications. An example of identification in a dynamic situation (see Chapter 8) is the estimation of the characteristics of a dynamic process, such as the coefficients of the process' differential equation, so that some measure of the process' performance can be kept invariant. In this chapter, our interest is in the latter type of identification; hence, in the sequel, *identification shall refer to identification in the dynamic situation.*

Most of the early identification procedures are of a nonsequential nature because they were historically directed toward use by the analog computer. These procedures (Braun and Mishkin, 1961, for example) often require large amounts of data which have to be accumulated over relatively long periods of time, and artificial test signals which may destabilize the system. In addition, many of the early procedures do not permit identification during the normal operation of the system; therefore, they usually are not useful in those dynamic situations, such as a reinforcement-learning control system (see Chapter 8), in which decisions must be continually reevaluated.

Sequential identification procedures make use of information as it becomes available. These procedures have been developed as a result of the availability of today's high-speed digital computers. It is becoming common, for example, to include a digital computer as part of a system's controller. The subject of this chapter is sequential identification procedures (algorithms) in which estimates of a feature vector (parameter vector), $\boldsymbol{\theta}_k$, are obtained at time t_{k+1} ($k = 1, 2, \ldots$) from the preceding estimate at time t_k and from the gradient of a performance function that provides a measure of identification error. Our discussion is limited to identification for linear systems; however, many of the concepts discussed herein are also useful in understanding the behavior of identification algorithms when the identified system is nonlinear (see Aizerman *et al.*, 1964, for example). By a linear system we mean a system with output which can be expressed as a linear combination of its input signals. Although the linearity constraint is quite restrictive, there are many important applications, as we shall see in Section II, which fit within its associated theoretical framework.

Sequential identification algorithms are closely related to pattern-recognition training algorithms. Different information is available, however, in the identification and pattern-recognition problems. In the former problem, the actual value (or a noisy version) of a function (system output) is known at a training sample (system input at time t_k); in the latter problem, only some property about a function is known at a training sample. When perfect information about a system's inputs and output is known, the gradient identification algorithms (described in Sections III and IV) are closely related to the training algorithms in Chapter 3. On the other hand, when inputs or output are known imperfectly, the gradient algorithms are closely related to the stochastic approximation algorithms in Chapters 9 and 10. Just as it is important to demonstrate convergence for the training and stochastic approximation algorithms so they can be used with confidence, it is also important to demonstrate convergence for identification algorithms; therefore, convergence questions occupy a large portion of this chapter. The emphasis is on determining conditions that can be satisfied before identification takes place (a priori conditions), so that convergence is almost always guaranteed. In addition, because of space limitations our attention will be directed primarily toward the identification of stationary and time-varying features from perfect input-output measurements. Identification in the presence of noisy input and output measurements is discussed briefly in Section V and in Chapter 10.

II. System Description

The discussion in the first half of this chapter is for the system depicted in Fig. 1, and is taken in part from Mendel (1968). Noise-free measurements are assumed. The double lines in Fig. 1 denote the

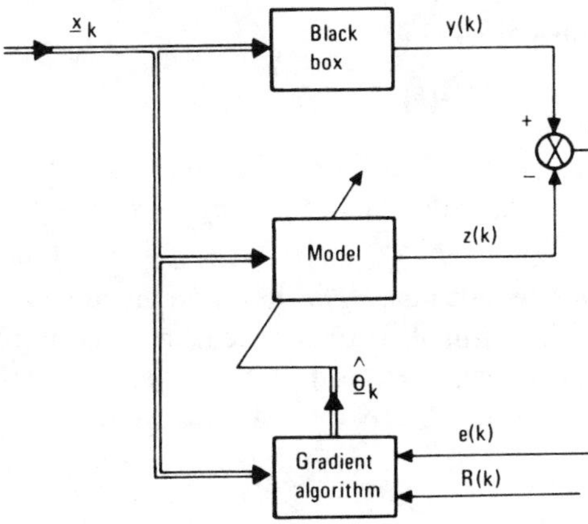

FIGURE 1. Identification system

transmission of vector quantities, and the single lines denote the transmission of scalars. Although Fig. 1 looks like a block diagram for what one customarily thinks of as a plant and its model, the signals, $\mathbf{x}_k$ and $y(k)$, do not necessarily correspond to the input and output of a real plant; hence, the nomenclature black box is used rather than plant. The examples at the end of this section show how a number of identification problems can be interpreted in the manner of Fig. 1. The development throughout the chapter is in the discrete domain for the convenience of digital-computer application.

It is assumed herein that the output of the black box is some linear but unknown combination of the components of its input, $\mathbf{x}_k$. The kth sample of the output or *actual signal*, $y(t)$, denoted $y(k)$, is assumed to be given, therefore, by an expression of the form

$$y(k) = \sum_{i=1}^{n} \theta_i(k)\, x_i(k) = (\boldsymbol{\theta}_k, \mathbf{x}_k) \tag{6.1}$$

where $k = 1, 2,..., \boldsymbol{\theta}_k = (\theta_1(k),..., \theta_n(k))'$ is an unknown, time-varying feature (parameter) vector, and $\mathbf{x}_k = (x_1(k), x_2(k),..., x_n(k))'$ is an input vector of perfect measurements. In the case of stationary features, $\boldsymbol{\theta}_k = \boldsymbol{\theta}$. The following approximation to $y(k)$ is assumed:

$$z(k) = \sum_{i=1}^{n} \hat{\theta}_i(k)\, x_i(k) = (\hat{\boldsymbol{\theta}}_k, \mathbf{x}_k) \tag{6.2}$$

where $\hat{\boldsymbol{\theta}}_k = (\hat{\theta}_1(k),..., \hat{\theta}_n(k))'$ is the kth approximation of $\boldsymbol{\theta}_k$. The error between $z(k)$ and $y(k)$, $e(k)$, is

$$e(k) = y(k) - z(k) \tag{6.3}$$

A direct approach to obtain $\hat{\boldsymbol{\theta}}_k$ is to minimize some measure of the error between $\hat{\boldsymbol{\theta}}_k$ and $\boldsymbol{\theta}_k$ at t_k, such as $\| \boldsymbol{\theta}_k - \hat{\boldsymbol{\theta}}_k \|^2$, where $\| \boldsymbol{\theta}_k - \hat{\boldsymbol{\theta}}_k \|$ is the Euclidean norm $[\| \mathbf{a} \| = \sqrt{\sum_{i=1}^{n} a_i^2} = (\mathbf{a}, \mathbf{a})^{1/2}]$. This approach is inapplicable in practice because $\boldsymbol{\theta}_k$ is not known ahead of time. A less direct approach for obtaining $\hat{\boldsymbol{\theta}}_k$ is to choose it in a manner that minimizes some measure of the error, $e(k)$, and to then demonstrate that, for that choice, $\hat{\boldsymbol{\theta}}_k$ converges to $\boldsymbol{\theta}_k$. Here we define a quadratic measure of the error $e(k)$,

$$J(\hat{\boldsymbol{\theta}}_k) = \tfrac{1}{2}e^2(k) \tag{6.4}$$

for $k = 1, 2,...$, and obtain $\hat{\boldsymbol{\theta}}_k$ by minimizing $J(\hat{\boldsymbol{\theta}}_k)$ with respect to each of the n components of $\hat{\boldsymbol{\theta}}_k$. The minimum value of $J(\hat{\boldsymbol{\theta}}_k)$ is obviously zero, which [see Eqs. (6.1)–(6.4)] occurs when $\hat{\boldsymbol{\theta}}_k = \boldsymbol{\theta}_k$ [unless $\boldsymbol{\theta}_k - \hat{\boldsymbol{\theta}}_k$ and $\mathbf{x}_k$ are orthogonal, in which case $J(\hat{\boldsymbol{\theta}}_k) = 0$, but $\hat{\boldsymbol{\theta}}_k \neq \boldsymbol{\theta}_k$]. The specific method used for minimizing $J(\hat{\boldsymbol{\theta}}_k)$ is the gradient descent procedure. It is well known (Blaydon, 1967; Tompkins, 1956) that from this procedure

$$\hat{\boldsymbol{\theta}}_{k+1} = \hat{\boldsymbol{\theta}}_k - R(k)\, \text{grad}_{\hat{\boldsymbol{\theta}}_k} [J(\hat{\boldsymbol{\theta}}_k)] \tag{6.5}$$

where $k = 1, 2,..., \hat{\boldsymbol{\theta}}_1$ is specified a priori, and it is assumed that $R(k)$ is an $n \times n$ symmetric gain matrix with elements remaining to be specified. It can be straightforwardly shown from Eqs. (6.1)–(6.4) that

$$\text{grad}_{\hat{\boldsymbol{\theta}}_k} [J(\hat{\boldsymbol{\theta}}_k)] = -e(k)\, \mathbf{x}_k \tag{6.6}$$

Hence, the *gradient identification algorithm* in Eq. (6.5) becomes

$$\hat{\boldsymbol{\theta}}_{k+1} = \hat{\boldsymbol{\theta}}_k + e(k)\, R(k)\, \mathbf{x}_k \tag{6.7}$$

The convergence of $\hat{\boldsymbol{\theta}}_k$ to $\boldsymbol{\theta}_k$, when $\hat{\boldsymbol{\theta}}_k$ is updated by means of this algorithm, is the subject of Sections III (Stationary Parameters) and IV (Time-Varying Parameters). Choices for $R(k)$ are discussed in Section IIIC.

The gradient identification algorithm in Eq. (6.7) has been applied to a variety of identification problems. Among the applications are: (1) determination of a plant's differential equation during its normal operation (Braverman, 1966); (2) determination of the sampled impulse response of a system (Nagumo and Noda, 1967); and (3) determination of the kernels of a Volterra representation for nonlinear systems (Roy and Sherman, 1967). Examples 1 and 2 below illustrate how Applications 1 and 2 can be formulated as in Fig. 1. Application 3 can also be formulated in this manner; however, it will not be discussed in this chapter.

Example 1. Assume that the plant is linear and time-invariant, and that its differential equation can be written in the form

$$g^{(n)}(t) + a_1 g^{(n-1)}(t) + \cdots + a_n g(t) = d_o w^{(m)}(t) + d_1 w^{(m-1)}(t) + \cdots + d_m w(t) \tag{6.8}$$

where m and n are known a priori; $g(t)$ and $w(t)$ are the plant's output and input (control), respectively; $g, \dot{g},\ldots, g^{(n)}$, $w, \dot{w},\ldots,$ and $w^{(m)}$ are measured perfectly at discrete instants of time $t_1, t_2,\ldots, t_k,\ldots$; and, $t_{k+1} - t_k = \Delta t$. Letting $g(k)$, $w(k)$,..., etc., denote the measured value of $g(t)$, $w(t)$,..., etc., at $t = t_k$, Eq. (6.8) is rewritten as

$$g^{(n)}(k) = -a_1 g^{(n-1)}(k) - \cdots - a_n g(k) + d_o w^{(m)}(k) + \cdots + d_m w(k) \tag{6.9}$$

This equation can now be written in the form of Eq. (6.1):

$$y(k) = \sum_{i=1}^{n+m+1} \theta_i x_i(k) \tag{6.10}$$

where

$$y(k) \triangleq g^{(n)}(k) \tag{6.11}$$

$$x_i(k) = \left.\begin{matrix} g^{(n-i)}(k) & (i = 1,\ldots, n) \\ w^{(m+n+1-i)}(k) & (i = n+1,\ldots, n+m+1) \end{matrix}\right\} \tag{6.12}$$

and

$$\theta_i = \left.\begin{matrix} -a_i & (i = 1,\ldots, n) \\ d_{i-n-1} & (i = n+1,\ldots, n+m+1) \end{matrix}\right\} \tag{6.13}$$

Although the goal has been achieved, the end result may not in itself be very useful because along the way the assumption had to be made that g, $\dot{g}$,..., $g^{(n)}$ w, $\dot{w}$,..., and $w^{(m)}$ are all measurable. This assumption can be relaxed considerably if the technique discussed in Lion (1967) is incorporated into the formulation. With Lion's technique, only $g(t)$ and $w(t)$ need to be measured; the additional $n + m$ signals, which are required for the identification, are obtained directly from $g(t)$ and $w(t)$.

Example 2. The plant is again assumed linear and time-invariant. Its impulse response, $f(t)$, is sampled every Δt units and is assumed to decay to zero in a finite duration; that is,

$$f(t) \simeq 0 \qquad \text{for} \quad t > N\Delta t \tag{6.14}$$

which means that $N\Delta t$ covers the significant duration of the impulse response. It is also assumed that the plant's sampled input, $w(k)$, and output, $g(k)$, are measured perfectly every Δt units of time.

For $k \geqslant N + 1$, the superposition summation that relates the input of the plant to the output (Friedland and Schwartz, 1965) is

$$g(k) = \sum_{i=1}^{N} f_i w(k - i) \tag{6.15}$$

This equation is put into the form of Eq. (6.1) by defining

$$y(k) = g(k) \tag{6.16}$$

$$x_i(k) = w(k - i) \tag{6.17}$$

and

$$\theta_i = f_i \tag{6.18}$$

where $i = 1, 2,..., N$, and $k \geqslant N + 1$. The weights, f_1 ,..., and f_N , can now be identified by means of Eq. (6.7).

III. Gradient Identification Algorithms: Stationary Parameters

A. *Convergence*

For notational convenience, let

$$\mathbf{u}_k \triangleq \boldsymbol{\theta} - \hat{\boldsymbol{\theta}}_k \tag{6.19}$$

It is well known (Vulikh, 1963) that for a finite-dimensional Euclidean space, $\hat{\boldsymbol{\theta}}_{k+1} \to \boldsymbol{\theta}$ if $\| \mathbf{u}_{k+1} \|^2 \to 0$ as $k \to \infty$. Here, an expression is obtained for $\| \mathbf{u}_{k+1} \|^2$ and conditions under which $\| \mathbf{u}_{k+1} \|^2 \to 0$ as $k \to \infty$, when $\hat{\boldsymbol{\theta}}_k$ is updated by means of Eq. (6.7), are obtained.

From Eqs. (6.7) and (6.19), and the fact that $e(k)$ in Eq. (6.3) can be written in terms of $\mathbf{u}_k$ and $\mathbf{x}_k$, as

$$e(k) = (\mathbf{u}_k , \mathbf{x}_k) \tag{6.20}$$

it follows, that

$$\hat{\boldsymbol{\theta}}_{k+1} = \hat{\boldsymbol{\theta}}_k + R(k)(\boldsymbol{\theta} - \hat{\boldsymbol{\theta}}_k , \mathbf{x}_k)\, \mathbf{x}_k = \hat{\boldsymbol{\theta}}_k + R(k)\, \mathbf{x}_k \mathbf{x}_k{}' \mathbf{u}_k \tag{6.21}$$

Subtracting $\boldsymbol{\theta}$ from both sides of this equation, one obtains

$$\mathbf{u}_{k+1} = Q(k)\, \mathbf{u}_k \tag{6.22}$$

where

$$Q(k) = I - R(k)\, \mathbf{x}_k \mathbf{x}_k{}' \tag{6.23}$$

The square of the norm of $\mathbf{u}_{k+1}$ is found from Eq. (6.22) as

$$\| \mathbf{u}_{k+1} \|^2 = (\mathbf{u}_k , Q'(k)\, Q(k)\, \mathbf{u}_k) \tag{6.24}$$

and, upon expanding the right-hand side of this equation, it becomes

$$\| \mathbf{u}_{k+1} \|^2 = \| \mathbf{u}_k \|^2 - 2(\mathbf{u}_k , R(k)\, \mathbf{x}_k \mathbf{x}_k{}' \mathbf{u}_k) + (\mathbf{u}_k , \mathbf{x}_k \mathbf{x}_k{}' R^2(k)\, \mathbf{x}_k \mathbf{x}_k{}' \mathbf{u}_k) \tag{6.25}$$

Making use of the identity

$$\mathbf{x}_k \mathbf{x}_k{}' \mathbf{u}_k = e(k)\, \mathbf{x}_k \tag{6.26}$$

it is straightforward to reduce Eq. (6.25) to

$$\| \mathbf{u}_{k+1} \|^2 = \| \mathbf{u}_k \|^2 - 2e(k)(\mathbf{u}_k , R(k)\mathbf{x}_k) + e^2(k)\, \| R(k)\mathbf{x}_k \|^2 \tag{6.27}$$

which can then be written as

$$\| \mathbf{u}_{k+1} \|^2 = (1 - \xi_k) \| \mathbf{u}_k \|^2 \qquad k = 1, 2, \ldots, \tag{6.28}$$

where

$$\xi_k = \frac{2e(k)(\mathbf{u}_k , R(k)\, \mathbf{x}_k) - e^2(k) \| R(k)\, \mathbf{x}_k \|^2}{\| \mathbf{u}_k \|^2} \tag{6.29}$$

Theorem 1. If $0 < \xi_k < 1$, and $\xi_k = 0$ almost never, then a necessary and sufficient condition that $\| \mathbf{u}_k \| \to 0$ as $k \to \infty$ is

$$\sum_{r=m+1}^{\infty} \xi_r = \infty \tag{6.30}$$

(m is chosen so that when $r > m$, $0 < \xi_r < 1$). In addition, if $\xi_k = 1$ for any value of k (say, k_1) then $\| \mathbf{u}_k \| = 0$ for all $k \geqslant k_1 + 1$.

Because the proof of this theorem is not essential to the rest of this chapter, it is omitted. (A complete proof is given in Mendel, 1968.)

Remark. If $e(k) = 0$, then $\xi_k = 0$; however, it is apparent from Eq. (6.20) that $e(k)$ can become of zero value in three distinct ways. If, for example, $\mathbf{u}_k = \mathbf{0}$, or $\mathbf{x}_k = \mathbf{0}$, then $e(k) = 0$. Also, as we pointed out in Section II, $e(k) = 0$ if $\mathbf{x}_k$ and $\mathbf{u}_k$ are orthogonal and, in this case, convergence of $\| \mathbf{u}_{k+1} \|^2$ to zero may not occur; for example, if $e(k)$ is identically equal to zero for all $k \geqslant k_1$, $\xi_k = 0$ for all $k \geqslant k_1$ and the condition in Eq. (6.30) is not satisfied. In this case, even though $y(k) = z(k)$ for all $k \geqslant k_1$, $\hat{\boldsymbol{\theta}}_k \nrightarrow \boldsymbol{\theta}$ (unless $\xi_k = 1$ for some $k < k_1$, which is unlikely). The orthogonality of $\mathbf{u}_k$ and $\mathbf{x}_k$ is discussed further in the next paragraph.

To make the best use of Theorem 1, we would like to know a priori conditions on the elements of $R(k)$, so that $0 < \xi_k < 1$.

Theorem 2. A necessary condition for $0 < \xi_k < 1$ is

$$e(k)(\mathbf{u}_k, R(k)\,\mathbf{x}_k) > 0 \tag{6.31}$$

for all k.

The proof of this result follows directly from Eq. (6.29).

Example 3. When $R(k)$ is chosen to be

$$R(k) = \frac{\alpha I}{\| \mathbf{x}_k \|^2} \tag{6.32}$$

where α is a positive constant and I is the $n \times n$ identity matrix, it is clear that Eq. (6.31) is statisfied because

$$e(k)\left(\mathbf{u}_k, \frac{\alpha I}{\| \mathbf{x}_k \|^2}\mathbf{x}_k\right) = \frac{\alpha e^2(k)}{\| \mathbf{x}_k \|^2} > 0$$

It is also simple to show for this choice of $R(k)$ that $0 < \alpha < 2$ is a sufficient condition for $0 < \xi_k < 1$.

During an identification, $\mathbf{u}_k$ is usually not available; hence, the condition in Eq. (6.31) generally is not physically realizable. It is not known how to obtain general necessary and sufficient conditions for ξ_k in Eq. (6.29) so that $0 < \xi_k < 1$; hence, Theorem 1 is not of much practical value since it cannot be used to indicate how $R(k)$ should be chosen a priori so that convergence is assured. In the next paragraph, a priori conditions on the elements of $R(k)$ are obtained for convergence of $\| \mathbf{u}_{k+1} \|^2$ to zero by means of a different approach.

B. *Convergence: A Priori Conditions*

$\hat{\boldsymbol{\theta}}_k$ is updated using Eq. (6.7); however, it is now assumed that

$$R(k) = c(k)\,\mathrm{diag}[h_1(k), h_2(k),\dots, h_n(k)] \tag{6.33}$$

where

$$0 < h \leqslant h_i(k) \leqslant H < \infty \qquad \text{for all} \quad i \text{ and } k \tag{6.34}$$

and the scalar $c(k)$ remains to be specified. In this paragraph, the convergence of the gradient identification algorithm is reexamined in the context of Lyapunov stability theory. It is assumed below that the reader is acquainted with Lyapunov stability theory for discrete, linear, time-varying systems (see Bertram and Kalman, 1960, for example).

In this paragraph, we work directly with Eq. (6.22) which is a discrete, vector difference equation, and determine conditions on $c(k)$ and $h_i(k)$ $(i = 1, 2,\dots, n)$ so that the *error system* [Eq. (6.22)]

$$\mathbf{u}_{k+1} = [I - R(k)\,\mathbf{x}_k\mathbf{x}_k']\mathbf{u}_k \tag{6.35}$$

is *uniformly asymptotically stable in the large*. Doing this is equivalent to showing that $\hat{\boldsymbol{\theta}}_k \to \boldsymbol{\theta}$ as $k \to \infty$, regardless of the initial estimate, $\hat{\boldsymbol{\theta}}_1$.

A scalar function, $V(\mathbf{u}_k, k)$, is defined here as

$$V(\mathbf{u}_k, k) \triangleq h_m(k) \sum_{i=1}^{n} \left\{ \frac{[\theta_i - \hat{\theta}_i(k)]^2}{h_i(k)} \right\} \tag{6.36}$$

where

$$h_m(k) \in \{h_i(k)\}_{i=1}^{n} \tag{6.37}$$

and

$$\frac{h_m(k) - h_m(k+1)}{h_m(k)} \geqslant \frac{h_i(k) - h_i(k+1)}{h_i(k)} \tag{6.38}$$

for all i and all k. The condition in Eq. (6.38) is easily met in practice; the reason for it will be given shortly.

$V(\mathbf{u}_k, k)$ has the following properties: (1) $V(\mathbf{0}, k) = 0$ for all k; (2) $V(\mathbf{u}_k, k)$ is positive definite if Eq. (6.34) is statisfied; (3) $V(\mathbf{u}_k, k)$ has an infinitely small upper bound if Eq. (6.34) is satisfied; and (4) $V(\mathbf{u}_k, k) \to \infty$ when $\|\mathbf{u}_k\| \to \infty$. From Theorem 1* in Bertram and Kalman (1960), $\mathbf{u}_k = \mathbf{0}$ is uniformly asymptotically stable in the large, and $V(\mathbf{u}_k, k)$ is a Lyapunov function of the system in Eq. (6.35) if, in addition to the above four properties that $V(\mathbf{u}_k, k)$ possesses,

$$V(\mathbf{u}_{k+1}, k+1) - V(\mathbf{u}_k, k) \triangleq \Delta V(\mathbf{u}_k, k) \leqslant -\gamma(\|\mathbf{u}_k\|) < 0 \tag{6.39}$$

for all $\mathbf{u}_k \neq \mathbf{0}$, and all k.

Letting

$$\Delta V_m \triangleq \frac{V(\mathbf{u}_{k+1}, k)}{h_m(k+1)} - \frac{V(\mathbf{u}_k, k)}{h_m(k)} \tag{6.40}$$

if follows from Eq. (6.36) that

$$\begin{aligned}\Delta V_m &= \sum_i \left\{ \frac{[\theta_i - \hat{\theta}_i(k+1)]^2}{h_i(k+1)} - \frac{[\theta_i - \hat{\theta}_i(k)]^2}{h_i(k)} \right\} \\ &= \sum_i \left\{ \frac{[\theta_i - \hat{\theta}_i(k+1)]^2}{h_i(k)} - \frac{[\theta_i - \hat{\theta}_i(k)]^2}{h_i(k)} \right\} \\ &\quad + \sum_i \left\{ [\theta_i - \hat{\theta}_i(k+1)]^2 \left[\frac{h_i(k) - h_i(k+1)}{h_i(k)\, h_i(k+1)} \right] \right\}\end{aligned} \tag{6.41}$$

The ith component of $\hat{\boldsymbol{\theta}}_{k+1}$ from Eqs. (6.7) and (6.33) is

$$\hat{\theta}_i(k+1) = \hat{\theta}_i(k) + c(k)\, e(k)\, h_i(k)\, x_i(k) \tag{6.42}$$

Substituting this expression into the first term on the right-hand side of Eq. (6.41), and making use of Eqs. (6.1)–(6.3), one finds

$$\begin{aligned}\Delta V_m &= \left\{ c^2(k)\, e^2(k) \sum_i [h_i(k)\, x_i^2(k)] - 2c(k)\, e^2(k) \right\} \\ &\quad + \sum_i \left\{ [\theta_i - \hat{\theta}_i(k+1)]^2 \left[\frac{h_i(k) - h_i(k+1)}{h_i(k)\, h_i(k+1)} \right] \right\}\end{aligned} \tag{6.43}$$

which, from Eqs. (6.38) and (6.40), reduces to

$$\Delta V(\mathbf{u}_k, k) \leqslant -2h_m(k)\, c(k)\, e^2(k) \left[1 - \frac{1}{2} c(k) \sum_{i=1}^{n} h_i(k)\, x_i^2(k) \right] \tag{6.44}$$

From this equation and simple inequality analysis, one can readily show that $\Delta V(\mathbf{u}_k, k) < 0$ for all k and $\mathbf{u}_k \neq \mathbf{0}$, as long as $\mathbf{u}_k$ and $\mathbf{x}_k$ are not orthogonal, if

$$c(k) > 0 \tag{6.45}$$

and

$$c(k) < \frac{2}{\sum_{i=1}^{n} h_i(k)\, x_i^2(k)} \tag{6.46}$$

When $\mathbf{u}_k$ and $\mathbf{x}_k$ are orthogonal, the error system in Eq. (6.35) is uniformly stable but is not uniformly, asymptotically stable in the large, meaning that $\hat{\boldsymbol{\theta}}_{k+1}$ may not converge to $\boldsymbol{\theta}$ as $k \to \infty$. This represents a limitation of the present identification algorithm. In practice, however, convergence of $\hat{\boldsymbol{\theta}}_{k+1}$ to $\boldsymbol{\theta}$ is almost always obtained. (This has been observed by the author and also by Shipley *et al.*, 1965, and Stefani, 1967.) The condition $(\mathbf{u}_k, \mathbf{x}_k) = 0$ when $\mathbf{u}_k \neq \mathbf{0}$ is strongly dependent upon the input sequence, $\mathbf{x}_k$. Additional discussions that relate the frequency content of $\mathbf{x}(t)$ to the nonorthogonality of $\mathbf{x}_k$ and $\mathbf{u}_k$ are found in Lion (1967).

The results obtained thus far in this paragraph are summarized for reference purposes in the following theorem:

Theorem 3. If $\hat{\boldsymbol{\theta}}_k$ is updated by means of Eqs. (6.7) and (6.33), where the elements of $R(k)$ are subject to the constraints in Eqs. (6.34), (6.38), (6.45), and (6.46), then almost always (unless $\mathbf{u}_k$ and $\mathbf{x}_k$ are orthogonal) $\hat{\boldsymbol{\theta}}_{k+1} \to \boldsymbol{\theta}$ as $k \to \infty$, regardless of the initial estimate, $\hat{\boldsymbol{\theta}}_1$.

Example 4. If

$$c(k) \triangleq \frac{c}{\sum_{i=1}^{n} h_i(k)\, x_i^2(k)} \tag{6.47}$$

where

$$0 < c < 2 \tag{6.48}$$

then

$$\Delta V(\mathbf{u}_k, k) \leqslant -\frac{c(2-c)\, h_m(k)}{\sum_{i=1}^{n} h_i(k)\, x_i^2(k)}\, e^2(k) < 0 \tag{6.49}$$

for all k and $\mathbf{u}_k \neq \mathbf{0}$, and the error system in Eq. (6.35) is uniformly, asymptotically stable in the large—as long as $\mathbf{u}_k$ and $\mathbf{x}_k$ are not orthogonal. We show in the next paragraph that the choice for $c(k)$ in Eq. (6.47) with $c = 1$ is important for practical considerations.

C. *An Optimum Choice for the Gain Matrix*, $R(k)$

In the following section, a gain matrix is derived from two completely different points of view: Lyapunov stability theory and an error-correction property. We show that the gain matrices obtained from the two approaches are one and the same.

1. *A Lyapunov-optimum gain matrix.* $\Delta V(\mathbf{u}_k, k)$ provides a measure of the rate at which $\hat{\boldsymbol{\theta}}_{k+1}$ converges to $\boldsymbol{\theta}$. Naturally, we desire rapid convergence. Setting the partial derivative of the right-hand side of Eq. (6.44), with respect to $c(k)$, equal to zero, leads to the following optimum choice, $c^*(k)$, for $c(k)$:

$$c^*(k) = \frac{1}{\sum_{i=1}^{n} h_i(k)\, x_i^2(k)} \tag{6.50}$$

Observe that $c^*(k)$ is of the form of $c(k)$ in Eq. (6.47), and that the condition in Eq. (6.48) is satisfied for $c^*(k)$; hence, convergence is assured for $c^*(k)$. $R^*(k)$, which is obtained by substitution of Eq. (6.50) into Eq. (6.33), is referred to as the Lyapunov-optimum gain matrix.

2. *An error-correction gain matrix.* The elements of $R(k)$ are chosen to satisfy an error-correction property. In this property, which is based on the error-correction training procedure (see Chapter 1), *the output of the adjusted model in Fig.* 1 *must equal the actual output if the same input is applied at the next sampling instant.* More precisely, one has the following error-correction property theorem:

Theorem 4. If $z(k) \neq y(k)$ and $\mathbf{x}_{k+1} = \mathbf{x}_k$, then $z(k+1) = y(k)$ if, and only if

$$(R(k)\,\mathbf{x}_k\,,\,\mathbf{x}_k) = 1 \tag{6.51}$$

Proof. (1) Under the conditions of the theorem and from Eqs. (6.2), (6.3), and (6.7), it follows that

$$\begin{aligned} z(k+1) &= (\hat{\boldsymbol{\theta}}_{k+1}\,,\,\mathbf{x}_k) = z(k) + e(k)(R(k)\,\mathbf{x}_k\,,\,\mathbf{x}_k) \\ &= z(k) + e(k) = y(k) \end{aligned}$$

which proves the sufficiency of Eq. (6.51).
(2) Assume $z(k) \neq y(k)$; then

$$\begin{aligned} z(k+1) &= z(k) + e(k)(R(k)\,\mathbf{x}_k\,,\,\mathbf{x}_k) \\ &= z(k)[1 - (R(k)\,\mathbf{x}_k\,,\,\mathbf{x}_k)] + y(k)(R(k)\,\mathbf{x}_k\,,\,\mathbf{x}_k) \end{aligned}$$

Upon setting $z(k+1) = y(k)$, one finds

$$[y(k) - z(k)][1 - (R(k)\,\mathbf{x}_k\,,\,\mathbf{x}_k)] = 0 \tag{6.52}$$

which must hold for all values of k. Since $z(k) \neq y(k)$, Eq. (6.52) can be satisfied for all k only if $(R(k)\,\mathbf{x}_k\,,\,\mathbf{x}_k) = 1$ which proves the necessity of Eq. (6.51).

Many choices of gain matrices that satisfy Eq. (6.51) are possible. In fact, $R^*(k)$ satisfies Eq. (6.51); hence, we have shown that:

Theorem 5. The Lyapunov-optimum gain matrix for the identification algorithm in Eq. (6.7),

$$R^*(k) = \frac{\operatorname{diag}[h_1(k), h_2(k), \ldots, h_n(k)]}{\sum_{i=1}^{n} h_i(k)\, x_i^2(k)} \tag{6.53}$$

subject to Eqs. (6.34) and (6.38), is also an error-correction gain matrix for that algorithm.

It is refreshing to observe that optimal step sizes which are derived from stability theory can also be derived from a physical principle, the error-correction property. Such a property seems basic when identifying parameters from perfect measurements.

D. *Stationary-Parameter-Identification Applications*

The theoretical development of the preceding sections has advocated weighting each element of the input sequence, $\mathbf{x}_k$, by a different amount; thus, a matrix of gains, $R(k)$, appears in the identification algorithm rather than the more usual scalar gain. Why should one use a matrix of gains instead of a scalar gain? If it could be demonstrated that the rate of convergence or some other meaningful performance measure is improved when the matrix of gains is used, it would definitely be more advantageous to use it in an online identification. Analytical results for this problem have not been obtained (to the author's knowledge); however, in every example studied by the author, the performance of the identification algorithm with the matrix of gains was superior to the algorithm with the scalar gain. This is demonstrated in the examples below.

1. *Impulse-response identification.* The sampled impulse response in Fig. 2 is to be identified. The input is the realization of a random sequence of zeros and ones, both of which are assumed to be equally likely. Input and output measurements are summarized in Table I. [The output sequence can be computed directly from Eq. (6.15) for $k \geqslant 4$.] Estimates of f_1, f_2, and f_3 are to be obtained when $R(k) = 1/\|\mathbf{x}_k\|^2$ (scalar gain) and also when

$$R(k) = R^*(k) = \frac{\mathrm{diag}[h_1(k), h_2(k), h_3(k)]}{\sum_{i=1}^{3} h_i(k)\, x_i^2(k)} \tag{6.54}$$

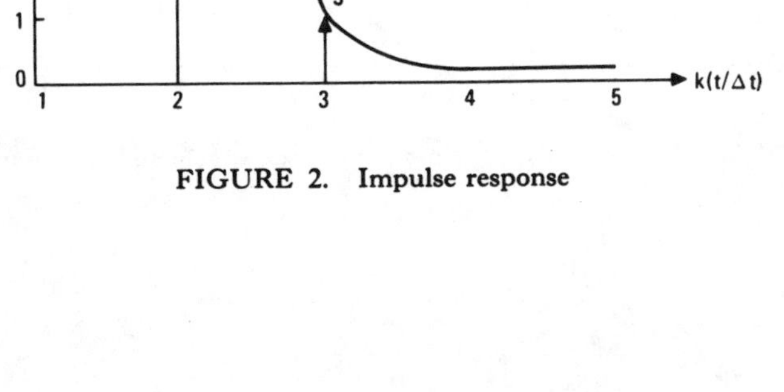

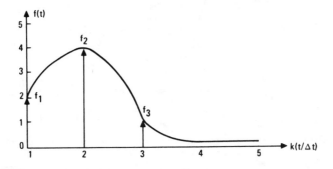

FIGURE 2. Impulse response

TABLE I

DATA FOR IMPULSE—RESPONSE IDENTIFICATION[a]

k	1	2	3	4	5	6	7	8
$w(k)$	0	0	0	1	1	0	0	1
$g(k)$				2	6	5	1	2
k	9	10	11	12	13	14	15	16
$w(k)$	1	1	0	1	0	1	1	0
$g(k)$	6	7	5	3	4	3	6	5

[a] The relations between $\mathbf{w}_k$ and $\mathbf{x}_k$, and $g(k)$ and $y(k)$ are given in Eqs. (6.17) and (6.16), respectively.

where

$$\left.\begin{aligned} h_1(k) &= 1 \\ h_2(k) &= 1/2 \\ h_3(k) &= 1/4 \end{aligned}\right\} \tag{6.55}$$

The meaning of the weightings in Eq. (6.55) is that past values of the input sequence are weighted less heavily than more recent values (Problem 4). Results for $R(k) = 1/\| \mathbf{x}_k \|^2$, when $\hat{\boldsymbol{\theta}}_1 = \hat{\mathbf{f}}_1 = \mathbf{0}$, are depicted in Fig. 3. Convergence to the correct values of f_1, f_2, and f_3 occurs and in relatively few iterations. Results for the matrix of gains

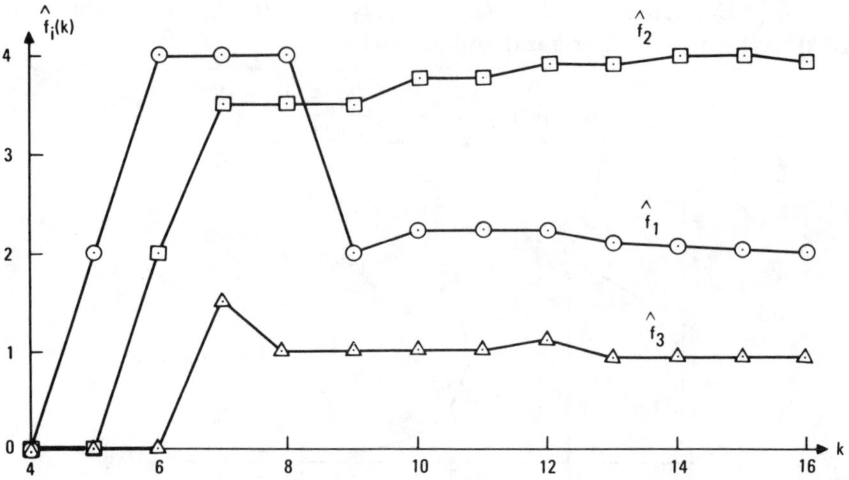

FIGURE 3. Estimates of f_1, f_2, and f_3 for a scalar gain and for the input realization in Table I

in Eqs. (6.54) and (6.55) are compared with those for the scalar gain in Fig. 4; $\| \mathbf{u}_k \|_M$ and $\| \mathbf{u}_k \|_s$ are associated with the matrix and scalar gains, respectively. It is clear that for $k \geqslant 9$, the identification for the matrix of gains becomes superior to the results for the scalar gain.

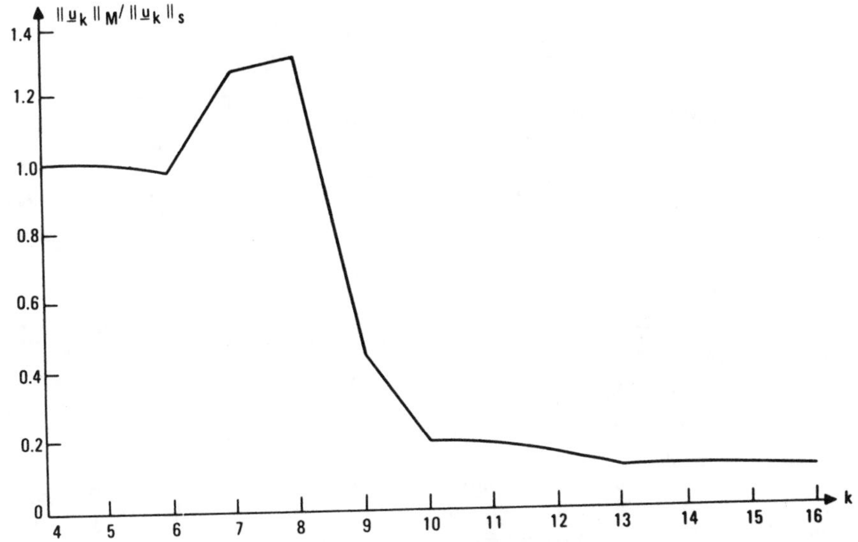

FIGURE 4. Comparison of estimates for matrix of gains and scalar gain

2. *High-performance, adaptive, normal acceleration control system.* Figure 5 depicts simplified third-order pitch-plane dynamics for a typical, high-performance, aerodynamically controlled aerospace vehicle. Cross-coupling and body-bending effects are neglected. Normal acceleration control is considered with feedback on normal acceleration and angle-of-attack rate. In Stefani (1967), it is shown that if the system gains are chosen as

$$K_{Ni} = \frac{C_2}{100 M_\delta Z_\alpha} \tag{6.56}$$

$$K_{\dot{\alpha}} = \frac{C_1 - 100\left(\dfrac{Z_\alpha 1845}{\mu}\right) + M_\alpha}{100 M_\delta} \tag{6.57}$$

and

$$K_{Na} = \frac{C_2 + 100 M_\alpha}{100 M_\delta Z_\alpha} \tag{6.58}$$

then

$$\frac{N_a}{N_i}(s) = \frac{C_2}{s^3 + 100 s^2 + C_1 s + C_2} \tag{6.59}$$

Stefani (1967) assumes $Z_\alpha 1845/\mu$ is relatively small, and chooses $C_1 = 1{,}400$ and $C_2 = 14{,}000$. The closed-loop response resembles that of a second-order system with a bandwidth of 2 cps and a damping ratio of 0.6 that responds to a step command of input acceleration with zero steady-state error.

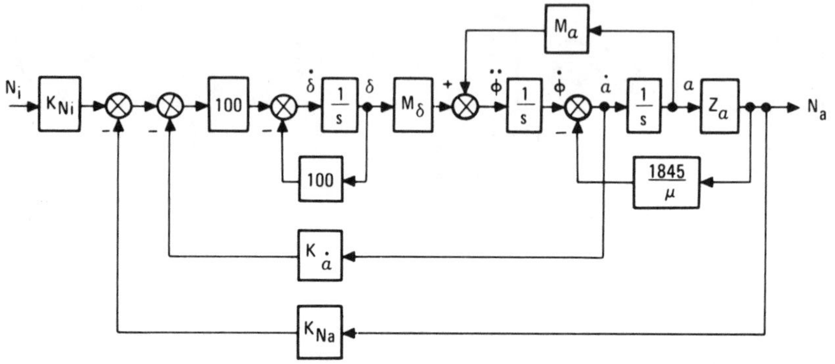

N_i	Input normal acceleration along the negative Z-axis
K_{Ni}	Gain on N_i
δ	Control-surface deflection
M_δ	Control-surface effectiveness
$\ddot{\phi}$	Rigid-body acceleration
α	Angle-of-attack
M_α	Aerodynamic moment effectiveness
$K_{\dot{\alpha}}$	Control gain on $\dot{\alpha}$
Z_α	Normal acceleration force coefficient
μ	Axial velocity
N_a	System-achieved normal acceleration along the negative Z-axis
K_{Na}	Control gain on N_a

FIGURE 5. Pitch-plane dynamics and nomenclature

If system response is to remain the same for all values of M_α, M_δ, and Z_α, it is necessary to estimate these parameters so that K_{Ni}, $K_{\dot{\alpha}}$, and K_{Na} can be adapted to keep C_1 and C_2 invariant at their designed values. In general, M_α, M_δ, and Z_α are dynamic parameters and all vary through a large range of values. Also, M_α may be positive (unstable vehicle) or negative (stable vehicle). It is assumed in the present paragraph that these parameters are frozen at specific values (see Section IVC for the more general situation in which M_α, M_δ, and Z_α are time-varying). From Fig. 5,

$$\ddot{\phi}(t) = M_\alpha \alpha(t) + M_\delta \, \delta(t) \tag{6.60}$$

and

$$N_a(t) = Z_\alpha \, \alpha(t) \tag{6.61}$$

It is assumed here that $\alpha(t)$ [which is approximately equal to $\dot{\phi}(t)$ under the assumption of small $Z_\alpha 1845/\mu$], $N_a(t)$, and $\ddot{\phi}(t)$ are measurable (perfectly, that is) and are sampled every $\Delta t = 0.01$ unit of time; hence, Z_α is considered to be known always from $N_a(k)/\alpha(k)$. Estimates of M_α and M_δ in Eq. (6.60) are obtained from Eqs. (6.7) and (6.53). When these equations are combined, one obtains the following expressions for $\hat{M}_\alpha(k+1)$ and $\hat{M}_\delta(k+1)$:

$$\hat{M}_\alpha(k+1) = \hat{M}_\alpha(k) + \frac{h_1(k)\, e(k)\, \alpha(k)}{h_1(k)\, \alpha^2(k) + h_2(k)\, \delta^2(k)} \tag{6.62}$$

and

$$\hat{M}_\delta(k+1) = \hat{M}_\delta(k) + \frac{h_2(k)\, e(k)\, \delta(k)}{h_1(k)\, \alpha^2(k) + h_2(k)\, \delta^2(k)} \tag{6.63}$$

where

$$e(k) = \ddot{\phi}(k) - \hat{M}_\alpha(k)\, \alpha(k) - \hat{M}_\delta(k)\, \delta(k) \tag{6.64}$$

Observe that the estimates in Eqs. (6.62) and (6.63) depend only upon the ratio of $h_2(k)$ and $h_1(k)$ and not upon their absolute values. The system in Fig. 5 was simulated along with Eqs. (6.62)–(6.64), and identification of M_α and M_δ was accomplished for different settings of these parameters. The objective of the study was to compare $\hat{M}_\alpha$ and $\hat{M}_\delta$ for different choices of $h_2(k)/h_1(k)$.

In order to remove some of the subjectivity from these comparisons, the following indexes of performance were used as the basis for rating the different identifiers:

$$(IP)_1 \triangleq J(N) \tag{6.65}$$

$$(IP)_2 \triangleq \sum_{k=1}^{N} J(k) \tag{6.66}$$

and

$$(IP)_3 \triangleq \sum_{k=1}^{N} W(k)\, J(k) \tag{6.67}$$

where

$$J(k) = \sqrt{\left(\frac{\hat{M}_\alpha(k) - M_\alpha}{M_\alpha}\right)^2 + \left(\frac{\hat{M}_\delta(k) - M_\delta}{M_\delta}\right)^2} \tag{6.68}$$

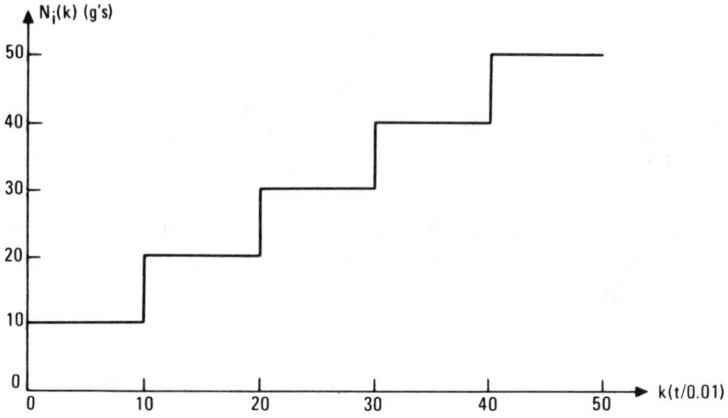

FIGURE 6. Command history for input normal acceleration

TABLE II

RESULTS FOR $M_\alpha - M_\delta$ IDENTIFICATION

$M_\alpha = 500, M_\delta = 1{,}000; \hat{M}_\alpha(1) = 250, \hat{M}_\delta(1) = 500$

$h_2(k)/h_1(k)$	Normalized Performance Index $(\overline{IP})_i$			Ranking of Identifier		
	$(\overline{IP})_1$	$(\overline{IP})_2$	$(\overline{IP})_3$	$(\overline{IP})_1$	$(\overline{IP})_2$	$(\overline{IP})_3$
0.01	0.236	0.367	0.443	2	2	2
0.10	0.200	0.219	0.232	1	1	1
1.00	1.000	1.000	1.000	5	5	5
10.00	1.340	1.425	1.440	6	6	6
100.00	0.526	0.840	0.956	3	3	4
$(0.9)^k$	0.928	0.926	0.930	4	4	3

$M_\alpha = -100, M_\delta = 500; \hat{M}_\alpha(1) = -250, \hat{M}_\delta(1) = 750$

$h_2(k)/h_1(k)$	$(\overline{IP})_1$	$(\overline{IP})_2$	$(\overline{IP})_3$	$(\overline{IP})_1$	$(\overline{IP})_2$	$(\overline{IP})_3$
0.01	0.265	0.656	0.800	1	2	2
0.10	0.378	0.555	0.615	2	1	1
1.00	1.000	1.000	1.000	4	4	4
10.00	2.810	2.040	1.848	5	5	5
100.00	5.750	3.340	2.850	6	6	6
$(0.9)^k$	0.910	0.936	0.945	3	3	3

and $W(k)$ is a weighting function given by the expression

$$W(k) = 1 + \left(\frac{N_a(k) - N_i}{N_i}\right)^2 \tag{6.69}$$

This weighting weights the performance of the identifier more heavily over the interval of time immediately preceding a command, N_i, and approaches unity as $N_a(k) \to N_i$. $(IP)_3$ provides a measure of performance for the identifier in operation in the control system, whereas $(IP)_1$ and $(IP)_2$ provide open-loop measures of performance for the identifier. In Eqs. (6.62)–(6.64), $N = 50$; hence, a 0.5-sec flight was considered. The command history shown in Fig. 6 was used throughout.

Some results of this study are tabulated in Table II. In this table, the values of $(IP)_1$, $(IP)_2$, and $(IP)_3$ have been normalized by the value of the respective index of performance for the unity $h_2(k)/h_1(k)$ case. Identifiers for which $\overline{IP} < 1$ are better than those for which $\overline{IP} \geqslant 1$. It is clear that weighting angle-of-attack (α) more heavily than control-surface deflection (δ) leads to better identifiers for this application.

IV. Gradient Identification Algorithms: Time-Varying Parameters

A. *Convergence*

It is assumed that at t_{k+1}, each component of the time-varying parameter vector, $\boldsymbol{\theta}_{k+1}$, can be expressed in the following form:

$$\theta_i(k+1) = \theta_i(k) + \Delta\theta_i(k; k+1) \tag{6.70}$$

in which $\Delta\theta_i(k; k+1)$ denotes the change in the ith parameter from $t = t_k$ to $t = t_{k+1}$. Here, just as in Section IIIB, $\boldsymbol{\theta}_{k+1}$ is estimated using Eq. (6.7) in which $R(k)$ is as in Eq. (6.33). We seek conditions on $c(k)$ and $h_i(k)$ ($i = 1, 2,..., n$) so that the error system in Eq. (6.35) is uniformly, asymptotically stable in the large. Our development is similar to the development in Section IIIB; however, it is complicated considerably by the time-varying nature of the parameter vector, $\boldsymbol{\theta}_k$.

A scalar function, $V(\mathbf{u}_k, k)$, is defined here as

$$V(\mathbf{u}_k, k) \triangleq h_m(k) \sum_{i=1}^{n} \left\{\frac{[\theta_i(k) - \hat{\theta}_i(k)]^2}{h_i(k)}\right\} \tag{6.71}$$

where $h_m(k)$ and $h_i(k)$ are constrained as in Eqs. (6.37), (6.38), and (6.34). In order to determine if $V(\mathbf{u}_k, k)$ is a Lyapunov function for the error system, we need to investigate the condition in Eq. (6.39); thus, we shall now obtain an expression for $\Delta V(\mathbf{u}_k, k)$. Defining ΔV_m as in Eq. (6.40), it follows from Eq. (6.71) that

$$\Delta V_m = \sum_i \left\{ \frac{[\theta_i(k+1) - \hat{\theta}_i(k+1)]^2}{h_i(k+1)} - \frac{[\theta_i(k) - \hat{\theta}_i(k)]^2}{h_i(k)} \right\}$$

$$\Delta V_m = \sum_i \left\{ \frac{[\theta_i(k+1) - \hat{\theta}_i(k+1)]^2}{h_i(k)} - \frac{[\theta_i(k) - \hat{\theta}_i(k)]^2}{h_i(k)} \right\} + \sum_i \left\{ \frac{[\theta_i(k+1) - \hat{\theta}_i(k+1)]^2}{h_i(k+1)} - \frac{[\theta_i(k+1) - \hat{\theta}_i(k+1)]^2}{h_i(k)} \right\}$$

$$\Delta V_m = \sum_i \left\{ \frac{1}{h_i(k)} [\theta_i^2(k+1) - \theta_i^2(k)] \right\} + \sum_i \left\{ \frac{1}{h_i(k)} [\hat{\theta}_i^2(k+1) - 2\hat{\theta}_i(k+1)\,\theta_i(k+1) + 2\theta_i(k)\,\hat{\theta}_i(k) - \hat{\theta}_i^2(k)] \right\} + \sum_i \left\{ [\theta_i(k+1) - \hat{\theta}_i(k+1)]^2 \left[\frac{h_i(k) - h_i(k+1)}{h_i(k+1)\,h_i(k)} \right] \right\} \tag{6.72}$$

Upon factoring $[\hat{\theta}_i(k) - \hat{\theta}_i(k+1)]$ from the second term in Eq. (6.72), this term, which is denoted $T2$ for notational convenience, becomes

$$T2 = -\sum_i \left\{ \frac{1}{h_i(k)} [\hat{\theta}_i(k) - \hat{\theta}_i(k+1)][\hat{\theta}_i(k) + \hat{\theta}_i(k+1) - 2\theta_i(k)] \right\} - 2\sum_i \left\{ \frac{1}{h_i(k)} \hat{\theta}_i(k+1)[\theta_i(k+1) - \theta_i(k)] \right\} \tag{6.73}$$

whereupon ΔV_m becomes

$$\Delta V_m = \sum_i \left\{ \frac{1}{h_i(k)} [\hat{\theta}_i(k+1) - \hat{\theta}_i(k)][\hat{\theta}_i(k) + \hat{\theta}_i(k+1) - 2\theta_i(k)] \right\} + \sum_i \left\{ \frac{1}{h_i(k)} [\theta_i(k+1) - \theta_i(k)][\theta_i(k+1) + \theta_i(k) - 2\hat{\theta}_i(k+1)] \right\} + \sum_i \left\{ [\theta_i(k+1) - \hat{\theta}_i(k+1)]^2 \left[\frac{h_i(k) - h_i(k+1)}{h_i(k+1)\,h_i(k)} \right] \right\} \tag{6.74}$$

The first term in Eq. (6.74)[denoted T1] is, as is easily shown, the same as the first term in Eq. (6.41); hence [see the development that precedes Eq. (6.43)],

$$T1 = c^2(k)\,e^2(k) \sum_i [h_i(k)\,x_i^2(k)] - 2c(k)\,e^2(k) \tag{6.75}$$

The second term in Eq. (6.74) [denoted $T2'$] is simplified by means of Eq. (6.70), and is rewritten as

$$T2' = -\sum_i \frac{1}{h_i(k)} \{2\Delta\theta_i(k; k+1)[\hat{\theta}_i(k+1) - \theta_i(k+1)] + [\Delta\theta_i(k; k+1)]^2\} \tag{6.76}$$

Substituting Eqs. (6.75) and (6.76) into Eq. (6.74), ΔV_m becomes

$$\Delta V_m = -2c(k)\, e^2(k) \left[1 - \frac{1}{2} c(k) \sum_i h_i(k)\, x_i^2(k)\right]$$
$$+ \sum_i \left\{[\theta_i(k+1) - \hat{\theta}_i(k+1)]^2 \left[\frac{h_i(k) - h_i(k+1)}{h_i(k+1)\, h_i(k)}\right]\right\}$$
$$- \sum_i \frac{1}{h_i(k)} \left\{2\Delta\theta_i(k; k+1)[\hat{\theta}_i(k+1) - \theta_i(k+1)] + [\Delta\theta_i(k; k+1)]^2\right\} \tag{6.77}$$

Observe that the first two terms in Eq. (6.77) do not depend upon $\Delta\theta_i(k; k+1)$, and are, in fact, the same as the two terms in Eq. (6.43). From Eqs. (6.77), (6.38) and (6.40), it follows that

$$\Delta V(\mathbf{u}_k, k) \leqslant \Delta V(\mathbf{u}_k, k)\,|_{\Delta\boldsymbol{\theta}(k;k+1)=\mathbf{0}} + h_m(k)\, T2' \tag{6.78}$$

where $\Delta V(\mathbf{u}_k, k)|_{\Delta\boldsymbol{\theta}(k;k+1)=\mathbf{0}}$ means $\Delta V(\mathbf{u}_k, k)$ in Eq. (6.44), and $T2'$ is defined in Eq. (6.76).

We see, from Eq. (678), that *sufficient conditions for satisfying the requirement of Eq.* (6.39) *are*:

$$\Delta V(\mathbf{u}_k, k)\,|_{\Delta\boldsymbol{\theta}(k;k+1)=\mathbf{0}} < 0 \tag{6.79}$$

and

$$T2' \leqslant 0 \tag{6.80}$$

If both of these conditions are satisfied, then the estimate will be tracking the unknown parameter vector satisfactorily. Unfortunately, Eq. (6.80) is not of much help in practice, because it depends upon knowledge of $\boldsymbol{\theta}_{k+1}$, $\Delta\boldsymbol{\theta}(k; k+1)$, and $\hat{\boldsymbol{\theta}}_{k+1}$; such knowledge is usually not known ahead of time.

If nominal trajectories (time-histories) are known for the n parameters, $\theta_1(k)$, $\theta_2(k)$,..., and $\theta_n(k)$, then conservative stability boundaries can be obtained for the identifier from Eq. (6.80); however, because Eq. (6.80) is only a sufficient condition for convergence, its violation is not indicative of anything, even when nominal trajectories are available ahead of time.

Because the rate of change of the Lyapunov function can be partitioned as in Eq. (6.78), it is possible to conclude that, for *small variations in the unknown parameters, the second term in Eq.* (6.78) *can be neglected.* Hence, for slowly varying parameters, Eq. (6.78) reduces (approximately) to Eq. (6.44), and convergence of $\hat{\boldsymbol{\theta}}_k$ to $\boldsymbol{\theta}_k$ is almost always assured upon satisfaction of the conditions in Theorem 3.

B. *Making Use of Additional Information*

1. *A priori and a posteriori identification.* We have seen that it is theoretically difficult to guarantee satisfactory identification of time-varying parameters unless these parameters are slowly time-varying. Often, a time-varying parameter is actually a product of two other parameters, one of which is rapidly time-varying but is known a priori, and the other of which is slowly varying but is unknown. For example, $M_\alpha(t)$ and $M_\delta(t)$ [Section IIID2] can be written as

$$M_\alpha(t) = q(t)\, M_{\alpha q}(t) \tag{6.81}$$

$$M_\delta(t) = q(t)\, M_{\delta q}(t) \tag{6.82}$$

In these equations, $q(t)$ is dynamic pressure; it varies by large amounts from one sampling instant to the next, but is either known ahead of time from guidance information or can be measured online by means of a pressure probe. $M_{\alpha q}(t)$ and $M_{\delta q}(t)$ vary over smaller ranges of values and usually at slower rates than do $M_\alpha(t)$ and $M_\delta(t)$.

In this paragraph it is assumed that $\boldsymbol{\theta}_k$ is related to another set of parameters, $\boldsymbol{\beta}_k$, in a known manner; that is, it is assumed

$$\boldsymbol{\theta}_k = P(k)\, \boldsymbol{\beta}_k \tag{6.83}$$

where $P(k)$ is an $n \times n$ invertible *information matrix* whose elements are either measurable, or specified a priori, at t_k.

Estimates of parameters at t_{k+1} that only make use of information at t_k will be referred to as a priori estimates, whereas estimates at t_{k+1} that make use of information at t_k and t_{k+1} will be referred to as a posteriori estimates. $\hat{\boldsymbol{\theta}}_{k+1|k}$ and $\hat{\boldsymbol{\theta}}_{k+1|k+1}$ will denote the a priori and a posteriori estimates of $\boldsymbol{\theta}_k$ at t_{k+1}, respectively. Obviously, the unknown parameter vector must be time-varying, or else there is no need to distinguish a priori and a posteriori estimates.

In order to put our preceding results in the perspective of a priori and a posteriori identification, we rewrite the identification algorithm in Eq. (6.7) in terms of a priori estimates

$$\hat{\boldsymbol{\theta}}_{k+1|k} = \hat{\boldsymbol{\theta}}_{k|k-1} + e(k)\, R(k)\, \mathbf{x}_k \tag{6.84}$$

where

$$e(k) = y(k) - (\hat{\boldsymbol{\theta}}_{k|k-1}, \mathbf{x}_k) \tag{6.85}$$

Rewriting Eq. (6.7) as in Eq. (6.85) emphasizes the fact that the known information at t_k and t_{k+1}, contained in $P(k)$ and $P(k+1)$, has not been used. Intuitively, not having used this information is bad. The next two subsections show how one may use $P(k)$ and $P(k+1)$ to obtain the a posteriori estimate of $\boldsymbol{\theta}_{k+1}$, $\hat{\boldsymbol{\theta}}_{k+1|k+1}$.

2. *A posteriori identification: first approach.* Two assumptions —both of which are quite reasonable and basic to our development of an a posteriori identifier—are:

$$\hat{\boldsymbol{\theta}}_{k+1|k+1} = P(k+1)\,\hat{\boldsymbol{\beta}}_{k+1|k+1} \tag{6.86}$$

and

$$\hat{\boldsymbol{\beta}}_{k+1|k+1} = \hat{\boldsymbol{\beta}}_{k+1|k} \tag{6.87}$$

Equation (6.86) follows directly from Eq. (6.83), and provides the recipe for making the transition from an estimate of $\boldsymbol{\beta}_k$ to the desired estimate of $\boldsymbol{\theta}_k$. Because the known information about $P(k+1)$ is used to obtain $\hat{\boldsymbol{\theta}}_{k+1|k+1}$ from $\hat{\boldsymbol{\beta}}_{k+1|k+1}$, there is no need to distinguish a priori and a posteriori estimates of $\boldsymbol{\beta}_k$; hence, Eq. (6.87).

We shall now indicate how the theory in Sections III and IVA can be used to estimate $\boldsymbol{\beta}_k$. Observe from Eqs. (6.1) and (6.83) that

$$y(k) = (\boldsymbol{\theta}_k, \mathbf{x}_k) = (\boldsymbol{\beta}_k, P'(k)\,\mathbf{x}_k) \tag{6.88}$$

where $P'(k)$ denotes the transpose of $P(k)$. We see that $\mathbf{x}_k$ acts as the system input (Fig. 1) with respect to the identification of $\boldsymbol{\theta}_k$, and $[P'(k)\,\mathbf{x}_k]$ acts as the system input with respect to the identification of $\boldsymbol{\beta}_k$. Hence, replacing $\mathbf{x}_k$ by $P'(k)\,\mathbf{x}_k$ in Eq. (6.84), assuming that $R(k)$ is given by Eq. (6.53), we have the following algorithm for obtaining $\hat{\boldsymbol{\beta}}_{k+1|k}$:

$$\hat{\boldsymbol{\beta}}_{k+1|k} = \hat{\boldsymbol{\beta}}_{k|k-1} + e_\beta(k)\frac{H(k)[P'(k)\,\mathbf{x}_k]}{[\mathbf{x}_k'P(k)]\,H(k)[P'(k)\,\mathbf{x}_k]} \tag{6.89}$$

where

$$e_\beta(k) = y(k) - (\hat{\boldsymbol{\beta}}_{k|k-1}, P'(k)\mathbf{x}_k) \tag{6.90}$$

and

$$H(k) = \operatorname{diag}[h_1(k),\ldots, h_n(k)] \tag{6.91}$$

If $\boldsymbol{\beta}_{k+1}$ is slowly time-varying, then, from our discussions in Section IVA, we are fairly confident about convergence of $\hat{\boldsymbol{\beta}}_{k+1|k}$ to $\boldsymbol{\beta}_k$. The elements of $H(k)$ should be chosen according to the conditions in Theorem 3 (Section III).

Combining Eqs. (6.89), (6.87), and 6.86), we obtain the following a posteriori identification system for $\hat{\boldsymbol{\theta}}_{k+1|k+1}$:

$$\hat{\boldsymbol{\beta}}_{k+1|k+1} = \hat{\boldsymbol{\beta}}_{k|k} + e_\beta(k) \frac{H(k)[P'(k)\,\mathbf{x}_k]}{[\mathbf{x}_k'P(k)]\,H(k)[P'(k)\,\mathbf{x}_k]} \tag{6.92}$$

$$\hat{\boldsymbol{\theta}}_{k+1|k+1} = P(k+1)\,\hat{\boldsymbol{\beta}}_{k+1|k+1} \tag{6.93}$$

In the sequel, this system is referred to as the "$\beta - \theta$ a posteriori identifier." For theoretical purposes, we have found it useful to view $P'(k)\,\mathbf{x}_k$ as the input to the identification system in Fig. 1. In practice, however, because $e_\beta(k) = y(k) - (\hat{\boldsymbol{\beta}}_{k|k-1}, P'(k)\,\mathbf{x}_k) = y(k) - (\hat{\boldsymbol{\theta}}_{k|k}, \mathbf{x}_k)$, $\mathbf{x}_k$ does does not actually have to be modified before it is transmitted to the black box and model.

Naturally, it is possible to combine Eqs. (6.92) and (6.93) into a single expression for $\hat{\boldsymbol{\theta}}_{k+1|k+1}$ as a function of $\hat{\boldsymbol{\theta}}_{k|k}$. A less direct, but more interesting approach for achieving the same result is discussed next.

3. *A posteriori identification: second approach.* We postulate the following "mixed a posteriori identifier":

$$\hat{\boldsymbol{\theta}}_{k+1|k} = \hat{\boldsymbol{\theta}}_{k|k} + e_\theta(k)\,R(k)\,\mathbf{x}_k \tag{6.94}$$

$$\hat{\boldsymbol{\theta}}_{k+1|k+1} = \Gamma(k)\,\hat{\boldsymbol{\theta}}_{k+1|k} + \boldsymbol{\nu}_k \tag{6.95}$$

where

$$e_\theta(k) = y(k) - (\hat{\boldsymbol{\theta}}_{k|k}, \mathbf{x}_k) \tag{6.96}$$

and the $n \times n$ matrix, $\Gamma(k)$, and $n \times 1$ vector, $\boldsymbol{\nu}_k$, remain to be determined. Equation (6.94) is a mixed equation because it contains a priori and a posteriori quantities. Equation (6.95) relates the a priori estimate of $\boldsymbol{\theta}_{k+1}$ to the a posteriori estimate. After $\Gamma(k)$ and $\boldsymbol{\nu}_k$ have been determined, Eqs. (6.94) and (6.95) can be combined to give a single equation that relates $\hat{\boldsymbol{\theta}}_{k|k}$ to $\hat{\boldsymbol{\theta}}_{k+1|k+1}$.

In order to determine $\Gamma(k)$ and $\boldsymbol{\nu}(k)$, we shall require

$$\begin{aligned} &\hat{\boldsymbol{\theta}}_{k+1|k+1}, \text{ from "}\beta - \theta \text{ a posteriori identifier"} \\ &\quad = \hat{\boldsymbol{\theta}}_{k+1|k+1}, \text{ from "mixed a posteriori identifier"} \end{aligned} \tag{6.97}$$

Under the assumptions of Eqs. (6.86) and (6.87), and for $e_\theta(k)$ and $e_\beta(k)$ defined in Eqs. (6.96) and (6.90), respectively, one can easily show that

$$e_\theta(k) = e_\beta(k) \tag{6.98}$$

for all k.

Theorem 6. Under the assumptions of Eqs. (6.86) and (6.97),

$$\hat{\boldsymbol{\theta}}_{k+1|k+1} = P(k+1)\, P^{-1}(k)[\hat{\boldsymbol{\theta}}_{k|k} + e_\theta(k)\, R_2(k)\, \mathbf{x}_k] \tag{6.99}$$

where

$$R_2(k) = \frac{P(k)\, H(k)\, P'(k)}{\mathbf{x}_k' P(k)\, H(k)\, P'(k)\, \mathbf{x}_k} \tag{6.100}$$

Proof. From Eqs. (6.94), (6.95), and (6.86),

$$\hat{\boldsymbol{\theta}}_{k+1|k+1} = \Gamma(k)\, \hat{\boldsymbol{\theta}}_{k|k} + e_\theta(k)\, \Gamma(k)\, R(k)\, \mathbf{x}_k + \boldsymbol{\nu}_k \tag{6.101}$$

and, therefore,

$$\begin{aligned} P^{-1}(k+1)\, \hat{\boldsymbol{\theta}}_{k+1|k+1} = {} & P^{-1}(k+1)\, \Gamma(k)\, P(k)\, P^{-1}(k)\, \hat{\boldsymbol{\theta}}_{k|k} \\ & + e_\theta(k)\, P^{-1}(k+1)\, \Gamma(k)\, R(k)\, \mathbf{x}_k + P^{-1}(k+1)\, \boldsymbol{\nu}_k \end{aligned} \tag{6.102}$$

Hence,

$$\begin{aligned} \hat{\boldsymbol{\beta}}_{k+1|k+1} = {} & P^{-1}(k+1)\, \Gamma(k)\, P(k)\, \hat{\boldsymbol{\beta}}_{k|k} \\ & + e_\theta(k)\, P^{-1}(k+1)\, \Gamma(k)\, R(k)\, \mathbf{x}_k + P^{-1}(k+1)\, \boldsymbol{\nu}_k \end{aligned} \tag{6.103}$$

Under the assumption of Eq. (6.97), $\hat{\boldsymbol{\beta}}_{k+1|k+1}$ in Eqs. (6.103) and (6.92) must be identical; hence,

$$P^{-1}(k+1)\, \Gamma(k)\, P(k) = I \tag{6.104}$$

and

$$e_\theta(k)\, P^{-1}(k+1)\, \Gamma(k)\, R(k)\, \mathbf{x}_k + P^{-1}(k+1)\, \boldsymbol{\nu}_k = e_\beta(k)\, P^{-1}(k)\, R_2(k)\, \mathbf{x}_k \tag{6.105}$$

From Eq. (6.104) it follows that

$$\Gamma(k) = P(k+1)\, P^{-1}(k) \tag{6.106}$$

and from Eqs. (6.105), (6.106), and (6.98), it follows that

$$\boldsymbol{\nu}_k = e_\theta(k)\, P(k+1)\, P^{-1}(k)[R_2(k) - R(k)]\, \mathbf{x}_k \tag{6.107}$$

Equation (6.99) is obtained upon substitution of Eqs. (6.106) and (6.107) into Eq. (6.101). This completes the proof of Theorem 6.

Because of the ways in which the a posteriori identifiers were derived, their convergence is assured if $\boldsymbol{\beta}_{k+1}$ is slowly time-varying, and if the elements of $H(k)$ are chosen according to the conditions in Theorem 3.

Example 5. The cases (1) $P(k)$ diagonal with unequal diagonal elements, and (2) $P(k)$ diagonal with equal diagonal elements, are interesting and important in practical applications.

When $P(k)$ is diagonal, with unequal diagonal elements, each element of $\boldsymbol{\beta}_k$ is scaled by the appropriate element of $P(k)$ to obtain the respective element in $\boldsymbol{\theta}_k$. In this case, $P'(k) = P(k)$, and it is a simple matter to obtain $P^{-1}(k)$ for Eq. (6.108).

When $P(k)$ is diagonal, with equal diagonal elements, $p(k)$, each element of $\boldsymbol{\beta}_k$ is scaled by the same amount to obtain the respective element in $\boldsymbol{\theta}_k$. In this case, $R_2(k) = R(k)$, and Eq. (6.99) simplifies to the expression

$$\hat{\boldsymbol{\theta}}_{k+1|k+1} = \frac{p(k+1)}{p(k)} [\hat{\boldsymbol{\theta}}_{k|k} + e_\theta(k)\, R(k)\, \mathbf{x}_k] \tag{6.108}$$

C. *Time-Varying Parameter Identification Application*

In this application, which is a continuation of the application in Section IIID2, it is assumed that $M_\alpha(t)$, $M_\delta(t)$, and $q(t)$ [see Eqs. (6.81) and (6.82)] vary as shown in Fig. 7. The parameter variations correspond to an hypothetical vehicle reentering the atmosphere. Observe that $M_\alpha(t)$ and $M_\delta(t)$ vary over a wide range of values, whereas $M_{\alpha q}(t)$ and $M_{\delta q}(t)$, which were computed by means of Eqs. (6.81) and (6.82), respectively, vary over a much narrower range. In fact, $M_{\alpha q}(t)$ is constant for the first 4 sec of the flight.

Estimates of $M_\alpha(t)$ and $M_\delta(t)$ are depicted in Figs. 8 and 9, respectively. The a priori estimates were obtained from Eqs. (6.62) and (6.63), in which $h_2(k)/h_1(k) = 1/10$, whereas the a posteriori estimates were obtained from Eq. (6.108), in which $p = q$ and $h_2(k)/h_1(k) = 1/10$. In all cases, a sequence of step commands in input normal acceleration, similar to the sequence depicted in Fig. 6, was applied. The command was incremented by 10 g's every second during the 10-sec flight. Note how much better the a posteriori identifier is able to track both $M_\alpha(t)$ and $M_\delta(t)$.

V. Noisy Measurement Situation

A. *Modified Identification System*

In the presence of measurement noise the Fig. 1 identification system must be modified to the structure shown in Fig. 10. The various quantities in the modified identification system are: *actual input*, $\mathbf{x}_k(n \times 1)$ which is *inaccessible*; *input noise*, $\mathbf{n}_k(n \times 1)$, with properties given in Theorem 7 below; *measured input*, $\mathbf{r}_k(n \times 1)$, where

$$\mathbf{r}_k = \mathbf{x}_k + \mathbf{n}_k \tag{6.109}$$

actual output, $y(k)$, which is *inaccessible* and is related to $\mathbf{x}_k$ as in Eq. (6.1);

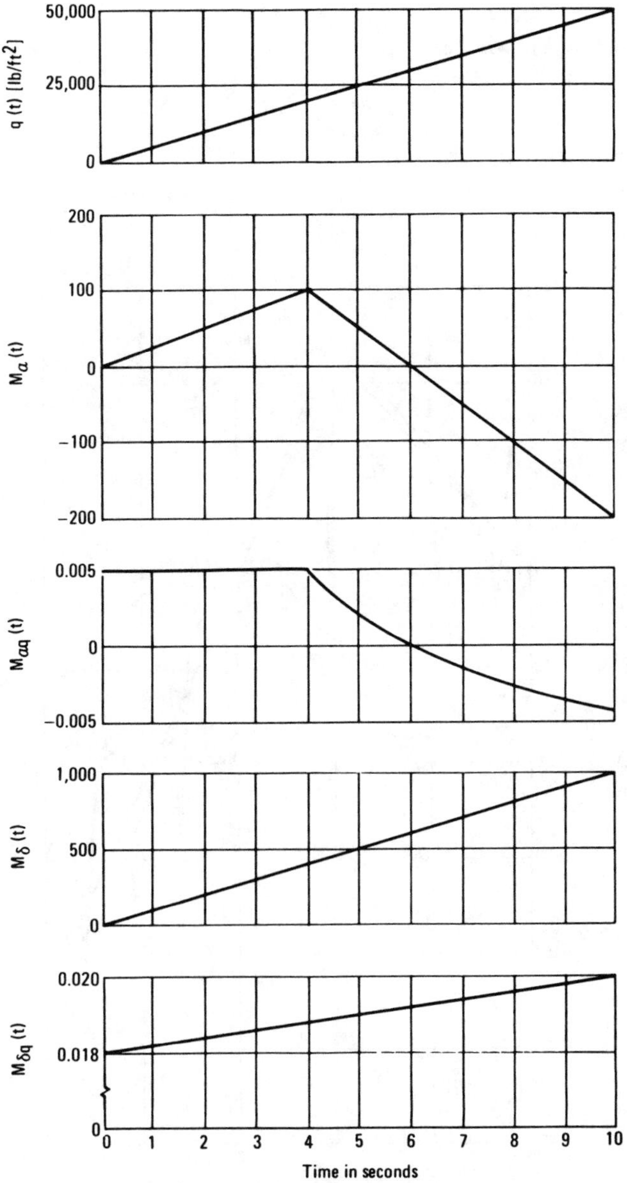

FIGURE 7. Typical time-varying aerodynamic parameters

output noise, $v(k)$, with properties given in Theorem 7; *observed output*, $y_o(k)$, where

$$y_o(k) = y(k) + v(k) \tag{6.110}$$

model output, $z(k)$, where

$$z(k) = (\hat{\boldsymbol{\theta}}_k , \mathbf{r}_k) \tag{6.111}$$

and *error signal*, $e(k)$, where

$$e(k) = y_o(k) - z(k) \tag{6.112}$$

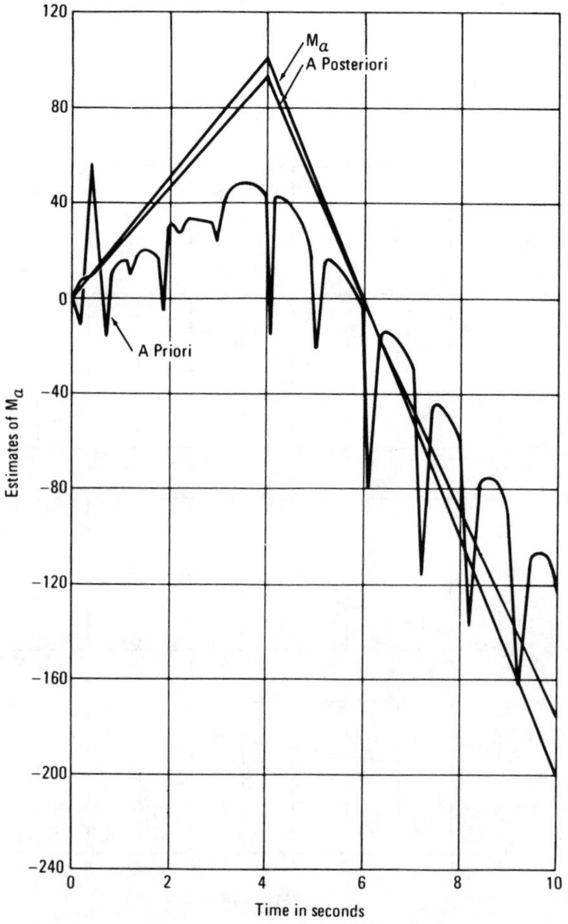

FIGURE 8. Comparison of a priori and a posteriori estimates of $M_\alpha(t)$

Different algorithms for obtaining $\hat{\boldsymbol{\theta}}_k$ are briefly described in the paragraphs below.

B. *Noisy Measurements and Stationary Parameters*

Theorem 7. The sequence $\hat{\boldsymbol{\theta}}_{k+1}$, defined by

$$\hat{\boldsymbol{\theta}}_{k+1} = [I + R(k)\,\Sigma_n]\,\hat{\boldsymbol{\theta}}_k + R(k)\,e(k)\,\mathbf{r}_k \tag{6.113}$$

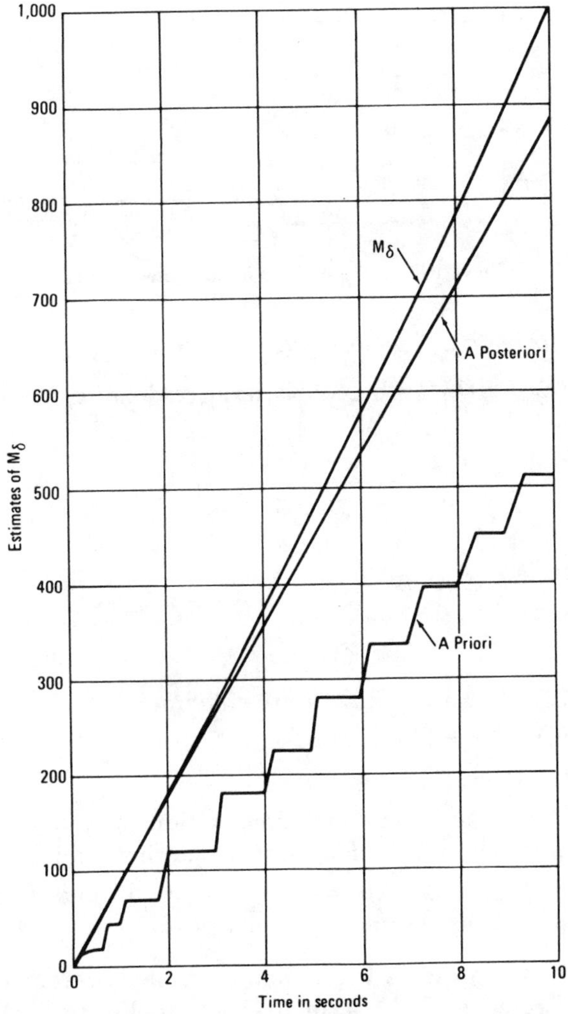

FIGURE 9. Comparison of a priori and a posteriori estimates of $M_\delta(t)$

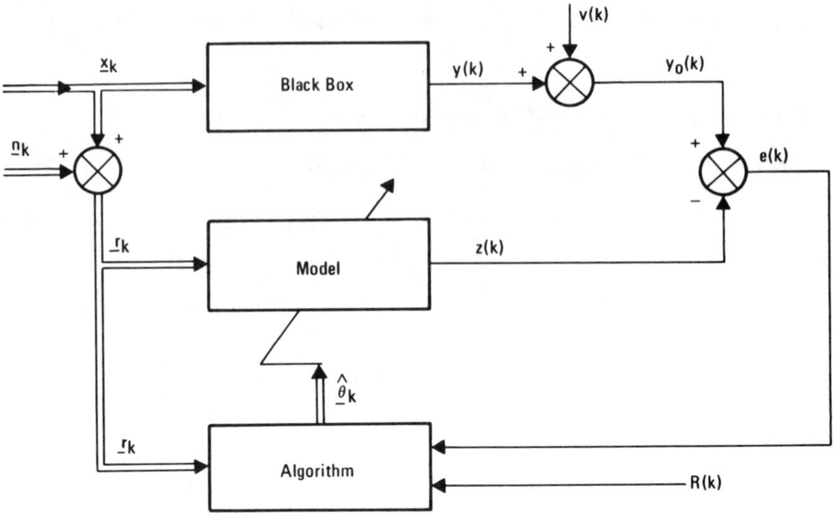

FIGURE 10. Modified identification system

$(k = 1, 2, \ldots)$ converges in mean-square to $\boldsymbol{\theta}$, if:

(i) $R(k) = \rho(k)H$ where H is positive definite,

$$\rho(k) > 0,$$

$$\sum_{k=1}^{\infty} \rho(k) = \infty,$$

and

$$\sum_{k=1}^{\infty} \rho^2(k) < \infty;$$

(ii) $E\{\mathbf{x}_k\mathbf{x}_k' \mid \hat{\boldsymbol{\theta}}_k\} = \Omega$, Ω positive definite;

(iii) $E\{\| \mathbf{r}_k \|^2 \, \mathbf{r}_k\mathbf{r}_k' \mid \hat{\boldsymbol{\theta}}_k\} < \infty$ and $E\{v^2(k)\| \mathbf{r}_k \|^2 \mid \hat{\boldsymbol{\theta}}_k\} < \infty$;

(iv) $\mathbf{x}_k$, $\mathbf{n}_k$, and $v(k)$ are time-stationary sequences, and are statistically independent of one another; and

(v) $E\{\mathbf{n}_k\} = \mathbf{0}$, $E\{v(k)\} = 0$, $E\{v^2(k)\} \leqslant V$, and $E\{\mathbf{n}_k\mathbf{n}_k'\} = \Sigma_n$, where Σ_n is assumed known a priori.

This theorem represents a generalization of Theorem II in Holmes (1968). The presence of the term $R(k)\Sigma_n\hat{\boldsymbol{\theta}}_k$ in Eq. (6.113) is necessary if the estimate of $\boldsymbol{\theta}$ is to be unbiased (Problem 5). Once again, it is possible to choose $R(k)$ a priori to satisfy the conditions of this theorem so that convergence occurs (see Chapter 9).

C. *Noisy Measurements and Time-Varying Parameters: A Posteriori Identification*

1. $\beta - \theta$, *a posteriori identifier.* It can be observed from Eqs. (6.1), (6.111), (6.83), (6.86), and (6.87), that

$$y(k) = (\boldsymbol{\theta}_k , \mathbf{x}_k) = (\boldsymbol{\beta}_k , P'(k)\, \mathbf{x}_k) \tag{6.114}$$

and

$$z(k) = (\hat{\boldsymbol{\theta}}_{k|k} , \mathbf{r}_k) = (\hat{\boldsymbol{\beta}}_{k|k} , P'(k)\, \mathbf{r}_k) \tag{6.115}$$

It can be seen that $\mathbf{x}_k$ and $\mathbf{r}_k$ act as the system and model inputs (Fig. 10) with respect to the identification of $\boldsymbol{\theta}_k$, and $P'(k)\, \mathbf{x}_k$ and $P'(k)\, \mathbf{r}_k$ act as the system and model inputs with respect to the identification of $\boldsymbol{\beta}_k$. By analogy with Theorem 7, the following algorithm is obtained for $\hat{\boldsymbol{\beta}}_{k+1|k}$:

$$\hat{\boldsymbol{\beta}}_{k+1|k} = [I + R(k)\, N(k)]\, \hat{\boldsymbol{\beta}}_{k|k-1} + e_\beta{}^*(k)\, R(k)[P'(k)\, \mathbf{r}_k] \tag{6.116}$$

where

$$N(k) = P'(k)\, \Sigma_n P(k) \tag{6.117}$$

and

$$e_\beta{}^*(k) = (\boldsymbol{\beta}_k , P'(k)\, \mathbf{x}_k) + v(k) - (\hat{\boldsymbol{\beta}}_{k|k-1} , P'(k)\, \mathbf{r}_k) \tag{6.118}$$

Combining Eqs. (6.116), (6.86), and (6.87), the "$\beta - \theta$ a posteriori identifier" is obtained. For reasons similar to those discussed at the end of Section IVB2, it is not necessary, in practice, to modify $\mathbf{x}_k$ to $P'(k)\, \mathbf{x}_k$ and $\mathbf{r}_k$ to $P'(k)\, \mathbf{r}_k$ before these signals are transmitted to the black box and model, respectively, in Fig. 10.

2. *Mixed a posteriori identifier.* The following "mixed a posteriori identifier" is postulated:

$$\hat{\boldsymbol{\theta}}_{k+1|k} = [I + R(k)\, N(k)]\, P^{-1}(k)\, \hat{\boldsymbol{\theta}}_{k|k} + e_b{}^*(k)\, R(k)\, P'(k)\, \mathbf{r}_k \tag{6.119}$$

$$\hat{\boldsymbol{\theta}}_{k+1|k+1} = \Gamma(k)\, \hat{\boldsymbol{\theta}}_{k+1|k} + \boldsymbol{\nu}_k \tag{6.120}$$

where

$$e_b{}^*(k) = y_0(k) - (\hat{\boldsymbol{\theta}}_{k|k} , \mathbf{r}_k) \tag{6.121}$$

In order to determine $\Gamma(k)$ and $\boldsymbol{\nu}_k$, we require

$$E\{\hat{\boldsymbol{\theta}}_{k+1|k+1} , \text{from "}\beta - \theta \text{ a posteriori identifier"}\}$$
$$= E\{\hat{\boldsymbol{\theta}}_{k+1|k+1} , \text{from "mixed a posteriori identifier"}\} \tag{6.122}$$

After lengthy calculations, it can be shown (Problem 7) that

$$\Gamma(k) = P(k+1) \tag{6.123}$$

and

$$\boldsymbol{\nu}_k = \mathbf{0} \tag{6.124}$$

Hence,

$$\begin{aligned}\hat{\boldsymbol{\theta}}_{k+1|k+1} &= P(k+1)[I + R(k)\,N(k)]\,P^{-1}(k)\,\hat{\boldsymbol{\theta}}_{k|k} \\ &\quad + e_b{}^*(k)\,P(k+1)\,R(k)\,P'(k)\,\mathbf{r}_k\end{aligned} \tag{6.125}$$

which is obtained by combining Eqs. (6.119), (6.120), (6.123), and (6.124), and is analogous to Eq. (6.99).

VI. Conclusions

A theoretical basis for the identification of a collection of unknown parameters by means of a gradient algorithm has been demonstrated. Two cases were considered: identification of (1) stationary parameters, and (2) time-varying parameters.

In the case of identification of stationary parameters, conditions under which the identification error approaches zero (in the limit) are given. These conditions can be satisfied by careful design of the matrix of gains, $R(k)$; hence, special attention was directed at choosing the gain matrix. The matrix was obtained in two distinct ways, with the same result. In the first way, it was found as a consequence of an error-correction property. This property was given a rigorous mathematical basis in this chapter. In the second way, it was found by maximizing the rate of change of a Lyapunov function. Examples that illustrate applications of the gradient algorithm to identification of stationary parameters have been presented. In these examples, it was shown that it is often better to use a matrix of gains rather than a scalar gain in the algorithm; hence, the additional complexity introduced by the matrix of gains in the theoretical development is justified.

In the case of identification of time-varying parameters, we distinguished between rapidly and slowly varying parameters. The convergence of the gradient algorithm was studied and was demonstrated for the class of slowly varying parameters; however, the study was inconclusive for the class of rapidly varying parameters. Often, though, an unknown rapidly varying parameter vector can be decomposed into the product of a known matrix, the elements of which are rapidly time-varying, and an unknown but slowly varying vector. It has been shown how to make use of the additional known information in an algorithm for estimating the original rapidly varying parameter vector. We have distinguished a priori and a posteriori identifiers and have derived gradient algorithms for both. The a posteriori identifiers make use of additional known information (if it is available), whereas the a priori identifiers do not. When such information is not present, the two identifiers become the same. An example was given which demonstrated the superiority of a posteriori identification when additional information is present.

Identification algorithms for the noisy measurement situation were given in Section V. Because of the stochastic nature of the resulting error system, analysis of convergence is more complex in the noisy situation than it is for the case of no noise. When the input vector is known perfectly (see Fig. 10) and only the output is contaminated with noise, the analysis of the gradient algorithm is identical to the analysis of conventional stochastic approximation algorithms (Chapters 9 and 10). If, on the other hand, input and output measurement (or disturbance) noises are both present, and an unbiased estimate is desired, the structure of the gradient algorithm must be changed (Holmes, 1968). Even in this case, conditions can be obtained for the elements of the gain matrix so that convergence (in mean-square) is achieved.

References

Aizerman, M. A., Braverman, E. M., and Rozonoer, L. I., The method of potential functions for the problem of restoring the characteristic of a function generator from randomly observed points. *Automation and Remote Control 25*, No. 12, pp. 1546–1556 (1964).

Bertram, J. E. and Kalman, R. E., Control system analysis and design via the "second method" of Lyapunov, II Discrete-time systems. *J. Basic Engin., Ser. D, 82*, pp. 394–400 (1960).

Blaydon, C. C., Recursive algorithms for pattern classification. Rept No. 520. Division of Engineering and Applied Physics, Harvard Univ., Cambridge, Mass., March 1967.

Braun, Jr., L. and Mishkin, E. (eds.), "Adaptive Control Systems." McGraw–Hill, New York, 1961.

Braverman, E. M., Determination of a plant's differential equation during its normal operation. *Automation and Remote Control 27*, No. 3, pp. 425–431 (1966).

Friedland, B. and Schwartz, R. J., "Linear Systems." McGraw–Hill, New York, 1965.

Holmes, J. K. Two stochastic approximation procedures for identifying linear systems. *IEEE Proc. 7th Symp. on Adaptive Processes* (68C62–ADAP), paper 5–b (1968).

Lion, P. M., Rapid identification of linear and nonlinear systems. *AIAA J. 5*, No. 10, pp. 1835–1842 (1967).

Mendel, J. M. Gradient, error-correction identification algorithms. *Info. Sciences 1*, No. 1, pp. 23–42 (1968).

Nagumo, J., and Noda, A., A learning method for system identification. *IEEE Trans. Auto. Control 12*, No. 3, pp. 282–287 (1967).

Roy, R. and Sherman, J., System identification and pattern recognition. *Interntl. Federation on Automatic Control Symp. on Identification in Automatic Control Systems, Prague, Czechoslovakia, 1967*. Paper 1.6.

Shipley, R. P., Engel, A. G., and Hung, J. W., Self-adaptive flight control by multivariable parameter identification. Rept. No. AFFDL–TR–65–90. Wright–Patterson Air Force Base, Dayton, Ohio, May 1965.

Stefani, R. T., Design and simulation of a high performance, digital, adaptive, normal acceleration control system using modern parameter estimation techniques. Rept. No. DAC–60637. Douglas Aircraft Co., Santa Monica, Calif., May 1967.

Tompkins, C. B., Methods of steep descent. *In* "Modern Mathematics for the Engineer" (E. F. Beckenbach, ed.), Chap. 18, pp. 448–479. McGraw–Hill, New York, 1956.

Vulikh, B. Z., "Introduction to Functional Analysis for Scientists and Technologists." Pergamon Press, New York, 1963.

7

G. J. McMurtry

ADAPTIVE OPTIMIZATION PROCEDURES

I. Introduction

The problem of seeking the optimum of a function which is more or less unknown to the observer has resulted in the development of a large variety of search techniques. Two general types of systems for which such techniques are useful in optimization are: (1) systems whose state and/or output is observed to be dependent upon the input but the functional relationship between input and output is not readily available in mathematical form; and (2) systems whose effectiveness is measured by an index of performance (*IP*) so complicated that a mathematical solution is not feasible. The availability of digital computers has increased the attention devoted to such problems, and the resultant techniques have been applied in such diverse fields as adaptive and optimum control systems, economics, operations research, pattern recognition, engineering design, and many others (Alexsandrov *et al.*, 1968; Pierre, 1969).

Many problems requiring search procedures arise in operations research including optimum military strategy, economic and business decision processes, and problems in planning and predicting for long and short term investments. In economics an optimum combination of business factors may be sought such that maximum profits are realized. In engineering design work, the engineer must often determine the best design according to a specified design criterion. Certain problems in radar applications, where methods are required for locating lost objects in the sky, have resulted in search procedures which, though not normally of the type discussed here, are related and may be useful in other fields.

Adaptive and learning control systems may be designed to search automatically for the set of parameters which minimizes the measured error as environmental factors change. In addition, a search may be conducted to find the parameters of a model used for identification of an unknown system. Just as mathematical models are constructed for reinforcement-type learning in order to provide an organized form of adaptivity, search techniques are models by which the consecutive steps taken in seeking an optimum control law are organized in a logical, efficient, and effective manner. In pattern recognition, search techniques may be applied in order to adjust the thresholds or weights used in classification, or to aid in selecting the best n features to be used in a classifier.

In this chapter, the problem of interest is the minimization of an unknown function of several parameters

$$IP = I(\mathbf{y}) = I(y_1, y_2, \ldots, y_n) \tag{7.1}$$

where

$$\mathbf{y} = (y_1, y_2, \ldots, y_n)' \tag{7.2}$$

is a vector consisting of n controllable search parameters. The vector, $\mathbf{y}$, with all its parameters, and a measured value of IP are assumed known at all times, but the functional relationship between IP and $\mathbf{y}$ is unknown. Single dimensional ($n = 1$) searches may be considered as special cases of this general formulation. The minimum value of $I(\mathbf{y})$, generally assumed unknown, is designated as I_o and assumed to be a function of an unknown input vector, $\mathbf{y}_o$, or

$$\min I(\mathbf{y}) = I_o = I(\mathbf{y}_o) \tag{7.3}$$

A. *Types of Search Methods*

Search problems, and the corresponding applicable techniques, may be classified according to whether the function (surface) to be optimized is:

unimodal or multimodal
single or multi-dimensional
deterministic or noisy
discrete or continuous

A deterministic surface is one on which $I(\mathbf{y})$ can be measured exactly at each point, $\mathbf{y}$, while a noisy surface is subject to random disturbances or experimental error. A unimodal function is one which exhibits a single minimum (maximum) point. Consider a straight line passing from any point, $\mathbf{y}_2$, through any other point, $\mathbf{y}_1$, to $\mathbf{y}_o$. If

$$I_o = I(\mathbf{y}_o) < I(\mathbf{y}_1) \leqslant I(\mathbf{y}_2) \tag{7.4}$$

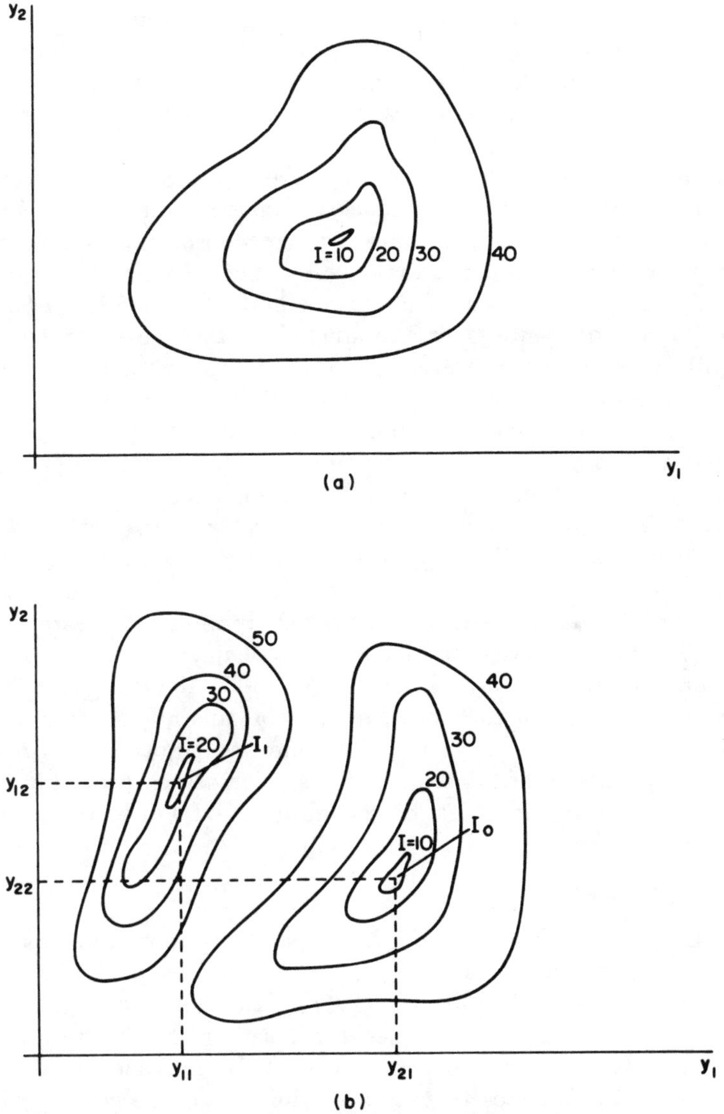

FIGURE 1. (a) Unimodal surface, (b) Multimodal surface

then the surface is unimodal. Otherwise, the surface is multimodal. If the function is multimodal, the search procedure should be capable of finding the true optimum and not terminating on a local optimal point (minimum or maximum). Figure 1a represents contours of constant values of $I(y_1, y_2)$ and it is seen that this is a unimodal, two-dimensional surface. Figure 1b shows the contours of a multimodal surface with a local minimum of I_1 at (y_{11}, y_{12}) and the global minimum of I_o at (y_{21}, y_{22}) where $I_o < I_1$. The rate of convergence is an important consideration in applying any search procedures and the required searching time obviously increases with dimensionality, modality, and noise.

Search techniques may also be classified as being either simultaneous or sequential. Simultaneous searches use parameter combinations (inputs) which are independent of any measured response, and thus may be completely predetermined prior to the conduct of the search. An example of a simultaneous search is the factorial method (Brooks, 1958; Idelsohn, 1964) in which trial inputs are conducted at the center of each cell of a grid covering the parameter space. If the problem is multidimensional, with the trial inputs having n parameters $(y_1, y_2, \ldots, y_n)$ and each parameter quantized into Δ levels, then Δ^n trials must be conducted and the one yielding the minimum (or maximum) response is considered optimum. Polynomial expressions may be fitted to the response values thus obtained in order to develop mathematical models of the unknown surface. Such an approach may be useful in conducting the opening phase of a multimodal search and various modifications of this technique have been used. Another simultaneous search is the purely random search discussed later in this chapter.

Sequential searches utilize information obtained during the search and base the location of each new input upon this information. Search variables such as step length and direction are adjusted in order to improve the efficiency of the search. Thus, such search procedures may be labeled as adaptive optimization techniques, and will be the principal subject of this chapter.

B. *Strategy of Search*

The strategy of search should be dependent upon the designer's knowledge or estimate of the type of surface involved. For example, it has been suggested by Brooks (1958) that most unimodal search methods are refinement techniques for locating the maximum of a local peak, and in the multimodal case must be preceded by a global search. Wilde (1964) states that in a multidimensional search problem, the search strategy consists of three phases. In the opening phase, if little or nothing is known about the surface, an exploratory search should be conducted in order to find the region of the surface most likely to contain the optimum. A second, or middle, phase is then entered during which the strategy is to climb the hill as rapidly as possible toward the optimum. Finally, in the end phase, an intensive search is conducted in order to converge to the desired optimum. Many multidimensional search problems are solved by methods which automatically adjust their step size and alter the search direction as the search proceeds and more information is gained about the surface. Although these methods may be used from the initiation of a search to the final convergence, it is usually possible to show that they also proceed through the three phases suggested by Wilde.

C. *Other Considerations*

In applying any search procedure, consideration must be given to many factors which may influence either the choice of the method to be employed or the modification of a chosen technique. The adjustment of the step size when adjusting the parameters of the search will directly affect the rate of convergence. Stopping rules must be provided, particularly in those cases of interest here where the mathematical function describing the surface is not generally known and the optimum value is presumably unknown. Proper scaling of parameters is desired in order to normalize the sensitivity of the surface to each controllable parameter, but this usually proves to be a difficult, if not impossible, task when little or nothing is known about the surface. Constraints on the search (controllable) parameters may be imposed, thus setting boundaries on the search space and often introducing local minima into an otherwise unimodal system. These and other factors must obviously be evaluated in order to determine the most effective search procedure.

II. Unimodal Techniques

In the unimodal case, only one minimum point is assumed to exist and there is no concern that the search will terminate on a local minimum rather than the global optimum. Most search techniques developed to date are unimodal methods.

A. *Fibonacci Search*

The Fibonacci search (Wilde, 1964) is a method for finding the minimum of a one-dimensional $[I(\mathbf{y}) = I(y)]$, unimodal, deterministic surface. If only a specified number, K, of trials is permitted, this method sequentially locates the K trials so that $\mathbf{y}_o = y_o$ is known to lie in an interval of minimum length; i.e., the method is optimal for a specified number of trials.

Consider Fig. 2a in which it is assumed that $K - 1$ trials have been conducted and it is known that $y_a \leqslant y_o \leqslant y_b$. The "interval of uncertainty" is defined as the shortest interval in which y_o is known to lie; i.e., in Fig. 2a, this interval is between y_a and y_b and has length

$$L_{K-1} = y_b - y_a \tag{7.5}$$

Assume that a previous trial is located inside this interval at y_c, or a distance $(L_{K-1})/2 - \epsilon/2$ from y_a, where ϵ is the shortest distance between two trials for which a difference in $I(y)$ can be observed. If only one more trial (and thus a total of K trials) is permitted, the optimum placement of this last trial is at y_K located symmetrically with y_c about the midpoint of the "interval of uncertainty" and a distance ϵ from y_c. Now if $I(y_c) < I(y_K)$, then $y_a \leqslant y_o \leqslant y_K$, or if $I(y_c) > I(y_K)$, then

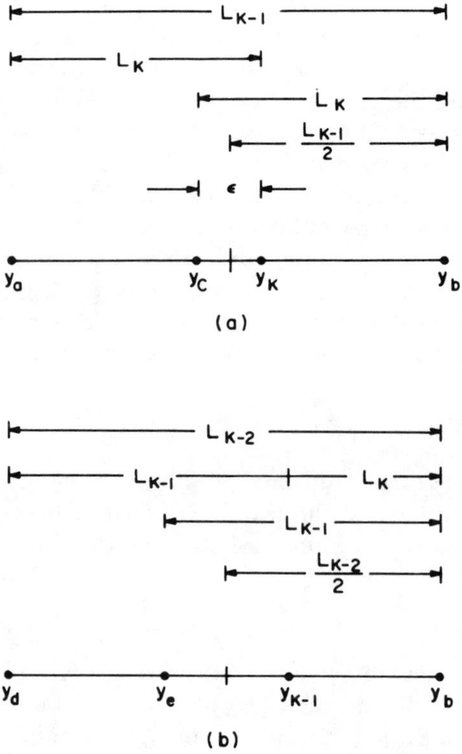

FIGURE 2. Optimal trial location

$y_c \leqslant y_o \leqslant y_b$. In either case, the final "interval of uncertainty" has been reduced by almost 1/2 of the "interval of uncertainty" after $K-1$ trials and has length

$$L_K = \tfrac{1}{2}L_{K-1} + \tfrac{1}{2}\epsilon \tag{7.6}$$

or

$$L_{K-1} = 2L_K - \epsilon \tag{7.7}$$

Now it is necessary to make sure that y_c is located at the proper position in Fig. 2a. Consider Fig. 2b in which the "interval of uncertainty" after $K-2$ trials has length L_{K-2}, or $y_d \leqslant y_o \leqslant y_b$, and y_e is the location of a previous trial lying in this interval. If y_{K-1} is located symmetrically with y_e about the midpoint of L_{K-2}, and if $I(y_{K-1}) < I(y_e)$, then the "interval of uncertainty" after $K-1$ trials is between y_e and y_b, as assumed in Fig. 2a. Thus y_{K-1} becomes y_c, y_e becomes y_a, and

$$L_{K-1} = L_{K-2} - L_K \tag{7.8}$$

If $I(y_{K-1}) > I(y_a)$, the "interval of uncertainty" would be between y_d and y_{K-1} but would have the same length as given in Eq. (7.8). Then a figure similar to Fig. 2a would have been used with y_d and y_{K-1} as the endpoints of the interval, y_e would be located a distance $\epsilon/2$ to the right of the midpoint of this interval, and y_k would be placed a distance ϵ to the left of y_e. Thus, no generality is lost in the example given here.

Continuation of this backward development leads to the general recursive relation

$$L_{K-i} = L_{K-(i-1)} + L_{K-(i-2)} \qquad i = 2, 3, \ldots, K \tag{7.9}$$

If Eqs. (7.7), (7.8), and (7.9) are combined, the result is

$$\begin{aligned} L_{K-2} &= L_{K-1} + L_K = 3L_K - \epsilon \\ L_{K-3} &= L_{K-2} + L_{K-1} = 5L_K - 2\epsilon \\ L_{K-4} &= L_{K-3} + L_{K-2} = 8L_K - 3\epsilon \\ L_{K-5} &= L_{K-4} + L_{K-3} = 13L_K - 5\epsilon \end{aligned} \tag{7.10}$$

Thus,

$$L_{K-i} = F_{i+1}L_K - F_{i-1}\epsilon \qquad i = 0, 1, 2, \ldots, K-1 \tag{7.11}$$

where F_i is the ith Fibonacci number given by

$$\begin{aligned} &F_i = F_{i-1} + F_{i-2} \qquad i = 2, 3, \ldots \\ &F_0 = F_1 = 1 \qquad F_{-1} = 0 \end{aligned} \tag{7.12}$$

It is observed that if $i = K - 1$

$$L_1 = F_K L_K - F_{K-2}\epsilon \tag{7.13}$$

or

$$L_K = \frac{L_1 + F_{K-2}\epsilon}{F_K} \tag{7.14}$$

Thus the length, L_K, of the final "interval of uncertainty" is given by Eq. (7.14) as a function of the length, L_1, of the initial "interval of uncertainty," and the number, K, of trials to be conducted. (Note that $L_1 = L_0$ since the initial interval of uncertainty of length L_0 cannot be reduced with only one trial.)

From Eq. (7.11) it is known that

$$L_2 = F_{K-1} L_K - F_{K-3}\epsilon \tag{7.15}$$

where L_K is found from Eq. (7.14). Thus the search is started by placing the first two trials symmetrically about the midpoint of the initial "interval of uncertainty" at a distance L_2 from each end of this interval. If $i = K - k$ in Eq. (7.11) then the "interval of uncertainty" after the kth trial is given by

$$L_k = F_{K-k+1} L_K - F_{K-k-1}\epsilon \qquad k = 1, 2, \ldots, K \tag{7.16}$$

and the kth trial should be placed at a distance L_k from the appropriate end of the "interval of uncertainty" after $k - 1$ trials.

The Fibonacci search is thus a one-dimensional, deterministic, unimodal optimization method that is the optimal search plan for a specified number of trials. It requires only a minimum amount of calculation and storage. It does require, however, that K and ϵ are known before starting the search.

B. *Golden Section Search* (Wilde, 1964)

It is frequently desirable to begin a search without specifying the total number of trials, K, or determining the minimum interval, ϵ. In this case, the "Golden Section" algorithm may be used to keep the ratio of successive "intervals of uncertainty" constant; that is,

$$\frac{L_{k-1}}{L_k} = \frac{L_k}{L_{k+1}} = \tau \tag{7.17}$$

Then if Eq. (7.9) is rewritten as

$$L_k = L_{k-1} - L_{k+1} \tag{7.18}$$

and combined with Eq. (7.17), it is easily shown that

$$\tau^2 = 1 + \tau \tag{7.19}$$

The positive root of Eq. (7.19) is

$$\tau = \frac{1 + \sqrt{5}}{2} = 1.618033989 \tag{7.20}$$

which is the "Golden Ratio" that results when an interval is divided into two unequal parts such that the ratio of the whole interval to the larger part is equal to the ratio of the larger part to the smaller part.

Search by the "Golden Section" thus requires that the first two trials be placed at a distance $L_2 = L_1/\tau$ from either end of the initial "interval of uncertainty." In general, the $(k + 1)$st trial is placed symmetrically in the kth interval so that Eq. (7.17) is satisfied and therefore,

$$L_{k+1} = \frac{1}{\tau^k} L_1 \tag{7.21}$$

Although this method is not optimal, it results is an interval reduction ratio that is near optimal and does not require knowledge of either K or ϵ. It has been suggested (Wilde, 1964) that early trials in a search could be located by the "Golden Section" and after several trials the search could be changed to the Fibonacci method when it becomes desirable to stop the search after K more trials.

C. *Univariate Method*

The univariate method is a multidimensional method which searches along each parameter sequentially (Brooks, 1958). Initially parameters $y_2, \ldots, y_n$ are fixed and y_1 is varied either a specified number of times or until no further improvement can be found by varying y_1. Then y_1 is held constant, as are y_3, $y_4, \ldots,$ and y_n, while y_2 is varied in the same manner as y_1. Each parameter is searched in turn and the entire procedure may be repeated until the appropriate stopping rule is executed (e.g., the magnitude of the decrease in $I(\mathbf{y})$ is less than $\epsilon > 0$ over the last complete repetition of the search). The variation of each parameter may be conducted in steps of fixed length, or the length may be reduced as the search proceeds toward the optimum.

This technique has the advantage of great simplicity of implementation since it requires only the measurement of the response, $I(\mathbf{y})$, at each step and stores only the best value yet found for each parameter, y_i. No calculations of gradients are required. It may be very inefficient if the parameters are strongly interdependent and may not converge if the step size is not reduced properly.

D. *Unidirectional Method of Steepest Descent*

In order to improve the efficiency of the search, methods of steepest descent attempt to descend the surface in the direction of steepest slope. A simple variation of this approach measures the gradient at the initial point and then moves in the direction of the negative of that gradient. The search is continued in this direction by taking fixed-length steps until no further reduction in $I(\mathbf{y})$ results. Then a new gradient is measured and the search is continued along the negative of this gradient. This sequence is repeated until the search converges to I_o or a stopping rule is executed. The length of the steps may be varied as the search progresses. This method has the advantage of only requiring the measurement or calculation of the gradient when no improvement is observed in $I(\mathbf{y})$ as opposed to measuring the gradient at each step as in the steepest descent method described below. It is more efficient than the univariate method with only a moderate increase in complexity. The principal disadvantage of this method is its failure to allow for a possible change in the gradient direction at each step. It steps in the same direction until no further change in $I(\mathbf{y})$ is observed, when another direction might yield greater improvement in $I(\mathbf{y})$ after the first step.

E. *Method of Steepest Descent*

The method of steepest descent (Tompkins, 1956; Eveleigh, 1967) measures the gradient of $I(\mathbf{y})$ at each trial and the next step is in the negative gradient direction. The gradient of $I(\mathbf{y})$ is defined as the vector

$$\nabla I(\mathbf{y}_k) = \left(\frac{\partial I}{\partial y_1}, \frac{\partial I}{\partial y_2}, \ldots, \frac{\partial I}{\partial y_n}\right)' \tag{7.22}$$

where $\partial I/\partial y_i$ is the partial derivative of $I(\mathbf{y})$ with respect to y_i evaluated at the kth trial, $\mathbf{y}_k$, of the search. The gradient is normal to the contour of constant $I(\mathbf{y})$ at each point on the surface. Since it is assumed that the expression for $I(\mathbf{y})$ is not known, the gradient components, $\partial I/\partial y_i$, may be measured at each step by making a small test step in each direction, Δy_i, and observing the resultant change in $I(\mathbf{y})$, ΔI. Then $\partial I/\partial y_i$ is estimated by $\Delta I/\Delta y_i$. It has also been shown (Narendra and Baker, 1968) that for certain linear time-invariant systems, the gradient may be determined by using a single perturbation signal, thus obtaining all the components of $\nabla I(\mathbf{y}_k)$ simultaneously.

The next step is given by

$$\Delta \mathbf{y}_k = -c_k \nabla I(\mathbf{y}_k) \tag{7.23}$$

or

$$\mathbf{y}_{k+1} = \mathbf{y}_k - c_k \nabla I(\mathbf{y}_k) \tag{7.24}$$

where c_k is an arbitrary value which may or may not change with k. Thus the step size, $| \Delta \mathbf{y}_k |$, decreases with a reduction in the gradient magnitude, and in the limit when $\nabla I(\mathbf{y}) = 0$ at the minimum, I_o, no change is made in $\mathbf{y}$. Normally, it is not expected that complete convergence will be achieved, and some stopping rule is checked at each step. The most common rule is to stop the search when

$$0 \leqslant \| \nabla I \|^2 = \sum_{i=1}^{n} \left(\frac{\partial I}{\partial y_i} \right)^2 \simeq \sum_{i=1}^{n} \left(\frac{\Delta I}{\Delta y_i} \right)^2 < \epsilon \tag{7.25}$$

The method of steepest descent is a more rapidly convergent scheme than those discussed above and will always proceed toward the minimum of a convex, time-invariant surface. If the system is time-varying, the method will follow the optimum as long as the system is not shifting faster than the time required to make several search steps. The procedure has the disadvantage of requiring the measurement of the gradient at each step and each test step made in this measurement presumably requires as much time as each gradient search step. Thus, the steps in the direction of the gradient must decrease $I(\mathbf{y})$ sufficiently to warrant the additional time spent in measuring the gradient. This implies that the value of c_k should be relatively large, but if c_k is too large the search may not converge at all.

A method of controlling c_k is suggested as follows by Eveleigh (1967): let

$$\delta I_p = \nabla I' \Delta \mathbf{y} = -c_k \nabla I' \nabla I = -c_k \| \nabla I \|^2 \tag{7.26}$$

where δI_p is the predicted change in $I(\mathbf{y})$. Then the actual change in $I(\mathbf{y})$ is measured as

$$\delta I_A = I(\mathbf{y}_{k+1}) - I(\mathbf{y}_k) \tag{7.27}$$

and an algorithm is used to reduce c_k if

$$| \delta I_p - \delta I_A | > \alpha | \delta I_A | \qquad 0 < \alpha < 1 \tag{7.28}$$

that is, if the difference between the predicted and actual change in I is greater than some arbitrary percentage of the actual change, then c_k should be reduced. Similarly, if

$$|\,\delta I_p - \delta I_A\,| < \beta|\,\delta I_A\,| \qquad 0 < \beta < \alpha < 1 \tag{7.29}$$

then c_k should be increased. In this manner, a value of c_k is continuously sought such that

$$\beta \leqslant \frac{|\,\delta I_p - \delta I_A\,|}{|\,\delta I_A\,|} \leqslant \alpha \tag{7.30}$$

Eveleigh suggests that $\beta = 0.2$ and $\alpha = 0.5$ are reasonable values.

F. *Mathematical Programming Methods*

Mathematical programming techniques have become very popular with the availability of modern high-speed computers (Lasdon and Waren, 1967). Such procedures maximize or minimize a given function, I, by proper selection of the variables, y_i, where I is assumed unimodal. Many of these methods have been developed to handle nonlinear functions with constraints imposed on the variables. Although these techniques normally assume knowledge of the function, I, being optimized, several have been adapted to the search of unknown surfaces and some of the more prominent ones are discussed below.

1. *Conjugate gradient method.* The conjugate gradient technique is a quadratically convergent method based on the concept of conjugate directions (Hestenes and Steifel, 1952). Two unit vectors, $\mathbf{u}_i$ and $\mathbf{u}_j$, are said to represent A-conjugate directions if

$$\mathbf{u}_i' A \mathbf{u}_j = 0 \qquad (i \neq j) \tag{7.31}$$

where A is positive definite and symmetric. The function to be minimized is assumed to be described by a quadratic equation

$$I = I_o + \tfrac{1}{2}[\mathbf{y} - \mathbf{y}_o]' \, G[\mathbf{y} - \mathbf{y}_o] \tag{7.32}$$

where $I_o = I(\mathbf{y}_o)$, G is the (nxn) positive definite, symmetric Hessian matrix of second-order partial derivatives having elements $G_{ij} = \partial^2 I / \partial y_i \, \partial y_j$, and the expression for I has been expanded about the minimum, $\mathbf{y}_o$, in Taylor series form.

From Eq. (7.32), the gradient is

$$\nabla I(\mathbf{y}_k) = G[\mathbf{y}_k - \mathbf{y}_o] \tag{7.33}$$

Now if $\mathbf{y}_k$ represents the parameter vector, $\mathbf{y}$, at the kth trial or iteration, then let

$$\mathbf{y}_{k+1} = \mathbf{y}_k + \alpha_k \mathbf{s}_k \tag{7.34}$$

where α_k is a scalar parameter to be computed and $\mathbf{s}_k$ is a specified direction discussed below. If the $\mathbf{s}_k$ ($k = 0,1,..., n - 1$) are G-conjugate, i.e., if

$$\mathbf{s}_k' G \mathbf{s}_j = 0 \qquad k \neq j \tag{7.35}$$

then α_k is chosen so that

$$\nabla I(\mathbf{y}_{k+1})' \, \mathbf{s}_k = 0 \tag{7.36}$$

that is, α_k is the value that yields, from Eq. (7.34), a step in the $\mathbf{s}_k$ direction to the point $\mathbf{y}_{k+1}$ which has a zero slope (minimum) in the $\mathbf{s}_k$ direction. At this point, $\mathbf{s}_{k+1}$ is computed as a G-conjugate direction to $\mathbf{s}_k$ and the procedure is repeated. It has been shown by Hestenes and Steifel (1952) that this iterative process yields I_o in n steps or less. However, this procedure requires the knowledge of G which is assumed unknown in this chapter.

Fletcher and Reeves (1964) have shown how to apply the conjugate gradient method to problems where G is unknown. Assuming an arbitrary starting point, $\mathbf{y}_0$, let

$$\mathbf{s}_0 = -\nabla I(\mathbf{y}_0) \tag{7.37}$$

It is assumed that the kth search step terminates at $\mathbf{y}_k$ ($k = 0,1,..., n - 1$) and that $\mathbf{y}_{k+1}$ is determined by Eqs. (7.34) and (7.36). Fletcher and Reeves suggest that α_k be determined by cubic interpolation so that $\mathbf{y}_{k+1}$ satisfies Eq. (7.36). At $\mathbf{y}_{k+1}$, $\nabla I(\mathbf{y}_{k+1})$ is measured or computed and used to compute

$$\beta_k = \frac{\| \nabla I(\mathbf{y}_{k+1}) \|^2}{\| \nabla I(\mathbf{y}_k) \|^2} \tag{7.38}$$

where

$$\| \nabla I(y_k) \|^2 = \sum_{j=1}^{n} \left(\frac{\partial I}{\partial y_j} \right)^2 = \nabla I(\mathbf{y}_k)' \, \nabla I(\mathbf{y}_k) \tag{7.39}$$

The next direction of search, $\mathbf{s}_{k+1}$, is given by

$$\mathbf{s}_{k+1} = -\nabla I(\mathbf{y}_{k+1}) + \beta_k \mathbf{s}_k \tag{7.40}$$

Fletcher and Reeves report that on surfaces that are not quadratic, convergence was not as rapid as desired and the procedure was modified every $(n + 1)$ iterations by letting $\mathbf{s} = -\nabla I$, that is, repeating the entire procedure after every n iterations.

This method has the advantage of taking into account the nonlinearity of the surface, $I(\mathbf{y})$, as opposed to the steepest descent method. The method is efficient, does not require the storage of any matrices, and only three vectors need to be stored for the computations involved. It does require more calculations than the steepest descent procedure.

The method of Fletcher and Reeves has been applied to optimal control problems by Lasdon, Mitter, and Waren (1967).

2. *Fletcher–Powell method* (Fletcher and Powell, 1963). The Fletcher–Powell method is perhaps the most powerful method available for minimizing a unimodal function, I. This method also assumes a quadratic surface described by Eq. (7.32). Assuming G to be a nonsingular matrix, Eq. (7.33) may be rearranged as

$$[\mathbf{y}_o - \mathbf{y}_k] = -G^{-1} \nabla I(\mathbf{y}_k) \tag{7.41}$$

Then a symmetric positive definite matrix, H, is assumed (initially H is chosen as the unit matrix) and the direction of change in $\mathbf{y}$ is

$$\mathbf{s}_k = -H_k \nabla I(\mathbf{y}_k) \tag{7.42}$$

where H_k is the matrix H after the kth iteration. Now if α_k is again chosen so that $I(\mathbf{y}_{k+1})$ is a minimum along the direction $\mathbf{s}_k$ from $\mathbf{y}_k$, and $\mathbf{y}_{k+1}$ is determined by Eq. (7.34), then

$$\boldsymbol{\sigma}_k = [\mathbf{y}_{k+1} - \mathbf{y}_k] \tag{7.43}$$

is an eigenvector of the matrix $H_{k+1}\,G$ and as the procedure converges, $H = G^{-1}$ at the minimum. The matrix H is modified at each step as follows

$$H_{k+1} = H_k + A_k + B_k \tag{7.44}$$

where

$$A_k = \frac{\boldsymbol{\sigma}_k \boldsymbol{\sigma}_k'}{\boldsymbol{\sigma}_k' \boldsymbol{\gamma}_k} \tag{7.45}$$

$$\boldsymbol{\gamma}_k = \nabla I(\mathbf{y}_{k+1}) - \nabla I(\mathbf{y}_k) \tag{7.46}$$

$$B_k = -\frac{H_k \boldsymbol{\gamma}_k \boldsymbol{\gamma}_k' H_k}{\boldsymbol{\gamma}_k' H_k \boldsymbol{\gamma}_k} \tag{7.47}$$

Fletcher and Powell (1963) show that if $I(\mathbf{y})$ is indeed quadratic, this procedure converges in n steps. In the general case where G is unknown, the value of α_k may again be computed using cubic interpolation and the condition that $I(\mathbf{y}_{k+1})$ be a minimum along $\mathbf{s}_k$ from $\mathbf{y}_k$ is not a requirement for convergence.

This method has been shown (Fletcher and Reeves, 1964; Fletcher and Powell, 1963) to be more rapidly convergent than the methods above and requires the same measurements as needed for the conjugate gradient method at each step. It does, however, require considerable matrix computation at each iteration and storage of the matrices A, B, and H.

Another method based on the concept of conjugate directions is that of Powell (1964) in which each parameter is varied one at a time and it is not necessary to determine the gradient at each step.

3. *Constrained optimization methods.* In the previously discussed methods it has been assumed that the parameters, y_i, could take on any finite value. Many problems however, introduce constraints such that the y_i may have only certain allowable values. A problem may have equality or inequality constraints which may be linear or nonlinear. In addition, if the allowable parameters are contained within a constraint set that is not convex, then local minima may be introduced and it will not be possible to prove convergence of nonlinear programming methods to the global minimum. A scalar function, $I(\mathbf{y})$, is said to be convex (Zoutendijk, 1960; Wilde and Beightler, 1967) if the function is never underestimated at any point by linear interpolation between any two other points. Thus, for any two vectors, $\mathbf{y}_1$ and $\mathbf{y}_2$, $I(\mathbf{y})$ is convex if

$$I[(1-\alpha)\,\mathbf{y}_1 + \alpha\mathbf{y}_2] \leqslant (1-\alpha)\,I(\mathbf{y}_1) + \alpha I(\mathbf{y}_2) \tag{7.48}$$

where

$$0 < \alpha < 1 \tag{7.49}$$

A set of constraints

$$f_i(\mathbf{y}) \leqslant 0 \qquad i = 1, 2, \ldots, m < n \tag{7.50}$$

is said to be a convex constraint set if all $f_i(\mathbf{y})$ are convex functions. A concave function is one whose negative is convex.

Zoutendijk (1960) uses the method of "feasible directions" for problems with inequality constraints and a convex constraint set. A direction is determined to be feasible if a small step in that direction does not violate any constraints. If such a step also decreases $I(\mathbf{y})$, the direction is called a usable feasible direction. A starting point is assumed which satisfies one or more of the constraints and the procedure causes the next step to be made inside the constraint set. The succeeding steps are all chosen in usable feasible directions until the optimum is reached.

Problems with inequality constraints may often be converted to an unconstrained form by introducing penalty functions which "punish" the search method as the constraints are violated. Fiacco and McCormick (1964) use the function

$$R(\mathbf{y}, r) = I(\mathbf{y}) + r \sum_{i=1}^{m} \frac{1}{f_i(\mathbf{y})} \tag{7.51}$$

with $r > 0$ and where there are m inequality constraints, $f_i(\mathbf{y}) \geqslant 0$. Initially, a value of $\mathbf{y}$ is chosen inside the constraint set and the next step is chosen to reduce R (which has now become the IP to be minimized). If $\mathbf{y}$ is very near the constraint boundaries and r is large, the resulting R will be very large. Thus, the method forces the search to stay away from the boundaries initially. An algorithm in which r is reduced sequentially at each step then results in convergence to the minimum, and the search may approach the constraint boundaries as closely as desired.

G. *Stochastic Approximation Methods*

All of the techniques discussed thus far have not considered the possibility of noise in either the system being minimized or in any measurements required. Random signals of either type may be very detrimental to any search procedure not designed to operate on noisy surfaces. Small errors may not be serious and some methods, e.g., steepest descent, have been shown to be effective in moderately noisy systems. Most of the procedures discussed later in this chapter will operate satisfactorily in noise, but they were not developed with noise specifically in mind. However, there is a class of search techniques specifically designed to converge to a unimodal optimum when noise is present. These are called stochastic approximation methods, and though they are not discussed here because other chapters of this book consider them separately in detail, it is felt that they are of sufficient importance in search problems to bring them to the attention of the reader. (See Wilde, 1964; Hill and Fu, 1965; Fu and Nikolic, 1966).

H. *Rastrigin's Random Scanning Method*

Rastrigin (1960) introduced a type of controlled random search which varies from the usual search procedure in that the rate of change of parameters is chosen randomly rather than the parameters themselves. Consequently, this method varies the search parameters continuously, in contrast to the previous methods which change the parameters only at discrete time intervals. This multiparameter technique is easily implemented and is suitable for optimization of a time-varying noisy surface.

Let

$$\mathbf{v} = (\dot{y}_1, \dot{y}_2, ..., \dot{y}_n)' = \frac{d}{dt}(\mathbf{y}) \tag{7.52}$$

be the vector used to perform the search, i.e., the rate of change of the parameters will be controlled. Then the derivative of $I(\mathbf{y})$

$$\frac{dI}{dt} = \frac{\partial I}{\partial y_1}\dot{y}_1 + \frac{\partial I}{\partial y_2}\dot{y}_2 + \cdots + \frac{\partial I}{\partial y_n}\dot{y}_n = \nabla I(\mathbf{y})'\mathbf{v} \tag{7.53}$$

is evaluated for a given $\mathbf{v} = (\dot{y}_1, \dot{y}_2, ..., \dot{y}_n)'$, and the vector $\mathbf{v}$ is retained for as long as

$$\frac{dI}{dt} < 0 \tag{7.54}$$

If Eq. (7.54) no longer holds, a new $\mathbf{v}$ is selected at random until Eq. (7.54) is again satisfied and the search continues. If $\mathbf{v}_k$ is the vector chosen at time t_k, then

$$\mathbf{y}(t) = \mathbf{y}_k + \mathbf{v}_k t \qquad (t_k \leqslant t \leqslant t_{k+1}) \tag{7.55}$$

Realization of this algorithm, however, requires that Eq. (7.53) be calculated continuously. In addition to the computational requirements, the calculation of Eq. (7.53) reduces the noise stability, since noise in the system could cause $\nabla I(\mathbf{y})$, and consequently dI/dt, to change sign at any instant. Eq. (7.54) would no longer be satisfied and a new $\mathbf{v}$ would be sought.

Therefore, the method is modified to an even simpler algorithm which is reliable and does not require the calculation of Eq. (7.53). Rastrigin (1960) states that the rate of convergence is reduced somewhat, but the noise stability is improved. In this algorithm $\mathbf{v}_k = (\dot{y}_1, \dot{y}_2, ..., \dot{y}_n)'$ is selected at random, as before, at the kth step. Now consider the *IP* as a changing quantity so that for $t_k \leqslant t < t_{k+1}$

$$I = I(\mathbf{v}_k, \mathbf{y}_k, t) = I(\mathbf{y}_k) + \int_{t_k}^{t} \frac{dI(\mathbf{v}_k, \mathbf{y}_k, t)}{dt}\,dt \tag{7.56}$$

where $I(\mathbf{v}_k, \mathbf{y}_k, t_k) = I(\mathbf{y}_k)$ is the value of $I(\mathbf{y})$ at t_k (the time $\mathbf{v}_k$ was applied). Compare I with a time-varying threshold

$$\eta(t) = I(\mathbf{v}_k, \mathbf{y}_k, t_k) - q(t - t_k) \tag{7.57}$$

where $q > 0$ is an arbitrary threshold control term. Continue the search using $\mathbf{v}_k$ as long as

$$e(t) = I(\mathbf{v}_k, \mathbf{y}_k, t) - \eta(t) < 0 \qquad (7.58)$$

When $e(t) = 0$, or $I(\mathbf{v}_k, \mathbf{y}_k, t) = \eta(t)$, then $t = t_{k+1}$, the parameter rate vector, $\mathbf{v}_k$, is switched to a new vector, $\mathbf{v}_{k+1}$, chosen at random to satisfy

$$\frac{dI}{dt} < -q \qquad (7.59)$$

and the procedure is repeated.

Consider Fig. 3 in which $I(\mathbf{y})$ is plotted versus time for two vectors $\mathbf{v}_k^{(i)}$ $(i = 1, 2)$.

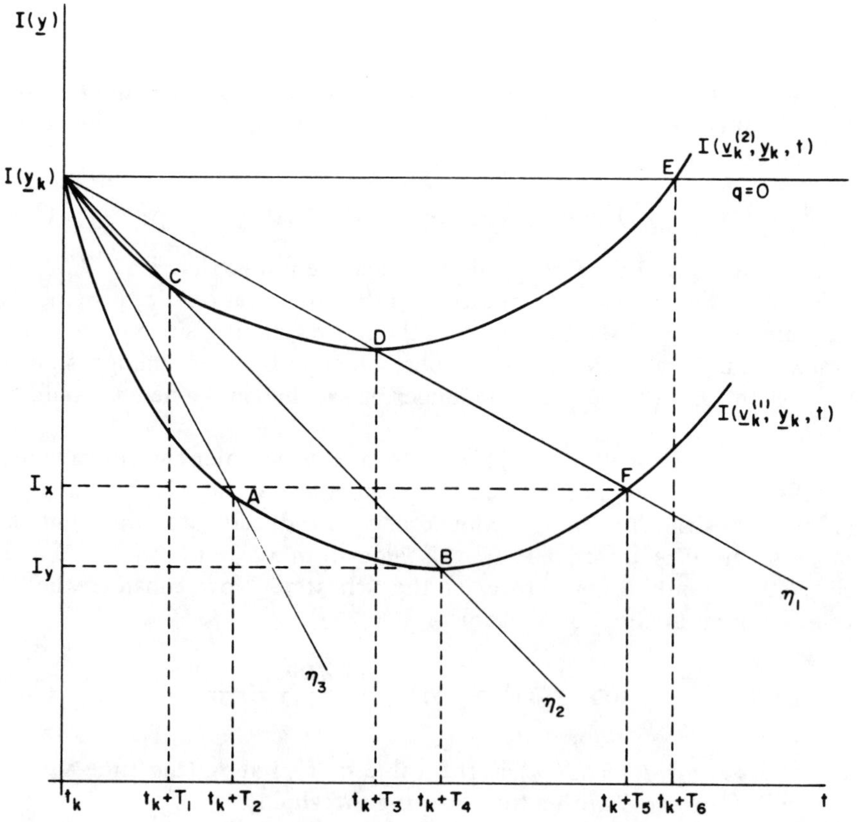

FIGURE 3. I vs. t for various $\mathbf{v}_i$ and 0

At time, t_k, the *IP* had value

$$I(\mathbf{y}_k) = I(\mathbf{v}_{k-1}, \mathbf{y}_{k-1}, t_k) = \eta(t_k) \tag{7.60}$$

and therefore a new value of **v** is sought which will satisfy Eq. (7.59). Thresholds, η, are shown for various q as follows:

$$\eta_i = I(\mathbf{y}_k) - q_i(t - t_k) \qquad i = 1, 2, 3 \tag{7.61}$$

where $q_3 > q_2 > q_1 > 0$.

Given $\eta = \eta_3$, then if $\mathbf{v}_k = \mathbf{v}_k^{(2)}$ is the next search vector selected randomly, it will be rejected immediately since Eq. (7.59) is not satisfied at t_k. However, $\mathbf{v}_k = \mathbf{v}_k^{(1)}$ satisfies Eq. (7.59) for η_3 and would be used until (A) $t = t_k + T_2$ when a new $\mathbf{v} = \mathbf{v}_{k+1}$ would need to be chosen.

If $\eta = \eta_2$, however, both $\mathbf{v}_k^{(1)}$ and $\mathbf{v}_k^{(2)}$ satisfy Eq. (7.59) at t_k and either one could be accepted, if selected at random as $\mathbf{v}_k$, and used until (B or C), $t = t_k + T_4$ or $t = t_k + T_1$, respectively. For the case $q = 0$ the modified procedure has the same criterion as the first algorithm described, as can be seen by observing Eq. (7.54) and Eq. (7.59). However, $q = 0$ is not suitable in the modified procedure and some $q > 0$ must be used. This can be demonstrated by considering Fig. 3 once again. Assume first that $q = q_2(\eta = \eta_2)$ and that $\mathbf{v}_k = \mathbf{v}_k^{(2)}$ is found acceptable at $t = t_k$. The search using $\mathbf{v}_k^{(2)}$ is continued until (C) $t = t_k + T_1$ where $\eta_2 = I(\mathbf{v}_k, \mathbf{y}_k, t_k + T_1) < I(\mathbf{y}_k)$. Now if $\eta = \eta_1(q_2 > q_1)$ is used and again $\mathbf{v}_k^{(2)}$ is selected, the *IP* reaches its lowest value for that $\mathbf{v}_k$ and intersects with η_1 at (D) $t_{k+1} = t_k + T_3$. If q is decreased still further until $q = 0$ $[\eta = I(\mathbf{y}_k)]$ then the search continues until (E) $t = t_k + T_6$ where $I(\mathbf{y}) = \eta$ again, but no net improvement in the performance is achieved. Thus, some value of $q > 0$ must be used with this procedure if convergence is to result.

Figure 4 suggests a possible search sequence using Rastrigin's method. Here a constant $q = q_o$ is assumed over all steps. Some delay is shown in the form of preparation time between steps. During this time the system is assumed to maintain a constant $I(\mathbf{y}_k)$ while seeking a suitable $\mathbf{v}_k$ at random. The search continues until no acceptable **v** can be found $(t = T_s)$. At this point, the search can be terminated or q may be decreased to q_1. The latter choice may result in a **v** being found which satisfies Eq. (7.59) for q_1 but not q_o.

It may be assumed that for small values of q the probability of selecting a $\mathbf{v}_k$ that satisfies Eq. (7.59) is approximately one-half. As q is increased this probability decreases accordingly and for some $q > 0$ no acceptable $\mathbf{v}_k$ will be found. However, as q is increased the *IP* is decreased more rapidly once an acceptable $\mathbf{v}_k$ is found. Also if q is decreased, the method

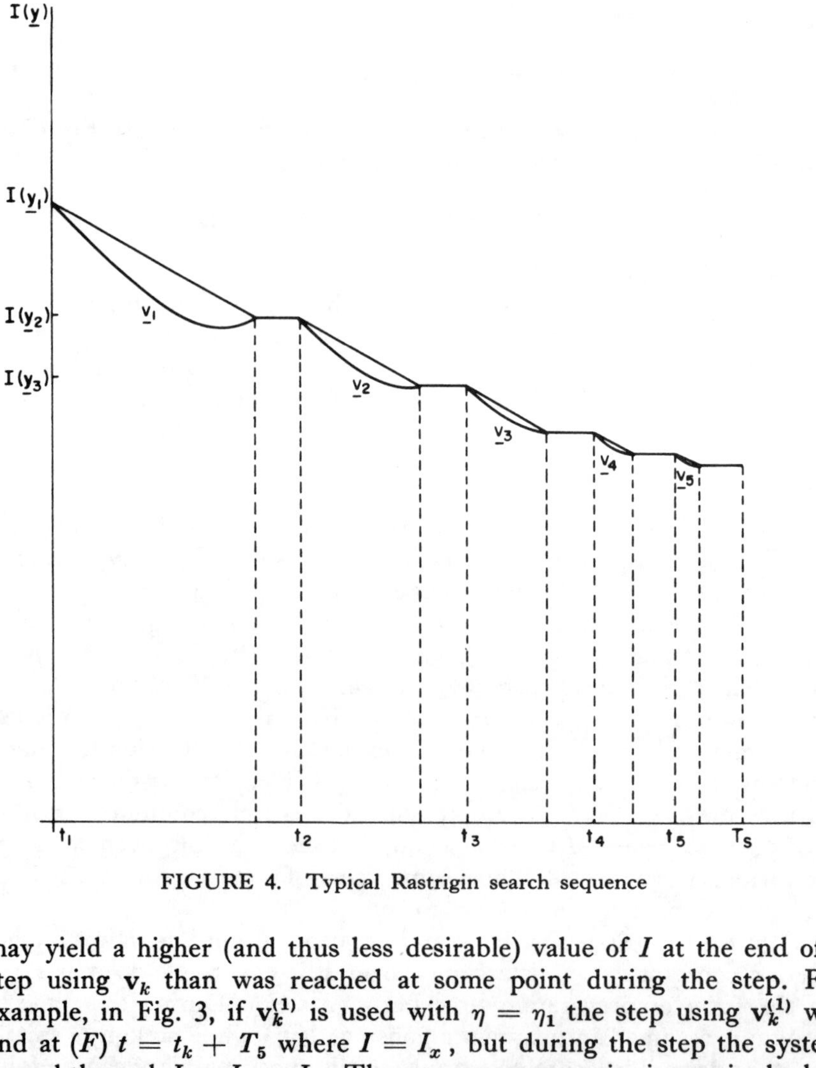

FIGURE 4. Typical Rastrigin search sequence

may yield a higher (and thus less desirable) value of I at the end of a step using $\mathbf{v}_k$ than was reached at some point during the step. For example, in Fig. 3, if $\mathbf{v}_k^{(1)}$ is used with $\eta = \eta_1$ the step using $\mathbf{v}_k^{(1)}$ will end at (F) $t = t_k + T_5$ where $I = I_x$, but during the step the system passed through $I = I_y < I_x$. Thus, some compromise is required when attempting to meet the requirements of rapid convergence and relatively large probability of finding a suitable $\mathbf{v}$. In fact, Rastrigin suggests that there exists an optimum $q = q^*$ which optimizes the system with respect to rate of convergence. Determination of q^* deserves further attention.

A possible modification of this method is now suggested. At the beginning of the search, when it may be assumed that the system is not near I_o, q is chosen to be quite large so that only sizeable improvements in I are accepted. As the search continues (and I approaches I_o) the value of q is decreased and smaller improvements are tolerated. Thus an adaptive type of control on q is exerted and the rate of convergence should improve.

Rastrigin's method requires very simple equipment for implementation without the need for a large computing capability. The good noise stability makes it very useful in searching noisy surfaces. Some modification of the procedure would be necessary for multimodal search since this method varies the parameters continuously and no provision is made for discrete parameter jumps once any minimum is found.

Rastrigin (1963) compared this method with a gradient method for rate of convergence in a multiparameter noisy system and demonstrated that for the deterministic case, the random search is better than the gradient technique when the number of parameters (n) is greater than 3 and when the system is not near I_0. In the noisy case, Gurin and Rastrigin (1965) showed that the random procedure is better than the gradient technique for $n > 6$. The random method is also found to have greater noise stability. Both methods were compared using a linear index of performance [corresponding to η in Eq. (7.61)].

I. *Adaptive Step Size Random Search*

Schumer and Steiglitz (1968) consider the unimodal search problem when the only significant cost is the evaluation (measurement or calculation) of $I(\mathbf{y})$ at each step. Thus, the method that requires the fewest total steps is the least expensive in its operation. Inspired by the comparison between the gradient method and the random search mentioned above (Rastrigin, 1963; Gurin and Rastrigin, 1965), Schumer and Steiglitz consider a hypothetical random search method that uses the optimum step size at each step. The operation of this hypothetical method is analyzed on a hyperspherical surface only. An adaptive step size random search is then proposed and shown to approximate the optimum step size random search (OSSRS).

Consider the fixed step size random search (FSSRS) in which

$$\mathbf{y}_{k+1} = \mathbf{y}_k - \rho_k \boldsymbol{\zeta}_k + \boldsymbol{\zeta}_{k+1} \tag{7.62}$$

where $\boldsymbol{\zeta}_k$ ($k = 1, 2, \ldots$) is a random vector of length s which is distributed uniformly over the n-dimension hypersphere of radius s centered at the origin. The penalty function, ρ_k, is defined by

$$\rho_k = \begin{cases} 0 & \text{if } I(\mathbf{y}_k) < I(\mathbf{y}_{k-1}) \\ 1 & \text{if } I(\mathbf{y}_k) \geqslant I(\mathbf{y}_{k-1}) \end{cases} \tag{7.63}$$

Thus, the kth step is negated if it was unsuccessful in finding a lower value of $I(\mathbf{y})$. For the hyperspherical surface given by

$$I(\mathbf{y}) = \mathbf{y}'\mathbf{y} = \sum_{i=1}^{n} y_i^2 = r^2 \tag{7.64}$$

where r is the distance to the minimum (at the origin), and a search loss defined as

$$L = \frac{2I(\mathbf{y})}{E\{\Delta I\}} \tag{7.65}$$

where $E\{\Delta I\}$ is the expected value of the improvement in I per step, Schumer and Steiglitz show that the search loss for the FSSRS is

$$L_r(n, \eta) = \frac{2\int_0^{\pi/2} \sin^{n-2}\phi \, d\phi}{\eta \int_0^{\phi_o} \cos\phi \sin^{n-2}\phi \, d\phi - \frac{\eta^2}{2}\int_0^{\phi_o} \sin^{n-2}\phi \, d\phi} \tag{7.66}$$

where

$$\eta = \frac{s}{r} \qquad \phi_o = \cos^{-1}\left(\frac{\eta}{2}\right) \tag{7.67}$$

Similarly, for the gradient (steepest descent) technique using the same fixed step size, s, as in FSSRS, the search loss is

$$L_g(n, \eta) = \frac{2(n+1)}{2\eta - \eta^2} \tag{7.68}$$

where n steps are assumed necessary to evaluate the gradient at each step. A comparison of L_g and L_r shows that for $n < 4$, the gradient method is superior, but for higher dimensions the FSSRS is superior for small η.

Although the probability of improvement using FSSRS is approximately one-half for a very small step size, the magnitude of the improvement, on the average, will also be very small. If the step size is too large, however, the probability of improvement will be small. Therefore, Schumer and Steiglitz maximize the expected improvement for a hyperspherical surface and show that the probability of success is 0.27 if an optimum step size could be chosen at each step. This, of course, requires unknown information, e.g., distance to the minimum, and the optimum step size cannot be analytically determined.

The adaptive step size random search (ASSRS) makes no attempt to find the optimum step size. On the first step, an arbitrary value, s_1, is chosen for the step size, and at each succeeding step the step size is adjusted. Two steps in random directions, one of length s_k and one of length $s_k(1 + \alpha)$ are taken on the kth iteration $(1 > \alpha > 0)$ and the resulting improvements are compared. The step size that yielded the greater improvement is selected as s_{k+1}. If neither step gives improvement, $s_{k+1} = s_k$. If several iterations yield no improvement, then the step size is reduced. In addition, after some arbitrary, large number of iterations (steps), α is made much larger than one so that s_k is compared with a very large step. This is done to insure that s_k has not become too small.

Schumer and Steiglitz tested ASSRS on three quadratic or quartic surfaces and compared the results with deterministic methods (Newton–Raphson and simplex). The results indicated that ASSRS is superior on high-dimensional problems without narrow valleys or ridges. If ridges and valleys are expected, it is advisable to introduce some directional adaptation as in Matyas' method to be described next. Perhaps the most significant result of these tests is that the number of steps required by ASSRS increases directly proportional to n. The optimum step size random search (OSSRS) also requires a number of steps which becomes asymptotically proportional to n as n is large. Thus, the ASSRS is found to be a practical random search algorithm that has some characteristics of the OSSRS.

J. *Matyas' Method*

Matyas (1965) has proposed a method of adaptive optimization in which parameters that very randomly in both magnitude and direction are used. The convergence of a random sequence of parameters to a unique optimum in a stationary hill-climbing situation is proven and Matyas provides an algorithm for increasing the rate of convergence by incorporating memory into the procedure and introducing the concept of directional adaptation.

Consider first the simple random optimization method applied to a stationary IP with a unique minimum, I_o. Let the parameter vector after the kth step be $\mathbf{y}_k$, as before. A random vector, $\boldsymbol{\zeta}_{k+1} = (\zeta_1, \zeta_2, \ldots \zeta_n)'_{k+1}$ is selected from a multivariate normal distribution with zero mean and unit correlation matrix. Then the next parameter vector is, as in ASSRS, given by

$$\mathbf{y}_{k+1} = \mathbf{y}_k - \rho_k \boldsymbol{\zeta}_k + \boldsymbol{\zeta}_{k+1} \tag{7.69}$$

where the penalty function, ρ_k, is defined by

$$\rho_k = \begin{cases} 0 & \text{if } I(\mathbf{y}_k) < I(\mathbf{y}_{k-1}) - \epsilon \\ 1 & \text{if } I(\mathbf{y}_k) \geqslant I(\mathbf{y}_{k-1}) - \epsilon \end{cases} \tag{7.70}$$

Eq. (7.70) is the same as Eq. (7.63) except for the term, ϵ, which represents the minimum acceptable improvement in performance. The procedure is repeated until the optimum state, $\mathbf{y}_o$, is reached, or until a suitable stopping rule is executed; e.g., the value of $I(\mathbf{y}_k)$ is considered satisfactory.

Mendel and Zapalac (1968) have reformulated this algorithm to relate the kth trial, $\mathbf{y}_k$, to the starting point, $\mathbf{y}_0$. It is easily shown that

$$\mathbf{y}_k = \mathbf{y}_0 + \sum_{i=1}^{k} f_i \boldsymbol{\zeta}_i \qquad k = 0, 1, 2,... \tag{7.71}$$

where

$$f_i = \begin{cases} 1 - \rho_i & i = 1, 2,..., k-1 \\ 1 & i = k \end{cases} \tag{7.72}$$

If $\mathbf{y}_0$ is considered to be a random starting point, $\mathbf{y}_0 = \boldsymbol{\zeta}_0$, and $f_0 = 1$, then Eq. (7.71) may be rewritten as $\mathbf{y}_k = \sum_{i=0}^{k} f_i \boldsymbol{\zeta}_i$. Matyas proves the convergence of this algorithm for a stationary performance surface. In general, the probability of a successful step at the kth stage is near 0.5, but Matyas suggests a modified method in which the results of preceding steps are taken into consideration in order to accelerate the search. This accelerated algorithm, which is described next, is called adaptive random optimization.

In the simple random search procedure the step vector, $\boldsymbol{\zeta}_{k+1}$, is randomly chosen from a multivariate normal distribution with mean zero and unit correlation matrix. The adaptive random optimization procedure attempts to speed up the search by using the information gained in previous trials to bias each new step.

The step vector now becomes

$$\boldsymbol{\delta}_{k+1} = \mathbf{d}_{k+1} + T_{k+1} \boldsymbol{\zeta}_{k+1} \tag{7.73}$$

where T_{k+1} is a variable correlation matrix and $\boldsymbol{\zeta}_{k+1}$ is the same as before. Now the vector $\mathbf{d}_k$ serves as the bias and is the mean of $\boldsymbol{\delta}_k$. If

$$\mathbf{d}_{k+1} = f_d[\boldsymbol{\delta}_k, \rho_k; \boldsymbol{\delta}_{k-1}, \rho_{k-1}; \cdots] \tag{7.74}$$

$$T_{k+1} = f_T[\boldsymbol{\delta}_k, \rho_k; \boldsymbol{\delta}_{k-1}, \rho_{k-1}; \cdots] \tag{7.75}$$

then $\mathbf{d}_{k+1}$ and T_{k+1} are dependent upon the directions and lengths of previous steps and upon the outcome of those steps (success: $\rho = 0$; failure: $\rho = 1$).

Initially it is assumed that no a priori information is available and therefore $\mathbf{d}_1 = \mathbf{0}$ and $\boldsymbol{\delta}_1 = T_1 \boldsymbol{\zeta}_1$ so that

$$\mathbf{y}_1 = \mathbf{y}_0 + T_1 \boldsymbol{\zeta}_1 \tag{7.76}$$

as in the simple random search. Now define

$$\begin{aligned} c_1(\mathbf{y}_1) &> 0 \qquad \text{for} \quad \rho_1 = 0 \\ c_1(\mathbf{y}_1) &\leqslant 0 \qquad \text{for} \quad \rho_1 = 1 \end{aligned} \tag{7.77}$$

and then let

$$\mathbf{d}_2 = c_1(\mathbf{y}_1)\, \boldsymbol{\delta}_1 = c_1(\mathbf{y}_1)\, T_1 \boldsymbol{\zeta}_1 = f_d[\boldsymbol{\delta}_1, \rho_1] \tag{7.78}$$

Thus, the outcome of the previous step (success or failure) determines $c_1(\mathbf{y}_1)$. If the first step was successful, then the next step is biased in that direction; but if the first step was unsuccessful, the second step may be either unbiased or biased in the opposite direction.

In general, the algorithm becomes

$$\begin{aligned} \mathbf{y}_{k+1} &= \mathbf{y}_k + \boldsymbol{\delta}_{k+1} \\ &= \mathbf{y}_k + \mathbf{d}_{k+1} + T_{k+1} \boldsymbol{\zeta}_{k+1} \end{aligned} \tag{7.79}$$

with

$$\mathbf{d}_{k+1} = c_0(y_k) \left[\mathbf{d}_k + \sum_{i=1}^{k-1} h_{i,k-1}\, \boldsymbol{\delta}_i \right] + c_1(y_k) \left[\boldsymbol{\delta}_k + \sum_{i=1}^{k-1} h_{i,k-1}\, \boldsymbol{\delta}_i \right] \tag{7.80}$$

or

$$\mathbf{d}_{k+1} = [c_0(y_k) + c_1(y_k)] \left[\mathbf{d}_k + \sum_{i=1}^{k-1} h_{i,k-1}\, \boldsymbol{\delta}_i \right] + c_1(y_k)\, T_k \boldsymbol{\zeta}_k \tag{7.81}$$

where $c_0(\mathbf{y}_k)$ and $c_1(\mathbf{y}_k)$ are functions of ρ_k as follows:

$$\begin{array}{lll} 0 \leqslant c_0(\mathbf{y}_k) \leqslant 1 & c_1(\mathbf{y}_k) > 0 & c_0(\mathbf{y}_k) + c_1(\mathbf{y}_k) > 1 \quad \text{if } \rho_k = 0 \\ 0 \leqslant c_0(\mathbf{y}_k) \leqslant 1 & c_1(\mathbf{y}_k) \leqslant 0 & |\, c_0(\mathbf{y}_k) + c_1(\mathbf{y}_k)| < 1 \quad \text{if } \rho_k = 1 \end{array} \tag{7.82}$$

and

$$h_{i,k-1} = \prod_{j=1}^{k-1} \rho_j = \rho_i \rho_{i+1} \rho_{i+2} \cdots \rho_{k-2} \rho_{k-1}$$

so that $h_{i,k-1} = 1$ if trials at $\mathbf{y}_i$ through $\mathbf{y}_{k-1}$, consecutively, have all failed. Otherwise, $h_{i,k-1} = 0$. Thus if $\rho_{k-1} = 1$ [the $(k-1)$st step is unsucessful], the summation terms in Eqs. (7.80) and (7.81) represent the sum of all steps since the last sucessful step. If $\rho_{k-1} = 0$, the summation terms are zero and drop out of the expression for $\mathbf{d}_{k+1}$. The significance of c_0 and c_1 is best illustrated by the assignment of specific values to these coefficients.

As an example, let

$$c_0(\mathbf{y}_k) = 1 - \tfrac{1}{2}\rho_k \tag{7.83}$$

$$c_1(\mathbf{y}_k) = 2(\tfrac{1}{2} - \rho_k) \tag{7.84}$$

where Eqs. (7.83) and (7.84) satisfy Eq. (7.82). Under this assignment when $\mathbf{y}_k$ is a successful trial, $c_0 = 1$ and $c_1 = 1$. From Eq. (7.81)

$$\mathbf{d}_{k+1} = 2\left[\mathbf{d}_k + \sum_{i=1}^{k-1} h_{i,k-1}\,\boldsymbol{\delta}_i\right] + T_k\zeta_k \tag{7.85}$$

and if the $(k-1)$st step was successful, the $(k+1)$st step is biased in the same direction as the kth step, with more emphasis upon the preceding mean, $\mathbf{d}_k$, than the random component, $T_k\zeta_k$. If the $(k-1)$st step was unsuccessful the $(k+1)$st step is biased in the direction of the last two steps combined, etc. If Eqs. (7.83) and (7.84) are used and $\mathbf{y}_k$ is an unsuccessful trial, then $c_0 = \frac{1}{2}$ and $c_1 = -1$. From Eq. (7.81)

$$\mathbf{d}_{k+1} = -\tfrac{1}{2}\left[\mathbf{d}_k + \sum_{i=1}^{k-1} h_{i,k-1}\,\boldsymbol{\delta}_i\right] - T_k\zeta_k \tag{7.86}$$

and if the $(k-1)$st step was successful, the algorithm eliminates the kth step $(-\boldsymbol{\delta}_k)$ and the $(k+1)$st step is biased, from $\mathbf{y}_{k-1}$, in the same direction as the kth step, but only half as far. If successive steps (that is, k, $k-1$) are unsuccessful, the bias of the $(k+1)$st step is halved for each successive failure. Thus, $\mathbf{d}_{k+1}$ may be viewed as a step in the opposite direction of the bias of the preceding step.

A succession of successful search steps will tend to increase the length of the bias vector, $\mathbf{d}_{k+1}$, since $|c_0 + c_1| > 1$ when $\rho_k = 0$, and a continued increase in this length is normally undesirable, particularly as the search approaches the optimum. Matyas suggests therefore, that a limit, D, be placed on the maximum length of $\boldsymbol{\delta}_k$.

It should be understood that Eqs. (7.85) and (7.86) are based on one choice of c_0 and c_1. Other choices that satisfy Eq. (7.82) have been used (Mendel and Zapalac, 1968).

Determination of the T_{k+1} matrix is left to the designer, but considering the computational difficulties it is suggested that T_{k+1} be formed as a diagonal matrix (elements of $T_{k+1}\zeta_{k+1}$ are thus uncorrelated). In fact, Matyas suggests that this be simplified even further to

$$T_{k+1} = b_{k+1}E \tag{7.87}$$

where E is the identity matrix and $b_{k+1} > 0$. Since b_{k+1} determines the standard deviation of all the components of ζ_{k+1}, b_{k+1} could be made adjustable in such a way as to reduce these deviations as the search approaches the optimum.

Figure 5 is an example in two-dimensional space of a possible sequence of steps using this method. Eqs. (7.83) and (7.84) are assumed for the choice of c_0 and c_1. The first step, during which the random vector, $T_1\zeta_1$, is tried, is a successful one. The second step is biased, $\mathbf{d}_2$, in the direction of the successful first step in accordance with Eq. (7.78) and the random vector, $T_2\zeta_2$ is added to $\mathbf{d}_2$. As a result, I is increased and $\rho_2 = 1$. From Eq. (7.86), $\mathbf{d}_3$ is determined by going back to $\mathbf{y}_1$ (eliminating ζ_2) and then stepping in the same direction as $\mathbf{d}_2$, but only half as far. Again a random vector, $T_3\zeta_3$, is added to $\mathbf{d}_3$ to obtain

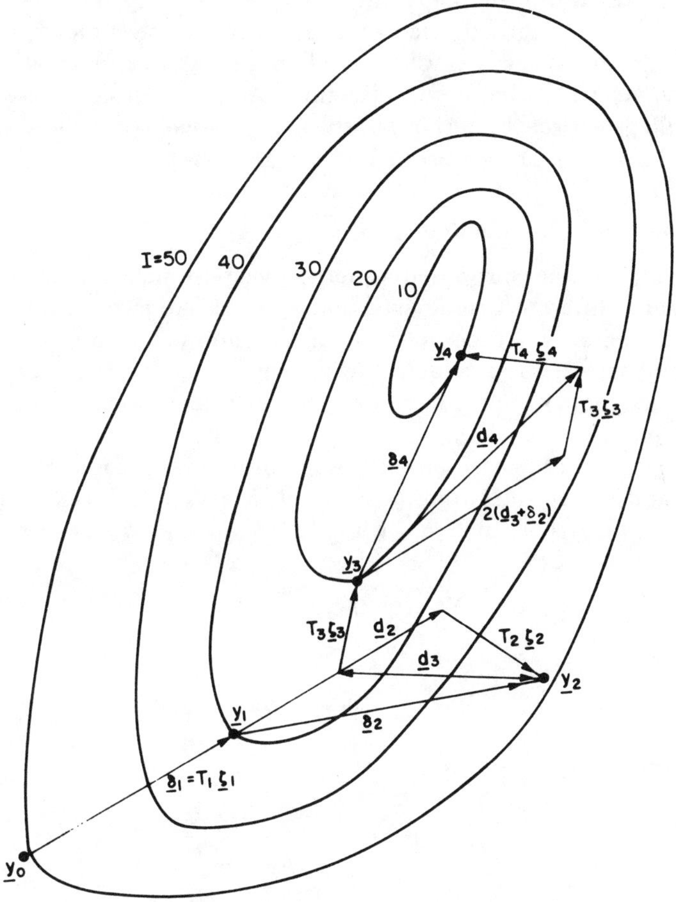

FIGURE 5. Adaptive random optimization

$\boldsymbol{\delta}_3$ and then $\mathbf{y}_3 = \mathbf{y}_2 + \boldsymbol{\delta}_3$ in accordance with Eq. (7.79). This yields a lower I, $\rho_3 = 0$, and $\mathbf{d}_4$ is obtained as a weighted combination of $\mathbf{d}_3$ and $T_3\boldsymbol{\zeta}_3$. (Note that the biased vector, $\mathbf{d}_3$, is weighted more heavily than the random vector, $T_3\boldsymbol{\zeta}_3$.) After addition of $T_4\boldsymbol{\zeta}_4$ to $\mathbf{d}_4$, then $\mathbf{y}_4 = \mathbf{y}_3 + \boldsymbol{\delta}_4$ and $\rho_4 = 0$. In this way it is seen that convergence to I_o occurs.

No specific stopping rules have been formulated for this search. Matyas assumes a knowledge of I_o and simply stops the search when $I \leqslant I_o + \Delta$ where Δ is an arbitrary small value. Another obvious stopping rule is to limit the number of total steps that are allowed.

This method has the advantageous property of using the results of previous steps to bias the direction of the next step. Although the method requires more computing capability and consequently more equipment than the Rastrigin method, the procedure seems to be somewhat simpler conceptually and is easily implemented on a computer. Several variables (T, c_0, c_1, b_k) are available for adjustment if it is desired to use a more sophisticated approach, although the assignement of values to these variables and their proper use is not straightforward.

K. *Absolute Bias Modification*

Bekey *et al.* (1966) proposed a method very similar to that of Matyas except that a different bias is used and a procedure is recommended for the global search after completion of the unimodal search. The rate of convergence is not available for this method, but it is very simply programmed and a hybrid computer implementation was shown by Bekey *et al.*

Consider first the local optimization (unimodal) problem. As in the simple random optimization method of Matyas, the next parameter vector, $\mathbf{y}_{k+1}$, is determined according to Eq. (7.69) which can be written as

$$\mathbf{y}_{k+1} = \mathbf{y}_k + \boldsymbol{\delta}_{k+1} \tag{7.88}$$

where

$$\boldsymbol{\delta}_{k+1} = -\rho_k\boldsymbol{\zeta}_k + \boldsymbol{\zeta}_{k+1} \tag{7.89}$$

In addition, define

$$r_k = \begin{cases} 0 & \text{if } \rho_k = 0 \\ r_{k-1} + 1 & \text{if } \rho_k = 1 \end{cases} \tag{7.90}$$

where r is a counter indicating the number of successive failures ($\rho = 1$).

Then

$$\begin{aligned} \boldsymbol{\delta}_{k+1} &= \boldsymbol{\delta}_k && \text{if } \rho_k = 0 \\ \boldsymbol{\delta}_{k+1} &= -2\boldsymbol{\delta}_k && \text{if } \rho_k = 1 \quad r_k < 2 \\ \boldsymbol{\delta}_{k+1} &= \boldsymbol{\zeta}_{k+1} && \text{if } \rho_k = 1 \quad r_k \geqslant 2 \end{aligned} \tag{7.91}$$

Thus, the algorithm repeats the last search step if it was successful. If not, then the next step is taken opposite to the last step. If a failure is determined in this opposite step also, then the algorithm requires that a new random step be taken and the process is repeated. The stopping rule for this local search is simply to stop the search after $r_k > M$ where M is an arbitrary number representing the maximum allowable number of successive failures.

An additional condition, similar to that used by Schumer and Steiglitz (1968), could be used to prevent this search algorithm from locking on to a very small step, $\boldsymbol{\delta}$. Define another counter, σ_k, and let

$$\sigma_k = \begin{cases} \sigma_{k-1} + 1 & \text{if } \rho_k = 0 \\ 0 & \text{if } \rho_k = 1 \end{cases} \tag{7.92}$$

Then, if $\rho_k = 0$ and $\sigma_k = R$, where R is arbitrary, let $\boldsymbol{\delta}_{k+1} = \boldsymbol{\zeta}_{k+1}$. Thus, if R consecutive successes have occurred, a new random vector is selected to insure that $\boldsymbol{\delta}$ is not too small.

After completion of the local search, a random search for the global optimum is commenced. The strategy initially selects random vectors originating at the local optimum. If no better values of I are found, the variance of the random vectors is increased. If an improved value of I is found at some point, $\mathbf{y}$, then the local search is again implemented starting at this new $\mathbf{y}$.

L. *Gradient Biased Random Search*

Pensa (1969) utilized the noisy gradient measurement as the bias vector in Eq. (7.79) of the biased random search. Optimization of the rate of convergence on a noisy unimodal surface is accomplished by specifying the covariance matrix, T_{k+1}, whereas Matyas did not prove convergence on a noisy surface nor specify the optimum T_{k+1}.

This gradient biased random search may also be considered as a Keifer–Wolfowitz stochastic approximation scheme with an n-dimensional random vector added to each step. Stochastic approximation search schemes guarantee convergence in the presence of measurement noise but have inherently slow convergence properties. Their operation is therefore poor in on-line applications. The addition of the random search vector to the Keifer–Wolfowitz algorithm will, under certain circumstances, significantly improve the rate of convergence.

III. Multimodal Techniques

In the multimodal case, no assurance can be provided that the techniques in Section II will converge to the global extremum. In fact, Karnopp (1963) suggests that most unimodal methods are refinement techniques which must be combined with some other search procedure when seeking the absolute minimum of a multimodal function. In this section, several random search techniques are discussed as global procedures, and it is shown how a variable structure approach may be used to determine the region most likely to contain I_o. Finally, a complete search procedure of a multimodal surface is outlined.

A. *Random Search Methods*

Karnopp (1963) investigated the use of random search techniques and suggests that their flexibility and efficiency make them useful in a wide range of applications. Pure random search may be defined as a method in which the trial points, $\mathbf{y}$, are chosen by means of a random process that has stationary characteristics throughout the search. The random process is defined by a probability density function, $p(\mathbf{y})$, representing the probability of choosing $\mathbf{y}$ in the parameter space to be searched. A sequence of trials is then conducted with trial points, $\mathbf{y}_k$, selected according to the scan distribution, $p(\mathbf{y})$. The result of the first trial, $I(\mathbf{y}_1)$, is recorded as the minimum I value, $I_1{}^*$, found thus far in the search. Let

$$\begin{aligned} I_{k+1}^* &= I(\mathbf{y}_{k+1}); \quad \mathbf{y}_{k+1}^* = \mathbf{y}_{k+1} \quad \text{if } I(\mathbf{y}_{k+1}) < I_k{}^* \\ I_{k+1}^* &= I_k{}^*; \quad\quad\; y_{k+1}^* = y_k{}^* \quad \text{if } I(\mathbf{y}_{k+1}) \geqslant I_k{}^* \end{aligned} \tag{7.93}$$

Then $I_k{}^*$ is the smallest value of I found in the first k trials, and the value of $\mathbf{y}$ at which $I_k{}^*$ occurred is recorded as $y_k{}^*$; that is, $I_k{}^* = I(y_k{}^*)$. [Note that $\mathbf{y}_k{}^*$ is not necessarily $\mathbf{y}_k$, since it may be that $\mathbf{y}_k{}^* = \mathbf{y}_j$ $(j < k)$, that is, the minimum value was found at trial j.]

The pure random search method could be used until the global minimum, I_o, is found, but it is usually desirable to combine the random multimodal search with a refinement, such as a unimodal technique, in order to obtain an accurate local minimum as the best estimate to the global minimum. Thus, the total search time is divided into a global search phase and a unimodal search phase. If there is no information available about the number of local minima, or if several are believed to exist, most of the toal search time should be spent on the global phase. However, if only two or three minima are believed to exist, it might be more efficient to find one minimum with a unimodal search and then use a global search to determine whether a lower minimum exists. This was suggested by Bekey and mentioned previously in this chapter.

Random search techniques have the distinct advantages of simple implementation, insensitivity to discontinuities in I, and high efficiency when little is known about I. In addition, much general information is gained about I (and the corresponding system) during a random search. If storage is not a significant problem, then this information may be recorded and used in other phases of the search or for other purposes in evaluating the system being optimized. The principal disadvantage of random search is the number of trials required, particularly in multidimensional cases, and, consequently, slow convergence.

Brooks (1958, 1959) considers the multidimensional random search problem in which success is defined as the determination of a combination of parameters $\mathbf{y}_s = (y_1, y_2, \ldots, y_n)'$ such that not more than a small fraction, μ, of the entire parameter space volume has a value of $I < I(\mathbf{y}_s)$. In addition, Brooks considers the probability of finding such a $\mathbf{y}_s$ in a fixed number of random trials.

If the parameter space is assumed finite with

$$0 \leqslant y_i \leqslant Y_i \qquad i = 1, 2, \ldots, n \tag{7.94}$$

then each Y_i is divided into Δ_i levels of equal length

$$w_i = \frac{Y_i}{\Delta_i} \tag{7.95}$$

Thus, there are

$$N = \prod_{i=1}^{n} \Delta_i \tag{7.96}$$

quantized regions or cells, each having an n-dimensional volume, v, where

$$v = \prod_{i=1}^{n} w_i \tag{7.97}$$

The value of the average I over the cell is assigned to the center of the cell. Then m trials are performed, each one at a cell chosen at random from the scan distribution, $p(\mathbf{y}) = 1/N$, with the $\mathbf{y}$ now restricted to be the centers of the N cells. The probability that at least one of these m independent trials will fall in one of the μN cells having the best performance is given by

$$p(\mu N) = 1 - (1 - \mu)^m \tag{7.98}$$

where $(1 - \mu)$ is the probability that a single trial will not fall in one of the μN best cells. Then

$$m = \frac{\log(1 - p(\mu N))}{\log(1 - \mu)} \tag{7.99}$$

Several observations are now pertinent to the above results. First of all, it is not necessary for the parameter space to be divided into cells as above; but m points, independently chosen from a uniform distribution over the entire parameter space, will yield, with probability $p(\mu N)$, at least one point in the fraction, μ, of the total parameter space having $I < I(\mathbf{y}_s)$. The number of trials required is extremely low when it is realized that m is independent of the number of parameters, n. However, Hooke and Jeeves (1958) pointed out that in a hyperspace where n is large, the range of each parameter, y_i, that is included in the fraction, μ, of the entire parameter space is still a very large proportion of y_i. Wilde (1964) also considers this problem of multidimensionality. In addition, even if the resulting hypervolume is acceptable, the results give no assurance that the best performance found, $I(\mathbf{y}_s)$, is within a fraction, b, of the absolute minimum, I_o, that is, that $I(\mathbf{y}_s) \leqslant (1 + b) I_o$.

Perhaps the most serious objection to the pure random search procedure is that it is conceptually a simultaneous search and therefore it does not take advantage of any previous results. It should also be noted that no noise due to experimental error or external disturbances is considered above.

The random method makes no assumptions about the form of the response surface; it is applicable when the surface is multimodal, and, if n is not too large (i.e., the problem of multidimensionality discussed above is not too severe), the random search may be employed until the searching algorithm has sufficient confidence that a region of unimodality has been found. Then one of the unimodal searches could be initiated.

Brooks suggested three variations of the random method, one of which is basically a simultaneous procedure while the others are sequential. In the stratified random method the parameter space is divided into N equal regions or cells as discussed above. Each cell is then subjected to one trial at a point randomly chosen within that region. This procedure is intuitively appealing, but the problem of quantizing a multidimensional parameter space into an optimum set of regions is not readily solved (Max, 1960; Bessarabova, 1968). In addition, the number of trials, m, needed to gain a specified confidence level is unknown.

A sequential procedure is suggested in which a pure random search is initially employed in a sequential manner. As each new point is randomly selected it is rejected as a test point if it is within a distance, d, of any previously selected point, or if it is less than $\frac{1}{2}d$ away from the boundary of the parameter space. Thus a set of nonoverlapping hyperspheres of diameter d are tested. The choice of d is a design problem which must consider the resulting number of hyperspheres (or trial points) and the need for a near-uniform coverage of the parameter space. A similar procedure called clustering is frequently utilized in pattern recognition (Sebestyen, 1962), while Waltz and Fu (1965) have used the clustering concept to partition a control system measurement space.

Finally, a sequential procedure, called the creeping random method, is proposed in which knowledge gained from previous trials is utilized. An initial trial is conducted at random and is followed by k trials selected from a normal scan distribution about the initial point. Of these $(k + 1)$ trials, the best one is selected as the center of the distribution for the next $(k + 1)$ trials and if the variance of the normal scan distribution is reduced every $(k + 1)$ trials, then after several such iterations of $(k + 1)$ trials, the method should converge to a local minimum.

B. *Variable Structure Method* (McMurtry and Fu, 1966)

In this section a global search of a performance surface quantized into several regions is discussed. The various quantization levels in the one-dimensional case, or regions in multidimensions, are searched in accordance with probabilities assigned on the basis of past relative performances. The search algorithm has a variable structure so that the system is able to adjust its search probabilities continuously. Linear reinforcement is used as an averaging technique. Thus the method is capable of performing on-line optimization of a nonstationary surface. The method is described here as a one-dimensional search, but it is readily extended to the multidimensional problem.*

Assume the IP curve is a nonnegative, continuous, and generally unknown function of a single parameter, y; that is, $IP = I(y) > 0$. The IP may be multimodal, and the admissible region of y is $0 < y \leqslant Y$ (Fig. 6). The admissible region is quantized into Δ levels, L_j $(j = 1, 2, \ldots, \Delta)$, of equal width

$$W = \frac{Y}{\Delta} \tag{7.100}$$

and each level is centered at u^j, where

$$u^j = W \cdot (j - \tfrac{1}{2}) \qquad j = 1, 2, \ldots, \Delta \tag{7.101}$$

* This method was developed using a stochastic automaton as a model of the search algorithm. For the automaton development, see McMurtry and Fu (1966).

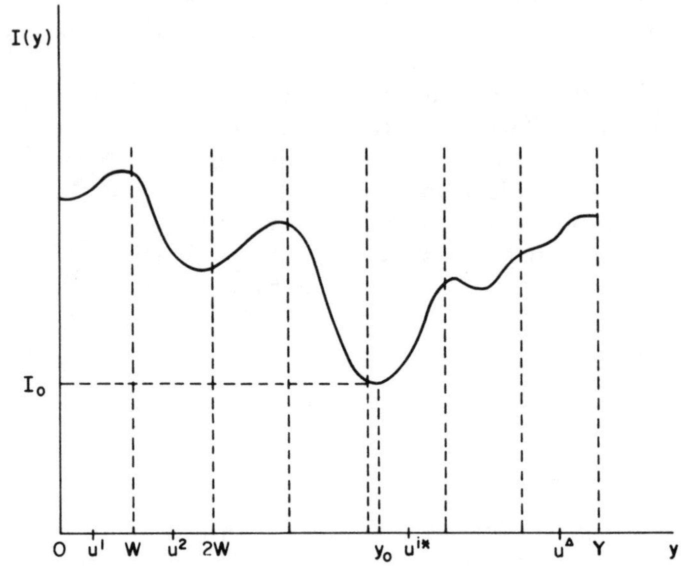

FIGURE 6. Multimodal hill

After the kth trial, a search distribution is formed in which P_k^i is the probability of selecting level L_i for the $(k+1)$st trial and

$$\sum_{j=1}^{\Delta} P_k^j = 1 \qquad (k = 1, 2, \ldots) \tag{7.102}$$

The actual $(k+1)$st search point, $\mathbf{y}_{k+1} = y(k+1)$, is then randomly located within L_i at

$$y(k+1) = u_{k+1}^i + r_{k+1} \tag{7.103}$$

where r_{k+1} is a continuous random variable

$$-\frac{W}{2} \leqslant r_{k+1} \leqslant \frac{W}{2} \tag{7.104}$$

with uniform distribution

$$f(r_{k+1}) = \frac{1}{W} \tag{7.105}$$

The selection of each trial point is thus similar to the stratified random method mentioned in Section IIIA of this chapter.

A new quantity, called the I-complement, is defined as

$$z^i_{k+1} = \left[\frac{1}{I(y(k+1))}\right]^\gamma \tag{7.106}$$

where γ is a constant which is determined later in this section, and $y(k+1)$ lies in L_i [Eq. (7.103)].

The reinforced average of the I-complement after the $(k+1)$st trial is given by the recursive relation

$$\begin{aligned} \overline{z^i_{k+1}} &= \theta\overline{z_k^{\,i}} + (1-\theta)\, z^i_{k+1} \qquad k = 1, 2,\ldots \\ \overline{z^j_{k+1}} &= \overline{z_k^{\,j}} \qquad j \neq i, \;\; j = 1, 2,\ldots, \Delta \end{aligned} \tag{7.107}$$

where $\theta < 1$. Thus, the I-complement is adjusted for the selected level, L_i, while the $\overline{z^j}$ for all other levels are unchanged. By proper choice of θ, the appropriate emphasis may be placed on recent and past observations, since the $(k+s)$th measurement is weighted θ^{-s} times heavier than the kth measurement. If $\theta = 1 - [1/(k+1)]$, this model simply represents the standard averaging procedure. If the *IP* surface is changing, the value of θ may be decreased in order to decrease the effects of measurements in the distant past.

Now let the probability of searching each level, L_j, on the $(k+1)$ trial be assigned as follows:

$$P_k^{\,j} = \frac{\overline{z_k^{\,j}}}{Z_k} \qquad j = 1, 2,\ldots, \Delta \tag{7.108}$$

where

$$Z_k = \sum_{j=1}^{\Delta} \overline{z_k^{\,j}} \tag{7.109}$$

and thus Eq. (7.102) is satisfied. The P^i are thus based on the relative weighted average measurements of I in all levels. Since $\overline{z^i}$ is inversely proportional to I, lower values of $I(y)$ in L_i result in larger $\overline{z^i}$ and therefore a higher probability, P^i, of searching L_i for the true minimum. It is shown that if γ is sufficiently large, the level, $L_i{}^*$, containing the true minimum, I_o, will have the highest search probability.

Assume a multimodal hill with a relatively flat surface about a local minimum, I_1, and a steep surface near the true minimum, I_o, as shown in Fig. 7. This represents a worst case condition in which $L_i{}^*$ may yield a lower $\overline{z^i}$ than some other relatively flat level of equal width which contains only a local minimum (or perhaps no minimum at all). If

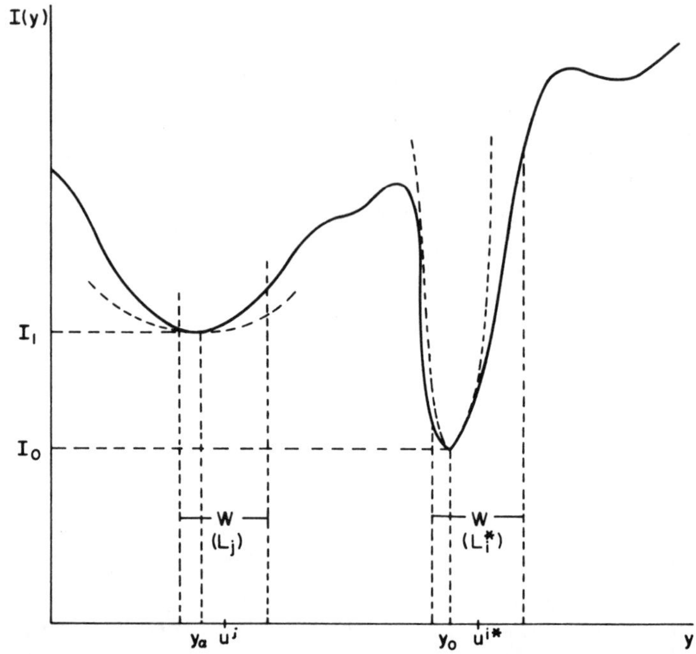

FIGURE 7. Worst case on a multimodal hill

$\gamma = 1$ in Eq. (7.106), the highest probability will then not be assigned to level L_i^*. It is therefore desired to find a sufficiently large γ so that $\overline{z^{i*}}$ in L_i^* is the largest average I-complement over all L_j ($j = 1, 2, \ldots, \Delta$) so that the corresponding P^{i*} is the highest search probability.

The expected value of z^j, using Eqs. (7.103)–(7.106), is

$$E\{z^j\} = \frac{1}{W}\int_{u^j-W/2}^{u^j+W/2} \frac{dy}{I^\gamma(y)} \qquad j = 1, 2, \ldots, \Delta \tag{7.110}$$

A value of γ, denoted G, is sought such that, even for large quantization widths,

$$\overline{Z^j} = \int_{u^j-W/2}^{u^j+W/2} \frac{dy}{I^\gamma(y)} \leqslant \int_{u^{i*}-W/2}^{u^{i*}+W/2} \frac{dy}{I^\gamma(y)} = \bar{Z}^* \qquad j \neq i^*; \quad \gamma \geqslant G \tag{7.111}$$

where u^{i*} is the center of L_i^*.

Approximate the curve in L_i^* and L_j, respectively, by

$$I = b(y - y_o)^2 + I_o \qquad \left(u^{i*} - \frac{W}{2} \leqslant y \leqslant u^{i*} + \frac{W}{2}\right) \tag{7.112}$$

and

$$I = e(y - y_\alpha)^2 + I_1 \qquad \left(u^j - \frac{W}{2} \leqslant y \leqslant u^j + \frac{W}{2}\right) \tag{7.113}$$

where

$$b > e, \quad I_o < I_1 \qquad I_1 = I(y_\alpha), \quad I_o = I(y_o). \tag{7.114}$$

and

$$u^j - \frac{W}{2} \leqslant y_\alpha \leqslant u^j + \frac{W}{2} \qquad u^{i*} - \frac{W}{2} \leqslant y_o \leqslant u^{i*} + \frac{W}{2}$$

Let Eqs. (7.112) and (7.113) describe curves above and below the true curve everywhere in L_i^* and L_j, respectively, as indicated in Fig. 7. The worst case, i.e., when $\bar{Z}^j$ is maximized, $\bar{Z}^*$ is minimized, and the ratio of P^{i*} to P^j is reduced, is easily shown to occur when

$$y_o = u^{i*} - \frac{W}{2} \qquad \text{and} \qquad y_\alpha = u^j \tag{7.115}$$

Substituting Eqs. (7.112), (7.113) and (7.115) into Eq. (7.111), rewriting and simplifying, yields

$$\bar{Z}^j = 2\int_0^{W/2} \frac{dy}{[ey^2 + I_1]^\gamma} \leqslant \int_0^W \frac{dy}{[by^2 + I_o]^\gamma} = \bar{Z}^* \tag{7.116}$$

which may be evaluated from standard tables to yield the following sufficient conditions:

$$W \leqslant \frac{\sqrt{I_1 - I_0}}{\sqrt{b - e/4}} = W_{\max} \tag{7.117}$$

and

$$\gamma \geqslant 0.5\left[1 + \frac{\ln 4b/e}{\ln I_1/I_0}\right] = G \tag{7.118}$$

Thus, if $W < W_{\max}$, there exists a value G given by Eq. (7.118) such that if $\gamma \geqslant G$, then $\bar{Z}^*$ is greater than $\bar{Z}^j$ and consequently $P^{i*} > P^j$ $(j \neq i^*)$. Determination of $W_{\max}$ and G requires knowledge of b, e, I_0 and I_1; that is, knowledge of the performance surface. However, it is shown below that it is possible to exceed $W_{\max}$, and by increasing γ sufficiently, L_i^* will still yield the maximum average I-complement.

Since the P^i are determined on a relative basis, consider

$$R = \frac{\bar{Z}^*}{\bar{Z}^j}$$

Thus, R must exceed unity in order that $P^{i*} > P^j$. McMurtry and Fu (1966) have shown that R may be rewritten as

$$R = R(K, K_1, K_2, \gamma) \tag{7.119}$$

where

$$K_1 = \frac{e}{b} < 1.0 \qquad K_2 = \frac{I_1}{I_o} \qquad \text{and} \qquad K = \frac{W}{W_{\max}} = \frac{W}{2}\sqrt{\frac{b}{I_o}}\sqrt{\frac{4-K_1}{K_2-1}}$$

so that R is not directly dependent on e, b, I_0, I_1, but rather upon the respective ratios of e to b, I_1 to I_0 and b to I_o. Thus the designer, without exact knowledge of I, may specify acceptable limits on these ratios and then choose a suitable γ as shown below.

Computer evaluation of R, as shown in McMurtry and Fu (1966), indicates that even if $W_{\max}$ is exceeded greatly, $K_1 \ll 1$, and K_2 is very near unity (worst case conditions), a value, G, of γ may be found, above which $R > 1$ and thus P^{i*} would be maximum.

An interesting observation of considerable practical importance is that if a constant is subtracted from the entire IP curve, then K_2 is increased and K_1 remains constant, as does $I_1 - I_0$; thux $W_{\max}$ remains constant, K does not change for a given W, and the value of γ required to keep $R > 1$ decreases. However, since it has been assumed that the surface is nonnegative, subtraction of such a constant could not be allowed to result in any negative values of I.

The time required to perform the search effectively is rather long and must be considered as an undesirable feature of this method. For on-line optimization, this method would be most applicable on those processes that operate over long periods of time, e.g., chemical process control. Then the long search time is not too restrictive since the algorithm continues to search each level according to the assigned probability distribution which is based on previous experience. The level with the lowest IP tends to be tested more frequently and the average IP is reduced while the algorithm is adjusting itself to indicate $L_i{}^*$.

This procedure has the advantage of being able to adjust its probabilities as the environment changes and is thus applicable in a nonstationary system where unmeasurable environmental factors are varying. The only calculation required during the search is the relatively simple adjustment of search probabilities. Storage is required only for the P^i and $\overline{z^i}$. The time required to search can be expected to increase significantly as the number of dimensions is increased.

For refinement of the IP, two possible alternatives are: (1) search until it may be assumed with confidence that the level of highest probability contains I_0 and then quantize that level into finer levels and repeat the search (this would be applicable when there is no assurance that the original quantized levels would be unimodal); or (2) after the global search, switch to a unimodal type search.

C. *Multimodal Stochastic Approximation*

Vaysbord and Yudin (1968) proposed an iterative method for finding the global extremum of the mathematical expectation of a multidimensional random function, $I(\mathbf{y})$, based on the results of the measured values of $I(\mathbf{y})$ at the points $\mathbf{y}_k$. The iterative sequence of $\mathbf{y}_k$ combines a modification of stochastic approximation with jumps of random amplitude and direction at random instants. The expectation of $I(\mathbf{y})$ is assumed to be bounded from below, have a finite gradient, bounded matrix of second derivatives in the search space, global minimum at some finite $\mathbf{y}$, and a positive norm of the gradient as $\mathbf{y}$ approaches infinity.

Let η_k be a random variable having as its value one of the integers from the interval $[1, N]$, for some large N. When $\eta_k \neq 1$,

$$\eta_{k+1} = \begin{cases} \eta_k - 1 & \text{with probability } p_k \\ \min(\eta_k + 1, N) & \text{with probability } q_k = 1 - p_k \end{cases} \tag{7.120}$$

where p_k is a monotonically increasing function of $I(\mathbf{y}_k)$ satisfying $0 < p_k < 0.5$. Thus a large value of $I(\mathbf{y}_k)$ increases the probability of making η_{k+1} smaller than η_k. If $\eta_k = 1$, then η_{k+1} is a random variable having one of the integer values $(2, 3, \ldots, N)$ with an arbitrary distribution law.

Now let

$$h_k = h(k - j)^{-(\frac{1}{2}+s)} \qquad c_k = c(k - j)^{-(\frac{1}{2}+r)} \tag{7.121}$$

where the jth step was the last step for which $\eta_j = 1$, h and c are constants, and

$$0 < r < s \qquad s + r < \tfrac{1}{2} \qquad s + 2r > \tfrac{1}{2} \tag{7.122}$$

In the algorithm below, h_k is the magnitude of the $(k + 1)$st step and c_k is the magnitude of the test step to determine the sign of the estimated gradient at $\mathbf{y}_k$. Next $\boldsymbol{\zeta}_k$ is a random vector which satisfies $\| \boldsymbol{\zeta}_k \| = 1$ and whose distribution function is independent of k and $\mathbf{y}_k$ such that $p\{| \boldsymbol{\zeta}_k, \boldsymbol{\zeta}_i | > \alpha\} > \beta$ where α and β are fixed constants independent of $\boldsymbol{\zeta}_i$. This latter condition is satisfied, for example, by choosing $\boldsymbol{\zeta}_k$ from a uniform distribution on the unit sphere of the n-dimensional search space.

The search algorithm is then given by

$$\mathbf{y}_{k+1} = \begin{cases} \mathbf{y}_k - h_k \boldsymbol{\zeta}_k \operatorname{sgn}[I(\mathbf{y}_k + c_k \boldsymbol{\zeta}_k) - I(\mathbf{y}_k)] & \text{for } \eta_k \neq 1 \\ \boldsymbol{\psi} & \text{for } \eta_k = 1 \end{cases} \tag{7.123}$$

where $\boldsymbol{\psi}$ is a random vector whose distribution density is nonzero everywhere in the search space and independent of k and $\mathbf{y}_k$.

Thus for $\eta_k \neq 1$, the algorithm proceeds as a unimodal stochastic approximation method. When $\eta_k = 1$, a random jump is taken and the unimodal search is repeated. [Note that $(k - j)$ in Eq. (7.121) represents the number of steps since the last jump.] Vaysbord and Yudin proved that $\mathbf{y}_k$ converges to an arbitrary small (ϵ) neighborhood of the global minimum $\mathbf{y}_o$, with probability greater than $(1 - \epsilon)$. An interesting area of research would be the investigation of increasing the rate of convergence of this algorithm by using information known a priori or gained during the search. A similar concept has been suggested for multimodal operation of a biased random search (Pensa and McMurtry, 1969).

D. *Combinational Search*

Multimodal search techniques are primarily designed to locate the region in which the global extremum lies and it is expected that they will be followed by a unimodal search technique. An adaptive search of a multimodal surface in which several of the above techniques are used has been reported by Hill (1968). Hill describes the difficulty in developing a single method which can be guaranteed to converge in the multimodal, multidimensional case in the presence of constraints. The search is divided into the opening, middle, and end phases discussed in Section IB of this chapter. In the opening phase, Hill suggests a factorial search be conducted and a specified number, N_f, of cells and the corresponding *IP* values of their centers be stored in memory. Only the N_f lowest values of *IP* and their cells are stored, while all other cells are eliminated from further search. Then the standard deviation of all measured *IP* values is computed and all cells having a measured *IP* greater than one-half standard deviation from the minimum *IP* are also eliminated.

In the middle phase of the search, each cell is assigned a probability that it contains the global extremum, in a manner similar to the variable structure method. Next a one-step steepest descent search is conducted in each remaining cell and the changes in the *IP* are computed. Those cells having a relatively large *IP*, with only a small change having been observed, are then eliminated and a credibility is computed for each remaining cell using Bayes Theorem. The credibility represents the program's confidence that a given cell contains the global minimum. Further one-step steepest descent searches are conducted with resulting elimination of cells until the credibility of the cell with the lowest *IP* approaches 1.0. This cell is then selected as the cell most likely to contain the global minimum.

The end phase is conducted in the selected cell and both steepest descent and random search methods are utilized. Constraints are constantly considered throughout the entire search procedure.

E. *Surface Model Methods*

The emphasis in this chapter has been placed on search methods which attempt to locate the optimum point, or region containing it, by sequential operations which utilize information gained during the search to help locate each succeeding trial point. There are methods which extend this concept and utilize such information to form a model of the surface being searched. Two such methods are mentioned briefly here.

Kushner (1963) assumes a Gaussian random function as a model for an unknown one-dimensional multimodal hill; in particular, a Brownian motion stochastic process is chosen as the model of the unknown function. The only available information is contained in noise-disturbed samples. Trials are made sequentially and a sequence of estimates of the optimum point is generated.

Hill (1964) proposed a piecewise cubic approximation as a model of the surface being searched. The method is applicable to multimodal multidimensional surfaces and may be used in low noise-level environments. The surface is quantized into fixed intervals and a cubic polynomial is formed for each interval on the basis of sample trials made at fixed locations. Once the model is constructed, it must be differentiated in order to locate the optimum.

IV. Conclusions

In this chapter some of the more prominent and popular adaptive optimization techniques have been discussed. Obviously, all such methods could not be included, but it is hoped that this chapter has provided an insight into the extent of the problem of optimization of an unknown function and some of the more effective methods for attacking it.

In conclusion, a few words seem in order regarding the assumption of unimodality versus multimodality. Wilde (1964) states that in his own experience, he has never seen an optimization problem in which $I(\mathbf{y})$ was not unimodal in the admissible range of $\mathbf{y}$. In addition, Eveleigh

(1967) states that in most applications of adaptive and learning control, only one extremum exists. It is suggested here that while this may indeed be true, it is at least partially due to the fact that *IP* are often purposely designed so that they will have only one minimum and can therefore be effectively searched. Wilde (1964) also comments that consideration of multidimensional problems weakens belief in the concept of unimodality. It is therefore suggested that if more effective multimodal techniques were available, more meaningful *IP* might be proposed and utilized without concern for either their analytical niceties or their desirable search properties. Consequently, the problem of multimodal search is considered to be an important area for continued serious research.

Evaluation of the cost of conducting a search by the various methods is worthy of more attention (Schumer and Steiglitz, 1968) and should be used as a basis for selection of a search method. Other areas needing additional research include the choice of stopping rules and methods of quantization of search parameters.

References

Aleksandrov, V. M., Sysoyev, V. I., and Shemeneva, V. V., Stochastic optimization. *Engineering Cybernetics 6*, No. 5, pp. 11–16 (1968).

Bekey, G. A., Gran, M. H., Sabroff, A. E., and Wong, A., Parameter optimization by random search using hybrid computer techniques. *Proc. Fall Joint Comp. Conf.*, 1966.

Bessarabova, A. A., Quantization of the normal random process using arbitrary thresholds and levels. *Engineering Cybernetics 6*, No. 5, pp. 162–166 (1968).

Brooks, S. H., A discussion of random methods for seeking maxima. *Operations Research 6*, No. 2, pp. 244–251 (1958).

Brooks, S. H., A comparison of maximum-seeking methods. *Operations Research 7*, No. 4, pp. 430–457 (1959).

Eveleigh, V. W., "Adaptive Control and Optimization Techniques." McGraw–Hill, New York, 1967.

Fiacco, A. V. and McCormick, G. P., The sequential unconstrained minimization technique for nonlinear programming, a primal-dual method. *Management Science 10*, No. 2, pp. 360–366 (1964).

Fletcher, R. and Powell, M. J. D., A rapidly convergent descent method for minimization. *British Comp. J. 6*, No. 2, pp. 163–168 (1963).

Fletcher, R. and Reeves, C. M., Function minimization by conjugate gradients. *British Comp. J. 7*, No. 2, pp. 149–154 (1964).

Fu, K. S. and Nikolic, Z. J., On some reinforcement techniques and their relation with stochastic approximation. *IEEE Trans. Auto. Control AC-11*, No. 4, pp. 756–758 (1966).

Gurin, L. S. and Rastrigin, L. A., Convergence of the random search method in the presence of noise. *Automation and Remote Control 26*, No. 9, pp. 1505–1511 (1965).

Hestenes, M. R. and Steifel, E., Methods of conjugate gradients for solving linear systems. *J. Research of the Natl. Bureau of Standards 49*, No. 6, pp. 409–436 (1952).

Hill, J. C., A hillclimbing technique using piecewise cubic approximation. Ph.D. Thesis, Purdue Univ., Lafayette, Ind., 1964.

Hill, J. D. and Fu, K. S., A learning control system using stochastic approximation for hill-climbing. *1965 Joint Auto. Control Conf. Proc.*, pp. 334–340 (1965).

Hill, J. D., A search technique for multimodal surfaces. *IEEE Trans. Systems Sci. Cybernetics SSC-5*, No. 1, pp. 2–8 (1969).

Hooke, R. and Jeeves, T. A., Comments on Brooks' discussion of random methods. *Operations Research 6*, No. 6, pp. 881–882 (1958).

Idelsohn, J. M., 10 ways to find the optimum. *Control Engin. 11*, No. 6, pp. 97–102 (1964).

Karnopp, D. C., Random search techniques for optimization problems. *Automatica 1*, pp. 111–121 (1963).

Kushner, H. J., A new method of locating the maximum point of an arbitrary multipeak curve in the presence of noise, *Preprints Joint Auto. Control Conf., 1963*, pp. 69–79.

Lasdon, L. S., Mitter, S. K., and Waren, A. D., The conjugate gradient method for optimal control problems, *IEEE Trans. Auto. Control AC-12*, No. 2, pp. 132–138 (1967).

Lasdon, L. S. and Waren, A. D., Mathematical programming for optimal design. *Electro-Technology 80*, No. 5, pp. 53–70 (1967).

Matyas, J., Random optimization. *Automation and Remote Control 26*, No. 2, pp. 244–251 (1965).

Max, J., Quantizing for minimum distortion, *IEEE Trans. Info. Theory IT–6*, No. 1, pp. 7–12 (1960).

McMurtry, G. J. and Fu, K. S., A variable structure automaton used as a multimodal searching technique. *IEEE Trans. Auto. Control AC-11*, No. 3, pp. 379–387 (1966).

Mendel, J. M. and Zapalac, J. J., The application of techniques of artificial intelligence to control system design. In "Advances in Control Systems, Vol. 6: Theory and Applications." Academic Press, New York, 1968.

Narendra, K. S. and Baker, T. S., Gradient generation using a single perturbation signal. *IEEE Trans. Auto. Control AC–13*, No. 3, pp. 298–299 (1968).

Pensa, A. F., Gradient biased random search. Ph.D. Thesis, The Pennsylvania State Univ., University Park, Pennsylvania, 1969.

Pensa, A. F. and McMurtry, G. J., Multimodal operation of biased random search. *Proc. 1969 Southeastern Symp. System Theory*, Blacksburg, Virginia.

Pierre, D. A., "Optimization Theory with Applications." Wiley, New York, 1969.

Powell, M. J. D., An efficient method for finding the minimum of a function of several variables without calculating derivatives. *British Comp. J. 7*, No. 2, pp. 155–162 (1964).

Rastrigin, L. A., Extremal control by the method of random scanning. *Automation and Remote Control 10*, No. 9, pp. 891–896 (1960).

Rastrigin, L. A., The convergence of the random search method in the extremal control of a many-parameter system. *Automation and Remote Control 24*, No. 11, pp. 1337–1342 (1963).

Schumer, M. A. and Steiglitz, K., Adaptive step size random search. *IEEE Trans. Auto Control AC-13*, No. 3, pp. 270–276 (1968).

Sebestyen, G., "Decision-Making Processes in Pattern Recognition." Macmillan, New York, 1962.

Tompkins, C. B., Methods of steep descent. *In* "Modern Mathematics for the Engineer" (E. F. Beckenbach, ed.), Chapt. 18, pp. 448–479. McGraw–Hill, New York, 1956.

Vaysbord, E. M. and Yudin, D. B., Multiextremal stochastic approximation. *Engineering Cybernetics 6*, No. 5, pp. 1–11 (1968).

Waltz, M. D. and Fu, K. S., A heuristic approach to learning control systems, *IEEE Trans. Auto. Control AC*–10, No. 4, pp. 390–398 (1965).
Wilde, D. J., "Optimum Seeking Methods." Prentice–Hall, Englewood Cliffs, New Jersey, 1964.
Wilde, D. J. and Beightler, C. S., "Foundations of Optimization." Prentice–Hall, Englewood Cliffs, New Jersey, 1967.
Zoutendijk, G., "Methods of Feasible Directions." Elsevier, New York, 1960.

8

J. M. Mendel
R. W. McLaren

REINFORCEMENT-LEARNING CONTROL AND PATTERN RECOGNITION SYSTEMS

I. Introduction

A. *Psychological Origins of Learning System Models*

Learning, as a pattern of both human and animal behavior, has long been a subject for experimentation and study by psychologists, physiologists, and others; however, the scientific study of learning, based on experimental and observational results, has been carried out primarily by psychologists over about the last 80 years. The importance of learning and learning-theories in psychology is due to their influence on describing so much of man's diverse behavior. Learning models and theories in psychology are primarily analytical in that they explain or predict behavior based on experimental results and observations. In this chapter, learning models are formulated and applied to the synthesis of control systems and pattern-recognition systems in such a manner that these systems may be said to possess attributes of learning.

In order to account, from a psychological viewpoint, for the wide diversity of behavior attributed to learning, we will define learning as *the process by which an activity originates or is changed through reaction to an encountered situation which is not due to "native" response tendencies, maturation, or temporary states of the organism.* Although this definition is inexact (which may detract from its usefulness in some situations), it implies the following sequence of events: (1) the organism interacts with an environment; (2) the organism undergoes a change as a result of its interaction; and (3) the organism responds in a new way because of the change that has occurred. The response itself indicates that a change has occurred.

Experiments with, and observations of, biological systems have resulted in many learning theories (Bower and Hilgard, 1966, and Mowrer, 1960). The stimulus-response and cognitive theories constitute two major classes of learning theories. The former includes Pavlov's conditioning, Thorndike's connectionism, Skinner's operant conditioning, and Hull's work; the latter includes the theories of Tolman and those based on Gestalt psychology. Theories which do not fall clearly into either of these two classes include those based on Woodward's functionalism and Freud's psychodynamics. In addition, mathematical models which represent a recent trend in American psychology (for example, Bush and Estes, 1959; Bush and Mosteller, 1955; Luce *et al.*, 1963; and Atkinson *et al.*, 1965) are not included within these two classes.

Mathematical learning models combine the mathematical properties and psychological concepts of learning. They are formulated from experimental results, and attempt to predict learning behavior quantitatively. These models have been developed for such diverse learning conditions as classical conditioning, operant conditioning, and associative learning.

Efforts have also been directed at developing and investigating learning theories derived from the simulation of learning models or situations; these are called *information processing theories*, and are useful in complex learning situations such as problem-solving or recognition.

One of the most important principles in all learning theory is the *law of reinforcement*. This law governs how rewards and punishments produce changes in behavior (response to stimuli), and assumes various forms in the different learning theories (Mowrer, 1960). In theories based upon mathematical learning models, reinforcement assumes the form of rewards and punishments that change response probabilities.

B. *Concepts of Reinforcement Learning*

The importance of reinforcement learning concepts in psychological learning theories has been recognized by engineers who are interested in incorporating learning properties into control and pattern-recognition systems. In order to incorporate these properties into such systems, it is necessary to be more precise about reinforcement and its properties. By *reinforcement learning* we will mean the process by which the response of a system (or organism) to a stimulus is strengthened by reward and weakened by punishment. In the former situation, *positive reinforcement* occurs and increases a response probability, whereas in the latter situation *negative reinforcement* occurs and decreases a response probability.

Rewards and punishments represent favorable and unfavorable environmental reactions, respectively, to a response. Such reactions are evaluated (in some sense) by a system in its effort to achieve its goals. A reinforcement learning system seeks its goals by strengthening some responses and suppressing others. Psychological evidence indicates that the effects of reward and punishment are opposite but are not equal. In engineering applications, the effects of reward and punishment are based on a continuous scale for rewards, with strict reward and strict punishment representing the upper and lower bounds, respectively, of this scale. The engineering system is then designed to extremize reward.

In order to explain latent learning (latent learning refers to any learning that is not displayed in conduct at the time of the learning), a distinction is often made between learning as a property, and performance which results from learning. In engineering systems, performance is always taken as a measure of learning.

Secondary reinforcement, in which a subgoal or secondary drive replaces the primary goal, occurs in certain two-factor learning theories (Mowrer, 1960). The displacement of primary goals by secondary goals in biological systems can be applied to engineering systems as well. This occurs when seeking the primary goal is difficult to implement or when the primary goal is not well-defined. Satisfaction of secondary goals must, however, be consistent with satisfaction of the primary goal. Reinforcement learning can also be applied to patterns of responses; this is useful when individual responses are numerous or are not well defined. In addition, reinforcement of a response to a stimulus may reinforce the response to a class of stimuli.

Psychological evidence indicates that in some situations, rewarding a response part of the time increases its resistance to extinction. In general, such a reward schedule could result from a "noisy" environment. By applying reinforcement-learning algorithms which utilize the results from such environments, engineering systems can achieve acceptable performance. To analyze and predict the behavior of an engineering system that incorporates reinforcement learning, it is first necessary to formulate a mathematical learning model. Not all of the properties of reinforcement learning that were discussed above can be included in the model if it is to retain a form that is reasonable for analysis. Only the essential properties of reinforcement learning can be included.

II. Formulation of a Stochastic, Reinforcement-Learning Model

Mathematical-learning theorists have devised mathematical-learning models which are often capable of concisely describing the results of learning experiments. In certain situations, such models may even be useful in predicting the outcome of a new experiment. These models are stochastic and are defined by parameters; probabilities are assigned to certain actions or responses, and these probabilities are assumed to be positively or negatively reinforced by the outcome of a learning experiment. The model parameters are functions of the results of a specific learning experiment and are usually estimated after-the-fact from experimental data.

One of the most well-known learning experiments, which demonstrates reinforcement learning, is the one in which a hungry rat enters a T-maze and must decide which way to turn at the fork in the T. If he turns to the left, he does not find food; if he turns to the right, he finds a piece of cheese. The probabilities, then, are that the rat will turn either to the left or to the right. Turning to the right positively reinforces that probability, whereas turning to the left negatively reinforces the other probability. As the rat is repeatedly exposed to the same T-maze or event, we can project that the rat will learn to find the cheese by turning to the right. This is indeed what happens, and it is predicted by the mathematical model once the parameters of the model have been determined.

One of the objectives of this section is to define what is meant by a learning experiment and to present a basic reinforcement equation. Mathematical subtleties and details are not treated here because they are beyond the scope of this section (see Bush and Mosteller, 1955; Bush and Estes, 1959; Luce *et al.*, 1963; Atkinson *et al.*, 1965).

Before defining a learning experiment, the following concepts must be understood: response classes, set of alternatives, probability of a response, trial, event, and outcome.

To describe behavioral changes, one must be able to distinguish types of responses or alternatives. In the T-maze experiment, for example, the alternatives of turning right or turning left were distinguished. Other alternatives might been included, depending on the objective of the experiment. At least two classes of responses are necessary. Also, it is always possible to make the response classes mutually exclusive and exhaustive (a complete set) by redefining the response classes. Both of these response-class properties are essential to the synthesis of a meaningful stochastic learning model. In the T-maze experiment, exhaustiveness of response classes is easily achieved by defining a residual class as "everything else." It may also be expedient to combine the two turning-classes into a single class—turning.

In general, there will be s finite-response classes or *alternatives*, (A_1, A_2,..., and A_s) and the set is referred to as the set of alternatives. The specific alternatives are a function of a specific learning experiment.

In the stochastic learning model, a probability, P_j, is associated with alternative A_j. Because the s-alternatives are mutually exclusive and exhaustive, some one alternative must occur on every trial. A *trial* is an opportunity for choosing among the s-alternatives. The conservation of probability implies that the total probability is the same on every trial; hence, it is conjectured that after each trial, probabilities move about in such a manner that the total probability remains the same (unity). Such a flow of probability from one class of responses to another is the basis for the mathematical-learning theorists' description of learning. The only quantities that the stochastic model can predict is the set of s-probabilities on every trial.

What factors change the set of probabilities? Whenever certain *events* occur, the probabilities are assumed to be altered in a determined way. In the experiment described, the event is the rat being in the T-maze. In another learning experiment, a rat may be directed to one of a group of different T-mazes. Each T-maze represents a different event. In general, one can define an abstract set of v-events as E_1, E_2,..., and E_v. Associated with each event is a set of alternatives; these alternatives do not necessarily have to be the same for each event, and there may be more alternatives for some events than for others. In this section, however, it is assumed that each event has the same number of alternatives. In order to distinguish alternatives and their associated probabilities for each event, the following event-oriented notation is used: A_j^l is the jth alternative for the lth event, and P_j^l is the probability associated with A_j^l.

Learning theorists assume that every time a response occurs (A_1^l, A_2^l,..., or A_s^l) it has an *outcome*. In the T-maze experiment, for example, if the rat turns to the right, the outcome is food. If he turns to the left, the outcome is no food. Generalizing, if a set of r possible outcomes (denoted O_1, O_2,..., and O_r) is assumed, every outcome will have some effect (including zero effect) on the s-probabilities associated with the s-alternatives. This effect may be conveniently viewed as an iteration of the probabilities; hence, from one trial to the next a transition in the probabilities occurs.

A *learning experiment* can now be defined as consisting of a sequence of trials with each trial having only one response. Each response occurrence has an outcome that alters the probabilities of all of the responses (Bush and Mosteller, 1955).

It is further assumed that if a set of probabilities (for a specific event) is given on trial k, the new set on trial $k + 1$ is completely determined by the response occurring on trial k, and its outcome. This is a Markov property.

Stochastic matrix operators—one for each event—are central to a stochastic learning model. Each operator, denoted T_l, contains as many rows and columns as the number of response classes. The elements of T_l indicate how to weight the probabilities of the various response classes for the lth event to obtain the new probabilities for these classes. Letting $\mathbf{P}^l(k)$ be the collection of probabilities for the s-classes at the kth trial, the following model can be defined:

$$T_l\mathbf{P}(k) \triangleq \mathbf{P}^l(k + 1) = \alpha_l\mathbf{P}^l(k) + (1 - \alpha_l)\boldsymbol{\lambda}^l \tag{8.1}$$

where $l = 1, 2,..., v$, $k = 0, 1,...,$

$$\sum_{j=1}^{s} \lambda_j{}^l = 1 \tag{8.2}$$

and α_l and $\boldsymbol{\lambda}^l$ remain to be determined or specified and depend on the nature of the learning experiment.

If α_l and $\boldsymbol{\lambda}_l$ are given, then it is straightforward to compute $\mathbf{P}^l(k)$ from the following expression:

$$\mathbf{P}^l(k) = (\alpha_l)^k\, \mathbf{P}^l(0) + [1 - (\alpha_l)^k]\boldsymbol{\lambda}^l \tag{8.3}$$

Note that, for $| \alpha_l | < 1$,

$$\lim_{k\to\infty} \mathbf{P}^l(k) = \boldsymbol{\lambda}^l \tag{8.4}$$

It is clear from these results that a state of complete learning exists in the subject when the probabilities of his response classes reach fixed values. His performance is then predictable in a probabilistic sense.

III. Reinforcement-Learning Control Systems

A. *Definitions*

Basically, there are two types of control systems: open-loop, and closed-loop (feedback). An open-loop control system (D'Azzo and Houpis, 1966) is a system in which the output has no effect upon the input signal. A closed-loop control system is a system in which the output affects the input quantity in a manner which maintains desired system performance. Our attention will be directed to closed-loop control systems because they make use of the well-known feedback principle which is important and useful in the formulation of advanced control systems.

Space limitations prevent extensive elaboration on closed-loop control systems (see D'Azzo and Houpis, 1966; Eveleigh, 1967; and Athans and Falb, 1966, for more comprehensive coverage). For our purposes, it is convenient to view a closed-loop control system as shown in Fig. 1. Examples of process- or plant-environment combinations are: a missile disturbed by gusts of wind, a spacecraft acted upon by the moon's gravity while orbiting around the moon, and a gun following the motions of targets while mounted on the deck of a ship. The control law may take the form of a shaping network, a decision surface, or a special-purpose digital computer. The output of the control law acts as input to a device or subsystem which is able to exert control over the process. In the missile, spacecraft, and fire-control examples given, the device might be a reaction-jet engine, an inertia wheel, and an hydraulic amplifier, respectively. The mechanization of control laws, however, will not be considered in this chapter. The design of control laws for poorly defined processes or environments will be explored.

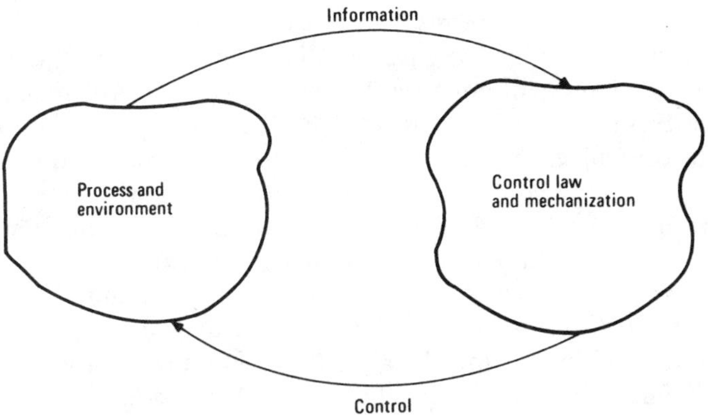

FIGURE 1. Representation of a closed-loop control system

If everything about the environment and process is known a priori, the design of the control law is straightforward and can be accomplished by means of proved techniques. On the other hand, if the environment or process is poorly defined, more advanced and sometimes less-proved techniques must be used to design the law. In the latter situation, control specialists have devised adaptive control systems and learning control systems.

An adaptive control system is one which is provided with: (1) a means of continuously monitoring its own performance relative to desired performance conditions, and (2) a means of modifying a part of its control law, by closed-loop action, so as to approach these conditions (Cooper *et al.*, 1960). The adaptive control law encompasses three major functions (Eveleigh, 1967): identification, decision, and modification. Identification is the process by which the plant or environment is characterized (see Chapter 6, for example), or by which the performance of the system is monitored. In the decision process, the performance measurements are used to decide how system performance relates to the desired performance conditions. If performance is inadequate, corrective adjustments are made according to an established strategy. Modification is the process of changing parameters—within the control law—toward their optimum settings. It is controlled by the identification and decision processes.

Conventional control systems are designed to meet certain performance specifications under known environment and process conditions; however, should these conditions change, performance will change as a result. In an adaptive control system, the system's actual performance is compared to the desired performance, and the difference is then used to drive actual performance toward desired performance.

If the environment is changing rapidly or is very poorly defined, the adaptive control law will not be able to drive actual performance toward desired performance. In this case, total adaptation will not be possible; hence, the control law must be broadened. This broadening is accomplished in a learning control law by localizing the adaptations to regions in a plant-environment space and by providing the control law with a long-term memory. In fact, it is often convenient to view a learning control system as an adaptive control system with memory.

Different principles have been the bases for different types of learning control systems (Mendel and Zapalac, 1968; Leondes and Mendel, 1969; Fu *et al.*, 1963). We will demonstrate in this section how principles from stochastic, reinforcement-learning theory can be used to design the control laws for these systems.

A class of learning-control systems—reinforcement-learning control systems—is one in which the plant or environment may not be known a priori. The control law is self-organizing; that is, it is able to change as a function of its experience and environment-plant. These changes can occur during the on-line operation of the system, and are based upon reinforcement-learning principles.

A representative learning control system is shown in Fig. 2. Learning occurs with the learning control law embedded in the control system during the (real-time) operation of the overall system. The learning

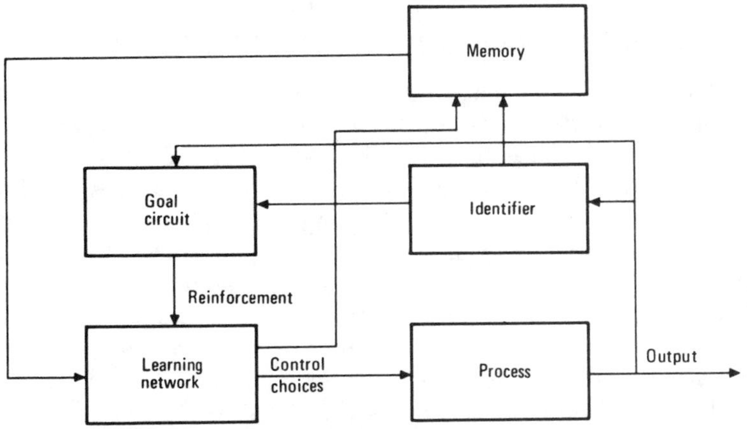

FIGURE 2. Representative learning control system

control law encompasses four major functions: identification, memory, decision, and modification. Learning (which occurs when the average performance history of the overall system—over a sequence of trials—indicates a trend toward improved performance) automatically improves the control law through the following functions: (1) evaluation of results of previous control choices (goal circuit in Fig. 2) made by the learning network for a given situation and according to a prescribed criterion, and (2) modification of the learning control law's memory store of parameters, its logic, or its physical structure, so that subsequent control-choices reflect the evaluation. In this section, we assume that modification is accomplished by means of a reinforcement technique.

Specifically, if present performance is an improvement upon recent past performance, the goal circuit generates a reward signal to the learning network which indicates that improvement has occurred. On the other hand, if present performance is worse than recent past performance, a punishment signal is generated which notifies the learning network of that fact. Loosely speaking, the reward signal positively reinforces those states of the network that contribute to improvement, while the punishment signal negatively reinforces the states that produced improper behavior.

To proceed further, it is necessary to demonstrate more precisely how one can interpret the learning control law as a learning experiment.

B. *Basic Notions*

Four basic notions are the heart of reinforcement-learning control systems: (1) mappings, (2) control situations, (3) subgoals, and (4) memory. (The material in this paragraph follows closely the material in Mendel and Zapalac, 1968; and Leondes and Mendel, 1968.)

1. *Mappings.* The mapping notion permits one to view problems of control-system design as collections of mappings: (1) from points in a plant-parameter space to respective points in a feedback-gain space (Fu *et al.*, 1963, 1964; Fu and Waltz, 1965), as in the design of a proportional control law for a slowly varying plant; (2) from points in state space to respective points in a control category space (Fu and Waltz, 1965), as in the design of a closed-loop, time-optimal control law; or (3) from points in an augmented state space (a state space with an additional dimension for each variable plant or environment parameter) to respective points in some control-choice space, as in the design of a closed-loop, fuel-optimal control law for a slowly-varying plant. This allows the control specialist to formulate his design problem in a form suitable for pattern-recognition interpretations.

Example 1. Consider the problem of designing a closed-loop, time-optimal control law for the linear, time-invariant system (Chapter 5).

$$\dot{\mathbf{x}}(t) = A\mathbf{x}(t) + \mathbf{b}u(t) \tag{8.5}$$

In this equation: $\mathbf{x}(t)$ is an $n \times 1$ state vector; A is an $n \times n$ matrix of constant coefficients; $\mathbf{b}$ is an $n \times 1$ control distribution vector; and $u(t)$ is a scalar control that is subject to the constraint

$$| u(t)| \leqslant L \tag{8.6}$$

It is well known (Athans and Falb, 1966) that the closed-loop, optimal control law is

$$u^*(\mathbf{x}) = -L \operatorname{sgn} f(\mathbf{x}) = \begin{cases} L, & \text{if } f(\mathbf{x}) < 0 \\ -L, & \text{if } f(\mathbf{x}) > 0 \\ \text{undefined if} & f(\mathbf{x}) = 0 \end{cases} \tag{8.7}$$

In practice, $f(\mathbf{x})$ is usually very difficult to determine [a technique for approximating $f(\mathbf{x})$ is described in Mendel's quasi-optimal control chapter]. A mapping-interpretation for this design problem is given in Fig. 3. In this figure, points from the n-dimensional state space are seen to be mapped into their respective control categories.

Control choices are analogous to alternatives in stochastic learning theory. In some problems, the control choices are well defined, as in Example 1. In other problems, however, there is as much freedom in designating control choices as there is in designating alternatives.

2. *Control Situations.* Control situations are regions in either plant-environment parameter space, state space, or augmented state space for which a single control choice (such as $+L$ or $-L$ in Example 1) leads to satisfactory performance for all points contained therein. Such regions may result from a pregridding of the respective spaces, or they may be

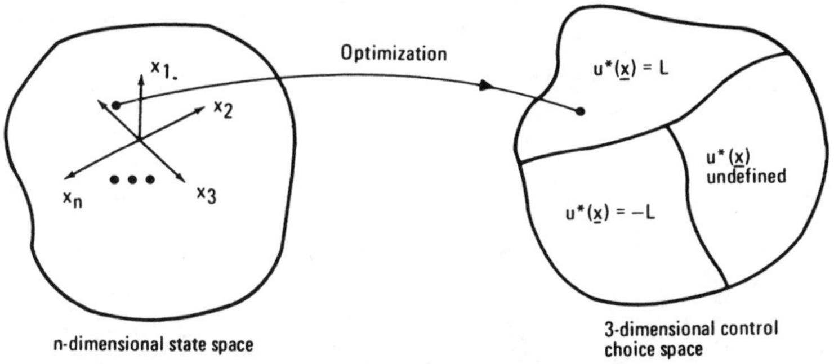

FIGURE 3. Mapping notion for system in Example 1

created on-line as the need for additional control situations manifests itself. The rationale for partitioning the different spaces into control situations is the assumption that neighboring points within a small region should have the same or similar control choices. Control situations permit localization of an optimization problem from the entire plant-environment parameter space, or augmented state space to regions in the respective spaces. They permit a broadening of the mapping notion. For example, one can imagine mapping regions of the state space in Example 1 into one of the three categories in the control choice space.

Control situations are analogous to events in stochastic learning theory. Consider the following modification of the T-maze experiment: The rat is directed to one of a group of different T-mazes on each trial (Fig. 4a). Each T-maze represents a different event; the purpose of the experiment is for the rat to learn which way to move in any one of the T-mazes to satisfy his hunger. To illustrate, assume that the rat is exposed to a systematic sequence of the events, in the order 123123123 and so forth. Such a learning experiment is analogous to the situation depicted in Fig. 4b, for the Example 1 system. In that figure, it is tacitly assumed that the system is continually restarted at the same initial condition, $\mathbf{x}_0$, and that, therefore, the system passes through the systematic sequence of control situations 123123123 and so forth. Also, the $u^*(\mathbf{x})$-undefined category has been combined into the category

$u^*(\mathbf{x}) = L$. (Combining categories or response classes is an essential part of the general, stochastic-learning theory model. See Bush and Mosteller, 1965.) Each control situation has either a $+L$ or $-L$ control choice, just as within each T-maze the rat has the two alternatives of turning right or turning left. As in the learning model, a probability is associated with each control choice. Initially, the probability of either a $+L$ or $-L$ control choice is assumed to be the same. For as long as

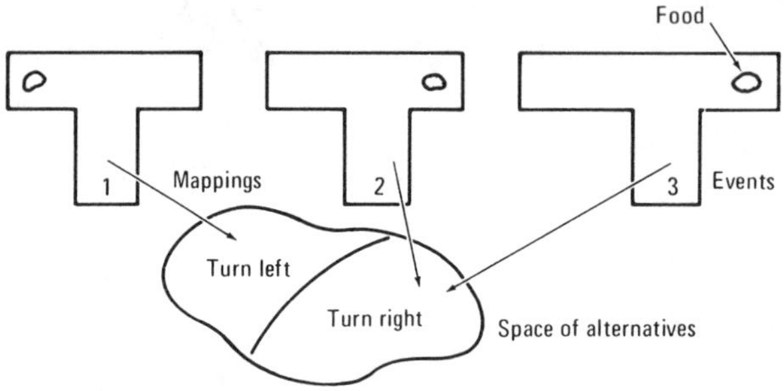

(a) Events and mappings

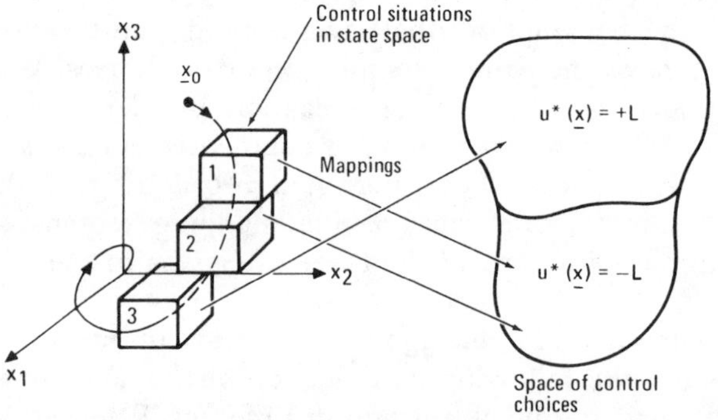

(b) Control situations and mappings

FIGURE 4. Comparison of control situations and events

the system is within a control situation, it responds in a dynamic manner. A measure of the system's response is obtained in the goal circuit and is used for altering the probabilities associated with the control choices in a reinforcement model. As learning proceeds, the probability for one of the control choices approaches a maximum in each control situation.

The close similarity between the updating of probabilities in control situations and the events that were described in the preceding section will be noted.

3. *Subgoals.* The subgoal notion has to do with the measure that is evaluated in the goal circuit and used for altering the probabilities associated with the different control choices.

Often, the true goal or objective for a control system cannot be formulated precisely. For example, in the fine attitude control of a laser communication satellite, as described in Mendel (1967), the overall objective was to contain attitude errors to within ± 0.20 arc sec. The actual performance requirements of the control system are related to the communication and information aspects of the problem; hence, whether containment implies that attitude errors must be contained at every instant of time or over intervals of time, in an absolute sense or in some probabilistic sense, depends upon information that may not be readily available or even known.

A quite common approach is to formulate a mathematically tractable index of performance (*IP*) and to associate desired or satisfactory system performance with the optimum value for the *IP*. This means, of course, that there must be compatibility between the *IP* and the overall objective.

Example 2. (Mendel and Zapalac, 1968) The overall objective for the laser satellite application described above is assumed to be containment of attitude errors in an absolute sense over fixed intervals of time; that is to say,

$$|x(t)| \leqslant \epsilon \qquad \text{for} \quad t_0 \leqslant t \leqslant t_0 + \tau \tag{8.8}$$

where $x(t)$ is the attitude error. Let the *IP* be defined as:

$$IP = \frac{1}{\tau} \int_{t_0}^{t_0+\tau} x^2(\xi)\, d\xi \tag{8.9}$$

Assuming that $x(t)$ is bounded from above, which seems reasonable for this application, it can be shown that Eqs. (8.8) and (8.9) are related by the following compatibility statement: If $IP \leqslant \delta(\epsilon)$, where $\delta(\epsilon) = \epsilon^2$, then $|x(t)| \leqslant \epsilon$, for $t_0 \leqslant t \leqslant t_0 + \tau$.

Although this example illustrates what is meant by compatibility between the *IP* and the overall objective, it is an oversimplification of reality. In practice, determining $\delta(\epsilon)$ is very difficult, and actually, very little is known about explicit compatibility relationships. If these relationships cannot be obtained by direct means, perhaps they can be synthesized, using pattern-recognition techniques.

The overall goal and IP provide a measure of the system's performance over a long interval of time—the time interval of interest. In learning control systems, decisions about the quality of the control law are usually made over short intervals of time. These decisions are determined, for the most part, by means of measures that provide an indication of the system's performance over these short-time intervals. Such performance measures are referred to as subgoals.

Subgoals might better be described as intermediate goals, whereas the overall goal is the primary goal. The subgoal is used to direct the learning process toward the optimal solution and satisfaction of the overall goal. It should have the following characteristics: (1) it must evaluate each decision separately, and (2) it must be related to the overall goal so that satisfying the subgoal with each decision leads to eventual satisfaction of the overall goal. This second characteristic is a compatibility requirement between the subgoal and overall goal. Because the overall goal and IP must be compatible, the subgoal and IP must be compatible also.

Example 3. Assume that the primary goal is to control a deterministic system in such a manner that a quadratic performance index of the form

$$IP(N) = \sum_{k=0}^{N-1} \mathbf{x}'_{k+1} Q \mathbf{x}_{k+1} + \rho u^2(k) \tag{8.10}$$

for a specified initial state $\mathbf{x}_0 = (x_1(0),..., x_n(0))'$, is to be minimized. Athans and Falb (1966), Lee (1964), and Tou (1964) discuss quadratic optimal control. The system is described by the following discrete version of Eq. (8.5):

$$\mathbf{x}_{k+1} = \Phi \mathbf{x}_k + \mathbf{h}u(k) \tag{8.11}$$

where $k = 0, 1,..., N - 1$.

The state transition matrix, Φ, and the control distribution vector, $\mathbf{h}$, are easily computed from A and $\mathbf{b}$ (Lee, 1964). Q is a positive-definite symmetric matrix and ρ is a constant multiplier. The first term in Eq. (8.10) is used to specify the deviation of the process from the origin at any time, kT, (for convenience, the sampling period, T, is set equal to unity), and the second term provides an energy constraint on the control signal. Appropriate weightings of these terms are achieved by specifying appropriate values for Q and ρ.

In a reinforcement-learning control system, the primary objective of minimizing $IP(N)$ is desired; however, the control is now constrained.

The constraints are that the control be chosen from a finite set of allowable actions

$$u(k) \epsilon \mathscr{U} = \{u_1, \dots, u_s\} \tag{8.12}$$

where $k = 0, \dots, N - 1$.
Probabilities are assigned to each element of $\mathscr{U}$, and the subgoal $SG(k)$,

$$SG(k) \triangleq \mathbf{x}'_{k+1} G(k) \mathbf{x}_{k+1} + \beta u^2(k) \tag{8.13}$$

is used in the reinforcement of these probabilities. How should $G(k)$ and β be chosen so that $SG(k)$ and $IP(N)$ are compatible? An answer to this question has been given by Jones (1967) and is briefly outlined below.

First, the optimum control law which minimizes $IP(N)$ is obtained. It can be found directly from calculus and the method of Lagrange multipliers or from the technique of dynamic programming. The details are not given here but can be found in Lee (1964) or Tou (1964). The optimum control law $u^*(k)$ is given by the following relationships:

$$u^*(k) = -K(N - k)\mathbf{x}_k \tag{8.14}$$

$$K(N - k) = \frac{\mathbf{h}'[Q + Z(N - k - 1)]\Phi}{\mathbf{h}'[Q + Z(N - k - 1)]\mathbf{h} + \rho} \tag{8.15}$$

$$Z(N - k) = [\Phi + \mathbf{h}K(N - k)]'[Q + Z(N - k - 1)][\Phi + \mathbf{h}K(N - k)] + \rho K'(N - k) K(N - k) \tag{8.16}$$

$$Z(0) = 0 \tag{8.17}$$

for $k = N - 1, N - 2, \dots, 0$. In these equations, $Z(N - k)$ is an $n \times n$ matrix and $K(N - k)$ is a $1 \times n$ row matrix. Observe that $K(N), K(N - 1), \dots,$ and $K(1)$ are required for generating the control sequence $u^*(0), u^*(1), \dots,$ and $u^*(N - 1)$, respectively, which means that Eqs. (8.15) and (8.16) must be solved backwards in time in order to generate this sequence.

Next, the control law that minimizes $SG(k)$ [assuming that there are no constraints on the control choices] is obtained. $u^{**}(k)$, to be distinguished from $u^*(k)$, is obtained by differentiating $SG(k)$ with respect to $u(k)$ after Eq. (8.11) is substituted into the expression for $SG(k)$, and setting the resulting expression equal to zero. The result is:

$$u^{**}(k) = \frac{-\mathbf{h}'G(k)\,\Phi\mathbf{x}_k}{\mathbf{h}'G(k)\,\mathbf{h} + \beta} \tag{8.18}$$

For $SG(k)$ to be the exact subgoal, $u^{**}(k)$ should be identical to $u^{*}(k)$ for all values of k; hence, $SG(k)$ is the exact subgoal if

$$\beta = \rho \tag{8.19}$$

and

$$G(k) = Q + Z(N - k - 1) \tag{8.20}$$

where $k = 0, 1, \ldots, N - 1$.
If β and $G(k)$ are chosen in this manner, $SG(k)$ and $IP(N)$ will be said to be compatible (see Problem 4).

This example illustrates what is meant by compatibility between the overall goal (or IP) and a subgoal. In practice, very little is known about primary-secondary-goal relationships. It is important to emphasize that the learning control system uses the subgoal, but does not use the analytical expression for the control law [Eq. (8.18), for example]. It uses the subgoal to update probabilities which have been associated with the elements of $\mathscr{U}$ in Eq. (8.12).

4. *Memory.* With the memory notion, a separate memory compartment is associated with each control situation. In the event that learning is not completed the first time a control situation is entered, pertitent information is stored in a memory compartment so that when the control situation is reentered, learning may continue. Memory, therefore, is essential to the meaning of learning.

There are two forms of memory: short-term and long-term memory. Short-term memory refers to the remembering of pertinent information for as long as the system is in the same control situation. Long-term memory, on the other hand, refers to the remembering of pertinent information out of the control situation. Consider, for example, the bang-bang system in Fig. 4b. As long as the system remains within a control situation, a short-term memory is required to facilitate the updating of the probabilities associated with the $+L$ or $-L$ control choice. The long-term memory remembers the last computed values for these two probabilities when the system leaves the control situation. In this way, when the control situation is reentered, the previously learned probabilities are recalled for subsequent trials.

The analogy is apparent between the short-term and long-term memory requirements in a control system, and the memory requirements of the rat in the learning experiment described in Section II.

The notions of mappings, control situations, subgoals, and memory are not, in themselves, unique to reinforcement-learning control systems. When combined, however, they are the essence of such systems.

C. *A Reinforcement-Learning Control Algorithm*

This paragraph postulates the structure of a reinforcement-learning control law or algorithm. The control algorithm makes use of the four basic notions of mappings, control situations, subgoals, and memory, and a reinforcement-type rule for modification of control actions. The control algorithm is heuristic in that no convergence proof is given for it (the basis for such a proof, when probability densities are stationary, is found in McLaren, 1967).

The control algorithm is summarized in Fig. 5. We assume that

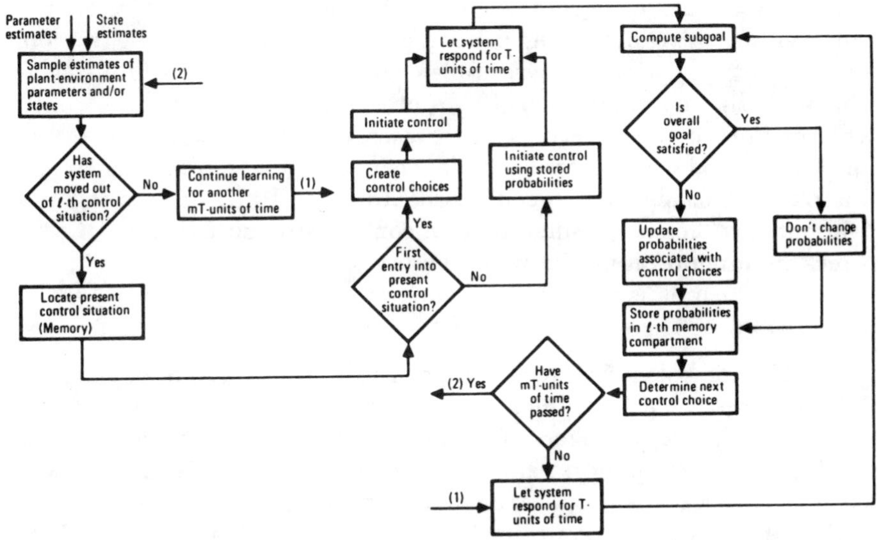

FIGURE 5. A reinforcement-learning control algorithm

control situations have been established a priori, although it is a simple matter to modify the flowchart if a capability for creating on-line control situations is desired. At the end of every mT-units of time, a control situation check is made. Information necessary for this check is assumed to be available from a general-purpose identifier which provides estimates of important plant-environment parameters and states. How much of this information is necessary depends on the specific application.

If the system is still in the same control situation, learning continues for that situation for another mT-units. If the system has moved out of a control situation, however, it locates which control situation it is presently in and ascertains whether it has been there before. If it has been in that control situation before, it makes use of information that has been stored in a memory bank to initiate the control action for the next T-units of time. The information stored is the set of learned probabilities of the control actions.

It is also assumed that all of the information available about the plant, environment, and desired system performance is used to design nominal control choices for each control situation. These choices can then be the basis for creation of control choices the first time a control situation is entered. In certain applications, the set of control choices is predetermined by the available actuator or by the performance requirement. If, for example, reaction-jet engines are used to control a missile, the only control actions available are full-forward thrust $(+L)$, full-reverse thrust $(-L)$, and engines-off (0). In other applications, a set of control choices must actually be created for each control situation. In the case of proportional control, for example, assume that a nominal control-gain matrix, $K_n{}^l$, has been designed for the lth control situation. In this case, when the system [Eq. (8.5)] enters the lth control situation for the first time, the nominal control law would be

$$u_n{}^l(\mathbf{x}) = K_n{}^l\mathbf{x} \tag{8.21}$$

A set of control choices for the lth control situation can be constructed. This is done by constructing a set of s gain-matrices which are uniformly distributed in a hypersphere of radius-η centered about the vector whose components correspond to all of the elements of $K_n{}^l$. Details of such a construction are given in Mendel and Zapalac (1968).

After the system responds for T-units, the subgoal is computed. If the primary goal is satisfied as determined by compatibility between the subgoal and the overall goal (IP), the probabilities remain unchanged for the next T-units. This does not mean that the same control action will be applied for the next T-units, since such action is chosen in probability. If the primary goal has not been satisfied, the probabilities are updated by means of a reinforcement rule such as the one in Eq. (8.2) in which $\boldsymbol{\lambda}^l$ is related to the subgoal.

Example 4. Assume that the control must be chosen from the finite set of allowable actions in Eq. (8.12), where N may be ∞. It is shown in Chapter 11, Section V that the conditional expected value of a normalized subgoal, $NSG(k)[\lambda_k(y)$ in Chapter 11], where

$$NSG(k) = \frac{SG(k)}{\sup_k[SG(k)]} \tag{8.22}$$

is minimized when the probabilities associated with the s-control choices are updated according to the following rule:

If the present control action is $u_j{}^l$, then

$$P_j{}^l(k+1) = \theta P_j{}^l(k) + (1-\theta)[1 - NSG(k)] \tag{8.23}$$

and

$$P_i{}^l(k+1) = \theta P_i{}^l(k) + \frac{(1-\theta)}{(r-1)} NSG(k) \tag{8.24}$$

where $i \neq j$, $i = 1, 2, \ldots, s$, and

$$0 < \theta < 1 \tag{8.25}$$

The notation $P_i{}^l(k+1)$ for the probability that $u^l(k+1) = u_i{}^l$ does not reflect the conditioning to $u^l(k)$. Additionally, it does not show the explicit dependance of $P_i(k+1)$ on measured system outputs, which affect $NSG(k)$. This notation is used throughout the rest chapter for convenience, and differs from the notation used in Chapter 11. There, the explicit dependence of $P^l{}_i(k+1)$ on inputs (to a stochastic automaton) is indicated parenthetically. The relationships between α_l and λ^l in Eq. (8.2) and θ and $NSG(k)$ in Eqs. (8.23) and (8.24) are obtained by comparing these equations.

Returning to our discussion of Fig. 5, probabilities are stored in memory compartments which are associated with respective control situations. These probabilities determine succeeding control actions.

We suggest that a time will be reached when one probability in each control situation will dominate the others; hence, after a sufficient amount of time, one control choice would be most likely to be applied each time the system reentered that control situation.

This reinforcement-learning control algorithm has been used by a number of investigators. It has been applied to the problem of precise attitude control for a satellite in Mars orbit (Mendel, 1967). In this application, proportional control [Eq. (8.21)] is used, and probabilities are associated with gain matrices which are constructed about a nominal gain matrix in the manner described. Control situations are formed in a plant-environment parameter space. Fu and Waltz (1965) have applied the control algorithm to the design of a time-optimal controller. Their application is quite similar to Example 1; control situations are formed in state space, and probabilities are associated with the two control choices, $+L$ and $-L$. Additionally, McLaren (1967) proposed a stochastic automaton model for the structure of a class of learning controllers using a reference model to control a stochastic plant of unknown statistics.

D. *Discussion*

A discussion of a reinforcement-learning control law has been presented. Correspondences have been established between elements of stochastic learning theory and elements of control theory. For example, it has been shown that: events are equivalent to control situations; a set of alternatives is equivalent to a set of allowable control actions; probability associated with each alternative is equivalent to probability associated with each control action; and reinforcement of probabilities associated with different alternatives is equivalent to reinforcement of probabilities associated with different control actions.

Once the associations between control-system and learning-theory concepts have been made, it is a rather straightforward task to develop a control algorithm which makes use of these associations. Providing a firm mathematical basis for these algorithms is yet another thing. Stochastic automata theory provides such a basis for a broad class of problems, and it is still being expanded to handle more situations (Chapter 11). In the not so distant future, we may expect additional support from game theory, heuristic programming, and other artifical intelligence disciplines.

IV. Reinforcement-Learning Pattern Recognition Systems

A. *Introduction*

The previous section considered the application of reinforcement learning to control systems. In this section, we will consider the application of reinforcement-learning models and concepts to a different class of systems—pattern recognition systems.

For the purpose of this section, it is convenient to view a pattern recognition system as a receptor or feature extractor and categorizer or classifier (Chapters 1 and 4). The receptor performs measurements on the input pattern and then generates a set of properties (features) for the pattern. The categorizer applies a decision scheme to the feature set of the pattern in order to estimate or recognize the pattern. From an engineering viewpoint, the basic problem of pattern recognition is to design a pattern recognition system that provides a specific upper bound on the average level of misrecognition (in general, a loss) for a given class of patterns. Often, the system is designed to minimize the average loss. This design includes selecting the decision scheme and the features.

Approaches to the design of pattern recognition systems are many and varied. Selection and manner of application of a particular recognition scheme for a particular set of pattern classes depend on (1) the nature of the patterns, and (2) the amount of a priori knowledge or assumptions concerning the patterns. The nature of the patterns determines whether the pattern recognition system is deterministic or stochastic, whether or not it interacts with its environment, and so forth. The nature of the decision scheme is determined to a certain extent by this information.

In order to obtain as high a performance level as possible, we utilize all a priori knowledge and assumptions about the input patterns in the design of the pattern recognition system. If the a priori knowledge implies that one or more of the pattern-class parameters is time-varying, then the system can be designed with adaptive properties so as to maintain acceptable performance. Such a pattern recognition system can change its own structure.

If knowledge or assumptions about the pattern classes is lacking or incomplete, a pattern recognition system with learning properties can be used to achieve long-term improvement in performance. In such systems, sufficient knowledge to improve performance is learned. This generally requires a long-term memory and a mechanism for providing iterative structural changes. Decision schemes with learning properties are usually obtained by modifying decision-schemes that have fixed structures.

Pattern recognition systems with learning properties can be classified as parametric or nonparametric, learning with or without a supervisor, and learning on-line or off-line (Chapter 1). The learning pattern recognition system must receive information concerning its performance for a given decision that is sufficient for it to adjust its parameters for the next decision; this information may be based on the system's own decision (with suitable assumptions) or on environmental feedback information.

Learning occurs when a structural change that is based upon the system's past experience effects an improvement in performance. Iterative structural changes are defined by a *learning algorithm*. Some learning algorithms are closely related to optimization procedures such as steepest descent or stochastic approximation (Chapters 7, 9, and 10); some are based on estimation techniques (Chapter 2 and Abramson *et al.*, 1963); others are based upon metric properties (Dwyer and Whitney, 1966).

The important role of learning theories and concepts in psychology has been the basis for many of the pattern-recognition learning algorithms. Many of these algorithms are closely related to psychological learning theories such as two-factor learning and mathematical models (see Section II). In the latter, reinforcement principles assume an important role.

Reinforcement-learning algorithms are useful in pattern recognition. They can be used in a predictive mode for on-line learning, or with a *noisy teacher* (a teacher that provides the system either with information which may be incorrect, or, a random performance measure) to recognize noisy patterns (McLaren, 1968). This class of algorithms generally represents a global learning method. In the application of reinforcement learning to pattern recognition, decision parameters (such as the coefficients for a set of hyperplanes) or the decisions themselves are reinforced by changing their probabilities of occurrence; hence, in reinforcement-learning pattern recognition systems, probabilities of occurrence are updated by means of reinforcement-learning algorithms. Properties of reinforcement-learning pattern recognition systems are discussed in the next paragraph.

B. *Basic Properties and Structure*

1. *Feature extraction.* A block diagram for a pattern recognition system interacting with its environment is depicted in Fig. 6. The receptor first generates a set of measurements, $\mathbf{y} = (y_1, y_2, ..., y_r)'$, from the pattern $\mathscr{S}$, and then extracts (calculates) a set of features (properties), $\mathbf{x} = (x_1, x_2, ..., x_{N'})'$, from the measurements. The features appear at the output of the receptor in either analog or digital form.

An important problem is the selection of the feature set for a given set of measurements. $\mathbf{x}$ should represent a set of important features. Another aspect of the feature-selection problem is how to choose a best subset of N'^* features from the set of N'-important features. Selection of the best features is based on which ones result in better performance. Compared to the decision problem, the feature-selection problem has not received much attention in the literature (Chapter 2; Green and Marill, 1963; Heydorn and Tou, 1967). Learning techniques, as described in this chapter, can be applied to the feature-selection problem. In applying these techniques, subsets of important features are considered to be responses, and probabilities associated with the feature subsets are updated by means of a reinforcement-learning algorithm (Section IVC).

2. *Mappings.* $\mathbf{x}$ represents a point in a N'-dimensional feature space, $\Omega_{\mathbf{x}}$. For a given $\mathbf{x}$, the decision process (Fig. 6) selects a decision, d_i, from a set of decisions, $\mathscr{D} = \{d_1, d_2, ..., d_s\}$; this may be done either

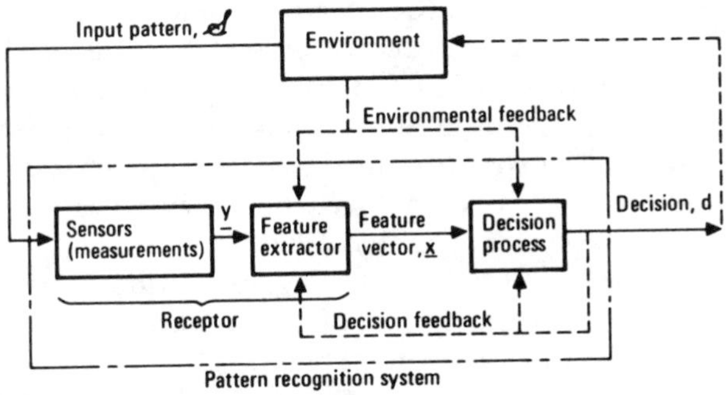

FIGURE 6. Block diagram showing different modes of interaction between a pattern recognition system and its environment (the broken lines denote the different modes; environmental feedback may include a "teacher")

by means of a fixed rule or probability distribution, $P(\mathbf{d} \mid \mathbf{x})$, defined over $\mathscr{D}$. The decision process defines a ***mapping*** from the feature space into the decision space. This mapping is usually a many–one mapping; that is, a mapping from a region, $\Omega_{\mathbf{x}}^{l}$, in $\Omega_{\mathbf{x}}$ into a single decision. The $\Omega_{\mathbf{x}}^{l}$ regions are formed by partitioning $\Omega_{\mathbf{x}}$; there is one mapping for each $\Omega_{\mathbf{x}}^{l}$ in $\Omega_{\mathbf{x}}$. It is implemented by means of discriminant functions. Selection of a specific mapping depends upon the amount of a priori information or assumptions available about the pattern classes.

Learning properties can be incorporated into decision schemes which are implemented by means of discriminant functions, by utilizing feedback information from the environment or the system's own decisions. Learning algorithms may be used to change the probability distributions assigned to the decision parameters, or they may be applied directly to the decisions assigned to each region $\Omega_{\mathbf{x}}^{l}$.

Of particular interest to us in the rest of this section is the class of pattern recognition systems which make use of reinforcement-learning concepts. For these systems, each response determines a decision for a given region of the feature space. The result (outcome) of the response (decision) occurs in the system's environment. The overall goal of the reinforcement-learning pattern recognition system is to achieve good performance; this is accomplished by positive reinforcement of those responses that lead to better performance, and suppression of the others. In order to implement this technique, some measure of system performance must be available to the system from the environment.

3. *Goals and Performance.* We have seen in Section II that learning behavior is closely related to the seeking of goals; hence, it is often appropriate to refer to learning behavior as goal-seeking behavior. Such

behavior is directed towards acquisition of some object, ideal, or set of conditions. In terms of the structure of the decision mechanism, this means that a structure is being sought that provides *best* performance for the overall system. As this best performance (e.g., smallest probability of error) is reached, the structure of the decision mechanism reaches its final (steady-state) form. The final structure may be said to represent a *stable structure* of the system (Ashby, 1960).

Learning corresponds to the mapping of a wide range of environmental conditions into a smaller set of conditions—the goal set. This is achieved through iterative structural changes of the decision mechanism. Performance measures the success or failure of this mapping; that is, the system uses a performance measure, such as a loss function, to provide it with a measure of its goal-seeking behavior and to change its structure.

Other examples of performance measures are: percentage of correct-recognition, probability of error, and entropy. Generally speaking, achieving the overall goal for the pattern recognition system is associated, by the engineer, with achieving the optimum value for a performance measure. An important design consideration is how to achieve compatibility between attaining the overall goal and optimizing a specific performance measure. The discussions in Section IIIB3 about such compatibility problems apply equally to the pattern-recognition and control-system problems; hence, our discussion of them in this section is brief.

Usually, the overall goal and performance measures provide a measure of the system's performance over a long time interval and for each of the elements in a region of the feature space, $\Omega_{\mathbf{x}}{}^{l}$. In reinforcement-learning pattern recognition systems, each successive decision is based on the short-term results of the previous decision(s). These decisions are determined by means of measures that provide an indication of the quality of the pattern recognition system's goal-seeking behavior over these short time-intervals. Such performance measures are subgoals.

The environment is often stochastic; hence, the pattern-recognition subgoal, $SG(k)$, is generally a random variable. In such cases, it is more appropriate to work with the expected value of the normalized subgoal, $NSG(k)$, and to associate goal-seeking behavior with the requirement, that either

$$E\{NSG(k+1)\} - E\{NSG(k)\} \leqslant 0 \tag{8.26}$$

or

$$E\{NSG(k+1)\} - E\{NSG(k)\} \geqslant 0 \tag{8.27}$$

for $k = 0, 1, \ldots$, depending upon the goal. In these equations the expected value is taken with respect to NSG. The primary goal, $IP(k)$, which is associated with the overall goal-seeking behavior of the system, is assumed to be that $E\{NSG(k)\}$ converges monotonically to its extremum. It is obvious, from Eqs. (8.26) or (8.27), and properties of $NSG(k)$, that the subgoal requirement is compatible with the overall-goal requirement.

In a reinforcement-learning pattern recognition system, the behavior of the probabilities associated with decisions should reflect the quest for achievement of the overall goal. This is accomplished (Section IVB5) by reinforcing these probabilities as a function of $NSG(k)$, in the manner, for example, of Eqs. (8.23) and (8.24). More specifically, the better the performance resulting from a given decision, the larger should that decision's average probability become [because the decision probabilities are a function of $NSG(k)$, they are, themselves, random variables]. If, for example, attainment of the overall goal implies a minimum $IP(k)$, then it is desirable for

$$E\{NSG(k)|\, d(k) = d_i\} \leqslant E\{NSG(k)|\, d(k) = d_j\} \tag{8.28a}$$

if and only if

$$E\{P_i(k)\} \geqslant E\{P_j(k)\} \tag{8.28b}$$

where $j = 1, 2,..., s$, and $j \neq i$ (and k is sufficiently large). In Eqs. (8.28a) and (8.28b), the expected values are with respect to NSG; $d(k)$ is the decision for $\mathbf{x} \in \Omega_{\mathbf{x}}{}^l$ at t_k (for notational convenience, the explicit dependence of the decisions on $\Omega_{\mathbf{x}}{}^l$, which was indicated in Sections II and III by superscript l, is omitted); and

$$P_j(k) = Pr\{d(k) = d_j \mid \mathbf{x} \in \Omega_{\mathbf{x}}{}^l \text{ at } t_k\} \tag{8.29}$$

where $j = 1, 2,..., s$ and $l = 1, 2,..., v$.

4. *Performance and feedback information.* It has been stated (Section IVA) that a pattern recognition system with learning properties is capable of continually improving its performance by utilizing its past experience. The experience may be obtained in various ways: from pattern or decision information without the intervention of a trainer (supervisor) [Spragins, 1966]; from a trainer (teacher, supervisor) as system parameters are adjusted during an off-line mode; or during an on-line mode from a *noisy* trainer, such as the reactions of an external environment. In a reinforcement-learning pattern recognition system, performance information is usually obtained as a result of interaction between the system and its environment. We see that, because of the closed-loop nature of this interaction (Fig. 6), performance is obtained from feedback information.

In one type of system-environment interaction, as a result of the response of the pattern recognition system, the environment provides sufficient feedback information for the system to compute its own performance. Initially, there might be a trainer to train the pattern recognition system, after which there could be a period during which the system would operate in its *natural environment* (the environment for which the system is designed to operate) and would learn by reinforcing its responses, using its own response to calculate performance.

A second type of system-environment interaction assumes the form of prediction in which successive patterns are utilized to predict the next (future) pattern (as in weather prediction, for example). In this case, feedback information is obtained from a direct comparison of the actual and predicted environmental conditions.

5. *Structural Change and Memory.* In a reinforcement-learning pattern recognition system, the nature of the system changes in the sense that decision probabilities change with the passage of time. It is these changes in probabilities that produce an improvement in the system's performance. Changing decision probabilities is, in effect, analogous to changing the *structure* of the decision mechanism.

Many other types of structural changes are possible, based upon information about the system's past performance. Performance information from training samples can be used to alter the positions of a set of decision hyperplanes. Reinforcement learning can be used to reinforce the probability distributions of the hyperplane's parameters. Similar performance information can also be used in clustering (Chapter 2), to reinforce decision probabilities that are associated with a k-nearest neighbor rule, and to update the boundaries associated with a sequential probability ratio test. We will not dwell upon these types of structural changes because in this chapter we are more interested in the former type of structural change. We are more interested in the approach in which s decisions are directly associated with a region of the feature space, and reinforcement learning (that makes use of past performance) is the basis for changing probabilities associated with these decisions. This type of structural change, motivated by psychological reinforcement-learning concepts (Section IVA), is describable by a stochastic, reinforcement-learning model.

Let us assume that, at the kth step (occurring at time t_k), the pattern is $\mathscr{S}_k$, the feature vector occurs in a region, $\Omega_{\mathbf{x}}{}^l$, of $\Omega_{\mathbf{x}}$, the response, $d(k)$, is d_i, and the outcome or performance is $NSG(k)$. The decision probabilities are defined in Eq. (8.29). Reinforcement learning can, in general, be defined by an expression of the following form:

$$P_j(k+1) = g_j[\mathbf{P}(k), d(k), NSG(k); \mathscr{P}] \tag{8.30}$$

for $j = 1, 2, \ldots, s$, where $\mathbf{P}(k) = (P_1(k), P_2(k), \ldots, P_s(k))'$ and $\mathscr{P}$ is a set of pattern-class parameters. The sequence of decisions which results from Eq. (8.30) defines a nonstationary, first-order Markov chain. By making $P_j(k+1)$ dependent upon several of the past decisions (finite memory), higher-order Markov chains can be obtained. Note that reinforcement learning can also be described by a set of response transition probabilities such as $Pr\{d(k+1) = d_i \mid d(k) = d_j\}$.

What are the desirable properties for the functions defined in Eq. (8.30)? If the outcome for decision d_i, as reflected by the normalized measured performance, $NSG(k)$, is good in some relative sense, then we want to choose the function, $g_i[\mathbf{P}(k), d(k), NSG(k); \mathscr{P}]$ in such a manner that $P_i(k+1) > P_i(k)$. On the other hand, if the outcome is bad, then we want to choose $g_i[\mathbf{P}(k), d(k), NSG(k); \mathscr{P}]$ such that $P_i(k+1) < P_i(k)$. In addition, the remaining $s - 1$ functions, $g_j[\mathbf{P}(k), d(k), NSG(k); \mathscr{P}]$ ($j = 1, 2, \ldots, s$, and $j \neq i$) must be chosen so that $\sum_{j=1}^{s} P_j(k+1) = 1$ (see Section II). The structural form chosen for these functions must be such that the better the performance resulting from a given decision, the larger the decision's average probability becomes. To accomplish this, the following conditions are imposed on g_i and g_j:

$$\partial g_i[\mathbf{P}(k), d(k), NSG(k); \mathscr{P}]/\partial NSG(k) < 0 \tag{8.31a}$$

and

$$\partial g_j[\mathbf{P}(k), d(k), NSG(k); \mathscr{P}]/\partial NSG(k) > 0 \tag{8.31b}$$

for all $j \neq i$. In addition, the structural form for the functions in Eq. (8.30) must lead to satisfaction of a requirement like the one in Eqs. (8.28a) and (8.28b). A specific structural form is described in Section IVC.

One difference between our reinforcement-learning model and the one described in Section II [Eq. (8-2)] is that, in the present model, the decision probabilities, $P_j(k)$, are random variables. Additionally, the present model need not be linear, although linear models are most frequently used.

In contrast to an adaptive system, a learning pattern recognition system requires a long-term memory to store its past experience. A separate memory compartment is associated with each region, $\Omega_{\mathbf{x}}{}^{l}$, of the feature space. Because it is impractical to store noisy patterns directly (except, perhaps, for fixed or deterministic patterns), average past experience, which appears in the form of the system's most recent structure, is stored. Hence, the s probabilities in Eq. (8.30) are stored for each $\Omega_{\mathbf{x}}{}^{l}(l = 1, 2, \ldots, v)$ in the system's memory. Structural information is retrieved from memory each time the overall system reenters $\Omega_{\mathbf{x}}{}^{l}$.

C. *A Class of Reinforcement-Learning Pattern Recognition Algorithms*

In this paragraph, our attention is focused on the decision process section of the interacting pattern recognition system depicted in Fig. 6. In relation to the decision process, the receptor may be looked upon as part of its environment; hence, in order to emphasize the decision process, Fig. 6 is redrawn as in Fig. 7. We see that the decision process is comprised of a *decision scheme* and a *learning system*. The learning system described below uses a reinforcement-learning algorithm to reinforce the parameters (or the decisions) of the decision scheme.

The learning system is comprised of two subsystems—the *evaluator* and the *learner*. The evaluator receives environmental information (e.g., the output of a comparator), $\mathbf{y}(k)$, and computes the performance measure, $SG(k)$ (e.g., a loss function), where $SG(k) \geqslant 0$. In some cases $SG(k)$ may not have to be computed because it may be available directly from the environment. The evaluator then normalizes $SG(k)$ as in Eq. (8.22); hence, the evaluator's output is $NSG(k)$.

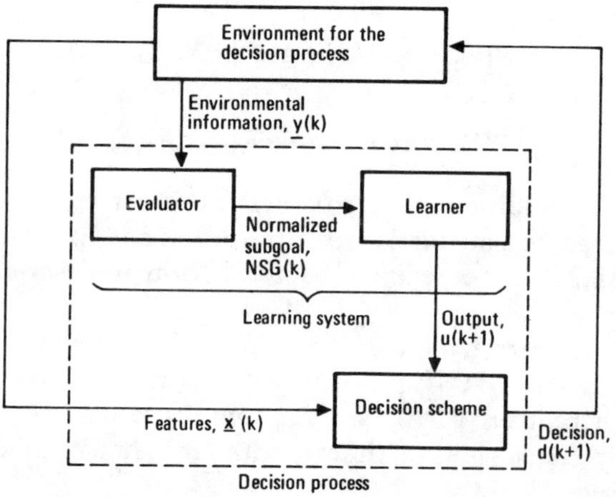

FIGURE 7. Interaction between the decision process and its environment

The learner subsystem selects an output, $u(k + 1)$, according to response probabilities $\Pi_1(k + 1)$, $\Pi_2(k + 1)$,..., and $\Pi_s(k + 1)$, which depend upon $NSG(k)$. The learner's output influences the decision made by the decision scheme, either directly or indirectly. In the latter situation, $u(k + 1)$ might determine the positions of a set of decision boundaries in $\Omega_{\mathbf{x}}$(e.g., hyperplanes [Highleyman, 1962]); whereas, in the former situation, $u(k+1)$ might correspond directly with the decision, $d(k+1)$, in which case the decision scheme serves only to implement $u(k+1)$. In the direct situation, the decision probabilities in Eq. (8.29) would be directly related (if not equal) to the response probabilities $\Pi_1(k+1), \Pi_2(k+1),\ldots,$ and $\Pi_s(k+1)$.

The overall goal of the learning system is to determine the best output, $u^*[u^* \in \mathcal{U}$, where $\mathcal{U} = \{u_1, u_2, \ldots, u_s\}]$—best in the sense that u^* optimizes an average performance measure for all $\mathbf{x} \in \Omega_{\mathbf{x}}{}^l$. It is assumed that interaction between the decision process and the environment can be described by an unknown but stationary probability density function, $P(NSG \mid u)$, for each $u \in \mathcal{U}$.

A stochastic automaton model is proposed for the structure of the learner subsystem. This model is comprised of s states, each of which corresponds to an element of the output set $\mathcal{U}$. At t_k, the learner exists in state u_j with probability $\Pi_j(k) = Pr\{u(k) = u_j\} (j = 1, 2,\ldots, s)$. At t_{k+1}, the structure of the learner changes according to the state-transition probabilities, $Pr\{u(k+1) = u_i \mid u(k) = u_j\}$, which generally depend upon both $NSG(k)$ and k. The behavior of the stochastic automaton model may be described by a sequence of stochastic matrices, $\| Pr\{u(k+1) = u_i \mid u(k) = u_j\}\|$ and $\mathbf{\Pi}_1(0) = (\Pi_1(0), \Pi_2(0),\ldots, \Pi_s(0))'$ [see Chapter 11]. The operation of the proposed automaton may also be described by a reinforcement-learning algorithm of the form in Eq. (8.30) for the output probabilities, $\Pi_j(k+1)$.

It is desirable that the learning algorithm provide the overall system with the following learning behavior: (1) $E\{NSG(k)\}$, where the expected value is with respect to $NSG(k)$, should converge to a global extremum monotonically; and (2) a criterion should exist for selecting the best output as the global extremum of $E\{NSG(k)\}$ is approached. As discussed in Fu and McLaren (1965), such behavior may be achieved by constraining the form of the algorithm in Eq. (8.30) in the following manner: the expected values of each of the $\Pi_j(k)$'s and their changes, $\Delta\Pi_j(k+1) = \Pi_j(k+1) - \Pi_j(k) (j = 1, 2,\ldots, s)$, must either increase or decrease in a monotonic fashion.

A particularly useful learning algorithm—useful for analytical studies—is the linear-reinforcement algorithm in Eqs. (8.23) and (8.24), in which $P_j{}^l(k)$ is replaced by $\Pi_j(k)$, and it is assumed that $1/s < \theta < 1$ and $\Pi_j(0) = 1/s$ for all j. Observe that as $NSG(k)$ decreases, $\Pi_j(k+1)$ increases (positive reinforcement), whereas all of the other output probabilities decrease (negative reinforcement). It can be shown (Chapter 11 and Fu and McLaren, 1965), that

$$E\{NSG(k) \mid u(k) = u_i\} \leqslant E\{NSG(k) \mid u(k) = u_j\} \tag{8.32a}$$

if, and only if

$$E\{\Pi_i(k)\} \geqslant E\{\Pi_j(k)\} \tag{8.32b}$$

where $j = 1, 2, \ldots, s$ and $j \neq i$; $E\{\Pi_j(k)\}$ converges monotonically to a value γ_j; and $E\{NSG(k)\}$ converges monotonically towards a minimum value. We see, therefore, that the best output (i.e., the output which minimizes $E\{NSG\}$) has the highest expected probability of occurring, which serves as a way for selecting u^*. $E\{\Pi_j(k)\}$ can be estimated by means of time averages (for sufficiently large k) because $E\{\Pi_j(k)\}$ becomes stationary for large k.

At $k = k'$, the learning process may be terminated by selecting the best value of u. The learning process can be accelerated by periodically discarding outputs that have low average probabilities, and continuing with the remaining smaller set of outputs.

As discussed above, the output from the learner subsystem influences the decision scheme either directly or indirectly. Indirectly, $u(k)$ can determine decision parameters such as the coefficients and thresholds of a set of hyperplanes which partition $\Omega_{\mathbf{x}}$. The recognition of English characters by means of such a technique is described in McLaren (1968).

Two different measures which may be useful in comparing the behaviors of different learning systems or in comparing the behaviors of the same system under different operating conditions, are the *learning rate* and the *step-by-step variation in performance*. Learning rate is defined as $E\{NSG(1)\} - E\{NSG(0)\}$. As shown by Fu and McLaren (1965), it decreases as either θ or s increases. A step-by-step variation in performance can be defined as the variance of the change in performance, given the response probabilities. It increases as θ increases or as environmental noise level increases. Hence, when choosing a value for θ, one trades learning rate for step-by-step performance variation, or vice versa.

An attribute of the proposed learning pattern recognition system is that its training sequence need not be known perfectly; that is to say, convergence will occur even if the teacher (environment) is a noisy one. Naturally, a noisy teacher reduces the learning rate. Other attributes of this system are its ability to function in an on-line mode, and its ability to attain a decision that is globally optimum.

D. *Discussion*

The basic properties of reinforcement-learning pattern recognition systems have been discussed. Just as for learning control systems (Section III), correspondences exist between elements of stochastic learning theory and pattern recognition systems. For example: events are equivalent to regions in feature space; a set of alternatives is equivalent to a set of outputs or decisions; probability associated with each alternative is equivalent to probability associated with each output or decision; and reinforcement of probabilities associated with different alternatives is equivalent to reinforcement of probabilities associated with different outputs or decisions.

A reinforcement-learning pattern recognition algorithm has been presented. The algorithm is based upon a class of linear stochastic automata, and provides a means for updating decision or output probabilities. It is quite similar to the algorithm depicted in Fig. 5 for a reinforcement-learning control system.

The discussions in this section have emphasized discrete, linear, pattern-recognition algorithms. We have seen that such algorithms are motivated by linear stochastic-learning models, and are easy to analyze. Although nonlinear algorithms are difficult to analyze, they should be considered because they may give greater noise immunity and may converge faster than the linear algorithms. Motivation for nonlinear pattern-recognition algorithms comes from nonlinear learning models which have been studied by psychologists (Atkinson *et al.*, 1965). In the not-so-distant future, we may expect to see not only nonlinear algorithms but also continuous-time algorithms (in which response probabilities are described by differential equations) and continuous-space algorithms (in which response probabilities are described by continuous probability density functions) [Fu and McLaren, 1965] applied to more and more important and difficult recognition problems.

References

Abramson, N., Braverman, D., and Sebestyen, G., Pattern Recognition and Machine Learning. *IEEE Trans. Info. Theory 9*, pp. 257–261 (1963).

Ashby, W. R., "Design for a Brain" (Second edition). Wiley, New York, 1960.

Athans, M. and Falb, P. L., "Optimal Control: An Introduction to the Theory and its Applications." McGraw–Hill, New York, 1966.

Atkinson, R. C., Bower, G. H., and Crothers, E. J., "An Introduction to Mathematical Learning Theory." Wiley, New York, 1965.

Bower, G. H. and Hilgard, E. R., "Theories of Learning." Appleton–Century–Crofts, New York, 1966.

Bush, R. R. and Estes, W. K. (eds.), "Studies in Mathematical Learning Theory." Stanford Univ. Press, Stanford, Calif., 1959.

Bush, R. R. and Mosteller, F., "Stochastic Models for Learning." Wiley, New York, 1955.

Cooper, G. R., Gibson, J. E., Eveleigh, V. W., Lindenlaub, J. C., Meditch, J. S., and Raible, R. H., A survey of the philosophy and state of the art of adaptive systems. Rept. No. PRF 2358, Purdue Univ., Lafayette, Ind., July 1960.

D'Azzo, J. J. and Houpis, C. H., "Feedback Control System Analysis and Synthesis" (Second edition). McGraw–Hill, New York, 1966.

Dwyer, S. J., III and Whitney, A. W., Performance and implementation of the *k*-nearest neighbor decision rule with incorrectly identified training samples. *Proc. 4th Annual Allerton Conf. Circuit and System Theory*, Univ. of Illinois, Urbana, Illinois (1966).

Eveleigh, V. W., "Adaptive Control and Optimization Techniques." McGraw–Hill, New York, 1967.

Fu, K. S., Gibson, J. E., Hill, J. D., Luisi, J. A., Raible, R. H., and Waltz, M. D., Philosophy and state of the art of learning control systems. Rept. No. TR–EE63–7, Purdue Univ., Lafayette, Ind., Nov. 1963.

Fu, K. S., Hill, J. D., and McMurtry, G. J., A computer-simulated on-line experiment in learning control systems. *Proc. Spring-Joint Comp. Conf. 25*, pp. 315–325 (1964).

Fu, K. S. and McLaren, R. W., An application of stochastic automata to the synthesis of learning systems. Rept. No. TR–EE65–17, Purdue Univ., Lafayette, Ind., Sept. 1965.

Fu, K. S. and Waltz, M. D., A heuristic approach to reinforcement-learning control systems. *IEEE Trans. Auto. Control 10*, No. 4, pp. 390–398 (1965).

Green, D. M. and Marill, T., On the effectiveness of receptors in recognition systems. *IEEE Trans. Info. Theory 9*, No. 1 (1963).

Heydorn, R. P. and Tou, J. T., Some approaches to optimum feature extraction. *In* "Computer and Information Sciences—II" (J. T. Tou, ed.), pp. 57–89. Academic Press, New York, 1967.

Highleyman, W. H., Linear decision functions with application to pattern recognition. *Proc. IRE 50*, No. 6, pp. 1501–1514 (1962).

Jones, L. E., On the choice of subgoals for learning control systems. *Proc. Natl. Electron. Conf.*, pp. 62–66 (1967).

Lee, R. C. K., "Optimal Estimation, Identification, and Control." M.I.T. Press, Cambridge, Mass., 1964.

Leondes, C. T. and Mendel, J. M., Artificial intelligence control. *In* "Survey of Cybernetics" (R. Rose, ed.). ILLIFE Press, London, England, 1969.

Luce, R. D., Bush, R. R., and Galanter, E. (eds.), "Handbook of Mathematical Psychology." Vols. I and II, Wiley, New York, 1963.

McLaren, R. W., A stochastic automaton model for a class of learning controllers. *Preprints Joint Auto. Control Conf., Philadelphia, Pa., June 1967*, pp. 267–274.

McLaren, R. W., The application of a stochastic automaton model to pattern recognition. *Proc. Hawaii Interntl. Conf. System Sciences*, Univ. of Hawaii, Honolulu, Hawaii, (1968).

Mendel, J. M., Applications of artificial intelligence techniques to a spacecraft control problem. *NASA Rept.* CR–755 (1967).

Mendel, J. M. and Zapalac, J. J., The application of techniques of artificial intelligence to control system design. *In* "Advances in Control Systems: Theory and Applications" (C. T. Leondes, ed.). Vol. 6, pp. 1–94, Academic Press, New York, 1968.

Mowrer, O. H., "Learning Theory and Behavior." Wiley, New York, 1960.

Spragins, J., Learning without a teacher. *IEEE Trans. Info. Theory 12*, No. 2, pp. 223–230 (1966).

Tou, J. T., "Modern Control Theory." McGraw–Hill, New York, 1964.

PART II PROBLEMS

Chapter 6 Problems

1. If $J(\hat{\boldsymbol{\theta}}_k) = 1/2[z(k) - y(k)]^2$, where $z(k)$ and $y(k)$ are defined in Eqs. (6.2) and (6.3), respectively, show that Eq. (6.7) can be written as

$$\hat{\boldsymbol{\theta}}_{k+1} = \hat{\boldsymbol{\theta}}_k - \frac{R(k)}{2c_k}\,\mathbf{d}_k$$

where

$$d_i(k) = J(\hat{\boldsymbol{\theta}}_k + c_k\mathbf{e}_i) - J(\hat{\boldsymbol{\theta}}_k - c_k\mathbf{e}_i)$$

and $\mathbf{e}_i (i = 1, 2, \ldots, n)$ are orthonormal unit vectors [for example: $\mathbf{e}_1 = (1, 0, 0, \ldots, 0)'$].

2. The sampled impulse response in Fig. 2 is to be identified. The input $w(k)$ is depicted below. Obtain $\hat{f}_1, \hat{f}_2$, and $\hat{f}_3$ for different values of $\hat{\mathbf{f}}_1$. Does convergence of $\hat{\mathbf{f}}_{k+1}$ to $\mathbf{f}$ occur? Explain.

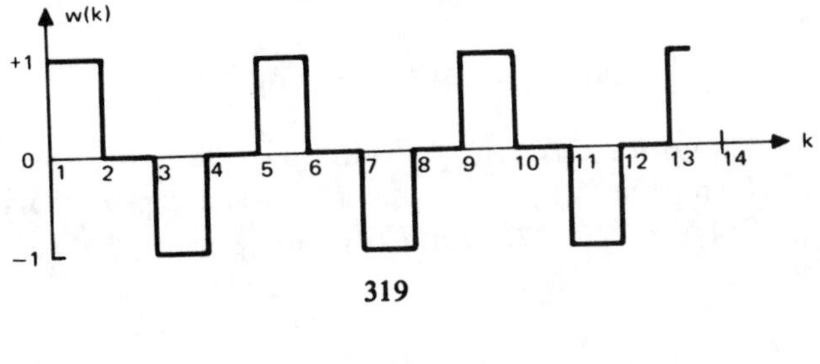

3. Let x_1, x_2,..., and x_n be independent random variables having the same symmetric distribution in time with respect to zero. Assume that $\boldsymbol{\theta}$ is estimated by Eq. (6.7) with $R(k) = I/\| \mathbf{x}_k \|^2$. Show that

$$E\{\| \mathbf{u}_{k+1} \|^2\} = \left(1 - \frac{1}{n}\right)^k E\{\| \mathbf{u}_1 \|^2\}$$

Letting

$$\bar{e}_k \triangleq \frac{\sqrt{E\{\| \mathbf{u}_k \|^2\}}}{\| \boldsymbol{\theta} \|^2}$$

show that

$$\bar{e}_k \leqslant \epsilon$$

when

$$k \geqslant 1 + \frac{2 \ln \epsilon}{\ln(1 - 1/n)}$$

4. Investigate the implications of Eq. (6.83) when $h_i(k) = \mu^{ik}$ where $i = 1, 2,\ldots,$ and n, and $0 < \mu < 1$.

5. (a) Show that $E\{\mathbf{r}_k \mathbf{r}_k' \mid \hat{\boldsymbol{\theta}}_k\} = \Omega + \Sigma_n$
(b) For the algorithm

$$\hat{\boldsymbol{\theta}}_{k+1} = \hat{\boldsymbol{\theta}}_k + R(k)\, e(k) \mathbf{r}_k$$

show

$$\lim_{k\to\infty} E\{\hat{\boldsymbol{\theta}}_k\} = (\Omega + \Sigma_n)^{-1} \Omega \boldsymbol{\theta}$$

(c) For the algorithm in Eq. (6.113), show

$$\lim_{k\to\infty} E\{\hat{\boldsymbol{\theta}}_k\} = \boldsymbol{\theta}$$

6. Outline a proof of Theorem 7.

7. (a) Show that (where the outer expectation is with respect to $\hat{\boldsymbol{\beta}}_{k|k}$)

$$EE\{e_\beta{}^*(k)\, P'(k) \mathbf{r}_k \mid \hat{\boldsymbol{\beta}}_{k|k}\} = \Phi(k) \boldsymbol{\beta}_k - [\Phi(k) + N(k)]\, E\{\hat{\boldsymbol{\beta}}_{k|k}\}$$

where

$$\Phi(k) \triangleq P'(k)\, E\{\mathbf{x}_k \mathbf{x}_k' \mid \hat{\boldsymbol{\beta}}_{k|k}\}\, P(k)$$

(b) Compute $E\{\hat{\boldsymbol{\beta}}_{k+1|k+1}$, from "$\beta - \theta$ a posteriori identifier"}
(c) Compute $E\{\hat{\boldsymbol{\beta}}_{k+1|k+1}$, from "mixed a posteriori identifier"}
(d) Solve Eq. (6.122) for $\Gamma(k)$ and $\boldsymbol{\nu}_k$.

Chapter 7 Problems

1. Find the minimum of

$$I(y) = 3 + 5y + 2y^2$$

in the interval $-2 \leqslant y \leqslant 2$ with all trials spaced at least 0.05 units apart. Restrict the search to K trials, where $K = 4, 6, 8, 10$.

   (a) What is the final interval of uncertainty for each K?
   (b) What is the lowest value of I found for each K?

2. Find the minimum of

$$I(\mathbf{y}) = \exp(y_1^2 + 4y_2^2 + 9y_3^2)$$

starting the search at (3, 3, 3). Use

   (a) steepest descent method with arbitrary initial c_k and adjust c_k according to Eq. (7.30) with $\beta = 0.2$ and $\alpha = 0.5$.
   (b) unidirectional method of steepest descent
   (c) univariate method

3. Given the two-dimensional surface

$$I(\mathbf{y}) = y_1^2 + 10y_2^2$$

Starting the search at (10, 10), use the steepest descent method with $c_k = 0.25, 0.5, 0.75, 1.0$ to find the minimum. Next let

$$\nabla I_k = \begin{bmatrix} 1 & 0 \\ 0 & 100 \end{bmatrix} \nabla I(\mathbf{y}_k) = U \nabla I(\mathbf{y}_k)$$

and change Eq. (7.24) to

$$\mathbf{y}_{k+1} = \mathbf{y}_k - c_k \nabla I_k$$

and repeat the search using the same values of c_k as above. Compare the two sets of results and observe the effect of the scale change introduced by the matrix, U.

4. (a) Using the definition of Eq. (7.65), derive the expression for the search loss, L_g, given in Eq. (7.68) for the *IP* of Eq. (7.64).
   (b) Evaluate L_g for $\eta = 1$ and $\eta = 2$. Interpret the results from a physical viewpoint.

*5. Derive the search loss, L_g, from Eq. (7.65) for the gradient technique using a fixed step size, s, when only one test perturbation is required for the gradient evaluation as outlined in Narendra and Baker (1968). Then compare this new L_g with L_r in Eq. (7.67). Plot a boundary line on the η^{-1} (0-20) vs. n(0-100) plane which shows the locus of $L_r = L_g$.

*6. Compare ASSRS and FSSRS experimentally on the IP of Eq. (7.64). Use several values of s and plot the results as the average number of steps versus dimension (n). Start all searches at $\mathbf{y} = (1,..., 1)'$ and stop each search when $I(\mathbf{y}) \leqslant 10^{-8}$.

*7. Given the Rosenbrock function

$$I(\mathbf{y}) = 100(y_2 - y_1^2)^2 + (1 - y_1)^2$$

Start a search for the minimum of this function at (−1.2, 1.0) and use the Fletcher–Powell, conjugate gradient, and the steepest descent methods. Compare the results and plot the search trajectories on the contours of this function.

*8. Given

$$I(\mathbf{y}) = I(y) = a_1 + \sum_{i=2}^{m} \left[a_i \cos \frac{(i-1)\,\pi y}{100} + b_i \sin \frac{(i-1)\,\pi y}{100}\right]$$

Let $a_1 = 50$ for $m = 8$ and generate three different $I(y)$ at random by generating three sets of random numbers (a_i, b_i) from a uniform distribution, $-10 \leqslant a_i, b_i \leqslant 10$. Let the admissible region be $0 \leqslant y \leqslant 100$ and quantize this region into ten equal levels, L_j.

(a) As a designer, you assume that $K_1 = e/b = 0.1$, $K_2 = I_1/I_0 = 1.10$ (i.e., a ten percent error in I_0 could result in a unimodal search), and $K = W/W_{max} = 5.0$. From McMurtry and Fu (1966) you select $\gamma = 18$ and conduct a search by the variable structure methods on each of the three $I(y)$.

(b) Plot $I(y)$ vs. y for each case and determine the actual K_1, K_2 and K.

(c) Compare the assumed K_1, K_2 and K with the actual values, and analyze the search results including the choice of γ.

9. Extend the variable structure method to multidimensions by assuming each component of $\mathbf{y}$ has an admissible region, $0 \leqslant y_i \leqslant Y_i$. Divide each Y_i into Δ_i levels as in Eq. (7.95) and devise a method for defining a scalar index to represent each quantized cell.

---

* Solution requires use of a digital computer.

Chapter 8 Problems

1. In the simplest learning experiment there is only one event with two alternatives: A_1 and A_2.

   (a) Denoting Pr (A_1) and Pr (A_2) as p and q, respectively, and the event operator, T, as

$$T = \begin{pmatrix} \mu_{11} & \mu_{12} \\ \mu_{21} & \mu_{22} \end{pmatrix}$$

show that

$$T\mathbf{P} = \begin{pmatrix} (1-b)p + aq \\ bp + (1-a)q \end{pmatrix}$$

where $\mathbf{P} = (p, q)'$, $a = \mu_{12}$, and $b = \mu_{21}$.

   (b) For convenience, $T\mathbf{P}$ can be written as

$$T\mathbf{P} = (\Gamma p, \tilde{\Gamma} q)'$$

where Γp, written in *fixed-point form*, is

$$\Gamma p = \alpha p + (1 - \alpha)\lambda.$$

Relate α and λ to a and b. Explain why the form for Γp is called fixed-point form.

   (c) Prove that λ is the fixed point of the operator, Γ, as well as its limit point.

2. Trace the historical development of control systems from open-loop to learning-control systems.

3. For the first-order system

$$\dot{x}(t) = -ax(t) + bu(t)$$

derive Eqs. (8.14)–(8.17) by means of calculus and the method of Lagrange multipliers. Obtain values for the control gains when $a = 5$, $b = 2$, and $N = 4$.

4. What are some difficulties associated with choosing $G(k)$ in Eq. (8.20)? How might they be resolved (see Jones, 1967)?

5. Due to large initial errors, it is sometimes useful to weight more recent observations more heavily than older observations. We define the *average subgoal*, $ASG(k)$, as

$$ASG(k+1) = \gamma ASG(k) + (1-\gamma)\, SG(k+1) \qquad (8.5.1)$$

for $k = 0, 1, \ldots,$ where

$$ASG(0) = SG(0) \tag{8.5.2}$$

For what values of γ are past values of the subgoal weighted less heavily than newer values? By what factor is $SG(k_1)/SG(k_1 + j)$ weighted (j is an arbitrary positive integer)? For what value of γ does the *linear reinforcement average* in Eq. (8.5.1) reduce to the *standard average*

$$\frac{1}{(k+1)} \sum_{i=0}^{k} SG(i)?$$

6. Sketch $ASG(k)$ [Problem 5] versus k and ζ for the first-order system

$$\dot{x}(t) = -ax(t) + bu(t)$$

$$u(t) = Kx(t)$$

when

$$\zeta = a - bK, \qquad SG(i) = \int_i^{i+1} x^2(t)\, dt,$$

and

$$ASG(k) = \frac{1}{(k+1)} \sum_{i=0}^{k} SG(i).$$

7. (Project) For the system and average subgoal in Problem 6, formulate a reinforcement-learning control law which begins with a nominal gain, K_n, for a nominal $a - b$ combination. Assume that $-2 \leqslant a \leqslant 7$ and $4 \leqslant b \leqslant 16$. If a digital computer is available, simulate the overall system and investigate convergence properties of the reinforcement-learning algorithm.

8. In a reinforcement-learning pattern recognition system, feature space is partitioned into disjoint regions, $\Omega_{\mathbf{x}}^l (l = 1, 2, \ldots, v)$. There is a set of decisions, $\mathscr{D} = \{d_1, d_2, \ldots, d_s\}$, associated with each region. Define a reinforcement scheme as follows:

    (a) If feature vector $\mathbf{x} \in \Omega_{\mathbf{x}}^l$ at step k, then apply the algorithm in Eqs. (8.23)–(8.25) to the decision probabilities for that region.

    (b) If feature vector $\mathbf{x} \notin \Omega_{\mathbf{x}}^l$ at step k, then let the decision probabilities for that region remain unchanged.

Letting $p_i^* = \Pr\{\mathbf{x} \in \Omega_{\mathbf{x}}^l\}$ use the results presented in Section IVC to show that the expected performance, $E\{NSG(k)\}$, converges monotonically toward a minimum value.

9. For the pattern recognition system described in the preceding problem, let $\mathbf{x} \in \Omega_{\mathbf{x}}^l$ at step k, and let the expected decision probabilities for $\Omega_{\mathbf{x}}^l$ be $E\{\Pi_1(k)\}$, $E\{\Pi_2(k)\}, \ldots,$ and $E\{\Pi_s(k)\}$, and, in addition, for some j let $P_j = \sup_i [E\{\Pi_i(k)\}]$. Show that making decision d_j will give an expected performance that is at least as good as that resulting from using a random decision rule that is defined by the decision probabilities $\Pi_1(k), \Pi_2(k), \ldots,$ and $\Pi_s(k)$.

PART III

SPECIAL TOPICS

9

R. L. Kashyap
C. C. Blaydon
K. S. Fu

STOCHASTIC APPROXIMATION

I. Introduction

The goal of many adaptive or learning systems is to find or "learn" the value of certain parameters which minimize a certain criterion function. If the criterion function is known precisely, the point of minimum can be found by any one of the standard numerical techniques. In many problems, the criterion function is not known explicitly. Even in such cases, we can determine the minimum of the function recursively by the steepest descent method if we are in a position to observe the *exact* value of the function for any given setting of the parameters by means of a suitable experiment. But in almost all experiments, the results are observed only after they have been corrupted by measurement noise. In such circumstances, the stochastic analogs of the steepest descent method may have to be used to obtain the minimum of the function. These analogs are the stochastic approximation methods.

In our discussion, we would like to minimize a deterministic function $J(\boldsymbol{\theta})$ where $\boldsymbol{\theta}$ is the parameter under our control. The function $J(\boldsymbol{\theta})$ is completely unknown; however, for every $\boldsymbol{\theta}$, we can observe a random variable $z(\boldsymbol{\theta})$ by performing a suitable experiment so that $E[z(\boldsymbol{\theta})|\,\boldsymbol{\theta}] = J(\boldsymbol{\theta})$. Sometimes, we may even be able to observe $\mathbf{y}(\boldsymbol{\theta})$, a noisy value of the gradient function where $\mathbf{y}(\boldsymbol{\theta})$ obeys the relation $E(\mathbf{y} \mid \boldsymbol{\theta}) = \boldsymbol{\nabla}_{\boldsymbol{\theta}} J(\boldsymbol{\theta})$. We have to devise a computing scheme to determine $\boldsymbol{\theta}^o$, the value of $\boldsymbol{\theta}$ which minimizes $J(\boldsymbol{\theta})$ based on the observed values of $z(\boldsymbol{\theta})$ or $\mathbf{y}(\boldsymbol{\theta})$. Since every experiment has a cost associated with it, it is important that our method should give a satisfactory result with as few observations as possible, by processing them in an optimal fashion. Moreover, if we make the scheme recursive so that it alternately involves the experimental evaluation of $z(\boldsymbol{\theta}_k)$ or $\mathbf{y}(\boldsymbol{\theta}_k)$ for a given value of $\boldsymbol{\theta}_k$ (the current estimate of $\boldsymbol{\theta}^0$ at the kth stage), and the updating of the estimate $\boldsymbol{\theta}_k$ on the basis of the additional information; then we can think of the scheme as possessing "learning" properties, since at each stage it gives an estimate of $\boldsymbol{\theta}^o$ which is superior to the one at the previous stage, and yields the true value $\boldsymbol{\theta}^o$ in the event of carrying on the computation for an infinite length of time.

To clarify the roles of $J(\boldsymbol{\theta})$, $z(\boldsymbol{\theta})$ and $\mathbf{y}(\boldsymbol{\theta})$, let us consider the following example in pattern classification. A random pattern $\mathbf{x}$ can be from one of two possible classes, ω_1 and ω_2. For every $\mathbf{x}$, define the class indicator variable $d(\mathbf{x})$ as follows:

$$\begin{aligned} d(\mathbf{x}) &= 1 \qquad \text{if} \quad \mathbf{x} \sim \omega_1 \\ &= 0 \qquad \text{if} \quad \mathbf{x} \sim \omega_2 \end{aligned}$$

For classifying any given pattern with unknown class, we need a decision rule. The decision rule which minimizes the probability of misclassification is given below in terms of the probability function $p(d(\mathbf{x}) = 1 \mid \mathbf{x})$:

$$\text{classify } \mathbf{x} \text{ in class } \omega_1 \text{ if } p(d(\mathbf{x}) = 1 \mid \mathbf{x}) > 0.5$$

$$\text{classify } \mathbf{x} \text{ in class } \omega_2 \text{ if } p(d(\mathbf{x}) = 0 \mid \mathbf{x}) < 0.5$$

Since we do not know the probability function $p(d(\mathbf{x}) = 1 \mid \mathbf{x})$, we might be willing to settle for an approximation $\boldsymbol{\theta}'\mathbf{x}$ for this function. The corresponding decision scheme is given below:

$$\text{classify } \mathbf{x} \text{ in class} \quad \begin{cases} \omega_1 \text{ if } \boldsymbol{\theta}'\mathbf{x} > 0.5 \\ \omega_2 \text{ if } \boldsymbol{\theta}'\mathbf{x} < 0.5 \end{cases}$$

where we want to choose the value of $\boldsymbol{\theta}$ to minimize the criterion $J_1(\boldsymbol{\theta})$

$$\begin{aligned} J_1(\boldsymbol{\theta}) &= E\{\boldsymbol{\theta}'\mathbf{x} - p(d(\mathbf{x}) = 1 \mid \mathbf{x})\}^2 \\ &= E\{\boldsymbol{\theta}'\mathbf{x} - E\{d(\mathbf{x}) \mid \mathbf{x}\}\}^2 \\ &= E\{\boldsymbol{\theta}'\mathbf{x} - d(\mathbf{x})\}^2 + E\{d(\mathbf{x}) - E\{d(\mathbf{x}) \mid \mathbf{x}\}\}^2 \end{aligned}$$

Let

$$J_2(\boldsymbol{\theta}) = E\{\boldsymbol{\theta}'\mathbf{x} - d(\mathbf{x})\}^2$$

Clearly, we may minimize $J_2(\boldsymbol{\theta})$ instead of $J_1(\boldsymbol{\theta})$. But $J_2(\boldsymbol{\theta})$ is not known to us explicitly. However, for any given value $\boldsymbol{\theta}$, we can evaluate the random variable $z(\boldsymbol{\theta})$ by observing a random pattern $\mathbf{x}$ with known classification $d(\mathbf{x})$

$$z(\boldsymbol{\theta}) = (\boldsymbol{\theta}'\mathbf{x} - d(\mathbf{x}))^2$$

$$E\{z(\boldsymbol{\theta}) \mid \boldsymbol{\theta}\} = J_2(\boldsymbol{\theta})$$

In this particular instance, we can observe, in addition, the noisy gradient value $\mathbf{y}(\boldsymbol{\theta})$,

$$\mathbf{y}(\boldsymbol{\theta}) = 2(\boldsymbol{\theta}'\mathbf{x} - d(\mathbf{x}))\mathbf{x} \qquad E\{\mathbf{y}(\boldsymbol{\theta}) \mid \boldsymbol{\theta}\} = \nabla_{\boldsymbol{\theta}} J_2(\boldsymbol{\theta})$$

If a sequence of pattern vectors $\{\mathbf{x}_1, \mathbf{x}_2, \ldots\}$ and their respective classifications $(d(\mathbf{x}_1), d(\mathbf{x}_2), \ldots)$ are available, then samples of $z(\boldsymbol{\theta})$ and $\mathbf{y}(\boldsymbol{\theta})$ are

$$z(\boldsymbol{\theta}) : \{(\boldsymbol{\theta}'\mathbf{x}_1 - d(\mathbf{x}_1))^2, (\boldsymbol{\theta}'\mathbf{x}_2 - d(\mathbf{x}_2))^2, \ldots\}$$

$$\mathbf{y}(\boldsymbol{\theta}) : \{2(\boldsymbol{\theta}'\mathbf{x}_1 - d(\mathbf{x}_1))\mathbf{x}_1, 2(\boldsymbol{\theta}'\mathbf{x}_2 - d(\mathbf{x}_2))\,\mathbf{x}_2, \ldots\}$$

Using the noisy gradient values, $\mathbf{y}(\boldsymbol{\theta})$, the gradient scheme for locating the minimum of $J_2(\boldsymbol{\theta})$ can be written as follows,

$$\begin{aligned}\boldsymbol{\theta}_{k+1} &= \boldsymbol{\theta}_k - \rho_k \mathbf{y}(\boldsymbol{\theta}_k) \\ &= \boldsymbol{\theta}_k - \rho_k(\boldsymbol{\theta}_k'\mathbf{x}_k - d(\mathbf{x}_k))\mathbf{x}_k\end{aligned}$$

where $\{\rho_k\}$ is a suitable scalar gain sequence. Based on the nature of the observations $\mathbf{y}(\boldsymbol{\theta})$ and $z(\boldsymbol{\theta})$ we divide the problems into three categories:

(i) For every $\boldsymbol{\theta}$, the samples of random variable $z(\boldsymbol{\theta})$ and $\mathbf{y}(\boldsymbol{\theta}) = \nabla_{\boldsymbol{\theta}} z(\boldsymbol{\theta})$ are available.

(ii) For every $\boldsymbol{\theta}$, the samples of $\mathbf{y}(\boldsymbol{\theta})$ are not directly observable. However, we can observe a related random variable $\bar{\mathbf{y}}(\boldsymbol{\theta})$ so that $\| E\{\bar{\mathbf{y}}(\boldsymbol{\theta})\} - E\{\mathbf{y}(\boldsymbol{\theta})\}\|$ goes to zero asymptotically.

(iii) For every $\boldsymbol{\theta}$, we can observe only samples of $z(\boldsymbol{\theta})$.

In this chapter, we will discuss stochastic approximation methods for minimizing $J(\boldsymbol{\theta}) = E\{z(\boldsymbol{\theta}) \mid \boldsymbol{\theta}\}$ for the three cases described above. Each case will be illustrated with a particular learning system. There are several surveys of stochastic approximation methods that give convergence conditions in all of their generality (Schmetterer 1961; Loginov

1966). In our discussion, we will only emphasize those sets of conditions which are easily verified in real situations. In addition to the review of stochastic approximation for minimizing functions, we will also discuss its application to recovering functions from noisy measurements of their values, and, describe the relationship of stochastic approximation to other techniques such as the potential function method.

II. Algorithms for Finding Zeroes of Functions

In some cases, the learning scheme can find the minimum of $J(\boldsymbol{\theta}) = E\{z(\boldsymbol{\theta})|\,\boldsymbol{\theta}\}$ by finding the zero of $\nabla_{\boldsymbol{\theta}} J(\boldsymbol{\theta})$. The problem treated in this section is the solution of Eq. (9.1) where $\mathbf{y}(\boldsymbol{\theta})$ is a random vector and $\mathbf{r}(\boldsymbol{\theta})$ is an *unknown function*

$$\nabla_{\boldsymbol{\theta}} J(\boldsymbol{\theta}) \triangleq \mathbf{r}(\boldsymbol{\theta}) \triangleq E\{\mathbf{y}(\boldsymbol{\theta})|\,\boldsymbol{\theta}\} = \mathbf{0} \tag{9.1}$$

Our first assumption is (A1).

(A1): For every $\boldsymbol{\theta}$, a random vector $\mathbf{y}(\boldsymbol{\theta})$ is observable where $\mathbf{r}(\boldsymbol{\theta}) \triangleq E\{\mathbf{y}(\boldsymbol{\theta})|\,\boldsymbol{\theta}\}$ has a unique zero at the value $\boldsymbol{\theta} = \boldsymbol{\theta}^o$ and $\boldsymbol{\theta}^o$ lies in the region given below

$$\theta_i^{(1)} \leqslant \theta_i^o \leqslant \theta_i^{(2)} \qquad i = 1,\dots n$$

If $\mathbf{r}(\boldsymbol{\theta})$ were known, the gradient scheme for finding the zero of $\mathbf{r}(\boldsymbol{\theta})$ would be:

$$\boldsymbol{\theta}_{k+1} = \boldsymbol{\theta}_k - \rho\mathbf{r}(\boldsymbol{\theta}_k) \tag{9.2}$$

Since $\mathbf{r}(\boldsymbol{\theta})$ is unknown, we replace $\mathbf{r}(\boldsymbol{\theta}_k)$ in Eq. (9.2) by the random variable $\mathbf{y}(\boldsymbol{\theta})$, using Eq. (9.1)

$$\boldsymbol{\theta}_{k+1} = \boldsymbol{\theta}_k - \rho_k\mathbf{y}(\boldsymbol{\theta}_k) \tag{9.3}$$

Instead of the fixed gain ρ in Eq. (9.2), we use the variable gain sequence ρ_k in Eq. (9.3) to compensate for the "error" involved in replacing the deterministic function $\mathbf{r}(\boldsymbol{\theta})$ by the random function $\mathbf{y}(\boldsymbol{\theta})$. The gain ρ_k in the algorithm must be chosen as in Eq. (9.4), where $\Sigma\rho_k^2 < \infty$ ensures that the sum of the squares of the correction terms in Eq. (9.3) is finite, but $\Sigma\rho_k = \infty$ assures that the sum of corrections terms may be infinite

$$\rho_k \geqslant 0, \qquad \sum_k \rho_k = \infty \qquad \sum_k \rho_k^2 < \infty \tag{9.4}$$

To make sure that the corrections applied in Eq. (9.3) drive $\boldsymbol{\theta}_k$ in the right direction on the average, culminating in the zero of $\mathbf{r}(\boldsymbol{\theta})$, we need the following assumption (A2), which says that $\mathbf{r}(\boldsymbol{\theta})$ behaves like a linear function for values of $\boldsymbol{\theta}$ near $\boldsymbol{\theta}^o$.

$$\text{(A2):} \qquad \operatorname*{Inf.}_{\epsilon < \|\boldsymbol{\theta} - \boldsymbol{\theta}^o\| < \epsilon^{-1}} [(\boldsymbol{\theta} - \boldsymbol{\theta}^o)' \, \mathbf{r}(\boldsymbol{\theta})] > 0 \qquad \forall \epsilon > 0$$

A further assumption (A3) on $\mathbf{y}(\boldsymbol{\theta})$ is necessary.

$$\text{(A3):} \qquad E\{\| \mathbf{y}(\boldsymbol{\theta})\|^2\} \leqslant h(1 + \| \boldsymbol{\theta} - \boldsymbol{\theta}^o \|^2) \qquad h > 0$$

The assumption (A3) assures that the variance of $\mathbf{y}(\boldsymbol{\theta})$ is bounded and that $\| \mathbf{y}(\boldsymbol{\theta})\|^2$ is bounded above by a quadratic function for all $\boldsymbol{\theta}$.

If all three assumptions are satisfied, then the algorithm in Eq. (9.3) with the gain as in Eq. (9.4) converges to the unique value $\boldsymbol{\theta}^o$ which makes $\mathbf{r}(\boldsymbol{\theta})$ zero in mean square and with probability one. In other words

$$\operatorname*{Lim}_{k \to \infty} E\{\| \boldsymbol{\theta}_k - \boldsymbol{\theta}^o \|^2\} = 0$$

and

$$\text{Prob.}\{\operatorname*{Lim}_{k \to \infty} \boldsymbol{\theta}_k = \boldsymbol{\theta}^o\} = 1$$

The proof of such convergence is given in Appendix 1; it is based on the proof of Theorem 1 of Gladyshev (1965).

It is important to note that we do not need the successive samples $\mathbf{y}(\boldsymbol{\theta}_1), \mathbf{y}(\boldsymbol{\theta}_2), \ldots$ to be independent of one another. The only restrictive assumption that has been made is (A3) and that can be relaxed. If this assumption is relaxed, an additional assumption about the independence of the samples must be made. In this case, replace (A3) with (A3)′ and (A4).

$$\text{(A3)}': \qquad E\{\| \boldsymbol{\eta}_k \|^2\} < k_1 \qquad \forall k > k_2 > 0$$

where $\boldsymbol{\eta}_k \triangleq \mathbf{y}(\boldsymbol{\theta}_k) - \mathbf{r}(\boldsymbol{\theta}_k)$

(A4): The random variables $\boldsymbol{\eta}_1, \boldsymbol{\eta}_2, \ldots$ are independent of one another.

Again, with the assumptions (A1), (A2), (A3)′ and (A4) the algorithm in Eq. (9.3) converges in mean square and with probability one to the unique zero of $\mathbf{r}(\boldsymbol{\theta})$. The convergence proof follows that of Theorem 3 of Venter (1966).

Finally, there is occasionally the case where the random variable $\mathbf{y}(\boldsymbol{\theta})$ cannot be directly observed. Even then, we can develop a scheme to locate the zero provided a random variable $\bar{\mathbf{y}}(\boldsymbol{\theta})$ can be observed, where

$$\bar{\mathbf{y}}(\boldsymbol{\theta}_k) = \mathbf{y}(\boldsymbol{\theta}_k) + \boldsymbol{\eta}_k$$

Here the random sequence $\{\eta_k\}$ is a "noise" masking the observation of $\mathbf{y}(\boldsymbol{\theta})$. The algorithm in Eq. (9.3) now has to use the observable $\bar{\mathbf{y}}(\boldsymbol{\theta})$ and becomes

$$\boldsymbol{\theta}_{k+1} = \boldsymbol{\theta}_k - \rho_k \bar{\mathbf{y}}(\boldsymbol{\theta}_k) \tag{9.3$'$}$$

Since the biases in the "noise" η_k could cause this algorithm to converge to values other than $\mathbf{0}^o$, some restrictions must be placed on η_k. Either of the following restrictions (A1)′ or (A1)″ will serve. They are

(A1)′: $$\lim_{k\to\infty} \| E\{\eta_k \mid \eta_{k-1}, \eta_{k-2}, ..., \eta_1\}\| = 0$$

or

(A1)″: $$\lim_{k\to\infty} E\{\| E\{\eta_k \mid \eta_{k-1}, \eta_{k-2}, ..., \eta_1\}\|^2\} = 0$$

Under the new assumptions (A1)′, (A2) and (A3)′, the algorithm in Eq. (9.3)′ with gains in Eq. (9.4), converges to the unique zero $\boldsymbol{\theta}^o$ of $\mathbf{r}(\boldsymbol{\theta})$ with probability one. If assumption (A1)′ is replaced by the stronger assumption (A1)″, then the algorithm/in Eq. (9.3)′ with gains in Eq. (9.4) converges both in mean square and with probability one. For a proof, see Venter (1966).

It is interesting to note that the condition $E\{\eta_k\} = \mathbf{0}$ is not sufficient to satisfy either assumption (A1)′ or (A1)″. However, the condition that $E\{\eta_k\} = \mathbf{0}$ and the additional condition that the sequence $\{\eta_k\}$ be independent is sufficient (but not necessary) to satisfy (A1)′ and (A1)″. This means that conditions (A1) and (A3)′ are special cases of (A1)′ and (A1)″.

III. Kiefer–Wolfowitz Schemes

In the previous section, we were interested in finding the extremum of the function $J(\boldsymbol{\theta}) = E(z(\boldsymbol{\theta})| \boldsymbol{\theta})$ based only on the observed samples of $\mathbf{y}(\boldsymbol{\theta}) = \nabla_{\boldsymbol{\theta}} z(\boldsymbol{\theta})$. In this section, we will determine methods for finding the extremum of $J(\boldsymbol{\theta})$ using only samples of the random variable $z(\boldsymbol{\theta})$. Such methods are called Kiefer–Wolfowitz (KW) algorithms.

The KW schemes use the estimates of the stochastic gradient $(\nabla_{\boldsymbol{\theta}} z(\boldsymbol{\theta}))$ computed from neighboring values of the function. To compute the stochastic gradient at a value $\boldsymbol{\theta}_k$, we need to observe $2n$ random samples of $z(\boldsymbol{\theta})$ which are $z(\boldsymbol{\theta}_k \pm c_k \mathbf{e}_j)$, $j = 1, ..., n$: where n is the dimension of $\boldsymbol{\theta}$; $c_1, c_2, ...$ is a suitably chosen positive sequence; and $\mathbf{e}_1, \mathbf{e}_2, ..., \mathbf{e}_n$ are the n-dimensional unit vectors,

$$\mathbf{e}_1' = (1, 0, ..., 0) \qquad \mathbf{e}_2' = (0, 1, 0, ..., 0) \cdots \mathbf{e}_n' = (0, 0, ..., 0, 1)$$

Thus,

$$\hat{\nabla}_{\theta} z(\theta_k) = \sum_{j=1}^{n} \mathbf{e}_j \frac{1}{2c_k} [z(\theta_k + c_k \mathbf{e}_j) - z(\theta_k - c_k \mathbf{e}_j)] \tag{9.5}$$

Using the estimate of the gradient, the computing scheme can be written as follows:

$$\theta_{k+1} = \theta_k - \rho_k \hat{\nabla}_{\theta} z(\theta_k) \tag{9.6}$$

The gains ρ_k and c_k decay to zero in the following manner:

$$\left.\begin{array}{l} \Sigma\rho_k = \infty \qquad \Sigma\rho_k c_k < \infty \qquad \Sigma\left(\dfrac{\rho_k}{c_k}\right)^2 < \infty \\ \rho_k < d_1 c_k^2 \qquad 0 < d_1 < \infty \end{array}\right\} \tag{9.7}$$

The condition $\Sigma(\rho_k/c_k)^2 < \infty$, as before, is imposed to ensure that the sum of the squares of the correction terms is finite. Moreover, if we expand the gradient $\nabla_{\theta} z(\theta)$ in Eq. (9.5) in a Taylor series about θ_k and retain only the first two terms, then the condition $\Sigma\rho_k c_k < \infty$ insures that the contributions of the second-order derivatives are finite.

The assumptions for the convergence given in the original pioneering paper by Kiefer–Wolfowitz (1952) are highly restrictive, especially the following condition of linear unimodality:

$$(\theta - \theta^o)' \frac{dJ}{d\theta} > 0 \qquad \forall \theta \tag{9.8}$$

We will give the assumptions used by Venter (1967b) in his proof of KW schemes:

(B1): $J(\theta)$ and its second-order derivatives are bounded over R^n.

(B2): θ^o is a local minimum of $J(\theta)$; i.e., for some $\epsilon > 0$, we have $J(\theta^o) \leqslant J(\theta)$ for all $\theta \neq \theta^o$ in the set $\{\theta : \| \theta - \theta^o \| < \epsilon\}$.

(B3): For every $\theta \in R^n$, $\nabla_{\theta} J(\theta) \neq \mathbf{0}$ if $\theta \neq \theta^o$; that is, θ^o is the only stationary point of $J(\theta)$.

(B4): $E[(\eta(\theta))^2] < \infty \; \forall \theta \in R^n$ where $J(\theta)$ has been redefined as

$$z(\theta) = J(\theta) + \eta(\theta) \qquad E\{\eta(\theta)\} = 0$$

If these conditions are met, then the algorithm in Eq. (9.6) with gains as in Eq. (9.7) converges with probability one to either θ^o or to infinity by Venter's theorem. There is no possibility of oscillation of infinite duration for θ_k.

The assumptions (B1) through (B3) are required for convergence even of the deterministic gradient algorithm in which $J(\boldsymbol{\theta})$ is explicitly known. The only auxiliary condition required for convergence of the stochastic algorithm is the assumption (B4) about the finiteness of the variance of the noise. The four assumptions assure the convergence of algorithm in Eq. (9.6) to the minimum of $J(\boldsymbol{\theta})$ or to $\pm\infty$.

Further, when $\boldsymbol{\theta}$ is scalar, we can show that $\| \boldsymbol{\theta}_k \| < \infty$ and thus prove convergence to the local minimum of $J(\boldsymbol{\theta})$ with probability one. If we want to rule out the possibility of $\| \boldsymbol{\theta}_k \| \to \infty$ when the dimension of $\boldsymbol{\theta}$ is greater than one, then we have to impose **one** of the following conditions (B5), (B5)′, or (B5)″.

(B5):
$$\lim_{t\to\infty} \inf_{\|\boldsymbol{\theta}-\boldsymbol{\theta}^o\|>t} \{\| \nabla_{\boldsymbol{\theta}} J(\boldsymbol{\theta})\|\} > 0$$

(B5) is not satisfied by such a simple function as $J(\boldsymbol{\theta}) = \{-\| \boldsymbol{\theta} - \boldsymbol{\theta}^o \|^2\}$. In such cases, we use condition (B5)′.

(B5)′: For some $t > 0$, $(\boldsymbol{\theta} - \boldsymbol{\theta}^o)' \nabla_{\boldsymbol{\theta}} J(\boldsymbol{\theta}) \leqslant 0$ for all $\boldsymbol{\theta}$ such that $\| \boldsymbol{\theta} - \boldsymbol{\theta}^o \| > t$

In many problems, the condition (B5) can be replaced by a weaker condition (B5)″.

(B5)″:
$$\lim_{t\to\infty} \inf_{\|\boldsymbol{\theta}-\boldsymbol{\theta}^o\|>t} \{\| \boldsymbol{\theta} - \boldsymbol{\theta}^o \| \, \| \nabla_{\boldsymbol{\theta}} J(\boldsymbol{\theta})\|\} > 0$$

Note that the condition (B5)′ is stronger than (B5)″.

Finally, we will comment briefly on the choice of the gains ρ_k and c_k. The usual choice is given below

$$\rho_k = \frac{\rho_1}{k} \qquad c_k = \frac{c_1}{k^\gamma} \qquad 0 < \gamma < 1/2 \qquad \rho_1, c_1 > 0$$

IV. Recovery of Functions from Noisy Measurements

In the previous two sections, we discussed the problem of finding the extremum of an unknown function when we had noisy observations of that function. In this section, we will discuss two related problems.

Problem (A): Let

$$z_k = f_k(\boldsymbol{\theta}^o) + \eta_k \qquad k = 1, 2, \ldots$$

where $f_1(\boldsymbol{\theta}), f_2(\boldsymbol{\theta}), \ldots$ are *known* functions of a parameter $\boldsymbol{\theta}$ whose true value $\boldsymbol{\theta}^o$ is unknown. The noise η_k is zero mean and independent. The problem is to recover $\boldsymbol{\theta}$ from the scalar measurements $z_1, z_2, \ldots$.

Problem (B): Let

$$z_k = f(\mathbf{x}_k) + \eta_k$$

where $f(\mathbf{x})$ is an *unknown* scalar function of the argument $\mathbf{x}$, which is a random m-vector. For every sample value of the argument (that is, $\mathbf{x}_k$), we can make a noisy measurement z_k of the function $f(\mathbf{x}_k)$. η_k is the corrupting additive noise. The problem is to estimate an approximation of $f(\cdot)$ from the sample pairs $\{z_k, \mathbf{x}_k; k = 1, 2,...\}$.

Problems (A) and (B) do not directly fit in the category of problems considered in Sections II and III. For example, in problems of type (A), the regression function $f_k(\boldsymbol{\theta})$ changes with the time index k (but θ remains the same), unlike Section II wherein the regression function did not change. Similarly, in problems of type (B) we deal with pairs of random variables $\{z_k, \mathbf{x}_k\}$ and not with only one random variable as in Section II.

A. *Estimation of the Parameters of a Known Time-Varying Function*

In this problem, the measurement at the kth stage is z_k and is given by

$$z_k = f_k(\boldsymbol{\theta}^o) + \eta_k$$

where $E(\eta_k) = 0$ and $f_k(\boldsymbol{\theta})$, $k = 1, 2,...$ are known functions of $\boldsymbol{\theta}$.

The unknown n-vector $\boldsymbol{\theta}^o$ has to be estimated. $\boldsymbol{\theta}_k$ is the estimate of $\boldsymbol{\theta}^o$ based on the measurements $z_1, z_2, ..., z_{k-1}$. We want to find a recursive relationship for finding $\boldsymbol{\theta}_{k+1}$ from the measurement z_k and $\boldsymbol{\theta}_k$ so that $\boldsymbol{\theta}_k$ tends to $\boldsymbol{\theta}^o$ as k goes to infinity.

Define the vector $\mathbf{g}_k(\boldsymbol{\theta})$ as

$$\mathbf{g}_k(\boldsymbol{\theta}) = \nabla_{\boldsymbol{\theta}} f_k(\boldsymbol{\theta}) \tag{9.9}$$

The expansion of $f_k(\boldsymbol{\theta})$ about $\boldsymbol{\theta}_k$ can then be written as

$$f_k(\boldsymbol{\theta}) = f_k(\boldsymbol{\theta}_k) + \mathbf{g}_k'(\boldsymbol{\xi}_k)(\boldsymbol{\theta} - \boldsymbol{\theta}_k) \tag{9.10}$$

where $\boldsymbol{\xi}_k$ is an n-vector whose tip lies on the line joining $\boldsymbol{\theta}$ and $\boldsymbol{\theta}_k$. We can define a "transformed" observation $\bar{z}_k$ as

$$\bar{z}_k \triangleq \mathbf{g}_k'(\boldsymbol{\xi}_k)\boldsymbol{\theta}^o + \eta_k \tag{9.11}$$

where

$$\bar{z}_k = z_k - f_k(\boldsymbol{\theta}_k) + \mathbf{g}_k'(\boldsymbol{\xi}_k)\boldsymbol{\theta}_k \tag{9.12}$$

Equations (9.11) and (9.12) form the basis for the recursion scheme.

There are two methods for the estimation of $\boldsymbol{\theta}$: a first-order method and a second-order method.

1. *First-order method.* One way of estimating $\boldsymbol{\theta}^o$ from the transformed observations in Eq. (9.11) would be to use a gradient algorithm to minimize the stochastic criterion function:

$$J_k(\boldsymbol{\theta}) = (\eta_k)^2 = (\bar{z}_k - \mathbf{g}_k'(\boldsymbol{\xi}_k)\boldsymbol{\theta})^2$$

The gradient algorithm is

$$\begin{aligned}\boldsymbol{\theta}_{k+1} &= \boldsymbol{\theta}_k - \rho_k \nabla_{\boldsymbol{\theta}} J(\boldsymbol{\theta})|_{\boldsymbol{\theta}=\boldsymbol{\theta}_k} \\ &= \boldsymbol{\theta}_k + \rho_k \mathbf{g}_k(\boldsymbol{\xi}_k)[\bar{z}_k - \mathbf{g}_k'(\boldsymbol{\xi}_k)\boldsymbol{\theta}_k] \\ &= \boldsymbol{\theta}_k + \rho_k \mathbf{g}_k(\boldsymbol{\xi}_k)[z_k - f_k(\boldsymbol{\theta}_k)]\end{aligned} \tag{9.13}$$

The two principal questions are how to choose the scalar sequence ρ_k and how to choose the points $\boldsymbol{\xi}_k$ at which to evaluate the derivatives $\mathbf{g}_k(\boldsymbol{\xi}_k)$. The choice of ρ_k can be made to depend on $\boldsymbol{\xi}_k$ by choosing the gain sequence to be

$$\rho_k = 1 \Big/ \sum_{j=1}^{k} \| \mathbf{g}_j(\boldsymbol{\xi}_j) \|^2 \tag{9.14}$$

This reduces the problem to the selection of $\{\boldsymbol{\xi}_k, k = 1, 2, \ldots\}$ which can be done in three ways.

(a) Deterministic gain sequence: Let $\boldsymbol{\xi}_k = \boldsymbol{\theta}_0$, a constant vector. In this case $\boldsymbol{\theta}_0$ is the a priori or nominal estimate of $\boldsymbol{\theta}^o$.

(b) Adaptive gain sequence: $\boldsymbol{\xi}_k = \boldsymbol{\theta}_k$. This is what is obtained by minimizing the criterion $J = (\boldsymbol{\xi}_k - f_k(\boldsymbol{\theta}))^2$ directly without linearizing about $\boldsymbol{\xi}_k$.

(c) Quasi-adaptive gain sequence: $\boldsymbol{\xi}_k = \boldsymbol{\theta}(j_k)$ where j_k is a nondecreasing sequence of integers with $j_k \leqslant k$. The corresponding gain ρ_k is between the deterministic and adaptive gains. One usually starts with $\boldsymbol{\xi}_k = \boldsymbol{\theta}_0$, but as $\boldsymbol{\theta}_k$ converges closer to $\boldsymbol{\theta}^o$, it is better to change (say at $k = n$) to an adaptive gain sequence. This will help speed up the convergence.

In many cases, we know that the $\boldsymbol{\theta}^o$ lies in the cube

$$c_i \leqslant \theta_i^o \leqslant d_i \qquad i = 1, \ldots, n \tag{9.15}$$

where θ_i^o is the ith component of $\boldsymbol{\theta}^o$.

In these cases, we can achieve faster convergence by modifying the algorithm in Eq. (9.13) so that $\boldsymbol{\theta}_k$ is never outside the cube for any k:

$$\boldsymbol{\theta}_{k+1} = \{\boldsymbol{\theta}_k + \rho_k \mathbf{g}_k(\boldsymbol{\xi}_k)(z_k - f_k(\boldsymbol{\theta}_k))\}_P$$

where $\{\mathbf{x}\}_P$ means the orthogonal projection of vector $\mathbf{x}$ onto the cube defined in Eq. (9.15); that is to say,

$$\{\mathbf{x}\}_P = \begin{bmatrix} \{x_1\}_P \\ \{x_2\}_P \\ \vdots \\ \{x_n\}_P \end{bmatrix}$$

where

$$\begin{aligned} \{x_i\}_P &= c_i && \text{if} \quad x_i \leqslant c_i \\ &= x_i && \text{if} \quad c_i \leqslant x_i \leqslant d_i \\ &= d_i && \text{if} \quad x_i \geqslant d_i \end{aligned}$$

2. *Second-order method.* Instead of just following the gradient of

$$J_k(\boldsymbol{\theta}) = (\bar{z}_k - \mathbf{g}_k'(\boldsymbol{\xi}_k)\boldsymbol{\theta})^2$$

it would be better to use an algorithm that minimizes

$$\sum_{j=1}^{k} J_j + \| \boldsymbol{\theta} - \boldsymbol{\theta}_0 \|_R^2$$

where $\boldsymbol{\theta}_0$ is the a priori value for $\boldsymbol{\theta}^o$ and R is a positive definite weighting matrix. The minimization algorithm is

$$\boldsymbol{\theta}_{k+1} = \left[\sum_{j=1}^{k} \mathbf{g}_j(\boldsymbol{\xi}_j)\, \mathbf{g}_j'(\boldsymbol{\xi}_j) + R\right]^{-1} \left[\sum_{j=1}^{k} \mathbf{g}_j(\boldsymbol{\xi}_j)\bar{z}_j + R\boldsymbol{\theta}_0\right]$$

which can be written recursively as

$$\begin{aligned} \boldsymbol{\theta}_{k+1} &= \boldsymbol{\theta}_k + P_k \mathbf{g}_k(\boldsymbol{\xi}_k)[\bar{z}_k - \mathbf{g}_k'(\boldsymbol{\xi}_k)\boldsymbol{\theta}_k] \\ &= \boldsymbol{\theta}_k + P_k \mathbf{g}_k(\boldsymbol{\xi}_k)[z_k - f_k(\boldsymbol{\theta}_k)] \end{aligned} \tag{9.16}$$

where the $n \times n$ matrix P_k obeys the following scheme

$$P_k = P_{k-1} - \frac{P_{k-1}\mathbf{g}_k(\boldsymbol{\xi}_k)\, \mathbf{g}_k'(\boldsymbol{\xi}_k) P_{k-1}}{1 + \mathbf{g}_k'(\boldsymbol{\xi}_k)\, P_{k-1}\mathbf{g}_k(\boldsymbol{\xi}_k)}$$

$$P_0 = R$$

The sequence $\boldsymbol{\xi}_k$ can also be chosen to be deterministic, adaptive, or quasi-adaptive as in the first order algorithm.

3. *Convergence conditions.* Albert and Gardner (1967) have described the sufficient conditions required for the convergence of the algorithms in Eqs. (9.13) and (9.16). Qualitatively, the most important condition concerns the direction and not the magnitude of the vectors $\mathbf{g}_k(\boldsymbol{\xi}_k)$. This condition requires that the vectors $\mathbf{g}_k(\boldsymbol{\xi}_k)$ repeatedly span the n-space ($\boldsymbol{\theta}$ has dimension n). If this condition is not met, the algorithm may converge but perhaps not to the true value $\boldsymbol{\theta}^o$. See Albert and Gardner (1967: 125–126) for the complete conditions and convergence proof.

B. *Estimation of Functions from Values Observed at Randomly Selected Points*

In the previous problem, the functions $f_k(\boldsymbol{\theta})$ were known and we wanted to estimate $\boldsymbol{\theta}^o$ based on noisy observations of $f_k(\boldsymbol{\theta}^o)$. In the present problem, the noisy observations are z_k, given by

$$z_k = f(\mathbf{x}_k) + \eta_k \tag{9.17}$$

where the function $f(\mathbf{x})$ is unknown and the argument $\mathbf{x}$ is a random vector. The problem is to obtain a suitable approximation for the function $f(\cdot)$ from the observations z_k. At each stage k we can observe z_k and the argument $\mathbf{x}_k$. We know nothing of the statistics of the random argument vector $\mathbf{x}$ or the noise η except that

$$E\{\eta_k \mid \mathbf{x}_k\} = 0$$

We will be content with seeking a "best" approximation to $f(\cdot)$. The approximation $\hat{f}(\cdot)$ will be chosen to have the form

$$\sum_{i=1}^{n} \theta_i \varphi_i(\mathbf{x}) = \boldsymbol{\theta}' \boldsymbol{\varphi}(\mathbf{x})$$

where $\varphi_1(\mathbf{x}), \varphi_2(\mathbf{x}),\ldots$ and $\varphi_n(\mathbf{x})$ are a set of n linearly independent functions (and $\boldsymbol{\theta}$ is an undetermined parameter). The problem is to find the value for $\boldsymbol{\theta}$ that makes $\hat{f}(\cdot)$ "best" in the sense that the mean square approximation error $E\{(f(\mathbf{x}) - \boldsymbol{\theta}'\boldsymbol{\varphi}(\mathbf{x})^2\}$ is a minimum. The value of $\boldsymbol{\theta}$ which minimizes this error is

$$\begin{aligned}\boldsymbol{\theta}^o &= \text{Arg.}[\underset{\boldsymbol{\theta}}{\text{Min.}}\ E\{f(\mathbf{x}) - \boldsymbol{\theta}'\boldsymbol{\varphi}(\mathbf{x})\}^2] \\ &= [E\{\boldsymbol{\varphi}(\mathbf{x})\, \boldsymbol{\varphi}'(\mathbf{x})\}]^{-1}\, E\{\boldsymbol{\varphi}(\mathbf{x})\, f(\mathbf{x})\}\end{aligned}$$

where we have assumed the indicated inverse to exist. The corresponding optimal approximation $\hat{f}(\mathbf{x})$ is

$$\hat{f}(\mathbf{x}) = \boldsymbol{\theta}^{o\prime} \boldsymbol{\varphi}(\mathbf{x})$$

We cannot calculate this expression explicitly because we do not know the function $f(\mathbf{x})$ or the statistics of $\mathbf{x}$. Instead note that $\boldsymbol{\theta}^o$ can be written as

$$\boldsymbol{\theta}^o = \text{Arg.}[\underset{\boldsymbol{\theta}}{\text{Min.}}\ E\{z - \boldsymbol{\theta}' \boldsymbol{\varphi}(\mathbf{x})\}^2]$$

In other words, $\boldsymbol{\theta}^o$ is the solution of the following equation:

$$E\{\boldsymbol{\varphi}(\mathbf{x})\, \boldsymbol{\varphi}'(\mathbf{x}) \boldsymbol{\theta}^o - \boldsymbol{\varphi}(\mathbf{x}) z\} = 0 \tag{9.18}$$

The algorithm of Section II, Eq. (9.3) for the solution of Eq. (9.18) for $\boldsymbol{\theta}^o$ can be written as

$$\boldsymbol{\theta}_{k+1} = \boldsymbol{\theta}_k + \rho_k \boldsymbol{\varphi}(\mathbf{x}_k)[z_k - \boldsymbol{\theta}_k' \boldsymbol{\varphi}(\mathbf{x}_k)] \tag{9.19}$$

with the gain sequence ρ_k obeying Eq. (9.4).

In addition to the conditions that $E\{\eta \mid \mathbf{x}\} = 0$ and that the samples $\mathbf{x}_1, \mathbf{x}_2, \ldots$ are independent, we also must assume that $E\{\boldsymbol{\varphi}(\mathbf{x})\, \boldsymbol{\varphi}'(\mathbf{x})\}$ and $E\{\boldsymbol{\varphi}(\mathbf{x})\, \boldsymbol{\varphi}'(\mathbf{x})\, \boldsymbol{\varphi}(\mathbf{x})\, \boldsymbol{\varphi}'(\mathbf{x})\}$ exist, are positive definite, and that $E\{\boldsymbol{\varphi}(\mathbf{x}) f(\mathbf{x})\}$ and $E\{\boldsymbol{\varphi}(\mathbf{x})\, \boldsymbol{\varphi}'(\mathbf{x})\, \boldsymbol{\varphi}(\mathbf{x}) f(\mathbf{x})\}$ exist. If these conditions are met, then $\boldsymbol{\theta}_k$ converges to $\boldsymbol{\theta}^o$ with probability one and in mean square (for a proof see Appendix 2).

Alternately, we can use a second order method to solve Eq. (9.18). Note that the derivative with respect to $\boldsymbol{\theta}$ of the left hand side of Eq. (9.18) is $E\{\boldsymbol{\varphi}(\mathbf{x})\, \boldsymbol{\varphi}'(\mathbf{x})\}$; hence, Newton's method for solving Eq. (9.18) can be written as

$$\boldsymbol{\theta}_{k+1} = \boldsymbol{\theta}_k + \rho_k [E\{\boldsymbol{\varphi}(\mathbf{x})\, \boldsymbol{\varphi}'(\mathbf{x})\}]^{-1}\, \boldsymbol{\varphi}(\mathbf{x}_k)\{z(k) - \boldsymbol{\theta}_k' \boldsymbol{\varphi}(\mathbf{x}_k)\} \tag{9.20}$$

At the kth stage, a good approximation for $E\{\boldsymbol{\varphi}(\mathbf{x})\, \boldsymbol{\varphi}'(\mathbf{x})\}$ is

$$\left\{\frac{1}{k} \sum_{j=1}^{k} \boldsymbol{\varphi}_j \boldsymbol{\varphi}_j' + B_0^{-1}\right\},$$

where B_0^{-1} is the a priori estimate of the covariance matrix of $\boldsymbol{\varphi}(\mathbf{x})$; hence, the algorithm in Eq. (9.20) can be written as

$$\boldsymbol{\theta}_{k+1} = \boldsymbol{\theta}_k + B_k \boldsymbol{\varphi}(\mathbf{x}_k)\{z_k - \boldsymbol{\theta}_k' \boldsymbol{\varphi}(\mathbf{x}_k)\} \tag{9.21}$$

where*

$$B_k = \left\{\frac{1}{k}\sum_{j=1}^{k} \boldsymbol{\varphi}_j\boldsymbol{\varphi}_j' + B_0^{-1}\right\}^{-1} \tag{9.22}$$

Equation (9.22) can be written in a form which does not involve the explicit inversion of a matrix at every instant

$$B_k = B_{k-1} - \frac{B_{k-1}\boldsymbol{\varphi}_k\boldsymbol{\varphi}_k' B_{k-1}}{1 + \boldsymbol{\varphi}_k' B_{k-1}\boldsymbol{\varphi}_k}$$

The same assumptions that assured convergence of the first-order algorithm, Eq. (9.18), also assure the convergence of algorithm (9.20) with probability one.

It has been observed experimentally that algorithm (9.21) has a faster rate of convergence than that of (9.20). We will elaborate upon this fact later.

If the function $f(\mathbf{x})$ did possess an expansion of the following type

$$f(\mathbf{x}) = \sum_{i=1}^{n} \alpha_i\varphi_i(\mathbf{x}) = \boldsymbol{\alpha}'\boldsymbol{\varphi}(\mathbf{x})$$

then $\boldsymbol{\alpha}$ and $\boldsymbol{\theta}^o$ would be identical; i.e., the best approximation to the function $f(\mathbf{x})$ is identical with the function $f(\mathbf{x})$ itself.

C. *The Method of Potential Functions*†

In the previous section, we developed algorithms for obtaining the best linear approximation to the unknown function $f(\mathbf{x})$. These algorithms do not lead to the unknown function itself, except in special cases. In this section we will treat the same problem as that treated in Section IVB and develop an algorithm to recover the function $f(\mathbf{x})$ itself from the noisy observations. These algorithms are obtained by the method of the potential functions, introduced by Aizerman *et al.* (1964). The method has been used for the recovery of unknown, uniformly bounded continuous functions which may be either deterministic or stochastic. The unknown function is recovered as an infinite sum of certain known functions.

With very little loss of generality, the unknown function $f(\mathbf{x})$ can be assumed to have the following infinite expansion

$$f(\mathbf{x}) = \sum_{j=1}^{\infty} \theta_j\varphi_j(\mathbf{x}) \tag{9.23}$$

---

* $\boldsymbol{\varphi}_j = \boldsymbol{\varphi}(\mathbf{x}_j)$.

† Additional discussions on the method of potential functions are given in Chapters 3 and 5.

where the functions $\varphi_1(\mathbf{x}), \varphi_2(\mathbf{x}),\ldots$ are orthonormal functions with a measure $\mu(\cdot)$ satisfying Eq. (9.24), and $\theta_1, \theta_2, \ldots$ are unknown parameters.

$$\int_{\Omega_x} \varphi_i(\mathbf{x})\, \varphi_j(\mathbf{x})\, d\mu(\mathbf{x}) = \delta_{ij} \tag{9.24}$$

In Eq. (9.23) Ω_x denotes the region where the function $f(\cdot)$ is defined. The unknown coefficients $\theta_1, \theta_2, \ldots$ must satisfy the condition in Eq. (9.25) so that $f(\mathbf{x})$ may exist:

$$\sum_{i=1}^{\infty} \theta_i^2 < \infty \tag{9.25}$$

We will introduce a known function $K(\mathbf{x}, \mathbf{y})$ of 2, n-vectors $\mathbf{x}$ and $\mathbf{y}$, the so-called potential function, which obeys the following conditions:

$$\begin{aligned} K(\mathbf{x}, \mathbf{y}) &= K(\mathbf{y}, \mathbf{x}) \\ \operatorname*{Max.}_{\mathbf{x}} K(\mathbf{x}, \mathbf{x}) &\leqslant c_2 \end{aligned} \tag{9.26}$$

and

$$K(\mathbf{x}, \mathbf{y}) = \sum_{i=1}^{\infty} \lambda_i^2 \varphi_i(\mathbf{x})\, \varphi_i(\mathbf{y}) \tag{9.27}$$

where

$$\lambda_i < \infty$$

A typical potential function obeying Eqs. (9.26) and (9.27) is $\exp[-c^2 \| \mathbf{x} - \mathbf{y} \|^2]$. We will have to return to the choice of the potential function later.

Let us define $f_k(\mathbf{x})$ as the estimate of the unknown function $f(\mathbf{x})$, at the kth stage using observations $\{\mathbf{x}_i, z_i, i = 1, 2,\ldots, k-1\}$ where z_i obeys Eq. (9.17). The estimate $f_k(\mathbf{x})$ is assumed to obey the following recursion equation:

$$f_{k+1}(\mathbf{x}) = f_k(\mathbf{x}) + \gamma_k K(\mathbf{x}, \mathbf{x}_k) \tag{9.28}$$

Thus, $K(\mathbf{x}, \mathbf{x}_k)$ represents the weighting function; it is based on $\mathbf{x}_k$, the point at which the latest measurement is made. The term γ_k is the (numerical) weight attached to the correction term $K(\mathbf{x}, \mathbf{x}_k)$; it incorporates the information about the latest observation pair $(\mathbf{x}_k, z_k)$. γ_k should be so chosen that $f_k(\mathbf{x})$ tends to the unknown $f(\mathbf{x})$ in some sense. Such a choice for γ_k for our problem is,

$$\gamma_k = \rho_k(z_k - f(\mathbf{x}_k)) \tag{9.29}$$

where ρ_k is the usual scalar gain sequence obeying Eq. (9.4). Thus, the estimate $f_{k+1}(\mathbf{x})$ is a weighted sum of $(k+1)$ known functions, $K(\mathbf{x}, \mathbf{x}_1),\ldots, K(\mathbf{x}, \mathbf{x}_k)$, and $f_0(\mathbf{x})$; that is to say,

$$f_{k+1}(\mathbf{x}) = f_0(\mathbf{x}) + \gamma_1 K(\mathbf{x}, \mathbf{x}_1) + \gamma_2 K(\mathbf{x}, \mathbf{x}_2) + \cdots + \gamma_k K(\mathbf{x}, \mathbf{x}_k)$$

The weights γ_k are recursively computed from Eq. (9.29). Braverman (1965) has shown that the algorithm in Eqs. (9.28) and (9.29) converges to the unknown function $f(\mathbf{x})$ in probability.

There are two methods for constructing the potential function. In the first method, we start with a set of functions $\psi_i(\mathbf{x})$, $i = 1, 2,\ldots$ which are complete in some sense and construct the series

$$K(\mathbf{x}, \mathbf{y}) = \sum_{i=1}^{\infty} \lambda_i^2 \psi_i(\mathbf{x})\, \psi_i(\mathbf{y}) \tag{9.30}$$

where the numbers λ_i , $i = 1, 2,\ldots$ are so chosen that the infinite series in Eq. (9.30) can be summed analytically.

The second method is to select a symmetrical function of two variables $\mathbf{x}$ and $\mathbf{y}$ and use it as a potential function as long as it can be expanded in an infinite series as in Eq. (9.27). It is convenient to regard $K(\mathbf{x}, \mathbf{y})$ as a distance between the points $\mathbf{x}$ and $\mathbf{y}$. According to Braverman (1965), the potential function can have the following form

$$K(\mathbf{x}, \mathbf{y}) = g(\| \mathbf{z} \|), \qquad \mathbf{z} = \mathbf{x} - \mathbf{y}, \qquad \| \mathbf{z} \| = \sqrt{z_1^2 + \cdots + z_n^2}$$

where $g(\| \mathbf{z} \|)$ can be any function which has a multidimensional fourier transform that is positive everywhere. Two typical examples of $K(\mathbf{x}, \mathbf{y})$ constructed in this manner are given below.

(i) $$K(\mathbf{x}, \mathbf{y}) = \exp[-c \| \mathbf{x} - \mathbf{y} \|^2] \qquad c > 0$$

(ii) $$K(\mathbf{x}, \mathbf{y}) = \frac{1}{1 + \| \mathbf{x} - \mathbf{y} \|^2} \qquad \text{if } \| \mathbf{x} - \mathbf{y} \|^2 < 1$$

The potential function method has the advantage that it imposes very few restrictions on the unknown function. The disadvantage is that it involves iteration in function space which gives rise to serious storage problems since the storage of the estimate $f_k(\mathbf{x})$ at the kth stage involves the storage of all the previous k potential functions $K(\mathbf{x}, \mathbf{x}_1),\ldots, K(\mathbf{x}, \mathbf{x}_{k-1})$. An infinite number of iterations (or an infinite sum of functions) finally converges to the correct form for the unknown function. The methods of stochastic approximation, instead, estimate parameters and they involve only a storage of an n-dimensional vector.

The potential function method reduces to the stochastic approximation when the function to be estimated can be exactly expressed as a finite sum

$$f(\mathbf{x}) = \boldsymbol{\theta}'\boldsymbol{\varphi}(\mathbf{x}) = \sum_{i=1}^{n} \theta_i \varphi_i(\mathbf{x}) \tag{9.31}$$

This will be demonstrated by chosing the potential function as follows

$$K(\mathbf{x}, \mathbf{y}) = \sum_{i=1}^{n} \varphi_i(\mathbf{x})\, \varphi_i(\mathbf{y}) = \boldsymbol{\varphi}'(\mathbf{x})\, \boldsymbol{\varphi}(\mathbf{y}) \tag{9.32}$$

Let

$$f_k(\mathbf{x}) = \boldsymbol{\theta}_k{}'\boldsymbol{\varphi}(\mathbf{x}) \tag{9.33}$$

Substituting Eqs. (9.31)–(9.33) in the algorithm of Eqs. (9.28) and (9.29) we get

$$\boldsymbol{\varphi}'(\mathbf{x})[\boldsymbol{\theta}_{k+1} - \boldsymbol{\theta}_k - \rho_k \boldsymbol{\varphi}(\mathbf{x}_k)(z_k - \boldsymbol{\theta}_k{}'\boldsymbol{\varphi}(\mathbf{x}_k)) = 0 \tag{9.34}$$

Removing $\boldsymbol{\varphi}'(\mathbf{x})$ from Eq. (9.34) gives us the stochastic approximation scheme in Eq. (9.19) for recovering the unknown parameter $\boldsymbol{\theta}^o$.

V. Convergence Rates

One measure of the rate of convergence of an algorithm is the mean square error $E\{\| \boldsymbol{\theta}_k - \boldsymbol{\theta}^o \|^2\}$ where $\boldsymbol{\theta}^o$ is the true unknown value and $\boldsymbol{\theta}_k$ is the estimate of $\boldsymbol{\theta}^o$ at the kth stage. This measure is convenient for evaluation in most of the algorithms discussed earlier. We will consider the algorithms of the Robbins–Munro type and those of Kiefer–Wolfowitz type separately.

A. *Algorithms of the Type of Robbins–Munro*

In this class we include not only algorithms mentioned in Section II, but also the algorithm in Eq. (9.19) in Section IV. We will consider only the case in which the gain ρ_k is of the form

$$\rho_k = \rho_1/k, \qquad \rho_1 > 0$$

Let $b_k = E\{\| \boldsymbol{\theta}_k - \boldsymbol{\theta}^o \|^2\}$

and $$E\{[\mathbf{y}_k - E\{y(\boldsymbol{\theta}_k)\}]^2\} = \frac{1}{k^{(d-1)}} \qquad d \geqslant 1$$

It is possible to show that b_k obeys the following difference equation

$$b_{k+1} \leqslant \left(1 - \frac{d_1}{k}\right) b_k + d_2 k^{-(1+d)}$$

where d_1 , $d_2 > 0$.
The above equation has the following asymptotic solution (Chung, 1954; Venter, 1966)*

$$\begin{aligned} b_k &= O(k^{-d}) && \text{if} \quad d_1 > d > 0 \\ &= O(k^{-d_1}) && \text{if} \quad d_1 = d > 0 \\ &= O(k^{-d_1}) && \text{if} \quad d > d_1 > 0 \end{aligned}$$

The usual value of d is unity. This is so in the case of the algorithm in Eq. (9.19) in Section IV when the variance of the measurement noise is constant.

B. *Algorithms of the Type of Kiefer–Wolfowitz*

In addition to the assumptions made in the propositions in Section III, we need the following conditions:

(i) Let $r(\boldsymbol{\theta}) = \nabla_{\boldsymbol{\theta}} J(\boldsymbol{\theta})$ where $J(\boldsymbol{\theta})$ is the criterion function being minimized. There exist two positive numbers k_0 and k_1 so that

$$k_0 \| \boldsymbol{\theta} - \boldsymbol{\theta}^o \|^2 \leqslant (\boldsymbol{\theta} - \boldsymbol{\theta}^o)' \mathbf{r}(\boldsymbol{\theta}) \qquad \text{and} \qquad \| \mathbf{r}(\boldsymbol{\theta}) \| \leqslant k_1 \| \boldsymbol{\theta} - \boldsymbol{\theta}^o \|$$

(ii) Let $J(\boldsymbol{\theta})$ possess derivatives of order not less than $(s + 1)$, $s \geqslant 2$; and

$$\rho_k = \frac{\rho_1}{k^\alpha} \qquad c_k = \frac{c_1}{k^\gamma}$$

$$\rho_1 > 0 \qquad c_1 > 0 \qquad 0 < \alpha \leqslant 1 \qquad 0 < \gamma < \alpha/2$$

$$2k_0\rho_1 > \beta \qquad \text{if} \quad \alpha = 1 \qquad \text{where} \quad \beta = \min\{2s\gamma, \alpha - 2\gamma\}$$

Then $E\{\| \boldsymbol{\theta}_k - \boldsymbol{\theta}^o \|^2\} = O(k^{-\beta})$.

Hence, the speed of Kiefer–Wolfowitz (KW) scheme is considerably less than that of Robbins–Munro (RM); therefore, KW should be used only if we cannot formulate the scheme as an RM procedure.

C. *Least Squares Algorithms*

We will consider only the algorithm in Eqs. (9.21) and (9.22). Experimentally this algorithm is observed to converge faster than the first order

---

* $g(n) \triangleq O(g(n))$ means Lim. Sup $| g(n)/h(n) | < + \infty$.

algorithm in Eq. (9.19). But the upper bound for the mean square error $E\{\| \boldsymbol{\theta}_k - \boldsymbol{\theta}^o \|^2\}$ is still of the form $1/k$, as before, and we cannot do better than this on account of the Cramer–Rao inequality. However, we can demonstrate the superiority of the scheme in Eqs. (9.21) and (9.22) in the following manner (Wagner, 1968):

Let us assume that there exists an integer $t > 1$ such that

$$E\{| \varphi_i(\mathbf{x})|^{2t}\} < \infty \qquad \forall i = 1,\ldots, n$$

$$E\{| f(\mathbf{x})|^{2t}\} < \infty$$

$$E\{| \eta_i |^t\} < \infty \qquad \forall i$$

Then the probability that $\boldsymbol{\theta}_k$ lies outside a sphere of radius ϵ centered around $\boldsymbol{\theta}^o$ obeys the following upper bound

$$\text{Prob.}[\| \boldsymbol{\theta}_k - \boldsymbol{\theta}^o \| \geqslant \epsilon] \leqslant \frac{\alpha_1(\epsilon)}{k^{t-1}}$$

$$\text{Prob.} \left\{\bigcup_{j=k}^{\infty} [\| \boldsymbol{\theta}_j - \boldsymbol{\theta}^o \| \geqslant \epsilon]\right\} \leqslant \frac{\alpha_2(\epsilon)}{k^{t-2}}$$

where $\alpha_1(\epsilon)$ and $\alpha_2(\epsilon)$ are positive constants depending on ϵ. In other words, the more moments which can be assumed to exist for the quantities $| \varphi_i(\mathbf{x})|$, $|f(\mathbf{x})|$ and $| \eta_k |$ the higher will be the convergence rate. When the above mentioned functions have moments of all orders (that is, $t = \infty$), then $\boldsymbol{\theta}_k$ tends to $\boldsymbol{\theta}^o$ at an exponential rate, i.e.,

$$\text{Prob.}[\| \boldsymbol{\theta}_k - \boldsymbol{\theta}^o \| \geqslant \epsilon] \leqslant b_1(\epsilon)(\rho(\epsilon))^k$$

$$\text{Prob.} \left[\bigcup_{j=k}^{\infty} \| \boldsymbol{\theta}_j - \boldsymbol{\theta}^o \| \geqslant \epsilon\right] \leqslant b_2(\epsilon)(\rho(\epsilon))^k$$

where $b_1(\epsilon)$, $b_2(\epsilon)$ are positive functions and $0 < \rho(\epsilon) < 1$.

VI. Methods of Accelerating Convergence

Two approaches have been suggested for accelerating the convergence of stochastic approximation procedures. The first approach is to accelerate convergence by selecting a proper weighting sequence $\{\rho_k\}$. The choice of the weighting sequence based on information concerning the behavior of the regression function, intuitively speaking, should improve the rate of convergence. We will limit our discussion to problems in which $\boldsymbol{\theta}$ is scalar. Historically, the first method of accelerating the convergence of a stochastic approximation procedure was proposed by Kesten (1958). The basic idea is that when the estimate is far from the sought quantity θ^0 there will be few changes of sign of $(\theta_k - \theta_{k-1})$. Near the goal, θ^0, one would expect overshooting to cause oscillation from one side of θ^0 to the other. Kesten proposed, using the number of sign changes of $(\theta_k - \theta_{k-1})$, to indicate whether the estimate is near or far from θ^0. Specifically, the gain γ_k is not decreased if $(\theta_k - \theta_{k-1})$ retains its sign. Mathematically, the Kesten algorithm is,

$$\theta_{k+1} = \theta_k - \gamma_k y(\theta_k) \tag{9.35}$$

where $\gamma_1 = \rho_1, \gamma_2 = \rho_2, \ldots, \gamma_k = \rho_{s(k)}$

$$s(k) = 2 + \sum_{j=1}^{k} \Phi[(\theta_k - \theta_{k-1})(\theta_{k-1} - \theta_{k-2})]$$

and

$$\Phi[x] = \begin{cases} 1 & \text{if } x < 0 \\ 0 & \text{if } x > 0 \end{cases}$$

The algorithm in Eq. (9.35) converges with probability one.

Fabian (1965) has proposed the following accelerated algorithms:

$$\theta_{k+1} = \theta_k + \rho_k \operatorname{sgn}[y(\theta_k)] \tag{9.36}$$

for RM schemes, and

$$\theta_{k+1} = \theta_k + \frac{\rho_k}{c_k} \operatorname{sgn}[z(\theta_k + c_k) - z(\theta_k - c_k)] \tag{9.37}$$

for KW schemes. Algorithms (9.36) and (9.37) converge to their sought quantities, respectively, only in a comparatively narrow class of problems in which the distribution function of the random variable y is symmetric with respect to θ. Another scheme of accelerating convergence proposed by Fabian is analogus to the steepest descent method.

The second approach for accelerating convergence is by taking more observations at each stage of iteration. Intuitively speaking, the additional observations made at each stage will help us in exploring the regression function in greater detail than the original stochastic approximation procedure, and, consequently, the extra information can be utilized to improve the rate of convergence. Venter (1967a) and Fabian (1965) have proposed accelerated algorithms for RM and KW procedures, respectively. For example, Venter's procedure estimates the slope of the regression function by taking two observations at each stage and using this information to improve the rate of convergence and the asymptotic variance of the Robbins–Munro procedure. The recursive algorithm is of the form

$$\theta_{k+1} = \theta_k - \rho_k \alpha_k^{-1} \tfrac{1}{2}(y_k' + y_k'') \tag{9.38}$$

where y_k' and y_k'' are random variables whose conditional distributions given y_j', y_j'', $j = 1, \ldots, (k-1)$ are identical to those of $y(\theta_k + c_k)$ and $y(\theta_k - c_k)$ respectively; $\rho_k = 1/k$, $c_k = ck^{-\gamma}$, $c > 0$, and $0 < \gamma < 1/2$; and, α_k is an estimate of the slope α of the regression function, $r(\theta)$, that is defined as follows:

Assume that $0 < a < \alpha < b < \infty$ with a and b known.

Let

$$b_k = k^{-1} \sum_{j=1}^{k} (y_k' - y_k'')/2c_k \tag{9.39a}$$

and

$$\alpha_k = \begin{cases} = a & \text{if } b_k \leqslant a \\ = b_k & \text{if } a \leqslant b_k \leqslant b \\ = b & \text{if } b_k \geqslant b \end{cases} \tag{9.39b}$$

The algorithm in Eq. (9.38) converges with probability one.

The same idea can be carried over to the KW procedures. In this case, three observations are taken at each stage of an iteration, and the appropriate second-order differences of the observations are used to estimate the second-order derivative of the regression function at the maximum (or minimum). This information would be utilized to determine the next estimate θ_{k+1} of the maximum (or minimum). In a similar manner, Fabian, showed that the KW procedure can be modified in such a way as to be almost as speedy as the RM procedure. The modification consists of taking more observations at every stage of an iteration and utilizing this information to eliminate (smooth out) the effect of all higher-order derivates of the regression function.

When the unknown parameter $\boldsymbol{\theta}$ is a vector, it is very hard to develop schemes which will yield a faster rate of convergence than the standard algorithms in Sections II and III. One suggestion is to use the stochastic approximation algorithms in conjunction with Monte Carlo schemes for optimizing the multivariate functions (Newbold, 1967).

One general comment regarding all accelerating schemes is in order. In all of them, the upper bound for the mean square error $E\{\| \boldsymbol{\theta}_k - \boldsymbol{\theta}^o \|^2\}$ cannot decay faster than $(c_1/(k + c_2))$ where $c_1, c_2 > 0$. This statement follows from the Cramer–Rao inequality. In essence, the different schemes lead to different values of c_1 and c_2 in the above bound.

VII. Conclusion

We have concentrated our attention on developing methods of finding the minimum of stochastic functions. Our algorithms need very little information about the measurement noise. The unknown quantity was always a finite dimensional vector which did not vary with time.

We can easily modify the algorithms (Dupac, 1965) so as to estimate parameters which are slowly time-varying and are varying in either a deterministic manner, or in a random fashion with their variances going to zero as time tends to infinity. However, if the parameter is a stochastic process, with variance not decreasing with time, then the problem is one in nonlinear estimation of stochastic processes and is, therefore, outside the scope of this chapter.

APPENDIX 1

Proof of the Convergence of the Basic Stochastic Approximation Scheme

In this appendix, we will demonstrate that the $\boldsymbol{\theta}_k$ given by the algorithm in Eq. (3) [rewritten below as Eq. (40)] will converge to the true value $\boldsymbol{\theta}^o$ under the assumptions (A1)–(A3) of Section II. The proof is based on a technique developed by Gladyshev (1965).

$$\boldsymbol{\theta}_{k+1} = \boldsymbol{\theta}_k - \rho_k \mathbf{y}(\boldsymbol{\theta}_k) \tag{9.40}$$

Let

$$\tilde{\boldsymbol{\theta}}_k = \boldsymbol{\theta}_k - \boldsymbol{\theta}^o \tag{9.41}$$

Subtract $\boldsymbol{\theta}^o$ from both sides of Eq. (9.40), square both sides of Eq. (9.40) and take expectations using Eq. (9.1) and assumption (A3).

$$\begin{aligned} &E\{\| \tilde{\boldsymbol{\theta}}_{k+1} \|^2 \mid \boldsymbol{\theta}_1, \ldots, \boldsymbol{\theta}_k\} \\ &\quad = \| \tilde{\boldsymbol{\theta}}_k \|^2 - 2\rho_k \tilde{\boldsymbol{\theta}}_k' \mathbf{r}(\boldsymbol{\theta}_k) + \rho_k^2 E\{\| \mathbf{y}(\boldsymbol{\theta}_k) \|^2 \mid \boldsymbol{\theta}_1, \ldots, \boldsymbol{\theta}_k\} \\ &\quad \leqslant \| \tilde{\boldsymbol{\theta}}_k \|^2 - 2\rho_k \tilde{\boldsymbol{\theta}}_k' \mathbf{r}(\boldsymbol{\theta}_k) + \rho_k^2 h(1 + \| \tilde{\boldsymbol{\theta}}_k \|^2) \end{aligned} \tag{9.42}$$

By assumption (A2), Eq. (9.42) becomes

$$E\{\| \tilde{\boldsymbol{\theta}}_{k+1} \|^2 \mid \boldsymbol{\theta}_1, \ldots, \boldsymbol{\theta}_k\} \leqslant (1 + h\rho_k^2) \| \tilde{\boldsymbol{\theta}}_k \|^2 + h\rho_k^2 \tag{9.43}$$

Let us define the scalar α_k to be

$$\alpha_k = \| \tilde{\boldsymbol{\theta}}_k \|^2 \prod_{j=k}^{\infty} (1 + h\rho_j^2) + \sum_{j=k}^{\infty} h\rho_j^2 \prod_{m=j+1}^{\infty} (1 + h\rho_m^2) \tag{9.44}$$

Using Eqs. (9.43) and (9.44), we can write a recursive inequality for α_k

$$E\{\alpha_{k+1} \mid \boldsymbol{\theta}_1, \ldots, \boldsymbol{\theta}_k\} \leqslant \alpha_k \tag{9.45}$$

Now let us take the conditional expectation on both sides of Eq. (9.45), given $\alpha_1, \ldots, \alpha_k$:

$$E\{\alpha_{k+1} \mid \alpha_1, \ldots, \alpha_k\} \leqslant \alpha_k \tag{9.46}$$

Inequality (9.46) shows that α_k is a semi-martingale where

$$E\{\alpha_{k+1}\} \leqslant E\{\alpha_k\} \leqslant \cdots \leqslant E\{\alpha_1\} < \infty \tag{9.47}$$

According to the theory of semi-martingales [Doob, 1953], the sequence α_k converges with probability one and, hence, by Eqs. (9.44) and (9.4), $\| \tilde{\boldsymbol{\theta}}_k \|^2$ tends to some random variable, say ξ, with probability one. It remains to show that $\xi = 0$ with probability one.

For this, we note that the boundedness of the sequence $E\{\| \tilde{\boldsymbol{\theta}}_k \|^2\}$ follows from Eqs. (9.47), (9.44) and (9.4). Further, let us take expectation over both sides of Eq. (9.42):

$$E \| \tilde{\boldsymbol{\theta}}_{k+1} \|^2 - E \| \tilde{\boldsymbol{\theta}}_k \|^2 \leqslant \rho_k^2 h(1 + E \| \tilde{\boldsymbol{\theta}}_k \|^2) - 2\rho_k E\{\tilde{\boldsymbol{\theta}}_k' \mathbf{r}(\boldsymbol{\theta}_k)\} \tag{9.48}$$

Repeated use of Eq. (9.48) gives us

$$E \| \tilde{\boldsymbol{\theta}}_{k+1} \|^2 - E \| \tilde{\boldsymbol{\theta}}_1 \|^2 \leqslant \sum_{j=1}^{k} h\rho_j^2(1 + E \| \tilde{\boldsymbol{\theta}}_j \|^2) - 2 \sum_{j=1}^{k} \rho_j E\{\tilde{\boldsymbol{\theta}}_j' \mathbf{r}(\boldsymbol{\theta}_j)\} \tag{9.49}$$

Equation (9.48), the boundedness of $E \| \tilde{\boldsymbol{\theta}}_k \|^2$, and Eq. (9.4) imply that

$$\sum_{j=1}^{k} \rho_j E\{\tilde{\boldsymbol{\theta}}_j' \mathbf{r}(\boldsymbol{\theta}_j)\} < \infty \tag{9.50}$$

Since $\tilde{\boldsymbol{\theta}}_j' \mathbf{r}(\boldsymbol{\theta}_j)$ is nonnegative by assumption (A2), Eq. (9.50) and the property of the $\{\rho_k\}$ sequence implies the existence of a subsequence $\{k_j\}$ such that

$$\tilde{\boldsymbol{\theta}}_{k_j}' \mathbf{r}(\boldsymbol{\theta}_{k_j}) \to 0 \text{ with probability one} \tag{9.51}$$

Equation (9.51), Assumption (A1) and the fact that $\tilde{\boldsymbol{\theta}}_k$ tends to some random variable imply $\tilde{\boldsymbol{\theta}}_k$ tends to $\mathbf{0}$ with probability one.

To prove mean square convergence, we note that by Assumption (A2) there exists a positive constant $d_2(\epsilon)$ so that

$$(\tilde{\boldsymbol{\theta}}_k)'\mathbf{r}(\boldsymbol{\theta}_k) \geqslant d_2(\epsilon)\| \tilde{\boldsymbol{\theta}}_k \|^2 \quad \forall \| \tilde{\boldsymbol{\theta}}_k \| < \epsilon, \qquad \epsilon > 0 \tag{9.52}$$

On account of the definition of the $\{\rho_k\}$ sequence, there exists an integer k, so that

$$2d_2(\epsilon) - \rho_k h \triangleq d_3(\epsilon) > 0 \qquad \forall k > k_1 \tag{9.53}$$

Using Eqs. (9.52), (9.53) and (9.47), it is easy to show

$$E \| \tilde{\boldsymbol{\theta}}_{k+1} \|^2 \leqslant E \| \tilde{\boldsymbol{\theta}}_k \|^2\{1 - \rho_k d_3(\epsilon)\} + \rho_k^2 h, \qquad \forall k > k_1 \tag{9.54}$$

Let us define the scalar sequence $\{\beta_k\}$,

$$\beta_k = (E \| \tilde{\boldsymbol{\theta}}_k \|^2 \prod_{j=k}^{\infty} (1 - d_3\rho_j)) + \sum_{j=k}^{\infty} h\rho_j^2 \prod_{m=j+1}^{\infty} (1 - d_3\rho_j) \tag{9.55}$$

From Eqs. (9.55) and (9.54), we get

$$\beta_{k+1} \leqslant \beta_k \qquad \forall k > k_1 ;$$

thus, β_k is bounded from above. We see in Eq. (9.55) that the second term is bounded as k tends to infinity, and that the term $\prod_{j=k}^{\infty} (1 - d_3\rho_j)$ tends to infinity with k; hence, if β_k is to be bounded, the term $E\{\| \tilde{\boldsymbol{\theta}}_k \|^2\}$ should tend to zero as k goes to infinity; thus completing the proof of mean square convergence.

APPENDIX 2

Convergence Proof of the Function Recovery Algorithm in Eq. (9.19)

The algorithm in Eq. (9.19) is rewritten here, as Eq. (9.56):

$$\boldsymbol{\theta}_{k+1} = \boldsymbol{\theta}_k + \rho_k \boldsymbol{\varphi}(\mathbf{x}_k)[z_k - \boldsymbol{\theta}_k{}'\boldsymbol{\varphi}(\mathbf{x}_k)] \tag{9.56}$$

where $z_k = f(\mathbf{x}_k) + \eta_k$.

Let

$$\boldsymbol{\theta}^o = [E\{\boldsymbol{\varphi}(\mathbf{x})\, \boldsymbol{\varphi}'(\mathbf{x})\}]^{-1} E[\boldsymbol{\varphi}(\mathbf{x}) f(\mathbf{x})] \tag{9.57}$$

We will show that the sequence $\{\boldsymbol{\theta}_k\}$ given by the algorithm in Eq. (9.56) tends to $\boldsymbol{\theta}^o$ defined above in the mean square sense and with probability one if the following conditions (i)–(v) are satisfied:

(i) The samples $\mathbf{x}_k$, $k = 1, 2, \ldots$, are statistically independent.
(ii) $E\{\boldsymbol{\varphi}(\mathbf{x})\, \boldsymbol{\varphi}'(\mathbf{x})\}$ and $E\{\boldsymbol{\varphi}(\mathbf{x})\, \boldsymbol{\varphi}'(\mathbf{x})\, \boldsymbol{\varphi}(\mathbf{x})\, \boldsymbol{\varphi}'(\mathbf{x})\}$ must be finite and positive definite.
(iii) $\| E\{\boldsymbol{\varphi}(\mathbf{x}) f(\mathbf{x})\}\| < \infty$.
$\| E\{\boldsymbol{\varphi}(\mathbf{x})\, \boldsymbol{\varphi}'(\mathbf{x})\, \boldsymbol{\varphi}(\mathbf{x}) f(\mathbf{x})\}\| < \infty$.
(iv) $E\{\eta_k^2\} < \infty$ and $E\{\eta_k\} = 0$.
(v) $E\{\| \boldsymbol{\theta}_0 \|^2\} < \infty$.

Let

$$\tilde{\boldsymbol{\theta}}_k = \boldsymbol{\theta}^o - \boldsymbol{\theta}_k, \qquad \boldsymbol{\varphi}_i = \boldsymbol{\varphi}(\mathbf{x}_i)$$
$$\xi_i = z_i - \boldsymbol{\theta}^{o\prime}\boldsymbol{\varphi}_i = f(\mathbf{x}_i) - \boldsymbol{\theta}^{o\prime}\boldsymbol{\varphi}_i + \eta_i \tag{9.58}$$

The algorithm in Eq. (9.56) can be written as

$$\tilde{\boldsymbol{\theta}}_{k+1} = (I - \rho_k \boldsymbol{\varphi}_k \boldsymbol{\varphi}_k')\tilde{\boldsymbol{\theta}}_k - \rho_k \boldsymbol{\varphi}_k \xi_k \tag{9.59}$$

Taking expectations on both sides of Eq. (9.59), noting $E(\boldsymbol{\varphi}_k \xi_k) = \mathbf{0}$ and using Condition (i), we get

$$E\{\tilde{\boldsymbol{\theta}}_{k+1}\} = [I - \rho_k E\{\boldsymbol{\varphi}_k \boldsymbol{\varphi}_k'\}]\, E(\tilde{\boldsymbol{\theta}}_k\} \tag{9.60}$$

Taking the Euclidean norm on both sides of Eq. (9.60), we get

$$\| E\tilde{\boldsymbol{\theta}}_{k+1} \| \leqslant (1 - d_4 \rho_k) \| E\tilde{\boldsymbol{\theta}}_k \| \tag{9.61}$$

where d_4 is the minimum eigenvalue of the matrix $E\{\boldsymbol{\varphi}\boldsymbol{\varphi}'\}$. Equation (9.61) in conjunction with the property of $\{\rho_k\}$ in Eq. (9.4) implies that

$$\operatorname*{Lim}_{k\to\infty} \| E\tilde{\boldsymbol{\theta}}_k \| = 0 \tag{9.62}$$

Let us scalar multiply Eq. (9.59) with itself and take the conditional expectation:

$$\begin{aligned} E\{\| \tilde{\boldsymbol{\theta}}_{k+1} \|^2 \mid \boldsymbol{\theta}_k\} &= E\{\| \boldsymbol{\theta}_k \|^2_{(I-\rho_1\boldsymbol{\varphi}_k\boldsymbol{\varphi}_k')^2} \mid \boldsymbol{\theta}_k\} \\ &\quad + \rho_k^2[E\{\xi_k^2 \| \boldsymbol{\varphi}_k \|^2 \mid \boldsymbol{\theta}_k\} + 2E\{\tilde{\boldsymbol{\theta}}_k' \boldsymbol{\varphi}_k \boldsymbol{\varphi}_k' \xi_k \mid \boldsymbol{\theta}_k\} \\ &\quad - 2\rho_k E\{\tilde{\boldsymbol{\theta}}_k' \boldsymbol{\varphi}_k \xi_k \mid \boldsymbol{\theta}_k\} \end{aligned} \tag{9.63}$$

Let us consider the various terms in Eq. (9.63) separately.*

* $\lambda_{\max}[A] \triangleq$ maximum eigenvalue of matrix A.

$$E\{\| \tilde{\theta}_k \|^2_{(I-\rho_k\varphi_k\varphi_k')^2} \mid \theta_k\} = \| \tilde{\theta}_k \|^2_{E\{(I-\rho_k\varphi_k\varphi_k')^2\}}$$

$$\leqslant \| \tilde{\theta}_k \|^2_{\lambda_{\max}[E\{(I-\rho_k\varphi_k\varphi_k)^2\}]}$$

$$\leqslant \| \tilde{\theta}_k \|^2_{\lambda_{\max}[I-(2-\epsilon_1)\rho_k E\{\varphi_k\varphi_k'\}]} \quad \forall k > k_1 \quad \text{and} \quad 0 < \epsilon_1 < 2$$

$$\leqslant \| \tilde{\theta}_k \|^2 (1 - d_5\rho_k) \tag{9.64}$$

where $d_5 = (2 - \epsilon_1)\, d_4$

By Conditions (i), (iii), and (iv),

$$E\{\xi_k^2 \| \varphi_k \|^2 \mid \theta_k\} \leqslant E\{(f(\mathbf{x}_k) - \theta^{o\prime}\varphi_k)^2 \| \varphi_k \|^2 + \eta_k^2 \| \varphi_k \|^2\} \leqslant d_6 < \infty \tag{9.65}$$

where d_6 is a constant.

Further,

$$E(\tilde{\theta}_k'\varphi_k\varphi_k'\varphi_k\xi_k \mid \theta_k) = (E\{\tilde{\theta}_k\})' E\{\varphi_k\varphi_k'\varphi_k\xi_k\} = 0 \tag{9.66}$$

Similarly,

$$E\{\tilde{\theta}_k'\varphi_k\xi_k \mid \theta_k\} = 0 \tag{9.67}$$

Substituting Eqs. (9.64)–(9.67) in Eq. (9.63), we get

$$E\{\| \tilde{\theta}_{k+1} \|^2 \mid \theta_k\} \leqslant \| \tilde{\theta}_k \|^2 (1 - d_5\rho_k) + d_6\rho_k^2 \tag{9.68}$$

Taking expectations on either side of Eq. (9.68), we get

$$E \| \tilde{\theta}_{k+1} \|^2 \leqslant (1 - d_5\rho_k) \| \tilde{\theta}_k \|^2 + d_6\rho_k^2 \tag{9.69}$$

We have already shown in Appendix 1 that the $E \| \tilde{\theta}_k \|^2$, given by Eq. (9.69), tends to zero with k, thus completing the proof.

The proof of convergence with probability one is omitted since it is given in Kashyap and Blaydon (1966).

References

Albert, A. and Gardner, L., "Stochastic Approximation and Nonlinear Regression." M.I.T. Press, Cambridge, Mass., 1967.

Aizerman, M. A., Braverman, F. M., and Rozonoer, L. I., The probability problem in pattern recognition learning and the method of potential functions. *Automation and Remote Control 25*, No. 9 (1964a).

Aizerman, M. A., Braverman, F. M., and Rozonoer, L. I., The method of potential functions in the problem of determining the characteristics of a function generator from randomly observed points. *Automation and Remote Control 25*, No. 12 (1964b).

Braverman, E. M., On the method of potential functions. *Automation and Remote Control 26*, No. 12 (1965).

Chung, K. L., On a stochastic approximation method. *Ann. Math. Stat. 25*, No. 4 (1954).

Dupac, V., A dynamic stochastic approximation method. *Ann. Math. Stat. 38*, Feb. (1967).

Fabian, V., Stochastic approximation of minima with improved asymptotic speed. *Ann. Math. Stat. 36*, Dec. (1965).

Gladyshev, E. A., On stochastic approximation. *Theory of Prob. and Appl. 10*, No. 2 (1965).

Kashyap, R. L. and Blaydon, C. C., Recovery of functions from noisy measurements taken at randomly selected points and its application to pattern classification. *Proc. IEEE 54*, pp. 1127–1129 (1966).

Kesten, H., Accelerated stochastic approximation methods. *Ann. Math. Stat. 29*, No. 1 (1958).

Kiefer, J. and Wolfowitz, J., Stochastic estimation of the maximum of a regression function. *Ann. Math. Stat. 23*, No. 3 (1952).

Loginov, N. V., Stochastic approximation methods. *Automation and Remote Control 27*, No. 4 (1966).

Newbold, P. M., A stochastic approximation scheme with accelerated convergence properties. Tech. Rept. No. 545, Division of Engineering and Applied Physics, Harvard Univ. Cambridge, Mass., 1967.

Robbins, H. and Monro, S., A stochastic approximation method. *Ann. Math. Stat. 22*, No. 1 (1951).

Schmetterer, L., Stochastic approximation. *Proc. 4th Berkeley Symp. Math. Stat. and Prob.*, Vol. I (1961).

Venter, J. H., On Dvoretzky stochastic approximation theorems. *Ann. Math. Stat. 37*, No. 4 (1966).

Venter, J. H., An extension of the Robbins–Munro procedure. *Ann. Math. Stat. 38*, No. 2 (1967a).

Venter, J. H., On the convergence of the Kiefer–Wolfowitz approximation procedure. *Ann. Math. Stat. 38*, No. 4, pp. 1031–1036 (1967b).

Wagner, T. J., The rate of convergence of an algorithm for recovering functions from noisy measurements taken at randomly selected points. *IEEE Trans. System Science and Cybernetics*, July (1968).

10

C. C. Blaydon
R. L. Kashyap
K. S. Fu

APPLICATIONS OF THE STOCHASTIC APPROXIMATION METHODS

I. Introduction

In this chapter we will describe some of the applications of the methods of stochastic approximation (SA) to some pattern classification, estimation, and control problems.

Recently, considerable success has been attained in the formulation and development of techniques for estimation and control of well-defined systems whether they be static or dynamic, deterministic or stochastic. Currently, however, the need is being felt for more robust methods which can tolerate greater ambiguity in the specification of the particular system under consideration. Such methods would be free of the narrow restrictions which can deter one from applying existing "optimal" techniques to a system about which only incomplete information is available. Stochastic approximation methods provide one means of approaching this problem. In many instances the (SA) schemes can operate with no information other than a set of observations from the process under consideration.

The stochastic approximation schemes have computational attractiveness since the computations involved are relatively straightforward and can be carried out in real time. The SA methods are valuable in processing data which arrives in such large quantities that its entire storage may pose problems.

In order to apply the SA methods, the problems under consideration are posed as extremum problems. We will deal here mainly with the mean square criterion function.

Each problem requires a slight modification of the theory to suit its peculiarities.

II. Pattern Classification Examples

In this section, the SA methods will be applied to a straightforward pattern classification problem. The problem is to model the decision mechanism by which the applicants to Harvard College are accepted or rejected.

When an applicant submits an application for admission to Harvard College, much of the information contained in the application is coded into a series of numbers. Each of these numbers will be considered to be a component of a pattern vector. The components of this vector are as follows:

x_1—public or private high school (either 1 or zero)
x_2—scholarship applicant or not (either 1 or zero)
x_3—coded rank in class (range: 20 to 80)
x_4—father's college (range: 1 to 5 with 1 being Harvard)
x_5—average verbal scholastic aptitude test score (range: 20 to 80)
x_6—average mathematical scholastic aptitude test score (range: 20 to 80)
x_7—average achievement test score (range: 20 to 80)
x_8—predicted rank list (range: 20 to 80)
x_9—predicted overall rating (range: 1 to 9)
x_{10}—predicted overall scholastic rating (range: 1 to 9)
x_{11}—academic rating (range: 1 to 6)
x_{12}—extracurricular activities rating (range: 1 to 6)
x_{13}—athletic rating (range: 1 to 6)
x_{14}—personal rating (range: 1 to 6)
x_{15}—first teacher's rating (range: 1 to 6)
x_{16}—second teacher's rating (range: 1 to 6)
x_{17}—principal's rating (range: 1 to 6)
x_{18}—staff personal rating (range: 1 to 6)
x_{19}—staff overall rating (range: 1 to 6)
x_{20}—alumni personal rating (range: 1 to 6)
x_{21}—alumni overall rating (range: 1 to 6)

It will be assumed here that the admissions committee makes a decision to accept or reject an applicant only on the basis of information represented in these numbers. This assumption is made in order to construct a mathematical model. The committee does not make actual decisions based solely on these numbers. The SA algorithm will be applied to the records of past decisions of the admissions committee in order to approximate a conditional probability function that describes the decisions of the committee. The probability function being approximated is the probability that an applicant will be accepted conditioned on the series of numbers that have been abstracted from his application. In other words, if the series of numbers abstracted from the application is taken to be the pattern vector $\mathbf{x}$, and if ω is the label assigned to the class of admitted applicants; then the algorithm is attempting to approximate the conditional probability function $P(\omega \mid \mathbf{x})$.

If the approximation $\hat{P}(\omega \mid \mathbf{x})$ to $P(\omega \mid \mathbf{x})$ is $\boldsymbol{\theta}'\mathbf{x} = \hat{P}(\omega \mid \mathbf{x})$, then the second-order SA algorithm below (see Section IV B of Chapter 9) will find the value $\boldsymbol{\theta} = \boldsymbol{\theta}^o$ that minimizes the MSE criterion $E\{\hat{P}(\omega \mid \mathbf{x}) - P(\omega \mid \mathbf{x})\}^2$.

$$\begin{aligned} \boldsymbol{\theta}_{k+1} &= \boldsymbol{\theta}_k + P_k\mathbf{x}_k(y_k - \boldsymbol{\theta}_k'\mathbf{x}_k) \\ P_{k+1} &= P_k - \frac{P_k\mathbf{x}_k\mathbf{x}_k'P_k}{1 + \mathbf{x}_k'P_k\mathbf{x}_k} \end{aligned} \tag{10.1}$$

where

$$y_k = \begin{cases} 1 & \text{if the applicant with pattern } \mathbf{x}_k \text{ is admitted} \\ 0 & \text{otherwise} \end{cases}$$

Example 1. In this example, the set of training samples consists of 500 patterns randomly selected from the applicants for admission to the Harvard Class of 1970. Applying the algorithm mentioned above to these patterns yields the following approximation for $P(\omega \mid \mathbf{x})$:

$$\begin{aligned} \hat{P}(\omega \mid \mathbf{x}) = 0.25 &- 0.084\, x_1 + 0.0089\, x_2 + 0.0042\, x_3 - 0.033\, x_4 \\ &+ 0.0038\, x_5 - 0.0026\, x_6 + 0.0064\, x_7 + 0.0078\, x_8 \\ &- 0.12\, x_9 + 0.0039\, x_{10} + 0.039\, x_{11} - 0.015\, x_{12} \\ &- 0.039\, x_{13} + 0.000091\, x_{14} - 0.013\, x_{15} + 0.0052\, x_{16} \\ &- 0.01\, x_{17} + 0.018\, x_{18} - 0.083\, x_{19} - 0.023\, x_{20} \\ &- 0.0014\, x_{21} \end{aligned}$$

Using this approximation as a discriminant function and applying it to both the 500 training samples and to a test set of 5,000 new, randomly selected patterns, the approximation function discriminates between accepted and rejected applicants in the manner displayed in the histogram in Fig. 1.

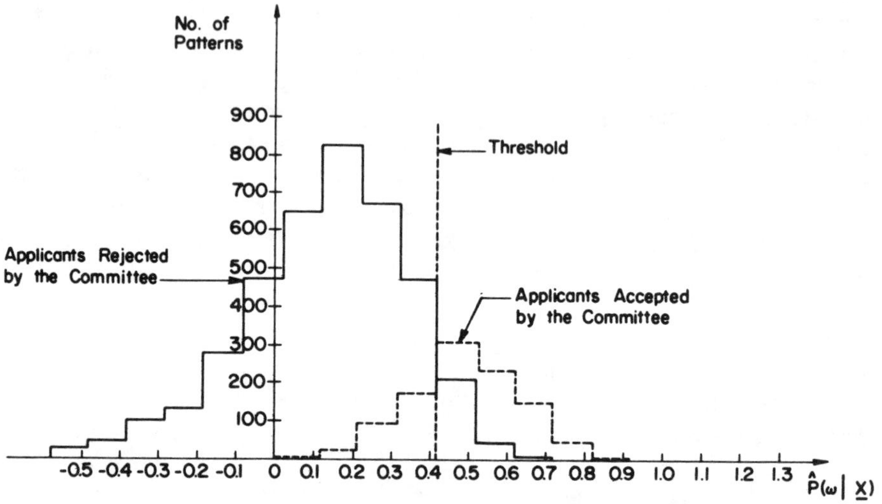

FIGURE 1. Pattern classification by $\hat{P}(\omega \mid \mathbf{x})$ trained on 500 samples

If a Bayesian decision rule were implemented using $\hat{P}(\omega \mid \mathbf{x})$, then the costs of misclassification would simply set a threshold value for the discriminant $\hat{P}(\omega \mid \mathbf{x})$. For example, if the cost of rejecting an applicant who should be accepted is the same as that for accepting one who should be rejected, then the threshold value for the discriminant is $\frac{1}{2}$ and the decision rule is as follows:

$$\text{if } \hat{P}(\omega \mid \mathbf{x}) > \tfrac{1}{2} \quad \text{classify } \mathbf{x} \text{ as "accepted"}$$

$$\text{if } \hat{P}(\omega \mid \mathbf{x}) < \tfrac{1}{2} \quad \text{classify } \mathbf{x} \text{ as "rejected"}$$

Adjusting the ratio of the cost of incorrect rejection to the cost of incorrect acceptance also adjusts the threshold of the discriminant. The threshold value which minimizes the number of incorrect decisions in the training sample is 0.422 which corresponds to a cost ratio of 0.73. With this threshold, $\hat{P}(\omega \mid \mathbf{x})$ misclassifies 6.6 percent of the training sample and 11.4 percent of the test sample.

Example 2. In this example the training set is increased to 1,000 randomly selected patterns, but the test set remains the same

5,000 patterns. The SA algorithm constructs the following approximation for $P(\omega \mid \mathbf{x})$.*

$$\begin{aligned}\hat{P}(\omega \mid \mathbf{x}) = 0.51 &- 0.67\,x_1 - 0.0073\,x_2 + 0.0042\,x_3 - 0.04\,x_4 \\ &+ 0.0037\,x_5 - 0.0029\,x_6 + 0.0053\,x_7 + 0.0079\,x_8 \\ &- 0.10\,x_9 - 0.0046\,x_{10} - 0.0069\,x_{11} - 0.0061\,x_{12} \\ &- 0.033\,x_{13} - 0.021\,x_{14} - 0.014\,x_{15} + 0.0017\,x_{16} \\ &- 0.0045\,x_{17} - 0.0014\,x_{18} - 0.084\,x_{19} - 0.0098\,x_{20} \\ &- 0.0099\,x_{21}\end{aligned}$$

The performance of $\hat{P}(\omega \mid \mathbf{x})$ as a discriminant function is displayed in the histogram of Fig. 2. The threshold which minimizes the number of incorrect decisions in the training sample is 0.327. With this threshold, the discriminant misclassifies 7.4 percent of the training sample and 10.9 percent of the test sample. Training on a larger sample set has improved the generalization property, i.e., the ability of the discriminant to classify new patterns that were not in the training set.

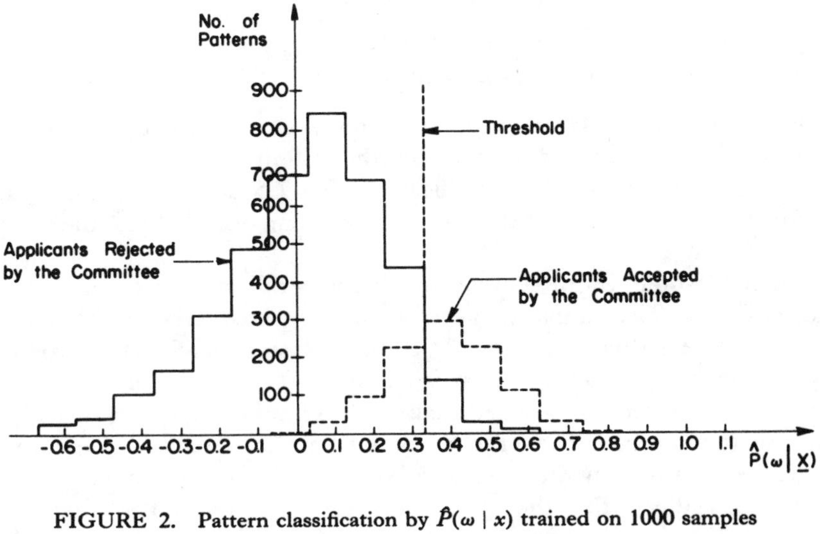

FIGURE 2. Pattern classification by $\hat{P}(\omega \mid x)$ trained on 1000 samples

* If the variables are normalized by their range, the coefficients would be respectively: 0.067, 0.0073, 0.252, 0.20, 0.222, 0.174, 0.318, 0.474, 0.8, 0.037, 0.041, 0.037, 0.20, 0.126, 0.084, 0.0104, 0.027, 0.0084, 0.504, 0.05888, 0.06. The three most significant variables turn out to be predicted overall rating, the staff overall rating, and the predicted rank list. The variables in the other two examples can be similarly normalized.

Example 3. In glancing at the list of components of the pattern vector, it can be noticed that some of the vector components are themselves discriminant functions derived by the admissions office staff. One such component is the predicted rank list. In this example we will take the discriminant function of Example 2 as the first component of a new pattern vector. In addition, the other components of the pattern vector will be father's college, verbal scholastic aptitude test score, and predicted overall rating, all of which appear to be reliable indicators. Using this pattern vector, a second-order approximation will be made to the probability $P(\omega \mid \mathbf{x})$. The approximation constructed for $P(\omega \mid \mathbf{x})$ using the second-order SA algorithm in Eq. (10.1) is:

$$\begin{aligned}\hat{P}(\omega \mid \mathbf{x}) = {} & -0.001 + 0.31\, x_1 + 0.12\, x_2 + 0.054\, x_3 - 0.11\, x_4 \\ & + 0.6\, x_1^2 + 0.084\, x_1x_2 + 0.24\, x_1x_3 - 0.091\, x_1x_4 \\ & + 0.02\, x_2^2 + 0.19\, x_2x_3 + 0.12\, x_2x_4 - 0.01\, x_3^2 \\ & + 0.16\, x_3x_4 + 0.16\, x_4^2\end{aligned}$$

where

$$\begin{aligned} & x_1 \text{ is } \hat{P}(\omega \mid \mathbf{x}) \text{ from Example 2} \\ & x_2 = \text{previous } x_5/75 \\ & x_3 = \text{previous } x_4/75 \\ & x_4 = \text{previous } x_9/75 \end{aligned}$$

The performance of this approximation is shown in Fig. 3 where the threshold that minimizes errors in the training sample is 0.49. This threshold gives incorrect classifications for 7.5 percent of the training sample and 9.8 percent of the test sample, using exactly the same samples as in Example 2.

Besides some improvement in the generalization property of the second-order discriminant, the most striking characteristic of this new discriminant is that it is actually coming close to having the properties of a probability function. That is, there are few values of $\hat{P}(\omega \mid \mathbf{x})$ that are less than zero or greater than one. This is not the case with the approximations constructed in Examples 1 and 2. The heavy weighting of the rejected applicants near zero and the spread of the accepted applicants seems to indicate that the coded variables accurately reflect the characteristics that cause a candidate to be rejected, but are less reliable in judging his acceptance. In accepting applicants, the committee evidently considers characteristics other than those reflected by these variables.

Because the SA algorithm is a least squares fit procedure, it can fall into the numerical difficulties that are common to such schemes. In particular, if all of the terms in the approximation are positive, it is very

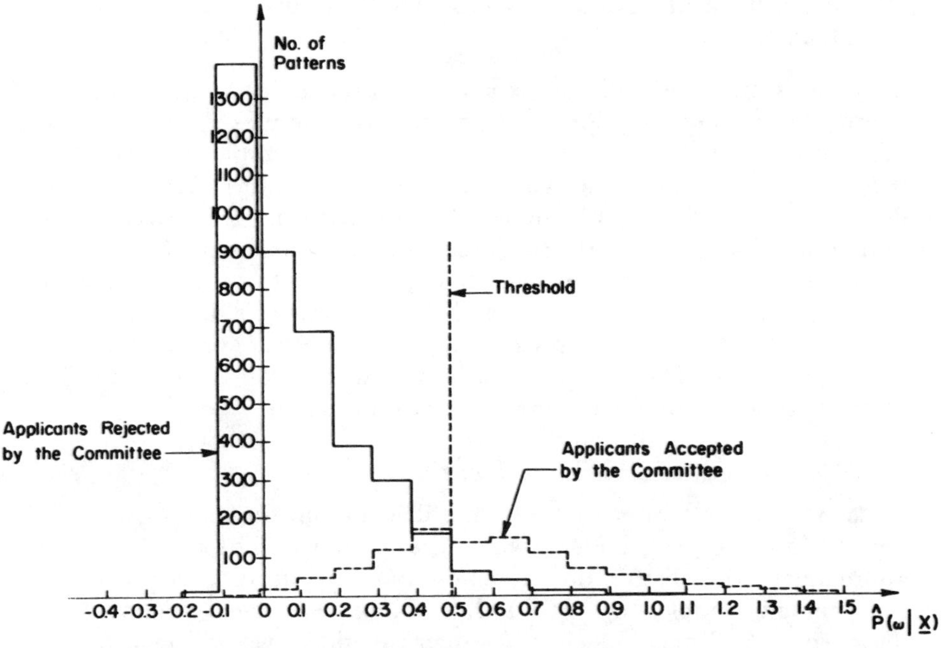

FIGURE 3. Pattern classification by a second order $\hat{P}(\omega \mid \mathbf{x})$

easy for the matrix P_k to become ill-conditioned with the consequent poor evaluation of P_k when using a computer. This difficulty can be avoided by a judicious normalization of the terms in the approximation, just as is commonly done in regression analysis. In Example 3, this ill-conditioning became apparent and was simply resolved, by dividing selected variables by their normalization constants.

For cases in which the probability function approximations are linear, it is not surprising that the results from the SA algorithms and the results from regression analyses are similar. Though regression analysis relies on assumptions of jointly Gaussian components in the pattern vectors, a close look at the computation involved shows that it is the same as the SA algorithm for the case where the conditional probability approximation is chosen to be linear in terms of the pattern components. Thus, the discriminant functions constructed by means of SA algorithms have the additional interpretation of being minimum-mean-square-error linear approximations to a conditional probability function. This approximation property, moreover, provides a justification for using nonlinear discriminants which are not often used in regression analysis.

III. Estimation of Probability Distribution and Density Functions

In this section we will approximate the probability distribution and density function of a random vector $\mathbf{x}$ from the samples $\mathbf{x}_1, \mathbf{x}_2, \ldots$ using SA methods. Such estimates are required, for example, in reliability theory for determining the conditional rate of failure. Traditionally, distribution and density functions are estimated using empirical distribution functions (Parzen, 1962). These estimates are numerical functions requiring large amounts of memory to compute and to store. One way of avoiding the numerical functions and their associated storage problems is to look for functional approximations which need not be stored in numerical form. These approximations will be constructed by SA methods so as to minimize suitable error criteria.

A. *Approximation of Distribution Functions*

Let $\mathbf{x}$ be a random m-vector with a distribution function $F(\mathbf{x})$ and a density function $f(\mathbf{x})$, both of which are unknown. The problem is to approximate the distribution function $F(\mathbf{x})$ by using a sequence of independent samples $\mathbf{x}_i$, $i = 1, 2, \ldots$. Since regression methods are designed to find parameters rather than functions, we will look for an approximation $\hat{F}(\mathbf{x})$ to $F(\mathbf{x})$ of the following form:

$$\hat{F}(\mathbf{x}) = \boldsymbol{\theta}'\boldsymbol{\varphi}(\mathbf{x}) = \sum_{i=1}^{n} \theta_i \varphi_i(\mathbf{x})$$

$\boldsymbol{\theta}$ is an n-vector of undetermined coefficients, $\{\varphi_i(\mathbf{x}); i = 1, \ldots, n\}$ is a set of known independent functions of $\mathbf{x}$ possessing moments up to the sixth moment, and the matrix $E\{\boldsymbol{\varphi}(\mathbf{x})\,\boldsymbol{\varphi}'(\mathbf{x})\}$ is positive definite. The number n denotes the memory needed to store the approximation. The larger the value of n, the closer will be the approximation $\hat{F}(\mathbf{x})$ to the true distribution function. The number n is chosen depending on the computational complexity and the amount of error that can be tolerated between the approximation and the true function.

The problem is to find the optimal value of $\boldsymbol{\theta}$, say $\boldsymbol{\theta}^o$, which minimizes a suitable function of the error, $(F(\mathbf{x}) - \boldsymbol{\theta}'\boldsymbol{\varphi}(\mathbf{x}))$, say, the mean-square-error,

$$J(\boldsymbol{\theta}) = E\{F(\mathbf{x}) - \boldsymbol{\theta}'\boldsymbol{\varphi}(\mathbf{x})\}^2$$

The value $\boldsymbol{\theta}^o$ of $\boldsymbol{\theta}$ which minimizes the criterion function is

$$\boldsymbol{\theta}^o = \operatorname{Arg}[\operatorname*{Min.}_{\boldsymbol{\theta}} J(\boldsymbol{\theta})] = (E\{\boldsymbol{\varphi}(\mathbf{x})\,\boldsymbol{\varphi}'(\mathbf{x})\})^{-1} E\{\boldsymbol{\varphi}(\mathbf{x})\,F(\mathbf{x})\}$$

so that

$$\begin{aligned}\hat{F}(\mathbf{x}) &= \text{optimal approximation to } F(\mathbf{x}) \\ &= \boldsymbol{\theta}^{o\prime}\boldsymbol{\varphi}(\mathbf{x})\end{aligned}$$

For applying the SA methods, we need an observable random variable whose expectation is the gradient $\nabla_{\boldsymbol{\theta}} J(\boldsymbol{\theta})$. Such a function, $\mathbf{y}(\boldsymbol{\theta}, \mathbf{x})$ is:

$$\mathbf{y}(\boldsymbol{\theta}, \mathbf{x}_k) = \boldsymbol{\varphi}(\mathbf{x}_k)(z_k(\mathbf{x}_k) - \boldsymbol{\theta}'\boldsymbol{\varphi}(\mathbf{x}_k))$$

where $z_k(\mathbf{x})$ is the empirical distribution function, defined as

$$z_k(\mathbf{x}) = \frac{1}{k-1} \Sigma_{j=1}^{k-1} \Omega_{\mathbf{x}}(\mathbf{x}_j) = F_k(\mathbf{x})$$

and

$$\Omega_{\mathbf{x}}(\mathbf{y}) = \begin{cases} 1 & \text{if} \quad x_k < y_k \; \forall \, k = 1, \dots, m \\ 0 & \quad \text{otherwise} \end{cases}$$

In other words,

$$z_i(\mathbf{x}) = \frac{\begin{array}{l}\text{The number of samples at the } i\text{th stage which} \\ \text{have all of their components less than the} \\ \text{corresponding components of } \mathbf{x}\end{array}}{\text{Total number of samples}}.$$

The empirical distribution function has the properties

$$\begin{aligned} E\{z_i(\mathbf{x}) | \; \mathbf{x}\} &= F(\mathbf{x}) \\ \text{Var}\{z_i(\mathbf{x}) | \; \mathbf{x}\} &= F(\mathbf{x})(1 - F(\mathbf{x}))/i \end{aligned}$$

This empirical distribution function requires that all samples from the first through the ith stages be stored. If we want to avoid this and store only the last N samples, then $z_i(\mathbf{x})$ can be redefined as

$$z_i(\mathbf{x}) = \frac{1}{N} \sum_{j=i-N}^{i-1} \Omega_{\mathbf{x}}(\mathbf{x}_j)$$

This function still has the property

$$E(z_i(\mathbf{x}) | \; \mathbf{x}) = F(\mathbf{x})$$

but now

$$\text{Var}(z_i(\mathbf{x}) | \; \mathbf{x}) = F(\mathbf{x})(1 - F(\mathbf{x}))/N \leqslant 1/4N$$

The first order SA algorithm for determining $\boldsymbol{\theta}^o$ can be written down as follows:

$$\boldsymbol{\theta}_{k+1} = \boldsymbol{\theta}_k + \rho_k \boldsymbol{\varphi}_k (z_k(\mathbf{x}_k) - \boldsymbol{\theta}_k' \boldsymbol{\varphi}_k) \tag{10.2}$$

The sequence $\boldsymbol{\theta}_k$ converges not only with probability one but also in mean square sense to the value $\boldsymbol{\theta} = \boldsymbol{\theta}^o$.

Alternatively, we can give a second order SA scheme, similar to Eq. (10.1), which also converges to $\boldsymbol{\theta}^o$

$$\left.\begin{aligned} \boldsymbol{\theta}_{k+1} &= \boldsymbol{\theta}_k + P_{k+1} \boldsymbol{\varphi}_k (z_k(\mathbf{x}_k) - \boldsymbol{\theta}_k' \boldsymbol{\varphi}_k) \\ P_{k+1} &= P_k - \frac{P_k \boldsymbol{\varphi}_k \boldsymbol{\varphi}_k' P_k}{1 + \boldsymbol{\varphi}_k' P_k \boldsymbol{\varphi}_k} \end{aligned}\right\} \tag{10.3}$$

where $\boldsymbol{\theta}_0$ is arbitrary and P_0 is an arbitrary positive definite matrix. For further details, see the paper by Kashyap and Blaydon (1968).

Example 4. $\mathbf{x}$ is a scalar ($m = 1$) whose distribution function is $\{1 - \exp(-x)\}$, $x \geqslant 0$. We choose $n = 3$ in the approximation. The storage number is $N = 400$. The functions $\varphi_i(x)$, $i = 1, 2, 3$ were chosen among the Laguerre polynomials.

$$\varphi_1(x) = 1$$

$$\varphi_2(x) = -x + 1$$

$$\varphi_3(x) = \frac{x^2}{2} - 2x + 1$$

The distribution function was approximated only in the region $0 \leqslant x \leqslant 4$. The sequence $\boldsymbol{\theta}_k$ was computed using both algorithms. The graphs of $\theta_{j,k}$ versus k for both algorithms are plotted for all $j = 1, 2, 3$ in Figs. 4, 5 and 6. As predicted, the second-order algorithm converges to the true value much faster than the first-order algorithm. $\hat{F}_1(x)$ and $\hat{F}_2(x)$, the estimates of the true $F(x)$ by first- and second-order algorithms, respectively, after 500 iterations, are given below. $\hat{F}(x)$ is the true minimum MSE approximation.

$$\hat{F}_1(x) = 0.493 - 0.202(-x + 1) - 0.216\left(\frac{x^2}{2} - 2x + 1\right)$$

$$\hat{F}_2(x) = 0.487 - 0.181(-x + 1) - 0.241\left(\frac{x^2}{2} - 2x + 1\right)$$

$$\hat{F}(x) = 0.480 - 0.186(-x + 1) - 0.239\left(\frac{x^2}{2} - 2x + 1\right)$$

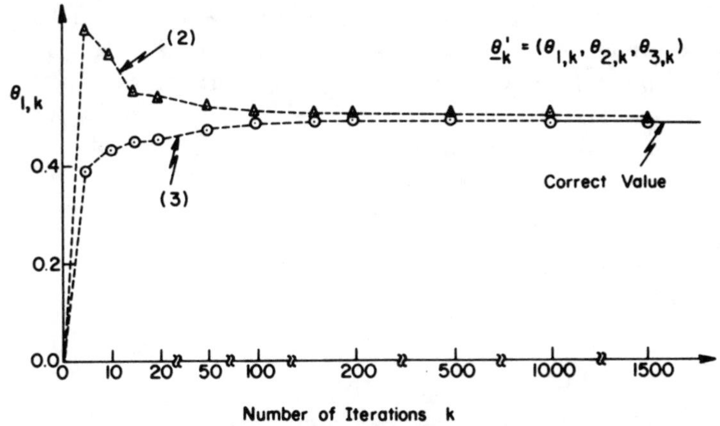

FIGURE 4. Graph of $\theta_{1,k}$ versus k using Eqs. (10.2) and (10.3)

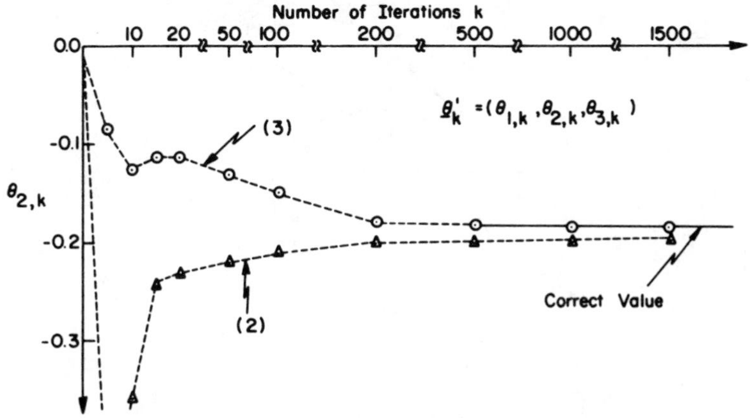

FIGURE 5. Graph of $\theta_{2,k}$ versus k using Eqs. (10.2) and (10.3)

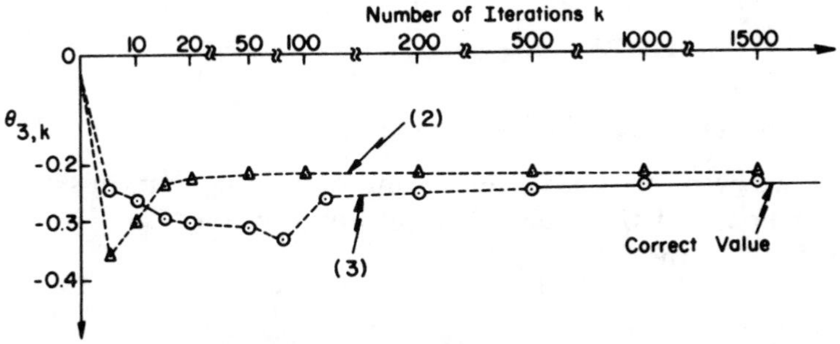

FIGURE 6. Graph of $\theta_{3,k}$ versus k using Eqs. (10.2) and (10.3)

To display the role of the number n, the graph of $\hat{F}(x)$ is plotted against x for various values of n in Fig. 7. In the same figure, $F(x)$ is also plotted against x displaying the error involved for various values of n.

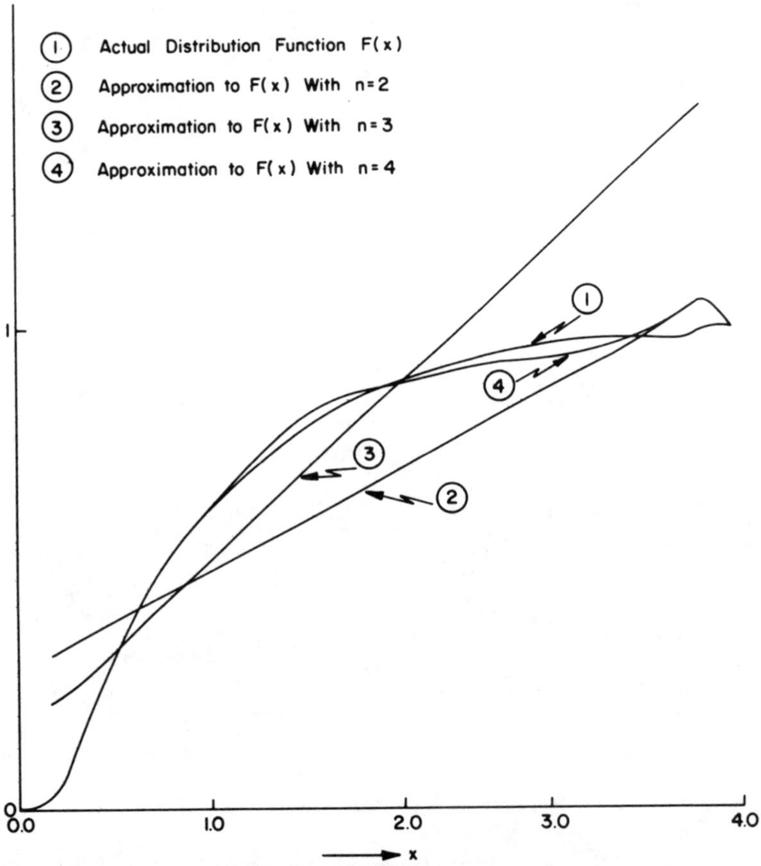

FIGURE 7. Graph of $F(\mathbf{x})$ and $\hat{F}(\mathbf{x})$ versus x

B. *Estimation of Probability Density Functions*

Again we want to find a linear approximation, but this time the approximation is of the probability density function $f(\mathbf{x})$. The approximation $\hat{f}(\mathbf{x})$ has the following form

$$\hat{f}(\mathbf{x}) = \boldsymbol{\theta}'\boldsymbol{\varphi}(\mathbf{x}) = \sum_{i=1}^{n} \theta_i \varphi_i(\mathbf{x})$$

We are looking for the value $\boldsymbol{\theta}^o$ which minimizes the mean-square-error criterion $J_1(\boldsymbol{\theta})$

$$J_1(\boldsymbol{\theta}) = E\{f(\mathbf{x}) - \boldsymbol{\theta}'\boldsymbol{\varphi}(\mathbf{x})\}^2$$

The minimizing value of $\boldsymbol{\theta}$ is

$$\boldsymbol{\theta}^o = [E\{\boldsymbol{\varphi}(\mathbf{x})\,\boldsymbol{\varphi}'(\mathbf{x})\}]^{-1}\,E\{\boldsymbol{\varphi}(\mathbf{x})\,f(\mathbf{x})\}$$

For recovering $\boldsymbol{\theta}^o$ we need, as before, an observable random vector $\mathbf{y}(\boldsymbol{\theta}, \mathbf{x})$ whose expectation is the gradient $\nabla_{\boldsymbol{\theta}} J_1(\boldsymbol{\theta})$.

For this problem however, an observable random vector $\mathbf{y}(\boldsymbol{\theta}, \mathbf{x})$ having the above property cannot be found. Instead, we have to settle for an observable vector having the property that

$$E\{\mathbf{y}(\boldsymbol{\theta}_k\,, \mathbf{x}_k) |\, \mathbf{x}_k\} = \nabla_{\boldsymbol{\theta}} J_1(\boldsymbol{\theta})|_{\boldsymbol{\theta}=\boldsymbol{\theta}_k} + c_k\,\mathbf{g}_k(\mathbf{x}_k)$$

with the bias term, $c_k\mathbf{g}_k(\mathbf{x}_k)$, vanishing as k tends to infinity. One such function is given below

$$\mathbf{y}(\boldsymbol{\theta}_k\,, \mathbf{x}_k) = \boldsymbol{\varphi}_k\{z_k(\mathbf{x}_k) - \boldsymbol{\theta}_k{}'\boldsymbol{\varphi}_k\}$$

where $z_k(\mathbf{x})$ is an approximation to a numerical derivative of the empirical distribution function; that is, $z_k(\mathbf{x})$ is an approximation to the empirical density function,

$$z_k(\mathbf{x}) = \frac{1}{2^m c_k{}^m} \sum_{\mathbf{e}} \left(\prod_{j=1}^{m} e_j \right) F_{k-1}(\mathbf{x} + c_k\mathbf{e}) \tag{10.4}$$

where

$$F_k(\mathbf{x}) = \text{empirical distribution function}$$
$$\mathbf{e}' = (e_1\,,..., e_m),\ e_i = +1 \text{ or } -1$$
$$(\mathbf{x} + c_k\mathbf{e})' = (x_1 + c_k e_1\,, x_2 + c_k e_2\,,..., x_m + c_k e_m)$$

and

$$c_k = \text{a positive scalar sequence to be defined.}$$

The summation in Eq. (10.4) is carried out over all 2^m possible combinations of $\mathbf{e}$. For example, if $m = 2$

$$\begin{aligned} z_k(\mathbf{x}) = \frac{1}{(2c_k)^2} \{ & F_{k-1}(x_1 + c_k\,, x_2 + c_k) \\ & - F_{k-1}(x_1 - c_k\,, x_2 + c_k) - F_{k-1}(x_1 + c_k\,, x_2 - c_k) \\ & + F_{k-1}(x_1 - c_k\,, x_2 - c_k)\} \end{aligned}$$

One can show that

$$E\{z_k(\mathbf{x})|\,\mathbf{x}\} = f(\mathbf{x}) + c_k g_k(\mathbf{x})$$

where $g_k(\mathbf{x})$ is a linear combination of the $(m+1)$st derivatives of $F(\mathbf{x})$ evaluated at various points inside a cube of side length $2c_i$ and centered at $\mathbf{x}$. Using the expression for $z_i(\mathbf{x})$ mentioned above, we can use the first-order algorithm in Eq. (10.2) to recover $\boldsymbol{\theta}^o$ with probability one—provided the gain P_k in the algorithm, and c_k mentioned above satisfy the following conditions:

$$\lim_{k\to\infty} \rho_k = 0 \qquad \sum_{k=1}^{\infty} \rho_k = \infty \qquad \sum_{k=1}^{\infty} \rho_k^2 < \infty$$

$$\lim_{k\to\infty} c_k = 0 \qquad \sum_{k=1}^{\infty} \rho_k c_k < \infty \quad \text{and} \quad \sum_{k=1}^{\infty} (\rho_k/c_k^m)^2 < \infty$$

We can also use the second-order algorithm in Eq. (10.3) to recover $\boldsymbol{\theta}^o$ with probability one, provided the gain c_k has the following properties

$$\lim_{k\to\infty} c_k = 0 \qquad \sum_k \frac{c_k}{k} < \infty \quad \text{and} \quad \sum_k \frac{1}{(kc_k^m)^2} < \infty$$

For further details of the method, such as convergence rates, approximation errors, and different error criterion functions, we refer to the paper by Kashyap and Blaydon (1968).

There are some advantages in using the SA methods instead of classical methods to estimate probability density and distribution functions. The highlights of the classical methods are:

(1) they require that all samples be stored during computation;

(2) the final result is in the form of a numerical function which is difficult to store in practice;

(3) the mean-square-error after j samples is proportional to K/j, $K > 0$; and

(4) they aim at getting the true distribution and density functions rather than their approximations.

The algorithms presented in this section do not suffer from disadvantages (1) and (2). In our case, not more than N samples need to be stored during computation, and the final estimate is an algebraic form rather than a numerical function; however, the algorithms of this section, in general, only *approximate* the true probability distribution and density functions. By choosing the number n sufficiently large, we can reduce the order of approximation to a desired level.

IV. State and Parameter Estimation Methods

Estimation of states in dynamical systems from noisy measurements is a popular subject. If the dynamical system is linear with known parameters and is excited by additive noise, and if only some components of the state are accessible for measurement, then the Kalman–Bucy filter gives an elegant method of computing the "best" linear estimate of the current state given all previous observations. If any of the assumptions just mentioned are not satisfied (such as if the system is not linear, or the parameters of the system are unknown, or the noise is correlated with the state) there is no general way of obtaining good estimates of the states given all the previous measurements. In such cases, it is convenient and practical to look for estimates which depend only on a finite number of past measurements. It is possible to compute such estimates using the SA algorithms. We will describe three types of problems: The first deals with state estimation in a stationary dynamical system with noisy measurements. In the second, we consider prediction in a nonstationary system, using dynamic stochastic approximation. In the third case, we consider the estimation of the parameters of a Markov chain when the only available information is the noise corrupted measurement of the state.

A. *State Estimation in Dynamical Systems*

The scalar signal x_k is assumed to obey the following difference equation:

$$\begin{aligned} x_{k+1} &= \psi_1(x_k, x_{k-1}, \ldots, \xi_k) \\ z_k &= x_k + v_k \\ v_{k+1} &= \psi_2(x_k, v_k, \eta_k) \end{aligned} \tag{10.5}$$

where z is the output that can be measured and v is the noise associated with the output measurement. We stress the fact that the functions ψ_1 and ψ_2 and the statistics of ξ and η need not be known explicitly. We assume that the system has reached steady state so that the random processes x, v and z can be regarded to be *stationary*.

The best estimate of x given all previous output measurements is $E(x_k \mid z_j, j \leqslant k)$. If the functions ψ_1 and ψ_2 are neither linear nor precisely known, there are no general techniques for computing the conditional mean $E(x_k \mid z_k, z_{k-1}, \ldots)$; hence, we would like to approximate the expression for the conditional mean of the state by a function involving only a finite number of output measurements, $z_k, z_{k-1}, \ldots,$ and z_{k-n} using the methods of stochastic approximation.

The time interval during which the approximating function is constructed is known as the training phase. The time interval during which the approximating function is used to construct the state estimates is known as the operating phase. In many problems, during the training phase we have additional information about the system besides the output measurement z. In particular we *assume* that the state x_k is *exactly* measurable (as it would be in a simulation of the system) during the training phase.

We would like to approximate the function $E[x_k \mid \mathbf{Z}_k]$ by a function

$$\sum_{i=1}^{n} \theta_i \varphi_i(\mathbf{Z})$$

where $\mathbf{Z}_k = (z_k, z_{k-1}, \ldots, z_{k-m+1})'$, a vector of m past measurements.

In many instances, we may choose

$$\boldsymbol{\varphi}(\mathbf{Z}) = \mathbf{Z}$$

The criterion function is

$$J(\boldsymbol{\theta}) = E\{\{E(x_k \mid \mathbf{Z}_k) - \boldsymbol{\theta}'\boldsymbol{\varphi}(\mathbf{Z}_k)\}^2\}$$

We can simplify this expression further, to

$$J(\boldsymbol{\theta}) = E\{x_k - \boldsymbol{\theta}'\boldsymbol{\varphi}(\mathbf{Z}_k)\}^2$$

Since both x_k and $\mathbf{Z}_k$ are accessible for exact measurement during the training phase, we can find the optimal value of $\boldsymbol{\theta}$ by the least squares algorithm in Eq. (10.1) with y_k replaced by x_k, and $\boldsymbol{\varphi}_k$ replaced by $\mathbf{Z}_k$

$$\begin{aligned} \boldsymbol{\theta}_{k+1} &= \boldsymbol{\theta}_k + P_{k+1}\mathbf{Z}_k(x_k - \boldsymbol{\theta}_k'\mathbf{Z}_k) \\ P_{k+1} &= P_k - \frac{P_k\mathbf{Z}_k\mathbf{Z}_k'P_k}{1 + \mathbf{Z}_k'P_k\mathbf{Z}_k} \end{aligned} \tag{10.6}$$

Because the observations are correlated, the SA convergence conditions that can be easily checked are not met; however, we will give a number of examples to demonstrate the reasonableness of the estimation scheme.

Example 5. The following stable second-order system was simulated on a digital computer:

$$x_{k+1} = 0.8\,x_k + 0.1\,x_{k-1} + 1.2\,\xi_k\,; \qquad \xi_k \sim N(0, 1)$$

where the measurement noise is correlated, with

$$v_{k+1} = 0.2\,v_k + (1.92)^{1/2}\,\eta_k\,; \qquad \eta_k \sim N(0, 1)$$

Both ξ and η are mutually independent noise processes. The sequences $\{\xi_k\}$ and $\{\eta_k\}$ are drawn from Gaussian random number generators. We chose $\varphi_i(\mathbf{Z}) = Z_i$ and $n = 6$. The filter constructed by the algorithm in Eq. (10.6), training on 200 samples is

$$\hat{x}_k = -0.22545 + 0.52049\, z_k + 0.12692\, z_{k-1} + 0.06621\, z_{k-2} + 0.02757\, z_{k-3} + 0.10717\, z_{k-4}$$

The sample steady-state error variance for this filter when tested on 200 new samples was 1.295. The steady-state error variance for a Kalman filter handling correlated noise, on the other hand, is 1.008.

Example 6. Consider the *unstable* system given by

$$x_{k+1} = 0.9\, x_k + 0.1\, x_{k-1} + 1.2\, \xi_k\,; \quad \xi \sim N(0, 1) \tag{10.7}$$

with measurements

$$z_k = 0.9\, x_k + v_k$$

The system can be simulated by using Gaussian random number generators where v_k is correlated noise given by

$$v_{k+1} = 0.2\, v_k + (0.96)^{1/2}\, \eta_k\,; \qquad \eta_k \sim N(0, 1)$$

ξ and η are mutually independent noise processes. Since Eq. (10.7) is unstable, the random process x is nonstationary. The filter constructed by the algorithm in Eq. (10.6) during a training phase of 200 samples with $n = 6$, is given by

$$\hat{x}_k = -0.68758 + 0.55108\, z_k + 0.14887\, z_{k-1} + 0.08541\, z_{k-2} + 0.041918\, z_{k-3} + 0.13496\, z_{k-4}$$

This filter had a sample error variance of 1.276 in a test phase of 200 samples. A plot of the state of this system and the corresponding estimates provided by the filter are shown in Fig. 8. In the test phase the standard deviation of the estimate was only about 3 percent of the mean value.

Example 7. Consider a system that has state dependent measurement noise, where the system is

$$x_{k+1} = 0.8\, x_k + 1.2\, \xi_k \qquad \xi \sim N(0, 1) \tag{10.8}$$

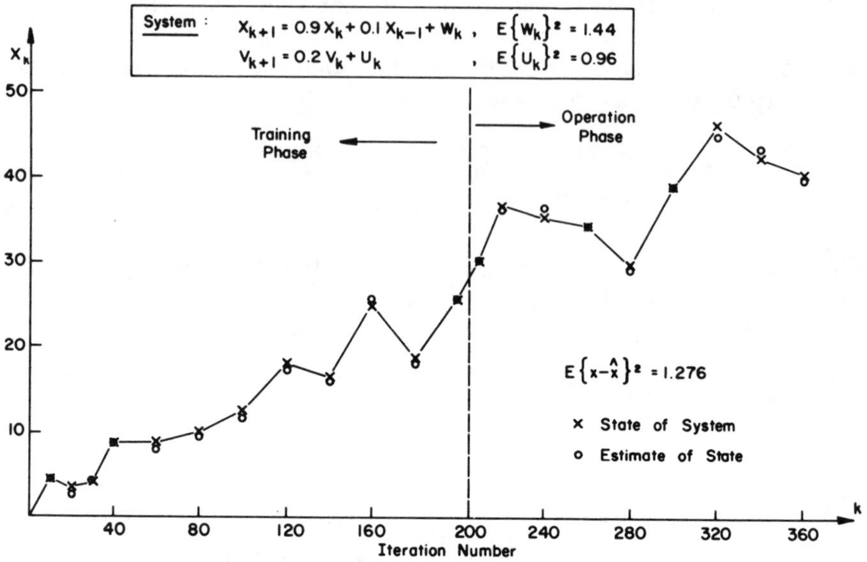

FIGURE 8. State estimation of unstable second-order linear system

with measurements given by

$$z_k = x_k + \left[\frac{x_k}{2} + 1\right]\eta_k \qquad \eta \sim N(0, 1)$$

In steady state, the variance of the state dependent noise term is

$$E\left[\left(\frac{x}{2} + 1\right)^2 \eta^2\right] = 2 \qquad \text{since} \qquad E(x^2) = 4$$

The linear approximation to the conditional expectation of the state constructed by the algorithm in Eq. (10.6) [with $n = 8$] is found to be

$$\begin{aligned}\hat{x}_k = {} & 0.09348 + 0.5209\, z_k + 0.21533\, z_{k-1} + 0.1033\, z_{k-2} \\ & + 0.002602\, z_{k-3} - 0.02908\, z_{k-4} + 0.003131\, z_{k-5} \\ & - 0.01946\, z_{k-6} + 0.05779\, z_{k-7}\end{aligned}$$

The sample variance of the error for this filter after 200 stages is 1.035. In steady state, if z_k alone were assumed to be the estimate of x_k then the error variance would be 6.0.

Example 8. To give an example with some physical motivation to it, consider the nonlinear integral servo whose stability was examined by

Jury and Lee (1964). The discrete version of this servo can be written as

$$x_{k+1} = 1.3\, x_{k+1} - 0.3\, x_k - F[0.60012\, x_{k+1} - 0.19986\, x_k] \qquad (10.9)$$

where $F(\cdot)$ is the nonlinear feedback function for the system. In this example, the nonlinearity is chosen to be a saturation function with

$$F(\sigma) = \begin{cases} \sigma; & \text{if} \quad |\sigma| < 3 \\ 3; & \text{if} \quad \sigma \geqslant 3 \\ -3; & \text{if} \quad \sigma \leqslant -3 \end{cases}$$

In addition, it is assumed that the position of the servo can be measured in the presence of additive correlated Gaussian noise. The measurement is

$$z_k = x_k + v_k$$

where

$$v_{k+1} = 0.2\, v_k + (1.92)^{1/2}\, \xi_j \qquad \xi \sim N(0, 1)$$

ξ is white noise. The linear approximation to the conditional mean of x_k, which is constructed by the algorithm in Eq. (10.6), yields the following filter with $n = 8$:

$$\begin{aligned} \hat{x}_k = {} & -0.01107 + 0.06782\, z_k + 0.01574\, z_{k-1} + 0.02659\, z_{k-2} \\ & - 0.00967\, z_{k-2} - 0.02871\, z_{k-4} - 0.01179\, z_{k-5} \\ & + 0.008438\, z_{k-6} - 0.01409\, z_{k-7} \end{aligned}$$

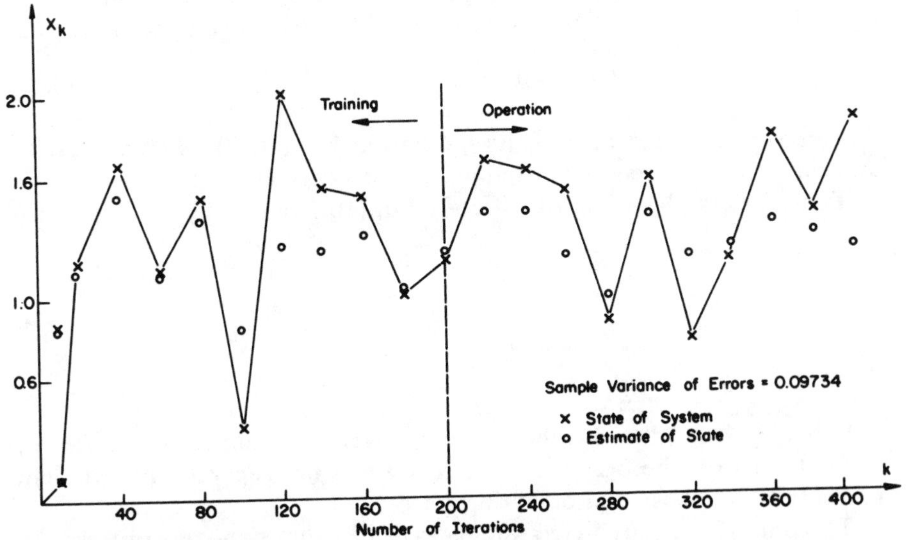

FIGURE 9. State estimation of second-order system with nonlinear feedback

This filter has a sample variance for errors that is 0.09734 calculated on a test sample of 200 stages. The performance of this filter is shown in Fig. 9. An error of one sample standard deviation is roughly 20 percent of the mean.

These examples clearly illustrate that *if it is possible* to measure the state of a system exactly during a training phase then stochastic approximation algorithms can be used to construct filters that are functions of a certain fixed number of past measurements. The filters that are so constructed are linear minimum-mean-square-error approximations to the conditional mean of the state even in cases where the system and measurements are nonlinear. In these cases, this approach can provide a reasonable filter without resorting to linearization about a nominal system path and using a Kalman filter.

B. *Prediction in Nonstationary Environment*

In this section, we are given a sequence of observations $z_1, z_2, \ldots$ arising from a stochastic process. The problem is to predict the value of z_{k+1} using only the history $z_k, z_{k-1}, \ldots$. The observed measurement z_k is assumed to be made up of a deterministic component (or trend) α_k and the random noise η_k,

$$z_k = \alpha_k + \eta_k$$

The sequence $\{\eta_k\}$ is a zero mean, noise sequence. The trend component α_k could be represented by the following Eq. (10.10) [Dupac, 1966].

$$\alpha_{k+1} = (1 + 1/k)\,\alpha_k + O(k^{-\mu}) \qquad \mu \geqslant 1 \tag{10.10}$$

The reason for the choice of the method in Eq. (10.10) is its simplicity and the apparent accuracy of the predictions derived from it.

Typical examples of α_k which obey Eq. (10.10) are

$$\alpha_k = \gamma_1 k$$

and

$$\alpha_k = \gamma_1 k + \gamma_2$$

where γ_1, γ_2 are unknown constants.

Let x_{k+1} = predicted value of z_{k+1} given measurement z_j, $j \leqslant k$. In contrast with the previous section, we will not separate the problem into a training phase and operating phase.

To compute the predicted value, we will use a two-step process. In the first step, we compute $\bar{x}_{k+1}$, the predicted value of $z(k+1)$ given x_k, the previous predicted value. We can write down the expression for $\bar{x}_{k+1}$ from Eq. (10.10).

$$\bar{x}_{k+1} = (1 + 1/k)\,\bar{x}_k + O(k^{-\mu}) \tag{10.11}$$

Then we can compute $x(k+1)$ from $\bar{x}_{k+1}$ using the standard stochastic approximation scheme

$$x_{k+1} = \bar{x}_{k+1} + \rho_{k+1}(z_k - \bar{x}_{k+1}) \tag{10.12}$$

where

$$\Sigma_k \rho_k = \infty \qquad \text{and} \qquad \Sigma_k \rho_k^2 < \infty \tag{10.13}$$

Using additional assumptions, the scheme in Eqs. (10.11)–(10.13) can be shown to converge in the following sense (Fa, 1968):

$$\operatorname*{Lim}_{k\to\infty} E\{(x_k - \alpha_k)^2\} = 0$$

and

$$\operatorname{Prob}[\lim_{k\to\infty} x_k = \alpha_k] = 1$$

Furthermore, we can choose the gain sequence $\rho_1, \ldots, \rho_k$ to minimize the mean sequence error $E\{(x_k - \alpha_k)^2\}$. The result is given below, where γ_k denotes the optimal value of ρ_k

$$\gamma_k = \frac{(k+1)^2}{\dfrac{(k+1)(k+2)(2k+3)}{6} + \left(\dfrac{\sigma^2}{V_1^2} - 1\right)} \tag{10.14}$$

where

$$\sigma^2 > E(\eta_k)^2$$

and

$$V_1^2 = E\{(x_1 - \alpha_1)^2\}$$

Very frequently, the results obtained by using the gain sequence in Eq. (10.14) are not satisfactory because of the rather large prediction error $|x_k - \alpha_k|$, when k is small; hence, we will accelerate the convergence by using the gains given by Kesten (1958), instead of those in Eq. (10.14):

$$\rho_1 = \gamma_1$$

$$\rho_k = \gamma_{t_k}$$

$$t_k = 1 + \sum_{i=2}^{k} f((x_{i+1} - \bar{x}_i)(x_i - \bar{x}_{i-1})) \tag{10.15}$$

with

$$f(x) = \begin{cases} 1 & \text{if} \quad x < 0 \\ 0 & \quad\quad x \geqslant 0 \end{cases}$$

and the gains γ_k are given in Eq. (10.14).

Example 9. We will use the theory developed above for prediction of atmospheric temperature variations. A typical record showing the average temperature of Hartford, Conn., during the period from March to July, 1966, is plotted in Fig. 10. The general linear trend in the graph suggests that the daily average temperature may be considered as a time-varying parameter obeying Eq. (10.10). The actual observations are denoted z and the one-step predictions by x_k (Chien and Fu, 1969).

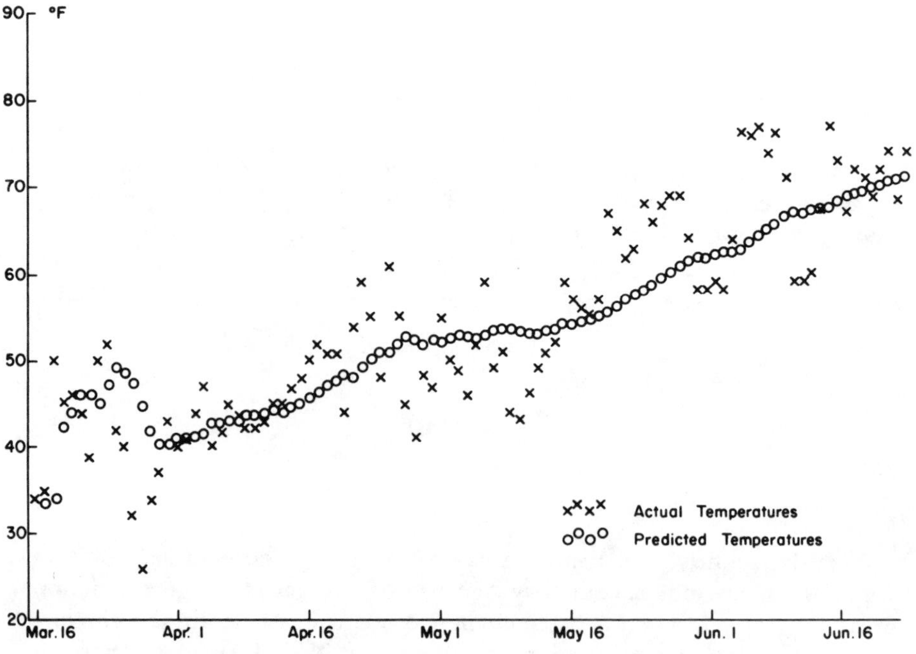

FIGURE 10. Average temperature °F (Hartford, Connecticut, 1966)

The predictions for Hartford, Conn., are plotted in Fig. 10. The predictions are obtained from Eqs. (10.11), (10.12) and the gains in Eq. (10.14). The average error, i.e., | Predicted value — Actual value | was found to be rather large. Hence, the prediction scheme was repeated using the gains in Eq. (10.15). The results are given in Fig. 11. The

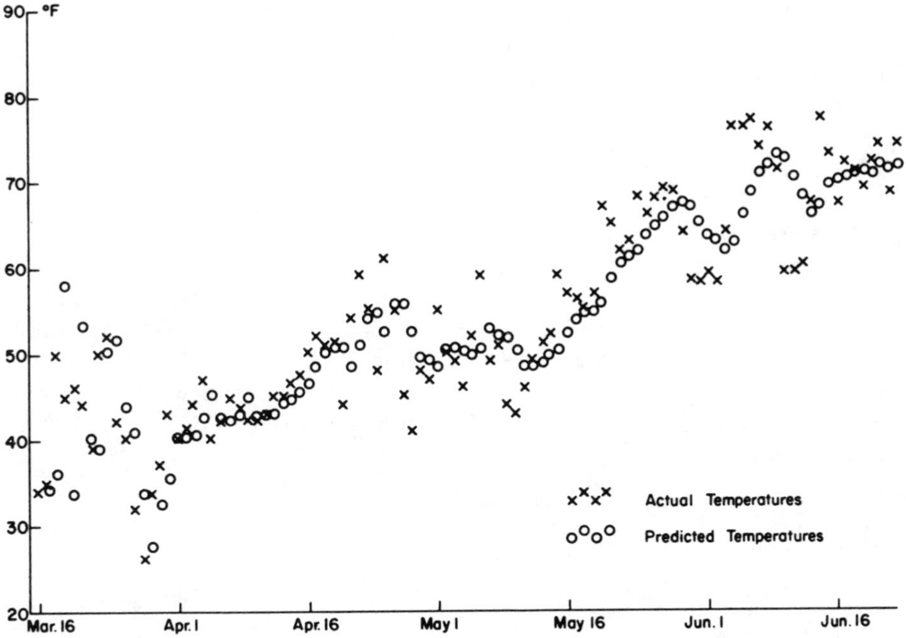

FIGURE 11. Average temperature °F (Hartford, Connecticut, 1966)

analysis of prediction error over a period of six years (1962–1967) is tabulated in Table I.

TABLE I

TEMPERATURE PREDICTIONS FOR HARTFORD, CONNECTICUT[a]

Prediction error (averaged over 6 years)		$\leqslant$ 5° F	$\leqslant$ 7°F	$\leqslant$ 10°F
Number of days	Dynamic SA. Eqs. (10.11) and (10.13)	43	94	121
	Modified Dynamic SA. Eqs. (10.11), (10.12), (10.14), and (10.15)	66	104	121

[a] Number of days predicted each year = 121 (March 17–July 15); Number of years averaged = 6 (1962–1967)

C. *Parameter Estimation in Markov Chains*

In this section, we will consider a system whose state x_k at instant k, for all k, can assume only a finite number of levels $s^{(1)},\ldots, s^{(N)}$ in the successive states $x_1, x_2, \ldots$ of a Markov chain; however, we cannot observe the state of the system directly. We can only observe a real-valued quantity z_k,

$$z_k = \varphi(x_k) + \eta_k \tag{10.16}$$

where η_k is an independent noise sequence which can only assume real values and $\varphi(\cdot)$ is a real valued function defined over the set of states $\{s^{(i)}\}$, so that $\varphi(s^{(i)}) \neq \varphi(s^{(j)})$ for all $i \neq j$. Given that the transition matrix $M(\boldsymbol{\theta})$ of the Markov chain depends on a unknown vector parameter $\boldsymbol{\theta}$, we want to recover the true value of $\boldsymbol{\theta}$ from the measurements $z_1, z_2, \ldots$.

Such a problem arises, for example, in the analysis of the random telegraph wave where there are two states. Additional examples can be constructed in connection with "learning" experiments involving responses to various types of stimuli. Below, we will consider the example of a chain having 2 states, $s^{(1)}$ and $s^{(2)}$. Let

$$\varphi(x_k = s^{(1)}) = -1$$
$$\varphi(x_k = s^{(2)}) = +1$$

Let the transition matrix $M(\boldsymbol{\theta})$ involve the vector parameter $\boldsymbol{\theta}$ whose true value $\boldsymbol{\theta}^o$ is unknown.

$$M(\boldsymbol{\theta}) = \begin{bmatrix} \theta_1 & 1 - \theta_1 \\ 1 - \theta_2 & \theta_2 \end{bmatrix} \qquad \boldsymbol{\theta} = \begin{pmatrix} \theta_1 \\ \theta_2 \end{pmatrix}$$

We will assume members of the noise sequence η have zero mean and finite variances, and are independent of one another and of x_k for all k. The Markov chain x_k, $k = 1, 2, \ldots$ is assumed to be (Chung, 1960) regular with steady state probabilities $p_1(\boldsymbol{\theta})$ and $p_2(\boldsymbol{\theta})$, where

$$p_1(\boldsymbol{\theta}) = \operatorname*{Lim}_{k\to\infty} \text{Prob.}[x_k = s^{(1)}] = \frac{1 - \theta_2}{2 - \theta_1 - \theta_2}$$

and

$$p_2(\boldsymbol{\theta}) = \operatorname*{Lim}_{k\to\infty} \text{Prob.}[x_k = s^{(2)}] = 1 - p_1(\boldsymbol{\theta})$$

From the given measurements z_k, $k = 1, 2, \ldots$ we will construct the following vector, $\mathbf{y}_k$, which is of same dimension as $\boldsymbol{\theta}$:

$$\mathbf{y}_k = \begin{pmatrix} y_{1k} \\ y_{2k} \end{pmatrix}$$

where

$$y_{1k} = \frac{1}{k} \sum_{j=1}^{k} z_j \tag{10.17}$$

and

$$y_{2k} = \frac{1}{k} \sum_{j=1}^{k} z_j z_{j-1}$$

Using the definition of z_k and the properties of x_k and η_k, one can show

$$f_1(\boldsymbol{\theta}) \triangleq \operatorname*{Lim}_{k\to\infty} E[y_{1k}] = p_2(\boldsymbol{\theta}) - p_1(\boldsymbol{\theta}) = \frac{\theta_2 - \theta_1}{2 - \theta_1 - \theta_2}$$

$$f_2(\boldsymbol{\theta}) \triangleq \operatorname*{Lim}_{k\to\infty} E[y_{2k}] = \operatorname*{Lim}_{k\to\infty} \frac{1}{k} \sum_{j=1}^{k} E(\varphi(x_j)\,\varphi(x_{j-1}))$$

$$= (2\theta_1 - 1)\,p_1(\theta) + (2\theta_2 - 1)\,p_2(\theta)$$

$$= \frac{4(1 - \theta_1\theta_2)}{2 - \theta_1 - \theta_2} - 3$$

Hence we can write

$$\mathbf{y}_k = \mathbf{f}(\boldsymbol{\theta}) + \bar{\boldsymbol{\eta}}_k \tag{10.18}$$

where

$$\mathbf{f}(\boldsymbol{\theta}) = \begin{pmatrix} f_1(\boldsymbol{\theta}) \\ f_2(\boldsymbol{\theta}) \end{pmatrix}$$

$\bar{\boldsymbol{\eta}}_k$ is a new vector noise sequence and it is possible to show that $\bar{\boldsymbol{\eta}}_k$ tends to zero with probability one. We have to find the true value of $\boldsymbol{\theta}$ by solving the regression Eq. (10.18). This can be done by the following SA algorithm:

$$\boldsymbol{\theta}_{k+1} = \boldsymbol{\theta}_k + \rho_k B(\boldsymbol{\theta}_k)[\mathbf{y}_k - f(\boldsymbol{\theta}_k)] \tag{10.19}$$

where

$$\boldsymbol{\theta}_k = \text{estimate of } \boldsymbol{\theta}^o \text{ at the } k\text{th stage}$$

$$= (\theta_{1k}, \theta_{2k})'$$

$$B(\boldsymbol{\theta}) = \begin{bmatrix} \dfrac{\partial f_1}{\partial \theta_1} & \dfrac{\partial f_2}{\partial \theta_1} \\ \dfrac{\partial f_1}{\partial \theta_2} & \dfrac{\partial f_2}{\partial \theta_2} \end{bmatrix}$$

It is possible to show (Kashyap, 1968) that $\boldsymbol{\theta}_k$ tends to $\boldsymbol{\theta}^o$ with probability one if the sequence of gains ρ_k is harmonic and the function $\|f(\boldsymbol{\theta}) - f(\boldsymbol{\theta}^o)\|^2$ has a unique minimum at $\boldsymbol{\theta} = \boldsymbol{\theta}^o$.

The same theory could be extended to the case when the number of states is more than two. In that case, let m be the dimension of vector $\boldsymbol{\theta}$. The corresponding m-vector $\mathbf{y}_k$ is constructed as shown below

$$y_k' = (y_{1k}, y_{2k}, \ldots, y_{mk})$$

$$y_{ik} = \frac{1}{k} \Sigma_{j=1}^{k} z_j z_{j-i+1} \qquad i = 1, \ldots, m$$

Apart from this change, the rest of the scheme is the same as before.

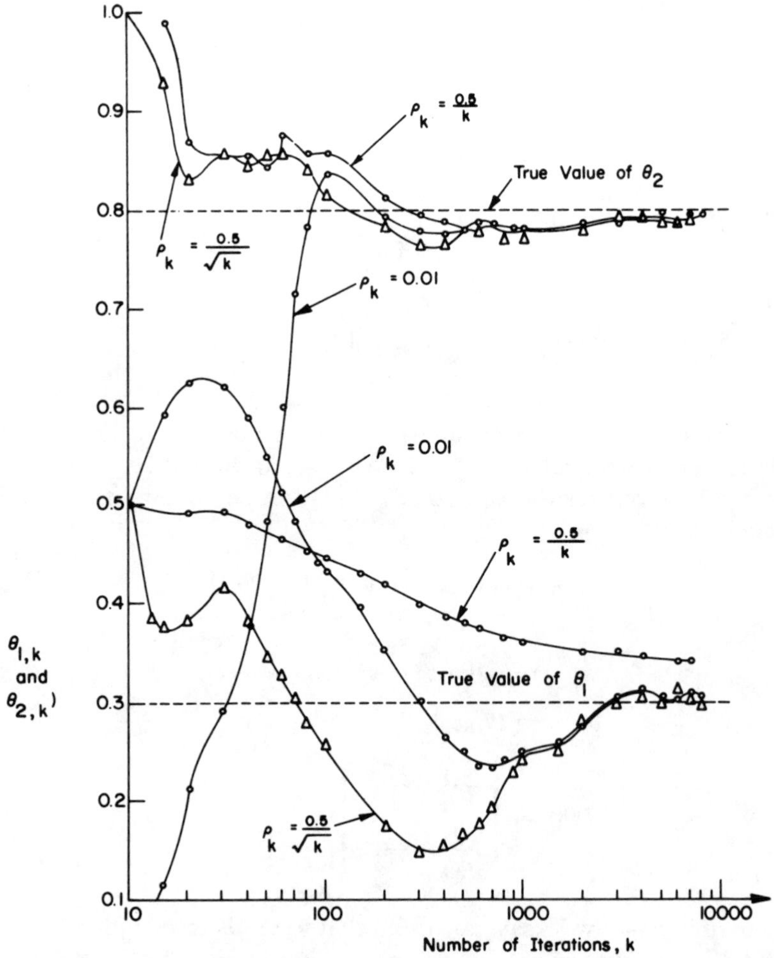

FIGURE 12. Graph of $\theta_{1,k}$ and $\theta_{2,k}$ versus k, the iteration number

Computational studies were performed with a simulated Markov chain having two states, where the true values of θ_1^o and θ_2^o were

$$\theta_1^o = 0.3 \qquad \theta_2^o = 0.8$$

The noise η_k was obtained from a Gaussian random number generator with zero mean and unit variance. Three types of gain references were used for ρ_k :

$$\text{(A)} \qquad \rho_k = 0.5/k$$

$$\text{(B)} \qquad \rho_k = 0.5/\sqrt{k}$$

$$\text{(C)} \qquad \rho_k = 0.01$$

The graphs of θ_{1k} and θ_{2k} versus k for the various gain sequences are depicted in Fig. 12. The cases (B) and (C) seem to have higher rates of convergence than case (A). This may be explained by the fact that in Eq. (10.18) the noise sequences η_k tend to zero not only with probability one, but also in the mean square sense. The decay of the variance of the effective noise $\bar{\eta}_k$ allows us to use gain sequences which decay more slowly than the harmonic sequence and to obtain higher rates of convergence.

V. Bang-Bang Feedback Control*

We will consider the control of dynamical systems in which the control variable u assumes only one of 2 values ± 1—the so-called bang-bang control. In many problems, such as transferring the state of a linear system from one value to another in minimum time, bang-bang control is the optimal control. It is not hard to see that in such problems, the crucial task is the switching of the control from one value to another at the correct instant. It is possible to show that the entire state-space can be divided into nonoverlapping regions in each of which the control assumes a constant value. The surfaces which separate those regions are known as switching surfaces. Thus, if we want to have practical implementation of the control scheme, we must store these boundaries in the controls, and switch the control whenever the state of system crosses the boundaries. This is the feedback control. Unfortunately, except in very simple problems, we cannot obtain the equation of the switching surface in an *explicit* form. Even if, after considerable computation, we succeed in approximating the switching surfaces in an explicit form, the inevitable

* Additional discussions on bang-bang control are found in Chapters 5 and 8.

errors in estimating the state from noisy measurements makes switching occur at the wrong moments; thus, degrading the level of performance.

In addition, if the mechanism of observation is incompletely known, then a state estimate could not even be made.

In these cases a switching function is needed which is given in terms of past measurements. The SA methods can be used to approximate such a function.

The SA methods cannot work unless there can be a training period during which the system is being controlled in the desired (optimal) manner and generating the correct data (i.e., the noisy state measurements) which will be used in the SA algorithm.

Example 10. A bang-bang control will drive the state $\mathbf{x}$ of a simple second-order system to zero in minimum time. The system is

$$\dot{\mathbf{x}} = A\mathbf{x} + \mathbf{b}u$$

with

$$A = \begin{bmatrix} 0 & 1 \\ 0 & 0 \end{bmatrix} \qquad \mathbf{b} = \begin{bmatrix} 0 \\ 1 \end{bmatrix}$$

There are measurements $z(t)$ available, where

$$z(t) = \mathbf{h}'\mathbf{x}(t) + v(t)$$

and

$$\mathbf{h}' = (1, 0)$$

where $v(t)$ is the measurement noise. Nothing is known about the statistics of $v(t)$.

The control, u, drives the state $\mathbf{x}$ to zero in least time by taking on values ± 1. For this simple problem, the bang-bang control can be a switching function expressed in closed form, as illustrated in Fig. 13. With such a closed-form expression, a knowledge of the state

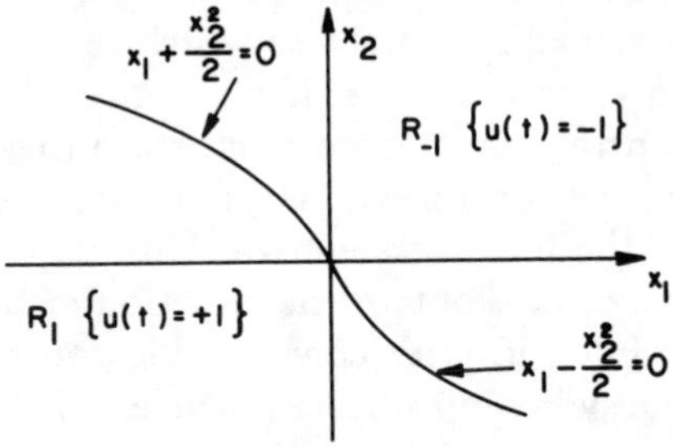

FIGURE 13. Optimal switching curve

vector will determine whether the control u should be $+1$ (that is, $\mathbf{x} \in R_1$) or -1 (that is, $\mathbf{x} \in R_{-1}$). From the noisy measurements in this problem, a Kalman filter could be used to estimate $\mathbf{x}(t)$. This estimate, used in conjunction with the switching curve of Fig. 13, then constitutes a feedback control program, which uses the measurement $z(t)$, from which $\mathbf{x}(t)$ is estimated, which, in turn, determines $u(t)$. Such a procedure may lead to rather unsatisfactory results, primarily because it uses the optimal Switching Curve, computed in the absence of all disturbances, to compute the control. The aspect of randomness calls for a different approach to the problem.

Using a pattern classification interpretation, the desired information for control is contained in the conditional probabilities $P[\mathbf{x}(t) \in R_1 \mid z(t)] = P_1$ and $P[\mathbf{x}(t) \in R_{-1} \mid z(t)] = P_{-1} = 1 - P_1$. It is true that the functional form of these conditional probabilities will depend on the statistics of $v(t)$ and on the form of the switching curve; but, since the SA algorithm does not need knowledge of P_1 in order to be able to construct an approximation, lack of knowledge about $v(t)$ and the switching curve presents no difficulty.

The only information required by the algorithm is a sequence of patterns of known classification. These can be obtained by simulating optimal open-loop trajectories where the measurements taken along these trajectories are the training patterns.

In many problems, the switching curve may be fairly complicated. This is particularly true in those problems where the switching curve cannot be expressed in closed form. In such cases, it is useful to employ knowledge concerning at which portion of the trajectory the system is currently located. A trajectory is easily broken up into portions separated by the switching points. In a second-order overdamped system, there is only one switch (Bellman *et al.*, 1956); thus, there are two portions of the trajectory, one before the switch and the other after the switch. In this case, for example, knowing that the system has not made its first switch and that u currently has the value, say $u = \pm 1$, then the required information for determining when to switch is contained in the probability $P_1[\mathbf{x}(t) \in R_1 \mid (z(t),\ldots, z(t - k\,\Delta t)) \triangleq \mathbf{Z}(t); u(t) = 1]$, which is the probability that $\mathbf{x}(t) \in R_1$ given that $u(t) = 1$ and given the vector of measurements $\mathbf{Z}(t)$. Thus, the approximation of P_1 is only concerned with the portion of the switching curve in the upper left-hand quadrant of Fig. 13.

It is clear, as shown in Fig. 14, that on a trajectory along which $u(t) = 1$ the question of interest is whether or not $\mathbf{x}(t)$ is to the right or left of that portion of the switching curve given by $x_1 + x_2^2/2 = 0$. This is a decision that can be made by using P_1.

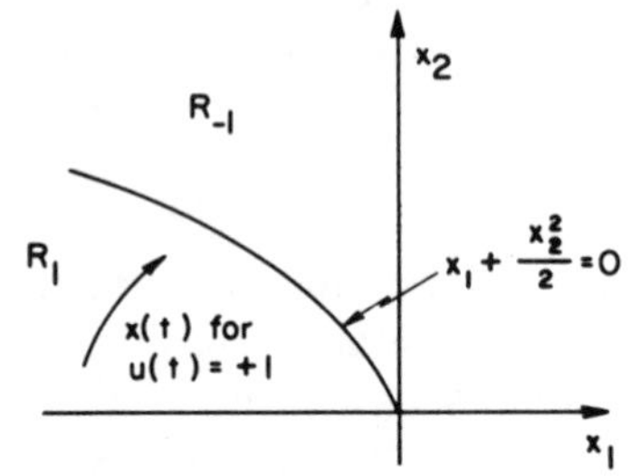

FIGURE 14. Trajectory for $u(t) = 1$

What happens when a switch is made at a point other than exactly on the switching curve? The trajectory then proceeds adjacent to the switching curve, but now $u(t) = -1$ (see Fig. 15). This is the second

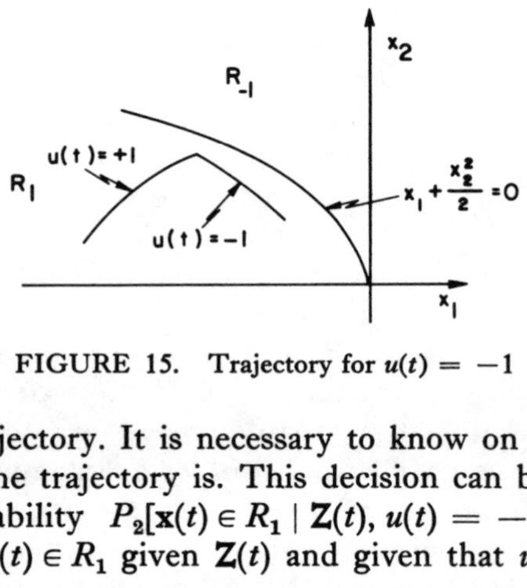

FIGURE 15. Trajectory for $u(t) = -1$

portion of the trajectory. It is necessary to know on which side of the switching curve the trajectory is. This decision can be made using the conditional probability $P_2[\mathbf{x}(t) \in R_1 \mid \mathbf{Z}(t), u(t) = -1]$ which is the probability that $\mathbf{x}(t) \in R_1$ given $\mathbf{Z}(t)$ and given that $u(t) = -1$. There are two cases:

(i) It can be decided that $\mathbf{x}(t)$ does lie in R_1 and then another switch can be made so as to get the trajectory closer to the switching curve (see Fig. 16); or

(ii) It can be decided that $\mathbf{x}(t) \in R_{-1}$, in which case nothing can be done to bring the trajectory closer to the switching curve. The system just has to wait until the trajectory approaches the second half of the switching curve and then use the decision functions associated with that portion of the switching curve, as is shown in Fig. 17.

Even if the trajectory is finally close to the switching curve, it will not, in all probability, go through the origin. Eventually then, even if $u(t)$ is

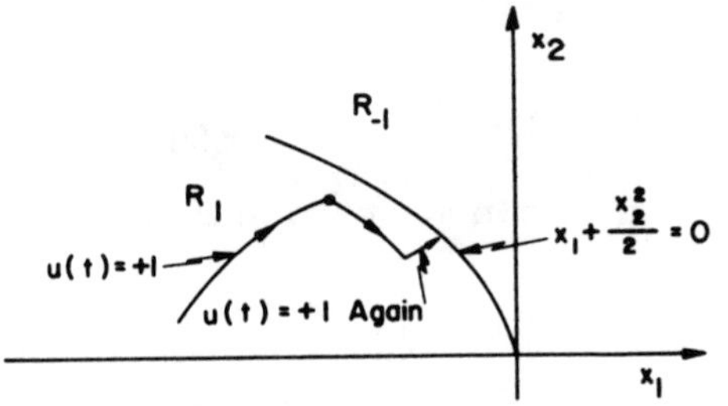

FIGURE 16. Trajectory with $u(t)$ switched back to $+1$

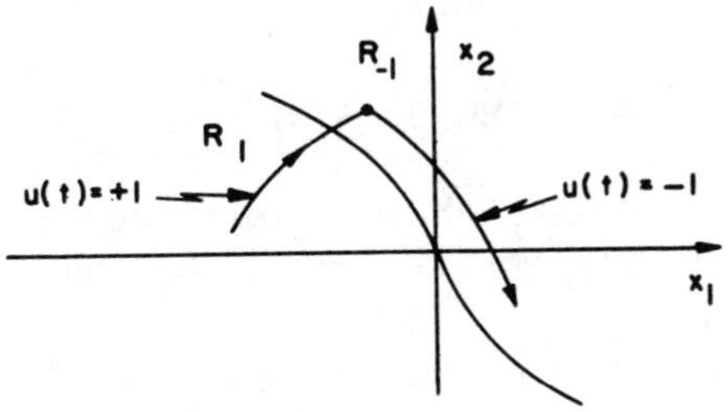

FIGURE 17. Trajectory with late switch

set equal to zero, the trajectory will travel away from the origin. Some feedback control function is necessary to keep the trajectory in the neighborhood of the origin. The neighborhood of the origin which is acceptable as being close enough to $\mathbf{x} = \mathbf{0}$ will be labelled R_0 (Fig. 18), which has associated with it the conditional probability

$$P_3[\mathbf{x}(t) \in R_0 \mid \mathbf{Z}(t), u(t) = -1]$$

Even if it has been decided that the trajectory has reached R_0, there must be a feedback controller to keep it in this region. For the present

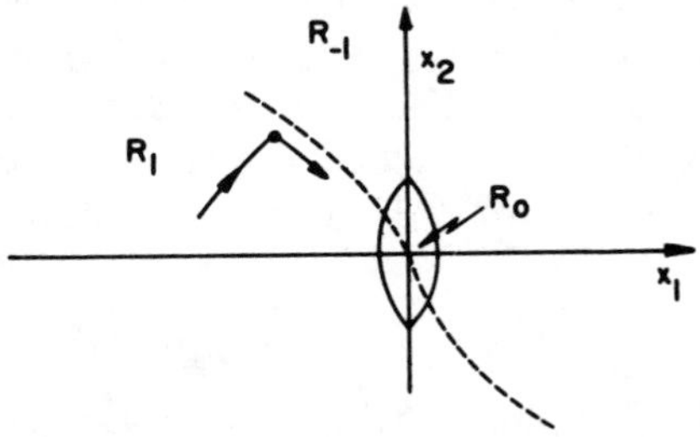

FIGURE 18. Definition of region R_0

problem, a stabilizing control is

$$u(t) = \begin{cases} +1 & \\ -1 & \text{if} \end{cases} \quad \begin{matrix} x_1(t) < 0 \\ x_1(t) > 0 \end{matrix}$$

which causes the system motion shown in Fig. 19.

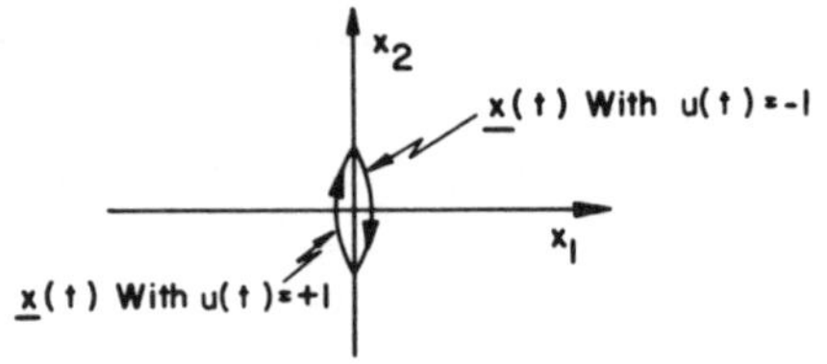

FIGURE 19. Stable trajectory in R_0

Switching decisions in R_0 can be made using the two conditional probabilities $P_4[x_1(t) < 0 \mid \mathbf{Z}(t), u(t) = 1, \mathbf{x}(t) \in R_0]$ and $P_5[x_1(t) > 0 \mid \mathbf{Z}(t), u(t) = 1, \mathbf{x}(t) \in R_0]$.

The conditional probability decision functions described above can be approximated using SA algorithms. The approximations are of the form $\hat{P}_1(\mathbf{Z}) = \boldsymbol{\theta}'\boldsymbol{\varphi}(\mathbf{Z}(t))$ where $\mathbf{Z}'(t) = (z(t), z(t - \Delta),..., z(t - (n - 1)\Delta))$. In particular we chose the 'φ' functions to be linear.

$$\boldsymbol{\varphi}(\mathbf{Z}) = \mathbf{Z}$$

The optimal value of $\boldsymbol{\theta}$ is found by minimizing $E\{(P_1 - \hat{P}_1)^2\}$.

To compute the optimal value of $\boldsymbol{\theta}$ using SA methods, we need a method for generating the pattern vectors $\mathbf{Z}(t)$ for various values of t. We can quite easily generate a field of optimal trajectories (optimal in the absence of noise) by the following equations;

$$\frac{d\mathbf{x}}{dt}(t) = A\mathbf{x}(t) + \mathbf{b}\,\text{sgn}(C_2 - C_1 t) \qquad \mathbf{x}(0) = \mathbf{0}$$

where C_1 and C_2 are arbitrary real constants. For each trajectory $\mathbf{x}(t)$, we can obtain the value of noise measurement $\mathbf{Z}(t)$ by simulation, where $v(t)$ is generated from a Gaussian random number generator with variance $\sigma_v^2 = 0.25$. To compute $\hat{P}_1(\mathbf{Z})$ we generate the pairs $\mathbf{Z}(t_k), y_{t_k}\}$, for $k = 1, 2, 3,...$ using only those optimal trajectories for which $u(t_k) = 1$:

$$\begin{aligned} \mathbf{Z}'(t_k) &= (z(t_k), z(t_{k-\Delta}),..., z(t_{k-7\Delta})) \qquad (\Delta = 10) \\ y(t_k) &= 1 \text{ if } \mathbf{x}(t_k) \in R_1 \\ &= 0 \text{ if } \mathbf{x}(t_k) \notin R_1 \end{aligned}$$

Using the pairs $\{\mathbf{Z}(t_k), y(t_k)\}$ we can compute the optimal value of $\boldsymbol{\theta}$ by using a second-order SA scheme as in Eq. (10.1) where $\mathbf{x}_k$ is replaced by $\mathbf{Z}(t_k)$ and y_k by $y(t_k)$. We can compute the approximate $\hat{P}_i(\mathbf{Z}), i = 2,..., 5$ in a similar manner.

Example 11. We will treat the same control problem as in Example 10, except that the measurement noise $v(t)$ will be dependent on the state of the system. This control problem cannot be handled by any of the existing methods. We will handle this problem by the SA approach.

The variance of the noise in this problem will be taken to be

$$\sigma_v^2 = \left(\frac{x_1^2 + x_2^2}{200}\right)^2$$

so that the variance ranges from ten to zero over the region of approximation. The coefficients of the five approximating functions as constructed by the SA algorithm are given in Table II. Trajectories using these decision functions are given in Figs. 20 through 22. The effect of the noise is represented in the diagrams by the error ellipse, whose equation is $\hat{\mathbf{x}}'\Sigma^{-1}\hat{\mathbf{x}} = \lambda^2$ where Σ is the covariance matrix of the estimate $\hat{\mathbf{x}}$ of state $\mathbf{x}$. The ellipses with $\lambda = 1, 2,...,$ etc. are known respectively as 1σ ellipse, 2σ ellipse, etc. If the expected value of the state is at the origin of 2σ ellipse, then the actual value of the state will stay inside the ellipse with probability $(1 - \exp(-2)) = 0.864$. The ellipses are drawn at various points on the trajectories. The various trajectories show the

TABLE II

COEFFICIENTS OF APPROXIMATING FUNCTIONS (STATE DEPENDENT NOISE)

	P_1	P_2	P_3	P_4	P_5
θ_0	0.594696	0.61459	−0.20122	0.72601	0.778612
θ_1	−0.0775262	−0.12829	+0.57671	−0.051767	0.12940
θ_2	−0.0491527	−0.04450	−0.18376	−0.053095	0.13964
θ_3	−0.0179626	−0.01035	−0.28098	−0.175842	0.10164
θ_4	−0.0105248	−0.01607	−0.36814	−0.28202	0.014877
θ_5	−0.00352893	+0.02341	−0.14556	+0.14006	−0.12078
θ_6	+0.014492	+0.02557	+0.03671	+0.45913	−0.304953
θ_7	+0.0471878	+0.02859	+0.04309	—	—
θ_8	+0.0513651	+0.02787	+0.05328	—	—

effect of switching the control, earlier or later than the optimal switching times.

How would this approach be applied to systems of higher dimension? When the system matrix A has only real roots, then the number of required switches is $n - 1$ where n is the dimension of the system. As the trajectory approaches a switching surface it requires a decision function to determine when to switch. After a switch has been made it requires another function to determine if the switch was made too soon or too late (this corresponds to P_2 in the previous discussions); thus, along each portion of a trajectory, two decision functions are required, the first to determine if the previous switch was accurate, the second to determine when to make the next switch.

It would be unrealistic to claim practicality of this method for very

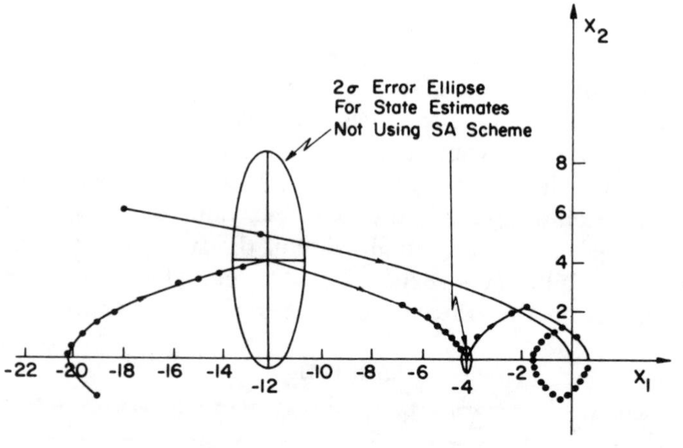

FIGURE 20. Sample trajectory 1

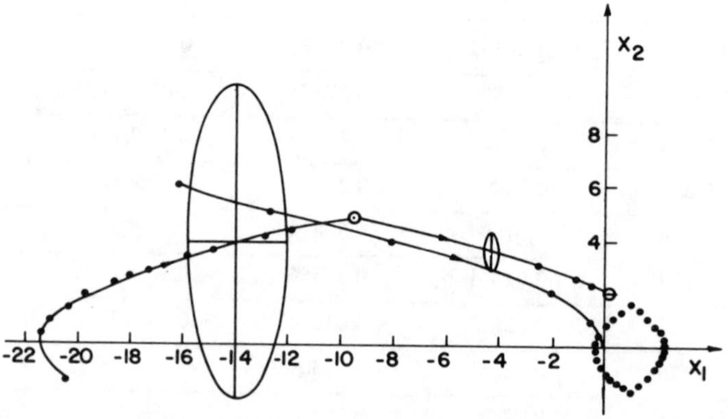

FIGURE 21. Sample trajectory 2

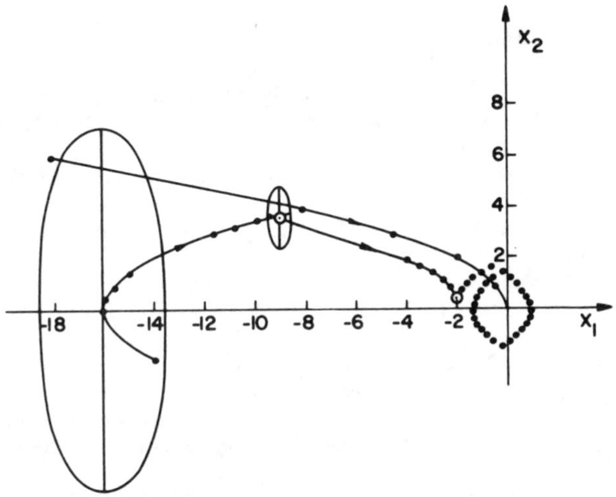

FIGURE 22. Sample trajectory 3

high-order systems, but the approach does have some advantages for low-order systems with bang-bang control. It does not require that the switching functions be known in closed form as a function of the state variables and it does not require that the statistics of the observation noise be known. Indeed, the noise can even be state dependent and correlated. The method only requires that one be able to simulate optimal trajectories during a training phase in order to approximate the optimal decision functions.

VI. Conclusions

In this chapter, we have shown the usefulness of stochastic approximation algorithms in the solution of a variety of problems. Most of the problems are characterized by the fact that they lack information about some parts of the system, such as the dynamics or noise statistics.

Stochastic approximation methods present one approach towards the solution of such problems. The attractiveness of the SA schemes is heightened by the fact that the algorithms are computationally simple and require very little storage.

References

Blaydon, C. C. Recursive algorithms for pattern classification. Rept. No. 520, DEAP, Harvard Univ., Cambridge, Mass., 1967.

Bellman, R. E., Glicksberg, I. and Gross, O. A. On the 'bang-bang' control problem. *Quart. Appl. Math. 14*, pp. 11–18 (1956).

Chien, Y. T. and Fu, K. S. Stochastic learning of time varying parameters in random environment. *IEEE Trans. System Science Cybernetics 5*, pp. 237–246 (1969).

Chung, K. L., "Markov Chains with Stationary Transition Probabilities." Springer-Verlag, Berlin, 1960.

Dupâc, V., A dynamic stochastic approximation method. *Ann. Math. Stat. 36*, pp. 1695–1702 (1965).

Fu, K.S., "Sequential Methods in Pattern Recognition and Machine Learning." Academic Press, New York, 1968.

Kalman, R. E., New methods in Wiener filtering. *Proc. 1st Symp. Engin. Appl. Random Function Theory and Prob.*, (J. L. Bogdanoff and F. Kozin, eds.). Wiley, New York, 1963.

Jury, E. I. and Lee, B. W. On the stability of a certain class of nonlinear sampled data systems. *IEEE Trans. Auto. Control 9*, No. 1, pp. 51–61 (1964).

Kashyap, R. L., Estimation of the transition matrix of a Markov chain from noisy measurements. *Proc. 2nd Annual Princeton Conf. Info. Sciences and Systems*, pp. 219–222 (1968).

Kashyap, R. L. and Blaydon, C. C. Information theory. *IEEE Trans. Info. Theory 14*, No. 4, pp. 549–556 (1968).

Kesten, A., Accelerated stochastic approximation. *Ann. Math. Stat. 29*, pp. 41–59 (1958).

Parzen, E., On estimation of probability density function and mode. *Ann. Math. Stat. 33*, pp. 1065–1076 (1962).

11

K. S. Fu

STOCHASTIC AUTOMATA AS MODELS OF LEARNING SYSTEMS

I. Introduction to Stochastic Automata

Finite automata can be used as mathematical models for systems with finite number of states which admit at discrete time intervals certain inputs and emit certain outputs. If the system is, at present, in a state q^i and the present input is y^α, then the system will move at the following instant into a new state (next state) q^j, which depends only on q^i and y^α, and will have an output u^l which depends on q^j. Thus, the system will transform a sequence of inputs into a sequence of outputs. The transformation is represented in terms of the intermediate quantities called "states," and it may be deterministic or probabilistic. There exists an extensive literature on deterministic (finite) automata. Recently, the investigations of stochastic or probabilistic automata have received increasing attention. The basic concept is that a stochastic automaton, when it is in state q^i and its input is y^α, could move into any (next) state q^j with probability $p^{ij}(y^\alpha)$ where $p^{ij}(y^\alpha)$ is a function of q^i and y^α.

Practical motivations for investigating stochastic automata are found in their possible applications to reliability problems (Rabin, 1963; Paz, 1966), theory of neural nets (Uttley, 1959), learning systems (Tsetlin, 1961; Varshavskii and Vorontsova, 1963; Fu, 1967), coding theory (Ott, 1966), and time-sharing computer systems (Kashyap, 1966).

This chapter is mainly concerned with the application of stochastic automata as models of learning systems. The relationships to other learning techniques are also discussed.

A stochastic automaton is a quintuple (Y, Q, U, F, G) where Y is a finite set of inputs, $Y = \{y^1,..., y^r\}$; Q is a finite set of states, $Q = \{q^1,..., q^s\}$; U is a finite set of outputs, $U = \{u^1,..., u^m\}$; F is the next state function

$$q_{k+1} = F(y_k, q_k) \qquad q_k \in Q \qquad y_k \in Y \tag{11.1}$$

and G is the output function

$$u_k = G(q_k) \tag{11.2}$$

y_k, q_k, and u_k are the input, state, and output (respectively) at the instant k. In general, the function F is stochastic and the function G may be deterministic or stochastic. For each input y^α applied to the automaton at instant k, the function F is usually represented as a state transition probability matrix $M_k(y^\alpha)$. The (i, j)-element $p_k^{ij}(y^\alpha)$ of $M_k(y^\alpha)$ is defined by

$$p_k^{ij}(y^\alpha) = P\{q_{k+1} = q^j \mid q_k = q^i, y_k = y^\alpha\} \qquad i, j = 1,..., s \tag{11.3}$$

that is, the probability of the next state q_{k+1} being q^j when the present state q_k is q^i and the present input is y^α. For all possible next $q^j, j = 1,..., s$,

$$\sum_{j=1}^{s} p_k^{ij}(y^\alpha) = 1 \tag{11.4}$$

thus, $M_k(y^\alpha)$ is a stochastic matrix. The probability distribution of the state q_{k+1} is determined by the probability distribution of q_k and y_k. In the stationary case $M_k(y^\alpha)$ is not a function of k; that is, $M_k(y^\alpha) = M(y^\alpha)$ for all k. It is easily seen that a deterministic finite automaton is a special case of a stochastic automaton of which the matrix $M(y^\alpha)$ consists of zeroes and ones, and each row of the matrix contains exactly one element which is equal to unity. The function G, if it is stochastic, can also be represented in a matrix form. The (i, j)-element of the matrix is the probability of the output being u^j if the state is q^i.

A combination of functions F and G can be expressed as an $rs \times ms$ stochastic matrix M which characterizes the input-output relationship of the automaton

$$M = \begin{bmatrix} M(u^1 \mid y^1) & M(u^2 \mid y^1) & \cdots & M(u^m \mid y^1) \\ M(u^1 \mid y^2) & M(u^2 \mid y^2) & \cdots & M(u^m \mid y^2) \\ \vdots & \vdots & & \vdots \\ M(u^1 \mid y^r) & M(u^2 \mid y^r) & & M(u^m \mid y^r) \end{bmatrix} \tag{11.5}$$

where $M(u^l \mid y^\alpha)$ is an $s \times s$ matrix with (i, j)-element

$$P\{q_{k+1} = q^j, u_{k+1} = u^l \mid q_k = q^i, y_k = y^\alpha\} \tag{11.6}$$

which denotes the probability of the next state being q^j and the output being u^l when the present state is q^i and the input is y^α. Equation (11.5) is especially useful when the states of the automaton are not observable. It is noted from Eq. (11.3) and Eq. (11.6) that

$$M(y^\alpha) = \sum_{l=1}^{m} M(u^l \mid y^\alpha) \tag{11.7}$$

For an input sequence of length n, $I = y^{\alpha_1} y^{\alpha_2} \cdots y^{\alpha_n} [y^{\alpha_i} \in Y]$, the corresponding output sequence $J = u^{k_1} u^{k_2} \cdots u^{k_n} [u^{k_i} \in U]$,

$$M(J \mid I) = M(u^{k_1} \mid y^{\alpha_1})\, M(u^{k_2} \mid y^{\alpha_2}) \cdots M(u^{k_n} \mid y^{\alpha_n}) \tag{11.8}$$

and

$$M(\varphi \mid \varphi) = \text{Identity matrix}$$

where φ is the empty sequence. Similarly, the n-step state transition matrix for an input sequence of length n, I, is

$$M(I) = M(y^{\alpha_1})\, M(y^{\alpha_2}) \cdots M(y^{\alpha_n}) \tag{11.9}$$

Let $\mathbf{\Pi}_0$ be the probability distribution of initial states, which is an s-component column vector with the ith component

$$\Pi_0^{\,i} = P\{q_0 = q^i\} \tag{11.10}$$

then the probability of producing output sequence J when the input sequence (with length n) is I can be computed by

$$P_{\mathbf{\Pi}_0}(J \mid I) = P\{J \mid I, \mathbf{\Pi}_0\} = \mathbf{\Pi}_0' M(J \mid I)\, \mathbf{e} \tag{11.11}$$

where $\mathbf{e}$ is an s-component column vector with unity elements. The final state distribution of the automaton after k steps of transitions can be determined by simply applying Bayes' theorem

$$\mathbf{\Pi}_k'(J, I) = \begin{cases} \dfrac{\mathbf{\Pi}_0' M(J \mid I)}{\mathbf{\Pi}_0' M(J \mid I)\, \mathbf{e}} & \text{if } \mathbf{\Pi}_0' M(J \mid I)\, \mathbf{e} \neq 0 \\ \mathbf{\Pi}_0' & \text{otherwise} \end{cases} \tag{11.12}$$

where $\mathbf{\Pi}_k(J, I)$ is an s-component column vector with the ith component

$$\Pi_k^{\,i}(J, I) = P\{q_k = q^i \mid I, J, \mathbf{\Pi}_0\} \tag{11.13}$$

which is the probability of the final state being q^i for input sequence I, output sequence J, and initial state distribution Π_0. From Eqs. (11.8) and (11.11), for an input sequence containing two subsequences I_1 and I_2,

$$P_{\Pi_0}(J_1 J_2 \mid I_1 I_2) = P_{\Pi_0}(J_1 \mid I_1)\, P_{\Pi_{\alpha_1}(J,I)}(J_2 \mid I_2) \tag{11.14}$$

where J_1 and J_2 are the corresponding output sequences when the input sequences are I_1 and I_2 respectively, and α_1 is the length of I_1. If the state transitions of a stochastic automaton are not observable, the probability that J is observed at the output when the input sequence I is applied with the automaton at initial state q^i is

$$P_i(J \mid I) = \sum_{q^j \in Q} P(q^j, J \mid q^i, I) \tag{11.15}$$

For initial distribution Π_0,

$$P_{\Pi_0}(J \mid I) = \sum_{q^i \in Q} \Pi_0{}^i P_i(J \mid I) \tag{11.16}$$

Stochastic automata for which the inputs are constant are called autonomous stochastic automata. An autonomous stochastic automaton can be interpreted as a finite-state Markov chain with the same state set Q. If a Bernoulli sequence or a Markov sequence of inputs is applied to a stochastic automaton with the function G being a one-to-one mapping between u and q, it can be shown that the automaton will operate as an autonomous stochastic automaton with an expanded state set (Booth, 1967). The new state set will be the combination of the input set and the original state set. That is, in the case of a Bernoulli input sequence with $P^\alpha = P\{y = y^\alpha\}$ the probability of the occurrence of y^α, let the new state set be $Q^* = Y \times Q$, then the state transition probability matrix of the equivalent autonomous stochastic automaton is an $rs \times rs$ stochastic matrix

$$M^*(y) = \begin{bmatrix} P^1M(y^1) & P^2M(y^1) & \cdots & P^rM(y^1) \\ P^1M(y^2) & P^2M(y^2) & \cdots & P^rM(y^2) \\ \vdots & \vdots & & \vdots \\ P^1M(y^r) & P^2M(y^r) & \cdots & P^rM(y^r) \end{bmatrix} \tag{11.17}$$

If the input sequence to the automaton is a Markov sequence with order d, let the states in the new state set be all possible $(d + 1)$-tuples of the following form

$$q^* = (q, y_n, y_{n-1}, \ldots, y_{n-d}) \tag{11.18}$$

Then the new state set will be

$$Q^* = \underbrace{Y \times Y \times Y \times \cdots \times Y}_{(d+1)\text{ terms}} \times Q \tag{11.19}$$

and the number of states in Q^* will be $(r)^{d+1}s$. It is noted that if $d = 0$, the case of a stochastic automaton with Markov input sequence reduces to that with Bernoulli input sequence.

The formulation of stochastic automata can also be employed to describe the behavior of deterministic automata with random inputs. Let the state transition matrices $M(y^\alpha)$, $\alpha = 1,\ldots, r$, corresponding to a deterministic finite automaton be denoted as $S(y^\alpha)$; i.e., the elements of $S(y^\alpha)$ are either zeroes or ones and each row contains exactly one element equal to unity. Let also $P^\alpha = P\{y = y^\alpha\}$, $\alpha = 1,\ldots, r$, be the probability of y^α occurring at the input. Thus, the behavior of a deterministic automaton with random inputs can be described by an equivalent autonomous stochastic automaton (or a Markov chain) with the state set $Q^* = Y \times Q$ and the state transition matrix

$$M^*(y) = \begin{bmatrix} P^1S(y^1) & P^2S(y^1) & \cdots & P^rS(y^1) \\ P^1S(y^2) & P^2S(y^2) & \cdots & P^rS(y^2) \\ \vdots & \vdots & & \vdots \\ P^1S(y^r) & P^2S(y^r) & \cdots & P^rS(y^r) \end{bmatrix} \tag{11.20}$$

The state and automata equivalence relations and minimization problems in deterministic finite automata can be extended to the case of stochastic automata. Several important results are summarized in this section (Carlyle, 1961, 1963; Bacon, 1964a, 1964b; Paz, 1967; Page, 1966; Ott, 1966).

The state q^i is said to be equivalent to the state q^j, written as $q^i \equiv q^j$ if

$$P_i(J \mid I) = P_j(J \mid L) \qquad \text{for all} \quad (I, J) \tag{11.21}$$

q^i and q^j may be referred to two different automata. The initial distributions Π_0 and $\Pi_0{}^*$ are equivalent, $\Pi_0 \equiv \Pi_0{}^*$, if

$$P_{\Pi_0}(J \mid I) = P_{\Pi_0{}^*}(J \mid I) \qquad \text{for all} \quad (I, J) \tag{11.22}$$

Similarly, Π_0 and $\Pi_0{}^*$ may be referred to two different automata. The states q^i and q^j are said to be k-equivalent, written as $q^i \overset{k}{\equiv} q^j$ if

$$P_i(J \mid I) = P_j(J \mid I) \tag{11.23}$$

for all I and J sequences of length k. In a similar manner, the k-equivalence can be defined for initial distributions Π_0 and Π_0^*.

The following theorems are given without proofs (Carlyle, 1961, 1963):

Theorem 1. Let M be any stochastic automaton, and suppose that Π_0 and Π_0^* are distinguishable (not equivalent) as initial distributions for M. Let the Π_0 and Π_0^* be k-equivalent but $(k + 1)$-distinguishable. Then, for any integer $l \leqslant k$, there exists a pair of distributions which are l-equivalent and $(l + 1)$-distinguishable.

Theorem 2. If M is an automaton with s states, and if Π_0 and Π_0^* are any two distributions on the states of M, then $(s - 1)$-equivalence of Π_0 and Π_0^* is a sufficient condition for $\Pi_0 \equiv \Pi_0^*$.

Theorem 3. If the automaton M has s states, the automaton M^* has s^* states, and Π_0 and Π_0^* are distributions on the states of M and M^* respectively, then $(s + s^* - 1)$-equivalence of M and M^* is a sufficient condition for their equivalence.

If to each state of a stochastic automaton M there corresponds an equivalent state of automaton M^*, and to each state of M^* there corresponds an equivalent state of M; then M and M^* are state-equivalent automata. Among the automata which are state-equivalent to a given automaton M, those having the smallest number of states are called reduced forms of M.

Theorem 4. Let M be an s-state stochastic automaton with at least one pair of equivalent states. Then there exist $(s - 1)$-state automata which are state-equivalent to M. In particular, if q^i and q^j are equivalent states of M, let $M^*(u \mid y)$ be the matrix formed from $M(u \mid y)$ be deleting row q^j and column q^j and replacing the column q^i with the sum of columns q^i and q^j; then M^* is an $(s - 1)$-state automaton which is state-equivalent to M.

It is noted that, in general, there is no uniquely reduced form of a stochastic automaton M. If to each distribution on the states of a stochastic automaton M there corresponds an equivalent distribution on the states of M^* and conversely, then M and M^* are distribution-equivalent automata. Evidently, if M and M^* are state-equivalent, then they are also distribution-equivalent, but the converse does not hold, in general. Among the automata which are distribution-equivalent to M, those with the smallest number of states are called minimal forms of M.

Theorem 5. Let M be in minimal form with s states and let M^* be distribution-equivalent to M; then M must have at least s states.

It is easy to see that for any deterministic automaton, the minimal form coincides with the (unique) reduced form.

II. Synthesis of Stochastic Automata

The basic idea used in the synthesis of stochastic automata follows the formulation of deterministic automata with random inputs; that is, autonomous stochastic automata are synthesized as deterministic automata with random inputs. Three synthesis procedures are discussed in the following paragraphs:

A. *Cleave's Procedure*

Cleave's (1962) synthesis procedure requires a set of deterministic finite automata and a random-signal generator (for the input) to synthesize an autonomous stochastic automaton through the decomposition of a state transition probability matrix $M(y)$ into a linear combination of $S(y^\alpha)$ matrices. Let

$$M(y) = \sum_{\alpha=1}^{r} P^\alpha S(y^\alpha) \tag{11.24}$$

For a given specification $M(y)$, P^α and $S(y^\alpha)$ can be determined from Eq. (11.24). The solution is not unique. The $S(y^\alpha)$ matrices specify the operation of the deterministic automaton and P^α, $\alpha = 1,\ldots, r$, will specify the random-signal generator. The deterministic automaton operates according to the matrix specified by $S(y^i)$ if y^i is generated by the random-signal generator as the input to the automaton.

Example 1. Given

$$M(y) = \begin{bmatrix} \frac{1}{3} & \frac{2}{3} \\ \frac{1}{4} & \frac{3}{4} \end{bmatrix} \tag{11.25}$$

Let

$$\begin{aligned} p^{11}(y) &= \tfrac{1}{3} = P^1 + P^4 \\ p^{12}(y) &= \tfrac{2}{3} = P^2 + P^3 \\ p^{21}(y) &= \tfrac{1}{4} = P^3 + P^4 \end{aligned} \tag{11.26}$$

and

$$p^{22}(y) = \tfrac{3}{4} = P^1 + P^2$$

By solving the equations in Eq. (11.26) simultaneously, we obtain

$$P^1 = \tfrac{1}{3} \qquad P^2 = \tfrac{5}{12} \qquad P^3 = \tfrac{1}{4} \qquad \text{and} \qquad P^4 = 0 \tag{11.27}$$

From Eq. (11.24)

$$M(y) = \frac{1}{3}\begin{bmatrix} 1 & 0 \\ 0 & 1 \end{bmatrix} + \frac{5}{12}\begin{bmatrix} 0 & 1 \\ 0 & 1 \end{bmatrix} + \frac{1}{4}\begin{bmatrix} 0 & 1 \\ 1 & 0 \end{bmatrix} \tag{11.28}$$

Thus, from Eqs. (11.27) and (11.28)

$$Y = \{y^1, y^2, y^3\} \qquad \text{and} \qquad Q = \{q^1, q^2\}$$

A general block diagram of the synthesized stochastic automaton is shown in Fig. 1.

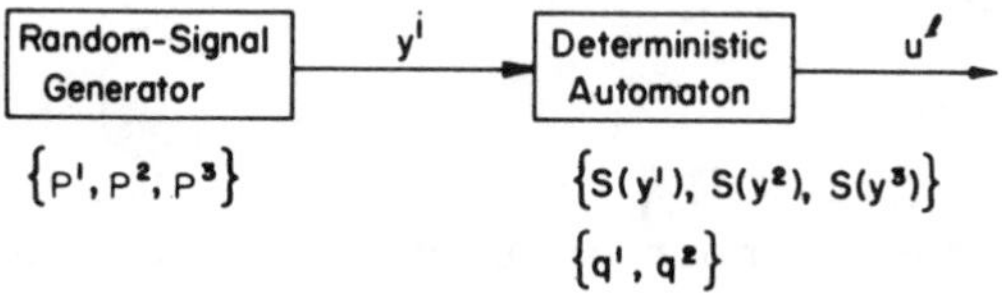

FIGURE 1. Synthesized stochastic automaton

The operations of the deterministic automaton for different inputs are given in Fig. 2.

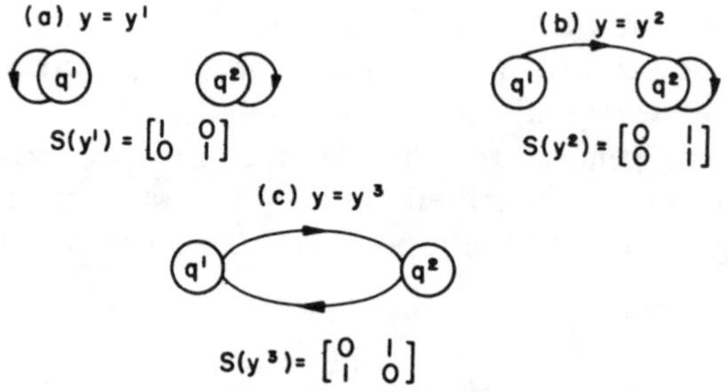

FIGURE 2. State transition—Example 1

B. *Murray's Procedure*

Murray (1955) has synthesized an autonomous stochastic automaton from a deterministic automaton with two inputs y^1 and y^2 and a random-pulse generator. In his synthesis procedure, the state of the deterministic automaton is only observed when y^2 appears at the input. The input sequence is generated by a random-pulse generator. The appearance of a pulse at the output of the generator corresponds to the appearance of y^2. If no pulse has appeared, the input is assumed to be y^1. Since the appearances of y^2 are random, the states of the deterministic automaton observed at these instants are also random. The deterministic automaton which is observed at random instants imitates the behavior of an autonomous stochastic automaton.

The synthesis procedure can be summarized as follows: For a given specification $M(y)$, let s_i be the least common denominator for the ith row of $M(y)$. Then, the deterministic automaton A will be specified by:

(i) $Y = \{y^1, y^2\}$

$$Q = \{q^1,..., q^N\} \qquad \text{where} \qquad N = \sum_{i=1}^{s} s_i \tag{11.29}$$

(ii) When the input $y = y^1$, s subautomata, $A_1, A_2, ..., A_s$, consisting of $s_1, s_2, ..., s_s$ states, respectively, are constructed. Each subautomaton operates as a closed (cyclic) automaton with equal transition probabilities (see Fig. 3).

(iii) When $y = y^2$, the modified skeleton matrix* of the automaton A_1, C_A, is obtained from $M(y)$ by letting

$$p^{ij}(y) = \frac{c^{ij}}{s_i} \qquad \sum_{j=1}^{s} c^{ij} = s_i \tag{11.30}$$

where c^{ij} is the (i, j)-element of C_A. The states of each subautomaton A_i are divided into groups G_{ij} with c^{ij} states each. If the present state $q_k \in G_{ij}$, then the next state $q_{k+1} \in Q_j$ where Q_j is the state set of subautomaton A_j. The probability $p^{ij}(y^2)$ from $q_k \in Q_i$ to $q_{k+1} \in Q_j$ is equal to c^{ij}/s_i if the assumption that the probabilities of the automaton A remaining in any of the states belonging to the same subautomaton are equal is made.

Example 2. Given

$$M(y) = \begin{bmatrix} \frac{1}{3} & 0 & \frac{2}{3} \\ 0 & \frac{1}{2} & \frac{1}{2} \\ \frac{1}{3} & \frac{1}{3} & \frac{1}{3} \end{bmatrix} \tag{11.31}$$

(i) For the automaton A,

$$Y = \{y^1, y^2\}$$
$$Q = \{q^1, q^2, ..., q^N\}$$

where $N = s_1 + s_2 + s_3 = 3 + 2 + 3 = 8$.

---

* The modified skeleton matrix of an s-state automaton is an sxs matrix of which the (i, j) element is l if l possible transitions exist from q^i to q^j, and is 0 if the transition does not exist (Gill, 1962).

(ii) For $y = y^1$,

$$A_1 : Q_1 = \{q^{1_1}, \ldots, q^{s_1}\} = \{q^1, q^2, q^3\}$$
$$A_2 : Q_2 = \{q^{1_2}, \ldots, q^{s_2}\} = \{q^4, q^5\}$$
$$A_3 : Q_3 = \{q^{1_3}, \ldots, q^{s_3}\} = \{q^6, q^7, q^8\}$$

(iii) For $y = y^2$, from Eqs. (11.30) and (11.31) $c^{11} = 1$, $c^{12} = 0$, $c^{13} = 2$, $c^{21} = 0$, $c^{22} = 1$, $c^{23} = 1$, $c^{31} = 1$, $c^{32} = 1$, and $c^{33} = 1$. Thus, the states of A_i, $i = 1, 2, 3$, are assigned as:

$$q^2 \in G_{11} \qquad \{q^1, q^3\} \in G_{13}$$
$$q^4 \in G_{22} \qquad q^5 \in G_{23}$$
$$q^6 \in G_{33} \qquad q^7 \in G_{31} \qquad q^8 \in G_{32}$$

The state transition diagram of A is shown in Fig. 3 where the solid line represents the operation when $y = y^1$, and the dotted line represents the operation when $y = y^2$.

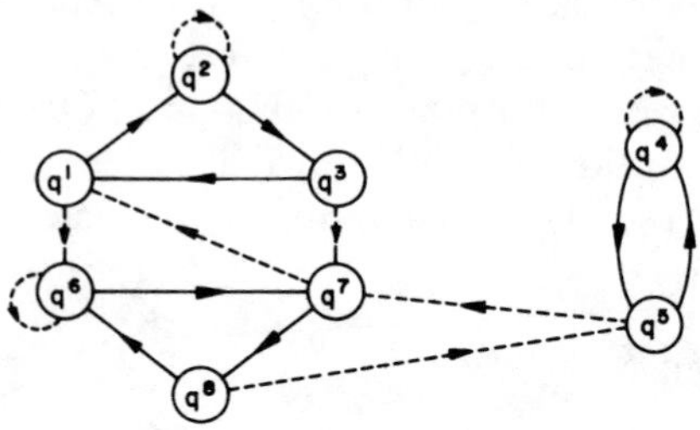

FIGURE 3. State transition—Example 2

Example 3. Nonautonomous stochastic automata
Given

$$M(y^1) = \begin{bmatrix} \frac{1}{4} & \frac{3}{4} \\ \frac{1}{2} & \frac{1}{2} \end{bmatrix} \qquad M(y^2) = \begin{bmatrix} \frac{2}{3} & \frac{1}{3} \\ \frac{1}{4} & \frac{3}{4} \end{bmatrix} \tag{11.32}$$

(i) For the automaton A,

$$Y = \{y^1, y^2\}$$
$$Q = \{q^1, \ldots, q^N\}$$

where

$$N = s_1 + s_2 = 12 + 4 = 16$$

Note: $s_i (i = 1, 2)$, in this case, is the least common denominator for the ith-row of both $M(y^1)$ and $M(y^2)$

(ii) Two cyclic subautomata are constructed:

$$A_1 : Q_1 = \{q^1, q^2, \ldots, q^{12}\}$$
$$A_2 : Q_2 = \{q^{13}, q^{14}, q^{15}, q^{16}\}$$

(iii) For $y = y^1$, from Eq. (11.30),

$$c^{11}(y^1) = 3 \qquad c^{12}(y^1) = 9 \qquad c^{21}(y^1) = 2 \qquad \text{and} \qquad c^{22}(y^1) = 2$$

Thus,

$$\{q^4, q^5, q^6\} \in G_{11}$$
$$\{q^1, q^2, q^3, q^7, q^8, q^9, q^{10}, q^{11}, q^{12}\} \in G_{12}$$
$$\{q^{13}, q^{14}\} \in G_{21}$$
$$\{q^{15}, q^{16}\} \in G_{22}$$

(iv) For $y = y^2$, from Eq. (11.25),

$$c^{11}(y^2) = 8 \qquad c^{12}(y^2) = 4 \qquad c^{21}(y^2) = 1 \qquad \text{and} \qquad c^{22}(y^2) = 3$$

Thus,

$$\{q^2, q^3, q^4, q^5, q^6, q^7, q^8, q^9\} \in G_{11}$$
$$\{q^1, q^{10}, q^{11}, q^{12}\} \in G_{12}$$
$$q^{14} \in G_{21}$$
$$\{q^{13}, q^{15}, q^{16}\} \in G_{22}$$

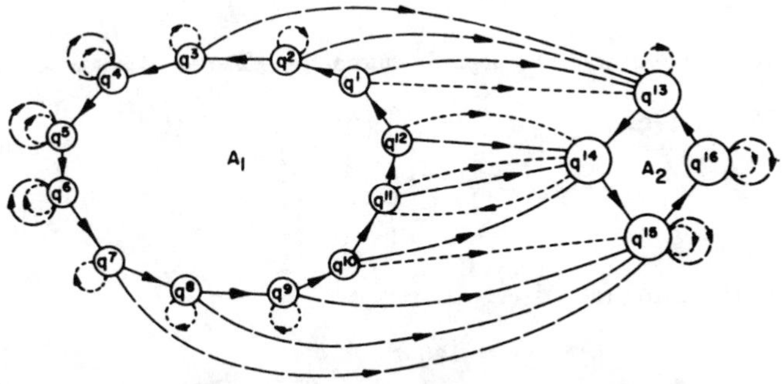

FIGURE 4. State transition—Example 3

According to the state assignment made in (ii), (iii), and (iv), the state transition diagram of A is shown in Fig. 4 where the solid line describes the operation in (ii), the dashed line describes (iii), and the dotted line for (iv).

C. *Tsertsvadze's Procedure*

Tsertsvadze (1963) modified Murray's procedure using a special configuration shown in Fig. 5. In Fig. 5, A is an autonomous, deterministic, cyclic automaton with N states where N is the least common denominator for all s rows of $M(y)$. Let

$$p^{ij}(y) = \frac{c^{ij}}{N} \tag{11.33}$$

φ_1 is a nonlinear convertor whose output represents the state of the stochastic automaton. Assume that the input to φ_1 is v^α, then the converter produces the output $q^{j'}$ if the state of A belongs to the group G_{ij} with c^{ij} elements. In other words, the function of φ_1 is also to achieve the subdivision of the states of A into groups G_{ij}. Each value of the input $v^\alpha(\alpha = 1,..., s)$ to the converter φ_1 corresponds to a particular subdivision. φ_2 is a coder which produces a fixed output v^α as long as its input generated from the random-pulse generator is y^1. When the input to φ^2 becomes y^2, say at the instant k, its output is changed from v^α to v^l if the state of A at the instant k belongs to the group $G_{\alpha l}$.

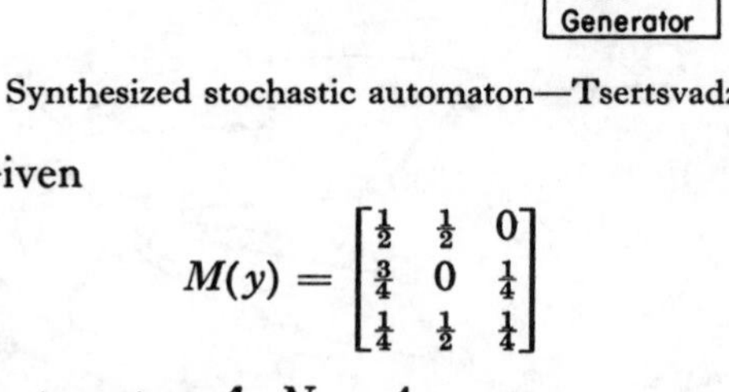

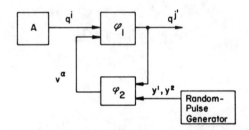

FIGURE 5. Synthesized stochastic automaton—Tsertsvadze's procedure

Example 4. Given

$$M(y) = \begin{bmatrix} \frac{1}{2} & \frac{1}{2} & 0 \\ \frac{3}{4} & 0 & \frac{1}{4} \\ \frac{1}{4} & \frac{1}{2} & \frac{1}{4} \end{bmatrix} \tag{11.34}$$

(i) For the automaton A: $N = 4$

$$Q = \{q^1, q^2, q^3, q^4\}$$

The state transition diagram of A is shown in Fig. 6.

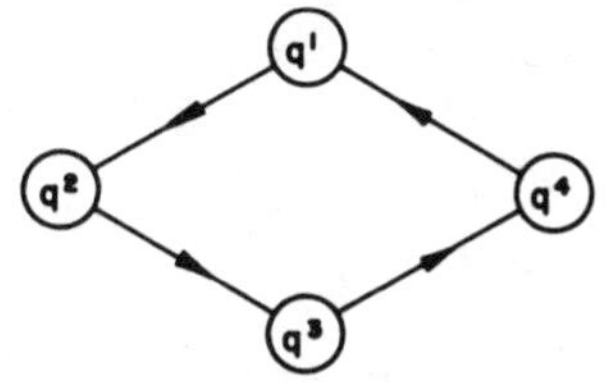

FIGURE 6. State transition—Example 4

(ii) For the converter φ_1, from Eqs. (11.33) and (11.34),

$$c^{11}(v^1) = 2 \qquad c^{12}(v^1) = 2 \qquad c^{13}(v^1) = 0 \qquad \text{for} \qquad v^\alpha = v^1$$

The input-output relationship can be represented by matrices of the following form:

When $v^\alpha = v^1$,

$$\varphi_1(v^1) = \begin{matrix} & q^{1'} & q^{2'} & q^{3'} \\ q^1 & 1 & 0 & 0 \\ q^2 & 1 & 0 & 0 \\ q^3 & 0 & 1 & 0 \\ q^4 & 0 & 1 & 0 \end{matrix} \qquad \{q^1, q^2\} \in G_{11} \qquad \{q^3, q^4\} \in G_{12} \tag{11.35}$$

The (i, j)-element of the matrix $\varphi_1(v^1)$ represents whether the conversion occurs from q^i to $q^{j'}$ when the input to the convertor φ_1 is v^1 (zero element means that no such a conversion occurs). Similarly, when $v^\alpha = v^2$,

$$c^{21}(v^2) = 3 \qquad c^{22}(v^2) = 0 \qquad c^{23}(v^2) = 1$$

$$\varphi_1(v^2) = \begin{bmatrix} 1 & 0 & 0 \\ 1 & 0 & 0 \\ 1 & 0 & 0 \\ 0 & 0 & 1 \end{bmatrix} \qquad \{q^1, q^2, q^3\} \in G_{21} \qquad q^4 \in G_{23} \tag{11.36}$$

When $v^\alpha = v^3$,

$$c^{31}(v^3) = 1 \qquad c^{32}(v^3) = 2 \qquad c^{33}(v^3) = 1$$

$$\varphi_1(v^3) = \begin{bmatrix} 1 & 0 & 0 \\ 0 & 1 & 0 \\ 0 & 1 & 0 \\ 0 & 0 & 1 \end{bmatrix} \qquad q^1 \in G_{31} \qquad \{q^2, q^3\} \in G_{32} \qquad q^4 \in G_{33} \tag{11.37}$$

(iii) For the coder φ_2, on the basis of the groups assignments in Eqs. (11.35), (11.36), (11.37), its operation, when the present input is y^2, can be described by the following matrices where $\varphi_2(q^i)$ denotes the operation matrix of φ_2 when the present state of A is q^i:

$$\varphi_2(q^1) = \begin{matrix} & v^1 & v^2 & v^3 \\ v^1 & 1 & 0 & 0 \\ v^2 & 1 & 0 & 0 \\ v^3 & 1 & 0 & 0 \end{matrix} \qquad \varphi_2(q^2) = \begin{bmatrix} 1 & 0 & 0 \\ 1 & 0 & 0 \\ 0 & 1 & 0 \end{bmatrix}$$

$$\varphi_2(q^3) = \begin{bmatrix} 0 & 1 & 0 \\ 1 & 0 & 0 \\ 0 & 1 & 0 \end{bmatrix} \qquad \varphi_2(q^4) = \begin{bmatrix} 0 & 1 & 0 \\ 0 & 0 & 1 \\ 0 & 0 & 1 \end{bmatrix} \tag{11.38}$$

III. Deterministic Automata Operating in Random Environments

The behavior of a finite (deterministic) automaton operating in a random environment was first studied by Tsetlin (1961). A simple block diagram of the overall system is shown in Fig. 7. At each instant k, the

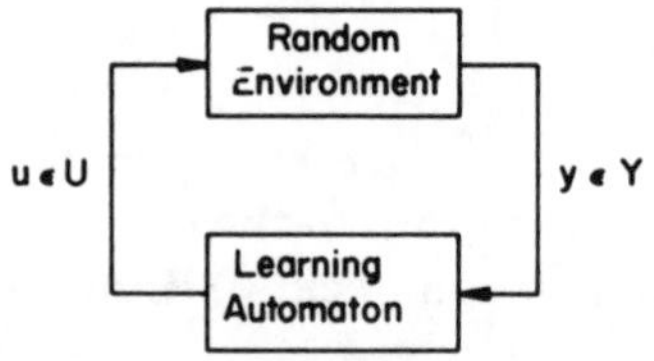

FIGURE 7. Automaton operating in a random environment

behavior of the automaton through the random environment is evaluated by either a penalty or a nonpenalty. The input set Y of the automaton contains only 1 and 0 where $y = 1$ is associated with penalty and $y = 0$ with a nonpenalty. The random environment C is assumed stationary and characterized by a set of probabilities $C(p^1,..., p^m)$ where

$$p^j = P\{y_k = 1 \mid u_k = u^j\} \qquad j = 1,..., m \tag{11.39}$$

Then, for $u^\alpha = G[q^i]$,

$$\begin{aligned} p_k^{ij} &= P\{q_{k+1} = q^j \mid q_k = q^i\} \\ &= p^\alpha p_k^{ij}(1) + (1 - p^\alpha)\, p_k^{ij}(0) \end{aligned} \tag{11.40}$$

Referring to Section I, since each row of $M_k(y^v)$, with elements $p_k^{ij}(y^v)$, contains exactly one element which is equal to unity, then

$$\sum_{j=1}^{s} p_k^{ij} = p^\alpha + (1 - p^\alpha) = 1 \qquad i = 1,..., s \tag{11.42}$$

and the matrix M_k with elements p_k^{ij}, is a stochastic matrix. Thus, the automaton operating in a stationary random environment is described by a finite Markov chain. Assuming that this chain is ergodic, let the final probability of state q^i which corresponds to the output u^α be

$$r^i(\alpha) = \lim_{k\to\infty} P\{q_k = q^i \mid G[q^i] = u^\alpha\} \tag{11.43}$$

and let σ^α denote the sum of the final probabilities for such states q^i which correspond to the output u^α. The overall measure of the performance of an automaton in a random environment is the expectation of penalty, that is,

$$I = \sum_{\alpha=1}^{m} p^\alpha \sigma^\alpha \tag{11.44}$$

If

$$I < \frac{1}{m} \sum_{\alpha=1}^{m} p^\alpha \tag{11.45}$$

the performance of the automaton is called expedient. Expediency is defined as the closeness of I to $I_{\min}$ where

$$I_{\min} = \text{Min}\{p^1,..., p^m\} \tag{11.46}$$

In the ideal case, $I = I_{\min}$, and the automaton is said to have optimal performance.

The state transition diagram for the automaton with "linear strategy," as defined by Tsetlin, with m branches and n states in each branch, is shown in Fig. 8. The state set of the automaton is

$$Q = \{q^{11}, q^{12},..., q^{1n}, q^{21},..., q^{2n},..., q^{m1},..., q^{mn}\}$$

where the superscripts represent the branch in which the state lies and the position in the branch, respectively. If $q_k = q^{ij}$ and $y_k = 0$, the state transitions are given by

$$q_{k+1} = \begin{cases} q^{i,j-1} & \text{for} \quad j \neq 1 \\ q^{i1} & \text{for} \quad j = 1 \end{cases} \tag{11.47}$$

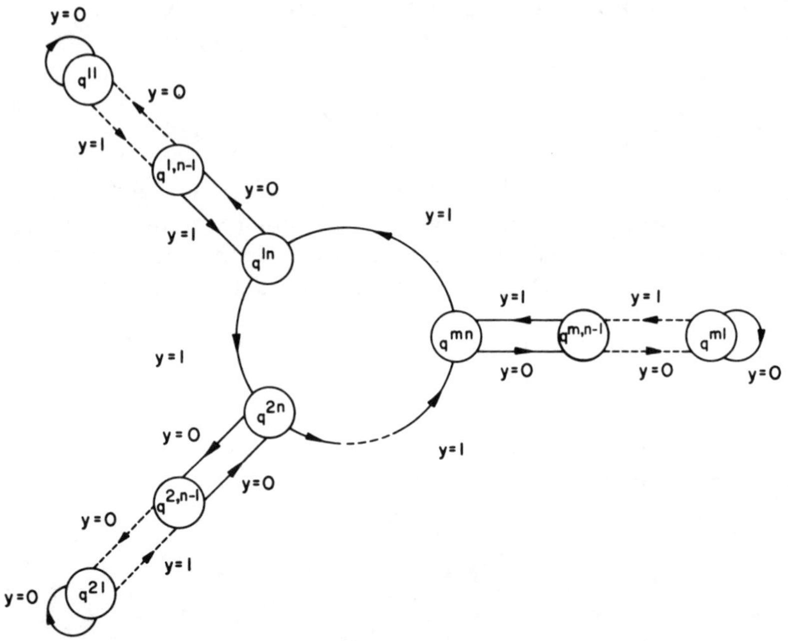

FIGURE 8. State transition for $L_{mn,m}$ model

If $q_k = q^{ij}$ and $y_k = 1$, then

$$q_{k+1} = \begin{cases} q^{i,j+1} & \text{for} \quad j \neq n \\ q^{i+1,n} & \text{for} \quad i \neq m \quad j = n \\ q^{1n} & \text{for} \quad i = m \quad \text{and} \quad j = n \end{cases} \tag{11.48}$$

The output set U is

$$U = \{u^1, \ldots, u^m\}$$

where

$$u_k = u^i = G[q_k = q^{ij}] \qquad 1 \leqslant i \leqslant m, \qquad 1 \leqslant j \leqslant k \tag{11.49}$$

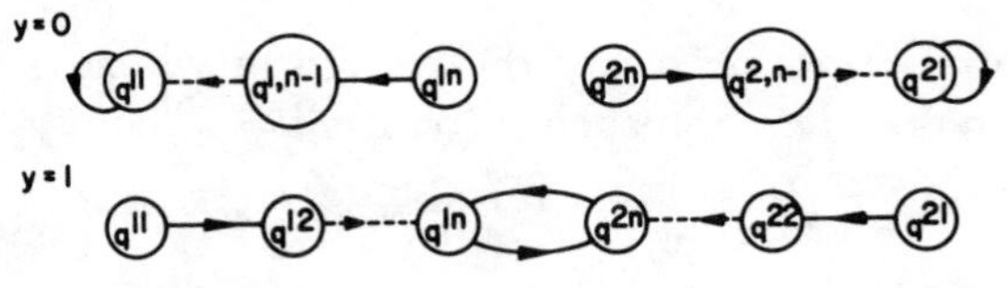

FIGURE 9. State transition for $L_{2n,2}$ model

For illustrative purpose, let $m = 2$. The random environment is characterized by $C(p^1, p^2)$. The state transition diagram of the automaton, designated as $L_{2n,2}$, is shown in Fig. 9. For computing the final state probabilities, the following system of equations is obtained (Tsetlin 1961)

$$\begin{aligned}
r^1 &= (1 - p^1)\, r^1 + (1 - p^1)\, r^2 \\
r^2 &= p^1 r^1 + (1 - p^1)\, r^3 \\
&\vdots \\
r^n &= p^1 r^{n-1} + p^2 r^{2n} \\
r^{n+1} &= (1 - p^2)\, r^{n+1} + (1 - p^2)\, r^{n+2} \\
r^{n+2} &= p^2 r^{n+1} + (1 - p^2)\, r^{n+3} \\
&\vdots \\
r^{2n} &= p^2 r^{2n-1} + p^1 r^n
\end{aligned} \tag{11.50}$$

and the normalization condition is

$$\sum_{i=1}^{2n} r^i = 1 \tag{11.51}$$

Solving for r^i, $i = 1,\ldots, 2n$ from Eqs. (11.50) and (11.51), we can compute σ^1 and σ^2. Hence, the performance of the automaton $L_{2n,2}$ operating in the random environment $C(p^1, p^2)$ can be computed from Eq. (11.44)

$$I(L_{2n,2}, C) = \frac{\dfrac{1}{(p^1)^{n-1}} \cdot \dfrac{(p^1)^n - (1 - p^1)^n}{(p^1) - (1 - p^1)} + \dfrac{1}{(p^2)^{n-1}} \cdot \dfrac{(p^2)^n - (1 - p^2)^n}{(p^2) - (1 - p^2)}}{\dfrac{1}{(p^1)^n} \cdot \dfrac{(p^1)^n - (1 - p^1)^n}{(p^1) - (1 - p^1)} + \dfrac{1}{(p^2)^n} \cdot \dfrac{(p^2)^n - (1 - p^2)^n}{(p^2) - (1 - p^2)}} \tag{11.52}$$

It is noted that $I(L_{2n,2}, C)$ is a decreasing function of the memory capacity n, and that for $I_{\min} \leqslant \frac{1}{2}$,

$$\lim_{n\to\infty} I(L_{2n,2}, C) = I_{\min} \tag{11.53}$$

That is, for a sufficiently large memory capacity n the automaton with linear strategy $L_{2n,2}$ produces almost exclusively the output for which the probability of a penalty is minimal. Automata which have this property are called asymptotically optimal. For a special case of $n = 1$, it can be easily seen that

$$r^1 = \frac{p^2}{p^1 + p^2} \qquad r^2 = \frac{p^1}{p^1 + p^2} \tag{11.54}$$

and

$$I(L_{2,2}, C) = p^1 r^1 + p^2 r^2 = \frac{2p^1 p^2}{p^1 + p^2} \tag{11.55}$$

Since $I(L_{2,2}, C) \leqslant (1/m) \sum_{\alpha=1}^{m} p^{\alpha}$, the automaton $L_{2,2}$ has expedient behavior. In general, for the automaton $L_{mn,m}$ operating in the random environment $C(p^1,..., p^m)$,

$$I(L_{mn,m}, C) = \frac{\displaystyle\sum_{\alpha=1}^{m} \frac{1}{(p^{\alpha})^{n-1}} \cdot \frac{(p^{\alpha})^n - (1 - p^{\alpha})^n}{p^{\alpha} - (1 - p^{\alpha})}}{\displaystyle\sum_{\alpha=1}^{m} \frac{1}{(p^{\alpha})^{n}} \cdot \frac{(p^{\alpha})^n - (1 - p^{\alpha})^n}{p^{\alpha} - (1 - p^{\alpha})}} \tag{11.56}$$

From Eq. (11.56), the automaton $L_{mn,m}$ is asymptotically optimal.

It is also noted that Tsetlin's linear-strategy automata models are very closely related to Robbins' finite memory strategy in two-armed bandit problems (Robbins 1956). In fact they are exactly the same strategy if the memory capacity n is equal to 1. In the case of automaton $L_{2,2}$, by using Robbin's approach it can be shown that the probability of receiving penalty at the kth trial is, for $k \geqslant 1$

$$p_k = (1 - p^1 - p^2)^{k-1} \left[p_1 - \frac{2p^1 \cdot p^2}{p^1 + p^2}\right] + \frac{2p^1 \cdot p^2}{p^1 + p^2}$$

For nontrivial case $| 1 - p^1 - p^2 | < 1$, the limiting expected penalty $I = 2p^1 \cdot p^2/(p^1 + p^2)$ which is the same result as that obtained in Eq. (11.55), but the assumption of ergodicity is not required here.

Krylov (1963) modified Tsetlin's linear-strategy model by making the automaton pseudo-probabilistic. Transition probabilities when $y_k = 1$ are

$$\begin{aligned} P\{q_{k+1} = q^{i,j+1} \mid q_k = q^{ij}; j \neq 1\} &= P\{q_{k+1} = q^{i,j-1} \mid q_k = q^{ij}; j \neq n\} \\ &= P\{q_{k+1} = q^{i+1,n} \mid q_k = q^{in}; i \neq m\} \\ &= P\{q_{k+1} = q^{i1} \mid q_k = q^{i1}\} \\ &= P\{q_{k+1} = q^{1n} \mid q_k = q^{mn}\} = \tfrac{1}{2} \end{aligned}$$

If $y_k = 0$, the transitions are specified as that of the linear-strategy model. This gives the effect of halving each p^i the optimal behavior, even with all $p^i > \frac{1}{2}$.

IV. Variable Structure Stochastic Automata As Models of Learning Systems

Because of the stochastic nature in state transitions and input-output relations, stochastic automata are considered suitable for modeling learning systems. A learning system (or automaton) can be considered as a system (or an automaton) which demonstrates an improvement of performance during its operation from a systematic modification of system's structure or parameter values. The algorithms which modify the system's structure or parameter values should provide certain properties to guarantee the necessary improvement of system's performance. One approach suggested is to modify input-output probabilities $p(u^l \mid y^\alpha)$ of a stochastic automaton in such a way that its performance can be improved during operation. Another approach is the modification of state transition probabilities or state probabilities if the unique relation between the output and the state is known deterministically. In both cases, the stochastic automaton has a variable structure due to the changes of input-output probabilities, state transition probabilities or state probabilities. Consequently, the feature of variable structure results in the learning behavior of the automaton.

Reinforcement algorithms have been proposed for modifying state transition probabilities or state probabilities. The amount of reinforcement is in general a function of the automaton's performance. The new transition probabilities or state probabilities reflect the information which the automaton has received from the input and consequently provide the ability to improve its performance. Varshavskii and Vorontsova (1963), following Tsetlin's approach for deterministic automata (Section III), have used the variable structure stochastic automata as models for learning systems operating in random environments.

In order to achieve expedient performance, transition probabilities $p^{ij}(y^\alpha)$'s are modified. The idea is to decrease $p^{ij}(y^\alpha)$ if the transition from q^i to q^j due to y^α is followed by a penalty. On the other hand, if a nonpenalty follows, $p^{ij}(y^\alpha)$ is increased. The remaining elements in the state transition probability matrix, $p^{ih}(y^\alpha)$, $h \neq j$, are also varied so as to keep the condition (11.4) satisfied. The stationary state of the transition probability $p^{ij}(y^\alpha)$ is defined as the value $p_k^{ij}(y^\alpha)$ that corresponds to one of the following two conditions:

(i) The expectation of $p_{k+1}^{ij}(y^\alpha)$ is equal to $p_k^{ij}(y^\alpha)$; that is,

$$E[p_{k+1}^{ij}(y^\alpha)] = p_k^{ij}(y^\alpha) = p^{ij}(y^\alpha) \tag{11.57}$$

(ii) $$\lim_{k\to\infty} [p_{k+1}^{ij}(y^\alpha) - p_k^{ij}(y^\alpha)] = 0 \tag{11.58}$$

and the sign of the difference in (ii) does not depend on the value of $p_k^{ij}(y^\alpha)$. The behavior of stochastic automata with variable structure in random environments can be described by means of inhomogeneous

Markov chains. For the reinforcement algorithms suggested, stationary values of the transition probabilities exist, and one can talk about final state probabilities of the system. Two illustrative examples are given in the following.

Example 5. The stochastic automaton M is characterized by:

$$Y = \{0, 1\} \qquad Q = \{q^1, q^2\} \qquad U = \{u^1, u^2\}$$

$$M(0) = \begin{bmatrix} p^{11}(0) & 1 - p^{11}(0) \\ 1 - p^{22}(0) & p^{22}(0) \end{bmatrix} \qquad M(1) = \begin{bmatrix} p^{11}(1) & 1 - p^{11}(1) \\ 1 - p^{22}(1) & p^{22}(1) \end{bmatrix}$$

If $q_k = q^i$ then $u_k = u^i$ for all i and k. The reinforcement algorithm for modifying $p^{ij}(y^\alpha)$, $i, j, \alpha = 1, 2$, is given as follows: If a transition occurs from q^i to q^j (that is, $q_k = q^i$ and $q_{k+1} = q^j$) due to the input $y_k = y^\alpha$ and has been penalized (that is, $y_{k+1} = 1$), then

$$p_{k+1}^{ij}(y^\alpha) = \theta p_k^{ij}(y^\alpha) \qquad 0 < \theta < 1 \qquad \alpha = 1, 2 \tag{11.59}$$

If $y_{k+1} = 0$, then,

$$p_{k+1}^{ij}(y^\alpha) = \theta p_k^{ij}(y^\alpha) + (1 - \theta) \tag{11.60}$$

Under these conditions,

$$E[p_{k+1}^{11}(0)] = p_k^{11}(0) - \Pi_k{}^1(1 - p^1)(1 - \theta)[p_k^{11}(0)(p^1 + p^2) - p^2] \tag{11.61}$$

$$E[p_{k+1}^{11}(1)] = p_k^{11}(1) - \Pi_k{}^1 p^1(1 - \theta)[p_k^{11}(1)(p^1 + p^2) - p^2] \tag{11.62}$$

$$E[p_{k+1}^{22}(0)] = p_k^{22}(0) - \Pi_k{}^2(1 - p^2)(1 - \theta)[p_k^{22}(0)(p^1 + p^2) - p^1] \tag{11.63}$$

$$E[p_{k+1}^{22}(1)] = p_k^{22}(1) - \Pi_k{}^2 p^2(1 - \theta)[p_k^{22}(1)(p^1 + p^2) - p^1] \tag{11.64}$$

From Eq. (11.57), for $E[p_{k+1}^{ij}(y^\alpha)] = p_k^{ij}(y^\alpha)$, Eqs. (11.61)–(11.64) result in following solution:

$$p^{11}(0) = p^{11}(1) = \frac{p^2}{p^1 + p^2} \quad \text{and} \quad p^{22}(0) = p^{22}(1) = \frac{p^1}{p^1 + p^2} \tag{11.65}$$

Thus, from Eq. (11.44),

$$I = \frac{2p^1p^2}{p^1 + p^2} \leqslant \tfrac{1}{2}(p^1 + p^2) \tag{11.66}$$

It is noted that Eq. (11.66) is identical to Eq. (11.55).

Example 6. In Example 5, instead of using Eqs. (11.59) and (11.60), the following reinforcement algorithm is used: If a transition occurs from q^i to q^j due to the input y^α and has been penalized, then

$$p_{k+1}^{ij}(y^\alpha) = p_k^{ij}(y^\alpha) - \theta p_k^{ij}(y^\alpha)[1 - p_k^{ij}(y^\alpha)] \qquad 0 < \theta < 1 \tag{11.67}$$

If, on the other hand, $y_{k+1} = 0$, then

$$p_{k+1}^{ij}(y^\alpha) = p_k^{ij}(y^\alpha) + \theta p_k^{ij}(y^\alpha)[1 - p_k^{ij}(y^\alpha)] \tag{11.68}$$

Under these conditions,

$$\begin{aligned} E[p_{k+1}^{11}(0)] = p_k^{11}(0) &+ \Pi_k{}^1(1 - p^1)\,\theta p_k^{11}(0)[1 - p_k^{11}(0)] \\ &\cdot [2(1 - p^1 - p^2)\,p_k^{11}(0) - (1 - 2p^2)] \end{aligned} \tag{11.69}$$

$$\begin{aligned} E[p_{k+1}^{11}(1)] = p_k^{11}(1) &+ \Pi_k{}^1 p^1 \theta p_k^{11}(1)[1 - p_k^{11}(1)] \\ &\cdot [2(1 - p^1 - p^2)\,p_k^{11}(1) - (1 - 2p^2)] \end{aligned} \tag{11.70}$$

$$\begin{aligned} E[p_{k+1}^{22}(0)] = p_k^{22}(0) &+ \Pi_k{}^2(1 - p^2)\,\theta p_k^{22}(0)[1 - p_k^{22}(0)] \\ &\cdot [2(1 - p^1 - p^2)\,p_k^{22}(0) - (1 - 2p^1)] \end{aligned} \tag{11.71}$$

$$\begin{aligned} E[p_{k+1}^{22}(1)] = p_k^{22}(1) &+ \Pi_k{}^2 p^2 \theta p_k^{22}(1)[1 - p_k^{22}(1)] \\ &\cdot [2(1 - p^1 - p^2)\,p_k^{22}(1) - (1 - 2p^1)] \end{aligned} \tag{11.72}$$

Case 1. If $p^1 < \frac{1}{2} < p^2$, then for $k \to \infty$, $p^{11}(0) \to 1$, $p^{22}(0) \to 0$, $p^{11}(1) \to 1$, $p^{22}(1) \to 0$ and $\Pi^1 \to 1$. Consequently,

$$I = p^1 = \text{Min}(p^1, p^2) \tag{11.73}$$

Case 2. If $p^1 > \frac{1}{2}$ and $p^2 > \frac{1}{2}$, then for $E[p_{k+1}^{ij}(y^\alpha)] = p_k^{ij}(y^\alpha)$,

$$p^{11}(0) = p^{11}(1) = \frac{1 - 2p^2}{2(1 - p^1 - p^2)}$$

and

$$p^{22}(0) = p^{22}(1) = \frac{1 - 2p^1}{2(1 - p^1 - p^2)} \tag{11.74}$$

which result in

$$I = \frac{p^1 + p^2 - 4p^1p^2}{2(1 - p^1 - p^2)} \tag{11.75}$$

It can be shown that in the cases treated in Examples 5 and 6, the expectation of a penalty I does not depend on the number of states of the automaton. (Varshavskii and Vorontsova, 1963). Also, from Example 6, it can be easily seen that, with the reinforcement algorithm, Eqs. (11.67) and (11.68), a stochastic automaton with a variable structure is equivalent to a linear-strategy automaton with an infinite number of states.

V. Generalizations of the Basic Reinforcement Learning Model

The basic linear reinforcement learning model described in Eqs. (11.59) and (11.60) has been extended to the cases where (i) instead of modifying $p_k^{ij}(y^\alpha)$, the modification of any convenient probability function is treated, and (ii) the performance of the learning automaton, instead of 0 (nonpenalty) or 1 (penalty), can be any value between 0 and 1 (Fu and McLaren, 1965; Fu and McMurtry, 1965; Nikolic and Fu, 1966). In the first case, the probabilities to be modified can be the probabilities at each state of the automaton, the probabilities of making each possible decision, or the probabilities of choosing each possible parameter value. In the second case, the reinforcement of the probabilities is related to a quantitative measure of the automaton's performance rather than just a qualitative measure (that is, 0 or 1). A generalized linear reinforcement algorithm based on the above-mentioned extensions is described in the following.

The performance of the automaton in a random environment, I, is used to direct the reinforcement learning process (see Fig. 10). In a

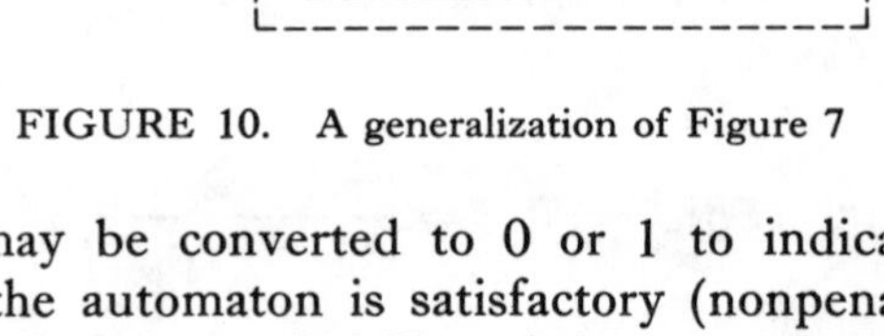

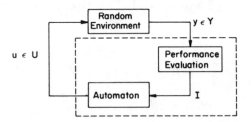

FIGURE 10. A generalization of Figure 7

special case, I may be converted to 0 or 1 to indicate whether the performance of the automaton is satisfactory (nonpenalty) or unsatisfactory (penalty). Let the probability of the automaton making the ith decision, choosing the ith parameter value, or being at the ith state be P^i, $i = 1,\ldots, s$, where s is the total number of possible decisions, the total number of possible (quantized) parameter settings, or the number of states of the automaton. The linear reinforcement algorithm which relates the P^i at the instant k and at the instant $(k + 1)$ respectively when the response from the environment is y can be expressed by the following equation:

$$P_{k+1}^i(y) = \theta P_k^i(y) + (1 - \theta)\,\lambda_k^i(y) \qquad i = 1,\ldots, s \tag{11.76}$$

where $0 < \theta < 1$, and $0 \leqslant \lambda_k^i(y) \leqslant 1$, $\sum_{i=1}^{s} \lambda_k^i(y) = 1$. If $\lambda_k^i(y) = \lambda^i(y)$, that is, $\lambda_k^k(y)$ is independent of k, then

$$P_k^i(y) = \theta^k P_0^i(y) + (1 - \theta^k)\,\lambda^i(y) \tag{11.77}$$

and hence,

$$\lim_{k\to\infty} P_k^i(y) = \lambda^i(y) \tag{11.78}$$

This means that $\lambda^i(y)$ is the limiting probability of $P_k^i(y)$, and it should be related to the information or performance measure evaluated from the response y through the random environment due to the ith decision of the automaton. In general, $\lambda_k(y)$ can be identified as a normalized performance index at the instant k, for example,

$$\lambda_k(y) = \frac{I_k(y)}{C} \tag{11.79}$$

where $I_k(y)$ is the performance of the automaton, I, evaluated at the instant k from the response y, and

$$C = \operatorname*{Max}_k I_k(y) \tag{11.80}$$

Thus, $0 \leqslant \lambda_k(y) \leqslant 1$ for all y and $k \geqslant 0$. In a special case, $\lambda_k(y)$ may be selected as

$$\lambda_k(y) = \begin{cases} 0 & \text{if} \quad I_k(y) > I_o \\ 1 & \text{if} \quad I_k(y) \leqslant I_o \end{cases} \tag{11.81}$$

where I_o is a prespecified threshold that indicates the satisfactory quality of the automaton's performance.

To illustrate the reinforcement algorithm for modifying the structure of the automaton and the subsequent properties, assume that the automaton will search for (or learn) the best decision or the best parameter setting in order to maximize the expectation of $\lambda_k(y)$. Specifically, if the decision at the instant k is the ith decision, then

$$P_{k+1}^i(y) = \theta P_k^i(y) + (1 - \theta)\, \lambda_k(y)$$

and (11.82)

$$P_{k+1}^j(y) = \theta P_k^j(y) + \frac{1-\theta}{s-1}[1 - \lambda_k(y)] \qquad j = 1,\ldots, s, \quad j \neq i$$

where $\lambda_k(y)$ is computed according to Eq. (11.79). Compare with Eq. (11.76), it is noted that, in this case,

$$\lambda_k^j(y) = \begin{cases} \lambda_k(y) & \text{if} \quad j = i \\ [1 - \lambda_k(y)]/(s-1) & \text{if} \quad j \neq i \end{cases} \tag{11.83}$$

Let the conditional expectation of $\lambda_k(y)$ given that the ith decision has been made be defined by

$$E_\lambda[\lambda_k^i(y)] = m_k^i \tag{11.84}$$

and then

$$E_\lambda[\lambda_k(y)] = \sum_{i=1}^{s} E_\lambda[P_k^i(y)] \cdot E_\lambda[\lambda_k^i(y)] = \sum_{i=1}^{s} m_k^i E_\lambda[P_k^i(y)] \tag{11.85}$$

Assume that the random environment is stationary; that is, $m_k^i = m^i$. From Eq. (11.76),

$$E_\lambda[P_1^i(y)] = \theta E_\lambda[P_0^i(y)] + (1 - \theta)\, E_\lambda[\lambda_0^i(y)] \qquad i = 1,\ldots, s \tag{11.86}$$

Since $P_0^i(y)$'s are preselected, $E_\lambda[P_0^i(y)] = P_0^i(y)$. Thus,

$$E_\lambda[P_1^i(y)] = \theta P_0^i(y) + (1 - \theta)\left[m^i P_0^i(y) + \sum_{\substack{j=1 \\ \neq i}}^{s} \frac{1 - m^j}{s-1} P_0^j(y)\right]$$

$$i = 1,\ldots, s \tag{11.87}$$

By iterating Eq. (11.87), it can be proved that (Fu and McLaren 1965)

$$\lim_{k\to\infty} E_\lambda[P_k^i(y)] = \gamma^i \qquad i = 1,\ldots, s \tag{11.88}$$

where

$$\gamma^i = \prod_{\substack{j=1 \\ \neq i}}^{s} (1 - m^j) \Big/ \sum_{j=1}^{s} \prod_{\substack{k=1 \\ \neq j}}^{s} (1 - m^k) \qquad i = 1,\ldots, s \tag{11.89}$$

Furthermore,

$$m^i \geqslant m^j \qquad \text{implies} \qquad \gamma^i \geqslant \gamma^j \tag{11.90}$$

and

$$m^i = \sup_j \{m^j\} \qquad \text{implies} \qquad \gamma^i = \sup_j \{\gamma^j\} \tag{11.91}$$

which means that the m^i's are of the same order of magnitude as the corresponding γ^i's in the limit as $k \to \infty$; the larger (better) m^i is, the higher the limit γ^i will be. In addition, the largest (best) m^i corresponds to the highest γ^i, consequently, to the decision or parameter setting with the highest expected probability. It can also be shown that

$$E_\lambda[\lambda_{k+1}(y)] \geqslant E_\lambda[\lambda_k(y)] \qquad \text{for} \qquad k \geqslant 0 \tag{11.92}$$

and

$$\lim_{k\to\infty} E_\lambda[\lambda_k(y)] = \sum_{j=1}^{s} m^j \gamma^j \tag{11.93}$$

which simply means that $E_\lambda[\lambda_k(y)]$ converges in a monotonic manner toward its maximum limit value. Similar results can be obtained for minimizing the expectation of $\lambda_k(y)$ in which Eq. (11.82) becomes

$$P_{k+1}^i(y) = \theta P_k^i(y) + (1-\theta)[1-\lambda_k(y)] \qquad 0 < \theta < 1 \tag{11.94}$$

and

$$P_{k+1}^j(y) = \theta P_k^j(y) + \frac{1-\theta}{s-1}\lambda_k(y) \qquad j = 1,\ldots, s, j \neq i$$

Equations (11.88) and (11.93) are still valid, but Eqs. (11.89), (11.90), and (11.78) become, respectively,

$$\gamma^i = \prod_{\substack{j=1 \\ \neq i}}^{s} m^j \Big/ \sum_{j=1}^{s} \prod_{\substack{k=1 \\ \neq j}}^{s} m^k \qquad i = 1,\ldots, s \tag{11.95}$$

$$m^i \leqslant m^j \qquad \text{implies} \qquad \gamma^i \geqslant \gamma^j \tag{11.96}$$

$$m^i = \inf_j \{m^j\} \qquad \text{implies} \qquad \gamma^i = \sup_j \{\gamma^j\} \tag{11.97}$$

and

$$E_\lambda[\lambda_{k+1}(y)] \leqslant E_\lambda[\lambda_k(y)] \qquad \text{for} \qquad k \geqslant 0 \tag{11.98}$$

VI. Automata Games

Automata operating in random environments can be viewed as the automata playing games against the nature. Based on this viewpoint, the problems treated in Section III, IV, and V can be extended to games between automata (Krylov and Tsetlin, 1963; Ginsburg, Krylov, and Tsetlin, 1964). In this section, two learning models for automata, having deterministic and probabilistic transition rules, are discussed and their application to automata games are demonstrated (Fu and Li, 1968).

A. *Formulation of Model $A_{r,m}$: Automata with Finite Memory*

In Section III, the automaton $L_{mn,m}$'s memory is embedded in the number of states associated with a particular output. Based on the two-armed bandit strategy proposed by Robbins (1956), the automata model $A_{r,m}$ is proposed. Referring to Fig. 7, the value of y can be either 1 (penalty) or 0 (nonpenalty). Similar to the $L_{mn,m}$ model, the automaton $A_{r,m}$ with m possible outputs or actions corresponds to mr states, and memory length r; that is,

$$G(q^{(i-1)r+1}) = G(q^{(i-1)r+2}) = \cdots = G(q^{ir}) = u^i, \quad i = 1, 2, \ldots, m.$$

The state transition diagram is shown in Fig. 11. It is noted, from Fig. 11, that after receiving a penalty ($y = 1$), $L_{mn,m}$ and $A_{r,m}$ have the same

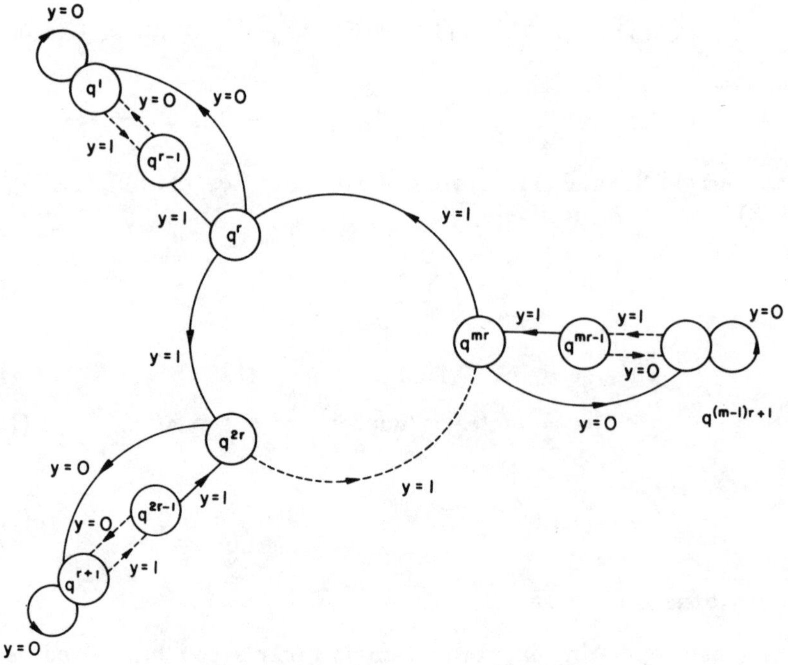

FIGURE 11. State transition for $A_{r,m}$ model

state transition. However, after receiving a nonpenalty, $A_{r,m}$ may have a jump in state transitions.

The behavior of the $A_{r,m}$ automaton operating in a random environment can be analyzed as follows*. Let a successive use of one particular action to be one "block." Then, for each block the expected number of trials required is

$$p^j + (1 - p^j)\left[1 + \frac{1 - (p^j)^r}{(1 - p^j)(p^j)^r}\right] = \frac{1}{(p^j)^r}$$

where p^j is the probability of receiving a penalty due to the automaton output u^j. Let l_i^j denote the length of the ith block of trials for state q^j; then, the overall trial sequence is, starting with q^1:

$$l_1^1, l_1^2, ..., l_1^m, l_2^1, l_2^2, ..., l_2^m, ..., l_n^1, l_n^2, l_n^m, ...$$

The proportion of time that $A_{r,m}$ stays in state q^j during the first mn blocks of trial is:

$$\begin{aligned} d^j &= \frac{l_1^j + l_2^j + \cdots + l_n^j}{l_1^1 + l_1^2 + \cdots + l_1^m + \cdots + l_n^1 + \cdots + l_n^m} \\ &= \frac{(l_1^j + l_2^j + \cdots + l_n^j)/n}{[(l_1^1 + \cdots + l_n^1)/n] + \cdots + [(l_1^m + \cdots + l_n^m)/n]} \end{aligned} \quad (11.99)$$

By strong law of large numbers, this tends to $[1/(p^j)^r]/\sum_{j=1}^m [1/(p^j)^r]$ in the limit. Then, the proportion of penalties in the first mn blocks of trials is $\sum_{j=1}^m p^j \cdot d^j$. Therefore, the expected penalty for automaton $A_{r,m}$ operating in random environment C is

$$I(A_{r,m}, C) = \sum_{j=1}^m p^j \frac{1/(p^j)^r}{\sum_{i=1}^m \frac{1}{(p^i)^r}} = \frac{\sum_{j=1}^m \frac{1}{(p^j)^{r-1}}}{\sum_{i=1}^m \frac{1}{(p^i)^r}} \quad (11.100)$$

It can be shown (Fu and Li, 1968) that $I(A_{r,m}, C)$ is a monotonically decreasing function with respect to r. Furthermore,

$$\lim_{r\to\infty} I(A_{r,m}, C) = \min(p^1, ..., p^m) = I_{\min} \quad (11.101)$$

asymptotic optimality is, therefore, established.

---

* The same result can be obtained by applying the theory of markov chains (Fu and Li, 1969). The analysis presented here is based on the strong law of large numbers (Robbins, 1956).

In comparing $A_{r,m}$ model with Tsetlin's linear-strategy $L_{mr,m}$ model, more generality is gained since the assumption $\min(p^1,..., p^m) \leqslant \frac{1}{2}$ is not required in the proposed model. But, if this assumption holds, then

$$\lim_{r\to\infty} I(A_{r,m}, C) = \lim I(L_{mr,m}, C) \tag{11.102}$$

Particularly, it can be shown by straightforward algebraic manipulation that:

$$I(A_{r,m}, C) \leqslant I(L_{mr,m}, C)$$

if

$$\min_i | 0.5 - p^i | = | 0.5 - \min_i p^i | \tag{11.103}$$

The most favorable situation for $A_{r,m}$ is when $\min(p^1,..., p^m) \geqslant \frac{1}{2}$ since Eq. (11.103) is automatically guaranteed in this case. Likewise, if

$$\min_i | 0.5 - p^i | = | 0.5 - \max_i p^i |$$

then

$$I(A_{r,m}, C) \geqslant I(L_{mr,m}, C)$$

B. *Formulation of Model $B_{r,m,b}$: Automata with Randomized Transition Rules (Stochastic Automata)*

Based on the work of Samuels (1966), an automata model $B_{r,m,b}$ is formulated by modifying $A_{r,m}$ model with a randomized transition rule. After the automaton receives a nonpenalty ($y = 0$), the state transition is the same as that for the automaton $A_{r,m}$. For $y = 1$, the state transition diagram is shown in Fig. 12, where $b(0 \leqslant b < 1)$ is the randomization factor. It is noted that, when $b = 0$, the automaton $B_{r,m,b}$ reduces to $A_{r-1,m}$.

The analysis of this model is similar to that of the deterministic case except for the randomized part. The number of trials in this long block with a particular state q^j is

$$\sum_{i=1}^{\tau} (Z_i + U_i + 1) - 1$$

where Z_i is the number of trials until r consecutive penalties occur in the ith cycle; U_i is the number of additional trials when the randomization device indicates "stay in q^j"; τ is the number of cycles until the randomization device finally indicates "change state." The 1 inside the parentheses represents the trial that the randomization device indicates

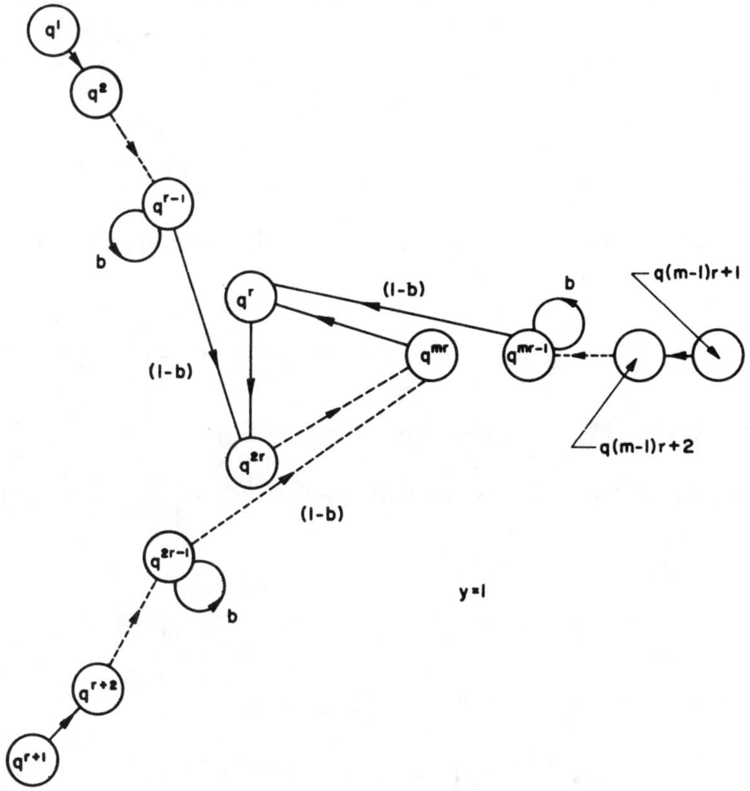

FIGURE 12. State transition for $B_{r,m,b}$ model

"stay in q^j" but nonpenalty result is obtained; the -1 is outside the parentheses because in the last cycle, there is no such case as "staying in state q^j and receiving a nonpenalty." Thus, the expected value of the number of trials in this long block is

$$\lambda^* = E\Big[\sum_{i=1}^{\tau}(Z_i + U_i + 1) - 1\Big] \tag{11.104}$$

Since Z_i's, U_i's and τ are all mutually independent and the Z_i's are identically distributed, so are the U_i's, then by Wald's identity (Wilks, 1962), Eq. (11.104) becomes

$$\lambda^* = E(\tau)\cdot[E(Z_i) + E(U_i + 1)] - 1 \tag{11.105}$$

with $E(Z_i) = [1 - (p^j)^r]/[(1 - p^j)(p^j)^r]$ as before. To calculate $E(U_i + 1)$, it is noted that

$$
\begin{aligned}
P\{U_i + 1 = k\} &= P\{U_i = k - 1\} \\
&= (b \cdot p^j)^{k-1} \cdot P\{U_i = 0\} \\
&= (1 - b \cdot p^j)(b \cdot p^j)^{k-1}
\end{aligned} \tag{11.106}
$$

Hence, the $U_i + 1$'s have geometric distribution with parameter $(1 - b \cdot p^j)$. Then, we have

$$E(U_i + 1) = \sum_{k=1}^{\infty} k \cdot (1 - b \cdot p^j) \cdot (b \cdot p^j)^{k-1} = \frac{1}{1 - b \cdot p^j} \tag{11.107}$$

To calculate $E(\tau)$, it is clear that

$$P\{\tau = 1\} = (1 - b)[1 + b \cdot p^j + b^2 \cdot (p^j)^2 + \cdots] = \frac{1 - b}{1 - b \cdot p^j} \tag{11.108}$$

But for $k > 1$,

$$P(\tau = k) = \frac{b(1 - p^j)}{1 - b \cdot p^j} \cdot P\{\tau = k - 1\} \tag{11.109}$$

By iteration, together with Eq. (11.108), we get

$$P\{\tau = k\} = \left(\frac{1 - b}{1 - b \cdot p^j}\right)\left[\frac{b(1 - p^j)}{1 - b \cdot p^j}\right]^{k-1} \tag{11.110}$$

Hence, τ is also geometrically distributed, but with parameter $(1 - b)/(1 - b \cdot p^j)$. Then we have

$$E(\tau) = \sum_{k=1}^{\infty} k \left(\frac{1 - b}{1 - b \cdot p^j}\right)\left[\frac{b(1 - p^j)}{1 - b \cdot p^j}\right]^{k-1} = \frac{1 - b \cdot p^j}{1 - b} \tag{11.111}$$

Combining Eqs. (11.105), (11.107), and (11.108), we get

$$\lambda^* = \frac{1 - b \cdot p^j}{(1 - b)} \cdot \frac{1 - (p^j)^r}{(1 - p^j)(p^j)^r} + \frac{1}{1 - b} \tag{11.112}$$

Then as in the deterministic case, for each block the expected number of trials required is

$$p^j + (1 - p^j)(1 + \lambda^*) = \left(\frac{1 - b \cdot p^j}{1 - b}\right)\frac{1}{(p^j)^r} \tag{11.113}$$

Therefore, the expected penalty for model $B_{r,m,b}$ operating in random environment $C = C(p^1,\ldots, p^m)$ is

$$I(B_{r,m,b}, C) = \frac{\sum_{i=1}^{m} (1 - p^i \cdot b) \frac{1}{(p^i)^{r-1}}}{\sum_{j=1}^{m} (1 - p^j \cdot b) \frac{1}{(p^j)^r}} \tag{11.114}$$

It can be shown (Fu and Li, 1968) that $I(B_{r,m,b}, C)$ is a monotonically decreasing function with respect to b. Thus, we may conclude:

(i) For the same random environment C, if $b \geqslant 1/(p^i + p^j)$ for all $i \neq j$, then $I(B_{r,m,b}, C) \leqslant I(A_{r,m}, C)$, $r \geqslant 2$.

(ii) $I(B_{r,m,b}, C)$ is a monotonically decreasing function with respect to both r and b.

(iii) For fixed value r, the least expected penalty one can attain is no less then

$$\frac{\sum_{i=1}^{m} (1 - p^i) \frac{1}{(p^i)^{r-1}}}{\sum_{j=1}^{m} (1 - p^j) \frac{1}{(p^j)^r}}$$

(iv) As in the deterministic case, a conservative strategy is a good policy.

C. *Computer Simulations*

1. *Games of $A_{r,m}$ automata against nature.* For the sake of experimental justification, consider the behavior of $A_{r,m}$ operating in an environment $C_7(p^1,\ldots, p^7)$ where $p^1 = 1$, $p^2 = 0.8$, $p^3 = 0.19$, $p^4 = 0.6$, $p^5 = 0.7$, $p^6 = 0.4$, $p^7 = 0.65$. In the simulation, 30,000 trials are performed for a particular value of memory length r. Average penalty is used to estimate the expected penalty. Both experimental and theoretical results are summarized in Fig. 13; their agreement with each other is clear. The behavior of the system is as expected: the expectation of penalty $I(A_{r,7}, C_7)$ decreases and D, the percentage of using the best policy, increases as r increases. Furthermore, $I(A_{r,7}, C_7)$ tends to $I_{\min}$ and D tends to 1 when r increases indefinitely.

2. *Games between $A_{r,m}$ automata.* For simplicity, consider only the "investment game" (Fig. 14) [Krylov and Tsetlin, 1963] between automata of $A_{r,m}$ type and study their group behavior.* The game is defined

* It should be remarked that both $A_{r,m}$ and $B_{r,m,b}$ have not been shown to be optimal strategies for investment games. The simulations presented here are mainly used to compare with the results obtained by Krylov and Tsetlin (1963).

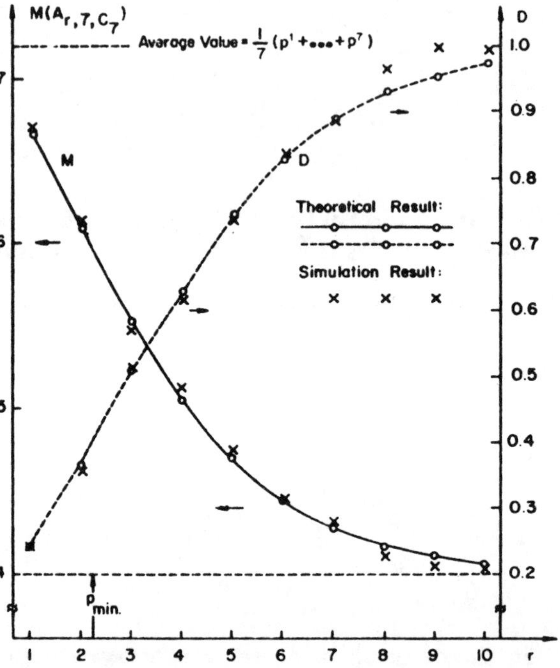

FIGURE 13. Simulation result of model $A_{r,7}$ in C_7

by a set of m constants $0 \leqslant a_i \leqslant 1$, called the value of the output u^i, $i = 1, 2, \ldots, m$. The pay-off I_β for player β equals the value of the action he uses divided by the total number of players using this action. Then the probability that player β will win ($\mu_\beta = +1$) is $\frac{1}{2}(I_\beta + 1)$, while the probability that player β will lose ($\mu_\beta = -1$) is $1 - \frac{1}{2}(I_\beta + 1)$. The objective is to minimize the average winning over N plays:

$$W_\beta(N) = \frac{1}{N} \sum_{k=1}^{N} \mu_\beta(k)$$

In the following, some simulation results are described and compared with that obtained by Krylov and Tsetlin (1963) under the same conditions.

(*a*) Five identical automata of $A_{r,m}$ type play the investment game: Each of them can select one of seven possible actions with the following values: $a_1 = 0.9$, $a_2 = a_3 = \cdots = a_7 = 0.33$. Since $2 \cdot a_i < a_1 < 3 \cdot a_i$ for $i = 2, 3, \ldots, 7$ it is natural for one to choose a distribution in which

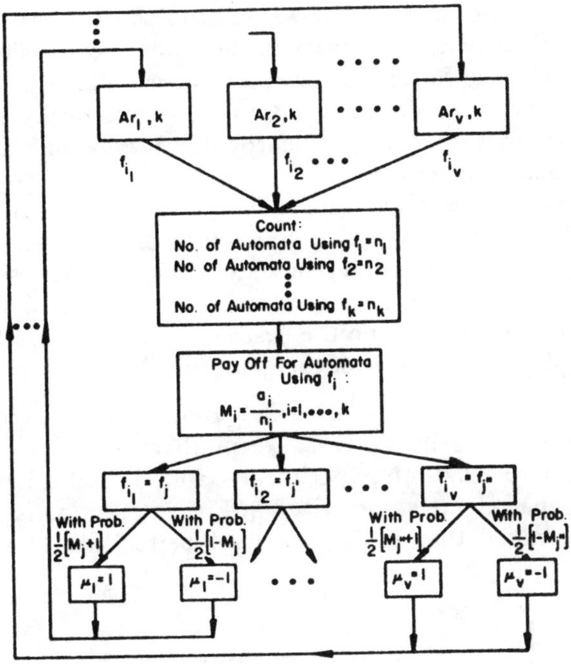

FIGURE 14. Flow diagram for investment game between automata

two automata use their first action and each of the remaining automata uses one of the remaining actions. Under this "best policy," the expected wining of each automaton should be $\frac{1}{5}(2 \times 0.45 + 3 \times 0.33) = 0.378$.

Table I shows the simulation result for the game between automata of $A_{r,m}$ type and that of $L_{mr,m}$ type for comparison. The fact that the

TABLE I

COMPUTER SIMULATION RESULTS FOR $A_{r,m}$ AND $L_{mr,m}$

r	1	2	3	4	5	6	7	8
Average Winning of $L_{mr,m}$	0.353	0.368	0.374	0.376	0.376	—	0.377	—
Average Winning of $A_{r,m}$	0.353	0.375	0.375	0.379	0.370	0.375	0.365	0.362
% of Using Best Policy	14.8	21.5	29.0	34.6	36.1	43.7	47.6	55.6

percentage of using the best policy increases as r increases indicates the learning behavior of the automata in the game. For smaller values of r, the average winning for $A_{r,m}$ is greater than that of $L_{mr,m}$. However, for both models the average winnings are not asymptotically optimal due to the nonstationarity viewed by a particular automaton when the other related automata changes states.

(*b*) The same game as that in (*a*) except that the values of the actions are $a_1 = a_2 = \cdots = a_7 = 0.33$: It is clear that the best policy is for each automaton to choose different actions. Simulation results show that for $r = 5$, starting with all automata in q^1, after 42 plays they are in different states. From then on the best policy was applied for 92.65 percent of the plays for the rest of the game.

3. *Games of $B_{r,m,b}$ automata.* The simulation procedure is similar to that in the deterministic case except that the model $B_{r,m,b}$ with b equal to 0.5 is used. Both experimental and theoretical results for the game against nature are summarized in Fig. 15. Comparing Fig. 15 with Fig. 13, it is noted that $B_{r,7,0.5}$ is always better than $A_{r,7}$ in the sense

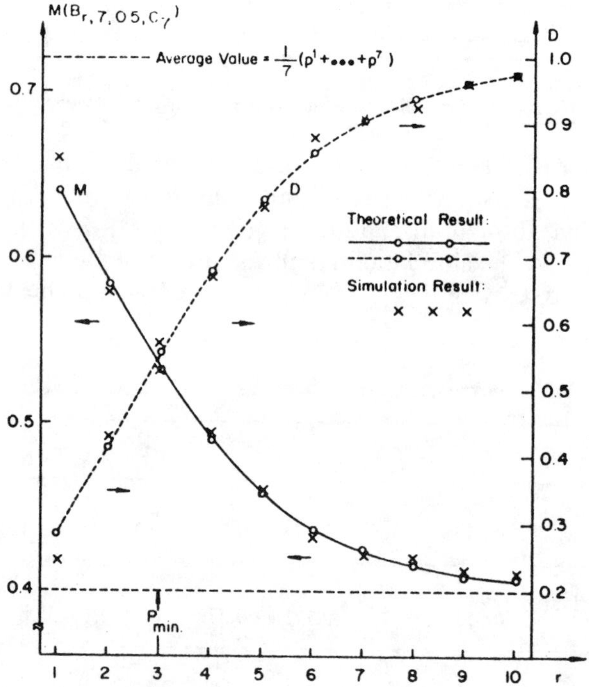

FIGURE 15. Simulation result of model $B_{r,7,0.5}$ in C_7

that the former has less average penalty but larger value of D. $I(B_{r,7,b}, C_7)$ is plotted in Fig. 16 as a function of randomization factor b with memory length r as a parameter; this agrees to the conclusions we have made previously. Also $I(B_{r,7,b}, C_7)$ is more sensitive to b for smaller value of r.

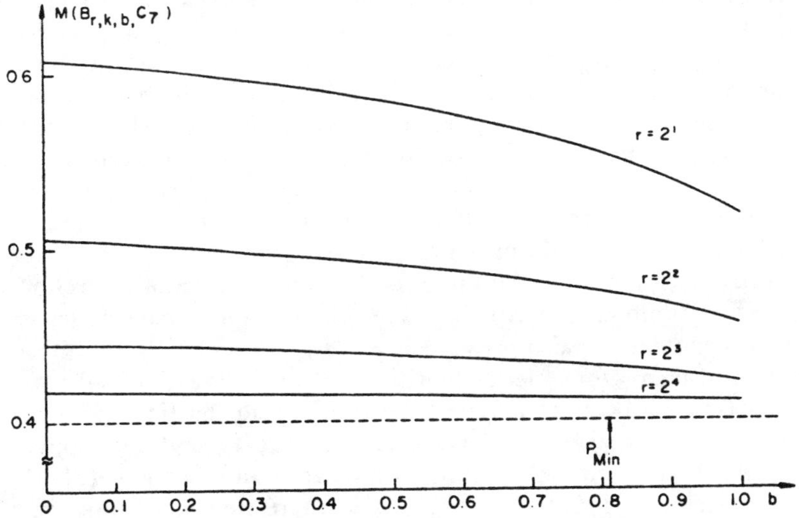

FIGURE 16. Expected behavior of $B_{r,7,b}$ in C_7

The same investment game as that in (2) is played by automata of $B_{r,m,b}$ type. With $b = 0.5$, the result shown in Table II is obtained.

TABLE II

COMPUTER SIMULATION RESULTS FOR $B_{r,m,b}$

r	1	2	3	4	5	6	7	8
Average winning of $B_{r,m,b}$	0.356	0.370	0.377	0.377	0.376	0.377	0.373	0.362
% of Using Best Policy	15.4	22.8	28.9	39.3	55.1	64.3	26.3	71.6

In comparison with the result for an automata game of $A_{r,m}$ type, it is noted that for smaller value of r, $B_{r,m,b}$ model has a better performance. For $r = 3,\ldots, 7$, $B_{r,m,b}$ model has a reasonably high average winning; the percentage of using the best policy also increases as a function of b and r.

VII. Conclusions and Further Remarks

The basic formulation and properties of stochastic automata have been briefly reviewed in this chapter. Three synthesis procedures of stochastic automata have been described. The use of stochastic automata as models of learning systems has been extensively discussed. Deterministic automata operating in random environments exhibit learning behavior of minimizing the expectation of penalty. Similar behavior can also be found in the case of stochastic automata operating in random environments using linear reinforcement algorithm. The learning model with penalty-nonpenalty has been generalized to the case where the performance of the system can be more qualitatively described by a normalized performance index. The convergence has been proved for the generalized model with linear reinforcement. Another generalization for automata operating in random environments is automata games. Preliminary results for automata games using deterministic and stochastic transition rules respectively are also presented.

The linear reinforcement algorithm can be shown to fall into the general framework of Dvoretzky's generalized stochastic approximation (Fu, 1968). Limited results have been obtained for automata operating in random environments using nonlinear reinforcement (Shen and Chanderasekran, 1966). It should be interesting and important to investigate the behavior of automata operating in nonstationary environments. Unfortunately, general results for learning in nonstationary environments have not yet been available. Most results obtained so far are mainly concerned with learning in switching environments (Tsetlin, 1961; Fu and Ackerson, 1968). Because the area of stochastic automata is relatively new, the applications to learning systems and other practical problems have not yet been fully investigated. However, the generality of the stochastic automata model has indicated a strong potential and a general model for learning systems may eventually be developed on the basis of stochastic automata theory.

The applications of the stochastic automata models to pattern recognition, multimodal search and learning control can be found in Chapter 7 and Chapter 8.

VIII. Nomenclature

q^i — ith state of the automaton
q_k — the state of automaton at instant k
u^l — lth output of the automaton
u_k — the output of automaton at instant k

y^α — αth input of the automaton
y_k — the input of automaton at instant k
Y — input set
Q — state set
U — output set
$p^{ij}(y^\alpha)$ — the transition probability of the next state being q^j when the present state is q^i and the present input is y^α
$M(y^\alpha)$ — the transition probability for the input y^α
M — the input-output matrix of an automaton
I — input sequence, expectation of penalty
J — output sequence
Π_0^i — the probability of the initial state q_0 being at q^i
$\mathbf{\Pi}_0$ — initial state distribution, a column vector with the ith element Π_0^i
p^α — the probability of the input being y^α
C_A — the modified skeleton matrix of automaton A
$P_k^i(y)$ — the probability of the state being q^i at instant k for input y
$\lambda^i(y)$ — the limiting probability of $P_k^i(y)$
l_i^j — the ith block of trials for state q^j

References

Bacon, G. C., The decomposition of stochastic automata. *Info. and Control 7*, pp. 320–339 (1964a).

Bacon, G. C., Minimal-state stochastic finite-state systems, *IEEE Trans. Circuit Theory, CT-11*, pp. 307–308 (1964b).

Booth, T. L., "Sequential Machines and Automata Theory." Wiley, New York, 1967.

Bruce, G. D. and Fu, K. S., A model for finite-state probabilistic system. *Proc. 1st Allerton Conf. Circuit and System Theory*, Univ. of Michigan Press, Ann Arbor, pp. 632–651 (1963).

Bryzgalov, V. I., Gel'fand, I. M., Pyatetskii–Shapiro, I. I., and Tsetlin, M. L., Homogeneous games for automata and their computer simulation. *Automation and Remote Control 25*, No. 11, pp. 1419–1427 (1964).

Carlyle, J. W., Equivalent stochastic sequential machines. Tech. Rept., Ser. 60 I 415, Electron. Research Lab., Univ. of California, Berkeley, Calif., 1961.

Carlyle, J. W., Reduced form for stochastic sequential machines, *J. Math. Analysis and Appl. 7*, pp. 167–175 (1963).

Chandrasekaran, B., Shen, D. W. C., On expediency and convergence in variable structure automata. *Proc. Natl. Electron. Conf. 22*, pp. 845–850 (1966).

Cleave, J. P., The synthesis of finite state homogeneous Markov chains. *Cybernetica 1*, pp. 38–47 (1962).

Fu, K. S., Stochastic automata as models of learning systems. "Computer and Information Sciences—II." Academic Press, New York, pp. 177–191 (1967).

Fu, K. S. and Li, T. J., On automata games. *Proc. Second Annual Princeton Conf. Info. Sciences*, pp. 200–203 (1968).

Fu, K. S. and McLaren, R. W., An application of stochastic automata to the synthesis of learning systems. Tech. Rept. EE, No. 17, Purdue Univ., Lafayette, Ind., 1965.

Fu, K. S. and McMurtry, G. J., A variable structure automaton used as a multi-modal searching technique. *Proc. Natl. Electron. Conf.*, 21, pp. 494–499 (1965).

Fu, K. S. and Nikolic, A. J., On some reinforcement techniques and their relation with stochastic approximation. *IEEE Trans. Auto. Control AC-11*, pp. 756–758 (1966).

Gill, A., "Introduction to the Theory of Finite-State Machines." McGraw–Hill, New York, 1962.

Ginsburg, S. L., Krylov, V. Yu., and Tsetlin, M. L., One example of a game for many identical automata. *Automation and Remote Control 25*, No. 5, pp. 608–622 (1964).

Harrison, M. A., "Introduction to Switching and Automata Theory." McGraw–Hill, New York, 1965.

Kashyap, R. L., Optimization of stochastic finite state systems. *Fifth Symp. Discrete Adaptive Processes*, Chicago, Ill., pp. 839–844 (1966).

Krylov, V. Yu., On one automaton that is asymptotically optimal in a random medium. *Automation and Remote Control 24*, No. 9, pp. 1114–1116 (1963).

Krylov, V. Yu. and Tsetlin, M. L., Games between automata. *Automation and Remote Control 24*, No. 7, pp. 889–899 (1963).

Mallows, C. L. and Robbins, E., Some problems of optimal sampling strategy. *J. Math. Analysis and Appl. 8*, pp. 90–103 (1964).

Maurer, H. E., An approach to the design of reliable radiation hardened integrated logic and sequential circuits. Ph.D. Thesis, Purdue Univ., Lafayette, Ind., 1965.

McMurtry, G. J. and Fu, K. S., On the learning behavior of finite-state systems in random environments. *Proc. 2nd Annual Allerton Conf. Circuit and System Theory*, Monticello, Ill., pp. 618–632 (1964).

Murray, F. J., Mechanisms and robots, *J. Assoc. for Computing Machinery 2*, pp. 61–82 (1965).

Nelson, R. J., "Introduction to Automata." Wiley, New York, 1968.

Nikolic, Z. J. and Fu, K. S., An algorithm for learning without external supervision and its application to learning control systems. *IEEE Trans. Auto. Control AC-11*, pp. 414–422 (1966).

Ott, E., Reconsider the state minimization problem for stochastic finite state systems. *Proc. 7th Annual Symp. Switching and Automata Theory* (1966).

Page, C. V., Equivalences between probabilistic and deterministic machines. *Info. and Control 9*, pp. 469–520 (1966).

Paz, A., Some aspects of probabilistic automata. *Info. and Control 9*, No. 1, pp. 26–60 (1966).

Paz, A., Minimization theorems and techniques for sequential stochastic machines. *Info. and Control 11*, pp. 155–166 (1967).

Rabin, M. O., Probabilistic automata. *Info. and Control 6*, pp. 230–245 (1963).

Robbins, H., A sequential decision problem with a finite memory. *Proc. Natl. Academy of Science 42*, pp. 920–923, (1956).

Salomaa, A., On *m*-adic probabilistic automata. *Info. and Control 10*, 215–219 (1967).

Samuels, S. M., Randomized rule for the two-armed-bandit with finite memory. Purdue Statistics Mimeograph Ser., No. 71, Purdue Univ., Lafayette, Ind. (1966).

Tsertsvadze, G. N., Certain properties of stochastic automata and methods for synthesizing them. *Automation and Remote Control 24*, No. 3, pp. 316–326 (1963).

Tsertsvadze, G. N., Stochastic automata and the problem of constructing reliable of unreliable elements. *Automation and Remote Control 25*, No. 4, pp. 458–464 (1964).

Tsetlin, M. L., On the behavior of finite automata in random media. *Automation and Remote Control 22*, No. 10, pp. 1210–1219 (1961).

Uttley, A. M., Conditional probability computing in a nervous system. *Proc. Symp. Mechanization of Thought Processes*, pp. 121–146 (1959).

Varshavskii, V. I. and Verontsova, I. P., On the behavior of stochastic automata with variable structure. *Automation and Remote Control 24*, No. 3, pp. 327–333 (1963).

Waltz, M. D. and Fu, K. S., A heuristic approach to reinforcement learning control systems. *IEEE Trans. Auto. Control AC-10*, pp. 390–398 (1965).

Wilks, S. S., "Mathematical Statistics." Wiley, New York, 1962.

PART III PROBLEMS

Chapter 9 Problems

1. Given a sequence of samples $\mathbf{x}_1, \mathbf{x}_2, \ldots$ from a n-variate normal distribution $N(\boldsymbol{\mu}, \Sigma)$ where both $\boldsymbol{\mu}$ and Σ are unknown, construct a converging SA algorithm to recover $\boldsymbol{\mu}$ given that $0 < a_1 \leqslant \| \Sigma \| \leqslant a_2$. If $\boldsymbol{\theta}_k$ is the estimate of $\boldsymbol{\mu}$ at the kth stage, find an asymptotic expression for $E\{\| \boldsymbol{\theta}_k - \boldsymbol{\mu} \|^2\}$.
2. Given a sequence of samples $x_1, x_2, \ldots$ from a Poisson distribution $[\exp(-\mu)\, \mu^x/x!]$ where $x = 0, 1, 2\ldots$ find a converging SA algorithm to estimate the scalar μ and obtain an asymptotic expression for $E\{(\theta_k - \mu)^2\}$ where θ_k is the estimate of μ at the kth stage.
3. Let $\mathbf{y}(\boldsymbol{\theta})$ be an observable random variable satisfying the assumptions (A1)–(A3). Suppose we are given the numbers c_i, d_i, $i = 1,\ldots, n$ bounding $\boldsymbol{\theta}^o$, the zero of $E\{y(\boldsymbol{\theta}) \mid \boldsymbol{\theta}\}$

$$c_i \leqslant \theta_i^o \leqslant d_i \qquad i = 1,\ldots, n$$

Consider the following algorithm where $\{\rho_k\}$ is defined in Eq. (9.4)

$$\boldsymbol{\theta}_{k+1} = \{\boldsymbol{\theta}_k - \rho_k y(\boldsymbol{\theta}_k)\}_{\mathscr{D}}$$

where

$$\{\mathbf{x}\}_p \triangleq (\{x_1\}_p, \ldots, \{x_n\}_p)'$$

and

$$\begin{aligned} \{x_i\}_p &= c_i \quad \text{if } x_i \leqslant c_i \\ &= x_i \quad\quad c_i < x_i < d_i \\ &= d_i \quad \text{if } x_i \geqslant d_i \end{aligned}$$

Show that $\boldsymbol{\theta}_k$ tends to $\boldsymbol{\theta}^o$ with probability one.

4. Using the results of Problem 3, estimate both $\boldsymbol{\mu}$ and Σ in Problem 1.

5. In a certain problem, for any given input $\boldsymbol{\theta} = (\theta_1, \theta_2)'$, we can observe an output $z_i(\boldsymbol{\theta})$,

$$z_i(\boldsymbol{\theta}) = \exp[-c_1(\theta_1 - \theta_1{}^*)^2 - c_2(\theta_2 - \theta_2{}^*)^2] + \eta_i$$

where c_1 and c_2 are unknown bounded positive constants, $\theta_1{}^*$, $\theta_2{}^*$ are known constants, and $\{\eta_i\}$ is a zero mean independent noise sequence with finite variance. Estimate $\theta_1{}^*$ and $\theta_2{}^*$ using KW scheme. Compare analytically the convergence rates when the gradients are approximated in the following manner

(i) $$\nabla_{\theta_i} z(\boldsymbol{\theta}) \approx \frac{1}{2c_i}\{z(\theta_1, \ldots, \theta_{i-1}, \theta_i + c_i, \theta_{i+1}, \ldots, \theta_n) - z(\theta_1, \ldots, \theta_{i-1}, \theta_i - c_i, \theta_{i+1}, \ldots, \theta_n)\}$$

(ii) $$\nabla_{\theta_i} z(\boldsymbol{\theta}) \approx \frac{1}{c_i}\{z(\theta_1, \ldots, \theta_{i-1}, \theta_i + c_i, \theta_{i+1}, \ldots, \theta_n) - z(\theta_1, \ldots, \theta_i, \theta_{i+1}, \ldots, \theta_n)\}.$$

Verify your results by simulation.

6. Consider the approximation of the function $f(x) = x^3$ by a linear form θx. Let x be a uniformly distributed random variable in $[-1, 1]$. Using a sequence $\{x_i\}$ of successively independent samples, let us construct the following algorithm with $\{\rho_k\}$ obeying Eq. (9.4).

$$\theta_{k+1} = \theta_k - \rho_k y_k$$

where

$$\begin{aligned} &\text{Case (i) } y_k = x_k(\theta_k x_k - f(x_k)) \\ &\text{Case (ii) } y_k = x_k \operatorname{sgn}(\theta_k x_k - f(x_k)) \\ &\text{Case (iii) } y_k = \operatorname{sgn}(x_k(\theta_k x_k - f(x_k)) \end{aligned}$$

Verify that the algorithm converges in all three cases and find the limiting value of $\{\theta_k\}$ in all the cases. Next suppose that $f(x_k)$ is not given to us; however, we are given $z(x_k)$ for every x_k where $\{\eta_k\}$ is a zero mean independent noise sequence

$$z(x_k) = f(x_k) + \eta_k$$

In which of the three cases does the above algorithm converge if we replace $f(x_k)$ by $z(x_k)$?

7. Consider the function $f(x) = \exp[-1/2(x_1^2 + x_2^2)], 0 \leqslant x_1, x_2 \leqslant 4$. Generate a sequence of samples $\mathbf{x}_i$, $i = 1, 2,..., N$ with $\mathbf{x} = (x_1, x_2)'$ obeying a uniform distribution in the region $0 \leqslant x_1, x_2 \leqslant 4$. Using only the values $f(\mathbf{x}_i)$, $i = 1,..., N$ obtain an approximation $f_N(\mathbf{x})$ for $f(\mathbf{x})$ in the region $0 \leqslant x_1, x_2 \leqslant 4$ using the method of potential functions. Study the effect of varying N on the mean square error $E\{\| f(\mathbf{x}) - f_N(\mathbf{x})\|^2\}$.
8. Suppose there are two classes ω_1 and ω_{-1} with a separating function $f^o(\mathbf{x})$

$$\begin{aligned} f^o(\mathbf{x}) &> 0 \quad \text{if } x \in \omega_1 \\ &< 0 \quad \text{if } x \in \omega_{-1} \end{aligned}$$

We are given a sequence of independent pairs $\{\mathbf{x}_k, z_k\}$, $k = 1, 2,...$ where

$$z_k = (\operatorname{sgn} f^o(\mathbf{x}_k))\, \eta_k \qquad E(\eta) = \hat{\eta} \neq 0$$

and $\{\eta_k\}$ is an independent sequence. Consider the algorithm

$$f_{k+1}(\mathbf{x}) = f_k(\mathbf{x}) + \frac{1}{\hat{\eta}} \rho_k(z_k - \hat{\eta} \operatorname{sgn} f_k(\mathbf{x}_k))\, K(\mathbf{x}, \mathbf{x}_k)$$

where $K(\mathbf{a}, \mathbf{b})$ is a potential function and ρ_k obeys Eq. (9.4). Given that $f^o(\mathbf{x})$ is mean square integrable, show that

$$\lim_{k\to\infty} E|\operatorname{sgn} f_k(\mathbf{x}) - \operatorname{sgn} f^o(\mathbf{x})| = 0.$$

Chapter 10 Problems

1. Consider the observations x_i, $i = 1, 2,...$ from a stationary dynamical system

$$x_{i+1} = ax_i + b\xi_i$$

where a is an unknown constant lying in the range $1 > a_1 \geqslant a \geqslant a_2$ and $\{\xi_i\}$ is a stationary Gaussian uncorrelated zero mean noise sequence with unknown variance q so that $0 < q_1 \leqslant q \leqslant q_2$. Develop a converging SA algorithm to estimate a and obtain an asymptotic expression for the mean square error.

2. Consider a sequence of random variables $\nu_1, \nu_2, \ldots$ with a common, but unknown, distribution function $F(\theta) = \text{Prob}(\nu_i \leqslant \theta)$. We cannot observe the variables ν_i directly. However, for any given value θ_i, we can observe a "response" variable y_i, where

$$\begin{aligned} y_i(\theta_i) &= 1 \quad \text{if } \nu_i \leqslant \theta_i \\ &= 0 \quad \text{otherwise} \end{aligned}$$

so that $E\{y(\theta) \mid \theta\} = F(\theta)$. Let θ^o be the value of θ so that $F(\theta^o) = 1/2$. Construct an SA algorithm to estimate θ^o using the measurements $y_1, y_2, \ldots$ (Robbins and Munro, 1951 in Chapter 9 References).

3. Given a function $f(\mathbf{x}) = \exp(-1/2(x_1^2 + x_2^2))$, $0 \leqslant x_1, x_2 \leqslant 4$, where the random variable $\mathbf{x}$ is uniformly distributed in the allowable region, construct a linear approximation $\hat{f}_n(\mathbf{x}) \triangleq \sum_{i=1}^{n} \theta_i \varphi_i(\mathbf{x})$ so as to minimize $J_n = E\{\|f(\mathbf{x}) - \hat{f}_n(\mathbf{x})\|^2\}$ for various values of $n = 1, 2, \ldots$ where $\varphi_i(\mathbf{x}), i = 1, 2, \ldots$ are orthogonal functions drawn from Legendre polynomials. Evaluate the minimum error J_n in each case. Study the effect of changing the distribution of $\mathbf{x}$ from uniform to normal $N(0, I)$.

4. Show that the algorithm in Eq. (10.12) converges with probability one.

5. Consider a sequence $\{x_k\}$ obeying the equation

$$x_{k+1} + x_{k-1} = \sin k\alpha \qquad k = 0, 1, 2, \ldots$$

where α is known and $x_0 \triangleq \theta_1$, $x_1 \triangleq \theta_2$ are unknown. $\{x_k\}$ are not directly observable. However, we can observe y_k where η_k are independent with zero mean and common variance and $y_k = \tan^{-1} x_k + \eta_k$. Estimate $\boldsymbol{\theta}' = (\theta_1, \theta_2)$ recursively from the $\{y_k\}$ (Albert and Gardner, 1967 in Chapter 9 References).

6. Consider the following second-order stable, time-invariant linear system

$$x_k + \theta_1 x_{k-1} + \theta_2 x_{k-2} = \frac{1}{\sqrt{2}}(1 + (-1)^k) + \sum_{l=1}^{2} \cos \omega_l k$$

where ω_1 and ω_2 are known numbers with $0 < \omega_1 < \omega_2 < \pi$. We can observe only the noisy measurements of x_k

$$y_k = x_k + \eta_k$$

where η_k are zero mean noise, not necessarily independent. Find a recursive method of estimating θ_1 and θ_2 (Albert and Gardner, 1967 in Chapter 9 References).

Chapter 11 Problems

1. Derive Eqs. (11.11) and (11.12) [Carlyle, 1961 in Chapter 11 References].
2. Prove Theorem 4 and Theorem 5 (Carlyle, 1961 in Chapter 11 References).
3. Given

$$M(y) = \begin{bmatrix} \frac{1}{5} & \frac{2}{5} & \frac{2}{5} \\ \frac{1}{3} & 0 & \frac{2}{3} \\ \frac{1}{4} & \frac{1}{2} & \frac{1}{4} \end{bmatrix}$$

synthesize a stochastic automaton for the specified $M(y)$ by
   (i) Cleave's procedure.
   (ii) Murray's procedure.
   (iii) Tsertsvadze's procedure.
4. Derive Eq. (11.56).
5. Verify Eq. (11.85) and derive Eq. (11.88).
6. Prove Eqs. (11.92) and (11.93).
7. Derive Eqs. (11.100) and (11.114) .
8. Study the behavior of the following modified Tsetlin's linear-strategy model:
   (i) for a nonpenalty, stay in the same state.
   (ii) for a penalty, change state in the same fashion as Tsetlin's model.

Index

A

Abstraction, 81
Adaptive control, *see* Control system
Adaptive optimization techniques, 246, *see also* Search techniques
Adaptive random optimization, 269
Alternatives, 290–291
Automata, 393, *see also* Stochastic automata and Automata games
  asymptotically optimal, 409, 410
  deterministic, operating in random environments, 406–410
  deterministic with random inputs, 397, 399, 400
  finite memory, 418–420
  model $A_{r,m}$, 418
  model $B_{r,m,b}$, 420
  randomized transition rules, 420–423
Automata games, 417–428
  model $A_{r,m}$, 418–423
  model $B_{r,m,b}$, 420–426
Average
  linear reinforcement, 324
  standard 324

B

Bernoulli sequence, 396

C

Centering, 119
Characterization, 81
Character recognition, 3
  decision rules for, 12–15
  features for, 4, 5–12, 15
Classes
  linearly separable, 85
  nonoverlapping, 82, 85–103, 107, 108–109
  overlapping, 82, 103–106, 107, 109–111
Classification
  backward sequential, 45–48, 48–50
  cloud pattern, 146
  forward sequential, 42–45
  lunar terrain, 144
  statistical, 13–15
Classification algorithms, 81, *see also* Convergence
  comparison, 111
  multiclass, 107–111
  nonoverlapping classes, 85–96, 96–103, 108–109
  overlapping classes, 103–107, 109–111
Classifiers, 4
  Bayes', 22, 35–39, 125
  iterative design of, 127–129
  sequential, 41
Cleave's procedure, 399–400
Cluster, 69
Cluster-seeking techniques (procedures), 30, 69
Code
  augmented multi-element, 187
  linear independent, 188
  multi-element, 187
  single-element, 187

Combinational search, 282–283
Conjugate gradient method, *see* Mathematical programming methods
Constrained optimization methods, *see* Mathematical programming methods
Control
  bang-bang, 383–391
  closed-loop, 166, 292
  feedback, 166, 383
  fuel-optimal, 166
  open-loop, 166, 292
  quadratic-optimal, 300
  time-optimal, 165, 296
Control choice, 296
Controllers
  multilevel, 164
Control situations, 297–299
  construction of, 304
Control system, 223
  adaptive, 293
  learning, 294
Convergence
  basic stochastic approximation scheme, 350–352
  classification algorithms, 86–88, 101–103
  function recovery algorithm, 352–354
  gradient identification algorithms, 214–219, 227–230
Convergence rates
  accelerating, 347–350
  Kiefer–Wolfowitz algorithm, 346
  least squares algorithm, 346–347
  Robbins–Munro algorithm, 345–346

D

Decision boundary
  based on Euclidean distance, 18–19
  based on Mahalanobis distance, 20–21
  estimation of parameters, 66–67
Decision process, 314
Decision rule
  Bayes', 14, 35–38
  maximum likelihood, 38
  nearest neighbor, 12
  sequential, 39–42
Discriminant analysis, 122, 129–133
Discriminant Analysis-Iterative Design (DAID), 126–133
Discriminant functions, 28, 38, 53, 129, 132, 309
  linear, 53, 126, 131
  polynomial, 179
  quadratic, 133
Distribution functions
  approximation of, 364–368
Divergence, 51
Dynamic programming, 45–46, 301

E

Encoding, 185
Enhancement, 118–119
Error-correction rule (scheme), 95, 125
  fixed-increment, 29
Estimation, *see also* Decision boundary, Distribution functions, Functions, Mixture distribution, Mode, Probability density functions, Parameter estimation, State estimation
  Bayesian, 61–68
Event, 291
Expediency, 407

F

Feasible direction, 257
Feature, 4 *see also* Feature selection
  augmentation, 154
  extraction, 23, 120–122, 172, 308
  extractor, 4, 15, 35, 306
  known, 121
  measurements, 39, 48
  ordering, 50–60
  processing, 169, 172, 177–190
  statistical, 121, 149
Feature selection, 23
  backward sequential procedure for, 48–50
  information theoretic approach for, 50–56
  Karhunen–Loéve expansion for, 56–60
Fibonacci number, 249
Fibonacci search, 247–250

Fletcher–Powell method, *see* Mathematical programming methods
Fourier transformation, 119
Functions, *see also* Convergence
  estimation of parameters, 337–340
  recovery from values observed at randomly selected points, 340–342

G

Gain matrix, 212, *see also* Gain sequence
  error-correction, 220
  Lyapunov-optimum, 219
  optimum choice for, 219
Gain sequence
  adaptive, 338
  deterministic, 338
  quasi-adaptive, 338
Games, *see also* Automata games
  $A_{r,m}$ automata against nature, 423
  between $A_{r,m}$ automata, 423–426
  $B_{r,m,b}$ automata, 426–427
  investment, 425
Generalization, 81, 175
Generalization test, 175
Generalized sequential probability ratio test, 40
Goals, 309, *see also* Subgoals
Golden ratio, 251
Golden section search, 250–251
Gradient, 212, 252
Gradient algorithms, *see also* Gradient identification algorithms
  first-order method, 338–339
  second-order method, 339–340
Gradient identification algorithms, 213, *see also* Convergence

H

Harvard College example, 358–364

I

Identification, 209, 294
  a posteriori, 230, 231–235, 239–240
  a priori, 230
  dynamic situation, 209
  sequential, 210
  static situation, 209
Identification algorithms, *see* Gradient identification algorithms
Identification applications
  high-performance, adaptive, normal acceleration control system, 223–227, 236–237
  plant's differential equation, 213–214
  sampled impulse response, 214, 221–223
Identification error system, 217
Identification system, 211, 237
Information matrix, 230
Interval of uncertainty, 248, 250
Invariance, 116
Iterative design, 158–161

K

Karhunen–Loéve expansion, 56–60
Kesten algorithm, 348
Kiefer-Wolfowitz, *see also* Convergence rates
  algorithm, 271, 334
  schemes, 334–336, 348

L

Laplacian filtering, 118
Learning, 61, *see also* Reinforcement learning
  algorithm, 115, 307, 309
  covariance matrix, 64, 65
  definition of, 287
  experiment, 291
  forced, 123, 124
  mean vector, 25, 63, 65
  models, 287
  nonparametric, 27–29
  nonsupervised (unsupervised), 29–31, 61, 66–68
  parametric, 24–27, 62
  properties, 330
  supervised, 61, 62
  system, 314
  theories, 288, 307
Learning control system, *see* Control system
Learning system, 410
Learning system models

formulation of, 290
psychological origins of, 287
Least-mean-square rule, 29
Least squares algorithm, *see* Convergence rates
Lyapunov function, 217
Lyapunov stability theory, 217

M

Madaline, 148
Mappings, 296, 308
Markov chain, 380, 396, 419
inhomogeneous, 411
Mathematical programming methods, 254
conjugate gradient, 254–256
constrained, 257–258
Fletcher–Powell, 256–257
Matyas, 265
Memory, 302, 312
long-term, 302, 313
short-term, 302
Mixture distribution
estimation of parameters, 67–68
Mode, 30, 69
estimation of, 68–75
Multimodal optimization techniques, 272–283, *see also* names of specific techniques and Random search techniques
Multimodal stochastic approximation, *see* Stochastic approximation
Multivariable polynomials, 179
examples of, 183–185
orthonormal, 184
properties of, 180–183
Murray's procedure, 400–404

N

Noisy gradient, 331
Noisy measurements, 237, 336
Noisy teacher, 308, 311

O

Optimization procedures, 243–286
Outcome, 291

P

Paradigms, 115
Parameter estimation in Markov Chains, 379–382, *see also* Identification
Pattern classification examples, 358–364
Pattern recognition
classical model, 22–31
elements of, 3–33
reinforcement learning, 306
statistical methods, 35–79
system, 306
Pattern recognition applications
quasi-optimal control, 163–194
sleep state classification, 133–141
video, 141–157
Perceptron, 121
algorithm, 87
modified, 91–92
Φ functions, 177
Potential functions, 177, 342
examples of, 95, 344
expandability of, 179
properties of, 95, 343
Preprocessing, 117–120, 136, 143–148
Probability density functions
estimation of, 368–371
Problems
Part I, 195–205
Part II, 319–325
Part III, 433–437
Punishment, 289

Q

Quantization, 185, 275
Quasi-optimal control, 164–168

R

Radmacher–Walsh expansion, 94
Random search techniques
absolute bias modification, 270–271
adaptive step size, 263–265
fixed step size, 263
gradient biased, 271–272
Matyas' method, 265–270
optimum step size, 263
pure, 272–275

Rastrigin's random scanning method, 258–263
Rastrigin, 258
Relaxation algorithm, 87
Reinforcement
negative, 289, 315
positive, 289, 315
secondary, 289
Reinforcement learning, 287
algorithm, 411, 414
control algorithm, 303
control systems, 292–306
definition of, 288
generalized model, 414–417
model, 290–292
pattern recognition algorithm, 314
pattern recognition systems, 306–317
Response classes, 290
Reward, 289
Robbins–Munro algorithm, 345, 348
Rosenbrock function, 322

S

Sample mean, 18
Search techniques, *see also* Unimodal techniques and Multimodal techniques
multidimensional, 251
sequential, 246, 274
simultaneous, 246
unidimensional, 247
Separability measure, 54
Separating function, 90
recovery of, 94
Sequential decision procedure, *see* Decision rule and Classification
Signal conditioning, *see* Preprocessing
Signature, 181
Signature problem, 181
State estimation, 371–376
State prediction, 376–379
Stationary parameters, 213, 214–227, 238–239
Steepest descent, 252–254, 329, *see also* Unidirectional steepest descent
Stochastic approximation, 93, 258, 329–355, *see also* Convergence
applications, 357–392
multimodal, 281–282
Stochastic automata, 393–431, *see also* Stochastic automaton
autonomous, 396, 399, 400
nonautonomous, 402
synthesis of, 399–406
variable structure, 410
Stochastic automation, 275, 393–398
autonomous, 396
cyclic, 404
distribution-equivalent, 398
model for learner subsystem, 315
state-equivalent, 398
Stopping boundaries, 39–40
time-varying, 42–45
Subgoals, 299–302, 310
average, 323
normalized, 304–305
Surface, *see also* Switching surface
deterministic, 244
multimodal, 246, 276
noisy, 244, 259
unimodal, 245
Surface model methods, 283
Switching function, 384
Switching surface, 167
quasi-optimal, 163, 167, 190

T

Template matching, 4
Time-varying parameters, 213, 227–237, 239–240
T-maze, 290
Trainable controllers, 168–170
application, 190–191
multilevel, 190
two-level, 190
Training, 168
samples, 96, 171
two-level, 170–172
Trial, 291
Tsertsvadze's procedure, 404–406

U

Unidirectional steepest descent, 252

Unimodal optimization techniques, 247–272, *see also* names of specific techniques and Random search techniques
Univariate search, 251

V

Variable structure method, 275–280

W

Wald's sequential probability ratio test, 39
Window function, 106, 119

Z

Zeroes of functions
  algorithms for finding, 332–334